CW00821739

An Illustrated History of the

NORTH CORNWALL RAILWAY

The Southern Railway Route between Okehampton, Launceston, Wadebridge and Padstow

Based on an original manuscript by the late David Wroe

The North Cornwall entered Launceston through the Kensey Valley from the east and St. Stephen's Church stands on the skyline to the north, providing the background to Bulleid Pacific's No. 34030 *Watersmeet* coming through the cutting at Ridgegrove with the 11.00am Padstow to Waterloo Atlantic Coast Express on 22nd August 1964. The coaches are in two sets of BR Mk1s supplied by the Southern region. Discernible through the smoke and steam are the ex-GWR shed (left, centre) and the 1943 inter-company spur joining the SR to the GWR (right). P. W. Gray.

Irwell Press Ltd.

An unidentified Bulleid Pacific crosses the magnificent Meldon Viaduct with a train for Wadebridge and the North Cornwall line. R. C. Riley, www.transporttreasury.co.uk

Copyright IRWELL PRESS LIMITED
ISBN-10-1-903266-89-0
13-978 1-903266-89-2

I first met David Wroe at a South Western Circle meeting in 1991. A charming man who I was to spend many a pleasant lunch with over the next three years. Irwell Press was an infant company in those days, so to be offered a book the size David was proposing was quite daunting. We eventually agreed that a certain amount of the material David had accrued was not essential and was therefore omitted from the original work. I remember too searching high and low for more photographs of the line which, at the time, were very scarce. His untimely death in October 1994 left a huge void and friends, and family, were able to finish off David's manuscript which saw publication in June 1995.

I remember joking with him only two days before his passing, that if the book went well enough we could consider a reprint, expanding on the original. Over a decade later and some eleven years after David's original work went out of print, we are able to present an updated and vastly expanded version of *The North Cornwall Railway*. This has only been possible through the good offices of many contributors who have spent many hours helping us to produce a book which David, I'm sure, would have approved.

I must first thank Chris Tooth who has spent literally hours writing additional material and weaving it into David's original text. He and a group of friends had been inspired by David's original book and had built an exhibition layout, Treneglos, a fictional station on the North Cornwall. Feeling there was more to learn about the North Cornwall Railway, Chris and his friends set out to research further the workings, history and locomotives of the line and have very kindly included all this material in the book. Chris would like to say a special thanks to those who helped him in the preparation of his work. Mike Watts, Stephen Austin, Graham Muspratt, Chris Knowles-Thomas, Brian MacDermott, David Lord, David Vidler, Peter Richards, Chris Osment, Glen Woods, John Wardle, Roger Whitehouse, Patrick Wainwright, Howard Sprenger, Rob McSweeney, Roger Merry-Price, John Isherwood, Paul Bartlett and a general catch-all being the SRG, LSWRR, SRLHCS and SeMG groups.

Some of the above have helped me too with various aspects of the book. I would therefore like to say a special thanks to Glen Woods and Chris Osment who have given help, time and material, especially with the additional information they were able to give on Carriage Workings and Signalling respectively. Roger Merry-Price, along with Peter Richards and Roger Whitehouse were able to supply us with the Working Timetable information and the Engine Diagrams - my sincere thanks to them.

Martin Smith put together the history of those very special locomotive, the Beattie Well Tanks and Barry Hoper, of The Transport Treasury, kindly allowed us to use not only the photos of Leslie Freeman, but his original diary notes too - again our sincere thanks to them both.

A chance call from a reader in Cornwall, Ian Barnes, inspired the chapter on *The North Cornwall Railway Today*. Ian set off with his friend Nikky Barton and recorded the remains of the line and interviewed the various occupants of the stations. A marvellous piece of work which again I am sure David would have approved - many thanks to them both and those residents who allowed us access.

Excluded from the original work were signalling diagrams, gradient profiles and a bridge and culvert log, the latter two being provided by Nick Pomfret. Nick my thanks to you, and the South Western Circle, who have very kindly allowed us to use the collection of the late John Eyres who meticulously recorded on film the entire line.

Lastly, and of course by no means least, Eric Youldon who patiently checked the entire manuscript correcting and suggesting alterations to the text - Eric as always our sincere and heartfelt thanks to you for your time and enthusiasm.

It remains for me to say that David's book has been inspirational to many Southern entusiasts over the years including myself. I hope therefore, that this expanded version of David's original work will be appreciated as a tribute to a man who was a loving husband, father, friend, railwayman and above all else, a thoroughly decent chap.

George Reeve

Cover top. **T9 4-4-0 No. 30710 pauses briefly at Halwill Junction with a train from Wadebridge and en-route for Okehampton in 1961.**
Cover bottom. **R. C. Riley's view of Wadebridge East signal box and O2 class No. 30203 in September 1954. www.transporttreasury.co.uk**

Back cover. **In 2003 three members of Stafford Railway Circle discovered a joint interest in the Southern's 'lost' lines West of Exeter. A copy of the original David Wroe North Cornwall Railway book and a new, highly detailed, model of a Bulleid Light Pacific from Hornby provided the catalysts and inspiration for building a OO gauge 'Withered Arm' exhibition layout 'Treneglos'. Modeller's licence was applied and Tresmeer station was 'transplanted' one mile west with the building constructed from stone as per those between Otterham and St Key Highway. Opting to model the proposed, but not built, viaduct instead of the viaduct at Treneglos the group operate prototypical trains as would be found on the line in summer seasons between 1958 and 1964. First exhibited in 2004 and now a regular on the exhibition circuit, the layout successfully captures the atmosphere of the North Cornwall line between Launceston and Wadebridge. If you'd like to see more of their representation of this forgotten part of the British railway network see their website** *www.treneglos.fotopic.net*

First published in the United Kingdom in 1995
Reprinted, updated and considerably expanded 2008
by Irwell Press Limited, 59A High Street, Clophill,
Bedfordshire MK45 4BE
Printed by Konway Press

CONTENTS

HALWILL FOR BEAWORTHY
JUNCTION FOR BUDE, NORTH CORNWALL &
TORRINGTON LINES
BRITISH RAILWAYS
EXCURSIONS
BRITISH RAILWAYS
TRAIN

All quiet at Halwill Junction in May 1961. Passengers are standing around awaiting the next Exeter train whilst others arrive on the left. A PW trolley is standing on the down line. Leslie Freeman, www.transporttreasury.co.uk

A general view of Wadebridge station and the magnificent signal gantry in 1960. T9 4-4-0 No. 30313 was allocated to Exmouth Junction at this time and carries the later style BR crest, one of the few T9s to do so. Behind the loco is a Maunsell corridor third (second) one of the 1935/6 variety built to Diagram 2008 with large corridor side windows and revised door locations (Body style Pattern 3 in the P-Set appendix). One of only 72 built. The second and third coaches are a Maunsell 2-Set P. The Brake Composite is leading (probably a Diagram 2401) and is followed by a Brake Third (second) (probably a Diagram 2113). At the rear appears to be a bogie newspaper van and an XP rated van. The train is probably the 3.13 departure from Padstow to Okehampton with the Newspaper van destined for Waterloo. Behind the train is Maunsell Brake Third (Second) No 2831 which was built to Diagram 2113 in December 1935. This was one coach of 2-Set P No 26 - the other being No 6586 which was built to Diagram 2401 in March 1930. R. C. Riley, www.transporttreasury.co.uk

461
30313
461
26
SHUNTING
BELL

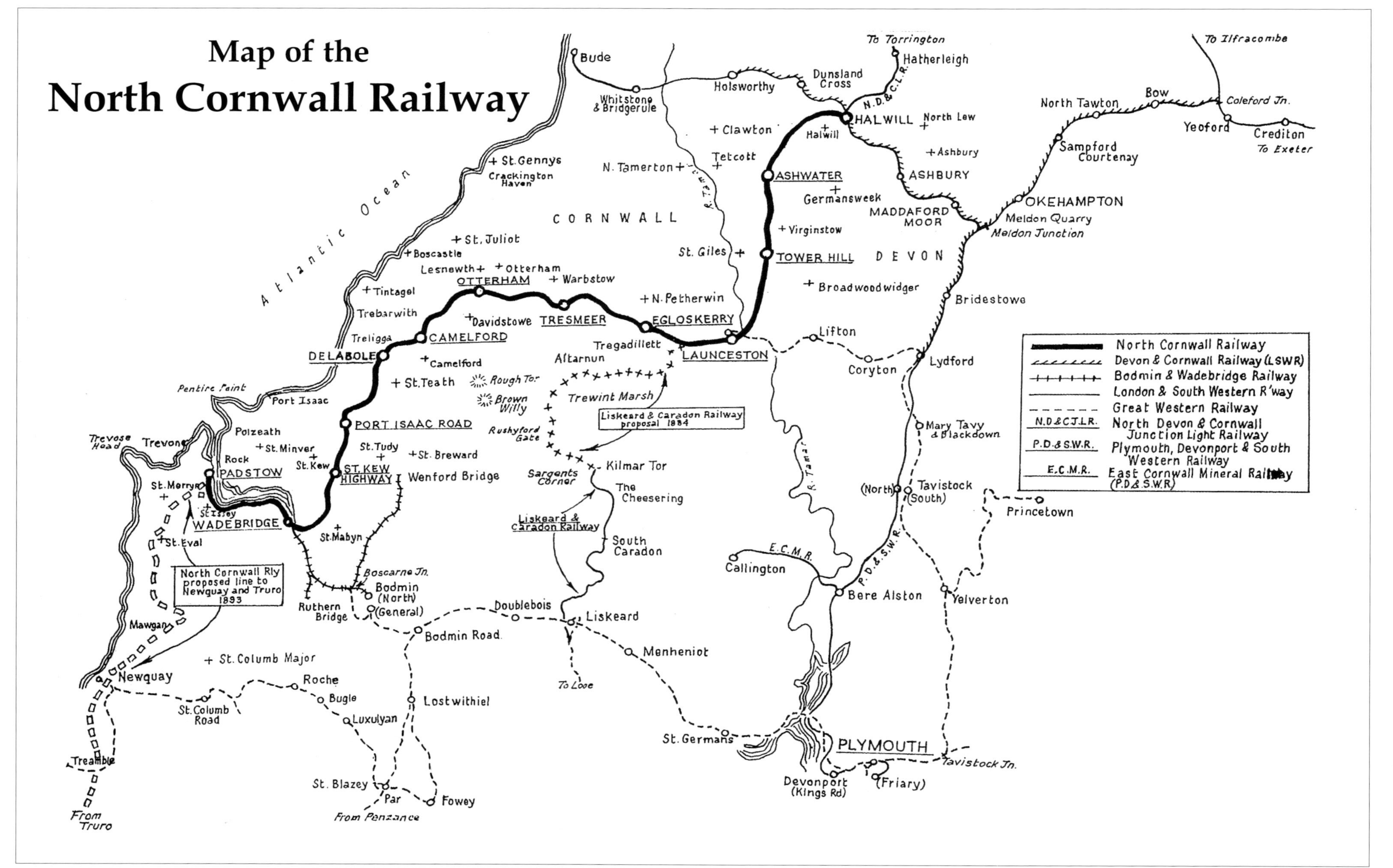
Map of the
North Cornwall Railway
North Cornwall Railway
Devon & Cornwall Railway (LSWR)
Bodmin & Wadebridge Railway
London & South Western R'way
Great Western Railway
N.D.&C.J.L.R. North Devon & Cornwall Junction Light Railway
P.D.&S.W.R. Plymouth, Devonport & South Western Railway
E.C.M.R. East Cornwall Mineral Railway (P.D.&S.W.R.)
To Ilfracombe
Coleford Jn.
Crediton
To Exeter
Yeoford
Bow
North Tawton
Sampford Courtenay
OKEHAMPTON
Meldon Quarry
Meldon Junction
To Torrington
Hatherleigh
N.D.&C.L.R.
HALWILL
North Lew
Halwill
Ashbury
ASHBURY
MADDAFORD MOOR
Germansweek
DEVON
Bridestowe
Bude
Whitstone & Bridgerule
Holsworthy
Dunsland Cross
Clawton
Tetcott
ASHWATER
Virginstow
TOWER HILL
Broadwoodwidger
N. Tamerton
R. Tamar
CORNWALL
St. Giles
N. Petherwin
EGLOSKERRY
LAUNCESTON
Lifton
Coryton
Lydford
Mary Tavy & Blackdown
Tavistock (North)
(South)
Princetown
Yelverton
Bere Alston
P.D.&S.W.R.
E.C.M.R.
Callington
R. Tamar
PLYMOUTH
Tavistock Jn.
(Friary)
Devonport (Kings Rd)
St. Germans
Menheniot
Liskeard
To Looe
Doublebois
Bodmin Road
Lostwithiel
Fowey
Par
St. Blazey
From Penzance
Luxulyan
Bugle
Roche
St. Columb Major
St. Columb Road
Newquay
Mawgan
Treamble
From Truro
Atlantic Ocean
St. Gennys
Crackington Haven
St. Juliot
Boscastle
Lesnewth
Otterham
OTTERHAM
Warbstow
Tintagel
Trebarwith
Treligga
TRESMEER
Davidstowe
DELABOLE
CAMELFORD
Camelford
St. Teath
Tregadillett
Altarnun
Rough Tor
Brown Willy
Trewint Marsh
Liskeard & Caradon Railway proposal 1884
Rushyford Gate
Sargents Corner
Kilmar Tor
The Cheesering
Liskeard & Caradon Railway
South Caradon
Pentire Point
Port Isaac
Polzeath
St. Minver
Rock
St. Kew
PORT ISAAC ROAD
St. Tudy
St. Breward
ST. KEW HIGHWAY
Wenford Bridge
Trevose Head
Trevone
PADSTOW
St. Merryn
St. Issey
WADEBRIDGE
St. Eval
St. Mabyn
North Cornwall Rly proposed line to Newquay and Truro 1893
Boscarne Jn.
Bodmin (North)
(General)
Ruthern Bridge

INTRODUCTION

The years now leave few memories of the 'North Cornwall', a meandering railway from Halwill Junction in West Devon to the River Camel Estuary at Padstow on the Cornish Coast. Some may recall a West Country Pacific edging its way round Slaughterbridge, by Brown Willy, with two or three coaches from the 11.00am 'Atlantic Coast Express' from Waterloo. Yet few now remember a pair of Adams 0-6-0s struggling up the Carey Valley with a cattle special for Halwill and Exeter. Photographs of recent years show T9 4-4-0s with the Up 'Perishables' at Camelford say, or Tresmeer. Empty platforms, guard looking at his watch. Rabbits for the London or Birmingham markets were a staple in the 1930s, until the myxomatosis of the 1950s. Fish from Padstow once vitalised the line.

Why did the North Cornwall come to exist? Railway politics of the 19th Century offer some clues. The London & South Western's ambitions west of Exeter, the Great Western guarding its territories, local promoters creating proposed lines with some certainty of support from one or both of those Companies. The North Cornwall seems to have made a good bargain with the LSWR and (unusually) maintained its

The Drummond T9 4-4-0s were relative latecomers to the North Cornwall although in later years they came to represent the very essence of motive power on the line. The 70ft 'table at Okehampton makes easy work of turning 30717 which was probably returning to Wadebridge on 14th July 1959. R. C. Riley, www.transporttreasury.co.uk

Below. **30338 is busying itself shunting some Meldon Quarry hoppers around Okehampton on the same day in 1959. R. C. Riley, www.transporttreasury.co.uk**

nominal independence until grouping in 1923. In the background were the railway contractors ever looking for business. How much lobbying occurred will never be known. The bigger contractors still had plenty of work in the 1870s when the North Cornwall was conceived. The great Settle & Carlisle project (Brassey's) was under way for instance, and in Devon the LSWR was forging its competitive way to Plymouth. Here the works were undertaken by lesser names such as Relf. It was he who was awarded the first link from Okehampton westwards to North Cornwall. He completed the Devon & Cornwall Railways (an LSWR protégé) line to Holsworthy, opened in January 1879.

Once the North Cornwall obtained its original Act of Parliament in the 1880s, nobody foresaw it would be nearly twenty years before it was completed. A peculiar situation had arisen at Wadebridge quite early, insofar as the LSWR was already there before

Top. **The N class 2-6-0s were a locomotive which arrived early on the lines to Bude and Padstow the U class not being seen here until 1943/44. Some were rebuilds of the original, and ill-fated, 'River' class 2-6-4Ts and were a rare commodity over the North Cornwall. Nos. 1635, 1638 and 1639 (built as 2-6-0s) and later 1795 were all observed working here at that time and later, in 1958/59, 31790 and 31791 were used sparingly on local turns. 31791 departs for Bude in July 1959. R. C. Riley, www.transporttreasury.co.uk**

Middle. **Mixed goods behind N 2-6-0 31860 in August 1961. The signal box at Meldon Quarry was really a rebuild of a box on the down side of the yard. This 1870s weather boarded cabin was in turn replaced by this brick built box of 1903. A unique feature was the iron grilling put in place during quarry blasting to prevent boulders smashing the cabin windows.**

Bottom. **An N class 2-6-0 heads a mixed train of a Maunsell brake composite, a Maunsell 3rd corridor, an SR parcels/mail van and what appears to be a flat wagon meat container, over Meldon Viaduct with a train for Okehampton in 1963. R. C. Riley, www.transporttreasury.co.uk**

The Southern's highest signal box on the standard gauge. Meldon Junction opened in 1878 as Meldon Loop and was on a lonely and isolated stretch of line near the summit at Sourton. Meldon Viaduct was singled at this time following concerns over its safety and here the signalman is handing the key to the driver of an up DMU.

T9 4-4-0 No.30719 waits patiently for an up train to pass hauled by Battle of Britain class No.34110 66 *Squadron* on a June day in 1960. The provision of extended loops along the line proved most useful in post-War summers when the North Cornwall trains multiplied. R. C. Riley, www.transporttreasury.co.uk

Halwill saw much attaching and detaching moves and would suddenly burst into life when the Padstow or Bude trains came in from either direction. T9 4-4-0 No.30712 arrives from Padstow in August 1958 with a Maunsell 3 coach set. R. C. Riley, www.transporttreasury.co.uk

its North Cornwall satellite arrived. The ancient Bodmin & Wadebridge Railway of 1834 was acquired by the South Western Directors, not quite legally in the Parliamentary sense, in 1845. The GWR was most annoyed, knowing it to be a pawn in the LSWR's designs in West Cornwall. By the time the NCR reached Wadebridge in 1895, however, much of the rancour had disappeared.

The prospect of tourist traffic emerged in the promoters' ideas for the line. Along the North Cornish coast only Newquay and Bude, which were to grow into resorts, actually fronted the Atlantic Ocean. Neither was of any size in the 1880s, the former a mineral outlet and a fishing port, the latter importing coal etc into a tiny harbour, and exporting sea sand inland by a canal. Both had attracted visitors of means, and although such people usually stayed put when on holiday, the germ of present-day restlessness was present. By the late 1890s, with the LSWR at Ilfracombe, Bideford, Bude and Padstow and the GWR at Newquay, the coaching companies, especially the 'North Cornwall' concern (no relation) were carrying several thousand passengers every summer between these places. The LSWR was excursion-minded and in the 1880s was encouraging, even subsidising, coach connections along the coast to view the scenery, and from inland railheads

Ivatt 2-6-2T No.41308 in the bay at Halwill with a goods off the Torrington line on 4th June 1960. The signal is in the off position so that the train can reverse to the run-round loop. Leslie Freeman, www.transporttreasury.co.uk

On Saturday 11th July 1964, the last year of steam on the North Cornwall and through coaches to Waterloo, N class No.31859 brings a Waterloo to Padstow train into Launceston. The signalman walks round to pick up the Tower Hill Tablet and hand the Egloskerry Tablet to the crew. R. A. Lumber.

The 45XX class tanks appeared not only on the Padstow-Wadebridge trains but on services out of Launceston SR station too, along the GWR branch to Plymouth. The GW station had closed in June 1952 requiring these Laira engines to use the SR facilities although they continued to use the GW shed and turntable. On 2nd April 1961 No.5541 is about to leave for Plymouth with a two-coach ex-GWR 'B' set. R. C. Riley, www.transporttreasury.co.uk

where desirable (such as Launceston and Holsworthy).

It is not generally realised how close the railway came to Boscastle and Tintagel, although it would have been improbable for a line to have descended down, except by some fearsome gradients. The lure of the Arthurian legends was fanned in the LSWR advertising – the LSWR and the Southern after it went even further and named a whole class of engines after the Knights of the Round Table. Port Isaac beckoned at a 'Road' station, but beaches and cliffs were nearer to Padstow at Rock, over the water, and Harlyn Bay or Trevone.

The jewels in the North Cornwall crown were undoubtedly Launceston and Wadebridge, agriculture centres; market towns and exporters of cattle, sheep and pigs. Wadebridge was also a small port which was rail-served. Bodmin, inland and already connected by the B&WR, replaced Launceston as the County Town but continued to hold the Assizes and its attendant gaol, together with the Country Asylum. A line from Boscarne Junction and Bodmin GWR to Bodmin Road, opened in 1888, could also be regarded as a potential link to the North Cornwall. Camelford town, rather in decline since the 1832 Reform Act abolished its two Parliamentary seats, nevertheless contributed revenue, though the station was some miles to the east. The line did go through Delabole (Pengelly village) and here lay the huge defile of the slate quarry, the result of joining several

With hardly a tree in the landscape, which directly faces the Atlantic Ocean, the North Cornwall breasted the summit at Trewanion, 860 feet above sea-level. The 1.00pm Padstow to Okehampton had come up over from Camelford and was coasting into Otterham behind N class No.31859 on a hot August afternoon in 1964. The train comprises Southern 4 wheel luggage van (PMV) to Diagram 3103, BR Mk1 bogie van (GUV to Diagram 811 which brought the national newspapers and is now being returned to Clapham Junction), Bulleid Open Saloon Third to Diagram 2017 (number series 1462-1506) and Bulleid 'loose' Brake Composite to Diagram 2406 (number series 6713-6752). P. W. Gray.

West Country Pacific No.34030 *Watersmeet* brings the Padstow portion of the Friday 11am ACE into Otterham on 15th July 1960. The leading vehicle is one of the Diagram 2668 Kitchen and Buffet Cars which were rebuilt from the original Diagram 2663 'pub' design in 1959/60 (not in use) for the next day's Padstow up ACE working. The second is a Diagram 2665 Composite Restaurant Car rebuilt from the original Diagram 2664 'pub' design in 1950/51. The bowler hatted Inspector Smith from Exmouth Junction is on the footplate of T9 No.30719 waiting to leave the up loop with the 3.13pm Padstow 'Perishables'. The wagons in the yard indicate the considerable fertiliser traffic to selected North Cornwall stations at this time. R. C. Riley, www.transporttreasury.co.uk

T9 4-4-0 No.30719 at Camelford with the all stations 9.56am from Okehampton, arriving at Padstow at 12.14pm. The train called at Halwill at 10.23am (where the rear two coaches were detached) and continued to Bude. Behind the loco are a parcel/mail van and a pair of Bulleid and Maunsell corridor coaches. R. C. Riley, www.transporttreasury.co.uk

All quiet at St. Kew Highway on a summer's day in 1961. It is debatable whether many people ever used this station; certainly very few did in later years. St. Kew village was about two miles away, as the crow flies, St. Mabyn was to the south along narrow twisting lanes and over to the east St. Trudy was again over two miles away.

together in the 1830s. Hitherto slates had been carried to Port Gaverne and Port Isaac by cart. The railway soon captured this traffic and expansion followed, maintained until the 1930s. The rest of the wayside stations promoted only modest business, with the exception of the rabbit-meat trade which increased tremendously in the 1920s, especially at Tresmeer and Otterham.

As found in many rural backwaters the two World Wars suddenly brought a lot of Government business to some unknown places. Thus Tower Hill, so quiet in the early 1920s that its loop was removed, burst into life again in 1943, with facilities restored, to handle ammunition trains in a new siding. Otterham yard, up on the summit and exposed to the Atlantic gales, hummed with activity following the opening of an airfield on Davidstow Moor to the south. Such activity was relatively short-lived, an artificial rise in fortune. Motor transport on the roads, not a real menace to rail in this part of the country until the 1950s, nevertheless established itself from the 1920s. Particularly the bus companies but the Southern Railway, by virtue of legislation in 1928, could buy into the local companies and so gain some control. It was surprising that the Southern Railway gave as much attention to the Devon and Cornwall

After Nationalisation in 1948 several of the Bodmin Road services were extended from Wadebridge down to Padstow. Hauling a GWR 'B' set 45XX tank 4568 arrives at Wadebridge in the evening sun. R. E. Vincent, www.transporttreasury.co.uk

The SR intended to use more powerful locomotives on the lines west of Exeter from the 1940s. Up to 1939 pairs of 4-4-0s hauled the heaviest holiday trains on the North Cornwall and Bude lines, but after 1945 Bulleid Pacifics could handle up to eight coaches with ease on the Devon and Cornish gradients. The battered headboard would have been attached at Exeter Central for the run to Padstow behind 34081 *92 Squadron* with its mixed train of Maunsell and Bulleid coaches. A. E. Bennett, www.transporttreasury.co.uk

lines as it did. One good reason was that a line stretching for 250 miles could generate revenue by distance alone. Worthwhile then to accentuate the less populated end for holiday traffic. So attention came in the form of, firstly, publicity for the resorts and comfortable corridor coaching stock. Secondly, most of the track was relaid in the 1930s, well in time for the increasingly heavy trains that did come, reaching a peak in 1939 (and again in the 1950s). One detects the hand of Sir Herbert Walker, the General Manager of the SR, preoccupied as he was with electrification of London routes at that time. After the contortion of traffic patterns in World War Two, when the lengthy 'Atlantic Coast Express' trains gave way to troop specials (even longer on many occasions!) there were great expectations for holidaymakers in 1946. The introduction of the 'West Country' light 4-6-2s in 1945 seemed to underline the restoration of trains, especially for North Cornwall and Bude. The names given to these Pacifics included 'Launceston', 'Wadebridge' and 'Padstow', 'Camelford'; even 'Rough Tor' came later. Travel on the 'Atlantic Coast', already famous since 1925 (although its predecessor the 'North Cornwall & Bude Express' started in 1907) again became the means of reaching Tintagel and Boscastle, the delights of Port Isaac, St Enodoc and Polzeath, and down to Padstow. John Betjeman was devoted to this part of the county and the 'North Cornwall' is reflected in one of his poems. The ACE, non-stop at times from Exeter to Halwill, and missing out the wayside stations, became more 'express' and enjoyed a restaurant car all the way to Padstow.

The winter months resulted in thinner receipts, depending on just local travel apart from the daily through coaches to London. The North Cornwall, though, provided a valuable communication into Wadebridge, Launceston, up to Okehampton, the shops and theatres in Exeter, even to Bideford over the lately-built Halwill to Torrington branch. Passengers were induced to go to Plymouth, via Okehampton, a lengthy detour compared with changing on to the GWR at Launceston. Both ways fell prey to the buses as they went more directly, not only the National Omnibuses but smaller concerns such as Blakes of Delabole, which ran almost daily into Plymouth. The Royal Blue long distance coaches expanded their services after 1950 and certainly shared the cream of the summer months by terminating at Bude and Polzeath.

In 1950, following nationalisation of the Southern Railway (in 1948) the commercial and civil engineering concerns passed to the Western Region of the new British Railways. The SR pattern of train services was maintained, passenger and goods, fed through Salisbury from Waterloo and Nine Elms, connected to the Midlands by the old Somerset & Dorset Joint Line via Templecombe and serviced by the yards and engine shed at Exmouth Junction. It seemed to be lasting for ever – the 'Woolworth' 2-6-0s plodding the length of the North Cornwall, shunting wagons at Halwill; the tang of tarpaulins, dust and straw in the goods yards, or the signalman/porter calling out 'Ot'tram' as the T9 and its train drew in from the Tresmeer in the dusk of a winter evening.

But the railway was secretly bleeding. Successive management changes and direction under nationalisation, rising costs against falling revenues, and misguided (as it turned out) understanding by the staff that they were providing a 'service' to the public, was leading to the Beeching era in the early 1960s. The feeding of trunk lines by branches and secondary lines was not part of the philosophy of the British Railways of the 1960s. When the 'Report' was published in 1963, sure

If Dugald Drummond, Chief Mechanical Engineer in the 1900s had got his way the three Beattie Well Tanks would have been scrapped and a piece of railway history lost forever. No suitable replacements were found so the trio were spared the torch and repaired to continue their work at Wadebridge and along the branch to Wenford. A. E. Bennett, The Transport Treasury.

T9 4-4-0 No.30709 arrives at Wadebridge from Padstow with a train consisting of an SR parcels/mail van and a pair of Maunsell and Bulleid coaches. Leslie Freeman, www.transporttreasury.co.uk

T9 in June 1960. 30338 is propelling the 12.58 train to Waterloo into the platform at Padstow. Leslie Freeman, www.transporttreasury.co.uk

enough, the North Cornwall was shown to be superfluous. BR put up its proposals for closure in 1964.

Road transport in the shape of the private car, the heavy lorry (but not yet the long distance 'juggernaut') and, to a lesser extent the bus, were already drawing off traffic from rail. The North Cornwall line meandering through Ashwater and St Kew Highway, its steam-hauled trains taking two hours to cover the sixty miles Okehampton-Padstow, already seemed an anachronism. Even the introduction of diesel railcars in 1965 did little to enhance the 'run down' atmosphere posed by rusty sidings and disheartened staff. The Western Region had full control from 1963. The severance of the SR's Devon and Cornwall network from Waterloo in September 1964 upset a long tradition. Henceforth Paddington became the London-traveller's destination, though it is fair to say there occurred some remarkable timesaving to Bude and Launceston by reason of the faster Paddington-Exeter trains.

At this time, 1964, the freight service was already slated for withdrawal. BR needed no approval to curtail or close down this operation. All goods trains ceased to run from 7 September 1964 despite appeals from local authorities. Launceston and Wadebridge were retained as railheads; they were otherwise connected than to the North Cornwall.

A stay of execution for the duration of the summer of 1966 only prolonged the inevitable date of passenger closure which duly took place on and from 3 October. The younger enthusiasts gave what cheer they could to the final day's services. The older generation sadly bought last tickets and thronged the trains. As always on these occasions, the last extinguishing of lamps, the locking of gates and doors and the final replacement of the single-line tokens in their machines, underlined the awful melancholy of those railway closedowns of the Beeching years.

In June 1960 a Drummond T9 4-4-0 sits well within the 70ft diameter turntable provided by the SR at Padstow in 1947 for the West Country Pacifics. Leslie Freeman, www.transporttreasury.co.uk

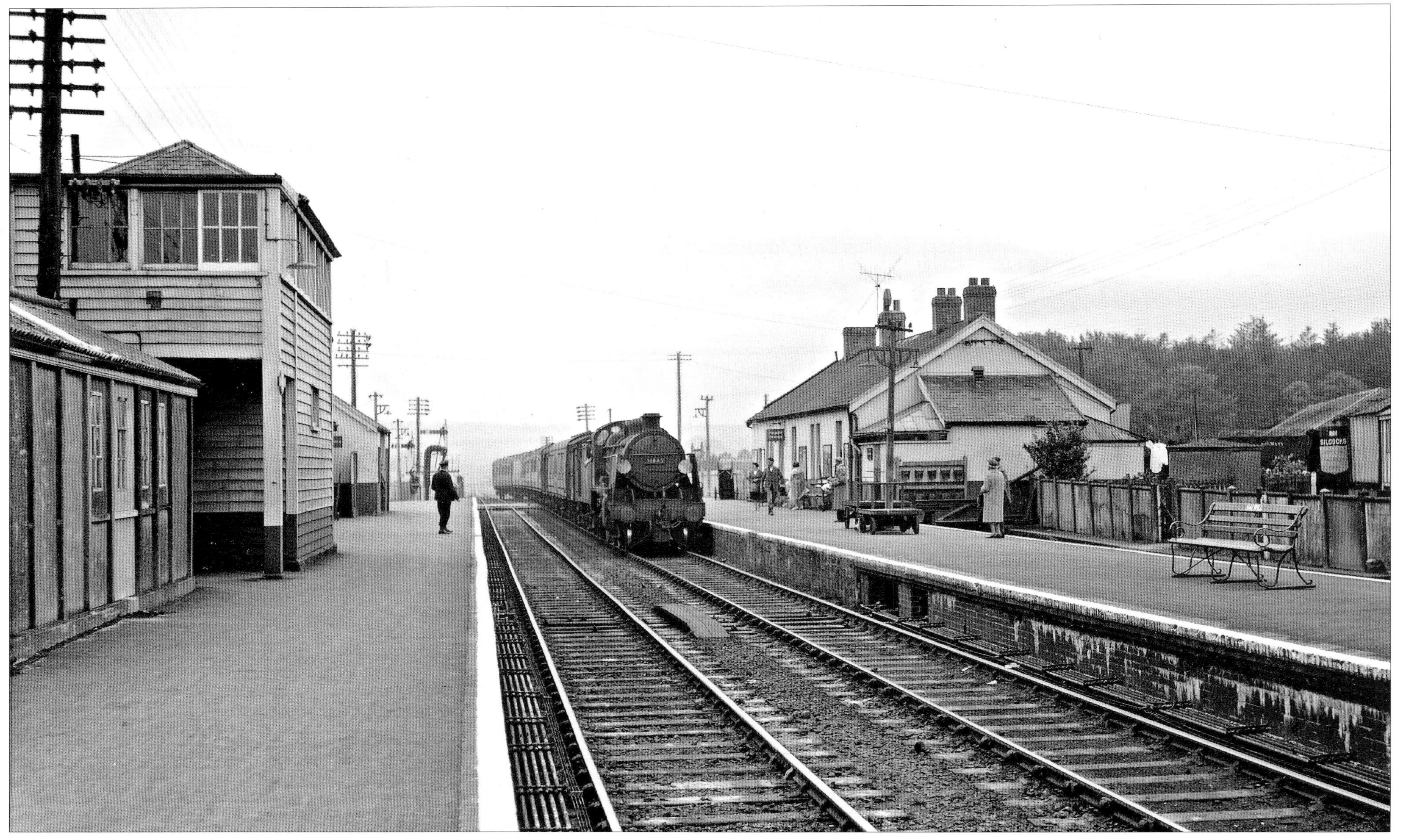

N class 2-6-0 No.31843 arrives at Halwill from Okehampton in August 1962. The extension to the signal box, to house the tablet apparatus for the Torrington line and the tablet machines for Hole, Dunsland Cross, Ashwater and Ashbury, can be seen clearly supported on wooden columns. R. C. Riley, www.transporttreasury.co.uk

Chapter One
THE LSWR IN WEST DEVON AND NORTH CORNWALL

The London & South Western Railway might well have arrived in Truro and Falmouth in the 1840s, such was the ambition, though at the time it was no nearer than Salisbury and Dorchester. Two projects were floated in 1845; one from Exeter via Okehampton, Launceston and Bodmin and the other, the nascent Cornwall Railway extending from the authorised South Devon Railway at Plymouth, via Liskeard to Falmouth. Neither came to pass in 1845, but the Cornwall Railway Bill succeeded in 1846. It was at this juncture that the Bodmin and Wadebridge was acquired by the LSWR directors, without Parliamentary sanction. The Cornwall and Devon Central Railway, as it was called, had been surveyed by the LSWR's engineer, Joseph Locke, though use of the B&WR in its existing form would have presented quite a problem. It was, however, significant that the Cornwall railway could be required to lay an additional rail to their broad gauge (7ft 0¼in) to Falmouth if a narrow gauge should join it at Truro. Another LSWR foothold, if minor, was gained at Plymouth when the company subscribed to the Sutton Harbour improvement works.

Building railways in Cornwall proved difficult. The Cornwall Railway, for instance, needed 42 viaducts en route to Falmouth. The proposed 'central route' would not have been an exception. The LSWR was behind a new Launceston, Bodmin and Wadebridge Junction Railway proposal in 1864. This involved a 630-yard tunnel between the Kensey and Inny valleys near Pipers Pool and a route through Camelford to join the B&WR's Wenford Branch. Turning itself into the 'Central Cornwall Railway' the following year, there was an eye on Falmouth again. Access to Truro would be via the B&W's Ruthernbridge Branch. Acts of Parliament were obtained in 1864 and 1865, but there was trouble arising from the latent agreement with the GWR over territorial expansions and the project was abandoned in 1871.

The region traversed eventually by the North Cornwall Railway had not escaped previous speculation. As far back as 1836 a dubious 'Launceston & Victoria Railway' was aimed at Tremoutha Haven in St Gennys Parish on the North Coast. A 'Plymouth and North Cornwall Railway' would have followed a circuitous route through Five Lanes, Davidstow (with a 946-yard

The Devon and Cornwall Railway's terminus at Holsworthy in 1882. The station was laid out as a future passing place on a through route to Bude or Wadebridge, but in the event the line was extended to the former in 1898. Beyer Peacock 4-4-0T No.320 with 4 or 6-wheel coaches is flanked by her driver and fireman, whilst the Station Master is surrounded by various staff and townsfolk. Mrs. G. Kendall.

Okehampton's station buildings have survived many years of closure, but not the LSWR's 1870 pattern signal box on the down side, which was demolished after the opening of the new one on the up side in 1935. The Station Master, in frock coat, his clerks and serge-uniformed platform staff pose for posterity in the period before 1914. Spiers & Pond held the general contract to run the LSWR's refreshment rooms for many years.

tunnel) to Delabole and Rock, opposite Padstow. After the demise of the LB&WJR two further lines were enabled by legislation in 1873. These were the Bodmin & Wadebridge & Delabole Railway via Wenford, and the Cornwall Mineral & Bodmin & Wadebridge Junction via Ruthernbridge. Both failed to materialise.

In 1860 the LSWR was at Exeter. After a foray with the Bristol & Exeter Railway, it succeeded in leasing the Exeter & Crediton Railway, linking to it through Exeter St Davids by narrow gauge from 1 February 1862. This Crediton line and a lease in 1862 of the North Devon Railway to Barnstaple provided a springboard for fresh incursions into West Devon, Plymouth and Cornwall. An Okehampton Railway Company obtained its Act in 1862 to build from Coleford near Yeoford, through North Tawton to that town.

By an Act dated 29 June 1865 the Okehampton Railway, now renamed the 'Devon & Cornwall Railway' was enabled to build from Sampford Courtenay to Bude. Another Act in 1867 would have made a line to Torrington and Bude, via Hatherleigh. Yet again, in 1873, an extensive proposal to go all the way to Wadebridge was contained in an Act signed on 7 July. One of several lines authorised under the Act was that from Meldon Junction, west of Okehampton, to Holsworthy. This was the limb from which sprang the North Cornwall Railway extensions of the 1890s. Another proposed Wadebridge line from Holsworthy, via North Tamerton (with a branch thence to Bude) and Camelford to Wenford Bridge was never built.

The nominally independent Devon & Cornwall Company's immediate role in the 1870s was to front the LSWR's attack on Plymouth, Stonehouse and Devonport. By way of a Lidford (sic) extension and a junction with the South Devon Railway's branch through Tavistock to Marsh Mills, South Western trains would enter the 'Three Towns' on mixed gauge rails in 1876. An important agreement in April 1874 empowered the LSWR to work the D&CR, to purchase lines as they were built and, more importantly perhaps, to decide what would be built. Thus the Holsworthy Branch, opened on 20 January 1879, was the only survivor of the 1873 authorisation.

Construction and Opening Okehampton, Meldon Junction and Holsworthy

The main line to Plymouth branched off from the North Devon line at Coleford Junction, west of Yeoford. On the opening to North Tawton in 1865 a single line ran next to the North Devon from Yeoford to Coleford, continuing on to 'Okehampton Road' (later Sampford Courtenay) in January 1867. Okehampton itself was reached in 1871, the public train service starting on 3 October. Already, as has been noted, an extension to 'Lidford' was authorised in 1863 but not until 1869 did contractor R.T. Relf start work beyond Okehampton. Meanwhile the temporary terminus was laid out in anticipation as a through station with two platforms. The site had to be excavated and earthworks left little room for expansion. A goods yard was established on the down side and quarrying provided stone for the new extension westward. The LSWR used large boulders in the sub-formations of their track. In 1879 a bay platform was established on the south side of the Down platform for the new Holsworthy trains.

The single line to Lydford was opened on 12 October 1874, under Devon & Cornwall Railway auspices. With running powers and a narrow gauge rail laid, the LSWR (working the D&CR) could enter Plymouth, though it was not until 17 May 1876 when the first South Western train arrived there. Following this opening, doubling from Coleford Junction was undertaken reaching Okehampton on 9 January 1879, along with the portion thence to Meldon Viaduct (east end) on the same day.

The massive viaduct, yet rather spindly in appearance when viewed from afar, was constructed during 1873-74 of Hughes wrought iron girders on piers of cast iron cylinders set in granite blocks. There was subsequent movement in these cylinders at the embanked ends and remedial walling was put in. Major General Hutchinson inspected the original viaduct in 1874, and again the widened structure, in

On 2nd August 1945 S11 class No.404 stands on the original 50ft turntable at Okehampton. She was one of ten in the class and had lately been loaned to the LMS (1941-44), hence the 21A Saltley code. Two S11s were allocated to Wadebridge pre-1914 and again in the 1920s to work the heavier trains from and to Exeter, and were seen on the Bude and Padstow Perishables in the 1930s. H. C. Casserley, courtesy R. M. Casserley.

The Drummond T9 4-4-0s will always be associated with the Bude and North Cornwall lines. On a hot summer day in July 1960 30719 crosses Meldon Viaduct with the 1.00pm from Okehampton. R. C. Riley, www.transporttreasury.co.uk

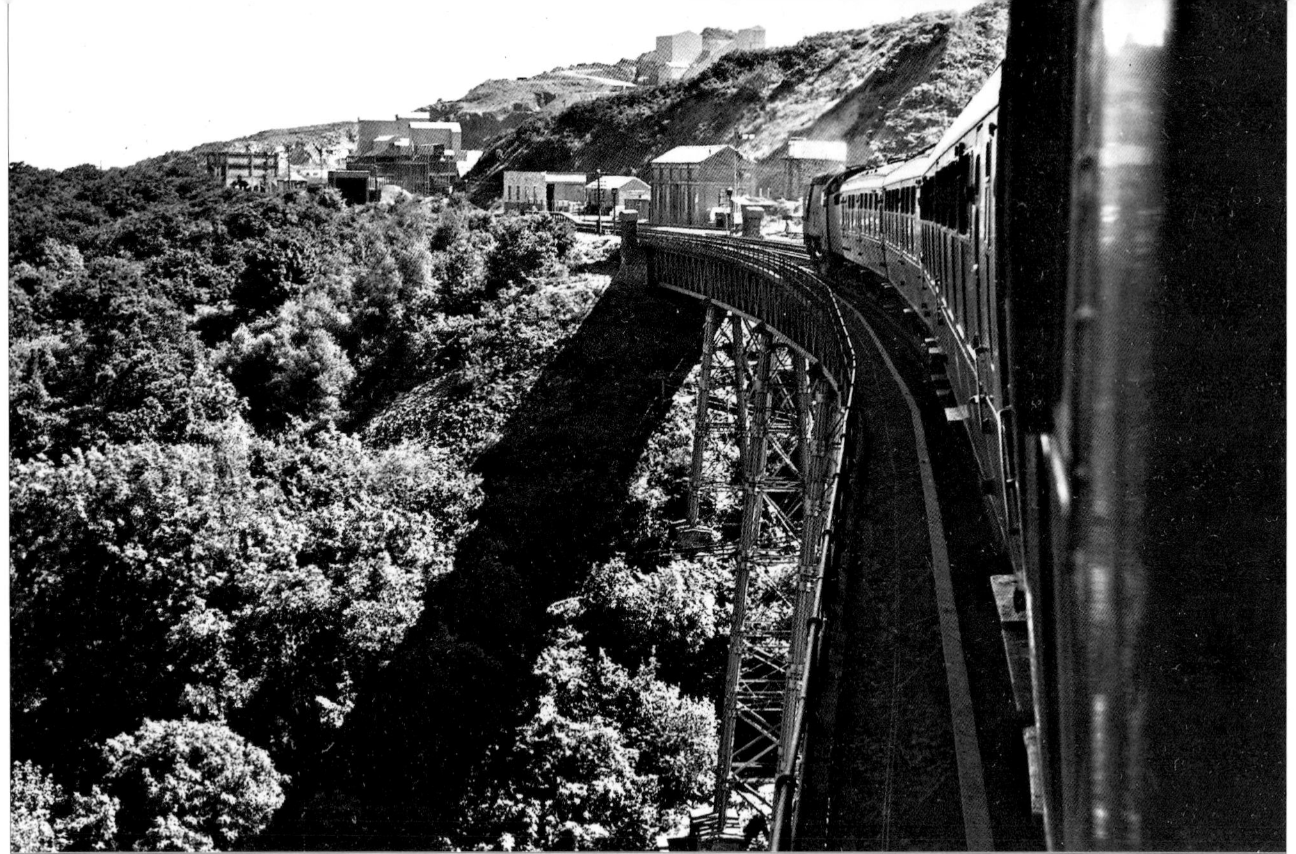

An unidentified Pacific coasts down the gradient from Meldon Junction over the spectacular Meldon Viaduct. Officially listed somewhat anonymously as Bridge No.613, the viaduct had been constructed in two parts. The older up side originated from the opening of the line in 1874 and was constructed in cast and wrought iron with six 85½ foot trusses supported on lattice trestles, the tallest being 120 feet. The line was doubled in 1879 and so was the viaduct, the new part more or less following the same construction and design as the earlier structure.

September 1879. It seems that the second structure (for the Up line) was welcomed by all parties as it was interlaced with the first. It may be remembered that the Tay Bridge at Dundee, a structure not entirely dissimilar to Meldon, later collapsed in a gale on 28 December 1879. The leg struts were connected into enlarged bases and steel was used this time. At the top the piers were connected with the originals, with cross-bracing 18ft below the carrying girders. Wheel timbers were placed directly above each girder and the top deck planked in from side to side. Major General Hutchinson ordered a test load of moving engines (at speed) and deflections of little more than a quarter of an inch were found. The final structure was of six spans of 85ft 6in and they were between 120 and 140 feet above ground. After a period of six weeks while the new structure served as the single line (from a temporary single box at the east end), the double line became available as from 1 November 1879. At present Meldon Viaduct is a 'listed' structure, though the rails now end at the Quarry.

In the meantime a junction on the single line at Meldon was formed for the new Holsworthy Branch at the 200 MP (to be). Relf, following completion of the Lydford extension, took up the Holsworthy contract, starting in August 1875. Extensive embankments had to be raised to carry the line across Bowerland on reversing 15-chain curves. It then climbed around the top of Thorndon Down and south of Venn Down before reaching Ashbury, the site of the only intermediate station to Beaworthy. The road from Bratton Clovelly to Ashbury village and North Lew occupied a gated level crossing at Venndown Gate. The long embankment thence to Broadbury can still be seen today from the adjacent road. Beyond Ashbury the line snaked on a falling gradient on 30 and 40 chain curves past Patchacott and Madworthy hamlets before emerging below Henderbarrow in sight of Beaworthy, or Halwill Junction as it eventually became. It then straightened for a mile to Beaworthy (209¾ MP). Here the railway was 600ft above sea level, having dropped 300 since Meldon. Beaworthy was equipped with a simple layout – crossing loop, two platforms, three sidings and a signal box – similar to the other two stations at Ashbury and Dunsland Cross. Holsworthy, the terminus, was more substantial. It had two platforms, again in anticipation of a future extension to Bude (not to come for 19 years!) and a handsome station house with a side office and large goods shed. Earthworks between Beaworthy and Holsworthy were considerable below Dunsland Cross and an eight span stone-built viaduct was necessary just east of Holsworthy. The total length of this branch was 17 miles and 64 chains.

The new line was ready in January 1879. Colonel Yolland, R.E. of the Railway Inspectorate travelled over it on the 5th. He stated in his report that he could recommend opening subject to certain omissions being rectified. He said the rails used were 75lb to the yard (double headed) and laid in cast iron chairs on Memel sleepers, averaging 2ft 8in centres. Interestingly the points were steel, only just being adopted in the 1870s. Turntables had been installed at Okehampton and Holsworthy. There were two level crossings, at Venn and Beaworthy. There were signal boxes at all four stations, each with 10 levers and the method of 'Absolute' Block by signal and telegraph was in force. Train Staff and Ticket was provided on only two sections, Meldon Junction to Beaworthy and Beaworthy to Holsworthy. (Trains were crossing at Ashbury in 1880, so it must be assumed that four Staff sections had then been introduced). Signalling was still somewhat primitive in the late 1870s, although locking frames and block telegraph working were now accepted for new passenger lines. Colonel Yolland had found only disc signals at the facing points. Semaphores should be erected, he said, so that drivers could see signals as far away as possible.

Beaworthy was renamed Halwill & Beaworthy in July 1879. It later became Halwill Junction, in March 1887, and Halwill (for Beaworthy) in 1923. Although agriculture had entered a depression in the late 1870s after a succession of wet summers and growing imports of North American corn, the railway was regarded as an encouragement for the future. Local landowners – Lord Stanhope, Lord Clinton and Mr W.J. Harris (of Halwill Manor) actually gave land for it. Many farmers were their tenants. Opening day was 20 January 1879 and Holsworthy was bedecked with festoons of evergreens and coloured streamers, not forgetting a triumphal arch in Chapel Street. The Directors of the LSWR and D&CR arrived at 11.45am in a saloon attached to the first down train. After an address by the Rail Committee Chairman, Dr Ash, a procession formed up and paraded through the town to the accompaniment of the Launceston, Bideford and Royal Marines Light Infantry bands. To a luncheon given in the Edgington Marquee were invited Lord and Lady Stanhope, two MPs, the Mayors of seven Devon towns, the Sheriff of Devon and the Chief Constable of Devon. R.H. Dutton, the LSWR Chairman said '...that the bracken, heather and gorse would disappear, and that agriculture would improve everywhere'. In due course the railway did indeed aid local agriculture, though not so much arable farming as beef herding. This increased in the late 1890s and the line supplied dealers to the east with store cattle and for slaughtering. Holsworthy itself gained a measurable prosperity through this, and a sizeable community subsequently grew in the vicinity of Halwill Junction. The down service in 1880 was five trains including one (the 9.10am from Okehampton) that was 'mixed' goods and passenger. The up service had two such 'mixed' with three passenger trains.

N class 2-6-0 No. 31857 heads a holiday extra train to Wadebridge in 1960 past Meldon Quarry. The resident works shunter DS3152 (ex-272, class G6 and renumbered in 1950) is on the right. Peter Tatlow.

The 1879 Devon & Cornwall station building at Halwill Junction is largely unaltered in 1963. Behind are the 1930s structures – a galvanised iron warehouse for Silcocks and a concrete version for the use of Bibbys – indicating an extensive traffic in cattle feeds and agricultural fertilisers which developed from that decade. Exmouth Junction's concrete products appear in the form of Bibby's traders store, lamp posts and informative name board. Peter Paye.

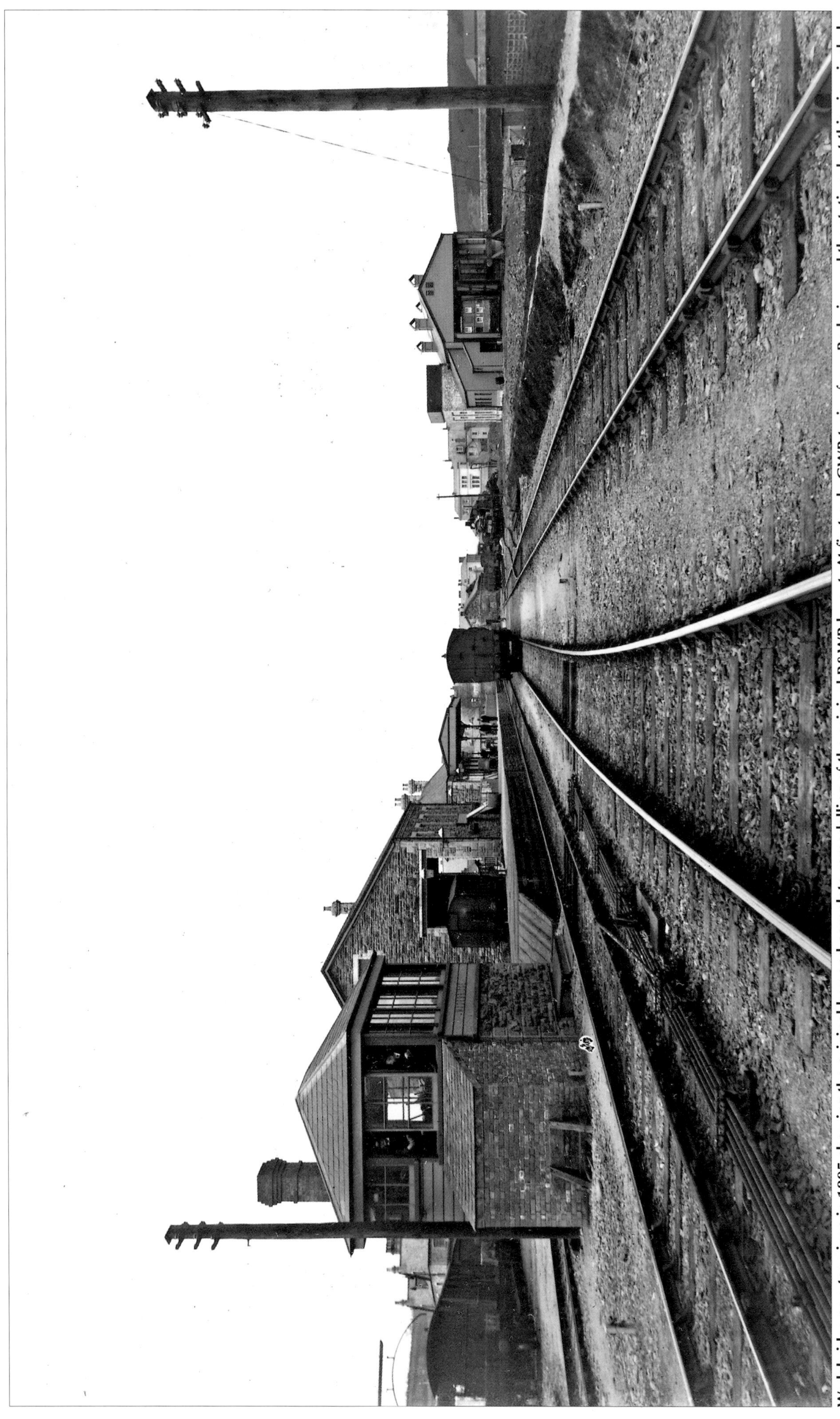

Wadebridge as a terminus in 1895 showing the original box and complete remodelling of the original B&WR layout. At first only GWR trains from Bodmin used the station, but this view includes the new LSWR 1895 engine shed (right). Access was from the turntable only, near the class 460 4-4-0 (centre). A run-round loop (with vehicle) is flanked to its right by the access siding to the quay. The station was remodelled again in 1899 for the Padstow extension.

Chapter Two
CONSTRUCTION OF THE NORTH CORNWALL RAILWAY

That the LSWR would back a route toward Launceston and Wadebridge seemed unquestionable – though going into Truro, as the NCR promoters had in mind, would obviously antagonise the GWR. Perhaps the choice of a Padstow terminus underlined this. In 1881 to the accompaniment of church bells and the local band a committee of Padstonians emerged from their meeting room offering to contribute to funds toward a survey of a line from Halwill to Padstow. Within a few months committees were set up at Wadebridge, Camelford and Launceston. Messrs Gilbraith and Church (the LSWR's Consulting Engineers) were engaged to find a suitable route. There seemed to be no argument about bringing a line down the Carey Valley from Halwill to Launceston, but the Launceston committee had designs on a station up in the town. They were told it would have to be in a tunnel in that case – the line emerging at Penygillam! Their desire for a route through Holloway Cross (Polyphant) and the Inny Valley to Davidstow was also turned down. The Padstow committee thought up an inland route from Wadebridge, via St Issey but as an extensive 1,000 yard tunnel at Tregella would be needed, the waterside route by the Camel was adhered to. It seems that the consultants, encouraged by the LSWR, were looking for an uncomplicated route with a ruling gradient of 1 in 73 and curves not generally less than 30 chains radius, and without long tunnels and viaducts.

Launceston had lost the Cornish Assizes to Bodmin in 1838 and the ancient Borough (with two seats in Parliament until 1832) was declining. Politics had played a strong part in bringing the broad gauge branch from Plymouth and Tavistock into the town in 1865. Local landowners, including the Dukes of Bedford and Northumberland, were won over to the railway cause. Such a roundabout route to Exeter and London and the need to tranship goods between the narrow and broad gauges at Lydford naturally irritated the natives of Launceston. A request for a narrow gauge rail from Lydford to Launceston was made to the GWR, but turned down. Hence the prospect of a narrow gauge line from Halwill was very encouraging. The Liberal Party cause was strong in North Cornwall. It stemmed from the Methodist Church (not then unified, but in various sects such as Wesleyans, Bible Christians and the 'Bryanites'). While Launceston was in the 'pocket' of the Duke of Northumberland until 1885 and usually returned a Conservative member, a Liberal invariably sat for 'Cornwall North'. Launceston, Camelford and Wadebridge were (and are) the political centres. A North Cornwall Railway would connect them nicely, and an extension to Truro, soon to become a 'city' and County Town in place of Bodmin even better.

Camelford was isolated and less important since it lost its two members

Connecting from the 1.00pm Waterloo to Plymouth, the 5.51pm Okehampton bowls along with two P Sets, one for Padstow and the other for Bude, approaching Maddaford Moor Halt on 8th May 196. After 62 years of service, long-term resident of Exmouth Junction shed T9 30709 was finally withdrawn in July 1961. As with the majority of the class running on the North Cornwall it is of the narrow cab/splasher variety, running with a 4,000 gallon watercart tender and early BR crest. Set 178, leading, comprised Diagram D2401 Brake Composite 6666 and Diagram D2113 Brake Third (Second) 2836. Second set unknown but is also a Maunsell P-Set. S. C. Nash.

Top. **In 1926 the M7 class 0-4-4Ts came to the Bude branch, released from the electrification of London suburban services. No. E35 is in the bay at Halwill waiting to back on to the rear pair of coaches of the Padstow train on the left. 460 class 4-4-0 No. E0417 is the engine there, while another 460, with square cab spectacles, waits in the yard. The latter is Barnstaple's No. E0473 which has arrived from the newly opened Torrington line, and has turned on the small turntable near the loan wagon in the distance. Beyond is the new police house under construction, indicating the growing importance of Halwill as a local centre as a result of the railway's arrival. The date is 26th June 1926. H. C. Casserley, courtesy R. M. Casserley.**

Middle. **T9 4-4-0 No. 719 pauses briefly at Halwill with a train for Bude. Note the signalman peering out of the signal box extension constructed in 1925 for the arrival of the Torrington line.**

Bottom. **An early view of Halwill Junction, probably around 1908. The signal box is in its original condition as is the Devon and Cornwall station building on the down side. A single bogie coach stands in the bay and may be the one for the 'regrators' (dairy product buyers) for attachment to Launceston trains on market days.**

of Parliament in 1832. The population numbers stayed the same for years, but its market and shops, and position on the main road to Wadebridge kept it fairly prosperous. Also it had its share of benefactors, like the Duke of Bedford (the town hall) and James Smith (a school).

Wadebridge (and Egloshayle) grew up around the medieval 14-arch bridge

An Adams class 395 0-6-0 waits at Halwill Junction's up platform about 1905, with a goods train for Okehampton. The nameboard shows Halwill & Beaworthy although it had been renamed in 1886. No. 442 was renumbered 0442 in 1907, 3442 in the 1930s and lasted until 1957 (latterly as BR No. 30578). The class shared goods workings with the Jubilee 0-4-2s until the First World War, but one of them could still be seen at Okehampton up to the 1950s, and occasionally with engineer's trains on the North Cornwall or Bude lines.

over the Camel. Coastal shipping could reach the quay, which was served by the B&WR. Again, the market drew numerous farmers into the town and regular imports of coal and merchandise enabled Wadebridge's population to rise considerably in the 19th century. There were several foundries and manufacturers as well, supplying local needs.

Padstow presented a quite different scene. Intensely proud, its fierce fishing and seagoing population dated from a borough period in the 16th century. Strangely the port was in better communication with Canada than perhaps London, through its connection with Nova Scotia and Prince Edward Island and it was an emigrant port to those colonies in the 1840s and 1850s. Along the North Coast of Cornwall, Padstow offered the only reasonably accessible harbour, though potentially dangerous due to the Doom Bar across the mouth of the Camel. At the time of promotion in 1882, the fishing was a local endeavour, but by the opening of the NCR in 1899 the scene was changing. Brixham men had been exploiting the North Coast, though taking their catches elsewhere. In the mid-1890s, however, East Coast of England sailing trawlers had appeared. Already fish was being carted to the Wadebridge railhead (via the GWR) and in 1899 the LSWR started express services from Padstow. The extensive works started by the Padstow Harbour Commissioners, then taken over and largely financed by the LSWR, will be described.

Apart from the final five miles to Padstow which hugged the south side of the wide Camel estuary, the chosen route for the North Cornwall Railway commenced and ended in sylvan valleys, in reality almost half in such surrounds. The remainder traversed the almost treeless uplands above the 300ft contour from Egloskerry to Port Isaac Road. It would there skirt the northern edge of Bodmin Moor, not closely, except where an outlier extended into Otterham and Davidstow Parishes, reaching 1,000ft above sea level at Hendraburnick. Just below here trains in the future crawled over the line's 860ft summit at Otterham. Yet only three miles away to the north-west the surging Atlantic Ocean spends itself against the cliffs at Boscastle. The Moor with its two prominent tors, Brown Willy (1,375ft) and Rough Tor (1,312ft) lies only a few miles to the east. Its granite mass and peaty bogs contrast with the Upper Devonian rock of which Delabole slate quarry is an outcrop, with possibilities of mineral extraction such as copper, lead etc. The land is quite

An Edwardian view of Hawill Junction from the down end. On the left can be seen the Junction Inn and on the right, nearest the camera, the slaughterhouse.

Top. **For the first few years of the newly opened Torrington-Halwill line, Barnstaple supplied elderly Adams 460 class 4-4-0s Here, No. E0470 with ex-rail motor coach, waits in the bay on 6 August 1926. The LSWR fresh meat vans are alongside the wooden slaughterhouse.**

Middle. **Adams A12 class 0-4-2 No. E643, built in 1893, prepares to depart from Halwill with the 5.48pm Okehampton – Padstow train on 4th August 1928. Ken Nunn Collection, LCGB**

Bottom. **Halwill station in 1931 from the Torrington bay. The North Devon & Cornwall Junction Light Railway had arrived in 1925 and terminated in a self contained part of the station layout. It had its own short bay and a run-round loop controlled by a ground frame. Thus the branch to Torrington could literally work independently from the North Cornwall and Bude lines.**

different again from Halwill, through Launceston to Egloskerry where the Middle Culm Measures project from West Devon. Here the NCR would share the Carey and Kensey valleys draining into the Tamar at Launceston. The countryside was given over to grassland, hence cattle raising, thereby contributing importantly to the LSWR's and SR's coffers in due course. In the 1880s farms existed at near-subsistence levels, with oats and barley grown to feed livestock. Sea sand obtainable from the Camel estuary, and Bude, was spread on fields as a dressing. It was considered that the NCR might carry 65,000 tons a year producing a revenue of £5,000. From Bude, a canal opened in 1823 distributed sand almost as far as Launceston and the B&WR was built largely for this purpose. Wheat was grown in the area below Port Isaac at this time, but increasing imports from North America discouraged farmers from this crop.

Leaving aside the possibilities of extending to Newquay and Truro (a distinct option in the early 1890s) what other prospects were there of actually opening a railway across the apparently unpromising and thinly populated countryside between the four principal towns? Delabole slate quarry, for one, with its 1880s production of about 1,400 tons a year, but estimated to rise to 20,000. At that time lead and silver mining adventures occurred in the St Teath area, even for manganese ore near Launceston. Then there was the potential tourist and holiday trade which, in the end, would become the seasonal mainstay of the North Cornwall line. Already the coach companies were feeding the established rail terminals at Bideford, Holsworthy, Launceston and Newquay and serving Bude, Boscastle and Tintagel along the coast. The attractions of Polzeath,

A destructive runaway in February 1905 at Halwill Junction. A goods train coming down from Ashwater became parted, the rear portion crashing into the front near the crossing gates. A pig sty (on the left) was demolished and the wagons spread over the track.

Trevone, Harlyn Bay and Mawgan Porth also beckoned.

While the NCR's promotion materialised another scheme was launched to connect Padstow, this time to the south. The Mid-Cornwall Railway was proposed to connect St Dennis on the Cornwall Minerals Railway through St Columb. The NCR saw no objection but the Bill got no further than the House of Lords Select Committee in May 1882. Once effect was to galvanise the GWR into obtaining powers to build their branch from Bodmin Road to Bodmin, and to Boscarne Junction on the B&WR. The Padstow committee was naturally upset at the loss of the Mid-Cornwall and then having to witness future piecemeal building of the NCR.

Overcoming GWR objections, the LSWR made Agreements with the NCR to work its line. The Act of Parliament authorising the North Cornwall Railway was passed and received Royal Assent on 18 August 1882. It was to run from a junction with the LSWR's Holsworthy Branch at Halwill & Beaworthy to Padstow South Quay (not including the existing Bodmin & Wadebridge as between Pendevy Bridge and Wadebridge). The authorised railways were:

	Railway	m	ch
No.1	Padstow South Quay to Wadebridge	5	41
No.2	Pendevy Bridge to Launceston	29	54
No.3	Spur near Pendevy Bridge towards Bodmin		26
No.4	Junction with L&SDR at Launceston		15
No.5	Launceston to a point 16 chains NW of Halwill & Beaworthy station	13	31

The authorised capital was to be £600,000 in shares, with powers to borrow £220,000. Included in the original NCR Bill was a requirement for the acquisition of the Bodmin & Wadebridge and extensive deviations were proposed for it, with a new station at Bodmin, also at Wadebridge. (In the event the LSWR did these itself). The B&WR had been held in trust by the LSWR directors since 1846, to the GWR's annoyance, so much so that the 1882 Act omitted Amalgamation clauses. Thus the LSWR Co legally bought it in. A cash payment of £35,000 and extinguishment on an Exchequer loan of £8,000 settled the matter, sealed by Acts dated 25 January and 1 July 1886. The 1882 Agreement with the LSWR carefully outlined the conditions regarding the NCR's association with the B&WR. There were also strictures on any future connection made at Launceston with the GWR (Railway No.4).

The working Agreements with the LSWR provided for working and maintaining the line in perpetuity, retaining 55% of the gross receipts after retaining Government duty. Thus with its 45% balance the NCR was ensured income to pay dividends from the opening date. An intricate rebate payment was also agreed by the LSWR. This was based on 10% of all gross receipts from lines east of Exeter passing to Launceston and Padstow. It also included all slate traffic from Delabole. The upward limit was £12,000 per annum, although if receipts were sufficient to pay 4½% on the share capital and 4% on the borrowed capital the rebate would be less (or cease) but could be revived. The Agreements allowed the LSWR to purchase the whole of the 4% Debenture stock, Debenture Bonds and Preference Stocks. In the event of these agreements the construction capital was reduced to £550,000 and £183,000 borrowing powers.

The first meeting of the North Cornwall Board of Directors was held at Bodmin on 17 October 1882. A Secretary, Edward Bellamy (London) was appointed at a salary of £400 p.a. The first general meeting was held at Bodmin (Town Arms Hotel) on 26 July 1883. In the Chair was Mr John Tremayne (who was to hold this office until his death in 1901) of Heligan, St Austell. The meeting confirmed the directors to be: J. Tremayne, the Earl of Wharncliffe, Viscount Torrington, Charles Glyn Prideaux-Brune, Lewis Charles Foster, Charles Gurney, T. Martin, Sir W.W. Onslow, C. Bainbridge Rendle (Devonport), Capt. W. Teague and J. Oag. Lord Wharncliffe, elected

Ashwater in the 1900s. A train for Okehampton is pulling away from the up platform whilst a team of men from R. H. Moon unload a consignment of timber in the loading dock.

deputy chairman, owned estates in the Camelford and Delabole areas; he and others were to be generous in their assignment of land to the NCR. James Oag Esq. of Thorndon, Ashwater, served as a director for many years until his death in 1912 and his estate was still a large shareholder in 1922. Foster (Chairman after Tremayne died in 1901) was a director of Robbins, Foster, the Liskeard Bank. On the death of Lord Torrington in 1885, Lord Halsbury (formerly Sir H.S. Giffard) was elected. The Molesworth family was represented in the 1890s by Sir Lewis William, Bart. of Penacarrow, Bodmin. Last, but not least, were the Prideaux-Brunes, Lords of the manor at Padstow. Charles G. Prideaux-Brune was succeeded by Colonel C.R. Prideaux-Brune in 1908. At the first meeting

Top. Ashwater in 1919, an LSWR cattle wagon standing in the head-shunt. The road dropped down from the village of Ashwater half a mile to the west by Ash Mill to the station which opened in March 1886. Consisting of station buildings, small goods shed and yard, signal box, passing loops and a shunting neck, Ashwater essentially represented the general pattern for these North Cornwall wayside stations.

Middle. The station staff take time out from their duties to pose for the camera in 1907.

Bottom. Pre-First World War photo of Ashwater, viewed from the road bridge. A three coach train is about to leave for Okehampton whilst a train of cattle wagons is being shunted by the locomotive in the background.

Top. **An early view of Ashwater, looking towards Meldon Junction, with a 460 class 4-4-0 and a train bound for North Cornwall entering the down loop. Passengers used the steps down from the road to cross the line, for footbridges were rarely provided at rural stations. The large post and arm of the down starting signal is noteworthy, also the duplicated up starting signals. Eric Youldon collection.**

Middle. **Ashwater Station house is evident on the right of this early view of the Carey Valley with Ash Mill to the left. Local merchant R. A. Moon's stores lie in the centre of the hill leading to Germansweek. After closure of the line the road was straightened to its original course. J. T. E. Spry.**

Bottom. **Tower Hill in the 1920s after the down loop had been removed, leaving the up as a single line. The nameboard is a new SR concrete and enamel example, the station appearing to have received a face lift, including Southern Railway advertising boards. Staff cottages beyond were provided by the LSWR and they remain in situ today although the station buildings were demolished after closure in 1966. The World War Two ammunition sidings were laid down in the field visible between the houses. R. L. Goodman collection.**

Messrs. W.R. Galbraith and R.T. Church were confirmed as Consulting Engineers, J.V.H. Drew of Exeter appointed Surveyor and Robbins, Foster as Bankers together with Williams, Deacon & Co (London). Solicitors were to be: Goode, Shilton & Co (St Austell), Venning & Goldsmith (Plymouth) and Burchall & Co.

It was soon realised that financing the complete line from Halwill to Padstow was out of the question. Thus a separate Launceston & Halwill Section Act was obtained, receiving Royal Assent on 28 July 1884. Financial arrangements with the LSWR had been agreed on 18 May 1883. From now on the North Cornwall Railway would be made in several sections and it is useful here to note how it was eventually capitalised, quoting the 'Statement of Authorised Capital 30 June 1896' and after completion to Padstow in 1899 *(see Table 1 overleaf)*.

The dual Role of the NCR and LSWR while the line was under construction, and up to 1922, needs explanation. The employment of the LSWR's engineering consultants Messrs. Galbraith and Church ensured the big company's practices and standards throughout the building periods. The rental and leasing arrangements meant that the LSWR managed just about everything else from payment of Parish rates to staffing. The NCR directors could only suggest, complain, dispose of surplus land, and finally receive monetary payments from

Table 1

North Cornwall Railway Financial structure

Section of Line	Main Act	Stocks & shares	Debenture stock (£)	Expenditure (As noted to 31 Dec 1900)	Commencing rebate (£)
Launceston & Halwill	28 July 1884	150,000	50,000	200,000	2,600
Launceston & Delabole	21 July 1891	187,000	62,000	249,000	4,000
Delabole & Wadebridge	27 July 1893	150,000	50,000	200,000	3,230
Padstow line	20 July 1896	88,000	nil	88,000	2,650

the LSWR, thus fixing dividends payable to their shareholders. Their involvement with the Padstow Harbour developments was more complicated, as will be seen.

Although references are made to 'standard' NCR buildings, it was really an LSWR design evolved during the 1870s (e.g. Mortehoe 1874). Similarly the goods sheds and signal boxes followed current LSWR practice as did the permanent way materials. In all other respects the LSWR (and the NCR) had to comply with the 1845 Railway Clauses and Consolidation Act, the significant 1889 Act regarding train braking and signalling and consequent government departmental (in this period the Board of Trade) regulation. The Southern Railway Company became the sole owner and operator from 1923.

Halwill to Launceston(1st Section) 1884-1886

The first issue of shares for the Launceston to Halwill Section (15,000 shares of £10 each) was advertised in 1883 and raised over the next two years without much trouble. Interest was payable at 4% on fully paid-up shares. Several local notables subscribed, including J.C. Williams (Werrington Park, Launceston), Sir Harding S. Giffard, MP for Launceston, and the Duke of Bedford. Under the agreement with LSWR, as well as the 45% portion of the gross receipts there would be £3,000 per annum from the rebate arrangements. In addition the LSWR purchased £50,000 Debentures at 2½% premium and by virtue of this appointed a Director to the NCR Board. He was Arthur Mills Esq. of Efford Down, Bude. The terms for the Engineers were set at £350 per mile, 2½% commission on all buildings and 3% on the value of measured quantities of the works. The Surveyor was to be paid at £50 per mile. All this was agreed at the October 1883 meeting and a contract (revised in May 1884) for the construction was sealed with Messrs. Curry & Reeve & Co. The following month the first Certificates amounting to £20,270 (part cash, part shares) were issued to them to start work. The shares, and those which followed over the next two years were for 'nominees'. It was usual for a contractor to borrow on them. On the Second Section, Curry & Reeve were paid on their Certificates by means of Lloyds Bonds, an alternative borrowing source.

Construction work on the Halwill to Launceston line started with ceremony on the afternoon of Monday 20 June 1884. The Chairman, Mr John Tremayne and several directors, arrived on the 3.29pm train to be met by Mr W.J. Harris of Winsford, Halwill (who gave land for the construction), The Mayor of Launceston and Messrs. Church (Consulting Engineer), Manning (of Curry & Reeve), J. Oag and Charles Gurney (directors) amongst others. Everyone walked down to the field owned by Mr Harris where the junction was to be formed. The Rector of Halwill offered prayer and Mr Tremayne cut the first sod with an 'ordinary spade' the handle of which was covered with dark blue velvet. Mr Harris, too, tried his hand with it to the ringing cheers of the assembly. Stations were to be sited at Ashwater and Tower Hill (though Boldford Bridge, nearer Launceston, had been considered).

Curry & Reeve started work and by October an engine and a good quantity of plant were to hand. The Surveyor had established six miles of line in the Company's possession after the first 'notices to treat' were issued in the summer. Some 250 workmen were employed by December 1884, but by February very wet weather had retarded the works and masonry was

Opening day at Launceston of the 1st. Section of the North Cornwall Railway. Tuesday 20th July 1886. The Directors' train stands in the down platform waiting to return to Exeter. The Adams 445 class 4-4-0 No. 448 appears to have been specially chosen for the event, although its driving wheels would not normally be regarded as suitable for local gradients. On the left is Beattie 2-4-0 No. 0195, rebuilt as a tender engine from a tank, likely to be Launceston's own motive power. Other interesting items are the pw pump trolley and the broad gauge GWR carriage (right).

Looking down on Launceston LSWR station; the GWR station is beyond. The lengthy bank of cattle pens is flanked by an end loading dock (with horse box) and a contemporary non-corridor North Cornwall local train (44ft. guards van, 46ft. Composite and a 42ft. Third in salmon pink and brown livery is in the up platform. Newport lies to the left and St. Stephen's on the hill above.

particularly behindhand. A further blow fell in April 1885 when it was reported that a major outbreak of smallpox made it difficult to keep the men together. More woe befell the project as September brought floods, and the River Tamar rose an incredible 15ft in just a few hours, bringing some anxious moments at the new Tamar overbridge site at Launceston. Curry & Reeve asked for an advance of £10,500 on the security of their plant and a lien on all shares. The North Cornwall board approved in June 1885. It was repaid during the autumn, the contractors having now acquired nearly 10,000 shares. By then four miles of track were in and the girder bridge over the GWR at Launceston was in place. As often happened, a clergyman asked for a grant to open a Navvy Mission. This time the Rev Mr Gough received £25. Presumably uplifted, the Navvies produced a line of rails nine miles from Halwill, and Galbraith had no reason to complain of progress in February 1886.

In March 1886 the station at Ashwater was complete, including the house. The iron framing Launceston engine shed, and the turntable, were on site. Curry's engine 'General Don' came down into Launceston with materials in May. Ashwater platforms, yard etc were finished and Tower Hill nearly so in April. Launceston Station was being roofed (the subcontractor here was Burt, a local builder). Bridging works below Netherbridge (222 miles) were considerable. The River Tamar was crossed by a double span of six wrought iron mainplates and the River Kensey needed three 28ft masonry arches. The GWR's Launceston Branch was crossed by a single girder span of 31ft on the skew. The contractor was quickly laying the permanent way by April, but ballasting was behind. The LSWR loaned two 'Lion' class 0-6-0s (Nos.102 'Lioness' and 108 'Ruby') to assist.

Unfortunately there were casualties on the works. A boy of 13, John Thomas Veale, died of injuries received at Tower Hill. He was employed to put tip chains on the wagons and to uncouple, and was walking between the horse and wagon when he caught his foot and fell within the rails. The wheels passed over him.

The station at Ashwater was sited where the road came down from the village, half a mile to the west, by Ash Mill. There was a small goods yard with two sidings, one to the goods shed and the other to an end loading dock, both fed from a shunting neck. This and the passing loop with two platforms, signal box and station buildings would be the general pattern for all the minor stations on the North Cornwall line. The other intermediate station, Tower Hill, was on a straight alignment where the Carey valley opened out in Broadwoodwidger Parish. It was situated where the road from St Giles-in-the-Heath crossed the adjacent Carey and went on to Broadwood and Lifton. Arrangements were similar to Ashwater. Both layouts were to be altered over the following years, and Tower Hill would lose its down loop between the Wars. There had been a gradual depopulation in rural West Devon over the years due to the agricultural depression from the 1870s, but the new railway would contribute to a quiet revival. Access to the markets for dairy products and cattle, the establishment of fertiliser, seeds and corn stores provided the stimulant.

The site for the narrow (4ft 8½in) gauge station at Launceston was to lay alongside the GWR terminus about 100 yards to the south. There would be no connection to the existing 7ft 0¼in broad gauge in spite of the authorisation for such a link ('Line No.4'). The GWR was narrowed in 1892 and a connection was considered in 1910, but it was wartime pressures in 1943 which eventually warranted a junction.

With the intention of forging westward the new line hugged the foot of the steep hill below the town and castle. At first the contractor ramped up a temporary line from the west of St Thomas's Road to carry spoil from the Priory side to earthworks at Ridgegrove. It would appear that the cutting at the Priory (towards New Mills) and the bridge to carry St Thomas's Road was undertaken by 1886. Recent finds by the Launceston Steam Railway under this ramp (near the engine shed) include a gauge rod and contractor's rail. The road overbridge was formed on a 1 in 12 gradient. This and the sharp bend into the station brought considerable criticism from the local Board of Health, so the parapet was modified.

The twin platforms with their loops were surprisingly short and not subsequently lengthened as others

Top. Launceston Square in the 1930s; it was well above the two railway stations in the Kensey Valley but buses were available at times. The White Hart Hotel ran its own, first a horse bus, later a motor vehicle. Private motoring was not a serious competitor until the 1950s as this scene suggests, and although the town has been expensively by-passed, there is little room in its narrow streets to linger or park.

Middle. The crew of this A12 0-4-2 No. 614 attend to their loco before moving off with a train for Okehampton.

Bottom. Launceston Castle dominates the town and the two railways in the valley below at Newport. In this early view the GWR station is in the foreground and the LSWR (North Cornwall Railway) station platforms and building beyond. Extreme left is the engine shed, slightly obscured by the GWR water tank, turntable and goods shed. In the centre are the enlarged cattle pens, flanked by a traders store. The prominent villa (above the brake van on the right) was the Station Master's house, and the steep path to the town may be seen leading up behind the quarried faces. R. L. Goodman collection.

were. The standard style of signal box of the 1880s and a waiting shed were situated on the up platform, while a medium sized, but not 'standard' station building was erected in stone blocks and decorative quoining, with a slate roof. A wide awning fronted this building. The footbridge beyond the country end of the platforms was a rather steep affair, another cause for local criticism.

Egloskerry and staff in 1905. The signalman/porter holds the Egloskerry-Launceston tablet and is about to hand it to the crew of the train approaching behind. The Station Master is in the middle, in frocked coat, and to the right of the signalman/porter can be seen the level crossing gates, the only set between Halwill Junction and Wadebridge.

With an eye on cattle traffic a set of pens and a side loading dock was placed against No.2 siding; it was extended in 1891. Between the pens and the down platform was a short end-loading dock. Both these sidings led directly into a long shunting neck on the down side of the single line from Tower Hill, paralleled by a second siding. Engine requirements were satisfied by a shot siding with coal stage, shed, and a 50ft turntable. More substantial was the stone goods shed with its slat roof. Two more sidings fed this area, one within the shed. Some excavation of the hillside seems to have occurred at this time (1880s) to accommodate sundry stores, a mill and later a cart weighbridge. The quarry beyond pre-dated the railway, but undoubtedly stone was taken for construction work.

Just where the stopblocks stood at Launceston from 1886 is not clear. It is known that the Launceston Gas Co was provided with a loading bank soon after, just west of St Thomas's Road Bridge. Trood, the local agricultural and seed merchant, asked for an extension into his new premises in July 1892. The LSWR provided materials and the NCR did the work at a cost of £300, probably using the contractors currently extending the line to Tresmeer. A formal agreement was concluded in 1893. The connection to these sidings was resited in 1904. Opposite, the LSWR, in due course, built eight dwellings for its employees.

Colonel J.H. Rich R.E. made an inspection of this 'First Section' of the North Cornwall Railway on 15th July 1886. His train left Launceston at 9.30am, preceded slowly by two engines to test the bridges. He noted in his subsequent report that the 13½ miles were wide enough for a double line but it would be single line signalled by Train Staff and block telegraph. The LSWR would work the line and the permanent way was to that Company's standard (at that time 82lb/yard double-headed steel rails, 24-foot lengths). All the 44 bridges were substantially constructed. Most were built entirely of dressed stone blocks, but some were of wrought iron rolled beams or girders. Interestingly, as a condition for public opening, Colonel Rich asked the LSWR to provide a turntable at Halwill within four months, although one had been provided at Launceston. Until that time trains would have to be restricted to 25mph and stop at all stations. He also stipulated that rails should be moved so that the steps would 'not be more than 2ft 3in from the edges of the platforms in stations' (this would appear to refer to the dimension from rail to platform wall). The home signals at Ashwater and Tower Hill should be raised so as to be seen from the signal cabins and clocks should be provided in those cabins, wrote Colonel Rich. The turntable at Halwill was installed (for £170) and the speed restriction removed in February 1887. The actual line of rails sanctioned for public trains ran from the junction with the Holsworthy Branch at 209m 71ch to a point under St Thomas's Road Bridge at 223m 42ch (i.e. 13m 51ch). Under an agreement made with the LSWR on 3 March 1888 a side line at Halwill extended 17 chains from the 'junction' (in reality end-on) into the bay platform. The NCR paid £1 per annum for the use of the LSWR land.

The opening day was set for Tuesday 20 July 1886. The LSWR provided a decorated Adams '445' class 4-4-0, No.448, for the Officers' special which left Exeter at 8.45am. On board were Arthur Mills MP (director), C. Scotter (General Manager), Messrs Gardner (Assistant Superintendent), White (Divisional Superintendent), Fisher (Engineer) and also the Mayor of Exeter. On arrival at Launceston, the engine was turned and the train left at 11.0am for Halwill. NCR directors were aboard this time, including Chairman J.C. Tremayne and the Mayor of Launceston, Dr Andrews. At each of the stations the train stopped – and at Boldford Bridge an old man fired a gun! At Halwill Mr J Oag declared the line

The North Cornwall line, rising from the 1 in 330 in the platforms to the 1 in 73 towards the 860ft. summit three quarters of a mile away, passes under the main coast road at Otterham where co-acting arms were provided for the down starting signal aspects. This station was the main railhead for Crackington Haven and St. Juliot (of Thomas Hardy fame) but Otterham village itself lay a mile away by footpath. The waiting shed was built in dressed Delabole stone with Portland stone quoins, as was the station main building. In this 1920s view the nameboard retains black lettering on white background in the LSWR style.

open. Back to Launceston about noon, the train was met by a vast throng and more speeches were heard. A procession formed up and, led by the Devon Volunteer Engineers Band, climbed the stiff hill to the White Hart Hotel and Central Rooms for Luncheon and still more speeches. This was not all for the day, as a 'Fancy Fayre' was staged on the Castle Green and in the evening a ball was held in a marquee and the Castle illuminated. Money raised from these events (and on the Wednesday) was used to build a new Town Hall. The direct narrow (standard) gauge to the east of the country was welcomed. It was said that the luncheon 'that recently at Lydford, 160 cattle from Launceston to Cheshire had to be changed from the broad gauge to the narrow gauge, taking an hour causing great difficulty and delay'.

Curry & Reeve maintained the permanent way for the first year after opening, the LSWR paying £14,000 to the NCR towards the cost. The public train service commenced on 21 July 1886. Trains left Halwill at 10.33am, 12.25pm, 3.25pm, 4.52pm and 9.00pm; at first the Launceston line was treated as a branch of Okehampton to Holsworthy. The latter three departures connected through from the Waterloo to Plymouth/Devonport trains at 9.00am, 11.00am and 2.30pm. Upwards the local trains left at 7.50am, 10.20am, 1.50pm, 2.50pm and 6.45pm, the first four connecting to Waterloo. An additional 8.24am from Okehampton was put on from 1887, a coach attached to the goods train on the first Wednesday of each month, to serve Launceston Market. An early goods left Launceston at 5.45am with wagons for Devonport and Exeter and another at 3.30pm to Okehampton. During the next few years Nine Elms/Launceston 'road boxes' were running overnight affording delivery of merchandise, but it was not until the turn of the century that passengers were given through coaches from and to Waterloo. Excursionists soon appeared, encouraged by LSWR fares offers, and the Padstow coach-and-two was arriving at Launceston at 1.40pm and

Currie & Reeve's navvies were working in large numbers on the construction of the line during the winter of 1892-93, reaching Otterham by December. Situated on the Bideford to Wadebridge main road on the edge of the escarpment of Wilsey Down and nearly 900 feet above sea level, this was a very exposed place. Trees were later planted to afford some shelter from the Atlantic gales. Although a goods shed was not provided, a store was eventually built, coming in very useful for the rabbit trade which burgeoned in the 1930s and 1940s. This was said to be more valuable than cattle (or even passengers!) at some stations.

The original awning over the up platform at Camelford's 1893 station was replaced by a more substantial version by 1900, Camelford being regarded as the railhead for Tintagel and Boscastle and thus uniquely endowed for a wayside station. No further luxuries were provided and passengers had to use the adjacent road bridge or (unofficially) the foot crossings at the platform ends, lit on their way at night by glimmering oil lamps.

departing at 4.15pm, going via Camelford. Mr Downing, of Launceston, organised an excursion to London on 19 October 1886 at a 12/- fare.

Over the next eighty years Launceston remained a valuable source of traffic, acting as a railhead to a wide area, especially to the south parishes, North Hill, Lewannick, Alternun (as far out as Bolventor) and northwards to Boyton. Yeolmbridge, North Petherwin and North Tamerton.

A dividend of 1½% on Ordinary shares was paid in 1887. The rentals amounted to £868.2.4 in August and it would rise to £2,426 (final half-year payment) based on the 45% gross receipts and the full annual rebate of £3,000 by 1896. The 'Halwill Line' remained separate until the 1913 capitalisation. As well as the Debenture stocks, valued at £50,000, the Ordinary stocks (£10) were divided into halves at 4% Preferred and a further 2% Deferred on the £150,000 capital.

Launceston to Delabole (2nd Section) 1890-1893

Contemplation of the remainder of the route to Padstow followed the establishment of the '1st Section' in 1884. The existing NCR powers would expire in 1885. Negotiation began with the LSWR and all seemed well, extra time being obtained in 1885. Relations with the GWR over the Bodmin & Wadebridge, as already mentioned, caused the LSWR to tread warily. The GWR was connected to the B&WR at Boscarne Junction from 3 September 1888, with GWR running powers into Wadebridge. Agreement between the two main line companies in 1884 had delineated the areas to which they might, or might not, extend. Thus the LSWR, although actually supporting the NCR did not, as might be expected, absorb the Halwill to Launceston line. In fact the NCR remained a separate company until 1922, probably (given its desire to extend to Truro in the 1890s and even in this century) to avert strain with the GWR.

With these considerations and a realisation that available local investment would be thin, the LSWR decided that another 'separate undertaking' from Launceston to Delabole should be formed. Extra time on the original Act was obtained in 1888. The LSWR came to an agreement with the NCR on 13 October 1891 to lease and work this section at an annual rental of £4,750 which would give a 3½% return on the £250,000 capital construction costs. A sum of £4,000 was to be awarded as the rebate. The £187,000 Share Capital was issued, together with Debentures to cover a further £62,000 (which could be borrowed). The NCR's Liskeard Bankers agreed to take £100,000 and the contractors (Curry & Reeve) were issued (by the NCR) with Lloyds Bonds affixed to previous Engineer's Certificates, on which they could borrow. The necessary Act was obtained on 21 July 1891. Work ('Railway No.2') had already started before March 1890 under original powers, material having been taken from the Priory area to the Ridgegrove bridge site in 1885.

Launceston to Tresmeer 1890-1892

Curry & Reeve assembled plant at Launceston, with station works sub-contracted again to Burt of Launceston. As has been seen, the line was already in place to the west of St Thomas's Road at Launceston, serving the Gas Works. The course thereafter was to follow the Kensey Valley for nearly six miles to Lanzion (below Tresmeer). From there a rather tortuous route had been surveyed for the 400ft climb to the Statton-Wadebridge road at Otterham, to pass over a summit 860 feet above sea level at Trewanion, in Lesnewth Parish. The Atlantic Ocean, only a few miles to the west at this point, is in full view. This high elevation was maintained through Melorne (Camelford).

Staking out commenced in March 1890 with surveyor Drew on the ground buying the freehold, but there was no earth moving until November. 'Much delay was being caused in the acquisition of land for the Launceston and Delabole by the exorbitant demands of landowners for accommodation works ... delay ... numerous stops for compulsory possession'. It is interesting to note that in 1892 Miss Gurney of Treybursye was awarded only £789.5s by the Board of Trade's arbitration, instead of her claim for £1,998.2s.6d.

By the turn of the year a line of rails ran through two fields but, needless to say, conditions were a 'veritable quagmire' due to the recent rains. During the frosty month of February 1891 work was going on in five cuttings with 200 men. The men, largely itinerant navvies, fluctuated in numbers throughout the NCR's construction. A proportion of local men were employed, but the heavy earth moving was the province of the navvy. There was a shortage of 'lodgings' at this time, but many navvies built their own shanties, some housing their families. The Great Blizzard of March 1891 (it was reported that snow was at rooftop level in Camelford) must have had its effect. The Engineer, Baron, reported slack progress in July and, although the number of men had increased to 445, only a quarter mile of permanent way was down on works extending 9¾ miles. A vast pile of timber and rails was accumulating at Launceston and, with great difficulty, the contractor's engine 'General Don' was transferred by road to Splatt. The Cornish & Devon Post described the scene: 'On Monday 'General Don', which had been repainted and had its name re-lettered by Mr John Hawkins of Launceston, was moved from Launceston to Splatt (Tresmeer) by road. The flanges of the wheels had been packed level by means

***Top*. Two members of Parliament sat for Camelford before the 1832 Reform Act, and the Town Hall dates from 1805, a gift of the Duke of Bedford. There were associations with the Pitt family, but by 1893 when the North Cornwall opened its station at Melorne a mile and a half to the west, the former borough had declined. The new railway brought tourists as well as cheaper foodstuffs and merchandise for local shops from London and the Midlands and prosperity returned.**

***Middle*. The Wharncliffe Hotel in Trevena village (Tintagel) was named after the 1st Earl, a landowner in the area and Deputy Chairman of the North Cornwall Railway. The Fry family established their own hotel here and developed a valuable transport business to Camelford in conjunction with the LSWR.**

of an iron tyre, tightened and wedged with wood and iron. A traction engine of Pearce's (Tavistock) did the hauling, steam, however, being also used by 'General Don'. A difficulty occurred at St Thomas's Road from the Station Road turning, the weight of the locomotive (20 tons) forcing out the wedges, something often repeated before the end of the journey, the whole proceedings watched by a large crowd.'

It is not always clear today why sites for stations were thus chosen. The North Cornwall was showered with letters and 'memorials' from individuals and local authorities. A public road intersection obviously called the tune, and at Badharlach Bridge a Mr Simcol was willing to give land. The station there became Egloskerry. A second station might have been called Splatt but of course Tresmeer, a mile to the south, sounded better. Two miles of land were offered on 'favourable terms if a station was fixed at Tinks House' in October 1891 and the following month a station was ordered to be built at Melorne. Neither of these names was adopted. The former was to become Otterham ('Boscastle Road' had been suggested) some way off but in that Parish, and the latter Camelford. Camelford itself was 1½ miles to the south, but roads radiated to Boscastle (four miles) and Tintagel (five miles). The alleged weakness, or lack of, stone resulted in all the masonry bridges being brick-arched. The mill leat aqueduct, half a mile beyond Launceston, built with stone obtained from Langdon's Quarry at Truscot, was a masonry arch supporting a cast iron trough. The line kept to the north side of the River Kensey, but crossed it four times below the steep escarpment of Red Down and Tregear at Egloskerry. Two miles of permanent way were down in September 1891. More and more men were brought in, some loaned by the LSWR, the numbers rising to 616 in March 1892. An accident occurred by blasting at Dyers Cutting

(Splatt) in November when a man called Bloom field received a blowback in the face after recharging a hole and a G. Harvey was killed by a material fall in Red Down cutting. By April 1892 five miles had been laid.

Trouble with subcontractors forced Curry & Reeve to build Tresmeer station themselves. Nearly all the bridges were complete thus far in May 1892, and a June opening was in prospect. However it was late July before the Board of Trade's Inspecting Officer was invited to approve the works and signalling. A train with a 'heavy luggage engine to test several wrought iron underbridges was provided for him, and his party, which left Launceston at 9.30am on 27 July'.

That evening Colonel H.A. Yorke, R.E., penned a long document to the Board of Trade. The line he inspected was 7m 69ch from the 13m 55ch point at Launceston (based on the installed mileposts this appears to have been from 223m 46ch to 231m 35ch). It would be worked by Train Staff and Ticket, he wrote, with crossing places at Egloskerry and Tresmeer. New track for the permanent way was 80lb/yd double-headed steel rails in 30ft lengths, laid in 40lb chairs. He described 23 bridges with special mention of the mill leat in cast iron; though 'somewhat peculiar in design', it showed 'no sign of leakage'.

There was a public level crossing at Egloskerry, hand-operated and properly interlocked. (Notice that this station was fully signalled as a passing loop, but could not be opened at this time). Tresmeer had 300ft platforms, 2ft 6in high. Special working was observed by Colonel Yorke at Launceston and Tresmeer. At Launceston up trains could depart from the Down platform to 'save a good deal of shunting'. This facility was abolished in later years. The signalling at Tresmeer also allowed up trains to start from the Down, although an original LSWR plan omits reference to this. The signal box, on the Down platform, had 17 levers, including 1 push and pull and 4 spare levers. As construction work was proceeding towards Otterham by then, a catchpoint was provided at the west end of Tresmeer to protect the new passenger trains. Egloskerry Signal Box frame also had 17 levers (1 push and pull). One lever locked the crossing gates, and three were spare. Once again there were strictures regarding tender-first working. As there was to be a turntable at Delabole, twelve miles further on, Colonel Yorke suggested allowing such a practice for the time being, from or to Launceston, but at a maximum speed of 25mph. Otherwise, provided the Gas Works siding received proper stopblocks and Egloskerry gates discs and handlamps, passenger working would commence to Tresmeer.

Opening day, without much ceremony, was Thursday 28 July 1892 to coincide with the Launceston Agriculture Society's Show. The new Station Master at Tresmeer was Mr W. Stacey, lately chief booking clerk at Okehampton. A special train left Launceston with Mayor and Mrs Treleaven aboard. It returned as a normal service at 10.15am with 250 passengers 'many of them never having sat behind an engine before' as the local press put it. As stated before, Egloskerry was not yet open. The erring subcontractor (Burt) had not been discharged and even Tresmeer goods shed was unfinished. Both were built of red brick (though to standard design), the only ones so treated on the NCR. Egloskerry was opened on 3 October 1892. The North Cornwall Coach Co's conveyance serving Wadebridge and Newquay was diverted to Tresmeer, via Launceston. In August there were complaints of insufficient accommodation on the coach, though a separate daily omnibus service was running to Tintagel and Boscastle. From this opening the LSWR started paying a proportional rental of £2,750, with £4,000 of the allotted rebate already reimbursed to the NCR.

The layout at Launceston was altered for the opening insofar as the Down loop at the St Thomas's Road end was connected to the signal box and protected by signals. A ground frame, worked on the push-and-pull principle and signal box-released, now controlled the Gas Works siding. Egloskerry's up side yard was of simple design, not even having a goods shed or shunt neck, though a cattle pen was provided. Tresmeer's two sidings, on the down side, followed the standard layout.

A nasty accident happened the following December when John Skinner, aged 34 (a 'travelling guard') from Exeter, was knocked off the footboard of his shunted van as it

Bottom left and above. **A class 460 4-4-0 waits at Delabole station with a goods train for Wadebridge in the early 1900s. The station was in close proximity to the cavernous slate quarry, top left in the photo above. The Old Delabole Slate Quarry Company siding was extended in 1899, thereafter directly serving the splitting sheds. The Company's narrow gauge system was converted to steam in the 1890, a Bagnall 0-4-0ST, *Sir J. T. Firbank*, arriving in 1902.**

Although a standard type of LSWR building the otherwise dour appearance was softened by overhanging eaves at Port Isaacs Road (and St. Kew). The 1880s style of signal box again denotes the LSWR influences and the SR produced an enamel nameboard, but the date is 5th May 1966. Diesel railcars (this one is single car No. W55026 on the 10.45am Halwill to Wadebridge) introduced by British Railways would not be able to save the line from closure the following October. R. A. Lumber.

About to depart from St. Kew Highway for Wadebridge early last century is a K10 4-4-0, No. 341, with a train consisting of 1880s low arc-roofed bogie non-corridors led by a 6-wheel luggage brake. 341 was built at Nine Elms in 1901 and is equipped with Drummond's cross-tube firebox, later removed. R. L. Goodman collection.

passed the goods shed stanchions. Four wagons passed over him and he died of his injuries in Launceston Hospital. Six cottages were erected by the LSWR for its employees, to the east of the station, but there was no water supply, except by delivery churn.

Another 'might have been' railway affecting the NCR was the Liskeard & Caradon's authorised extension from Sargent's corner, just south of their existing line to Kilmar Tor, to Trewint Marsh. Work started on 6 May 1884 but reached only 1½ miles, to Rushyford Gate. The avowed goal was either Camelford or Boscastle, presumably as an outlet for the mineral traffic from Caradon. In July 1884 the L&CR obtained an Act, however, to build a line from Trewint Marsh to Launceston. It would have trailed into the NCR towards Launceston close to the Priory. The South Caradon Mine closed in 1885, but as late as 1892 the L&CR requested that the NCR work its proposed Launceston line for 15% of the gross receipts.

Tresmeer to Camelford 1892

The navvies building the line were housed in an encampment at Splatt – reference has been found to a Mission Room there – but by November 1892 the Launceston Weekly News was moved to report that 'Otterham Station is very exposed, no houses within one mile. Navvies with wives and children living in huts, some single men in lodgings'. Construction work was following acquisition of land in the summer of 1892 as far as Delabole; excavations were taking place in all the cuttings during September and October and a start had been made on Otterham station. Argument as to the naming of the next station was resolved by the Directors when Camelford (for Tintagel and Boscastle) was chosen for Melorn. Considerable diversion of the main road at Otterham station with a sharp turn at the bridge, was authorised in 1891.

An embankment instead of a proposed viaduct at Treneglos, where the Scarsick tributary flows in a deep defile northwards to the River Ottery, required extra land, purchased in May 1891. Lack of suitable stone and a hard foundation was the reason cited. Earthworks were considerable anyway, because the line needed cuttings and embankments to claw its way round the north side of Wilsey Down on 25 and 30 chain reversing curves. This was in order to obtain a ruling gradient of 1 in 73, to climb from 550ft to 860ft, the summit of the North Cornwall Line at Trewannion a mile beyond Otterham. Overbridges, as before, were brick-arched masonry structures. These uplands on the edge of Davidstow Parish are bare of trees and exposed to whatever weather the Atlantic Ocean produces, be it blinding sunshine to gales, mist and rain. Rainfall here is the heaviest in Cornwall. The line fell slightly towards Camelford station (750ft) and briefly accompanied the Camel headwater by Worthy Vale and the legendary Slaughterbridge.

The name Delabole strictly belonged to the famous slate quarry. The 1890-period hamlets were Medrose and Pengelly; the original line would have bisected both their two streets, but the deviation allowed under the 1891 Act brought the line nearer the quarry, and only Pengelly suffered some demolitions. Apparently there had been lengthy negotiations with the Slate Company to build so near to the quarry perimeter, and the latter conveyed land to the NCR, free of charge. Possession of land was taken for the deviation in mid-1892. Progress was slow, and neither Camelford nor Delabole had been started by December. Concentrating east of Camelford, the number of men employed gradually increased from 602 in December to 768 in April (1893). There was trouble in June 1893 when a navvy was charged with seriously assaulting the wife of a

Three views of Delabole and its quarry. Behind the station in the top picture can be seen the steam powered cableway, slate splitting sheds and a raft of wagons for loading. The lamp room, with oil barrels within, shares the down platform with the Station Master's house. The rear side has a wash house and WC (left) in his open court yard, and the gentlemen's WC court opening on to the platform. In the middle picture an Adams 380 class 4-4-0 is about to depart with a 'special'. In the picture above is Delabole's Bagnall 0-4-0ST *Sir J. T. Firbank*.

missionary following her visit to a lodging hut. Curry & Reeve were going all out in this difficult section and by July 7 out of the nine miles to Camelford were laid. With a gang of platelayers from the LSWR, 852 men were working, thus encouraging a Directors' request for a BoT inspection for August 1893. Otterham was nearly complete and track laid in to Camelford with the signal and telegraph work well in hand. However, when Major Marindin R.E. came down he noted that the line from Camelford to Delabole was 'unfinished and quite unfit for traffic'.

He arrived in a special train on Tuesday 8 August with Messrs J.B. Fisher of the NCR and Church, the LSWR's Engineer. Tresmeer to Camelford was, he reported, 9 miles and 26 chains (apparently 231m 35ch to 240m 61ch). Steeper gradients resulted from the substitution of a 90ft embankment for the 110ft viaduct at Treneglos. The line needed lifting and straightening at several places, especially near this embankment. Camelford lacked its veranda and was 'unfinished'. The catchpoints at Tresmeer should be moved to Camelford, he said, and the points and crossings at the latter connected up! Otterham signal box had 13 levers (4 spare), Camelford 17 and 4 spare. Signalling was by Train Staff and Ticket, and Block Telegraph.

The new station at Otterham and Camelford again followed the LSWR's format and design. The Station Master's house and office buildings were on the up side at both, but Camelford, as befitted its status, received a veranda or awning. The light grey of the local stone contrasted with the red bricks used at Egloskerry and Tresmeer. Otterham was unusual for the NCR in not having a goods shed, a strange omission, though in due course its up side yard filled out with other stores and sheds. Adequate siding lengths were laid, and at Camelford too, where more pointwork connected to the Down loop. Along with Delabole and St Kew Highway the pressures of working the single lines and longer holiday trains caused the LSWR to lengthen the Camelford loops in 1911.

The opening day was set for Monday 14 August 1893. The Cornish & Devon Post headlines included 'Great Rejoicings' and it appears the weather that day was hot. Many of the thousand people who came from far and wide sought out cool hedgerows to await the opening ceremony. An excursion train from Okehampton took up to 200 passengers from Launceston alone at 9.30am. The Director's special followed, arriving at Camelford at 1.15pm. It was met by Sir William Onslow and Colonel Hawker, the latter presenting an illuminated address to Mr Tremayne the NCR Chairman. A large marquee had been erected in a field down the road to Camelford carrying a large board declaring 'Success to Agriculture'. The procession of Directors, LSWR officials and members of the Camelford Committee proceeded thence behind the Holsworthy Military and the Camelford Volunteer Bands. Long speeches followed, during which Drew, the NCR Surveyor, alluded to the acquisition of land which he said, was not so onerous as getting accommodation works. If he had given way on the Launceston to Camelford section, costs would have increased by 30%. In a sports field 1,200 school children were each given a bun and a bottle of ginger beer and a medal bearing the Cornish motto 'One and All'. At the Pain's firework display latter, the illuminated motto was 'Prosperity to Camelford'.

Passenger trains left Camelford at 7.20am, 9.40am, 1.10pm, 3.05pm and 5.40pm, running to Okehampton, all except the last connecting directly to

The North Cornwall made a junction with the Bodmin & Wadebridge line (right) from June 1895 and a signal box was provided. It lasted until 3rd February 1907 when a separate line was formed into Wadebridge. The upper storey is an LSWR 1860s type of construction probably from a block post superseded elsewhere. The ground part was converted to a pw hut.

Waterloo. The latter also ran on Sundays from December 1894. Downwards the 5.50am Waterloo connection arrived at 2.26pm, the 9.00am at 5.00pm, the 11.00am at 6.16pm and the 3.00pm at 10.30pm. There was also a 9.05am from Exeter Queen Street (10.19am from Okehampton) coming into Camelford at 12.18pm. The midnight goods from Exeter, limited to 25 wagons from Yeoford as it carried mails and newspapers and calves, reached Camelford at 6.50am. It commenced in December 1894, also running on Sundays. Remarkably, the overnight Nine Elms to Plymouth 'fast' goods dropped off wagons to the 5.00am Exeter, which in turn left them at Meldon Junction for the second goods for delivery at Camelford at 10.52am. Wagons for London left Camelford at 1.50pm and there was a second goods from there at 7.25pm.

Delabole Slate Quarry before 1893

At the time of the North Cornwall's arrival at Delabole in late 1893, the centuries-old quarry workings covered an area of 25 acres. Five individual working faces had been combined from the 1830s to create one pit, then about 400 feet deep. The Old Delabole Slate Quarry Company came to dominate, by acquiring leases and freeholds. Upwards of 500 men and boys were employed in the quarry and the flooring yard. The principal outlet for finished slates up to 1893 was Port Gaverne.

Farmers carted the slate to Port Gaverne, also to Bodmin Road GWR, though to Launceston when the broad gauge branch opened in 1865. The North Cornwall Co obtained a guarantee from the Slate Co in 1884 to send slates and bricks by standard gauge to Plymouth, Stonehouse (where they had a yard), Devonport and also to Exeter, at a maximum rate of 6s 8d a ton. With the opening to Launceston (NCR) in 1886 many tons were diverted thence, and the Slate Co, only too anxious to forward their products to all parts of the country, supplied land free at Delabole for the NCR's forthcoming route. Within the quarry premises 1ft 11in replaced a 3ft gauge system from 1890. Originally worked by horses, as the sidings spread it was soon served by 0-4-0 saddle tank locomotives.

Camelford to Delabole 1892-1893

A large embankment at Delabole (Medrose) on to the very edge of the quarry, still required 2,000 cubic yards of fill in September 1893. The Contractors had run short of rail chairs, thus 50 chains of route and half Delabole's yard remained to be done. The turntable had not arrived from the makers, though it had been promised. The route below Camelford was again most tortuous; three curves of 30 chains (left-hand), 30 (right) and 30 (left) radii and a final sweep at 50 chains around the north side of the quarry, brought the line into a straight for the Delabole platforms. The gradients, not so severe here, nevertheless fell at 1 in 74 round the last curve. Achieving this required continuous cuttings and embankments.

Colonel Hutchinson, R.E., arrived to inspect the work he had found unfinished the previous August, on 17 October 1893. The length to be inspected was 2m 29ch from Camelford (exclusive) to Delabole. The latter-day mileage system appears to place this between 240m 61ch and 243m 10ch. The embankment at Delabole was 66 feet high and four overbridges (Camelford Station and Delabole Barton) were brick-arched masonry as before. There was one section, Camelford to Delabole, worked by Train Staff and Ticket and with Absolute Block Telegraph. Delabole signal box had 17 levers with 4 spare. Colonel Hutchinson required the protective catchpoint to be placed at Delabole (work was continuing towards Port Isaacs Road) and he had no objections to Up trains starting from Delabole's Down platforms, so long as No.12 points (trailing from the yard) received locking appliances and a starting signal was provided.

Opening day was declared for Wednesday 18 October 1893. A public train left Launceston at 11.20am, two engines hauling 11 coaches. This was followed by the Directors' train ('two very handsome saloons and carriages, and several 1st Class carriages') and a lot of noise was created at Delabole by the letting off of fog signals. The celebrations that day were extensive and a general holiday was declared. A procession of the local committee, quarrymen and 'all Male Adults of the villages' headed by the Delabole Brass Band, marched from Lower Pengelly to a field near the new station. A free luncheon was provided for them (but for the women and children, a free tea in the afternoon). For the Directors, on the arrival of their train at 1.00pm, there was an address by the Chairman (Mr Edward Allen) of the Old Delabole Slate Company, a short visit to the quarry and luncheon in the Co-operative Hall. For the enjoyment of all, the Plymouth Royal Marines Band played during the afternoon, while 'Athletic Sports' took place. A Grand Concert at 6pm (2/-, 1/- and 6d) and fireworks at 8.30pm completed the day's jollifications. The North Cornwall Railway train service terminated here for nearly two years. Although the line to Port Isaac Road was inspected on 1 August 1894 the LSWR, working the NCR, would not open it.

Delabole was provided with a comparatively large goods yard in anticipation of the increased slate traffic. In addition to the engine shed and turntable siding, another served the cattle pen and goods shed, both joining and running northward into a long shunting neck. As at Camelford, crossovers joined the Down loop in both directions. In due course more sidings and a loading bank were added on the south-east side as the slate trade grew in volume.

Speeds were still limited at first to 25mph from Launceston to Tresmeer and 20mph thence to Delabole. In the summer of 1894 the seed of future holiday expresses was sown when the connection from the 1.00pm Waterloo, the 6.00pm from Okehampton, called only at Launceston, Tresmeer and Camelford, with a Delabole arrival at 7.55pm. An 11.45am from Delabole provided a similar up service. The North Cornwall Coach service started running via Camelford to Newquay on

2 July 1894. The LSWR authorised installation of Train Tablet signalling in early 1894 the whole way from Meldon Junction to Delabole (and to Holsworthy) but it was some years before conversion from Staff and Ticket was completed. There was expenditure on cottages for its employees at Tower Hill, Egloskerry and Otterham. At a cost of £9.12s.0d, shrubs were planted at Otterham, Camelford and Delabole.

In November 1893 250 Delabole quarrymen and friends took a train to Launceston on a Saturday afternoon, returning at a late hour. As well as the awe-inspiring castle, they were surprised at the size of the shopping area at Launceston. Launceston traders, however, were complaining that the cheap fare from Delabole was 2s 5d while from more distant Holsworthy and Tavistock it was only 2s 0d.

The rental and rebate of this '2nd Section' was superseded from 26 July 1894. The existing arrangement was dropped in favour of a 999-year lease by the LSWR at £8,750 annually, payable half-yearly. 3½% was paid on the Deferred and Ordinary Shares of the 'Launceston & Delabole' until the 1913 rearrangements.

Delabole to Wadebridge (3rd Section) 1893-1895

The NCR Act of 27 July 1891 included extra time for all unfinished works, excluding the Pendevy eastern spur toward Bodmin. For this '3rd Section' agreement was concluded with the LSWR for working and finance, by Acts of 1 May and 27 July 1893. The St Kew tunnel (Trelill) could be constructed as for a single line instead of double (nearly all the NCR overbridges were for double line, but many fewer under the railway). The rebate for this Section was to be up to £3,250 annually from the LSWR, payable half-yearly. The ordinary share capital of £150,000 was confirmed. In the event over half of this was issued to the Contractors (Curry & Reeve again) in the form of Lloyds Bonds payable to their nominees, the rest taken up locally. £50,000 could be borrowed and the LSWR took £45,000 of this as 3½% Debentures ('Wadebridge Guaranteed'). It would appear that for this Section the LSWR applied the 1882 arrangement for work, i.e. for 55% of gross receipts, the NCR receiving the balance. In after years 3% was paid on the ordinary shares. A further Act (17 August 1894) permitted a 2m 23ch deviation north of Wadebridge, in Egloshayle Parish. This put the line on the west side of the River Allen through Treworder (252 miles).

Extension to Truro?

A Parliamentary Bill was prepared in 1893 to authorise a line from Padstow to Truro; four 'Railways' were proposed. No.1 was to run from a trailing junction at Padstow station via St Merry, St Eval and Mawgan to a new station at Newquay, No.2 from Newquay to a terminus south of Truro city, with a spur at Padstow for direct running to Newquay from Wadebridge. Railway No.3 was to be a spur from the north of Truro to the existing line and station. Nos.3 and 4, together, allowed a line from the NCR's terminus, around the south side of Truro to Penwithers Junction. The LSWR would not support it and the preamble of the Bill was not proved by the House of Commons Committee; even though the House reversed this, it was not proceeded with. The Chairman of the NCR, J.C. Tremayne, however, met the GWR Chairman Greirson, in November 1894 to ask for assistance. The NCR proposal had been strongly supported by Falmouth Town Council, the Newquay Local Board, St Agnes interests and the Truro Merchants Association. The GWR was not forthcoming. Further LSWR, or NCR, ambitions toward Truro seemed to end here and Waterloo passengers, such as there were, completed their journey to Newquay by horse coach.

Delabole to Port Isaac Road 1894

Before work continued beyond Delabole toward Wadebridge on this Third Section of the North Cornwall Railway the site of Port Isaac Road station was settled on a contrived level stretch at Reddiford on the Trewarne Estate. St Teath villagers asked for their station at Trekee, or better still at Treroosal, only a mile to the west, but were told that the gradients were not right. Only 210 men were working between Delabole and Port Isaac Road in November 1893. The amount of earth working to be done, though not heavy, was continuous as the upper end of the route followed the east side of the high ground facing the coast. The curvature was not as sinuous as further east, except for a complete half circle traversed (at 30 chains radius) between Trekee and Reddiford. Over all this distance the gradient was formed at 1 in 73, falling from a height of 650ft to 400ft above sea level. With 790 men employed in June 1894, and Port Isaac Road nearly ready, the line was sufficiently advanced for the Railway Inspector to visit in August 1894.

Major Yorke was appointed to view 4m 10chs (243m 10ch to 247m 20ch). He counted five overbridges of stone (brick faced arches) and ten underbridges. Port Isaac Road signal box had 13 levers, four of them spare. Once again, without a turntable at Port Isaac Road, engines would have to run tender first in one direction. Major Yorke therefore ordered a 20mph restriction for all trains. Neither could goods trains be brought to a stand on the steep gradients west of Delabole. The safety trap points were to be moved to Port Isaac Road. However this subsection was to remain unused by public trains for another 11 months, the LSWR declining to open it. The now-authorised Electric Tablet signalling system was installed immediately.

Port Isaac Road to Wadebridge Junction

A fairly easy alignment was possible over the three miles from Port Isaac Road to St Kew Highway, including a rare straight near Trequite, with the gradient but 1 in 110. An early start was made on the tunnel at Trelill where a ridge of high ground to the south of Port Isaac Road had to be breached. A heading of 100 yards was achieved in January 1894, but progress proved to be very slow due to the hard rock and a drill was brought in during May; the bore was just about through in June. Of its course of 350 yards, 108 were opened out to full size by August 1894. The navvies were now working below Port Isaac Road, about 600 in that month, but down to 575 in November. Having taken a high position on the west side

A view along Fernleigh Road Wadebridge with the station and goods yard in the distance. Eight cattle wagons occupy the cattle dock and along the line of chimneys the engine shed roof can just be seen. The house on the extreme left is the back of the Station Master's house.

A spendid view across the Camel estuary to Wadebridge station and goods yard. To the left can be seen the engine shed with what appears to be a Beyer Peacock 0-6-0 Ilfracombe Goods class (possibly No. 394) stabled outside whilst the offices, carriage and engine sheds of the Bodmin and Wadebridge railway can be seen to the right.

of the Allen Valley and still to west of the Delabole to St Kew Road, it was necessary to drop from the 400ft contour to near sea level at Wadebridge. The surveyors pegged out the line (as deviated) to enter the Allen Valley at Lemail, after the tunnel at Trelill and the site of St Kew Highway station on the Camelford to Wadebridge road. Earthworks were particularly heavy (a high embankment at Hingham Mill) and more hard rock was encountered as the line steadily dropped to the level of the river.

In November 1894 the tunnel was full size (though single bore) and three quarters of a mile of permanent way had been laid on the south side. 513 men were on the works in February 1895 and the first piles were being driven into the bed of the River Camel. This and the Allen were to be bridged, also the adjacent Wadebridge to Bodmin road at Sladesbridge. In March two miles of permanent way were down and by April only 1¾ miles remained to be laid. The following month the girders for the river bridges were in place and the tunnel lined throughout. The number of men had dropped to 430. A decision had been made early in the year to make a junction, and not form a side line parallel to the B&WR for the last half mile into Wadebridge.

A junction with the reconstructed Bodmin and Wadebridge line was made therefore, at 0m 78ch (zero at Wadebridge Quay) or at what was to be 253m 15ch on the North Cornwall. A new signal box named 'Wadebridge Junction' was placed in the 'V' of the junction. A siding laid in for construction works trailed from the up side into the NCR line, its pointwork unconnected (though secured) to the box.

The NCR asked the Board of Trade in November 1894 for the Delabole-Port Isaac Road section to be opened, but was told that the LSWR would not do this until the line was completed to Wadebridge. The works were completed by the end of May 1895 and the Government Inspector, Colonel Yorke, arrived at Delabole on the 28th instant. According to the 'West Briton' two heavy engines, one fitted with inspection seats on the front, had been prepared for him. After traversing the unopened section to Port Isaac Road labourers with flares preceded this train at walking pace through Trelill tunnel. The first day ended at St Kew Highway. Next day the inspection train started at Wadebridge. The two engines (40 tons each) and two coaches were run up and down over the two iron river bridges at Pendevy.

Following this, Colonel Yorke reported only on the 5m 76ch between Port Isaac Road (exclusive) and Wadebridge Junction (apparently covering 247m 20ch and 253m 17ch). The sharpest curve was at 20 chains, across the embankment to the Junction. Trelill tunnel was lined throughout, had recesses, and there were 10 overbridges and 12 underbridges. The Camel bridge was of wrought iron girders and masonry abutments. St Kew's platforms were 3ft (compared to Tresmeer's 2ft 6in) with 'accommodation and amenities for both sexes'. St Kew Highway signal box contained 16 levers with three spare. Wadebridge Junction had 14 levers, all in use, though the diagram shows 16 in 1905. The turntable at Wadebridge not being ready, only tank engines were to be used from here to Delabole. The Electric Tablet system was to be used for signalling on this single line. Colonel Yorke was not pleased with the situation at Wadebridge station. The single platform was altogether insufficient for the additional trains from the North Cornwall line. The serious attention of the LSWR was called for and remedial measures to be made at an early date. (The LSWR was quite unrepentant! In a letter to the BoT in October 1895 it said the station was 'quite sufficient').

Additionally, 'no goods train' Colonel Yorke declared, should be 'brought to a stand outside St Kew's up home signal.' The LSWR questioned this too, offering to use two brake vans on goods trains. Colonel Yorke replied it would mean two brakesmen, but if the LSWR was confident that would obviate all risks of runaways towards

The 1886 Wadebridge station, then a terminus from Bodmin and Bodmin Road, was enlarged in 1899 on the opening of the Padstow extension. In this 1910 view the advertising signs for coffee, etc show how proprietary goods became widely available after the railway arrived.

Wadebridge then it was acceptable. The Board of Trade was never happy about this junction and was pleased to approve its abolition in 1907, when two separate lines were laid into Wadebridge. Provision of two brake vans, with a guard in each, except where a 20-ton van could be substituted, was ordered by the LSWR and a limit of 20 loaded wagons imposed on all up trains. The contractor's siding (retained as a runaway?) at the junction was removed by the LSWR, however, at the BoT's request. Looking ahead a little, Wadebridge station was reconstructed in time for the Padstow opening in March 1899. However, the LSWR provided a new two-road engine shed and 50ft turntable in 1895 on reclaimed ground to the north of the station.

Wadebridge Opening 1895

The LSWR lost no time in starting trains. On Friday 31 May several trucks with 50 cattle were taken up to Delabole for attachment to the 2.00pm goods. They had been bought by Mr Pearce of Camelford for sale at Chichester Market – a foretaste of what was to come on the North Cornwall! Saturday 1 June saw the 7.00am passenger train away from Wadebridge surrounded by a large crowd. Meanwhile the first down train, starting from Launceston at 8.23am, included Mr Oag, an NCR director. The second, from Okehampton, took Mr Tremayne (the Chairman), Mrs Tremayne and others, arriving at Wadebridge at 12.37pm. All repaired to the Molesworth Arms Hotel for lunch. Later in the day, what was to be the very first 'through' coach arrived at 6.00pm. Hired by Mr Chapman, the London builder, a saloon arrived with a party of 23 to go to Padstow (taken thence on a fleet of horse brakes by Messrs Pope & Son).

The initial passenger service was 7.00am, 9.18am, 10.20am, 1.15pm, 2.36pm and 6.05pm from Wadebridge. The 5.50am train from Waterloo connected at 2.32pm, the 9.00am at 5.22pm, the 11.00am at 5.59pm and the 1.00pm at 8.36pm. The Exeter 1.00am mail and goods was extended to Wadebridge as was the 5.30am goods from Exeter (Queen Street). Stopping goods trains left at 12.46pm and 4.55pm, thus putting Wadebridge into the 'road box' system, as well as opening up direct narrow (standard) gauge access for cattle, fish, coal and merchandise with the rest of Britain. Manual transfer of goods had been necessary through the broad gauge break at Bodmin Road up to 1892. The following Monday was the Whitsun Bank Holiday and many took to riding in the new train service to Wadebridge. Back at Otterham a special from Exeter and Plymouth, organised by Mr Rundle Brendon, the Bude coaching proprietor, set down 500 excursionists for conveyance to Boscastle and Tintagel. To celebrate at Port Isaac village, field and water sports were held. Sir William Onslow, Bart of Hengar and an NCR director, was presented with an address by Henry Symons, Chairman of the local 'Demonstration Committee'. It was Wednesday 12 June before the Official Opening from Delabole to Wadebridge took place, delayed to coincide with the Royal Cornwall Show at the latter, held at Trevanyon Road. The directors' special of LSWR saloons came through Launceston at 9.35am, picking up Mr and Mrs Tremayne and Colonel Byng. There were ten ordinary coaches as well, possibly bogies and, if so, a formidable load for the 'special and large' engine. It arrived at the single Wadebridge platform at 11.10am. Once everybody had gathered together the inevitable address was read by the acting secretary of the Wadebridge Representative Council. As well as the NCR directors, that Company's Secretary (Price), London Agent (Birchall), Solicitor (Venning), Surveyor (Drew) and Auditor (Hare) were present, together with Major Hext and Mark Symons of the North Cornwall Coach Company. The Exeter District Superintendent of the LSWR (Vallance), the District Engineer (Fisher) and Crouch, their Resident Engineer on the works, were joined by many notables. However, the Mayor of Truro arrived somewhat late,

Wadebridge and its ancient wooden footbridge some time after 1906. The footbridge was eventually replaced by a standard Southern Railway concrete structure prepared at Exmouth Junction works in 1927. In the distance Railcar No. 10 has moved on from the down platform to cross over to the up loop before preparing to return to Bodmin. The comparatively short life of these railcars was an indication of their failure in service. Lack of power and difficult firing were just two of several problems these vehicles suffered whilst working out of Wadebridge in the early years.

Two splendid views of the lifting bridge over a tidal creek at Wadebridge. It was eventually removed in October 1955 but was a remarkable piece of engineering. The four columns housed chains attached to counterbalancing weights which allowed the bridge to rise and fall with the tide. Various bolts and fishplates had to be removed by the Station Foreman when a high tide was expected; conversely, he was required to make sure they were in place before any movement of wagons over the bridge could take place.

his train (presumably from Bodmin Road) having been delayed. After the ceremony and speeches, the party proceeded to the Town Hall, headed by the Royal Marines (Plymouth) Band, for refreshment.

The Bodmin & Wadebridge Railway Reconstruction and a new Terminus at Wadebridge 1888

Opened in 1834, the primitive sand railway from the quay at Wadebridge to Bodmin, and its mineral branches to Wenford and Ruthernbridge was, as we have seen, acquired by the LSWR in 1846. The latter operated it at arm's length, supplying materials, including engines, by sea through Wadebridge. Track was relaid in places (there were 6ft stone sleepers and 'T' section rails) in 1866 and 1879. The passenger service to Bodmin, such as it was, was suspended from 1 November 1886. The arrival of the GWR at Boscarne Junction, by a standard gauge branch from Bodmin Road/Bodmin, and with running powers by agreement with the LSWR (5 June 1886), found the B&WR's Wadebridge terminus wholly inadequate to receive its trains. A new station building and 230ft platform was placed 12ch to the east of the old B&WR premises. It was provided by the LSWR under an agreement with the GWR, which was to share the running expenses (the GWR retained its own booking office here until 1915).

The NCR's partnership in this 1886 agreement remained muted until 1895. In 1899 the LSWR tried, unsuccessfully, to charge the NCR a proportion of the re-signalling costs. A single line to Boscarne Junction was instituted, ready for use from 3 September 1888. Alignment improvements to the B&WR (undertaken by Curry & Reeve in 1894/95) included a new terminus at Bodmin. So, only the GWR was operating passenger and mixed trains into Wadebridge until 1895. Even more unusually, its local system from Bodmin Road, standard gauge from the start, was an enclave in a broad gauge area until conversion of the Cornwall Railway in 1892. LSWR services from Boscarne Junction into its own Bodmin terminus did not reopen until 1 November 1895.

New Layout at Wadebridge

As related elsewhere, efforts by the NCR in the early 'nineties' to extend to Truro were thwarted and instead a separate Act obtained in August 1896 confirmed Padstow as the terminus. Meanwhile the LSWR overcame its coolness to the BoT's structures on Wadebridge station, and further reconstruction work, in view of the Padstow extension, was taken in hand. It included Molesworth Street Level Crossing, a new junction with the quay sidings, virtual doubling between there and the east end of Wadebridge, a new island platform with loop, and two signal boxes. The total LSWR (ex-B&WR) line involved extended from Wadebridge Junction 253m 15ch to the 1888 terminal stopblocks (at 253m 77ch), thence over a 10ch conversion of the B&WR's quay siding to an end-on junction with the new Padstow line at 254m 7ch. The two signal boxes and the new layout were brought into operation on 12 March 1899, in time for the Padstow opening on the 27th.

The island platform, 315ft long, faced the converted 1888 loop, and on its north side got an Up loop for Bodmin trains. The whole Up side layout, into the sand dock and engine shed, needed realignment for these works. The terminal stopblock disappeared under a realignment of the Down 'main' and points leading to the new Up 'main' and Up loop; this also allowed for westward lengthening of the Down platform. The B&WR engine and carriage shed sidings and the weighbridge loop were removed. A double line now existed to 253m 79ch from a point opposite a new East signal box at 253m 59ch. The sharply curved eastern exit from the old platform was straightened and then eased to a flatter 30 chain radius. Longer leads were provided to the goods shed, to a total of 460 feet. The island platform had a waiting room and veranda, with a period LSWR wooden footbridge to the down side. The 1888 'Wadebridge Signal Box' at the Bodmin end of the terminus platform was demolished.

Both the East and West signal boxes were constructed in stone with the LSWR's central 'pillar' style of the mid-1890s. Wadebridge West box (254m 4ch) was situated at Molesworth Street Crossing; lengthy rodding runs were necessary to work the west end of the station but shorter ones to the lead points and trap points at the quay.

Colonel Yorke inspected the Wadebridge station work in May 1899, two months after the Padstow opening.

Wadebridge in 1914 with what appears to be a group of men leaving to fight in the Great War.

It seems that the Molesworth Street Crossing was still exercising his mind, as he delayed submitting his Padstow report on the latter until 29 April. The East signal box held 29 levers (1 push and pull) and two spare; the signalman operated the adjacent occupation crossing to the river by a gate lock. The West box had 20 levers and three spare, and a wheel to operate Molesworth Street gates. After describing the new platforms, the boxes and the conversion of the B&WR quay line, the Colonel yet again referred to Molesworth Street. As this crossing exercised Wadebridge citizens for many years, it is worth recounting the story in more detail.

Molesworth Street Level Crossing

Only intermittent traffic passed on down to the quayside at Wadebridge and shunting was minimal, so in B&WR days the obstruction of Molesworth Street mattered little. Neither gates nor fences were provided. Under the 1882 proposals the line might have stopped short of it by 80 yards, a Padstow line circumventing Wadebridge to the south. Once it was realised that the 1890s route would really project over the crossing, there was great concern from the inhabitants. The newly-created County Council made representations, and an Inquiry was held in the Molesworth Hall on 20 March 1894, under the chairmanship of Major C.S. Hutchinson, R.E. Interestingly the proposed line was referred to as the 'Launceston to Truro'. On market days, '45 vehicles, 42 horses and cattle and 476 footpersons' crossed in one hour. In the event, the normal lie of the gates was to be against road traffic, though a footbridge was provided. In practice road traffic was given a fair chance in view of the few trains (about one an hour each way) to and from Padstow. Shunting was a different matter! The Urban District Council complained in 1904 about 'prolonged shunting' but Colonel Yorke in his report on the Wadebridge alterations of 1899 was adamant that road traffic preference against rail was 'rarely allowed'. He had been confronted by Council and Wadebridge UDC officers on his inspection of the Padstow extension in March, not only regarding Molesworth Street, but in connection with the Commissioner's Road several hundred yards to the west, the crossing at Harbour Lane (blocked) and 'encroachments' on Eddystone Road. Again, in 1908, the UDC complained that the gates were 'closed 15 minutes at a time'. An appeal to the BoT was met with the blank reply that it (BoT) 'does not appear to have any statutory authority in the matter' and that the 1863 Railway Clauses Act did not apply. The crossing was an obstruction, of course, and with the advent of the motor age matters got worse. It was additionally the main road from North to West Cornwall, later designated the A39 Trunk Road from Taunton to Fraddon.

Wadebridge Junction to Wadebridge Widening Works 1907

The single line from Wadebridge Junction to Wadebridge Station was proving inadequate for the ten or so North Cornwall passenger and goods trains each way, and a new Rail Motor service (1 June 1906) on the Bodmin Branch. There seems to have been a last-minute arrangement for a junction rather than two separate lines into Wadebridge, the Board of Trade having been unhappy about this since 1895, situated as it was at the foot of the long gradient from Delabole. The provision of two lines was covered by transferred powers from the NCR's original 1882 Act, and confirmed by LSWR Acts in 1883 and 1891 for the B&WR deviations.

Widening work commenced in 1906 to take two single lines in a width of 30ft. The overbridge at 253m 47ch (No 145A) was already built for double track (but at only 26ft). The east end of Wadebridge was remodelled so that the new single line (for North Cornwall) was aligned with the Up platform. A scissors crossover was laid in below Guineaport (253m 62ch) thereby permitting trains from Bodmin and North Cornwall to use the Down platform or to arrive in the Up loop, also to depart from the Up platform or Up Loop platform. New works were also undertaken at Wadebridge west end for the Rail Motors (a berthing siding) and provision made for trains to depart for Padstow from the Up Loop. Wadebridge West Signal Box frame was modified to suit.

Major Pringle, R.E. inspected the new arrangements in June 1907. He reported that a new single line 'about 65 chains' ran from the now separated junction (at 253m 15ch) to Wadebridge. The East Signal box frame was extended to hold 43 levers, including two spare. Tablet working was now in operation from here to St Kew Highway and Boscarne Junction. The rails used were second-hand, hard steel, 82lb/yard. Wadebridge Junction had been 'taken away' and the temporary connection (i.e. the original contractor's siding) removed. (It appears, however, that the LSWR had actually connected its points to the frame as late as 1905). Major Pringle was worried by the curvature, and asked for speed checks to be made for the exchange of Tablets. The 65 chains actually extended to the revised junction with the NCR's Padstow

The level crossing taking the North Cornwall's Padstow extension across Molesworth Street, Wadebridge, was under construction early in 1899. The imposition of fences and gates was unpopular with the Wadebridge citizenry and Col. Yorke, the BoT Inspecting Officer for railways, held a special meeting to discuss their grievances.

Molesworth Street and hotel, Wadebridge, in the 19th century. Some of the earlier meetings of the NCR Directors were held in the hotel, named after the Molesworth family whose seat was at nearby Pencarrow. Sir Lewis Molesworth was a director for many years.

extension at 254m 10ch. Wadebridge West Signal Box (254m 4ch) had not figured in Colonel Yorke's May 1899 Report (though Molesworth Street Crossing was scrutinised). The new Rail Motor facilities resulted in the West Box frame now holding 27 levers and two spare and its operation was now approved.

Wadebridge to Padstow

Deliberations in 1894 over extending to Truro rather held up action regarding the 1882 objective, Padstow. Time to construct that far, under the 1882 Act, had long run out; piecemeal arrangements had only just seen Wadebridge attained in 1895. The intermediate portion from the west of Wadebridge Junction to Wadebridge Quay being LSWR property, the fourth section would commence just beyond the quay at 254m 7ch.

In December 1895 the Delabole to Wadebridge section was still in the Capital account. £2,529 had been received in revenue and of the rebate from LSWR for the six months since opening, also £3,692 for the 1st section and £4,229 for the 2nd. The 1st Section ordinary shareholders were receiving 4% in 1895; for the other Sections it was 3½%.

The enabling Act to extend to Padstow received Royal assent on 20 July 1896, with the remaining £88,000 under authorised capital allocated. There were preferential shares this time. The NCR directors, however, asked Padstow citizens to guarantee £3,000. C.G. Prideaux-Brune put up £1,000; even so the first £1,000 was met by Foster's Bank. The LSWR promised the remaining £1,750 of the yearly rebate and agreed to work it for an annual rental of £2,650, again on a 999 year lease. The 'Padstow Leased Line Stock' was taken up by County backers, the Bolitho family, Michael Williams (a director), Coode (solicitor) and Grylls & Co Ltd (bankers). The latter also held £20,000 of the Wadebridge Guaranteed stock as nominees of Curry & Reeves. The North Cornwall Co had sealed Lloyds Bonds to the latter, which were now cancelled.

Once the Padstow extension Act was passed, the North Cornwall Co could choose their main contractor. Curry & Reeve were once again appointed, from

Wadebridge Quay in the 1880s, then owned by the LSWR after the legalities of 1886 confirmed its purchase of the B&WR in 1846. It had opened in 1834 and the siding emerging from between houses (left centre) curved sharply to each side of the two docks and to the river frontage (right). The two sheer-leg cranes were loading granite blocks from wagons to dockside, thence to ships holds. The terraces in Eddystone Road (centre right) echo the use of the De Lank granite for the lighthouse; it was even used for some of London's bridges, and smaller pieces were still being sent by rail up to the 1960s.

View from Egloshayle a line of B&WR trucks may be seen (centre) on the siding leading from the tidal bridge over the Treguddick brook (left). The Molesworth Exchange (later the Town Hall) appears new, placing the date in the late 1880s.

December 1896, piling starting straight away for a temporary bridge at Little Petherick. Acquiring the land proved rather complicated. Only 2½ miles were in possession in April 1897, and negotiations were started with the Duchy of Cornwall over the foreshore of the Camel. Then there was the proposed embankment at Wadebridge carrying the line from the quay area across the flats, together with a footpath to Polgammon Point. Twelve owners were involved and it was well into 1898 before the last piece of land was obtained. Discussions were held in May 1897 between the BoT's Harbour Department, the Padstow Harbour Commissioners and the North Cornwall Co regarding the establishment of a new quay at Padstow. The hillsides behind run steeply to the shore, divided by seven valleys or creeks. The widest creek to be crossed was Little Petherick. Here a 200 yard embankment, faced with massive concrete blocks, was linked to the Dennis Hill side by a long viaduct, all on a 20 chain curve. The 1882 submission proposed an opening bridge 30ft wide and ten arches of 30ft. By 1896 larger vessels were no longer trading to the Sea Mills inside the creek, and that site had been acquired earlier by the NCR, presumably to safeguard its situation. Other than crossing the creeks, room for the line was found by shelving into the hillside, with several deep cuttings. Heaviest were at Ball Hill and Dennis right outside Padstow with its 25 chain reverse curves. About halfway to Padstow it crossed the frontage of the Camel Quarries, with access to the beach by a path under No.149 bridge. There was just one overbridge, at Whitehouse, taking a narrow way down from Tregunna.

Progress was slowing by April 1897, for labour was scarce. The number of men gradually rose but only 294 were on the books in November. Material from the cuttings was forthcoming by then for the embankments at Dennis and Wadebridge. The station house at Padstow, followed by the buildings, were under way at the turn of the year. In February 1898 ironwork was being delivered by barge for the Petherick viaduct, from Wadebridge Quay, with the first cylinders sunk in March. The contractors were J.H. & N. Bell of London; erection was by subcontractors, Eastwood, Swingler & Co of Derby. The 133ft spans of pairs of 'N' truss wrought iron girders weighed 350 tons each. They rested on pairs of 8ft diameter cast iron cylinders which had to be driven through 53ft of mud before reaching solid rock. They were then filled with concrete. The abutments were masonry and stood 16ft above high water, and 30ft above the mud. Men arrived from completion of the Bude extension in August and 300 were

The headquarters of the Bodmin & Wadebridge Railway are partially visible on the right of this photograph as the line continues over the ungated Molesworth Street to the quay.

Top Town Quay with some coal wagons and, above, Padstow Harbour Commissioners Quay in 1961.

on the books in September. There was optimism for an early opening with 3½ miles of permanent way put down. Padstow station (but not the goods shed) was complete and the last of the bridge cylinders were in. Early in January 1899 rails were across Molesworth Street and the signal box completed. It was all too slow for the North Cornwall directors, however, who complained that the 'Engineers had stated they thought the position of affairs very discreditable to the Contractors'.

To accommodate the line between Eddystone Road and the quay sidings, the latter needed remodelling. The inner siding was shifted 15ft northwards, which sharpened the leads into four existing B&WR sidings, and a dividing fence was erected for security. To improve the Harbour Lane entrance, a corner of land was also purchased next to the Temperance Hotel. Eddystone Road was fenced off which caused local complaints that it had been 'encroached upon'. This short link was acquired by the NCR from the LSWR under authorisation in 1898, apparently from 254m 7ch to 254m 10ch.

To accommodate Padstow Station, the site of the old Higher Shipbuilding Yard was purchased, filled in, and the hillside cut back to form a level site. Two private roads, one rising to New Street (Station Road) and one towards the Inner Harbour were built. A small harbour, remnants of the yard, a dock wall and a shed formed the nucleus of the fishing port which was to come. A larger area of land (and foreshore) was not entirely used at first. The station consisted of a single platform 320ft long, served by the running line ending at stopblocks (259m 44ch), and a run-round loop. A standard North Cornwall Railway Station Master's house and offices, but with a fairly short awning. All walls were of stone, as were the signal box, station goods shed and cattle dock. The goods yard was equally unpretentious, no better than the wayside stations, but the goods shed was in the large (No.1) LSWR style, with side windows. No engine shed or turntable seems to have been contemplated by the LSWR (Wadebridge was nearby) but the Inspecting Officer thought otherwise. The Metropole Hotel which looms above Padstow station opened its doors in May 1901. At first called the 'South Western' it was built by the Cory family of ship owning and colliery owning fame, at a cost of £12,000. As a reminder of their Padstow origins, it remained in the family until sold to Trust Houses in 1936.

The bridges, station and permanent way were in a fit enough state by the end of February 1899 and Major Yorke was invited to inspect the new line on 20 March. The permanent way was second-hand 80lb rail (79lb worn). Even as late as this, one solid wooden trenail in three was used (the other two were iron spikes driven through hollow trenails).

A train of four engines and three coaches was employed to run up and down over Little Petherick Viaduct to test deflection. The latter was 'very modest'. The only station was Padstow; all was complete, with the platforms 3ft high. The signal box had 13 levers (including three push and pull) and five spare. The inspector recommended that the line could be opened subject to:

(1) A turntable installed at Padstow; until such time, tank engines to be used.
(2) A footbridge for the Harbour Commissioners' road be provided at Wadebridge.
(3) The signal wires to be cased.

A rider stated that speed should not exceed 20mph until the line was thoroughly consolidated. In the event the turntable was installed as well as, in due course, the footbridge at Wadebridge. The length of line inspected was 5m 37ch (i.e. 254m 7ch at Molesworth Street, to 259m 44ch the stop blocks at the end of the platform at Padstow). As noted, the NCR acquired the first three chains at Wadebridge from the LSWR in 1898. The 1882 authorised length was 5m 41ch (i.e. from 254m 10ch to 259m 51ch) but extended further towards the South Quay by arrangement with the Padstow Harbour Commissioners. For accountancy purposes the Quay Line was treated as a separate branch from a junction at 259m 28ch to 259m 54ch – actually the gate to the PHC's siding.

Padstow - Completion of the North Cornwall Railway

The opening ceremony was truly auspicious judging by the number of local and railway persons present. On Thursday 23 March the directors' special left Exeter at 9.30am, called at Launceston at 11.00am and reached Wadebridge at 12.10pm. The latter station was decorated for the occasion. On board were Messrs J.C. Tremayne (the NCR Chairman's son), L.C. Foster, C.G. Prideaux-Brune and three other Directors, Drew the Surveyor and Messrs Coode and Venning (Solicitors). For the LSWR, there were Chairman Colonel The Hon. W. Campbell, Owens

(General Manager), Andrews (Chief Engineer), Dugald Drummond (Locomotive Superintendent), Jacomb-Hood (District Engineer) and several other Officers.

Overnight light snow fell at Padstow, though it had largely disappeared by morning. Well wrapped up on the platform were local dignitaries including Messrs J. Hicks JP, G.A. Hellyar CC for Padstow, F. Bray Chairman of Padstow UDC, James Nicholls, F. Sluman and representatives from the parishes of Padstow, St Merryn, St Issey, St Eval, Little Petherick and no less than six local sea Captains. Joining them was the Lord of the Manor, C.G. Prideaux-Brune, who had backed the North Cornwall's entry to Padstow so admirably and it was Miss Prideaux-Brune who declared the new section open after the train pulled in at 12.30pm. It steamed slowly ahead and cut a tape which crossed the line, while the Padstow Artillery and Delabole Brass bands played 'See the Conquering Hero Comes' A royal salute of 21 rounds were fired from the big guns on the quay. Mr Hicks read an illuminated address to the directors – in the waiting room where it was doubtless warmer! In a marquee nearby luncheon was served for about 60, provided by Spiers & Pond at the behest of the NCR directors, followed by toasts and speeches. The special train left Padstow late in the afternoon.

After that two specials were run to Wadebridge and back. The first carried 600 children, who on their return were each given a Cornish pasty. The second was for adults, about 500 in all. At Padstow the new RNLI Lifeboat was demonstrated and opened for viewing, a free 'meat tea' was provided in the Institute for over a thousand locals and more salvoes of artillery were fired by Gunner Philip. Unfortunately the Lifeboat 'James Stevens' was lost on 11 April 1900 and eight Padstow lifeboatmen were drowned.

Public services started four days later on Monday 27 March. Passenger trains left at 6.50, 8.54, 10.20am, 1.04, 2.10, 5.40 and 8.12pm (all except the last two connected to London and the 8.12 terminated at Launceston). Downward the arrivals were at 9.31am (mixed from Wadebridge) 10.55am, 12.44pm, 2.45pm (off the 5.50am Waterloo), 5.07pm (9.15am Waterloo), 6.20pm (11.00am Waterloo) and 8.43pm (1.00pm Waterloo). No Sunday services were provided. A local goods, apart from the mixed train, ran in the afternoon from Wadebridge and the special fish train to Exeter has already been mentioned.

Padstow Harbour Developments

The Padstow Harbour Commissioners (PHC) were set up by an Act of Parliament in 1844; 24 were elected by parish ratepayers and one each appointed by the Duchy of Cornwall, the Prideaux-Brune estate and HM Customs & Excise. As Lords of the Manor, the Prideaux-Brunes leased the Inner Harbour to the Commissioners, which was used initially by Curry & Reeve to import some materials. One of the first sidings was laid from here towards Wadebridge and as we have seen the NCR's new property ended just short of the South Quay. It is worth noting that the Commissioners' writ extended to Polbeck Bridge, upstream from Wadebridge and so adjoined the LSWR again at the old B&WR quay. In 1897 the LSWR sought to obtain the freehold frontage of this Quay at Wadebridge, thus relations with the PHC here were not as friendly as at Padstow. The 1899 terminus was laid out on the site of the Higher Shipbuilding yard with parts incorporated into the river frontage.

Already in the 1890s Brixham and East Coast trawlers were fishing off Padstow, attracted by the herring shoals in the autumn. The arrival of the NCR in 1899 immediately opened up Padstow to all parts of Britain, and the LSWR was already approaching Lowestoft owners and buyers in 1900. The NCR itself was providing extra buoys that year and was lent £3,394 by the LSWR (at 3% interest) to fund the new fish shed, dock wall and extra sidings. From 1899 the LSWR put on a 3.30pm fast goods train calling only at Wadebrige, Camelford, Delabole and Launceston to Meldon Junction where it connected with the Plymouth-Nine Elms overnight goods. A sum of £600 was authorised for further moorings in 1903 showing that both companies were more involved with the increasing number of East Coast vessels now using the port.

By 1908 facilities were inadequate, and the existing jetty would shelter only

The steamer *Dunraven* brought merchandise from Bristol to Wadebridge Quay, some of it loaded to rail for Bodmin, but sea-borne trade declined after the North Cornwall arrived in 1895. The Padstow Harbour Commissioners built a 218ft wharf and siding, leasing the embankment and path on the right to the LSWR after the latter sought to acquire the whole river frontage in the 1870s.

On 5th May 1964 West Country class No. 34033 *Chard* crosses Little Pentherick viaduct at Padstow with two coaches of the ACE. The first coach is a Maunsell Diagram 2007 Open Saloon Third and the coach behind is likely to be a Bulleid 'loose' Brake Composite to Diagram 2406 (number series 6713-6752). The wrought iron supporting cylinders of the viaduct were drivern 53ft through mud to reach solid rock under the creek leading to the Sea Mills. The original 1882 plans included a bridge with an opening span for access to Tregaskes quay there. S. C. Nash.

a dozen trawlers. In 1909 the PHC sought powers to lengthen the short NCR quay to 780ft. The estimated cost of this (then known as the West Quay) together with the extension of the fish shed and sidings alterations, was £20,000, to be met by a Board of Trade grant, the NCR guaranteeing £3,000 and the LSWR £10,350. The PHC could issue Bonds on the strength of an Act of Parliament obtained in 1910. The LSWR extended the fish shed, on its own account, at a cost of £503. Work was in full swing in 1911. The PHC's contractor took infilling rock from behind the goods shed and from the river bed. The construction of the dock wall was taken over about 1910 by the LSWR who used three quarter ton concrete blocks brought by rail from Exmouth Junction. A steam crane was employed on a temporary track to lift these blocks in and move material for the wall foundations. The top was coped with granite blocks and the wall protected by vertical and horizontal timbers. The West Quay was largely completed in 1912.

The 1910 powers also provided for a massive new jetty 800ft long and 40ft wide, to parallel the West Quay. At the seaward end piers and a gate would close the gap thus forming a wet dock, the cost estimated at £40,000. Agreement between the NCR, LSWR and PHC was reached in August 1911 and a Provisional Order in 1912 enabled the PHC to sell or lease these undertakings. The LSWR took further Bonds up to £30,000 and in 1916 leased, and virtually ran, the port from then until 1966. These Bonds (then amounting to £86,000) were then renegotiated, the PHC repaying the debt to British Railways (the successor to the LSWR) and forthwith running Padstow themselves.

In the event the gate arrangement did not materialise and the dock remained (and remains) tidal. The tenders for the

It was a cold morning on 23rd March 1899. Light snow had fallen overnight, but a warm welcome awaits the special train at Padstow. An illuminating address is ready for presentation, bunting applied – and the word *Gentlemen* subsequently erased by the prudish photographer. Over on the right is the stock ready for use on the public specials to Wadebridge later in the day, together with an O2 0-4-4T. Train services started on 27th March. The white post is the 259½ milepost, but notice that the fish shed had not yet been constructed.

The deep cutting blasted out of the rock at Ball Hill (257m 60ch. Removal of spoil was entirely by hand, and no evidence of the use of a steam navvy (as on the contemporary Bude extension) has been found. The high construction costs of the Padstow extension is reflected in this cutting, that at Denis Hill and the expense of the Little Pentherick Viaduct.

new jetty were let in December 1912, together with a further extension of the West Quay. Some 2½ acres of foreshore were acquired by the LSWR and NCR and the existing short jetty demolished. Work continued into World War One and was probably completed in 1915, though some was still going on in 1920. The jetty was formed by two mass-concrete walls, strengthened by embedded rails, on rock foundations. They were 40ft wide and carried two sidings on grouted rubble infilling and a gravelled surface. The depth of water at ordinary neap tide was 12 to 13ft, and on completion sixty trawlers could be held between it and the West Quay. The jetty was referred to as the 'Railway Pier'.

The West Quay was again extended, by 160ft, in 1928 at a cost of £13,000. Yet more works by the Southern Railway in the 1930s saw the completion of a 'bull-nose' and breakwater at the extremity of the 'Railway Pier', and a breakwater protruding from the North Quay. The latter was 360ft long and constructed of concrete reinforced by old rails. These works were largely financed by Government grants (under the Public Works Facilities Act 1930) to alleviate unemployment; the total cost was about £40,000. It should be noted here that the 'West Quay' is now referred to locally as the 'Inner Dock Wall' and the long 'Railway Pier' as the 'Outer Dock Wall'.

Alterations to sidings, building work, ancillary services and rail services are described later. Before Word War One, the Government of the day wanted to improve the Cornish Fisheries and the LSWR, mindful to the revenue from high value fish traffic, could see the advantage of developing Padstow. The new General Manager, Herbert Walker and the Chairman, Sir Hugh Drummond, paid a visit to Padstow in July 1912 and the LSWR's ultimate controlling interest in the port stems from this time. The North Cornwall Company retained only a minor interest financially, though it was the landowner. The fortunes of the fish trade varied. In the 1910 season 1,735 tons were landed, increasing to 3,074 tons in 1911. Even in the First World War, when a large number of trawlers served as minesweepers, many of the remaining East Coast vessels fished out of Padstow summer and winter. In the post-war years the LSWR and SR still carried sizeable loadings – 1,747 tons in the 1931 season, with 70 boats working. By this time the trawlers were steam-powered thus requiring coal, most of it coming in by rail. Right up to 1938 the tonnage increased annually and, even in World War Two, fish trains were run on occasion. By the 1950s, however, catches had declined and only one or two East Coast vessels used the port. The trade was not helped by the ice factory burning down in 1950. The closure of the freight facilities at Padstow in 1964, and British Railways operations generally in 1966/67, sealed its fate. Or would have done. The role of the Commissioner's responsibilities changed dramatically in the following years, but this is not part of the railway story. Visitors to Padstow today can observe the new works subsequently undertaken, though the fish shed still stands as a memorial to the hectic dealing and loading that went on in advance of a fish special, timed to steam away from Padstow about 4.30pm of a winter's evening in the 1930s.

The Final Years 1900 to 1922

After the Padstow opening in 1899 the North Cornwall Railway Company settled down to a background existence as a distant satellite of the LSWR. The Board of Directors sat almost monthly in the first decade of the 20th Century, often at the South Western Hotel at Padstow. The Annual General Meetings took place there, as well, but as the shareholders were receiving regular dividends derived from the LSWR rentals, little dissent occurred. The Padstow Harbour Works were in full swing from 1910 and with the LSWR paying for most of them, the Company was even more satisfied!

Following the death in 1901 of John Tremayne, who had been Chairman since 1883, L.C. Foster was elected in his place. Tremayne owned estates in the Wadebridge area and had been an active and influential promoter of the Company's interests. His seat was at Croan, in Egloshayle Parish, and the family was related to that of Sir Trehawke H. Kekewich of Peamore,

The directors' special had just arrived at at Padstow at 12.30pm on 23rd March 1899. No record has emerged of the engine, which appears to be an Adams 4-4-0, but the train consists of LSWR 46ft First, Directors Saloon, 1877 Directors Saloon No. 9, 47ft 6in Eagle Saloon and a 30ft Brake. Notice the ribbon ready for cutting by Miss Prideaux-Brune.

Excavation of hard rock was necessary for the yard and goods shed (just out of picture to the left) while some gangers pose momentarily for the cameraman.

Exeter, who was elected to the Board in 1901. Lewis Charles Foster (1844-1923) was a partner in Robbins, Foster & Bolitho, bankers at Liskeard, also known as the East Cornwall Bank. He was Chairman of the Liskeard & Caradon Railway, County Councillor JP and a Deputy Lieutenant of the County. The Earl of Wharncliffe had been Deputy Chairman for many years. His estates in Tintagel and Delabole were disposed of before 1914. On his death in 1899 his son (the 2nd Earl) was elected in his place, but in 1913 Colonel the Hon. C.C.G. Byng became the Deputy. The Williams family of Scorrier, Redruth, who had large interests in mining and smelting in West Cornwall

A carriage siding was laid in at Padstow about 1905 occupied in this 1921 view by a rake of LSWR coaches in contemporary salmon pink and brown. The fish shed, behind, has by this time been extended. Facilities for cattle were no more than might be found at a country station; the wagons in the dock, behind the goods shed, being equipped with vacuum pipe or brake to run in passenger trains.

Above. Padstow about 1902 before redevelopment of the fish quays, but showing the new South Western Hotel. In the centre are the fish sidings, one lined with watering points for van washing. The O2 0-4-4T with a North Cornwall line train in the platform is unlikely to have worked beyond Wadebridge. The stock appears to be a six wheel first, a low arc-roofed 30ft bogie brake and a pair of 41ft bogie carriages of 1890s vintage. The open fish wagon on the right is one of a small fleet converted from carriage underframes (some were new) and equipped with vacuum brake for use on specials, or as tails on passenger trains.

Middle. Beattie tank No. 0298 awaits departure from Padstow with an Okehampton train on 16th June 1926. It is unlikely to have gone forward with it from Wadebridge. H. C. Casserley, courtesy R. M. Casserley.

Bottom. A very early view of Padstow showing the original jetty or breakwater, part of the old Higher shipyard. The 4-4-0 has a North Cornwall line train of two low arc-roofed bogies and guards brake, a high-roofed bogie coach and another guards brake. Passenger rated stock also occupies the fish sidings – a 42ft bogie guards brake and a 30ft example with a cupola lookout. The lack of accommodation at Padstow became acute at this time (a coach is stabled by the goods shed) and another siding was laid in next to the run-round loop about 1905.

Top. **Locals gather at Padstow in 1910 for the wedding party of Jack and Katie Stribley – Katie's aunt, Miss Emily Sleeman, is clutching a dog.**

Middle. **O2 0-4-4T No. 182 at Padstow with a train for Wadebridge. Lens of Sutton.**

Bottom. **From the beach on the north side of Padstow may be seen the new fish shed and the old semi-enclosed tidal dock (left) while a row of round ended fish wagons line the quay (centre). The year is c.1907 and within a few years substantial sums would be spent by the LSWR in redeveloping this frontage to accommodate 60 to 70 trawlers. The proposed gates for a wet dock, however, never materialised.**

and South Wales, later turned to banking. In 1905 the Liskeard bank (then Bolitho, Coode, Foster & Grylls – 'Consolidated Bank') was taken over by Barclay & Co. This bank, as we have seen, had backed the North Cornwall Company for many years. Michael Williams (1839-1907) was elected a Director in 1893. He had inherited estates in Davidstowe, Minster and Lesnewth (and a share in the East Cornwall Bank) subsequently making his home at Halwill Barton, Delabole. Bankers, again, the Bolitho family of Penzance, were large stockholders in the North Cornwall Railway Co until 1922.

During the lifetime of the North Cornwall Railway, the Molesworth and the Onslow family interests were represented by Sir Lewis of Pencarrow, Bodmin and Sir William of Hengar, St

Top. **Padstow from the east. Although a poor copy this photo is interesting in that it shows the original turntable in the process of being resited whilst work is progressing on the extension to the fish shed to the left.**

Middle. **Padstow station yard in the 1950s. Horse drawn carriages would wait here for the arrival of trains and in later years a local bus would convey passengers to the villages along the coast.**

Bottom. **Between the masts of the two Lowestoft-registered sailing trawlers (left) the new 800ft jetty can be seen under construction, whilst (centre) can be seen the fish shed and station buildings. The photograph would seem to date from about 1909.**

Tudy. The Molesworths were great benefactors of Wadebridge, while the Onslows – Sir William was a director from 1883 until 1899 – both gave land for construction of the line. Last, but not least, the Prideaux-Brunes of Padstow had pressed for the railway to extend there for many years, though it was 1899 before the family could look out from Prideaux Place and see steam rising from the new terminus in the town. Charles Glyn Prideaux-Brune was a Director from 1883 until his death in 1907. He was succeeded by his son Colonel Charles Robert and, appropriately, he was the last Chairman in 1922.

On the Devon side James Oag of Thorndon, near Ashwater, was for long

A steel hulled 100ft. schooner berthed by South Quay with a rake of china clay wagons behind.

Prideaux Place, the seat of the Prideaux-Brune family, is the scene of a wedding (presumably - see earlier) ceremony in this Edwardian photograph. C. G. Prideaux-Brune, a director of the North Cornwall Railway Company until his death in 1908, was succeded by his son Col. C. R. Prideaux-Brune until the end of the Company in 1923.

a Director (1883 until his death in 1912) as well as C. Bainbridge Rendle of Devonport (also a Director of the Delabole Slate Co). Lord Halsbury figured largely in the affairs of the NCR Co. The latter, as Sir Hardinge Stanley Giffard, sat as MP for Launceston from 1877 until becoming Baron Hardinge in 1885 to hold office as Lord Chancellor. With a seat at Pendruccombe House, Launceston, he was Constable of the Castle. A Director from 1885, following the death of Lord Torrington, and further created the Earl of Halsbury in 1898, he continued as such until his death in 1921.

The LSWR appointed Arthur Mills MP as their Director on the NCR Board and, on his death in 1899, F.J. Macauley and Sir F.C. Scotter (LSWR General Manager 1866-1898, thereafter a SWR Director).

In August 1912 there was a suggestion that the LSWR might absorb the North Cornwall Co or, at least, offer a reorganisation of the financial stockholding and existing rentals and rebates. The new General Manager, Herbert Walker, wrote to the NCR in October setting out the LSWR's proposals.

(a) A fixed rental of £25,250 per annum, paid half-yearly in place of the existing rentals and debates.

(b) Payment of Delabole to Wadebridge Section arrears of interest (£5,035).

(c) Payment of the £3,000 invested in the Padstow Harbour works.

(d) Necessary Parliamentary powers for consolidation of stocks.

So far as (d) was concerned, the existing issued capital (£574,000) and the Debentures (Launceston/Delabole 3½% = £62,000. Launceston/Halwill and Delabole/Wadebridge £50,000 each) would be converted to 'North Cornwall Line Stock' revalued at £801,000, the rental income paying about 3½% on the capital. Acceptance by the NCR shareholders came in 1913, agreement in April and ratification by an LSWR Act of 15 August.

Under the amalgamation powers for the new Southern Railway Company in 1922 the NCR would be absorbed by the LSWR in the first place. In the final count, at an extraordinary meeting held on 17 November 1922, the LSWR was already seen to be the largest shareholder (£130,308). Other large holdings were by the Curry interests (from the contracting years), the Oags and Bolitho interests, Colonel Prideaux-Brune and the Eastern Telegraph Co. These, and minor shareholders, received equivalent LSWR stocks totalling £161,309. The North Cornwall Railway Company was formally wound up at the last meeting at Finsbury Court, London on 6 March 1923. The four remaining Directors, L.C. Foster, H.D. Foster, Colonel Prideaux-Brune and Sir T.H. Kekewich, were compensated for loss of office, and the Secretary, E.C. Price, received a £250 testimonial.

Two views of 460 class No. 465 alongside the Fish Dock in 1909 and about to leave with a mixed goods train comprised largely of empty coal wagons. South Western Hotel, now the Metropole Hotel, behind.

Quotations by the SR, post-1923, recognised an 'actual' mileage from Waterloo, quoted in the timetables. The Engineer's Department employed the 'milepost' mileage for obvious reasons - bridges for example - and these are used in this book. The slacks in mileage on the North Cornwall were about 8 to 12 chains, so that the stopblock at Padstow, 259m 55ch, was seen locally as 259m 44ch.

The assets of the NCR comprised the land and permanent way, all structures and the stations. Not all buildings belonged to the Company; the staff cottages and the signalling system were LSWR for instance. The North Cornwall began at the boundary with the LSWR (17 chains beyond Halwill Junction station) and ended similarly short of Wadebridge Junction. The double line (as from 1907) to Wadebridge and through to Molesworth Street was LSWR. From the latter point to Padstow South Quay (but possibly not all sidings on the other quays) comprised the Padstow extension.

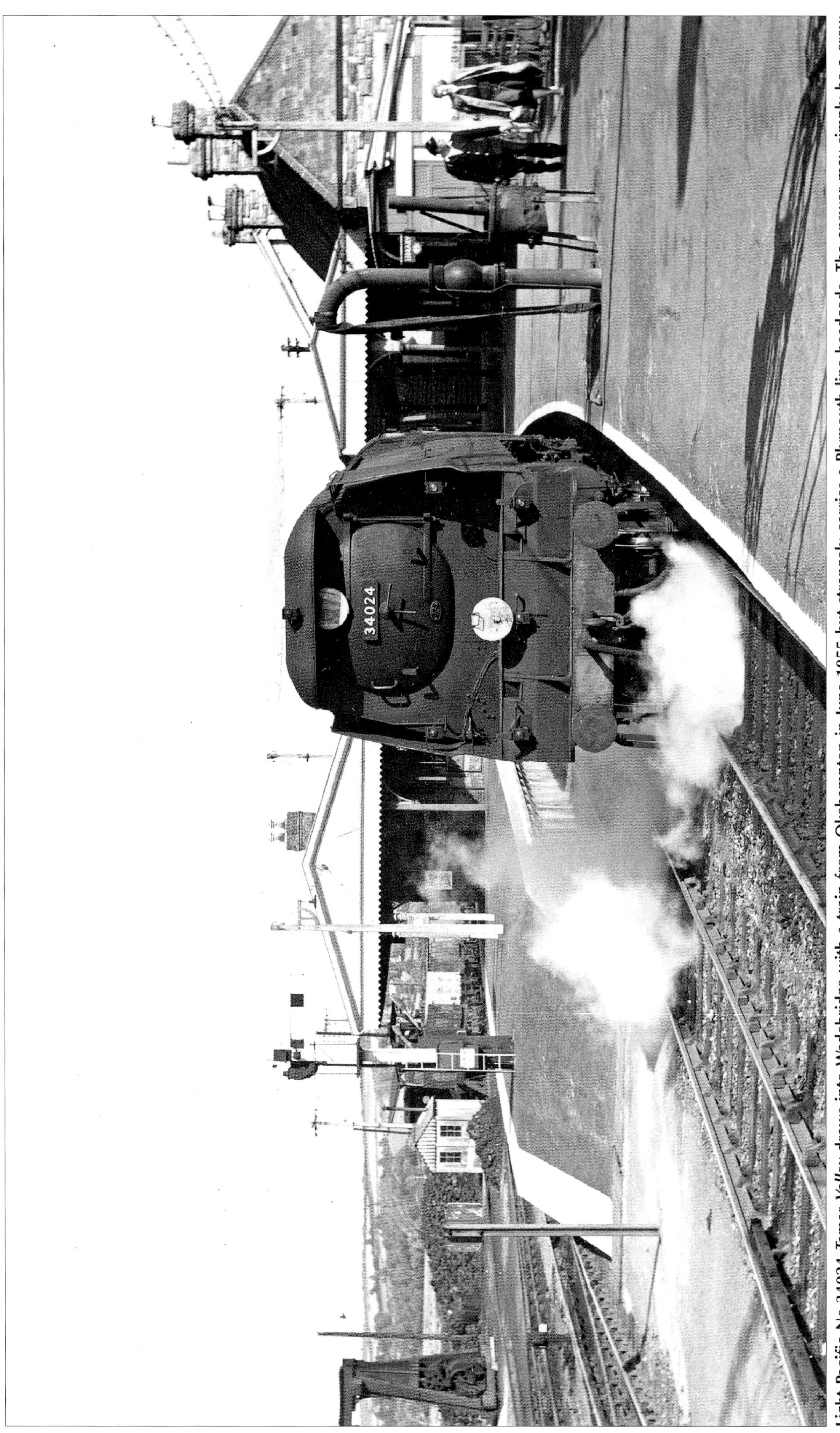

Light Pacific No.34024 *Tamar Valley* draws into Wadebridge with a train from Okehampton in June 1955 but strangely carries a Plymouth line headcode. The answer may simply be a crew oversight. Exmouth Junction duty 537 involved a light Pacific and the 1.45am freight to Plymouth Friary. It returned with the 10.57am freight to Okehampton and finally left Okehampton with a passenger train, the 3.55pm to Padstow. Note also the 'Library' sign behind! R. E. Vincent, www.transporttreasury.co.uk

Chapter Three
THE LINE DESCRIBED

Domesday Borough, Charter Town (James 1 – 1623), a cattle market and with a military presence from the Dartmoor training areas, Okehampton loomed large in railway developments. The station was well above the town to the south, a half mile steep climb for some, but horse and (later) motor buses served other users. Most local trains had portions for Bude and Padstow dividing and attaching further west at Halwill. The two-platform layout with a bay (departure only) on the Down side was restrictive, entailing carriage stock movements conflicting with shunting the goods yard. There was formerly a fifteen-lever signal box on the Down platform. There were rudimentary engine facilities on the Up side, for the Holsworthy tanks, but in 1894 proper accommodation came with a 50ft turntable and single road engine shed. Further sidings were required by the end of the 1880s for increased traffic.

To accommodate the Army an extensive loading bank served by three sidings was constructed by 1909 on the Up side to the west. As there was simply no room for long shunting necks, most moves from both sides required

N class mogul No. 31844 takes water at Okehampton shed in May 1964. The wagon was used to collect ash and clinker from the pit in front of the coal stage erected in 1947.

The elevated position of Okehampton station afforded fine views across the valley of the Okement River and the rolling Devon hills beyond. T9 4-4-0 No.30719 heads a Padstow bound train in July 1960. R. C. Riley, www.transporttreasury.co.uk

Plymouth and the North Cornwall lines beckon over the standard LSWR footbridge. In the North Cornwall bay, in the autumn of 1965 is a diesel railcar, likely to be a Plymouth Laira, BRC&W, 3-car set.

This North Cornwall line regular, a black-lined T9 No. 30717, stands on the coaling road at Okehampton shed in May 1953. W. Potter.

A gloomy wet Dartmoor day in 1955. David Wroe.

Several generations on from the early South Western 42ft. example installed in 1871, the turntable now had a vacuum motor and could turn the largest locomotives. Construction of the turntable and coaling stage began in May 1946 to coincide with the introduction of the powerful Bulleid Pacifics along the routes west of Exeter the following year. Similar examples were installed at Ilfracombe and Padstow. Alec Swain, www.transporttreasury.co.uk

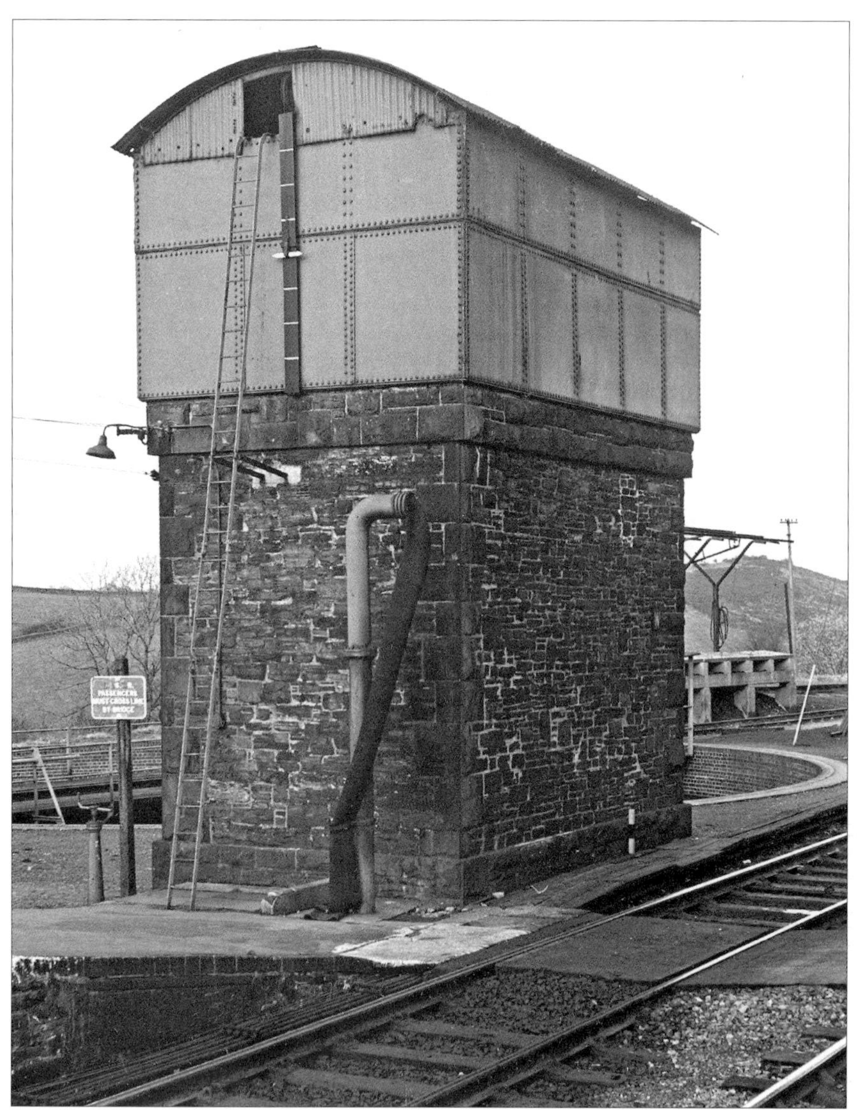

occupation of the running lines in the platforms. The underbridge at the west end was widened about 1886 to improve the exit from the bay, with a limited 'neck' for shunting the goods yard. The rising cattle traffic in the 1880s resulted in a landing with pens beyond the goods shed. Enlargement of the goods yard with three long sidings meant more quarrying out – and building up an embankment. The goods shed itself was a large country LSWR type, in local brown stone masonry.

The 1871 station building on the Up side originally comprised a large Station Master's house and single storey offices to the side. A large awning was provided – it can be rather wet at times in Okehampton! A waiting room was provided on the down platform and toilets in due course.

The SR undertook rebuilding and resignalling in the 1930s. A new signal box was erected on the Up side, opened on 12 May 1935, and Up side offices and a refreshment room built in brick, together with a steel-framed awning over the platform. Some alterations to the layout took place in 1935 and 1939. Okehampton was at full stretch in World War Two, especially from 1943 when the US Army built up for the Normandy invasion. There were yet more changes after the war. On its cramped ledge to the east of the station, the engine shed

Two structures at Okehampton dating from the opening of the station in 1871. Left, the sturdy water tower and, below, the goods shed, still intact today and in use as a youth hostel. Alec Swain, www.transporttreasury.co.uk

Okehampton in 1964. To the left is the signal box opened in May 1935 which in turn had replaced an earlier South Western example opened in 1871, sited on the down platform.

U class 2-6-0s were pretty scarce on the North Cornwall so the appearance of No. 31791 was worthy of note by R. C. Riley in July 1959. It stands in the North Cornwall bay and is destined for Bude. R. C. Riley, www.transporttreasury.co.uk

Okehampton to Halwill Junction

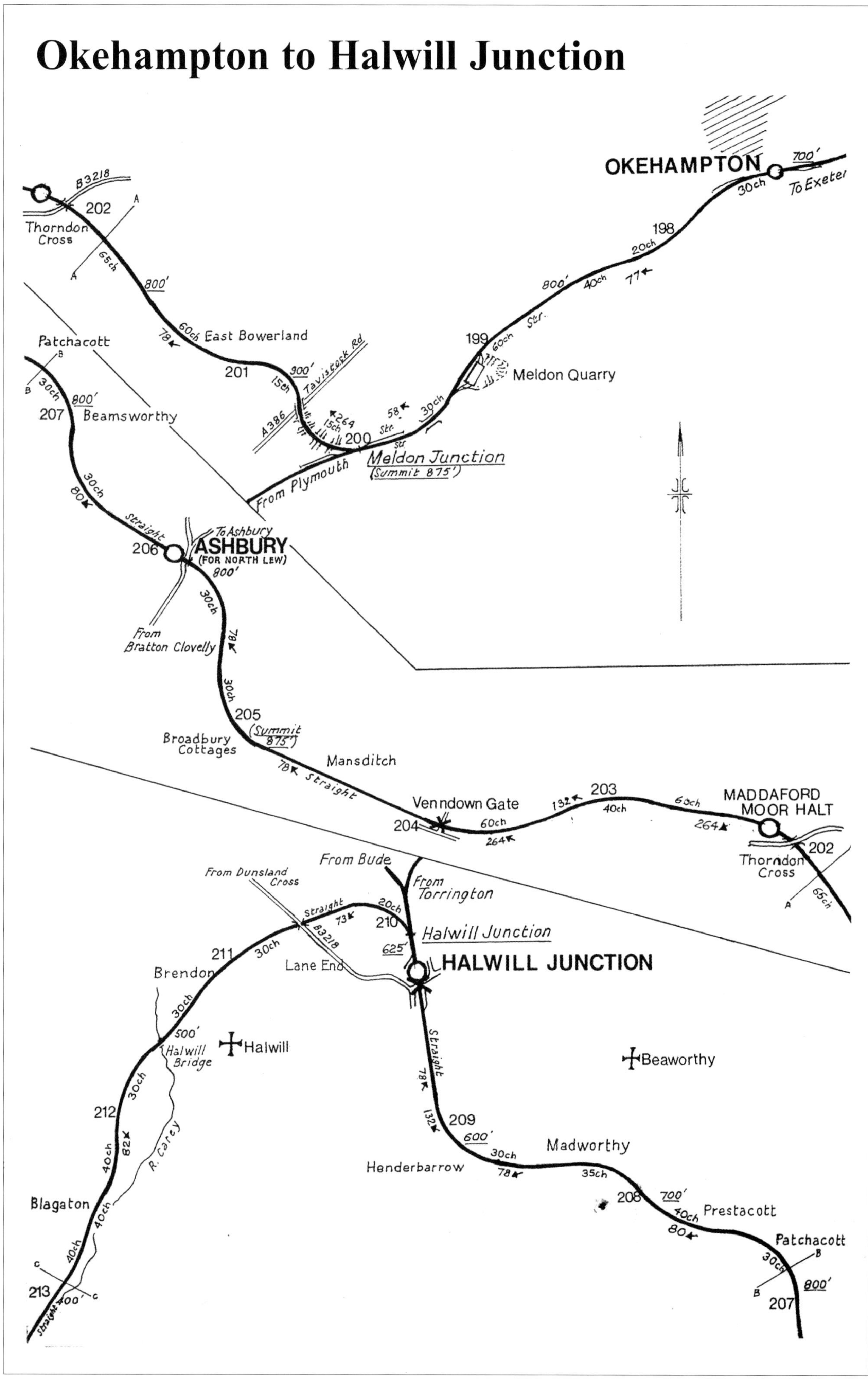

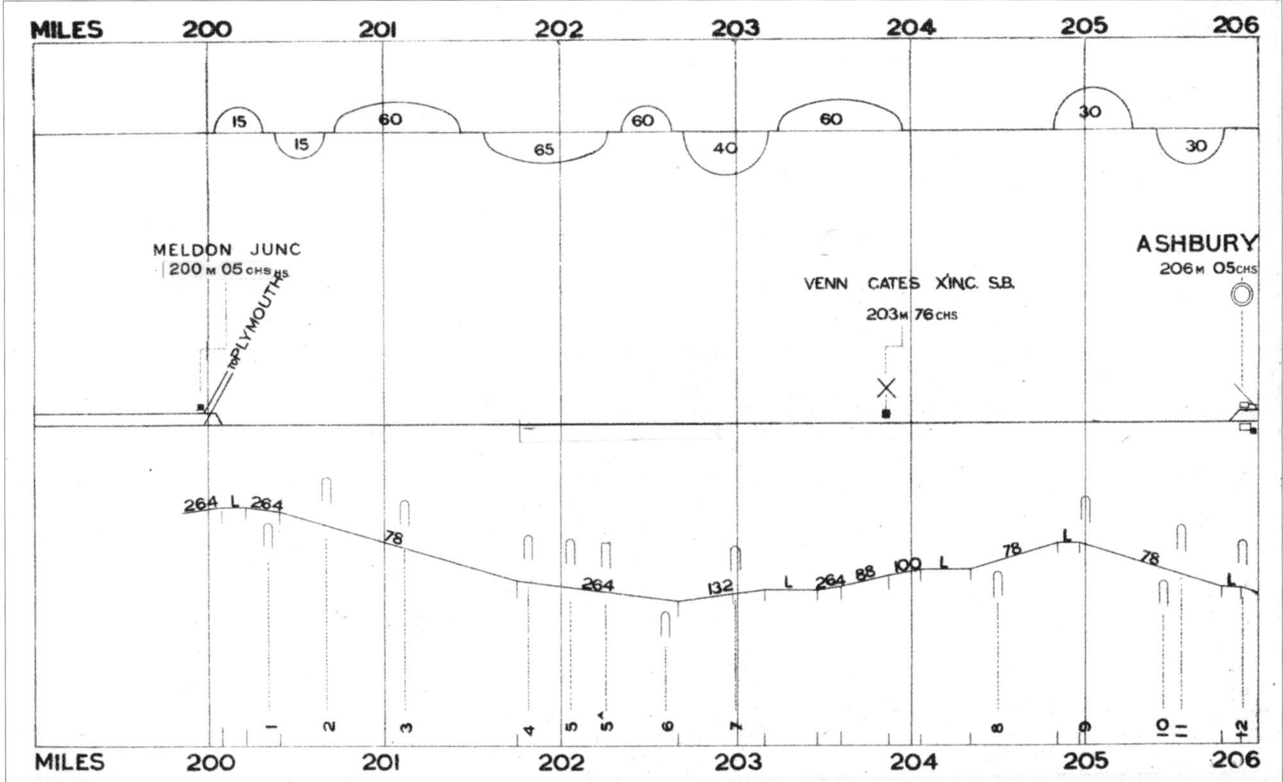

was completely revised. The new light Pacifics needed a longer turntable, so a new 70ft replacement was sited at one end, with a nest of three sidings between it and the engine shed. S15 4-6-0s working to Meldon Quarry could also now turn at Okehampton. At the height of the holiday season, however, the staff were hard-pressed to service engines in this restricted site.

The turn around of passenger trains was usually done by train engines, but a shunter/carriage pilot engine pottered about Okehampton most of the day. At one time '495' 0-6-0s or a K10 4-4-0 served but in the last years a Drummond '700' 0-6-0 (30691 for instance) filled this role. It could also push a snow plough shield kept here for clearing the way around Dartmoor. Certain North Cornwall goods trains also started and terminated at Okehampton, so there were invariably 'N' class 2-6-0s shunting as well. Over the years the siding accommodation increased to a capacity holding of over a hundred wagons. In addition to the box and open ordinary wagons, occasional empty ballast wagons for Meldon, army lorries and guns on flats, cattle wagons (for loading and transit), petrol and tar wagons were dealt with here. After the demise of Meldon Junction sidings in the 1920s, which had handled a lot of the Plymouth and Cornwall exchange traffic, Okehampton took on this role. Yeoford sidings were enlarged in the Second World War, thus some goods trains now passed Okehampton, en route there (or to Crediton) to the Western sorting yards at Exmouth Junction.

Okehampton and Meldon Junction

From a level stretch in the platforms at

The view from Park Road Bridge No. 610, as N mogul No.31847 drifts down the bank from Meldon Quarry and the summit of the line at Sourton with a train from Plymouth in July 1961. R. C. Riley, www.transporttreasury.co.uk

Top. The extensive sidings and quarry at Meldon in July 1963. To the left is the disused rock crusher and centre is the SR built Departmental loco shed, with USA 0-6-0T No.DS234 inside.

Middle. T9 4-4-0 No.30313 hauls a staff train from Okehampton to Meldon Halt in 1961. T. Gough.

Bottom. Unidentified mogul crosses Meldon Viaduct with a two coach train for Bude.

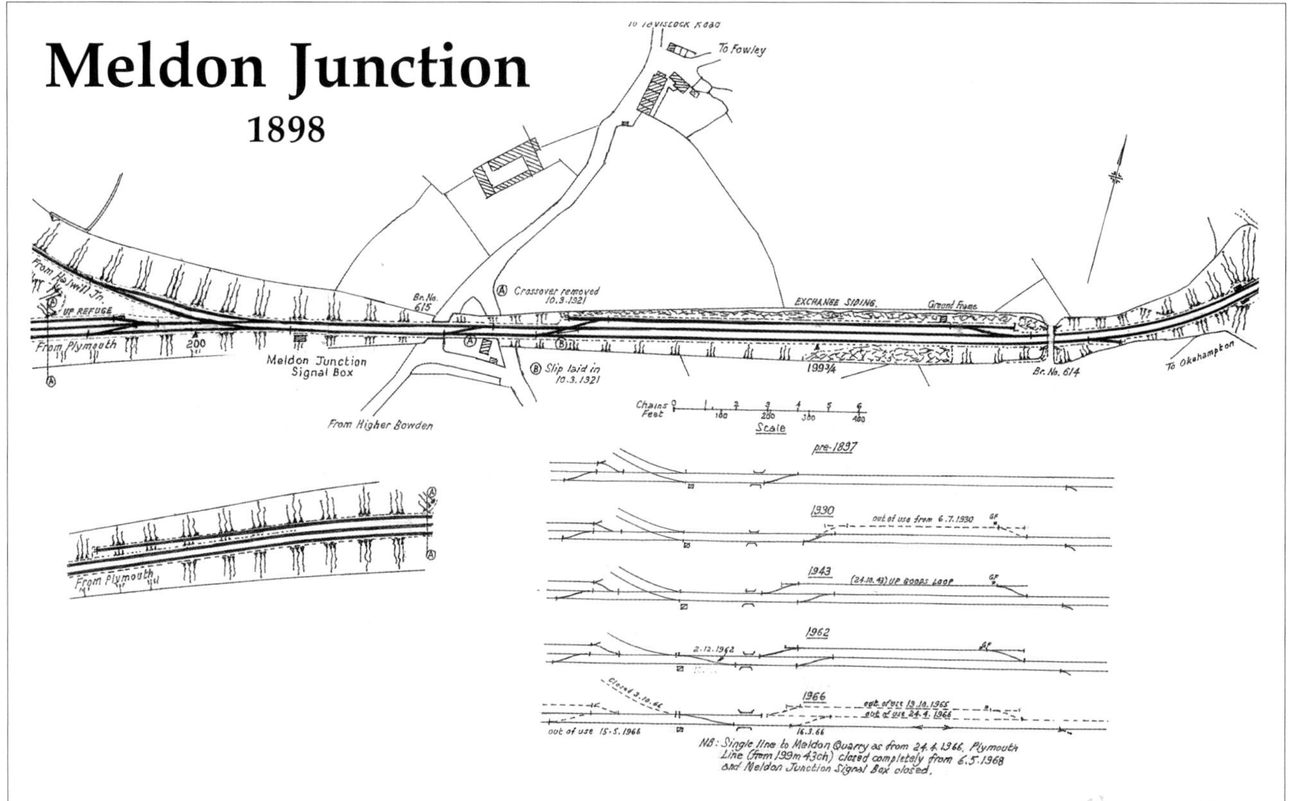

Okehampton, the Plymouth main line climbed 2½ miles at 1 in 77 to Meldon Quarry signal box, at 199m 22ch. The large quarry on the Down side, originated by the LSWR in 1882, had little to do with operations on the North Cornwall apart from such ballast as it required. However, some passenger trains did call at the tiny staff halt (199m 41ch), one being the Saturday afternoon working to and from Launceston. A special coach was taken by an Okehampton engine to and from Okehampton for the quarry staff. The Viaduct was difficult to maintain, but after repairs in the 1960s, the heavier axle-weight rebuilt light Pacifics were permitted to run to Plymouth. From 24 April 1966 the Up line was taken out of use and a single line instituted between Quarry signal box and Meldon Junction signal box.

Meldon Junction

The original layout of the junction at Meldon, where the Holsworthy branch turned off in 1879, comprised facing and trailing points in the double line converging to single towards Ashbury. It was more than just a simple junction. After 1897 there were two sidings on the Up side, one on each side. On the Plymouth end lay the 'refuge' latterly holding 30 wagons. On the viaduct side was a new 'exchange' and here sorting wagons for the Plymouth line and North Cornwall/Bude took place. At 900ft above sea level and on the 'weather side' of Dartmoor these operations must have been onerous, especially on dark winter nights. There was no lighting in that period, just handlamps and pinpoints from the

Two unusual views looking back to Meldon Junction from the North Cornwall line, in June 1963. The train, bound for Padstow, is crossing the A30 Launceston-Okehampton road. In the distance can be seen Meldon Junction signal box and the line sweeping in to meet the Plymouth main line. The white building to the left is the signalmans cottage. John Eyres, South Western Circle.

ground signals. The exchange siding was connected originally only to the Down line at the west or signal box end. The east end joined the Up and was controlled by a ground frame released from the box. The gradient here fell sharply at 1 in 58 towards the viaduct, so great care was necessary to avoid mis-shunts, and the resulting runaway wagons. The early morning Devonport to Launceston goods would set back over the ground frame points into the exchange. Brakes were pinned down and sprags applied to wheels to arrest wagons, while the engine went on down to Okehampton to deliver, collect and turn. On return, brake vans were left on the Down; many goods ran with two individual guards and vans, and a travelling shunter. The Launceston goods could draw directly out onto the Down line and set back on to the brake vans. Plymouth line goods would also leave wagons (secured as above) for collection by Halwill-bound trains.

Maddaford Moor (For Thorndon Cross) was opened in July 1926 by the Southern Railway. Only the barest facilities were provided at this remote outpost although some bungalows were erected in the surrounding area, before the War, which generated a modest traffic until the line's demise in the 1960s. A passing loop had existed here back in the 1800s, well before the halt was conceived, and was controlled by a small signal box. Left. The halt from the up ACE in July 1963 hauled at this time by Bulleid Pacific No. 34086 *219 Squadron* and below, a well know view of the halt in the early 1960s. John Eyres, South Western Circle.

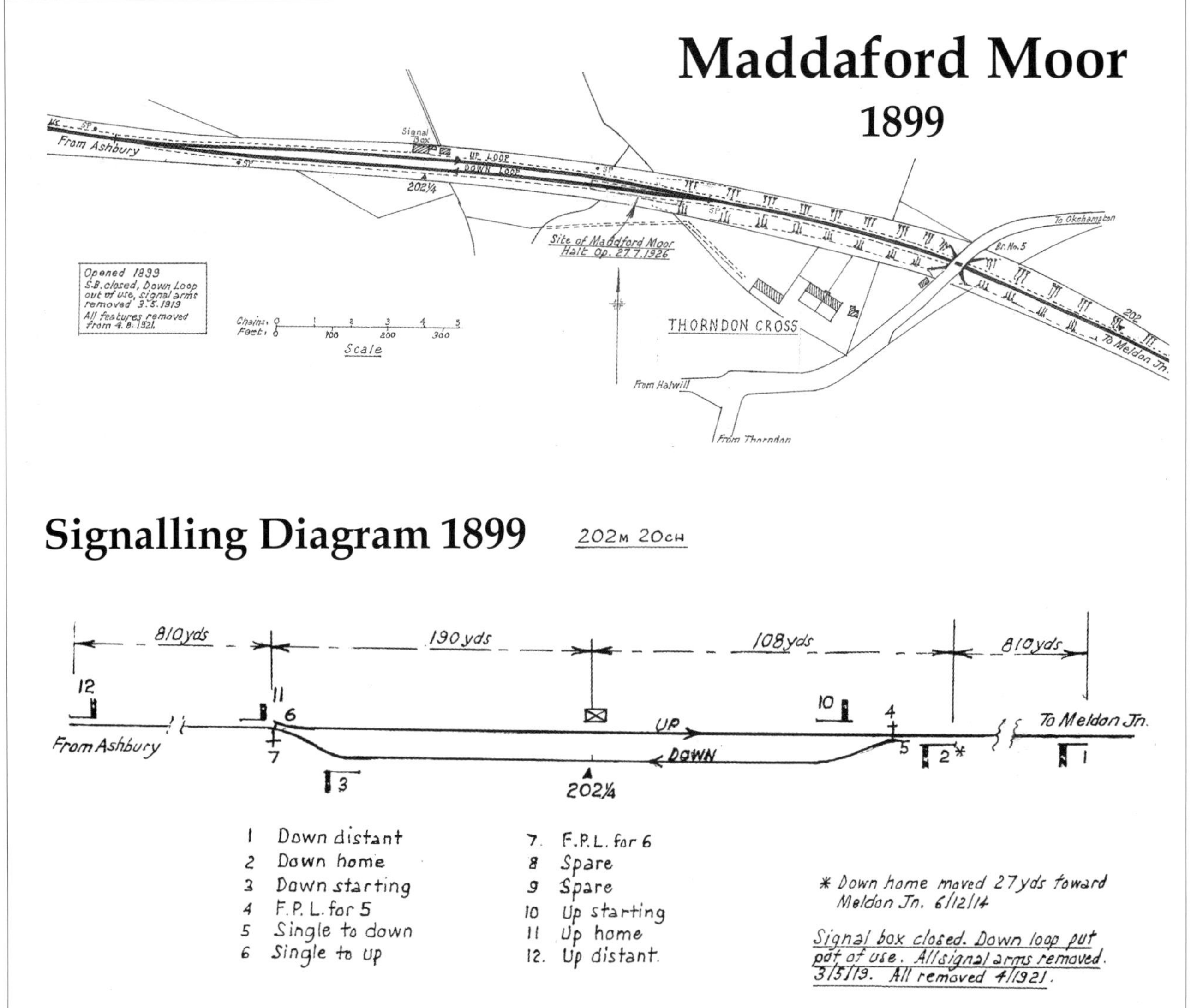

Until 1966 there were two trailing crossovers as well, each side of the junction points. They, and their ground signals, were operated by 'push-pull' levers. The gradual disuse of Meldon exchange siding in favour of Okehampton and Halwill caused its final abolition in July 1930 including the ground frame although it was not removed.

Meldon Junction signal box (199m 78ch) was rather a squat edifice of LSWR 1870s pattern. The signalling was concentrated at first, with no fewer than three bracketed junction signals in the Down direction: distants at 816 yards, outer homes at 144 yards and inner homes at 17 yards. 26 levers in the frame controlled them, those towards Bridestowe and Ashbury, as well as the pointwork and locking. At first the Ashbury single line was protected by a Staff, but from the 1890s a Tablet system was introduced (Tyers No.3) to the new block post at Maddaford Loop, but in BR days a returnable Token was substituted (to Ashbury). A 10mph restriction was imposed for exchange of Tablets. Two hundred yards towards Ashbury the Up and Down lines converged to single line. An interesting altercation between the Board of Trade and the LSWR occurred in 1897. The latter laid in a trailing runaway point in the Down line leading to Ashbury. Major Marindin did not like it at all. Nothing like it had ever been sanctioned before and it would be a danger to branch and main line, he said. The LSWR, under pressure, removed it in 1898.

For Up trains 'Regulation 5' applied, first from Maddaford Loop and then from Ashbury. This meant flagged signals to inform Up line drivers that Meldon Junction could not be assumed to be clear, with no protection from overrunning the Home signal. The previously mentioned down inner Homes at Meldon were subsequently removed due to the lack of sufficient overrun to the junction points.

The exchange siding was reactivated from 24 October 1943 but as an Up goods loop. The eastern end was still ground frame operated. This wartime provision appears to be associated with the new ASD yard at Halwill for ammunition trains. A new facing crossover came into use 2 December 1962 and henceforward North Cornwall down trains used this to gain the single line (the direct lead and diamond crossing being removed). Most connections and the goods loop were recovered in 1966 with the singling over the viaduct. The end of Meldon Junction and signal box in relation to the North Cornwall came on 30 October following withdrawal of passenger trains on the 3rd. To complete the story here, after withdrawal of services between Okehampton-Tavistock North-Bere Alston on 6 May 1968, a temporary stop block was placed on the single line at 199m 43ch (at the east end of the viaduct (199m 48ch) to better serve the ballast trains in Meldon Quarry. This has since been removed.

Meldon Junction to Ashbury and Halwill Junction

Leaving Meldon Junction on a double reverse curve of 15 chains on a high embankment (at 900 feet above sea level) set the line in a westerly direction. On this exposed plateau there are not many trees of size and hedges rise high to shelter livestock in numerous small fields. Two miles from the Junction lay Maddaford Moor Halt (202m 14ch). The sub-title 'For Thorndon Cross' originally referred to a proposed health resort. The Southern Railway was induced to open this halt on 27 July 1926. Development of bungalows continued into the 1930s, but no resort. Maddaford Moor survived, quite well used, until closure in 1966. The oil lamp by the waiting shed was placed there by train guards as required.

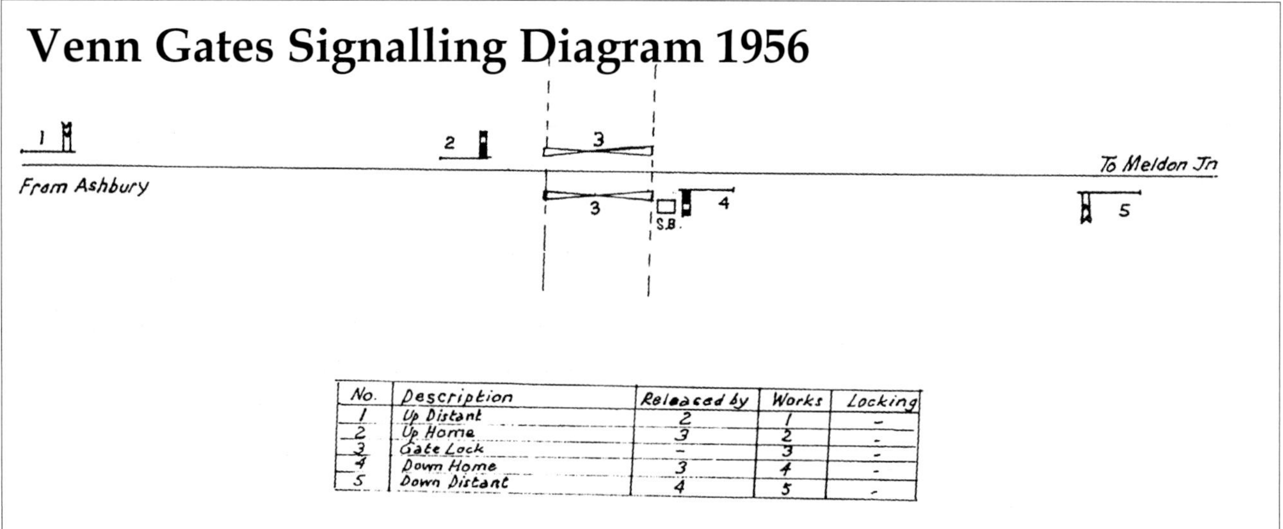

No.	Description	Released by	Works	Locking
1	Up Distant	2	1	-
2	Up Home	3	2	-
3	Gate Lock	-	3	-
4	Down Home	3	4	-
5	Down Distant	4	5	-

View from the cab of the 11.45am from Okehampton, about to enter Ashbury station under North Lew Road Bridge No. 12 in June 1966. John Eyres, South Western Circle.

Until 3 May 1919 a Down passing loop existed on the future site of Maddaford Moor Halt. Opened in 1899 it was fully signalled for passenger trains and controlled from a box centrally situated at 202m 28ch. Exceptionally long at over 1,000 feet and suitable for a 50 wagon, or 12 coach train, the requirement appeared to stem from increased traffic to Halwill Junction, now the North Cornwall was fully open. Not wishing to go to the expense of doubling, provision of this loop broke the long six-mile section from Meldon to Ashbury. The reason for closure is not known. Every train was required to slow to 10mph to exchange Tablets and it was not equipped to be by-passed by switching out. In the event the box and loop were kept in place until 1921.

Situated on a gently falling gradient of 1 in 260 and in a shallow dip between the summit at Meldon and the next station on the line, Ashbury, it was relatively safe from runaways. A mile and a half further on came Venn Gates Crossing. Protected by distant and home signals, it was not, however, a block post; the gateman received bell signals and acknowledged them, set his signals, but then only closed, and reopened, his gates by hand. The line then climbed, now on an embankment, to another summit at the 205 mile post. From here down to Halwill the gradient fell at 1 in 78/80 for five miles and was the scene of a spectacular runaway in February 1905, described elsewhere in this book.

ASHBURY (206M)

Just one mile down lay Ashbury 'for North Lew' Station. It was not very near either Ashbury (the population was only 54 in the 1920s) or North Lew (pop: 682) but it nevertheless served a wide area including Germansweek and Bratton Clovelly. It should be remembered from this distance in time that rural roads were unmetalled, atrocious in bad weather and public conveyance almost entirely absent. The arrival of the railway as a quick transit to market, or town, was a startling change of circumstance, and truly welcomed. Although it meant a long walk to a station for many people places like Ashbury could thus attract quite a few customers, certainly up to the 1930s.

The 1879 Ashbury (205m 75ch) barely altered until closure in 1966. On the Down platform was a bungalow-style station master's house and offices. There was no footbridge on these wayside stations, passengers using the road bridge at the east end, but there was a barrow crossing at rail level. Another squat signal box on the up platform dated from the opening. It was always manned by shift signalmen as

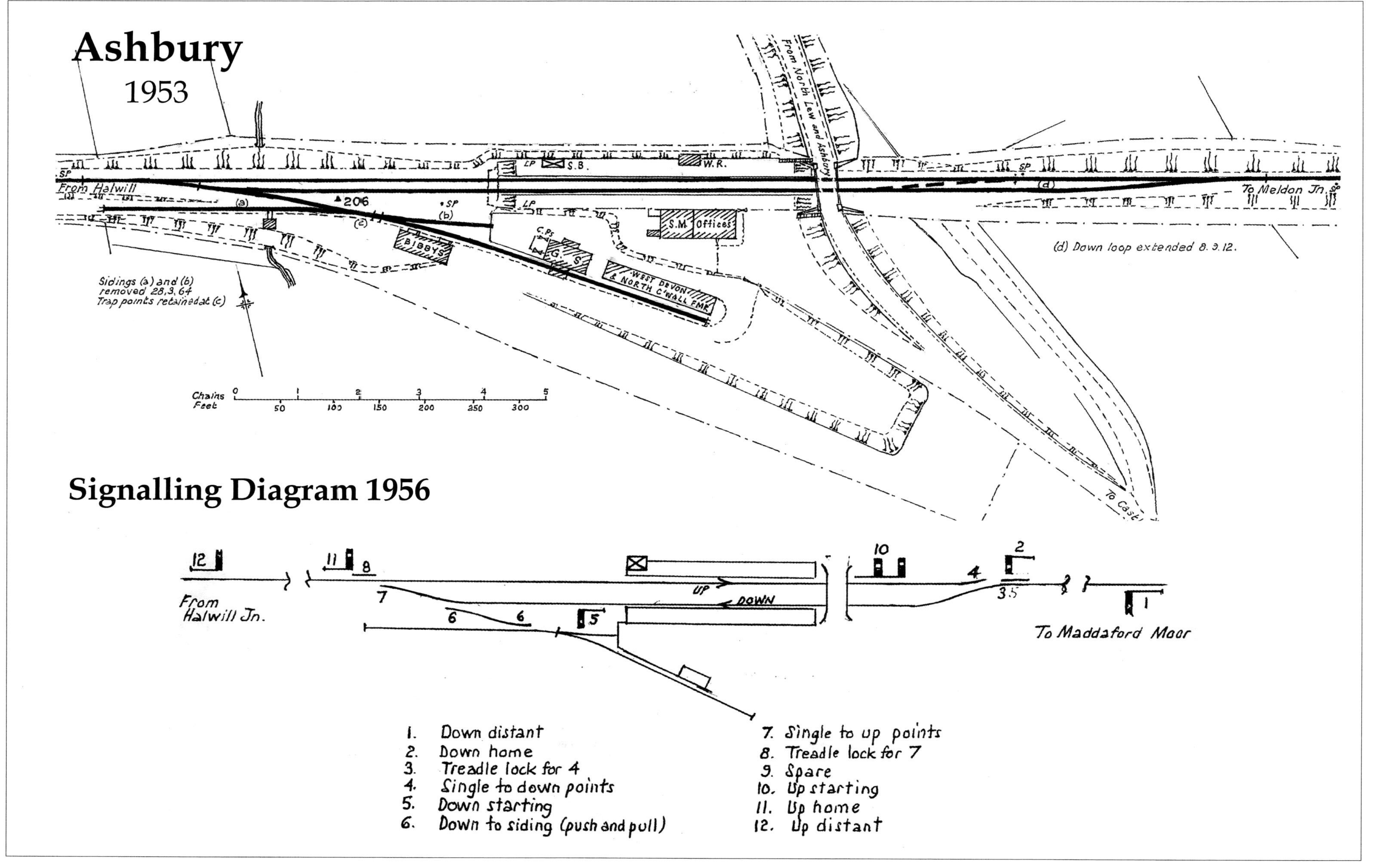
Ashbury
1953
From Halwill
206
(a)
(b)
(c)
SP
LP
S.B.
W.R.
From North Lew and Ashbury
(d)
To Meldon Jn.
S.M.
Offices
(d) Down loop extended 8.3.12.
BIBBYS
C.Ps
G
S
WEST DEVON & NORTH C'WALL FMR
Sidings (a) and (b) removed 28.3.64 Trap points retained at (c)
Chains
Feet
Signalling Diagram 1956
From Halwill Jn.
UP
DOWN
To Maddaford Moor
1. Down distant
2. Down home
3. Treadle lock for 4
4. Single to down points
5. Down starting
6. Down to siding (push and pull)
7. Single to up points
8. Treadle lock for 7
9. Spare
10. Up starting
11. Up home
12. Up distant

At some locations along the line a nearby road bridge would double as a footbridge. Access to Ashbury station for instance, was down a short flight of steps through the simple white gate.

Ashbury (for North Lew) could produce only one passenger on 16th May 1964 as the single coach and van, Bulleid 'loose' Brake Composite to Diagram 2406 (number series 6713-6752) and an ex-LMS 4 wheel CCT to Diagram 1929, of the 3.13pm Bude drew in behind AWS fitted N 2-6-0 No.31849. Both parishes lay to the north of the station, several miles away, and by this time only the occasional wagon of coal or fertiliser was shunted into the sidings. The poster on the left advertises the passenger closure proposals. R. A. Lumber.

After the short-lived passing loop at Maddaford Moor closed in 1919, Ashbury remained the only passing place on the line between Halwill and Meldon Junction. The station was oil lit even after the installation of a transformer for domestic use. John Eyres, South Western Circle.

T9 4-4-0 No.30709 at Ashbury with the 9.56am Padstow train, waiting to cross with the up ACE in May 1961. L. R. Freeman, www.transporttreasury.co.uk

traffic warranted their full time attendance (though a ticket office was later opened at the box end). Longer goods trains in this century necessitated lengthening the Down lop (from 1921, it is believed) and the equivalent wagon limit was raised to 34. The lever frame held twelve for the simple crossing loops and access to the goods siding (push/pull operation again). This siding was flanked by a goods shed and a cattle pen. In due course an agricultural store was established by West Devon & North Cornwall Farmers Ltd with an SR concrete unit store used by Messrs Bibby. This yard, on the down side, could be shunted by running onto the single line towards Halwill, but the original non-returnable Tablet had to be taken out and carried through as the Down starting signal was well inside the loop. In World War Two, Ashbury could be open 24 hours a day with Halwill handling numerous ammunition trains through 1943/44. The provision of a returnable Key Token to Halwill from this date was much more helpful.

Ashbury was the vital part of this line between Meldon Junction and Halwill with its passing loop. The evening goods trains from Halwill loaded heavily and needed a good clear run towards Meldon on the four mile climb at 1 in 78.

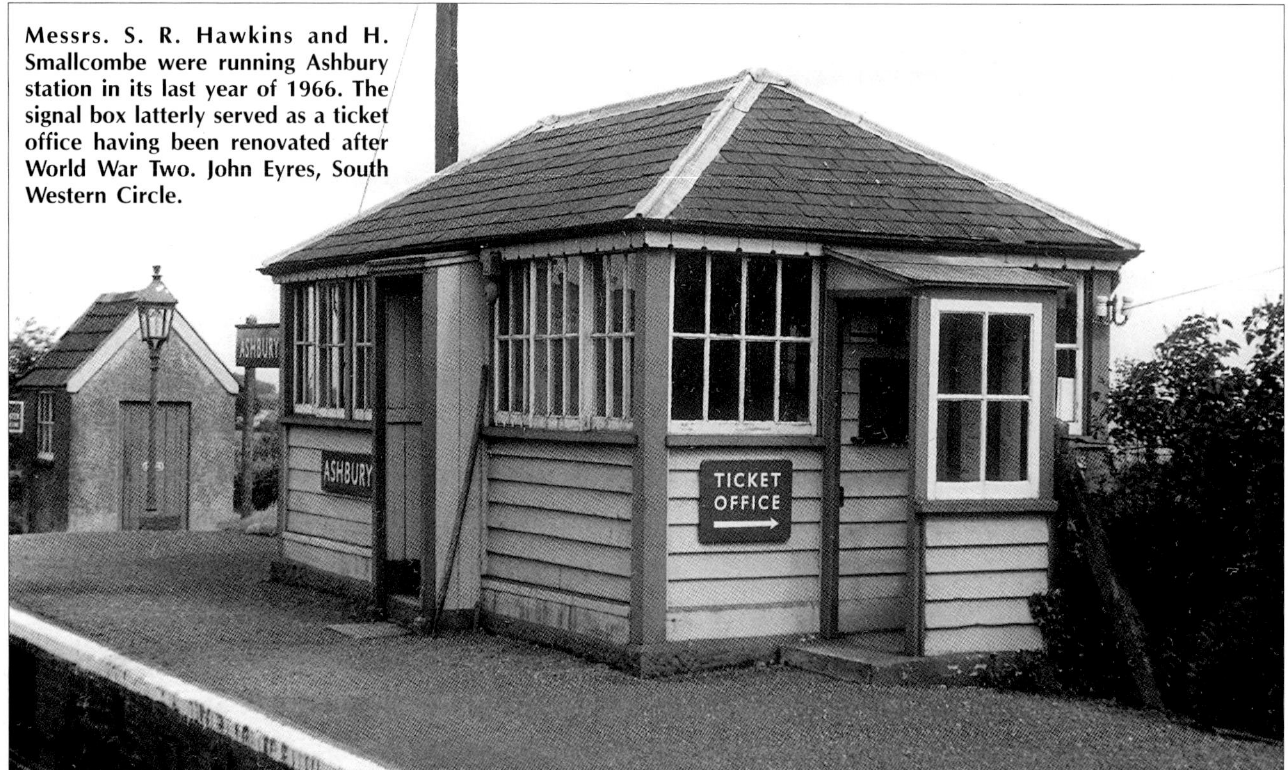

Messrs. S. R. Hawkins and H. Smallcombe were running Ashbury station in its last year of 1966. The signal box latterly served as a ticket office having been renovated after World War Two. John Eyres, South Western Circle.

Ashbury goods shed and end loading dock in June 1963. John Eyres, South Western Circle.

The sight and sound of a 'Woolworth' 2-6-0 charging up through Ashbury (hardly slowing for the Tablet) with 40 wagons on is not easily forgotten, the echoing bark from its chimney carrying back over the darkening winter landscape on the way up to Venn. On a summer Saturday, too, there was much activity from holiday trains (none stopped) and light engine movements in consequence of their various divisions at Halwill or Okehampton. The passing loop was retained in the diesel era, when many others lost them, and Ashbury remained a typical LSWR rural station of the 1880s period, retaining even its oil lamps to the end. From Ashbury the single line dropped steeply and sinuously by way of Patchacott and Madworthy. Quite extensive views could be obtained from this side of the plateau across Hatherleigh and further to Exmoor. Eventually Halwill could be seen in the distance, though there was a

The buildings differed completely from other stations on the North Cornwall line proper as Ashbury hailed from earlier times. Similar in appearance to the Devon and Cornwall buildings at Halwill and Dunsland Cross, they were constructed in 1879 with the line to Holsworthy. The view along the station approach shows, to the left, the agricultural store established by the West Devon and Cornwall Farmers Ltd. John Eyres, South Western Circle.

¼ mile climb on a rare straight, just before the Junction, for Down trains.

HALWILL JUNCTION (209m 60ch)
Along the Holsworthy Branch of 1879 a site for a station was chosen about half way between Halwill and Beaworthy, both 'churchtowns' as termed in Devon, but in reality mere hamlets. The road from Okehampton to Dunsland Cross had been improved in the 19th Century and the mail coach from Holsworthy and Stratton used it in due course, though earlier it followed the Hatherleigh Road to North Tawton and Exeter. This later road paralleled the Holsworthy Branch for most of the way and was thus rather too convenient for the bus substitution on closure in 1966.

As with many rural junctions, Halwill could be deceptively quiet for parts of the day, perhaps only the Bude branch tank doing some shunting in the yard between turns. Quite suddenly arrivals from all quarters brought forth much activity. Dividing and attaching coaches, exchanging wagons (especially around 5pm) with even the Torrington line contributing its quota. This latecomer, the North Devon and Cornwall Junction Light Railway (an independent concern until 1947 but worked by the SR) complicated the Halwill layout from its opening on 27 July 1925. It represented the last vestige of railway expansion. Despite dismissive remarks to the contrary, a fair-sized tonnage passed from it into Halwill over its 40 year life.

Right. **Halwill level crossing on 10th June 1963. The gradient from Ashbury down the hill, middle distance, is just visible beyond the points. The 1944 sidings were lower than those at the station and lay behind the hedge and cowslips on the left. John Eyres, South Western Circle.**

Halwill Junction is suddenly brought to life with a flurry on 8th August 1962. Light Pacific No. 34107 *Blandford Forum* draws slowly into the up platform from the single track North Cornwall line, crossing in front of N 2-6-0 No.31843 waiting to leave with a train for Bude. A lonely passenger makes his way along the diminutive single platform of the North Devon and Cornwall Junction Light Railway for a train bound for Torrington. R. C. Riley, www.transporttreasury.co.uk

B
Halwill Junction
1956
528
190
20½
TORRINGTON PLATFORM
L.P.
T.P.
S.B.
P.W.
G.S.
S.P.
W.Col.
BAY
'A'
209¾
Pump House
Slaughter House
Water Tank
E.P.
C.Pen
Goods Shed
Cattle
L.G.
'A' removed 1930
B
LOOP
SINGLE LINE
SINGLE LINE
MIDDLE SIDING
210 M.P.

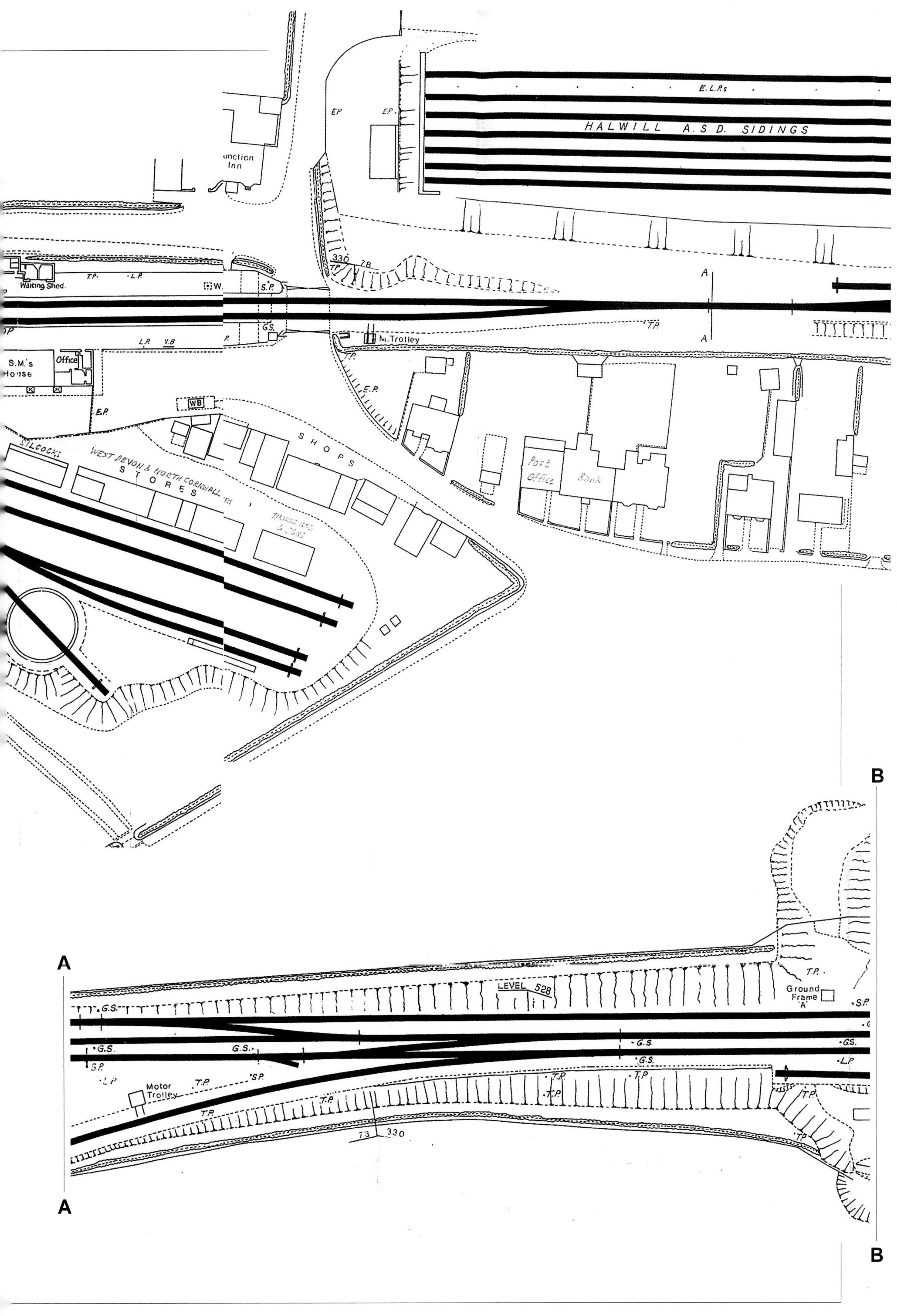
E.L.Ps
HALWILL A.S.D. SIDINGS
EP
EP
unction Inn
Waiting Shed
T.P.
L.P.
W.
S.P.
G.S.
330
T.P.
78
A
A
T.P.
L.P.
V.B
M. Trolley
T.P.
S.M.'s House
Office
E.P.
E.P.
WB
SHOPS
SILCOCKS
WEST DEVON & NORTH CORNWALL
STORES
Post Office
Bank
B
B
A
A
LEVEL
528
G.S.
G.S.
G.S.
G.S.
G.S.
GS.
S.P.
L.P.
S.P.
L.P.
Motor Trolley
T.P.
S.P.
T.P.
T.P.
T.P.
T.P.
T.P.
T.P.
T.P.
Ground Frame 'A'
S.P.
73
330

Signalling Diagrams 1900 and 1956

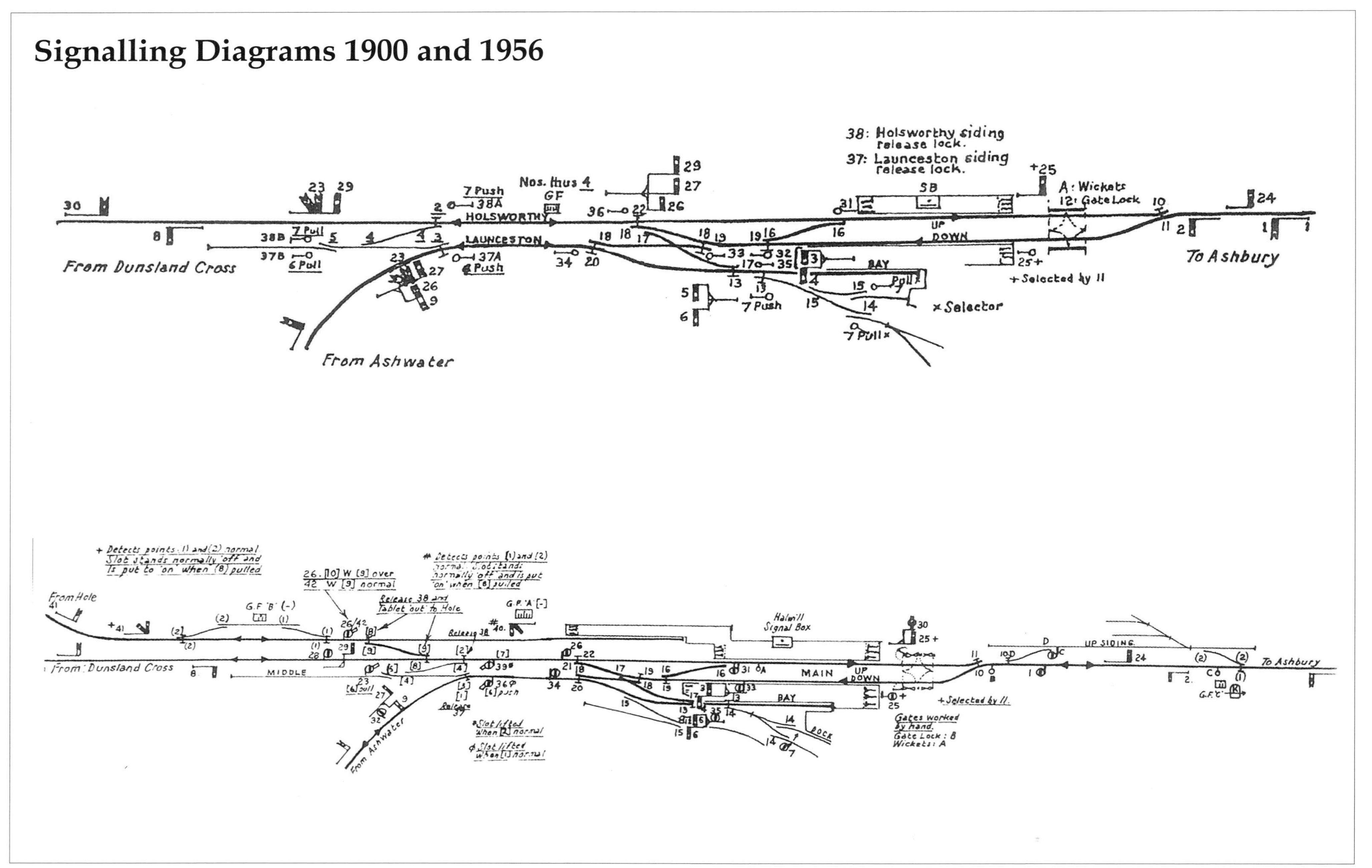

Although no plan has survived, it is likely that Halwill resembled Ashbury in 1879 as a simple crossing place – two loops and a goods siding. All three wayside stations to Holsworthy had the single storey station buildings on the Down side, signal box and waiting shed on the Up platform. This was to change in 1886 when Halwill's layout needed to cope with Launceston trains as well. The South Western Co allowed the North Cornwall 17ch 'mileage' which stretched from their land boundary to the centre of the station – a by-line as it were. The latter paralleled the Holsworthy Branch and joined the Down platform loop. New facing crossovers were provided between both lines and the existing loops. A bay was put in behind the Down platform, enough only for a tank engine and three six-wheel coaches. Slip points enabled this bay to be used for Holsworthy and Launceston trains in both directions. Extra sidings and a turntable were added to the yard. It is probable that the loops were extended at this time at the Ashbury end, extending two tracks across the level crossing.

***Top.* The Devon and Cornwall building at Halwill is largely unaltered, apart from the chimneys, in this 1965 view. The small white gate leads to the Station Master's accommodation. John Eyres, South Western Circle.**

***Left.* Halwill Junction was renamed Halwill for Beaworthy by the Southern in 1923, though it continued to be referred to as the 'Junction' and to this day the village signs say it! The 1879 station building, Station Masters house (at the far end) and the platforms were all electrically lit by 1963. John Eyres, South Western Circle.**

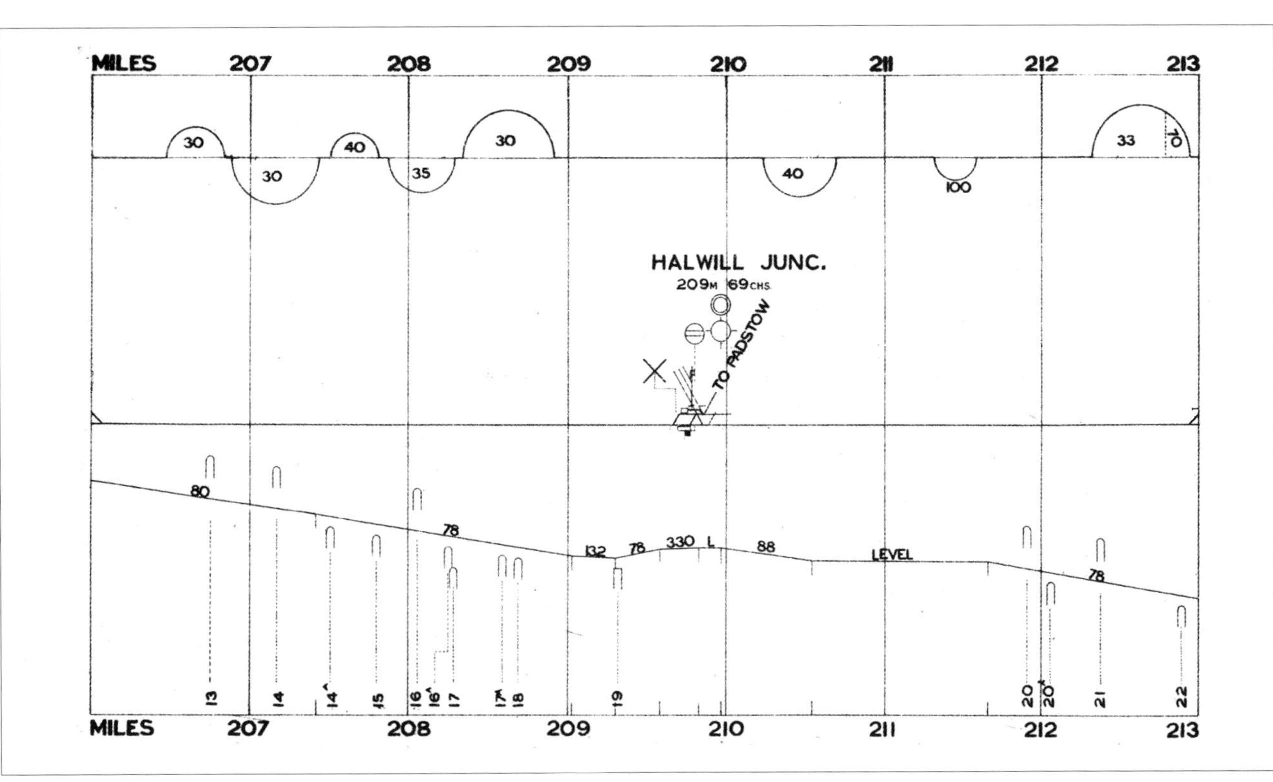

Top. In this 1930s view of the station a Maunsell brake composite, 1st/3rd, is about to be drawn back with the local two coach Bude branch set. They will go on through to Waterloo, attached to the up ACE from Padstow.

Middle. This substantial wooden structure seems to date from the opening of the Launceston section in 1886, as the original 1879 building only contained ten levers and would have resembled the latter-day Dunsland Cross box. It has by this time been extended and lost its ventilators along with its wooden name board HALWILL JUNCTION. Although largely controlled by ground levers, the arrival of the line from Torrington in 1925 necessitated an extension to house the tablet machines. The sympathetic work can be seen at the far end of the building. The small concrete hut to the left housed the PW inspector whose ground extended to Egloskerry, Hatherleigh, Bude and Meldon Junction. John Eyres, South Western Circle.

*Bottom.*The extensive goods yard in 1965. The bay is on the left and the end loading dock, its track removed in 1930, is in front of the goods shed. Five sidings sufficed for local goods traffic, which consisted largely of agricultural produce although there was a healthy cattle traffic too. The fresh meat trade grew considerably from the turn of the century and to the right of the photo is the old slaughter house. John Eyres, South Western Circle.

The signal box had to be enlarged; it appears to have been the existing structure raised much higher to accommodate a larger lever frame and to give a commanding view of the ¼ mile long layout. The levers now numbered 38. Trains from Holsworthy and Launceston could draw right up to Inner Home signals or be kept at the Outer Homes. With Staff and Ticket working, every yard of track inside the station limits (like the home and starting signals) was valuable. Even so, the tails of goods trains would often be well down the gradient towards Ashwater. Twice there were runaways through mis-shunts and failure to pin down wagon brakes.

It was always necessary to do a lot of shunting in the Halwill loops as goods trains exchanged wagons with the branches. A long 'middle' siding (costing the LSWR £846) was laid in, paralleling

Top. The little goods shed and traders' store in 1965. John Eyres, South Western Circle.

Middle. Tucked away behind the goods shed was Halwill's 50ft turntable but no other locomotive servicing facilities apart from water existed. It was much appreciated by crews who could avoid facing driving wind and rain on the run along the more exposed parts of the North Cornwall line up to Okehampton. John Eyres, South Western Circle.

Bottom. Halwill's water towers fed the goods yard, slaughter house and platform water columns, the station supply coming from a separate source. John Eyres, South Western Circle.

T9 4-4-0 N0.30710 arrives at Halwill Junction with the 6pm Padstow-Okehampton train in July 1958. A. E. Bennett, www.transporttreasury.co.uk

the Holsworthy line, in 1894. Now a goods could be safely berthed inside the signals, though it is doubtful if it was used as much as it should. The Tablet system (with interlocking of starting signals) may not have been introduced at Halwill until the early 1900s, probably at the same time as the Up inner homes (26/27/29) were removed. Nos.26 and 27 were for North Cornwall arrivals, and slotted to the outers; 29 was for Holsworthy trains. Henceforward the Bay would handle only Down departures, and it was lengthened at the inner end, to take an engine and three bogie coaches. The signalling remained unaltered until the Torrington line opened in 1925. Even then changes were only marginal, as the latter was self-contained and worked by ground frames. In 1934 wholesale replacement of ground signals took place and signal arm heights changed. The 'main' aspects were now for the North Cornwall line (the lower placed arms for the Bude Branch) on the Down main and Branch starting signals. Further signalling and layout alterations at the Ashbury end came in 1943 under wartime pressures.

The main platforms were gradually

The way west! From left to right, The North Cornwall single track swings away to the left whilst the 'Middle Siding' is to its right. The Bude single line is next and the Torrington line is to its right. Behind the signal, on the right, is the ground frame which controlled movements along the Torrington line. John Eyres, South Western Circle.

34086 *219 Squadron*, on the up ACE, drifts into Halwill in June 1963. The signal arms are worthy of note as they are of mixed lineage. Halwill's down advance starter to Ashwater was an ex-LSWR lower quadrant (left) and the up home from Ashwater (right) is of the ex-SR upper quadrant variety. The slender rail assembly needed strong 'guying' but a substantial steel bracket was erected to site the up home signal from Dunsland Cross (Bude) on the right. Also worthy of note was the new 109lb/yd flat bottom rail on pre-stressed concrete sleepers laid in by the Western Region at this late hour. John Eyres, South Western Circle.

lengthened over the years, the Down considerably so in 1886 to match the new Bay, the Ashbury ends (as noted) and the Up on the Torrington line opening in 1925. The latter extension fed a little pathway round to the Torrington platform. While the extensions were made in local stone, the Torrington platform was in reinforced concrete. Seven coaches could now be accommodated in the platforms, adequate for local traffic. The holiday trains in the 1930s were increasing in length to twelve coaches at times, troop trains even reached 16 in the Second World War and later pigeon specials to Bude frequently numbered the same, as bogie vans. From the 1900s local trains were usually in combination to and from Okehampton, with engine and Padstow train proceeding after detaching or attaching a Bude portion in the Halwill platforms. Halwill goods yard primarily served local traffic. Although some remarshalling occurred there, much wagon sorting took place out on the running lines, especially between 5 and 6pm when the up Bude and Wadebridge goods were in the loops. The final layout afforded four holding sidings for wagons of coal, agricultural supplies and products and cattle. A fifth siding served the 50ft turntable and a small coal stage. There was a cattle pen on the dock behind the Down platform (the direct end-loading siding here was removed in 1930). Cattle wagons were cleaned on the end of No.4 siding which was extended in 1912. Further along the goods shed siding, two more cattle pens were provided in the 1900s to cope with the expanding business. Farther on, national and local seed and fertiliser merchants established themselves in storehouses. Latterly Silcocks, West Devon and North Cornwall Farmers and Thomas Oke & Sons conducted business here.

Halwill was one of the main sources of cattle traffic and a market was opened a hundred yards or so down the road towards Halwill village. However, it was dead stock, slaughtered ex-market, which eventually dominated. A wooden slaughterhouse was built and a siding extended to it, at a date unknown but probably prior to 1900. From 1904 a direct connection was put from the North Cornwall side (No.15 points) and the siding lengthened to the west. In 1932 over 650 wagons arrived with livestock for slaughter, but 272 wagons of live cattle went to eastern destinations like Banbury and Sevenoaks. 22,855 sheep were slaughtered that year. A much larger brick building and long platform replaced the old one in 1938. It was closed under wartime conditions but reopened as the tonnage of meat increased tremendously. Insulated vans, used in the 1920s and 1930s and forwarded by overnight goods services via Exeter, gave way to demountable containers in the 1950s. The containers were rated as passenger traffic and were attached to the two afternoon 'perishable' trains from Bude and Padstow. Most went to Smithfield, by road from Nine Elms, though certain traffic was for the Midlands, via Templecombe. Apart from meat, there were tremendous quantities of eggs, 100,000 daily, it is said, along with 'day-old' chicks and butter.

Such merchandise as ordered locally was handled in the stone-built goods shed. It was medium sized, but unlike Holsworthy, had only a stanchioned 'port' over the siding. No crane was provided but the SR leased out a cart weighbridge in the station approach.

The growth of Halwill Junction as a railway centre in West Devon is reflected by the following establishment: Post Office ('Beaworthy'), police station, bank, public house ('The Junction Hotel'), a chapel (Baptist), a small cottage hospital, garage, cattle market, an egg packing station and some shops. The combined population of Halwill and Beaworthy was just over 600 in 1931 and grew perceptibly while other West Devon parishes declined. Since 1966 the name 'Halwill Junction' has survived, as the road signs declare, even though the site of the railway has been covered by a housing estate.

Although the area of the station grew, the original station master's house and offices remained unaltered. Houses built for railway employees by the LSWR were situated to the south of the goods yard. On the Up platform stood the enlarged signal box and the waiting room was rebuilt in 1905. The Permanent Way Inspector used an office on this side, and there was a small goods store. An electric pump fed a large tank (on the top of the cutting, down side) which supplied the two water columns on the platform, the slaughterhouse and the cattle wagon washdown. Even Holsworthy was supplied in drought periods (in a

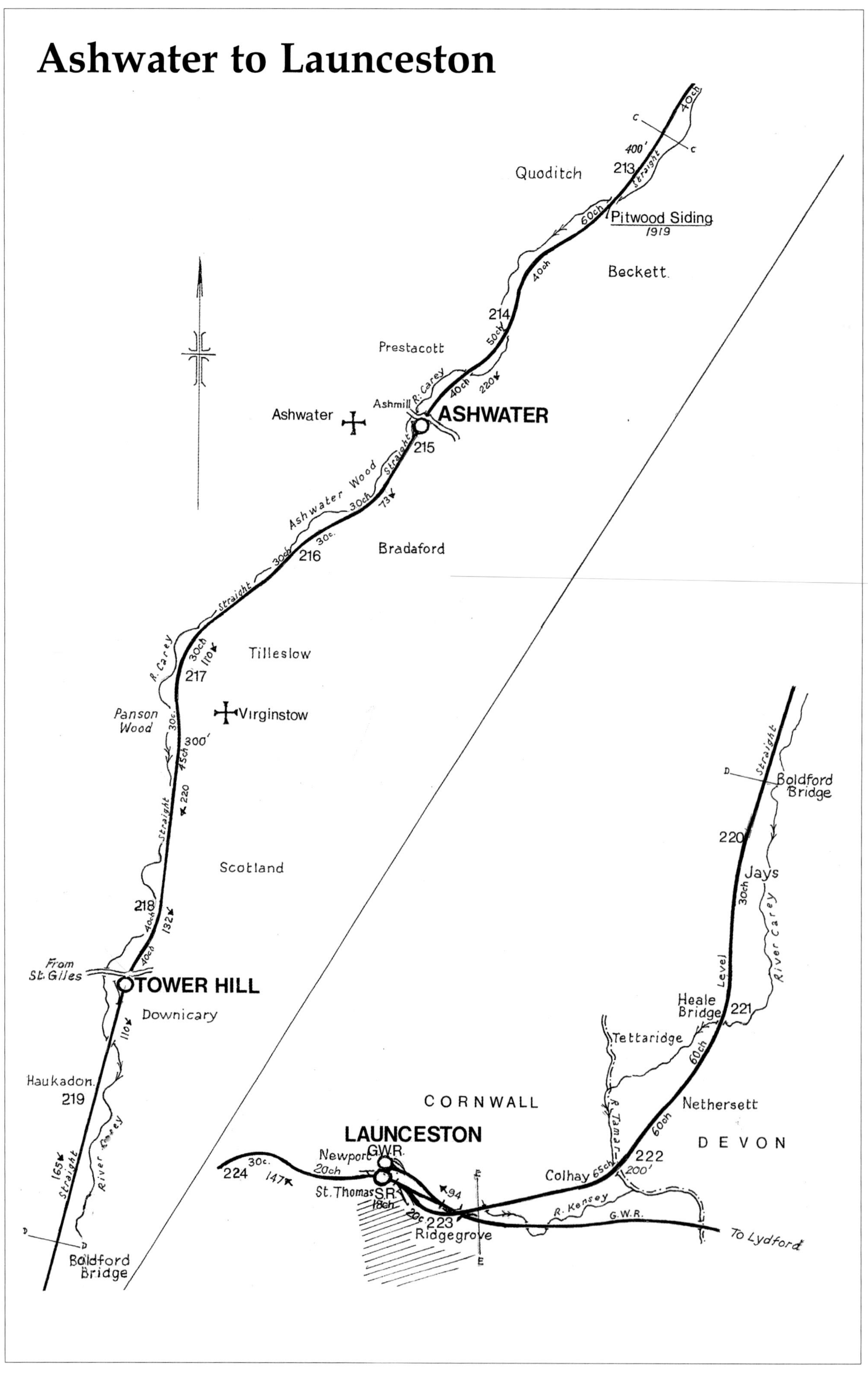
Ashwater to Launceston
Quoditch
Pitwood Siding
1919
Beckett.
Prestacott
Ashwater
Ashmill
R. Carey
ASHWATER
215
Ashwater Wood
Bradaford
216
Tilleslow
217
Virginstow
Panson Wood
Scotland
218
From St. Giles
TOWER HILL
Downicary
Haukadon.
219
River Carey
Boldford Bridge
Jays
220
221
Heale Bridge
Tettaridge
R. Tamar
Nethersett
CORNWALL
DEVON
LAUNCESTON
Newport
GWR.
St. Thomas
S.R.
224
223
222
Ridgegrove
Colhay
R. Kensey
G.W.R.
To Lydford
Straight
Level

Looking back towards Halwill, from Ashwater Station Road Bridge No.14. The ruling gradient of 1 in 73 is evident as the line winds its way down the River Carey valley. John Eyres, South Western Circle.

converted engine tender) and some of the Torrington line stations could also run dry.

Suddenly in 1943 Halwill entered the forward logistic planning for the invasion of France. The US Army, building up its ammunition supply, distributed it around the Devon countryside and extra yards were laid down at Tower Hill and Whitstone (on the Bude Branch). On the Ashbury and Up side at Halwill a large area of ground was levelled. The SR put down eight sidings capable of holding no less than 220 wagons. The outer siding faced hard standing for lorries of the Supply Service, often driven by coloured US troops. It is estimated that 35,000 tons were handled at these railheads, as well as Launceston, the yard here opening on 26 September 1943. After 'D' Day, 6 June 1944, only 4,000 tons of ammunition had still to be forwarded to the beach heads in Normandy. Operationally, a long loop siding (No.1) holding engine and 60 wagons was opened from 26 September 1943. It paralleled the line towards Ashbury. At that end a connection to the single line, protected by a spur, was controlled by a new ground frame 'C'. Trains could be 'shut in' by restoring the Halwill-Ashbury Token to an auxiliary machine at this end. At the station end the loop (and spur) were slotted into Halwill's main signalling and entry here indicated by a ringed-arm (30) bracketed to the Up starting signal. 'N' class 2-6-0s handled these trains and one of these, No.1833, was to be the cause of a spectacular rescue. On the 16 June 1944 1833 left the Up platform, gathering speed to rush the bank to Ashbury. Unfortunately the facing points to the new loop were left open, but the spur points at the far end closed. In spite of braking, the engine crashed through the stop blocks and nose-dived into the Beaworthy road. It was no problem to crane out the tender, but the engine's recovery was much more serious. A ship's hawser was obtained and two engines normally prohibited beyond Meldon, a S15 4-6-0 and a USA 'S160' 2-8-0 (probably No.2356), plus another 'N' together tried to pull her out. The second attempt also failed, the 2-8-0 suffering a buckled beam. On the third attempt a greased plate was laid under 1833's wheels and no less than three 'N' class and two N15s (including No.453) managed to do it. The 4-6-0s and the 2-8-0 were specially authorised to cross Meldon Viaduct.

Halwill Junction to Ashwater

From Halwill Junction, 600ft above sea level, a way was found to join the head of Carey River valley. From the junction at 209m 71ch a sharp 20ch curve took the line south-west, along a straight under the Dunsland road at Lane End, and then over a series of 30 chain reverses to join the infant river at Blagadon. Beyond the stone arch over the river at 213m 8ch there is little sign now of a siding which existed between 1919 and 1920. This faced Down trains and was worked by a 2 lever ground frame released by the Tablet. Paid for by the Pitwood Association Ltd (a consortium of Monmouthshire and South Wales Colliery owners) it could hold ten wagons and, as the title suggests, exported pit props, wood

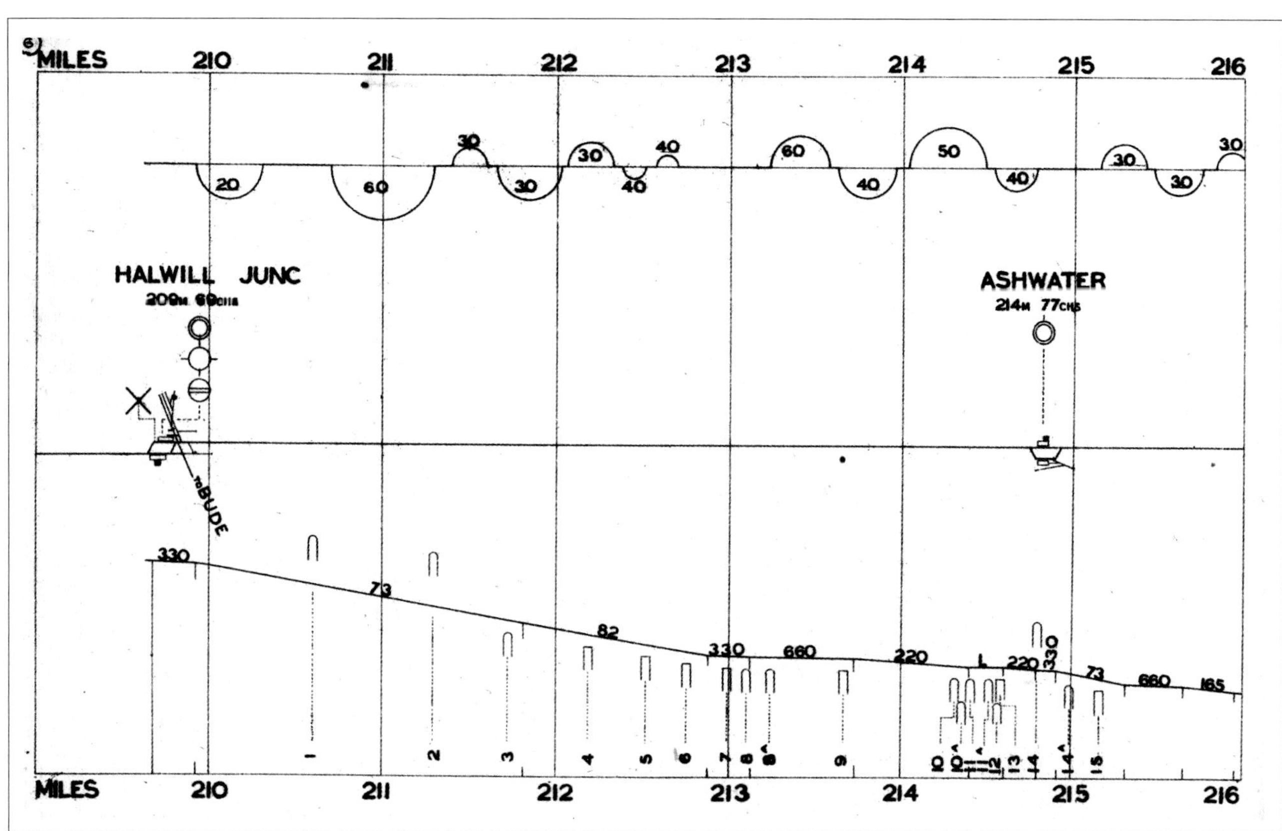

Above. **The crew of N 2-6-0 No.31837 pause briefly at Ashwater in May 1961 with their all stations train to Okehampton. R. C. Riley, www.transporttreasury.co.uk**

Middle. **The station was sited inconveniently at the bottom of a steep hill half a mile away from the village down a narrow lane. The layout at Ashwater could prove difficult operationally too, as the loops could only accommodate seven coach trains. A long goods, for instance, would need to set back partly into the sidings to allow a passing train to continue. John Eyres, South Western Circle.**

Bottom. **A much needed lengthening of the loops, therefore, was carried out in 1935 which allowed for 12 coach or 35 wagons trains to pass safely. John Eyres, South Western Circle.**

chocks etc. It is said to have been fed by an overhead cableway and worked by Belgian refugees. The wagons were sent to Yeoford to join wagon loads from the North Devon Line to South Wales.

Below this point the valley sides begin to steepen, but there is still room for the 28ft width of the North Cornwall Railway. All overbridges to Wadebridge, and abutments of some underbridges, were built for this double line if necessary. The ruling gradient of 1 in 73 and curves generally no sharper than 30 chains, adopted as a standard for the NCR, continued down to Ashwater. Early in December 1893 the

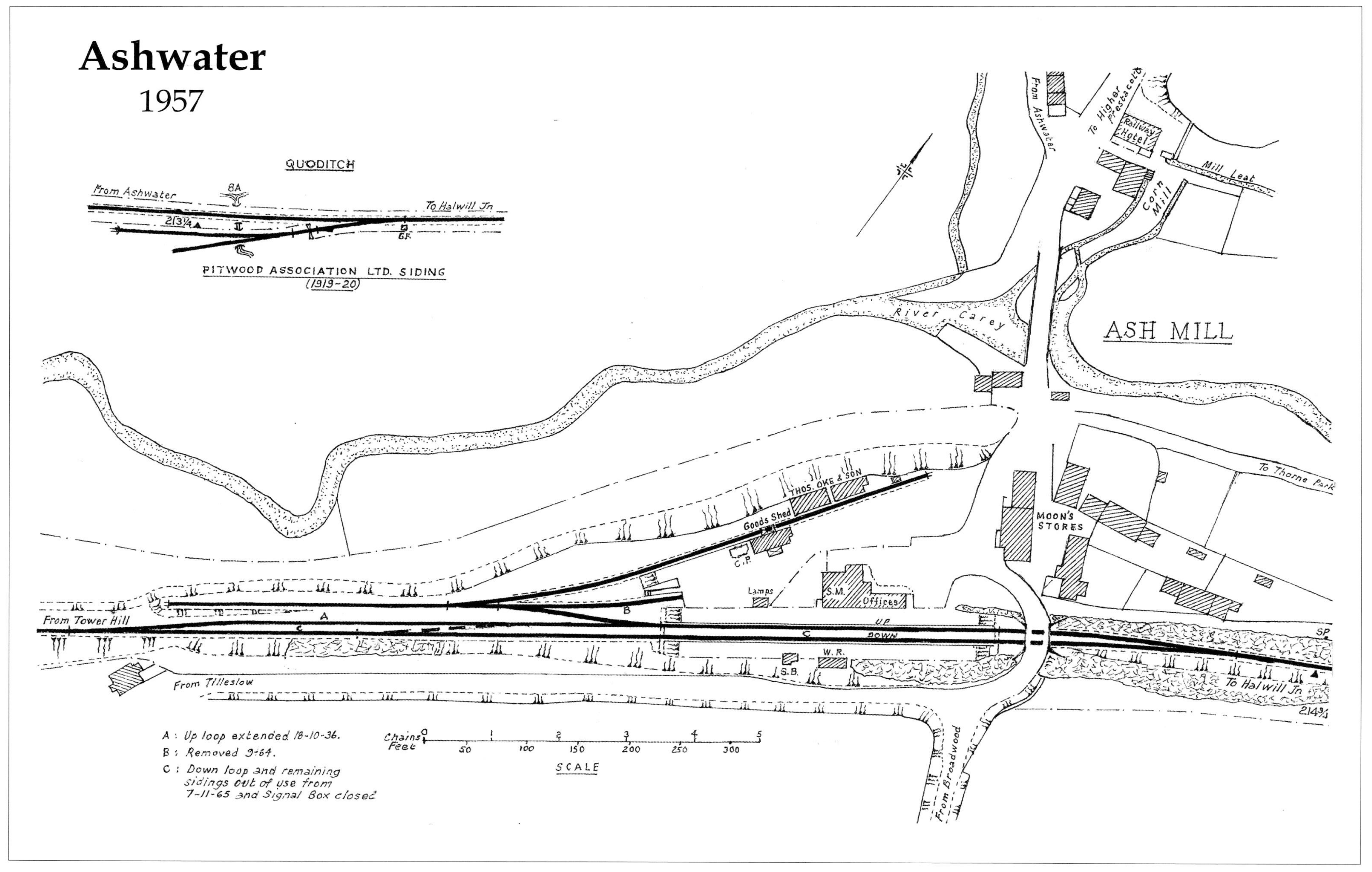
Ashwater
1957
QUODITCH
From Ashwater
8A
To Halwill Jn
213¼
G.F.
PITWOOD ASSOCIATION LTD. SIDING
(1919-20)
From Ashwater
To Higher Prestacott
Railway Hotel
Mill Leat
Corn Mill
River Carey
ASH MILL
To Thorne Park
THOS. OKE & SON
Goods Shed
C.P.
MOON'S STORES
Lamps
S.M. Offices
A
B
C
UP
DOWN
SP
From Tower Hill
W.R.
S.B.
From Tilleslow
To Halwill Jn
214¾
From Broadwood
A: Up loop extended 18-10-36.
B: Removed 9-64.
C: Down loop and remaining sidings out of use from 7-11-65 and Signal Box closed
Chains
Feet
SCALE

rear of an Up goods train (21 loaded cattle wagons, a meat van and the brake van) managed to run away backwards from Halwill. It had been left on the curve at the Junction and had, apparently, been nudged during shunting operations. The emergency bells rang to Ashwater, and further. Fortunately the line was clear. The runaways reached Tilleshow Woods, about seven miles away, in about eight minutes. Thankfully they came to a halt on a slight rise of 1 in 220 and no harm was done. In the aftermath (and there had been a previous runaway in 1887) the rules were tightened. If a goods train was left outside the Up Home signal it had to have two brake vans, or an engine, at the Ashwater end. The 1894 long (or 'Middle') siding at Halwill was part of this new protection.

Top. **The signal box on the down platform was a fully glazed pattern type adopted by the LSWR in the 1880s and accommodated, as well as the lever frame, the single line Tablet Apparatus. John Eyres, South Western Circle.**

Middle. **Ashwater's goods shed was constructed, unusually, of corrugated iron sheeting though it conformed to the LSWR No.2 pattern. The sagging corrugated iron building to the right was occupied by Thomas Okle and Sons who dealt in timber. John Eyres, South Western Circle.**

Below. **Ashwater station offices and Station Masters house in 1961. John Eyres, South Western Circle.**

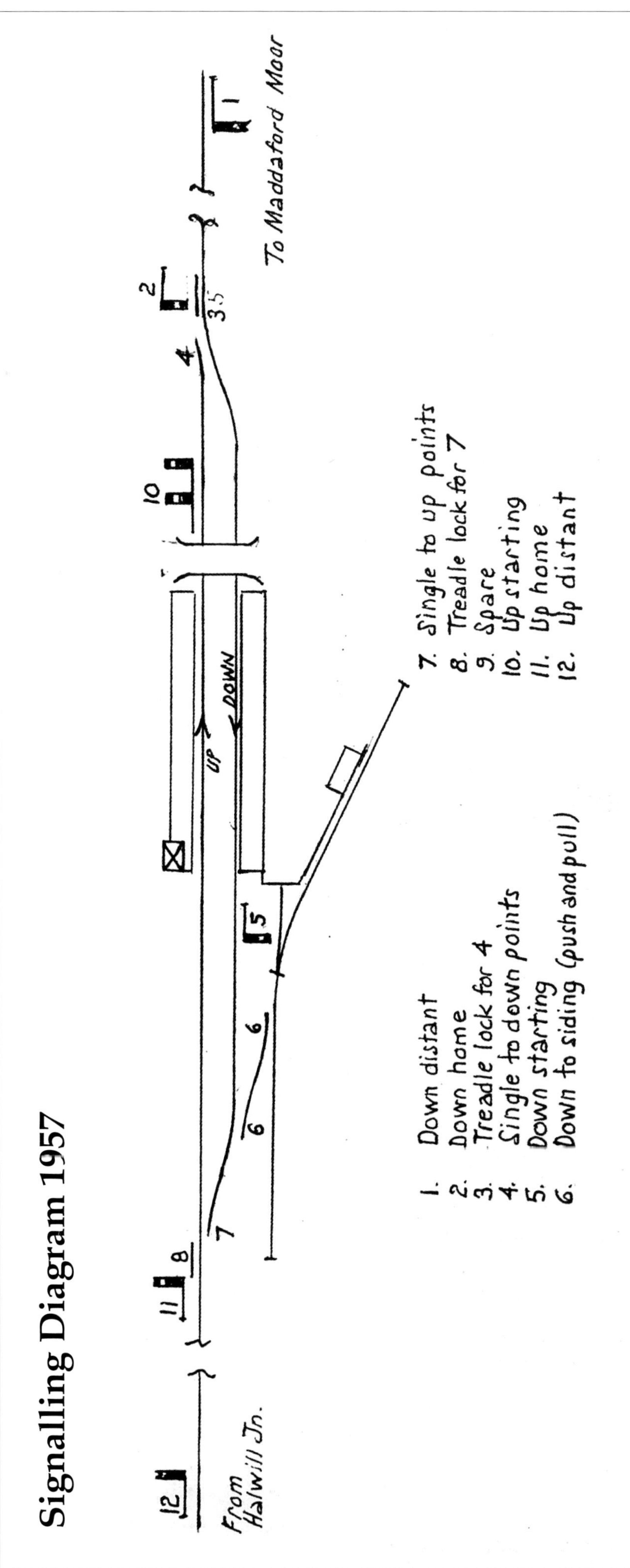

ASHWATER (214m 67ch)
Down the hill from Ashwater, with its pleasant green and church, was the North Cornwall station, in the vicinity of Ash Mill. Five miles from Halwill, it was 214m 67ch from Waterloo. It was approached from that direction by a 40 chain curve, under Bridge No.14 spanning a deep cutting, and into a straight on a 1 in 330 falling gradient. The platform would take only seven coaches, but the Up loop (lengthened from 18 October 1936) was suitable for 35 wagons or a twelve coach train. Before this date, a lengthy up goods, or cattle train, would have to shunt its tail into the yard. Ashwater yard could be quite busy at times; cattle forwarding was heavy before 1914 and again in the next war.

As in other stations, the SR built and leased a fertiliser, seed and agriculture store to a local firm. Thomas Oke & Sons of Holsworthy. The majority of business, however, was conducted by R.H. Moon & Sons, who ran an extensive store on the other side of the road at Ash Mill, for all manner of merchandise including coal. A small iron goods shed flanked the outer siding, the inner one ending in a side and ending loading dock. Quantities of timber on offer at Ashwater brought forward an extension of the loading dock in 1909. In the 1930s, Mr Harry Spry sent pig carcasses to Smithfield Market in London. They were brought by horse and cart from Prestacott Farm and loaded into a reserved van left in the platform by the 11.35am Up goods train from Wadebridge while the engine shunted the yard. Ashwater was a destination for roadstone from Wilminstone, a common material seen in Devon yards. Local farmers carried it further, under contract to the County Council. The rabbit trade was conducted locally by a Mr Dymond, who forwarded tremendous quantities over the years – this happened at most NCR stations, as we shall see.

The standard type of station building evolved by the LSWR in the West was repeated all the way down to Padstow. Ashwater was built of local brown stone, including a large station master's house with station offices adjacent, on the Up side. The Station Master's houses were quite commodious, 'comprised of' (as the estate agents say) three bedrooms, parlour, kitchen, WC and wash house. Within this block was the ladies' waiting room and WC, opening to the booking hall/waiting room. The latter, the booking office, staff room or parcels office and SM's offices were in the single storey extension. On the other side of the house adjacent to the enclosed SM's courtyard was the gentlemen's toilets. There were siting variations down the line (Camelford and Padstow were equipped with awnings) but room dimensions, door and windows were essentially similar. An LSWR signal box of the 1880s period,

Declining business saw the goods shed shut in 1964 and the station reduced to the status of a halt in 1965. Now unstaffed with the loop points clipped and padlocked on the up side line, trains no longer passed at Ashwater. John Eyres, South Western Circle.

Tower Hill looking back towards Ashwater with more of the Western Region's 109lb/yd flat bottomed rail evident in the distance. John Eyres, South Western Circle.

A glorious view across the Carey Valley from the hillside in 1964. The cottages are all that remain of the Tower Hill site today. John Eyres, South Western Circle.

with extensive glazing, stood on the Down platform. It had eleven levers, all in use. The last SM was Mr J.H. Lashbrook in 1926, when control passed to Launceston.

Alas, apart from seed, fertiliser and basic slag traffic, goods business declined and the goods yard closed with others from 7 September 1964. The station was reduced to an unstaffed halt on 7 November 1965 and all points were clipped and padlocked. The signal box was closed, leaving the former Up loop as a single line.

Ashwater to Tower Hill

Below Ashwater the line kept to the east side of the Carey. In places, due to the steep side of the valley, it was shelved into the lower hillside to maintain the 30 chain radii. The valley is well wooded through Ashwater to Tileshow (216 miles) but widens out at Virginstow (217 miles) and the curvature was less severe, including a long straight towards Tower Hill. The levels fall from 600ft at Halwill to the 300ft contour at Tower Hill, with gradients easing from the initial 1 in 73 to 1 in 110. Ashwater and Tower Hill served Broadwoodwidger and Virginstowe villages to the east and St Giles-in-the-Heath to the west. In 1921 the population of Ashwater parish was 659 and the combined inhabitants of the latter parishes 1,105, which demonstrates the low density in this part of West Devon.

In earlier times people walked to Ashwater or Tower Hill, and farmers would use a pony and trap. Dressed stone was available in quantity for this first section, but many of the cattle creeps were simply rows of old rails, and two

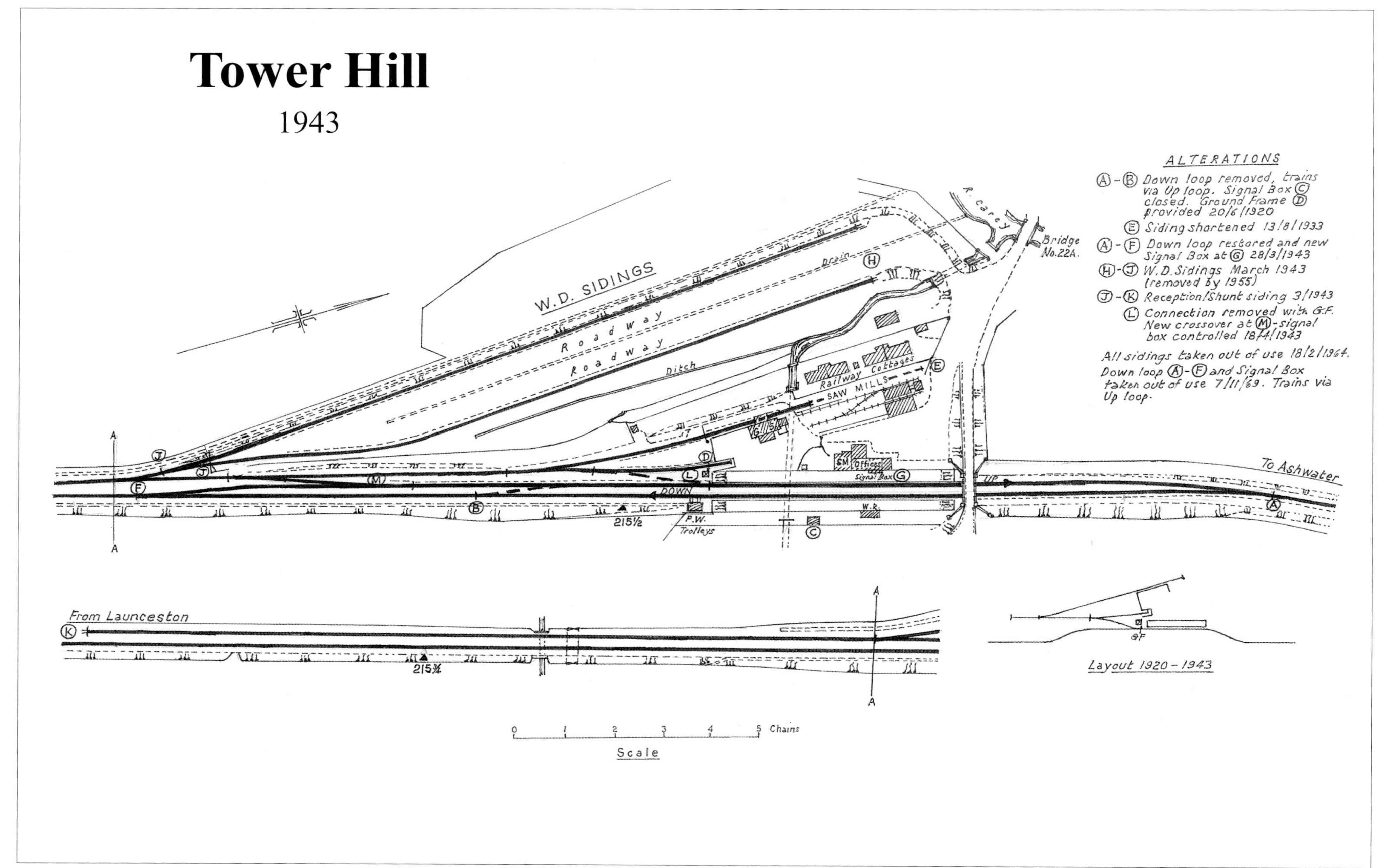

Tower Hill
1943
ALTERATIONS
Ⓐ-Ⓑ Down loop removed, trains via Up loop. Signal Box Ⓒ closed. Ground Frame Ⓓ provided 20/6/1920
Ⓔ Siding shortened 13/8/1933
Ⓐ-Ⓕ Down loop restored and new Signal Box at Ⓖ 28/3/1943
Ⓗ-Ⓙ W.D. Sidings March 1943 (removed by 1955)
Ⓙ-Ⓚ Reception/Shunt siding 3/1943
Ⓛ Connection removed with G.F. New crossover at Ⓜ-signal box controlled 18/4/1943
All sidings taken out of use 18/2/1964.
Down loop Ⓐ-Ⓕ and Signal Box taken out of use 7/11/69. Trains via Up loop.
W.D. SIDINGS
Roadway
Roadway
Ditch
Drain
R. Carey
Bridge No.22A.
Railway Cottages
SAW MILLS
SM
Offices
Signal Box
W.R.
P.W. Trolleys
DOWN
UP
215½
To Ashwater
From Launceston
215¾
Layout 1920 - 1943
GF
0 1 2 3 4 5 Chains
Scale

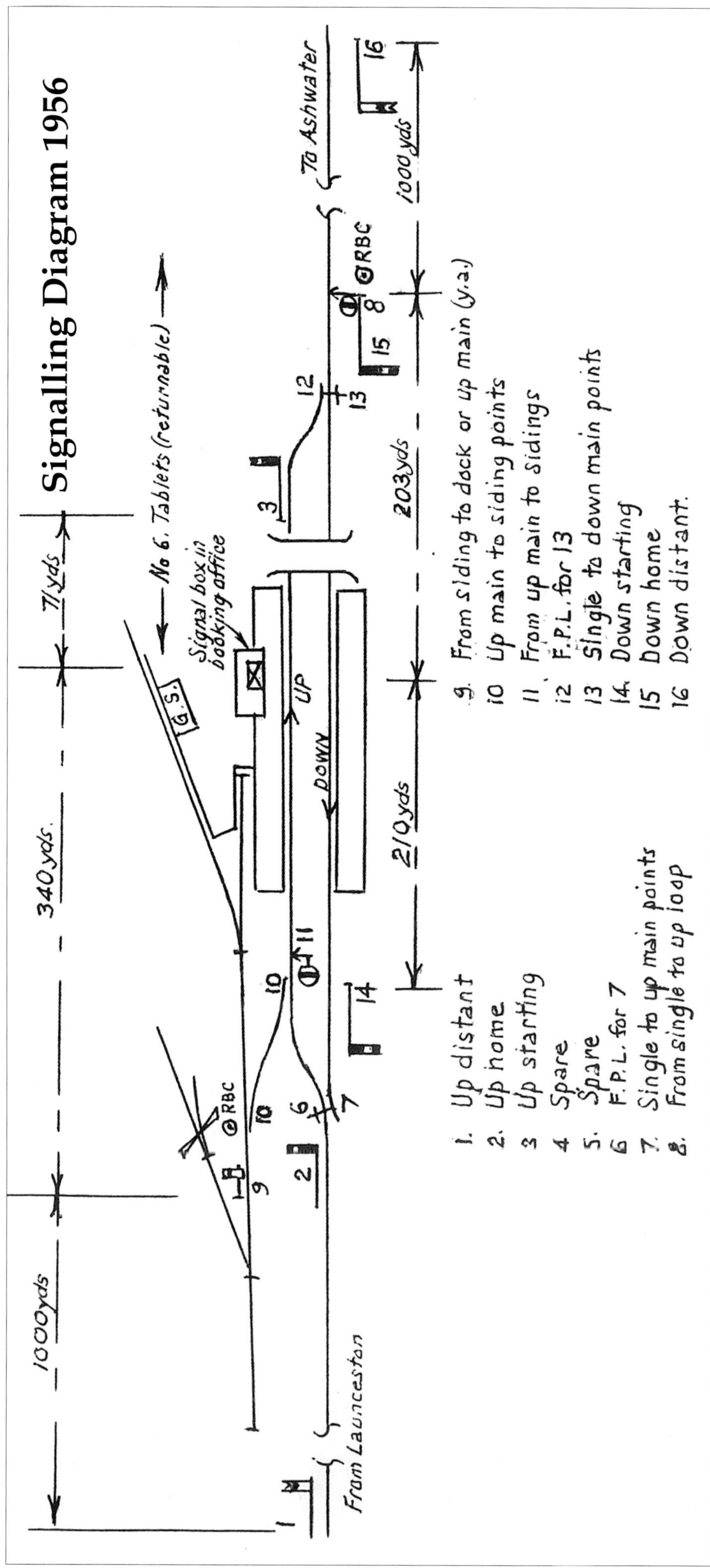

waybeams laid across stone abutments. In due course these (and Meldon Viaduct) would cause the prohibition of heavier engines. Where the line skirted the river, careful watch had to be kept for scouring, as water levels and volume could rise rapidly. In one wet winter, early on, slips were recorded within this section of the line.

TOWER HILL (218m 35ch)
Approached down a steep road from the east side, near the road bridge over the Carey leading to St Giles up a long hill to the west, Tower Hill was named after an adjacent farm. The stone-built station and the original goods layout, with the passing loops laid out on a straight, was identical to Ashwater. The first signal box stood on the Down platform, again in the roomy 1880s style. After the 1914-18 War the crossing facilities were abolished. From 15 June 1920 the Down loop was taken out of use and the signal box closed, thus creating a seven-mile section from Ashwater to Launceston. An amber light was displayed, thereafter, on the former Down distant signal as a marker for the approach to Tower Hill. At first the signal box levers were retained but later on a ground frame was substituted, released by the Section Tablet, to operate and lock the siding points on the push/pull principle.

The last stationmaster was Mr Dolby. From 1928 control came under Launceston. Tower Hill slept on through the 1930s, the goods yard moderately busy with incoming coal and agriculture products and the occasional cattle wagon for loading. The station house was occupied by one of the porters, while at the back of the yard were terraced houses (of LSWR origin) for the permanent way men. The end of the goods shed siding was shortened in 1933.

All this was to change in 1943 and at Tower Hill two sidings and hard standing for lorries were laid down on the up side to serve U.S. Army ammunition dumps in the surrounding countryside. As a preliminary, the Down loop was restored, longer by 150 yards than pre-1920, at the Launceston end. A signal box was established in the booking hall, protruding several feet on to the Up platform. All this was brought into use on 28 March 1943 and the following month points leading from the goods yard were moved 150 yards towards Launceston and connected to the new signal

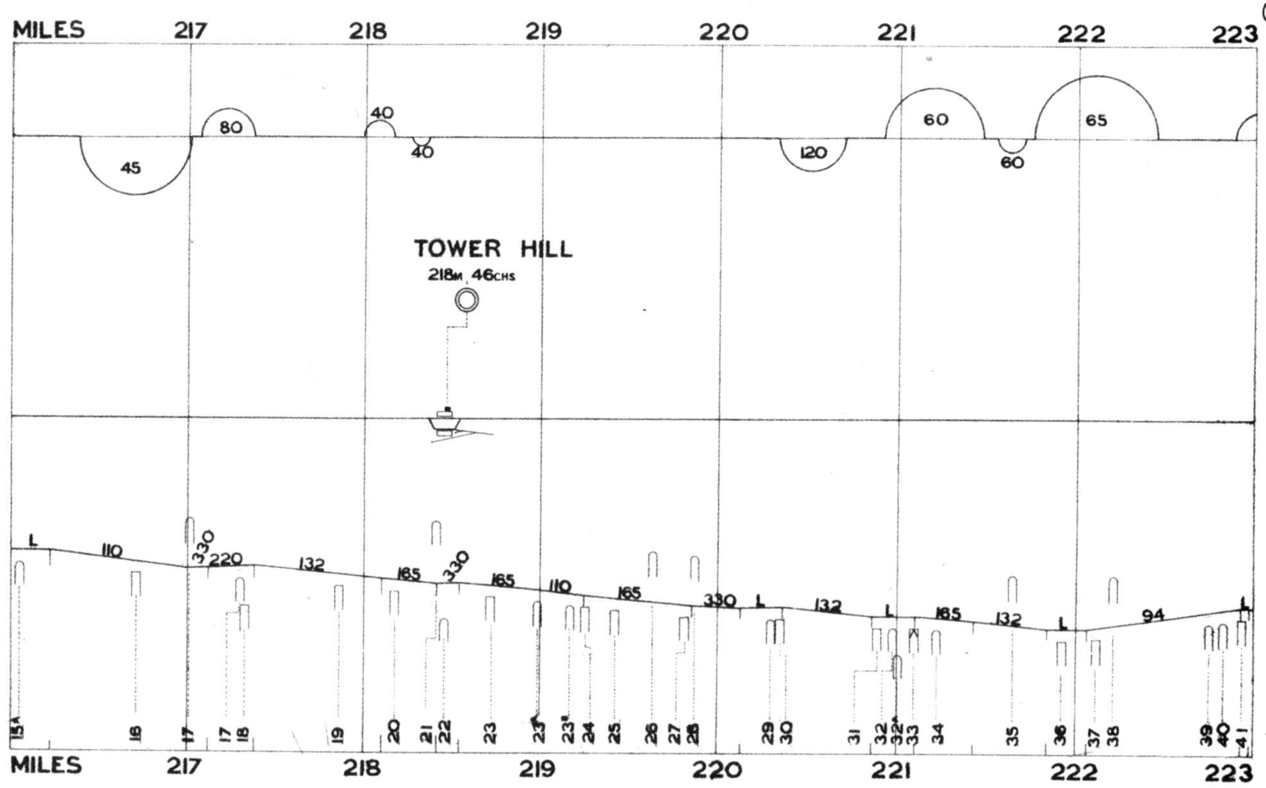

Left. The dressed stonework of Tower Hill Bridge No.21, station buildings and platform walls, are apparent on this damp day in the 1950s. *Below.* The new 1943 signal box was sited across the booking office frontage, can be seen nearest the camera. The Carey Valley widens considerably here, and the alignment through the station to Launceston started a rare straight section over two miles in length. John Eyres, South Western Circle.

Above. **Looking south west from Tower Hill Bridge and a fine view of the two mile straight section to Launceston. John Eyres, South Western Circle.**

Middle. **Some small protection from the elements was afforded here by the waiting shelter on the down side. One wonders how lonely a wait it would have been on a cold winter's night. John Eyres, South Western Circle.**

Below. **T9 4-4-0 No.30719 waits for a passing train to arrive at Tower Hill in July 1960. R. C. Riley, www.transporttreasury.co.uk**

Above. Tower Hill, (it was named after a nearby farm) station offices and Station Masters house in August 1961. Some Pres-flo wagons are trundling through the station beyond, probably being used to transport slate dust away from Delabole. John Eyres, South Western Circle.

Left and below. The goods shed at Tower Hill. In March 1943 two new sidings were laid down and the head shunt lengthened as part of the War effort. The down loop, removed in 1920, was reinstated, the booking hall was extended out onto the platform and a new signal box constructed. The points to the goods yard were also moved at this time allowing 40 wagon trains to be held in the loop. The sidings were sited beyond the hedge in the lower photo; they were removed after the War. John Eyres, South Western Circle.

The line from Tower Hill curves into Launceston station; the emergency wartime spur with the Great Western leaves to the left. John Eyres, South Western Circle.

frame. There were now sixteen levers (two spare). With room for a 40 wagon train (plus engine and van) in the loops, and another 40 in the shunt neck, Tower Hill could handle the thousands of tons of material brought into this end of Devon. By August 1944 most of the ammunition had gone to Normandy. The yard was removed in the 1950s but the long crossing loop remained. It would prove most useful as a passing place in post-war summers when the North Cornwall holiday trains multiplied. None ever called at Tower Hill and this rural corner of Devon lapsed into quietude again until closure in 1966, lit by oil lamps to the end. Services were withdrawn in February 1964 and the goods yard was lifted in 1965. Again the Down loop was placed out of use and the signal box closed, this time on 7 November 1965. Thus, with Ashwater signal box closure, a 12½ mile single line Section was created for the remaining diesel car trains from Halwill to Launceston. Tower Hill is the only station to have been demolished on the NCR since closure.

Tower Hill to Launceston

The valley widens below Tower Hill and the NCR engineers were able to project their line almost straight for about two miles towards Jay's Farm (220m 20ch) on a reasonable gradient of 1 in 165. However the Carey, meandering through the meadows, needed bridging twice more, at Hawkadon and at Heale. Here, a minor public road into Lifton and the river shared the two 15ft wrought iron spans taking the railway round a long 60ch curve towards Launceston. The town, surmounted by its spectacular Norman Castle, is clearly in view here. The Carey goes off to join the Tamar three quarters of a mile to the north, but the NCR skirted the hillside at Nethercott and then, supported on a shallow embankment beyond, headed towards the Tamar to cross the county boundary into Cornwall.

Crossing the Tamar by a double span wrought iron girder bridge on masonry piers at 222m 9ch, the North Cornwall's profile here 'bottomed out' at 200ft above sea level, before a rise at 1 in 94 towards Launceston. For the next fourteen miles engines of Down trains would work against the collar to climb 600ft to the Otterham summit. Past Colhay Farm the line made straight for its first crossing of the River Kensey (over a three arch masonry viaduct) then curved right across the GWR on a 31ft skew span of wrought iron lattice girders. At this point it came to the base of the hillside below Launceston, passed under the steep Ridgegrove Lane, and a few hundred yards on came to the eastern end of Launceston goods yard.

LAUNCESTON (223m 34ch)

Launceston stood as the 'gateway to Cornwall' for centuries. While rail travel was in the ascendancy this title waned, the GWR line over the Royal Albert Bridge at Saltash taking over. The rise of motoring in the 1920s re-established

Barely recognisable as Launceston engine shed, these sad remains are still in use in 1962 as a stabling and turning point. The shed opened with the station in 1886 and was an outstation of Wadebridge. M7 and O2 0-4-4Ts were regular visitors and by 1913 a small 48ft turntable was in place. John Eyres, South Western Circle.

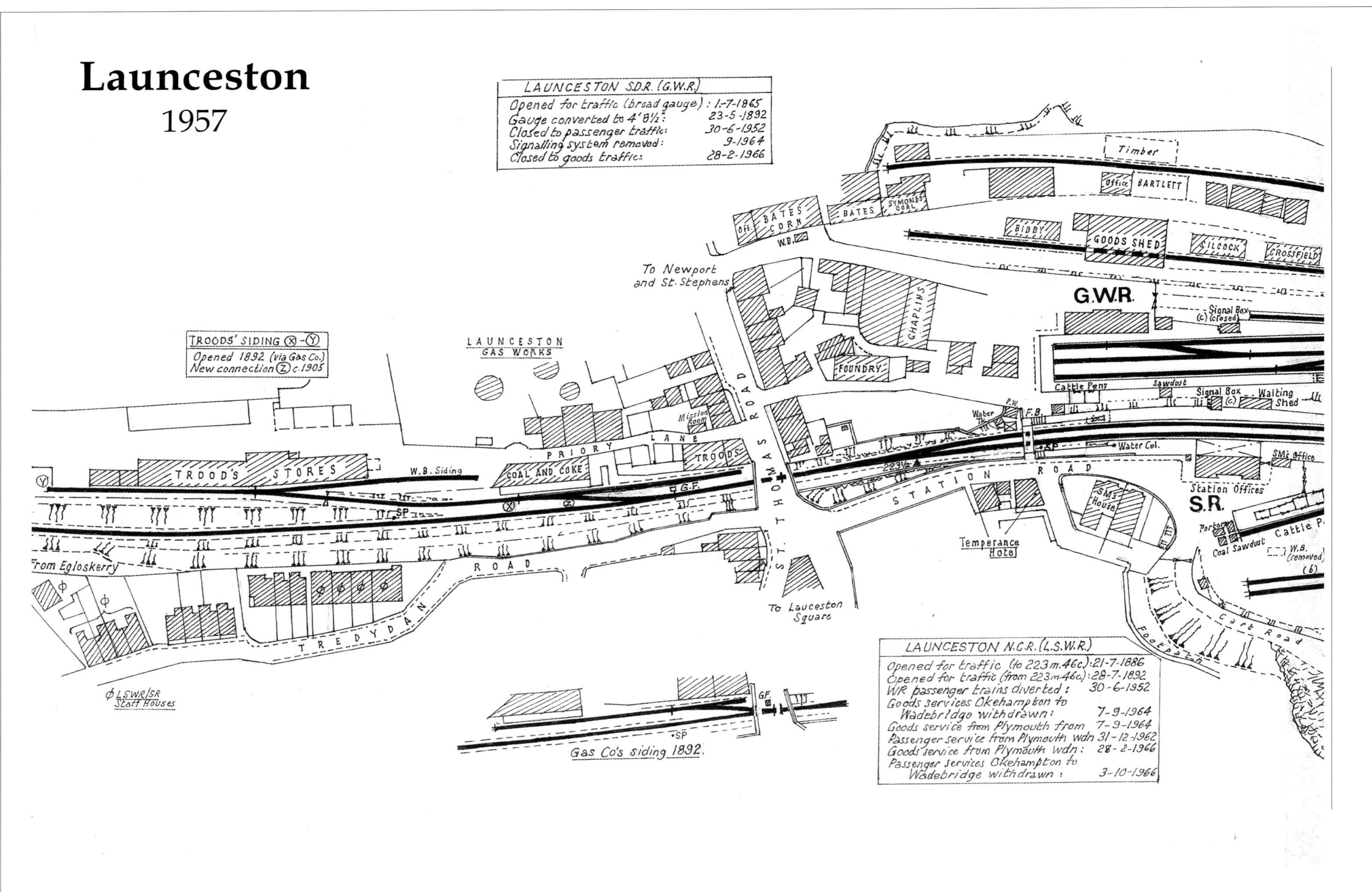
Launceston
1957
LAUNCESTON S.D.R. (G.W.R.)
Opened for traffic (broad gauge): 1-7-1865
Gauge converted to 4'8½": 23-5-1892
Closed to passenger traffic: 30-6-1952
Signalling system removed: 9-1964
Closed to goods traffic: 28-2-1966
TROODS' SIDING (X)-(Y)
Opened 1892 (via Gas Co.)
New connection (Z) c.1905
LAUNCESTON N.C.R. (L.S.W.R.)
Opened for traffic (to 223m.46c): 21-7-1886
Opened for traffic (from 223m.46c): 28-7-1892
WR passenger trains diverted: 30-6-1952
Goods services Okehampton to Wadebridge withdrawn: 7-9-1964
Goods service from Plymouth from 7-9-1964
Passenger service from Plymouth wdn 31-12-1962
Goods service from Plymouth wdn: 28-2-1966
Passenger services Okehampton to Wadebridge withdrawn: 3-10-1966
G.W.R.
S.R.
GOODS SHED
Station Offices
Signal Box (c) (closed)
Signal Box (c)
Walking Shed
Cattle Pens
Sawdust
Water Col.
Water Tk.
F.B.
SMs Office
SMs House
Temperance Hotel
STATION ROAD
ST. THOMAS ROAD
PRIORY LANE
TREDYDAN ROAD
LAUNCESTON GAS WORKS
COAL AND COKE
TROOD'S STORES
TROODS
W.B. Siding
FOUNDRY
CHAPLINS
BATES
BATES CORN
SYMONDS COAL
BIBBY
BARTLETT
SILCOCK
CROSSFIELD
Timber
Office
Mission Room
To Newport and St. Stephens
To Launceston Square
From Egloskerry
Gas Co's siding 1892.
LSWR/SR Staff Houses
Coal Sawdust
Cattle P
W.B. (removed)
Cart Road
Footpath

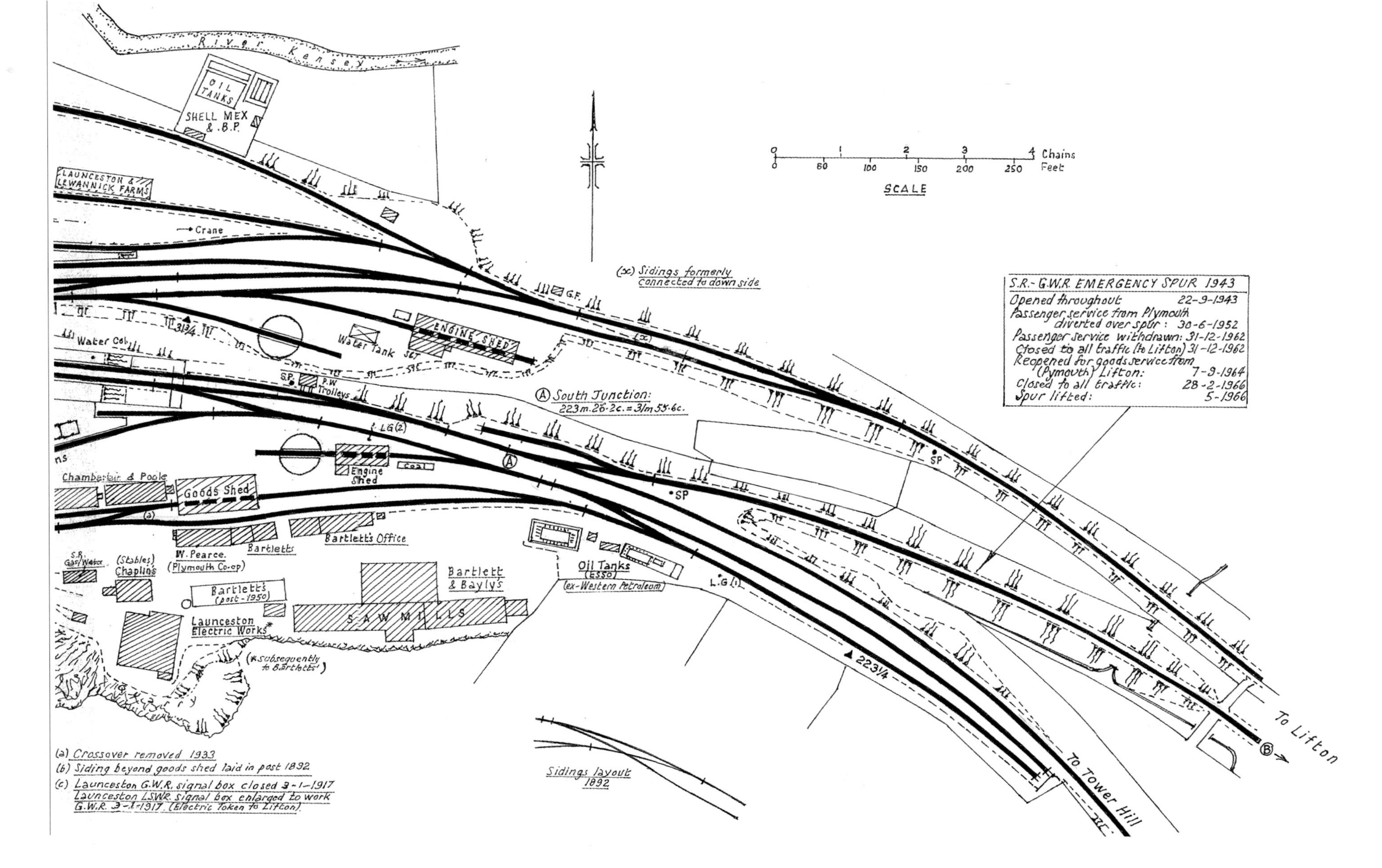
River Kensey
OIL TANKS SHELL MEX & B.P.
LAUNCESTON & LEWANNICK FARMS
Crane
0 1 2 3 4 Chains
0 50 100 150 200 250 Feet
SCALE
(x) Sidings formerly connected to down side
G.F.
S.R.- G.W.R. EMERGENCY SPUR 1943
Opened throughout 22-9-1943
Passenger service from Plymouth diverted over spur: 30-6-1952
Passenger service withdrawn: 31-12-1962
Closed to all traffic (to Lifton) 31-12-1962
Reopened for goods service from (Plymouth) Lifton: 7-9-1964
Closed to all traffic: 28-2-1966
Spur lifted: 5-1966
ENGINE SHED
Water Tank
Water Col.
SP
P.W Trolleys
Ⓐ South Junction: 223m. 26c. 2c. = 31m 55.6c.
L.G.(2)
Engine Shed
Coal
Chamberlain & Poole
Goods Shed
Bartletts
Bartlett's Office
S.R. Cart Weigher
(Stables) Chaplins
W. Pearce. (Plymouth Co-op)
Bartletts (post-1950)
Bartlett & Baylys
SAW MILLS
Launceston Electric Works*
(*subsequently to Bartletts)
Oil Tanks (ESSO) (ex-Western Petroleum)
L.G.(1)
223¼
To Lifton
To Tower Hill
Sidings layout 1892
(a) Crossover removed 1933
(b) Siding beyond goods shed laid in post 1892
(c) Launceston G.W.R. signal box closed 3-1-1917
Launceston LSWR. signal box enlarged to work G.W.R. 3-1-1917 (Electric Token to Lifton)

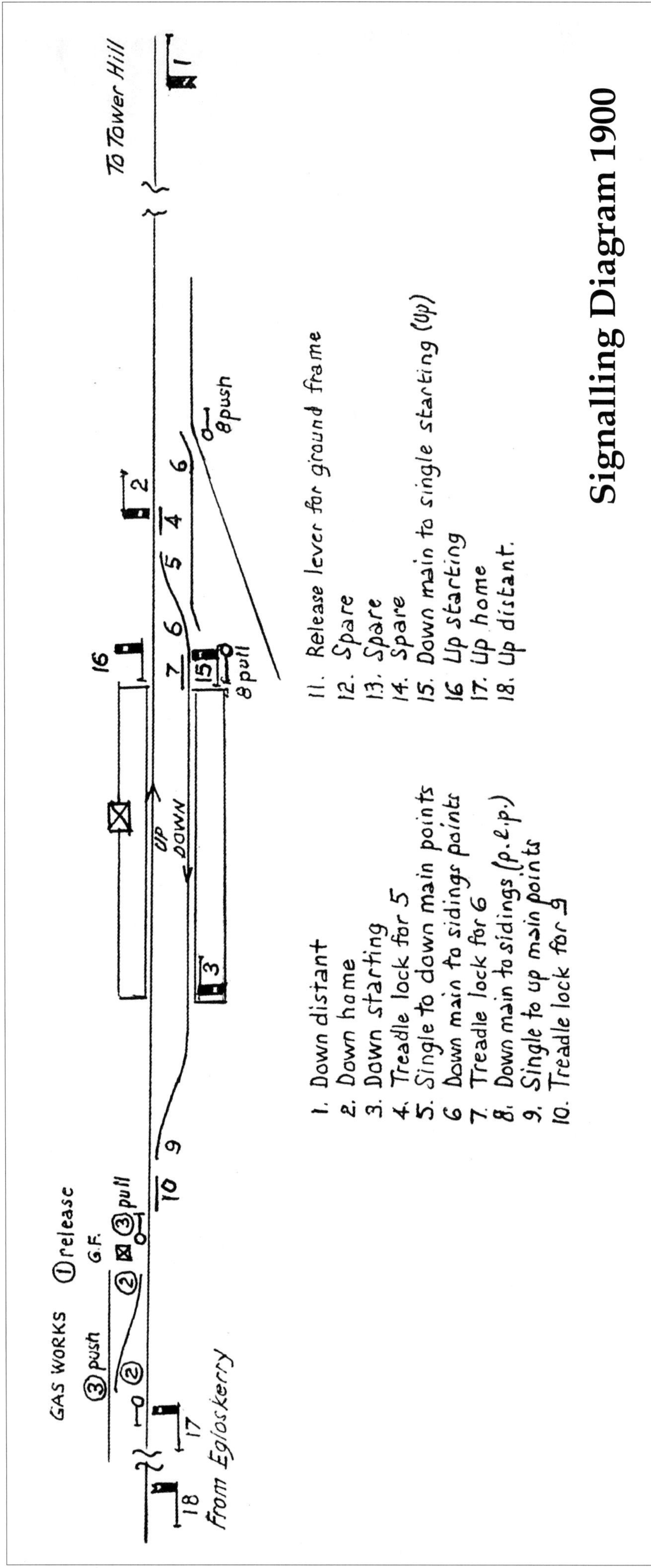

Signalling Diagram 1900

Launceston's 'gateway', though the town is now by-passed; the sheer volume of traffic is too much for the narrow streets, the tortuous turns and the Southgate arch. Down the hill from the town, for just over 100 years, the trains of the GWR, LSWR, SR and then BR, served the town. It grew considerably on the south side and in the Newport area, around the station. Tourists came to view the magnificently sited Norman castle, the richly decorated Church of St Mary Magdalene and some fine Georgian houses. Yet the main attractions of Launceston were the Markets, both Pannier (in the Square) and the important Cattle and Sheep Auctions, latterly at Race Hill. Although both were well away from the railway and down a very step hill, this did not deter country people of a former age, accustomed to walking. The Station Master (only one, as we shall see) actively canvassed for business for both, though this loyalty must have been strained! His station was the railhead for many miles around, from Byton and North Petherwin to the north and Lewannick, Lezant and North Hill in the south. For many years it was the lifeline to the numerous traders and manufacturers in the town.

Following the opening of the GWR in 1865 and the LSWR in 1886, the stations at the bottom of the steep hills leading down from Launceston Town and St Stephens village were simply referred to as the 'Great Western' and the 'South Western'. By earlier agreement, but under wartime circumstances, on 10th August 1915 most of the traffic working on the two stations was amalgamated; the pair thereafter were known as 'LSW & GW Joint' (SR & GW Joint after 1922). The Station Master was always an LSW/SR appointment, but his staff were employed by both companies. The GW passenger guards wore that company's uniform and buttons for instance, but the shunting staff were in LSWR uniforms and worked in both yards – their brass buttons, however, showed the joint status. Between 31 December 1916 and 3 January 1917 the GWR signalmen were transferred to the rear of an enlarged LSWR box, working a separate frame and the Electric Staff instrument to and from Lifton. The single-needle telegraph to Lifton was put into the LSWR booking office. Under war conditions again, in 1943, the two Launceston systems were joined by an 'emergency spur' giving direct running for Up SR and Down GWR trains. From 19 September 1943 the GWR completed its signalling arrangements (the SR the previous 30 May) and the spur was ready. It was used for munitions trains but not, at that time, for conventional transfers of traffic.

The spur saw continuous use, however, from 30 June 1952. After nationalisation in 1948, the GWR station was suffixed 'North' and the SR 'South'

Top. Launceston shed and goods yard in 1962. The shed was said to have been moved from Delabole to here in 1893 but this doesn't seem to have happened, the shed there being converted into a store. John Eyres, South Western Circle.

Middle. A mixed goods train is shunted around the yard in June 1963. John Eyres, South Western Circle.

Below. The standard type of country waiting shelter, rather larger as befitted Launceston, flanked by the extended signal box. The newer (1916) extension faced the opposite way towards the GWR station. John Eyres, South Western Circle.

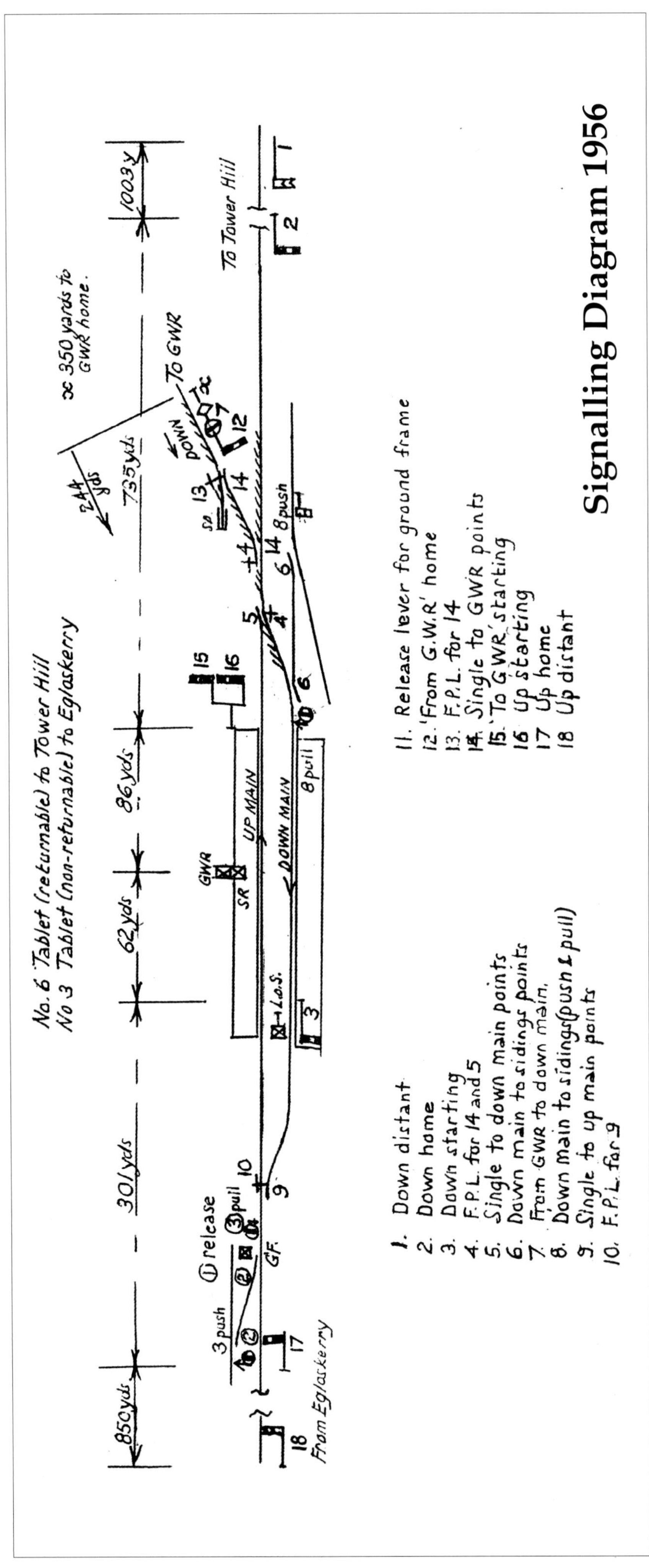

(1 January 1952). Within six months, the 'North' station was closed to passengers and the local WR Plymouth trains diverted into the Southern station. The Western side remained open for goods traffic, including engine servicing and was still fully signalled.

The Great Western station had been established in a side lane off the main road through Newport, opening on 1 July 1865. Although it appeared to be a typical GWR bywater for almost 100 years, this belied the fact that its goods business outstripped the LSW/SR in volume. The large goods shed was served by road boxes from Paddington and Plymouth and there was a considerable traffic in cattle feeds, fertilisers etc. This, in spite of the broad gauge (until 1892) and the shorter LSW route to Exeter and London from 1886.

The North Cornwall (LSWR) station platforms were on a slightly higher level, on the south of the GWR terminus. Access was from the main road, but just up the hill off St Thomas Road. Station Road sloped away to the buildings on the Down side, with the goods yard entrance opposite on the right. The sharp rise formed by St Thomas Hill Bridge was a hard test for horses hauling the station buses and cartage vehicles further up into town, several hundred feet above. An easier gradient than the St Thomas Hill was earlier found by a road skirting the west side of the Castle. No less steep was St Stephens Hill to the north, later relieved by Roydon Road further east. In the 1920s the White Hart Hotel ran its exclusive horse bus to the station, lesser folk using J.B. Smith's bus. Soon, motor buses were substituted by Truscott, then by the Western National's town service from 1938. Chaplins, the LSWR and SR cartage agent, had changed to lorries by the mid-1930s though Mr Gynn, agent, for some of the London wholesale houses, still used horse and cart until 1948.

The single storey building was unlike the usual NCR (LSWR) design. The Station Master lived in a large house opposite (only lately demolished) and the building was entirely devoted to offices (booking and parcels), staff room, waiting rooms and toilets. W.H. Smith & Sons ran a small bookstall on the platform side. The material used for construction was local stone with Portland stone quoining and Delabole slate for the steeply pitched roof. The building was backed with a generously wide cantilevered awning. The central stanchions supported the cross beams with gussets of most delicate tracery. The SM occupied a separate office at the east end. On the Up platform stood a large waiting shed again made of dressed stone, as were the platforms. The signal box of 1886, with its multiple glass panes, was almost duplicated rearwards for the additional GWR frame of 1917. Water columns on the departure ends of the platforms, a staff foot crossing

Top. Launceston's down side buildings in August 1964. The station lay at the foot of a steep hill with the ancient town and Norman Castle some 300ft above. John Eyres, South Western Circle.

Middle. Launceston looking east in 1961. The signal box was constructed in the style favoured by the South Western in the 1880s. The original structure was extended at the rear in 1916 for the GWR signalman, locking frame, levers and electric token apparatus to Lifton. John Eyres, South Western Circle.

Below. The station building in 1962. Like Wadebridge, Launceston did not have an integral Station Master's residence, just the booking and parcels hall, staff room, waiting rooms and toilets. Construction was in the usual dressed stone with Portland quoins. John Eyres, South Western Circle.

Top and middle. Some under-canopy detail and the station frontage in 1963. John Eyres, South Western Circle.

Below. The approach in 1963. The Great Western station, beyond the signal box, opened in 1865 prior to the arrival of the North Cornwall in 1886. Although it appeared to be a typical Great Western byway, for decades its goods business outstripped that of the South Western and latterly the Southern Railway. John Eyres, South Western Circle.

CAMELFORD (240m 56ch)
Mystery surrounds the hotels formerly adjoining this station. A 'North Cornwall Railway Hotel' was built on the Down side at the time of the opening, at the south-east corner, by the crossroads. It was destroyed by fire about 1900, rebuilt but again burned down about 1907. A new hotel, the 'Melorne' was erected on the opposite corner but slightly up the road towards Boscastle. Opened about 1908 it too succumbed in January 1917. The story goes that nothing was known of the last fire until the following morning, when the family was found huddling for shelter in a nearby barn. The shell was rebuilt into the present Melorne Farm. The presence of hotels signifies the relative importance of Camelford

***Top*. The station's down side goods yard was larger than many, but in July 1964 only a few fertiliser vans were in view. Crosfields, of Liverpool, established a warehouse in the former slaughterhouse (centre) distributing locally using a Bedford lorry.**

***Middle*. The slaughterhouse, established by the SR, provided enough traffic for two goods trains a day and the goods shed (No.2 style) saw a lively trade in rabbits, feed stuffs and agricultural merchandise.**

***Below*. Serving as the railhead for passengers from Tintagel and Boscastle, Camelford was provided with an awning, one of only two between Halwill and Wadebridge. The cast iron columns survive within the present Museum of Cycling. Photographs John Eyres, South Western Circle.**

Station. Tourists in the 1890s were not in such a hurry and commercial travellers found them useful. Apart from a Bible Christian Chapel there was little else at Melorne except the crossroads, re-aligned on top of the railway bridge. This dictated the siting of Camelford Station, with Boscastle and Bossiney to the north, Delabole and Tintagel to the west, Davidstow to the east and Camelford town to the south. The view to the east is dominated by the spectacular heights of Rough Tor and Brown Willy. It was one and a half miles down to Camelford, walkable enough although a horse bus met trains in earlier years. The LSWR subsidised another horse bus from Boscastle and Tintagel until withdrawal in 1920. Thereafter motor buses were run by Mrs Fry (Tintagel) and Mr Webber (Boscastle) until their contract with the SR ceased in 1930. Following this the Southern National bus company (part-owned by the SR) served this route, and into Camelford town. From 1935 the Southern National's 122 route

***Top and middle*. The up platform in August 1964. John Eyres, South Western Circle.**

***Below*. Camelford for Boscastle and Tintagel the Exmouth Junction name board proclaims in August 1964. John Eyres, South Western Circle.**

(Bude/Wadebridge) fairly comprehensively covered this area and connected with many trains at Camelford. Combined rail and road tickets were issued to Tintagel and Boscastle into BR days.

Not only the Melorne Hotel, but the opening of the large King Arthur's Castle Hotel (1899) at Tintagel and the continuing attraction of the earlier Wellington Hotel at Boscastle brought much business to Camelford; even royalty – Prince Albrecht of Prussia and his suite travelled by special train in 1895. Thomas Hardy came to St Juliot again in 1913 after the death of his wife Emma and again in 1916.

Camelford itself had not been well regarded for years. The new turnpike road from Launceston to Bodmin of 1769 by-passed it, and the Borough was disfranchised by the 1832 Reform Bill. Nevertheless the town was regarded as goal for several railway promotions; after all, the population was around 2,000, it retained the County Court and the surrounding area was quite well populated to the south, in St Breward and Michaelstow parishes, the Rural District numbering about 7,000. The Duke of Bedford who owned much estate hereabouts provided the distinctive Town Hall (1806) and a Grammar School derived from the native benefactor Sir James Smith (1679). Camelford town, though by-passed this time, actually derived some prosperity through the tourist trade and the business engendered by the new station – ready availability of general merchandise from London and wider selection of building materials was evident in new villas and terraces which appeared in the next decade.

Left. **The down side waiting shelter frames the signal box in August 1964. The box housed a Stevens 17 lever frame and was equipped in 1923 with a Tyers No.6 Tablet (returnable) for the section to Delabole. John Eyres, South Western Circle.**

Below. **Station approach in 1963. As we have seen at other locations, slating the walls of the house was an attempt to counter the effects of wind and rain in this exposed position high above the Atlantic coast. A good supply of household coal for the house, booking hall and offices was another essential. John Eyres, South Western Circle.**

The down side approach to the goods yard in August 1964. All traffic from this yard ceased in September 1964 although it was still operable until the following year. John Eyres, South Western Circle.

Two views from Station Bridge No.102. *Above*. Camelford, along with other stations on the line, received a coat of brown and cream paint after the original Western Region take-over in 1950. *Below*. The way west and Delabole beckons. The falling gradient of 1 in 123 is apparent as the line leans into the 40ch curve. The platform loop was extended in July 1911 allowing adequate room for 12 coach passenger or 35 wagon goods trains. John Eyres, South Western Circle.

Indicative of Camelford's status as a railhead was the provision of an awning over the Up platform, its original plain roof replaced by a more distinguished version before 1914. The building itself was constructed in faced Delabole stone, but the signal box and platform walls were in unfaced stone. Slate cladding was attached to the walls of the SM's house to keep out driving rain; like Otterham it can be very wet and windy up here at 700ft above sea level. A sea fog will also blank out visibility (it is also very wetting!) which made spotting signals difficult for enginemen. Camelford, from 1927, took control of Delabole, Port Isaac Road and St Kew Highway. John Wildish, a former SECR man, was appointed SM in 1928. What he made of his tenure, so different from his last station (Strood in Kent) can be gauged from the fact that he fitted in quite well. Being a Methodist and a good choir master at that, obviously helped! His staff at that time comprised booking clerk, goods checker, a leading porter (passed shunter) and two signalmen.

The platform loops were on a slightly easier 1 in 330 gradient, rising in the Delabole direction, and on a steady 40 chain curve reversing to 60 under the road bridge. After extensions at both ends were made in July 1911, these loops were adequate for passing 35 wagon goods trains or, at maximum, 12-coach passengers. The section towards Delabole was re-equipped with a No.6 Tyers Tablet ('returnable') in 1923, but the No.3 was not replaced by a WR Electric Key Token until 1961. The signal box was the square, well glazed, version of the 1880s period. The Stevens frame held 17 levers to work a slightly more complicated layout than usual. The down side goods yard was fed by facing and trailing points from the Down loop (push and pull).

Facing inner siding No.2 was a medium-sized country good shed, with ports both sides, in grey Delabole stonework, unfaced but with brick corners. In 1934 a new brick slaughterhouse opened at the extremity of the Up siding, later acquired from the Western Co-operative Society and used as a fertiliser store by Messrs Crossfields of Liverpool. Right to the end of freight working, a considerable tonnage was handled and distributed by lorry. Harry Bolt, formerly in the rabbit business here, at Otterham and Tresmeer and a member of a well-known railway family, latterly conducted Crossfield's distribution. Long before, Messrs Rush built a store for feedstuffs and agricultural merchandise at the other extremity of the long back siding. Olde of Boscastle also has a wooden store, next to the goods shed, and handled coal as well. It came through Wadebridge Quay or Plymouth in earlier years but later went direct from the collieries.

Blewitts of Marshgate ran the slaughterhouse (leased from the SR) and meat was forwarded to Nine Elms. There had been a fair quantity of cattle driven up from the Camelford monthly market and two pens were provided on the dock. Two goods trains in each direction during the day brought necessary wagons of coal, cattle, seeds (including potatoes from Scotland, though early potatoes from Boscastle were sent east in late May) and road boxes. In the 1930s the 'road boxes' from Exeter and Plymouth came in on the 6.00am goods from Okehampton, en route to Wadebridge. In the 40 minutes available, they were unloaded into the parcels store, or shunted over to the goods shed. The London (Nine Elms) box served only Launceston to St Kew Highway, having left at 9.30pm the previous night. In those days a telegram from a local grocer would have an ordered item (such as a special blend of tea) delivered within 24 hours, such was the role of these nominated wagons, though they carried most sundry merchandise, from beer to carpets. The 11.35am goods from Wadebridge returned the road boxes, through Camelford, in the early afternoon en route for Plymouth; there was also the overnight fast goods train from Exeter. Although the perishable and parcels traffic was diverted to the up afternoon passenger train from Padstow in the late 1920s, the road box system persisted until 1964. By this time BR was using railheads at Launceston and Wadebridge. From the opening years calves would be sent from East Devon stations to Camelford – very urgent, of course!

Mails arrived before 7.00am by goods trains from the 1890s. Camelford was the head Post Office for a wide area, and a contracted-out Mail Cart System extended from St Gennys in the north to Port Isaac in the south; also to St Breward, Boscastle, Tintagel, St Mabyn and St Tudy. This goods train also ran on Sundays, (terminating at Camelford) until 1917. Thereafter the Mails came by road from Launceston. In the Up direction the overnight despatch left by passenger train starting from Camelford at 6.30pm (again Sundays included until 1917).

Goods services ceased on 7 September 1964, but the yard remained connected until 30 November 1965, at the same time as the up block section was extended all the way to Egloskerry. Even after the passenger closure on 3 October 1966 wagons were stored in the Up loop. The station buildings survive as a residence and an extension now houses a cycle museum, while down the road to Worthyvale one can observe the LSWR staff cottages. The overbridge under the crossroads has been removed and the Chapel is a private house.

Camelford to Delabole

The road from Camelford Station to Delabole simply runs straight there, not to the route of the old North Cornwall line! As near Tresmeer, complete half-circles were plotted by the Engineers. Firstly by a 30 chains radius around Trethener Farm, then reversing to skirt the hillside about Deli, the route was brought by a 50-chain curve round to the top of the great quarry at Delabole. At least these contortions achieved a reasonable 1 in 123 falling gradient and a slight level beneath bridge No.106 carrying the Rockhead to Camelford Road. The two and a half miles between the stations was, even then, the shortest on the North Cornwall. The final curve ended in Delabole station after giving passengers a spectacular, almost frightening, glimpse into the tremendous depth of the quarry. Away to the south spread the slate spoil and on the further end of the pit ranged the quarry haulage machinery and storage buildings.

DELABOLE (243m 5ch)

The fortunes of Delabole depended mainly on the great slate quarry and the employment it gave to hundreds of men of the village, as well as the surrounding parishes of St Teath and Camelford, Stretching for about a mile between Rockhead through Medrose to Higher Pengelly, it may not have brought many tourists as did Tintagel or Boscastle, but the quarry itself was, and is, an attraction in its own right. After the railway opened, the output of slates and slate stone for building, rose considerably. This prosperity was reflected in new houses and an Anglican Church (St John's) though Chapel-going was strong, there being three at one time. Outside the quarrying community Delabole stayed rural, attracting a cattle market in due course.

The station and its goods yard sat to the north of the bridge under the street from Higher Pengelly down through

In the last year of steam in 1964, BR class 3 2-6-2Ts were taking turns on the North Cornwall trains. No.82030, built in December 1954 at Swindon and allocated to Exmouth Junction between June 1964 and May 1965, was one of the class repainted in BR lined green by Swindon Works in 1957. 82030 calls at Delabole on 19th September with the 11.05am Padstow with a train comprising BR Mk1 bogie van (GUV) to Diagram 811, BR Mark I Brake 2nd and on the up line a Southern 4-wheel general utility Van 'U' (CCT) to Diagram 3101. The goods yards connection into the down loop has already been spiked following closure on 7th September. R. A. Lumber.

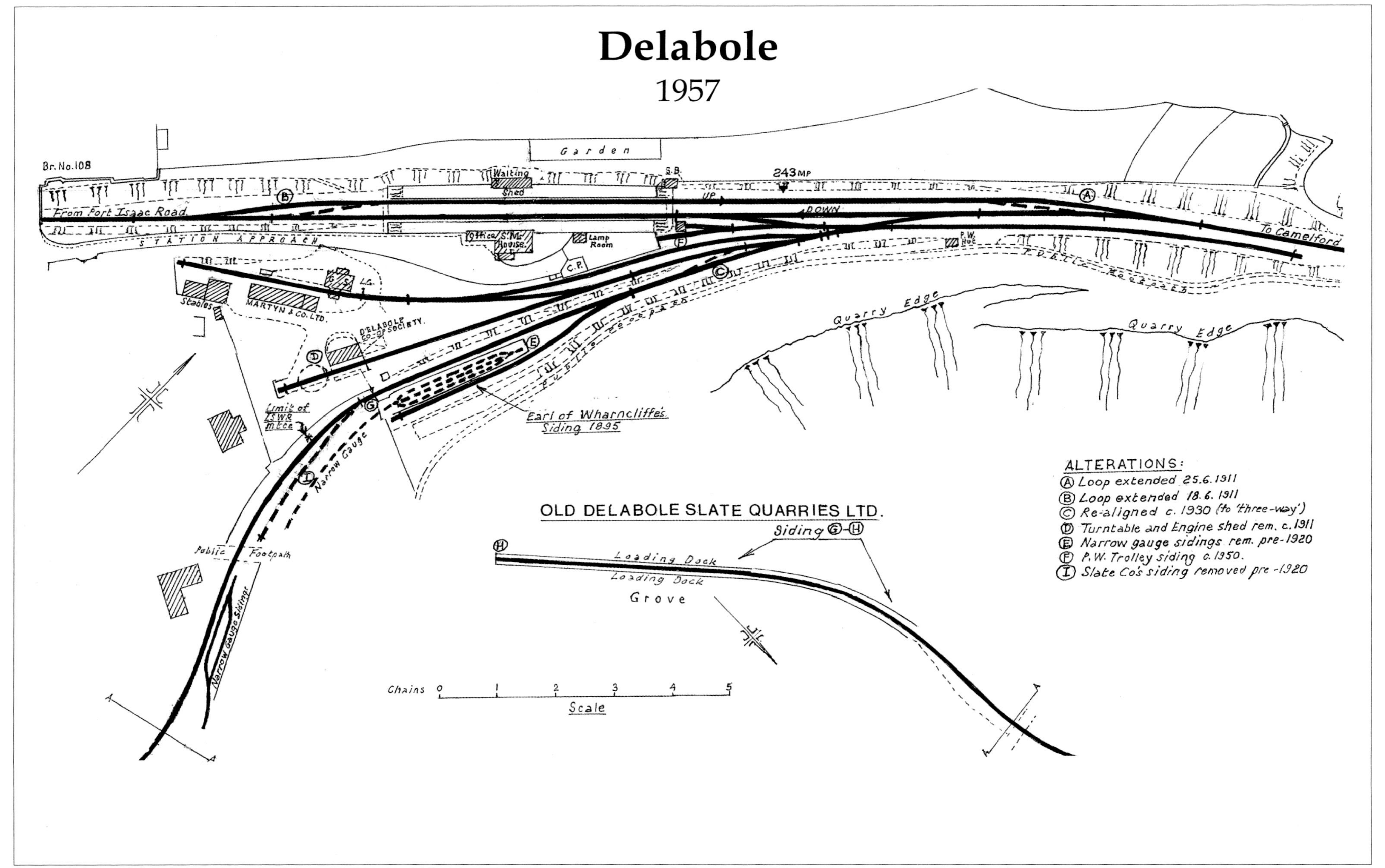
Delabole
1957
Garden
Br. No.108
From Port Isaac Road
STATION APPROACH
Waiting Shed
S.B.
243MP
UP
DOWN
To Camelford
Office/S.M. House
Lamp Room
C.P.
P.W. Hut
Stables
MARTYN & CO. LTD.
DELABOLE CO-OP SOCIETY.
L.G.
Limit of LSWR Mtce
Earl of Wharncliffe's Siding 1895
Quarry Edge
Quarry Edge
Narrow Gauge
Public Footpath
Narrow Gauge Sidings
OLD DELABOLE SLATE QUARRIES LTD.
Siding (G)-(H)
Loading Dock
Loading Dock
Grove
Chains 0 1 2 3 4 5
Scale
ALTERATIONS:
(A) Loop extended 25.6.1911
(B) Loop extended 18.6.1911
(C) Re-aligned c. 1930 (to 'three-way')
(D) Turntable and Engine shed rem. c.1911
(E) Narrow gauge sidings rem. pre-1920
(F) P.W. Trolley siding c.1950.
(I) Slate Co's siding removed pre-1920

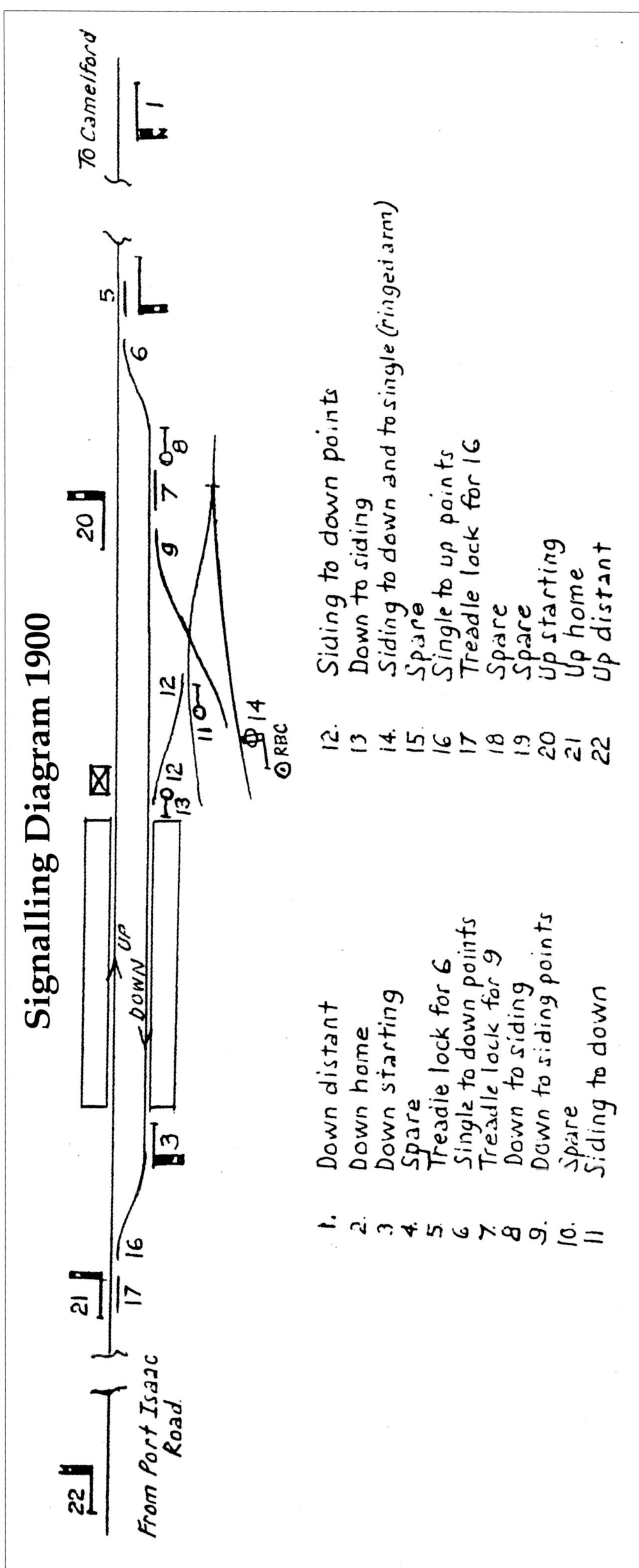

Signalling Diagram 1900

Pengelly to the quarry buildings and pit head at Grove. The goods yard, though fairly extensive, was hemmed in by the western face of the quarry. The LSWR expressed concern when this face began to be worked in 1904, though it was assured by the Slate Company that it was safe. The carriage of slates by rail directly to all parts of Britain was, of course, the prime reason for routing the NCR via Delabole. After a rather slow start (the LSWR complained!) tonnages rose steadily until the 1920s. At first only a short stub siding was provided but from 1895 the LSWR (not the NCR) built a wide loading bank to take three narrow gauge Slate Co sidings. Another siding was laid down in 1896 for the Earl of Wharncliffe's slate from his Trebarwith quarries. By 1899 the original short siding had been extended 400 yards to the Grove area, with a gate at the goods yard end. The loading bank gradually fell into disuse and the narrow gauge sidings were removed. Slates were packed in straw in 10 ton open wagons, whole trainloads being despatched in the years up to 1914. The firm was reconstituted as the Old Delabole Slate Co Ltd in 1898. After the Great War, the use of slate for roofing declined as clay tiles became popular. The main destinations in the 1930s were West Cornwall and the Continent (particularly Belgium). An interesting timetable note in 1927 required that slate from Delabole and Camelford to the LNER should be weighed at Woking, en route to Feltham Yard. By 1937 finished slate tonnage was down to 10,000, but uses for residual slate dust had been found, as will be seen.

The engine shed lasted until 1 July 1912. An iron-framed affair, it had been sold to the Delabole Co-operative Society for £20 in 1905. It was lifted sideways and became the Society's corn store. The 50ft turntable was removed. Apart from this siding and those for slate, a siding for about 35 wagons served a cattle pen bank and the goods shed (No.2 LSWR). A store for Martyns of Wadebridge lay beyond, with an end-loading dock siding and long shunt neck completing the accommodation. The 1893 signalling included a ringed-arm signal at the yard exit for slate trains to run directly out towards Camelford.

In similar fashion to Camelford, Delabole's standard station house was, in due course, slate clad on the upper storey. The darker dressed slate stone here contrasted well with the Bath stone quoining. This house and the offices were on the Down platform, the waiting shed and signal box on the Up. The frame held 22 levers, including four spare, housed in the 1880s-style wood and stone with multi-paned windows. Originally equipped with Tyers No.3 Tablets in both directions, in 1923 they were converted to No.6 (returnable) probably because of the lengthy shunt movements occurring at Delabole. From 1939 a new Up advanced starting

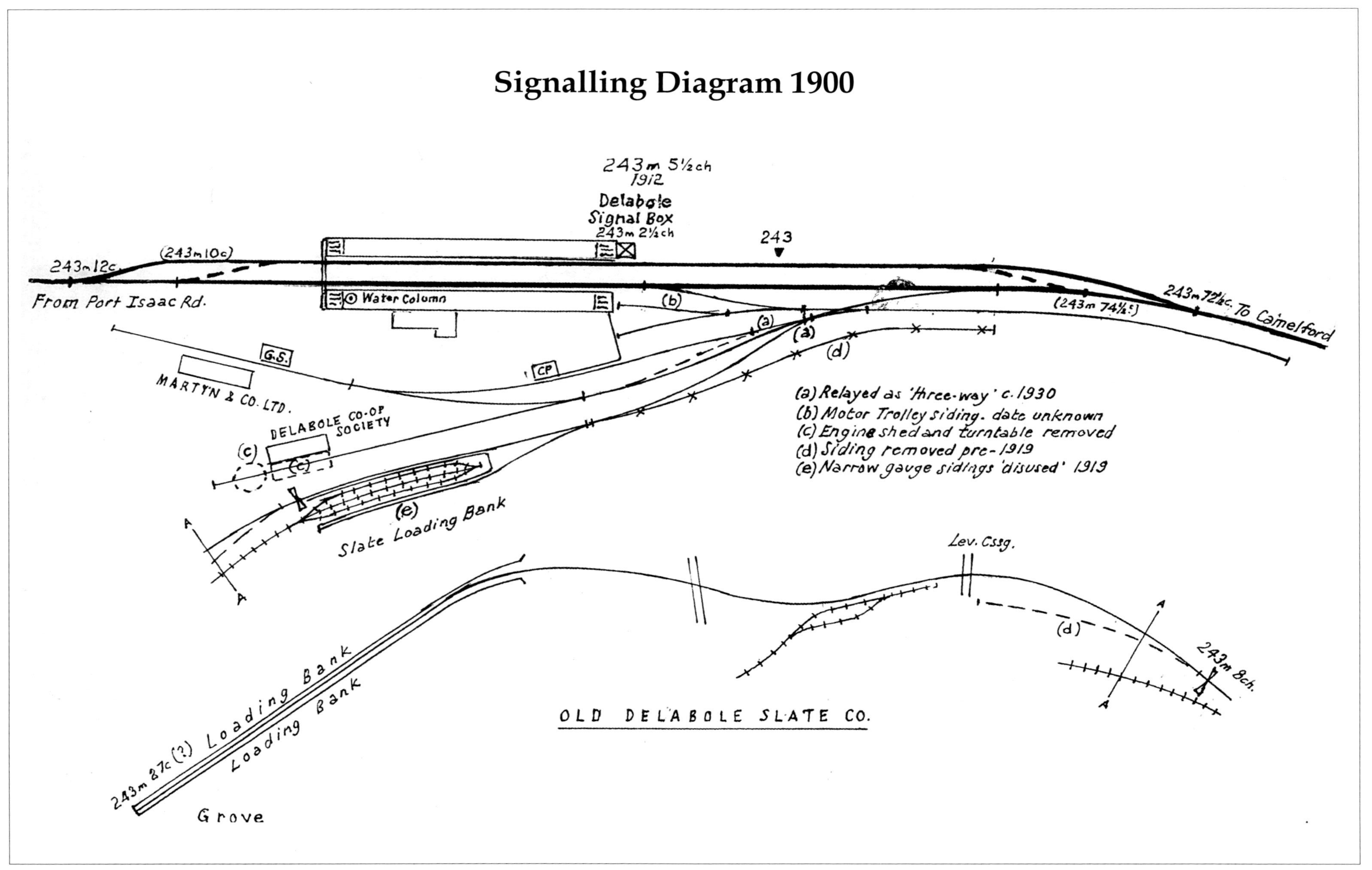
Signalling Diagram 1900
243m 5½ch
1912
Delabole
Signal Box
243m 2½ch
243
243m 12c
(243m 10c)
From Port Isaac Rd.
Water Column
(b)
(a)
(d)
(243m 74½c)
243m 72½c. To Camelford
G.S.
CP
MARTYN & CO. LTD.
DELABOLE CO-OP SOCIETY
(c)
(e)
Slate Loading Bank
(a) Relayed as 'three-way' c.1930
(b) Motor Trolley siding. date unknown
(c) Engine shed and turntable removed
(d) Siding removed pre-1919
(e) Narrow gauge sidings 'disused' 1919
Lev. Cssg.
243m 8ch.
243m 87c (?) Loading Bank
Loading Bank
OLD DELABOLE SLATE CO.
Grove

Delabole goods yard taken from the 8.48am Padstow to Okehampton train hauled by 4MT class 2-6-4T No.80059 in 1962. John Eyres, South Western Circle.

The down side platform of Delabole station looking back towards Camelford. The large corrugated building, almost identical to the one at Camelford, was for servicing the signals and station oil lamps. John Eyres, South Western Circle.

Top. **Standard North Cornwall building with the customary slate hung Station Masters house. The loops here were also extended in 1911 to accommodate, like Camelford and elsewhere, 12 coach and 35 wagon goods trains. John Eyres, South Western Circle.**

Above. **Delabole up platform and standard waiting shed on the left. LSWR 90lb/yd rail in 30ft lengths still existed here in the 1960s.**

signal (No.19) was installed towards Camelford, causing the Down home to be re-sited as well. In turn the Down distant was moved, ending up a mile and 86 yards from the box and (uncompensated) needing a tremendous pull by the signalman to get it 'off'.

After the 1911 loop extensions a twelve coach train could be held (seven against the platform) or 32 wagons, engine and van. On one occasion during the 1963 diversions from the WR, the signalman had four trains in his care – two in the platforms and two shunted back into the yard. The water column on the Down platform was the only one between Launceston and Wadebridge. Supply was restricted for many years until a better source was eventually found. On one occasion a ballast train engine working towards Otterham ran short of water, struggling up to the road overbridge there, for the crew to 'drop' the fire. Meanwhile a road tanker was quickly filled and brought down from Davidstow. The water fell by gravity into the engine tender from the road above. After 1935, at the other (Camelford) end of the Down platform a wooden shed sheltered the two local permanent way motor trolleys.

Jack Manning drove the light vehicle with Frank Bartlett (ganger) Bill Geach (sub-ganger), Bill Gregory and Claude Lee whilst on the Port Isaac side were Sid Keat, Bill Witheridge and Tom Stanbury. Later Ford-engined trolleys able to tow a trailer were substituted, but Tablets had to be drawn for movements outside station limits.

Stationmaster Caple had the Permanent Way men to pay as well as another half dozen traffic staff in the early 1920s. After 1927 Delabole came under the Camelford Station Master with two booking clerks, two signalmen and two porters in the 1930s, but the goods guard did the necessary shunting. LSWR houses for the staff were built in Pengelly, one of the reasons (with a certain stability of employment and wages above farm level) that attracted men to railway work.

Manufacturing of household goods in large towns had largely replaced locally made products by World War One. Rural water mills grinding the farmer's corn were less and less used. Before the rise of motor road transport the railway carried practically everything and Delabole's share would be handled in the yard and good shed. Overnight would come groceries from

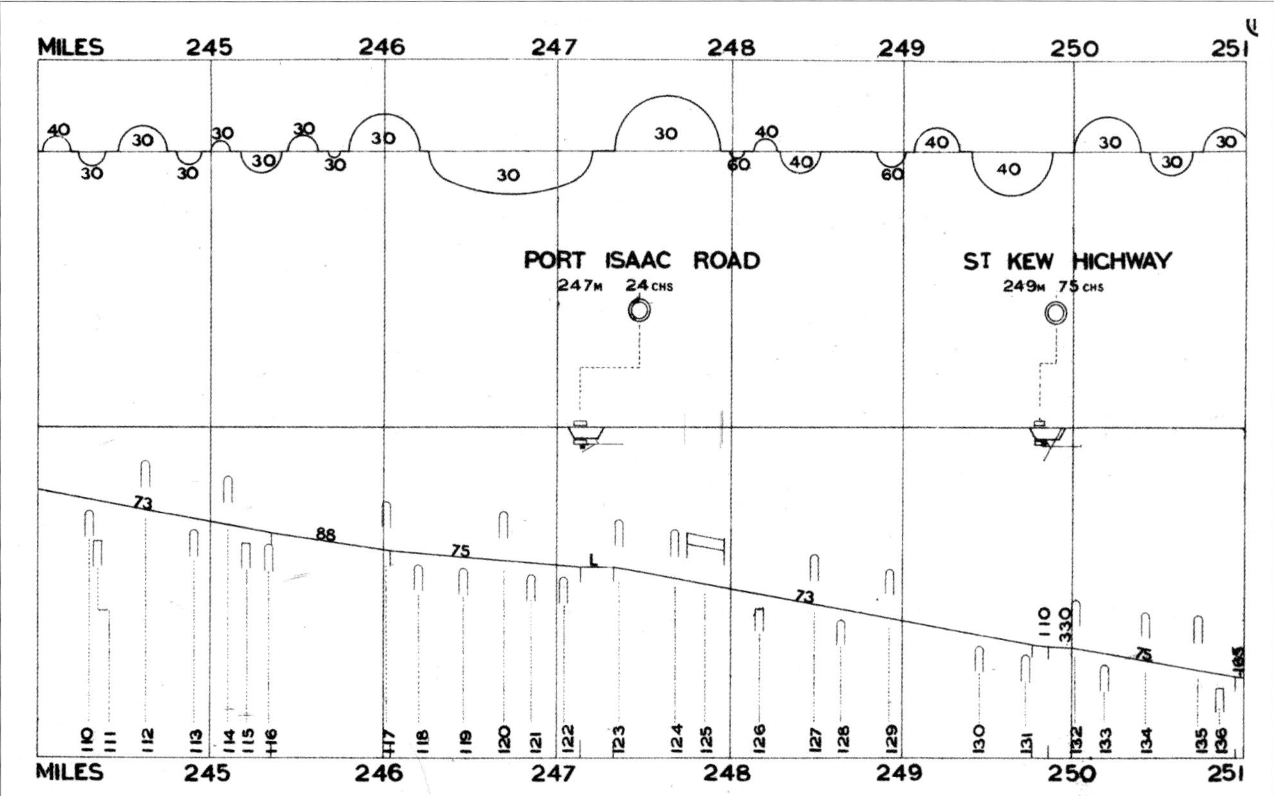

Exeter, Bristol and London in the ubiquitous road boxes, confectionery from Manchester and bags of flour from Avonmouth (milled from North American wheat) for local bakers. Iron and steel bars, bricks and timber would be taken straight from wagons to horse carts, later to steam wagons and, finally, to motor lorries for delivery south and west to Port Isaac, St Teath, even down to Polzeath. Coal, including the Slate Co's supplies, now came by rail instead of through Port Isaac. Some was transhipped from vessels at Wadebridge Quay and came northwards to Delabole. In 1940 a huge stack of coal was laid down in the yard as an emergency supply unloaded, it is said, by one man alone – Marnie Geach. The Co-operative Society traded in coal, corn and foodstuffs and West Cornwall Farmers in animal feeds and agriculture requirements, as did F.J. Martyn (of Wadebridge). Later Silcocks used an SR store for distributing their products. Thousands of rabbits (again!) were sent away from Delabole, a very lucrative trade. W. Pearce of Trewalder was the main trader.

Outwards a certain amount of wool went to Yorkshire in sacking bales, and in the 1940s to 1960s, sugar beet to Kidderminster. A cattle market came into its own from 1940. The Ministry of Food purchased animals brought in by Pearces, who then sent five or six wagons weekly. Easingwold in Yorkshire was one destination. Delabole, like Otterham, attracted military traffic during World War Two to the extent that redundant army tanks were imported to serve as targets for aircraft on the Treligga range, a mile or so to the west. With heavy traffic like this an O2 0-4-4T would be sent up from Wadebridge to shunt. About 40 wagons could be held in the yard and a train of 13 run-round inside. No wonder the Wadebridge foreman found Delabole's accommodation useful, though ten miles off! There was a breakaway on a goods train in 1949, the engine (No.34008) was well down towards Port Isaac Road with the leading wagons before it was discovered.

Mention of slate dust, once a by-product and then deliberately ground to powder in a large mill, has been made already. At first (from 1930) it went away in bags – 'Delafila' it was called – for use as a finish for rubber (690 tons in 1934 compared with 680 tons of slates). Bound for Brimsdown (Essex) via Feltham Yard, other loads went via the GWR to Hayes (Middlesex) to make the old '78' gramophone records. Then a 'Covhop' was tried out, confined to its own loading shed! This trial as a bulk carrier was followed by five (dedicated) 'Prestflo' wagons filled and emptied by air pressure, in the 1960s. Unfortunately the introduction of plastic 45 and 33 records from the mid-1950s badly affected business. When Delabole's freight facilities were closed the 'Prestflos' were loaded at Wadebridge from large bags taken by road, and this continued into the 1970s. Some powder was exported to Calcutta (a special load of 400 tons is recorded) via the docks at Newport (Mon) and once, 66 tons went to Rio de Janeiro. Finally, the diamond toothed saws used in the quarry were sent to Panmuir in Scotland for resetting. The present firm, Delabole Slate (1971) Ltd, a part of the RTZ Mining & Exploration Ltd since 1984, relies on road transport to export its powder and granules, reduced in a modern crushing plant installed in 1980. The pit is gradually being filled in by graders working on spiral tracks. The number of men now employed is much lower than the 350 in 1937. About 120 tons of slate block is currently quarried (sawn, not blasted) for floor slabbing, fireplace etc – but not for roofing!

Some alterations were made to the yard in 1930, and again in 1963, when the trailing connection to the down (No.12 points) were clipped out. Otherwise, after withdrawal of the freight services the yard remained in situ until 1965.

Delabole to Port Isaac Road

Below Delabole the line snaked its way on a series of 30 chain reversing curves at a ruling and mainly 1 in 73 gradient past Delamere and Benbole. At Treroosal Bridge (245m 7ch) the road leads to St Teath just over a mile away and this was where the inhabitants of 1892 would have preferred a station. On the Down side is the site of the once active Trewenham mine. Beyond, at Trekee, the NCR's surveyors laid out a complete semi-circle – a left-hand 30 chain curve to keep on the hillside above the deep valley at Trewarne. Down below, a quarry for blue stone had been worked over the years, but with the installation of a roadstone crusher at the railway level.

In 1922 the firm Tom Bros requested that the LSWR provide a siding. Served by facing points (Up) it was installed about half way round the mile-long curve at 246m 66ch; it was controlled by a two lever ground frame released by the Tablet. A key held in Port Isaac Road box unlocked the gate and a scotch block

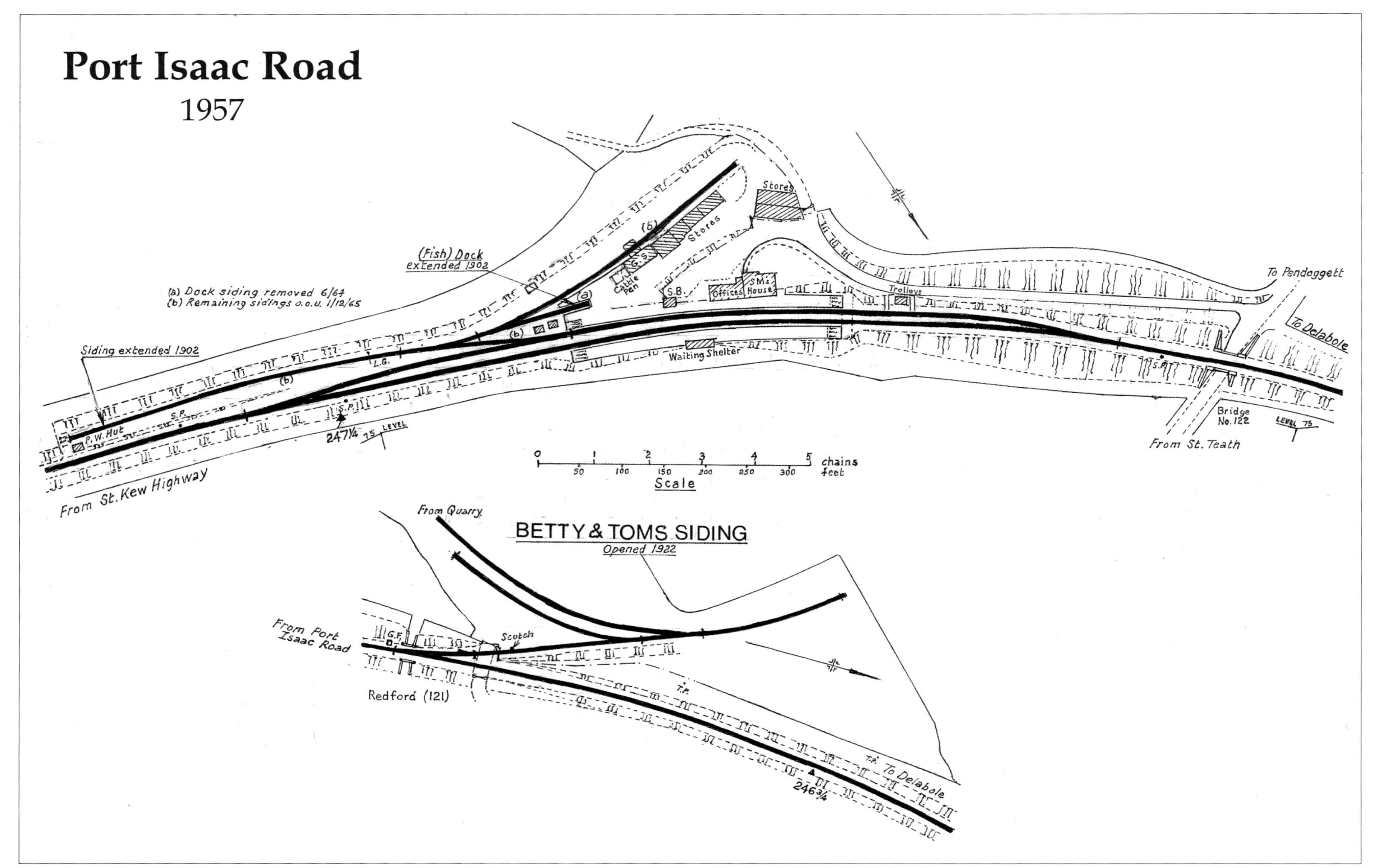
Port Isaac Road
1957
(Fish) Dock
extended 1902
(a) Dock siding removed 6/64
(b) Remaining sidings o.o.u. 1/12/65
Siding extended 1902
P.W. Hut
S.P.
L.G.
247¼
LEVEL
From St. Kew Highway
Stores
Stores
Cattle Pen
S.B.
Offices
S.M.'s House
Trolleys
Waiting Shelter
To Pendoggett
To Delabole
Bridge No. 122
From St. Teath
chains
feet
Scale
From Quarry
BETTY & TOMS SIDING
Opened 1922
From Port Isaac Road
G.F.
Scotch
Redford (121)
T.P.
To Delabole
246¾

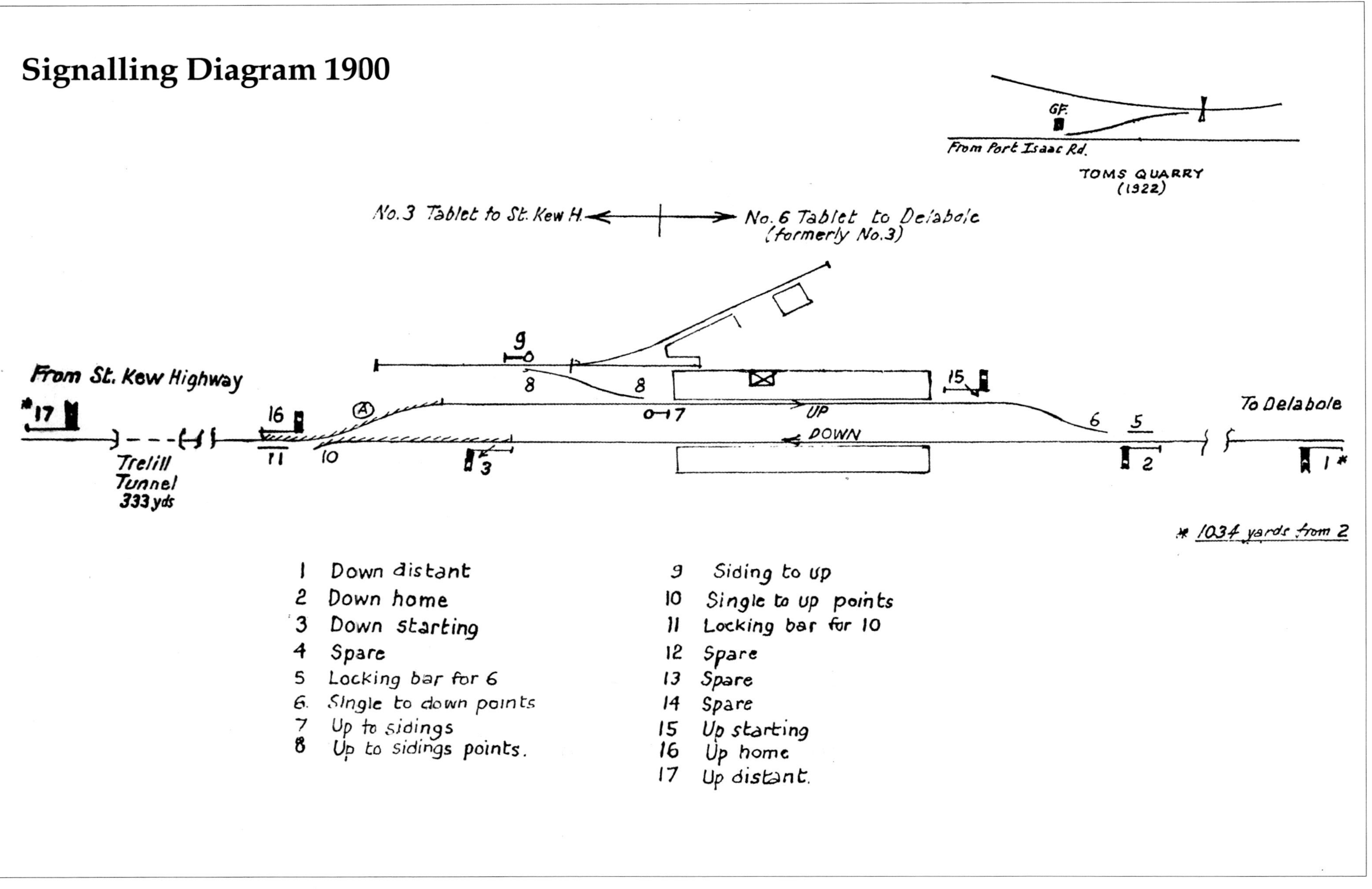
Signalling Diagram 1900
From Port Isaac Rd.
GF.
TOMS QUARRY (1922)
No. 3 Tablet to St. Kew H.
No. 6 Tablet to Delabole (formerly No. 3)
From St. Kew Highway
*17
Trelill Tunnel 333 yds
16
11
10
A
3
9
8
8
0-17
UP
DOWN
15
6
5
2
To Delabole
1*
* 1034 yards from 2
1 Down distant
2 Down home
3 Down starting
4 Spare
5 Locking bar for 6
6. Single to down points
7 Up to sidings
8 Up to sidings points.
9 Siding to up
10 Single to up points
11 Locking bar for 10
12 Spare
13 Spare
14 Spare
15 Up starting
16 Up home
17 Up distant.

inside. As it was not safe to work it by passing goods train, the siding was served by a special trip by an engine (off the pick-up goods) from Port Isaac Road. Empty wagons were propelled, brake van next to the engine, to just above the points. The engine then detached and, reversing, collected loaded wagons from inside the gate, coming back out and attaching to the brake and empties. The whole train was then drawn back clear of the points and then propelled into the siding. After leaving the empties inside the gate, the engine, loaded wagons and brake van returned to Port Isaac Road. The Tablet machine to Delabole was altered to No.6 (returnable) from 1923. After World War Two separate trip working was made between Wadebridge and (Betty &) Tom's siding, usually for wagons of ballast. It remained operational until 1964.

It was only another quarter mile thence to Port Isaac Road. Underbridge No.121 (247m 3ch) at the north end of the station has been, at the time of writing, proposed for listing as a 'scheduled' structure. Just below is a most awkward turn into the station access lane.

Top. **The line runs gently round the 30ch curve into Port Isaac Road in June 1963.**

Middle and below. **Four miles to the east of the fishing village by narrow lanes, Port Isaac Road was situated in St. Kew parish. Its remoteness did not prove an encouragement to passengers. John Eyres, South Western Circle.**

Even though in an exposed position it was not deemed necessary to clad the Station Masters house with additional slate protection. John Eyres, South Western Circle.

PORT ISAAC ROAD (247m 13ch)
Quite isolated, on a cross country road from St Teath to Pendogget which included several steep and narrow lanes, it seemed a most unlikely place for a station. Port Isaac itself was four miles to the west and St Teath was closer, at two miles. The Port Isaac fish trade was attractive and the prospects for tourism looked good. From opening the LSWR provided a good outlet for herring (which along with pilchards had declined) traded through Pawlyns, who brought in the mackerel and shellfish catches. Wagon loads were forwarded for overnight delivery to Billingsgate Market in London; in October 1897 for instance, 150 tons of fish brought by carts to the station was despatched to Exeter, Birmingham and London. The spur from the goods yard was lengthened in 1902 at some cost, to avoid 'tow roping', followed by extension of the dock in 1903. A shelf site was dug out to keep it level with the station, whereas the line to St Kew dropped sharply away at 1 in 73 in a cutting under Trewarne bridge. At one time a fair quantity of flowers and fruit also went away from this station. Growth in tourism and the building of hotels followed and Port Isaac was to draw a discerning clientele, not averse to the comparative isolation of this corner of the Atlantic Coast. John Prout started a road service from the village to Wadebridge and Bodmin Road from 1861. Subsequently his son John was the GWR cartage agent, while son Mark took on that for the LSWR/SR. Horse-drawn vehicles were replaced in the 1920s by motor buses, which also collected mail from pillar boxes. The SR withdrew its subsidy in June 1930 and a Southern National bus then served Port

Port Isaac Road and St. Kew Highway looked very much alike, but the former had its signal box on the up platform. To the south the line from Port Isaac Road falls away at 1 in 73 but the head shunt, in the background, kept to the level. Considerable amounts of fish were sent away from the station from the start, continuing in some measure until closure in 1966.

A delightful view across the fields north of the station in June 1963. John Ayres, South Western Circle.

Isaac. The Prout Brothers merged their businesses (which included carting, building materials and fish) and the firm still operates buses and coach tours to this day.

The standard house and offices were on the Up platform, a top-glazed signal box on the same side holding a frame of 17 levers (three spare). The buildings were in dressed local stone with slate roofs; slate slabs formed the platform coping. There was a standard waiting shed on the Down platform. The yard was awkward to shunt, and brake van(s) of Up goods trains were ordered at the Wadebridge end if wagons were left outside the home signal. Visibility was restricted by the 30-chain curve through the station and, noteworthy for the North Cornwall, there was a measure of track circuiting, covering the Up loop facing Down trailing (No.10) points, replacing a fouling bar. With an electrical release on the starting signal, shunting in the Down direction could be somewhat inhibited by the use of the non-returnable Tyers No.3 Table to St Kew. It was made easier in the Up direction after the substitution of a No.6 Tablet to Delabole in 1923 for working Tom's siding.

This wayside station prospered quietly up to the 1930s. As well as the fish, the inevitable rabbit business burgeoned after 1918 with much crating and barrowing to meet the arrival of the afternoon 'Perisher' from Padstow to Exeter. Inwards, calves from East Devon (also fish - the other way - plaice and cod from Grimsby) by passenger train, and sundry merchandise through the Road Box System, belied any notions that Port Isaac Road slumbered. A standard LSWR No.2 Goods Shed with a 2-ton crane inside dealt with larger consignments. Its stonework matched that of the station. Beyond, Messrs W.T. Tucker & Sons established a farm store for the usual corn, feeds and fertilisers, also coal and seed potatoes. The yard closed in September 1964 and was clipped out of use in December 1965.

The last Stationmaster was Mr Corrick in 1927. Thereafter it came under Camelford's control. The two signalmen, also acting as porters, manned the box, which here retained the Tablet apparatus (not transferred to the booking hall as elsewhere). Over the years Albert Vincent (1942-49) and others, like Arthur Beer and Ken Cory, operated the loops to the end of the service. A booking clerk attended, though the remoteness of the area discouraged applicants for this post!

Downward and to the sea. The line is now descending at 1 in 73 and in the background can be seen the headshunt, on the level as previously mentioned. The sidings were removed in 1964, the signal box closing in November 1965. John Eyres, South Western Circle.

Port Isaac Road to St Kew Highway

Below Trewarne Bridge the line went to the right on a continuous 30 chain curve, dropping at 1 in 73. Just after the road from Pengenna (where arsenic mining once was active) into Trelill village crossed the line, came the entrance to the short Trelill Tunnel, with its handsome stone/brick portal. The southern portal is plainer. The countryside from here to St Kew is less 'open' and the curvature was much less severe, in the 40 to 60 chain range. The line still fell at 1 in 73, however, from the 400 foot contour at Port Isaac Road to 250 at St Kew. On the left could be seen the farmlands of Bokelly, while on the right, well out of sight and nestling in a valley, is St Kew Churchtown, a

The seldom-photographed Trelill tunnel in 1963. Above is the more ornate northern portal whilst the more austere, southern portal is viewed from the window of the 8.48am Padstow to Exeter train. John Eyres, South Western Circle.

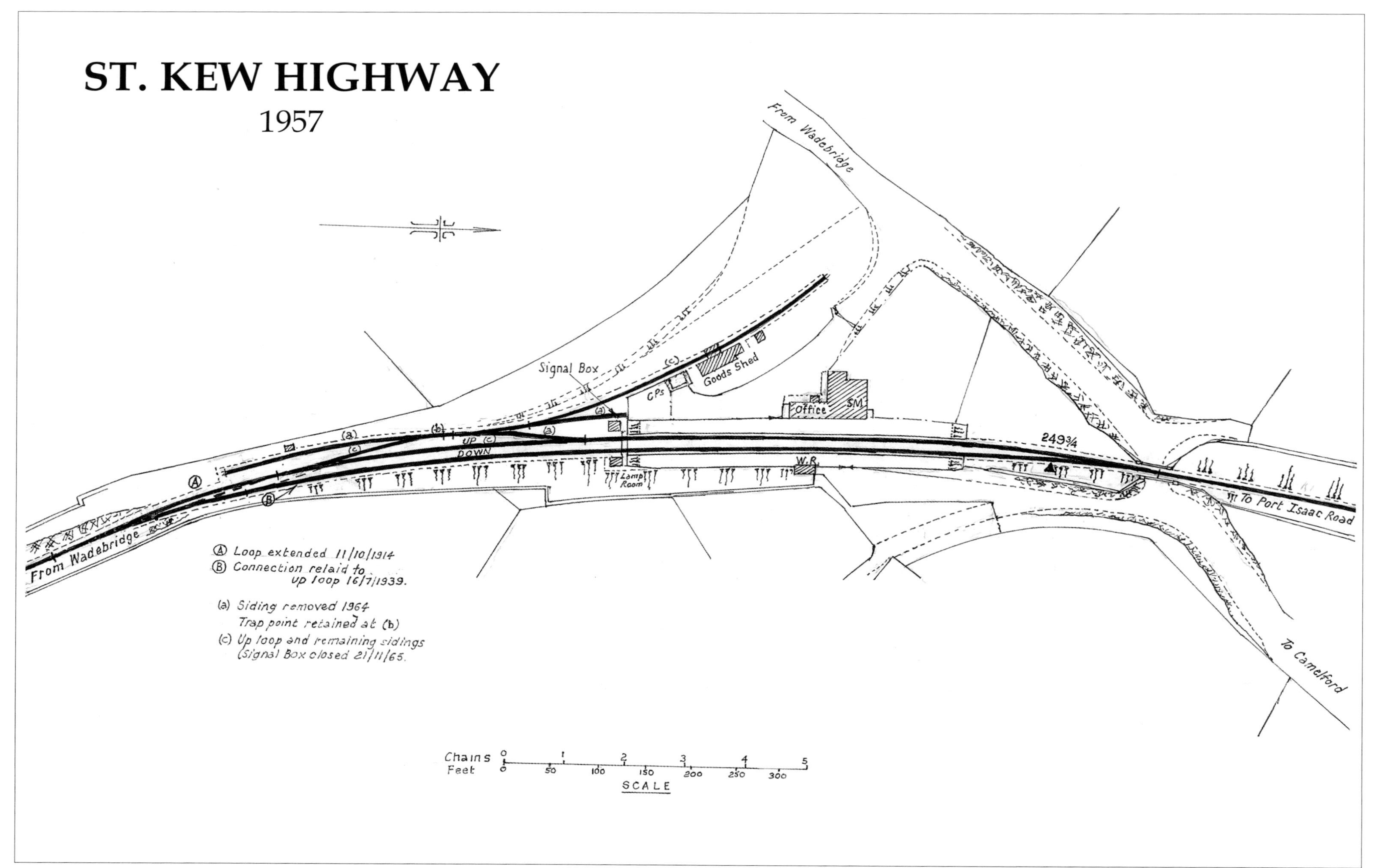
ST. KEW HIGHWAY
1957
From Wadebridge
To Port Isaac Road
To Camelford
From Wadebridge
249¾
S.M.
Office
W.R.
Goods Shed
CPs
Signal Box
Lamp Room
UP (c)
DOWN
Ⓐ Loop extended 11/10/1914
Ⓑ Connection relaid to up loop 16/7/1939.
(a) Siding removed 1964
Trap point retained at (b)
(c) Up loop and remaining sidings
(Signal Box closed 21/11/65.
Chains 0 1 2 3 4 5
Feet 0 50 100 150 200 250 300
SCALE

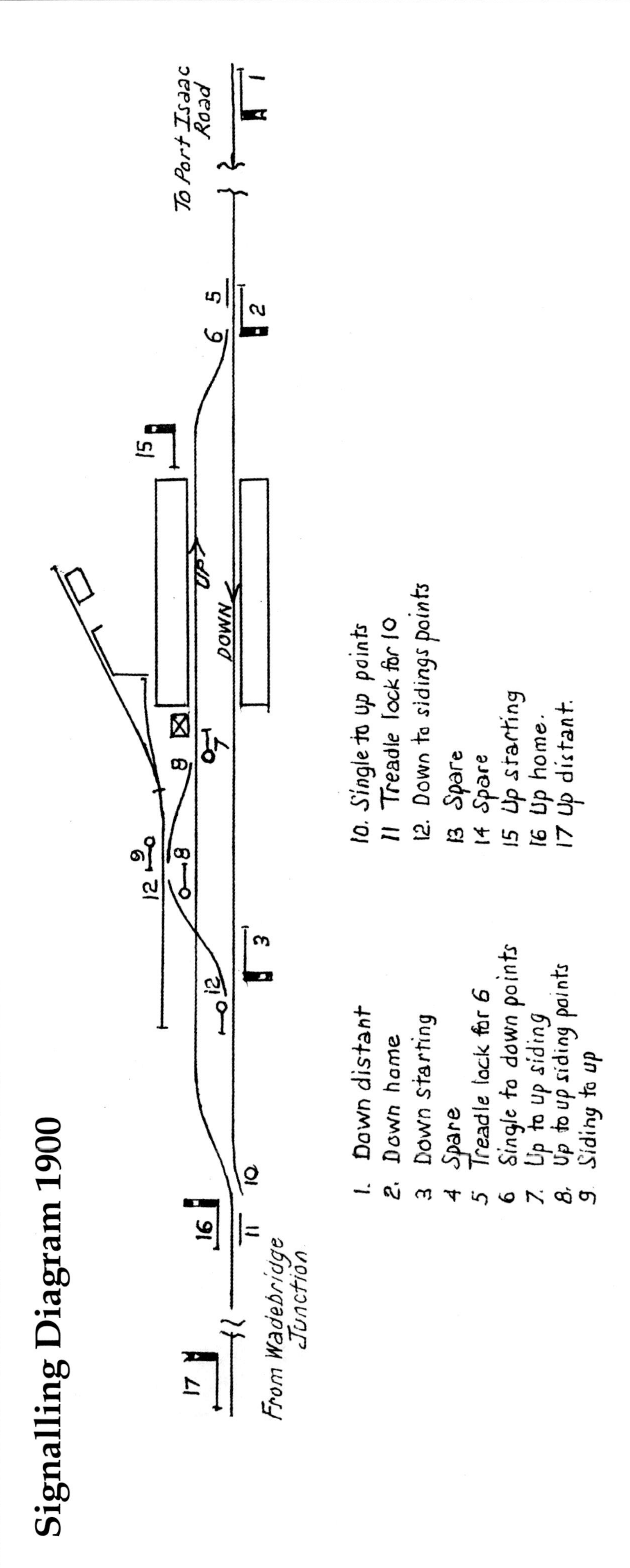

Signalling Diagram 1900

charming little place. The road from St Kew to Bokelly via Trequite crossed at 248m 51ch. Nearly into St Kew Highway another minor road came under the railway at the north end of the hamlet, the gradient easing to 1 in 330.

ST. KEW HIGHWAY (249m 64ch)
St Kew village lay to the north about two miles distant, though the road was indirect. St Mabyn village is southward by a tortuous road down to the Allen and up a long hill thereafter. Over to the east is St Tudy – walking distance about two and a half miles and beyond is St Breward on the edge of Bodmin Moor, at about six miles. How many local people used St Kew Highway, once opened, is a matter for conjecture. Certainly not very many in later years, and from the 1920s the motorbus served these communities better though only, perhaps, on one or two days a week. There was already a public house on the main road from Camelford to Wadebridge, with a small settlement (which grew somewhat after the railway opened) known as St Kew Highway. This road went under the railway just to the north of the station, with a very low headroom. The bridge still stands but the A39 now cuts a wide swathe through the adjacent embankment. Most holiday trains (and the ACE) called at St Kew Highway as it was the railhead for Polzeath on Padstow Bay and the straggling settlement of St Minver down to Rock. All these places, eight to ten miles to the west, attracted visitors who in the early days were quite prepared to ride in horse brakes to the quietest beaches and cliffs in the west country – and to the golf course at St Enodoc. Sir John Betjeman came to love this corner of Cornwall and travelled by train to St Kew or Wadebridge; not surprisingly, the North Cornwall Railway is commemorated in his prose and poems.

St Kew Highway was almost the double of Port Isaac Road in appearance and layout. The stations buildings were the same, though the approach road was much less sinuous and narrow. The signal box was off the platform though at the country end, almost four-square and fully glazed in the 1880s pattern. It held 17 levers and three spare to work the loop points, the 'push and pull' connections with the goods yard and the minimum number of semaphore signals needed to work these passing places; that is, six. Until 16 July 1939 there was a direct connection to the Down loop (resembling Whitstone on the Bude branch) as well as one trailing into the Up. As moves from the Down entailed working outside the starting signal (i.e. withdrawing the Tablet to Wadebridge) in later years a change was made to a Tyers No.6 (returnable to the St Kew machine). The loop points at the Wadebridge end were advanced 50 yards in October 1914. The signalling

Top. The gentle curve into St. Kew Highway from Port Isaac Road in June 1963. John Eyres, South Western Circle.

Middle. St. Kew Highway station took its name from the settlement on the Camelford to Wadebridge road, St. Kew village lying about a mile to the north. It also served St. Mabyn to the east and Minver (by Prout's buses). There were similar overhanging eaves on the station houses at Port Isaac Road and Padstow. John Eyres, South Western Circle.

The up starting signal raised for the mid-day train from Padstow to Okehampton will be lowered by the porter/signalman walking down to his box sited off the end of the up platform. He would have also restored the Tablet from Wadebridge East in the instrument located in the booking office. The rear two of the three coaches is a Maunsell 2-P Set whilst the third coach is probablty a Bulleid Brake 3rd. Lens of Sutton.

Above. Station approach at St. Kew Highway with a Vauxhall Velox parked outside in June 1963. John Eyres, South Western Circle.

Left and below. All quiet at the station in 1963 where a local topiarist has been at work. The buildings and layout here was almost identical to that at Port Isaac Road although the station approach road was far less narrow. John Eyres, South Western Circle.

Left. St. Kew Highway signal box in the 1950s. It was equipped with a 17 lever frame with three spare to work the loop points, the 'push-pull' connections with the goods yard and the signals. It was of the South Western's glazed style of the 1880s and was located off the end of the up platform equipped from the first with a Tyers single line Tablet apparatus. The North Cornwall line down to Delabole was originally provided with the old wooden staff and ticket system, though with telegraph and Absolute Block safeguard. It closed in November 1964.

Below. The line continues west downhill towards Wadebridge East whilst, like Port Isaac Road, the headshunt remains level. John Eyres, South Western Circle.

The goods shed in June 1963. Incoming coal and fertilizer, outgoing sugar beet, corn, rabbits and pigs were the staple work for the yard here, which closed in 1964. John Eyres, South Western Circle.

was modernised in 1939, the fouling bars exchanged for facing points lock and detectors and the wooden signal posts replaced by pairs of old rail latticed together and equipped with SR upper quadrant arms. At a late date the WR substituted Electric Key Tokens for No.6 Tablets to Wadebridge East. The first signalman was Joseph Vincent in 1895. The last, Peter Hamley, had followed his father-in-law into the box, working it as a relief man on closure in 1966.

The spur from the goods yard proved too short for shunting movements and was lengthened at some time. Otherwise only two sidings were provided, one for 15 wagons to the cattle pen and goods shed and a short stub to the end loading dock (removed in 1939). The goods shed was an LSWR standard No.2 with a two-ton crane. W.T. Tucker & Son traded here until the 1930s and again from the 1950s when they rented the goods shed as a fertiliser store. Several wagons per week brought Silcock's products in season and a certain amount of corn was sent away too. Sugar beet went to Kidderminster in 16-ton open wagons. In these days of mechanical handlers, it is difficult to visualise the amount of shovelling and forking necessary to shift beet, coal, bricks and, at one time, manure! St Kew served farmers' needs from St Mabyn, St Tudy and Chapel Amble to the east, also to the St Minver parishes to the west.

There were rabbits of course, to Birmingham and the Midlands and Messrs Inch forwarded live and carcassed pigs. Noteworthy was an early complete farm removal in pre-Second World War days, from Ashwater to St Kew Highway. The SR provided cartage to Pencarrow where Mr G. Daniel acquired a tenancy. But St Kew, very much a wayside station, was doomed by the rise of competing road transport. There had been no SM since Mr Dark in 1927, supervision passing to Camelford. The yard was taken out of use (after closure in September 1964), together with the Up loop on 21 November 1965 and the Signal Box closed.

St Kew Highway to Wadebridge

Down by Benbole the last stretch from St Kew to Wadebridge continued to fall at 1 in 75. Here the 'T9' and a down train skated along, leaning from one curve to the next en route to the sea. It was quite a pull the other way, needless to say, though a 'West Country' even with four or five on, made little of these gradients. The multiple exhaust beats would echo in the woods below Hingham, the scene in direct contrast to the open hillside near Otterham.

The entry into the Allen Valley could be effected only by more skilful engineering. A high embankment to cross a tributary at Bovehill, above Dinham, then under the road at Rocksea which was given a very tight diversionary curve from its original line, over another tributary before the railway arrived on a shelf built above the River Allen itself at the 251 MP. The NCR would have crossed the Allen here and come down its east side, but the 1894 deviation kept it higher up and above the west side of Lemail Wood and its old

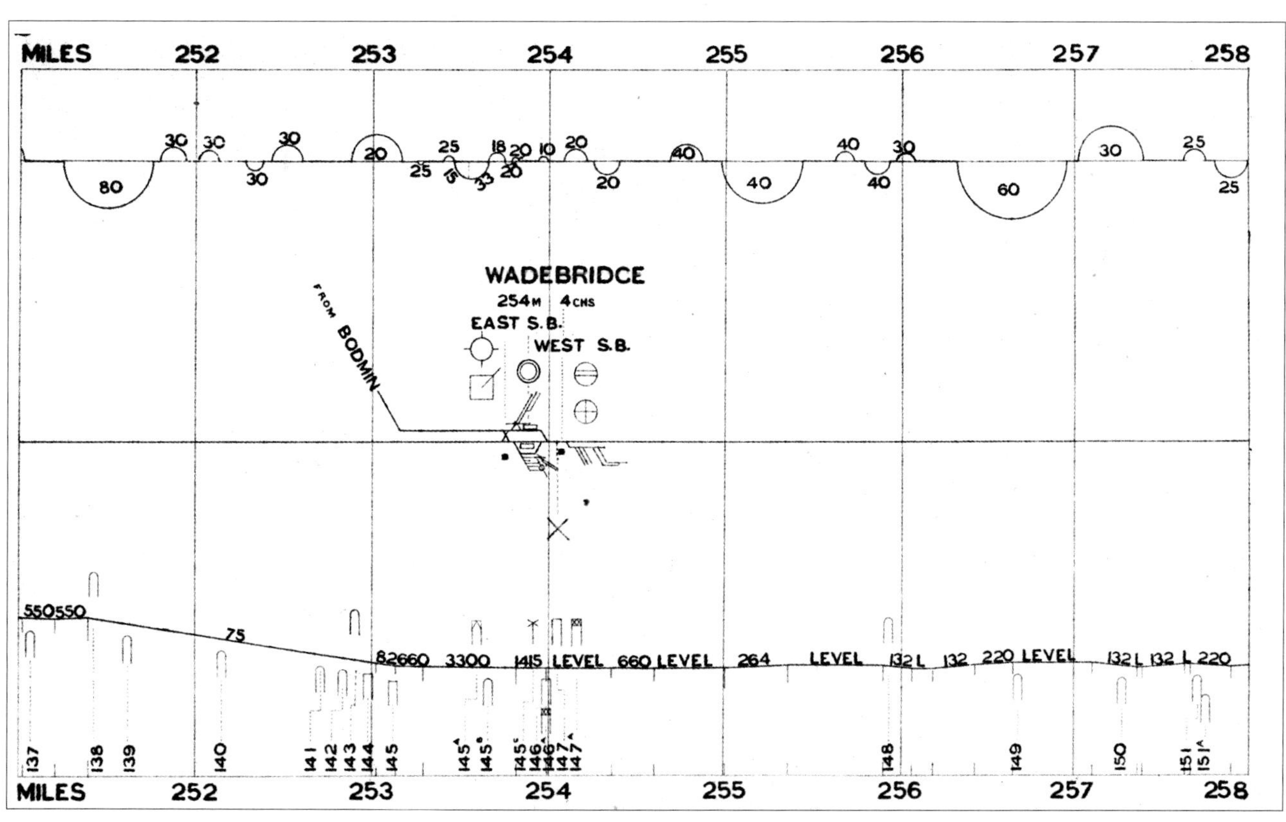

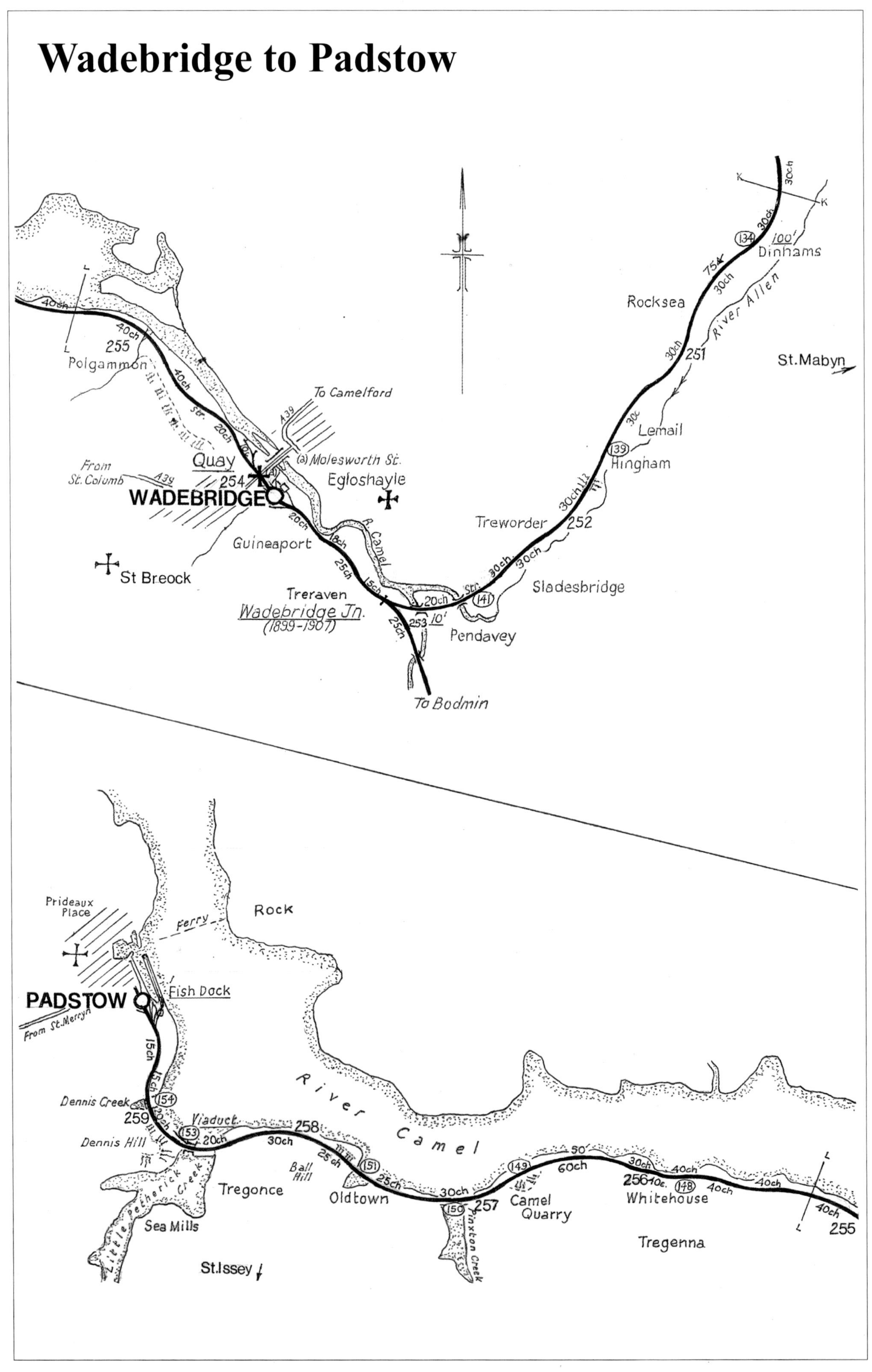
Wadebridge to Padstow
Polgammon
To Camelford
A39
(a) Molesworth St.
Quay
From St. Columb
WADEBRIDGE
Egloshayle
Guineaport
St Breock
R. Camel
Treraven
Wadebridge Jn.
(1899-1907)
Pendavey
Sladesbridge
Treworder
Hingham
Lemail
Rocksea
River Allen
Dinhams
St.Mabyn
To Bodmin
Prideaux Place
Ferry
Rock
PADSTOW
Fish Dock
From St.Merryn
River Camel
Dennis Creek
Dennis Hill
Viaduct
Little Petherick Creek
Tregonce
Sea Mills
St.Issey
Ball Hill
Oldtown
Camel Quarry
Whitehouse
Tregenna

Top. **A view across the meadows near Wadebridge Junction in 1963. *Above.* Not double track but two single lines. The North Cornwall is to the left and the Bodmin branch to the right. John Eyres, South Western Circle.**

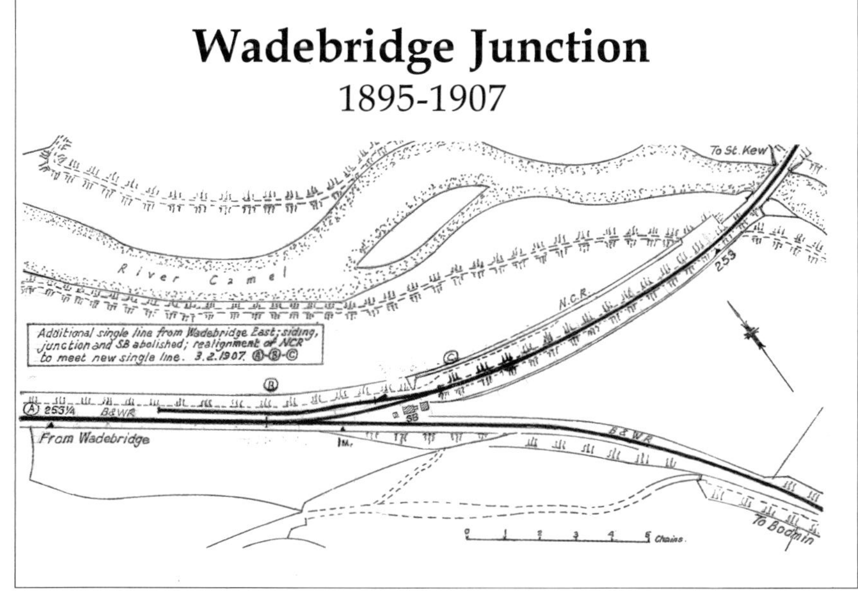

mill. There was another old mill at Hingham indicating the use made of the Allen for water power. A lot of grain was formerly grown in this area but by the time of the railway's arrival arable land had been converted to grass. The contractors had to blast their way through rock (granite) past Hingham, where once there was a hillside quarry.

Past the 252 milepost the level dropped nearer to that or the river and the one-time navigable limit at Sladesbridge. The line was carried over the Wadebridge to Bodmin Road by Bridge No.141, an all-masonry structure, not brick faced as was usual. This low headroom bridge has been removed in recent years and the road widened. Remaining on an embankment and in a straight alignment, the line was carried to the north bank of the Allen and then over it by a single arch bridge. Between the Allen and the Camel is the toe of the hillside rising above Pendavey Farm. A short, but deep, cutting was necessary to penetrate this before the North Cornwall line emerged over the Camel (bridge No.144) at 252m 78ch. It was rather unusual in that the main span was a pair of wrought iron hog back girders (over the river) and a 9ft plate girder over the river path. From here a sharp 20 chain curve rounded an embankment to the site of the former Wadebridge Junction, and the end of the North Cornwall Railway in 1895. All the NCR overbridges were constructed to double line standard (28ft in width) but only in a few cases, at stations, were any of them so utilised. As recounted, the original entry into Wadebridge was over the reconstructed single line Bodmin & Wadebridge Railway. The farm track to Treraven crossed at 253m 47ch by an overbridge made of two cast iron girders with only 26ft between its masonry abutments; this was just enough for the two single lines formed from 1907. The Camel Valley widens considerably below Pendavey but the B&W kept to the south side, hugging the edge of the hillside below Treraven on a near level profile. On the outskirts of Wadebrige the Camel meandered toward the railway, thus the 1907 widening works included retaining walls both against the river below and Guineaport Terrace above. The line curved left at 20 chains and reversed into an 18 chain radius at this point, an indication of its B&WR origins.

WADEBRIDGE (253m 72ch)
Wadebridge, until then part of St Columb Rural District Council, was granted Urban District status from April 1898. Situated each side of the ancient Camel river bridge, on the north side is the Parish of Egloshayle and on the other that of St Breock. Only part of Egloshayle was included in the new District and the railway was entirely on the south bank over the bridge. The population in 1901 was 3,470 and thus a most realistic goal

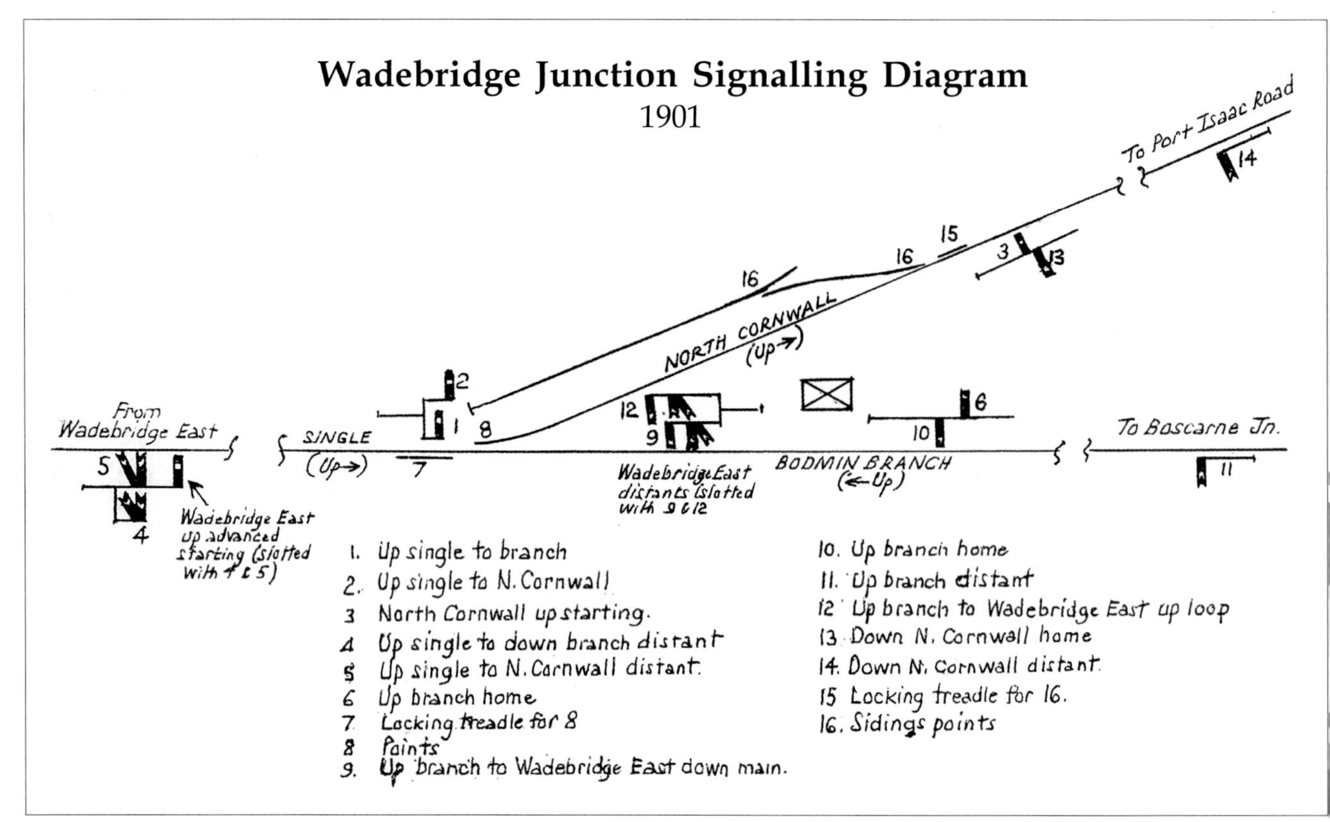
Wadebridge Junction Signalling Diagram
1901
To Port Isaac Road
NORTH CORNWALL
(Up→)
From Wadebridge East
SINGLE
(Up→)
BODMIN BRANCH
(←Up)
To Boscarne Jn.
Wadebridge East distants (slotted with 9 & 12
Wadebridge East up advanced starting (slotted with 4 & 5)
1. Up single to branch
2. Up single to N. Cornwall
3 North Cornwall up starting.
4 Up single to down branch distant
5 Up single to N. Cornwall distant.
6 Up branch home
7 Locking treadle for 8
8 Points
9. Up branch to Wadebridge East down main.
10. Up branch home
11. Up branch distant
12 Up branch to Wadebridge East up loop
13 Down N. Cornwall home
14. Down N. Cornwall distant.
15 Locking treadle for 16.
16. Sidings points

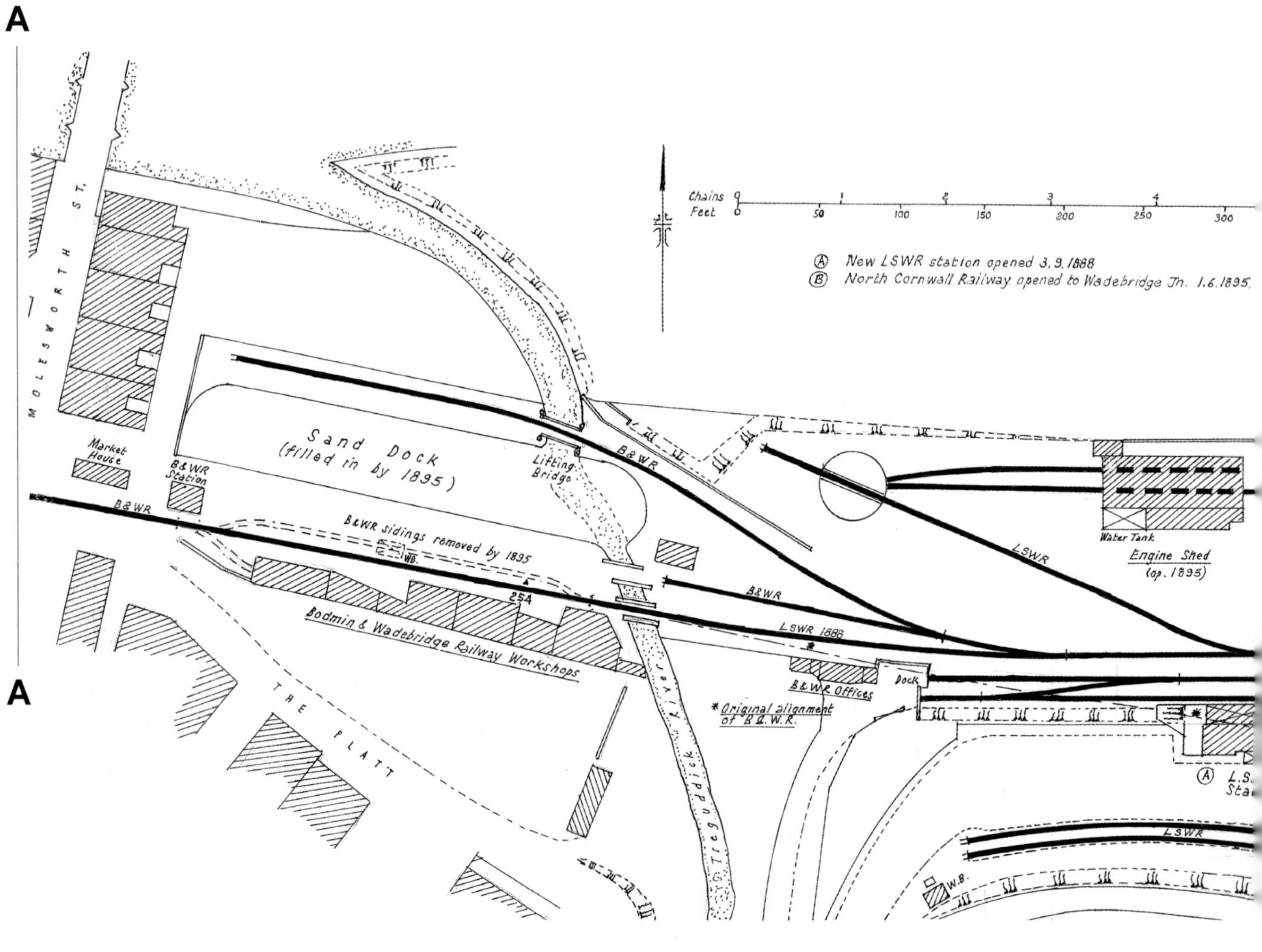

A

Chains 0 1 2 3 4
Feet 0 50 100 150 200 250 300
Ⓐ New LSWR station opened 3.9.1888
Ⓑ North Cornwall Railway opened to Wadebridge Jn. 1.6.1895.
MOLESWORTH ST.
Sand Dock (filled in by 1895)
Lifting Bridge
Market House
B&WR Station
B&WR
B&WR sidings removed by 1895
Bodmin & Wadebridge Railway Workshops
LSWR 1888
B&WR Offices
Dock
* Original alignment of B&W.R.
Water Tank
Engine Shed (op. 1895)
LSWR
THE PLATT
River Tiguddick
W.B.
Ⓐ L.S. Sta

A

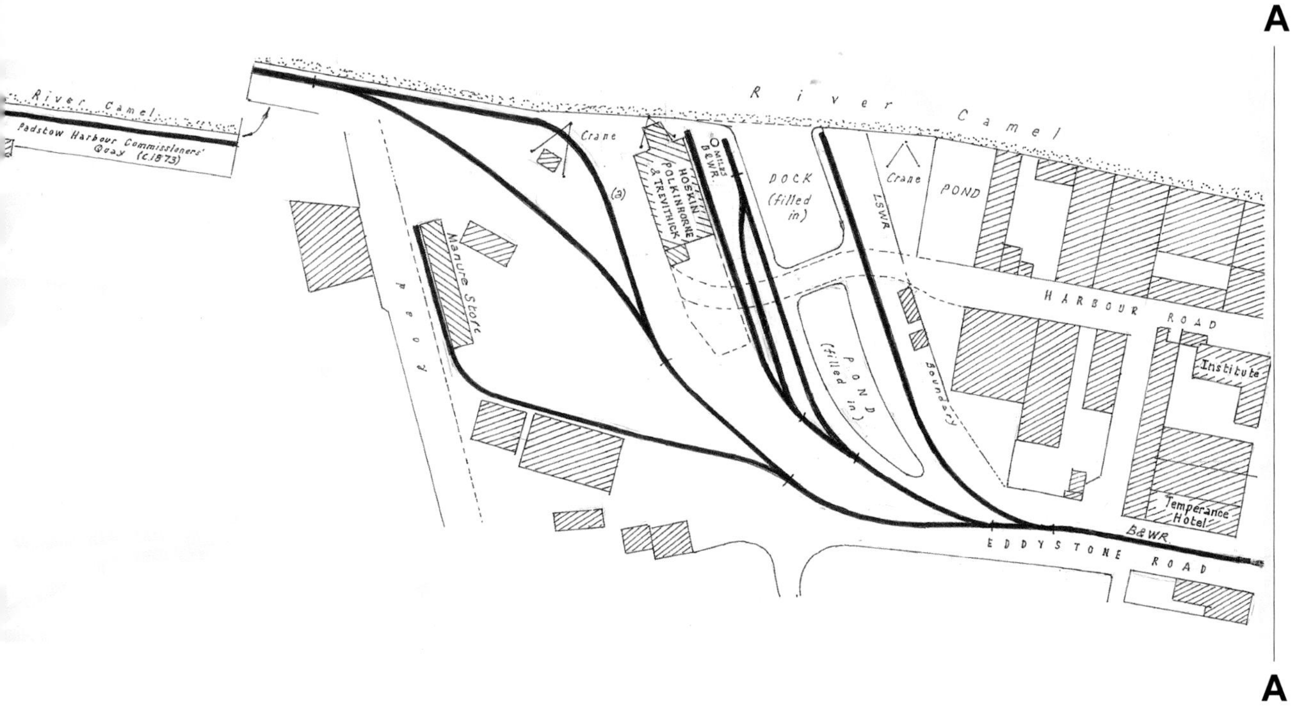

A

River Camel
Padstow Harbour Commissioners' Quay (C1873)
River Camel
Crane
(3)
HOSKIN POLKINHORNE & TREVITHICK
B&WR.
DOCK (filled in)
Crane
POND
LSWR
Manure Store
Road
POND (filled in)
Boundary
HARBOUR ROAD
Institute
Temperance Hotel
B&WR
EDDYSTONE ROAD

A

Wadebridge
1895

Scale

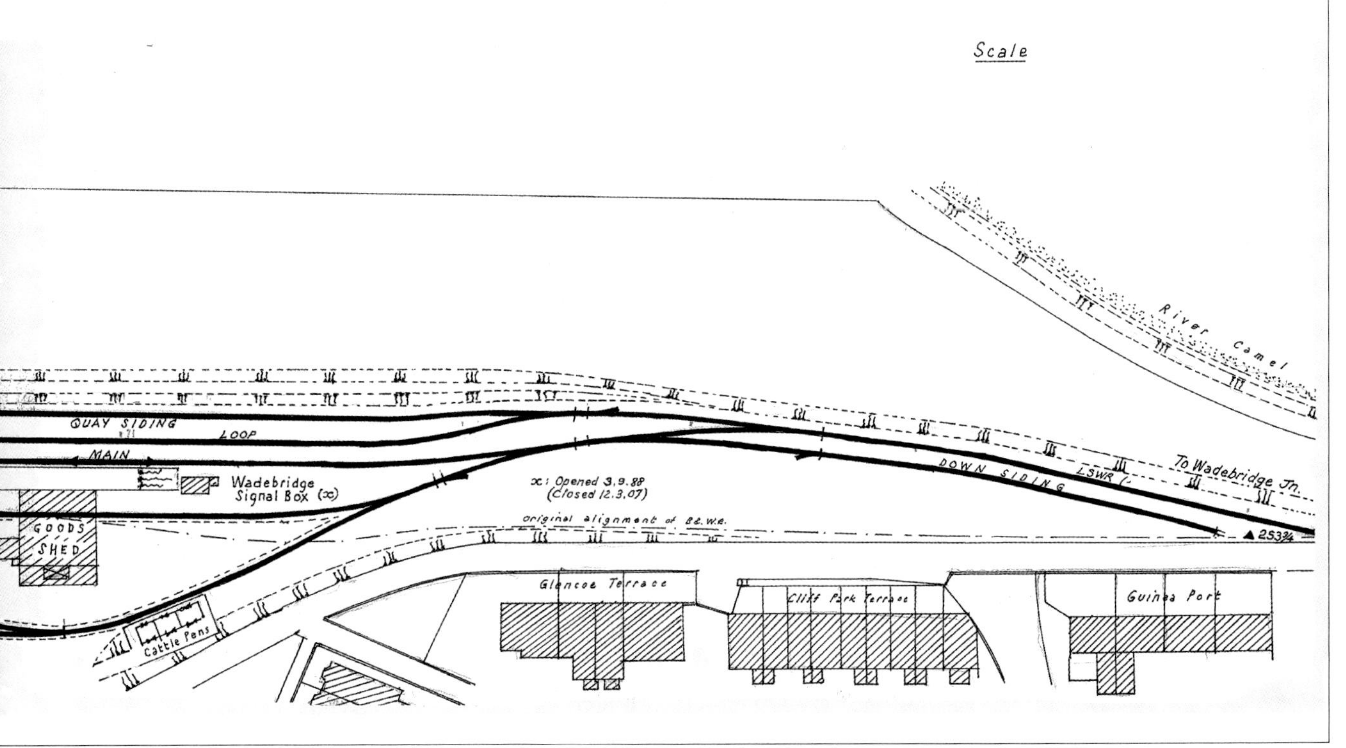

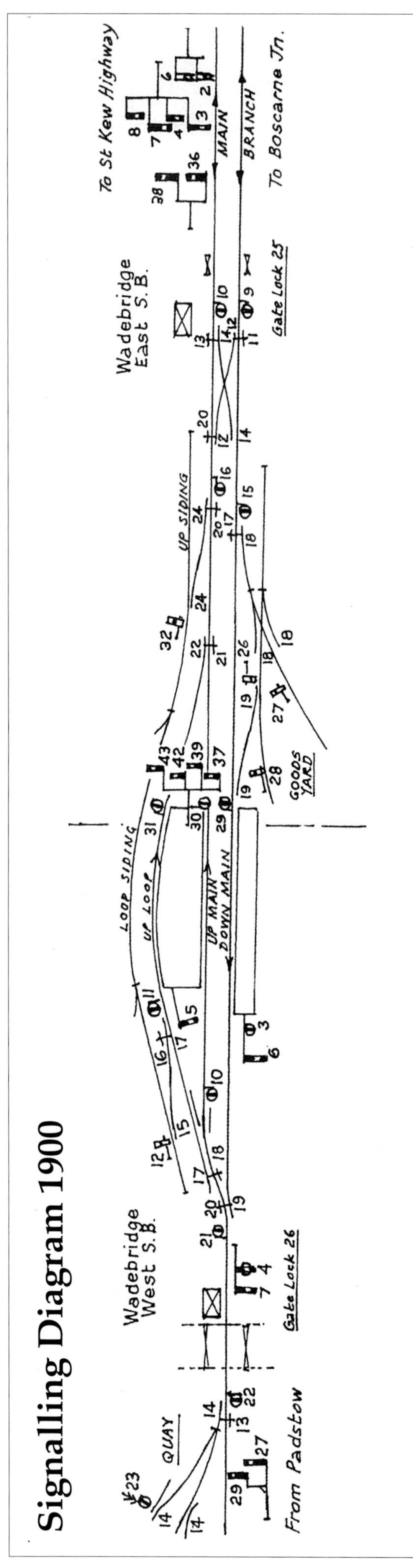

Signalling Diagram 1900

for the North Cornwall Railway, backed by the LSWR. Its railway inheritance has been noted – the primitive 1834 line to Bodmin, Ruthern Bridge and Wenford, also the 1888 connection from the GWR at Boscarne. Already a town of importance and of political influence, on the opening of the NCR in 1895 the way east was now by a direct standard gauge route for cattle shipment, granite, slates, manure and grain. Sea sand brought from Padstow was transferred to rail at the Quay and taken to inland destinations. Later a fair-sized forwarding of dairy products (not milk) fresh meat and rabbits was encouraged by the LSWR and SR. General merchandise, formerly brought by coaster from Bristol to the Quay, soon went to rail. The LSWR instituted their daily 'road box' system from London, Exeter and Plymouth; foodstuffs (including fresh fruit) were unloaded in the goods shed and distributed by cart around town and country. Soon to expand were inward loads of fertilisers, cattle feed and seeds. Two foundries in the town, Oatey & Martyn in Polmora Road and Iron Bros (1922, formerly Harris) relied on the railway for materials and coal, and despatching of finished goods. Timber arrived at the Quay from the Baltic. Granite and china clay came from Wenford – and (earlier) iron and copper ore – a continuation of the B&WR's traffic developed by the LSWR from the 1880s.

With its shops in Molesworth Street and weekly market (as well as the Monday Cattle Market) Wadebridge was well endowed to attract country people from North Cornwall stations, and from the Bodmin direction. Horse coaches plied from St Columb and Truro, replaced by motor buses in the 1920s. The LSWR encouraged tourist traffic by excursion fares, considering Wadebridge a railhead for New Quay! Even after the 1895 connection to the east it is doubtful if the LSWR attracted many long distance passengers to and from Bodmin, and thus away from the long-established GWR Cornish main line. In 1888 Truro became the County Town, and the centre of a Cornish Diocese and a new Cathedral, but Bodmin retained the Assizes, Gaol, Asylum and the Duke of Cornwall's Light Infantry Depot.

The 1888 station building and its single platform was transformed into a through layout with three platform faces in 1899, on completion of the North Cornwall Railway, but remained in LSWR ownership. The original platform was extended to a total of 460 feet by extensions at both ends, with a water column at the Padstow extremity. There was a cantilevered awning for about three quarters of the building. There was an ornate wooden footbridge for the new 1899 island platform but it had no cover for passengers. It was replaced by a stark concrete version in the 1920s. The 350ft island platform was wide enough for a large waiting room in brick with fireplace and chimney, the whole building surmounted by another cantilevered awning. The 3ft high platforms, a newer standard, originally supported by timber and iron struts, were gradually rebuilt in concrete pre-cast parts and lastly in BR's concrete blocks. At the east end stood two more water columns, essential for engines about to climb to Otterham (the next column was at Launceston) and to Bodmin Road. Built after the fashion of Launceston station building, single storeyed, with a steeply-pitched roof and dressed stone walls, there was no accommodation for the SM and his family. They lived in a house opposite, in residential developments dating from the 1888 opening from Bodmin. The Town Hall also dates from this period, though it opened as the 'Molesworth Hall', its cost largely borne by that family. The Platt (or Fair Plot) between the Hall and the Treguddick Brook and the railway accommodated a cattle market. With the North Cornwall's arrival it was to prove inadequate before long, for hitherto cattle dealing had been largely unorganised. There was now the prospect of much increased rail forwarding, mainly by dealers from Exeter and beyond, and a new site was found off the Polmora Road, again encouraged by the Molesworths who provided 8,000 loads of fill.

For the proposed Wadebridge station enlargement of 1895-98, land to the north was filled, the first structure to appear being a new engine shed, with turntable (50ft) and elevated water tank. It needed to be available for LSWR bigger engines arriving from June 1895. The Beattie well tanks had been housed in the old B&WR shed to the west. Although various other small-wheelbase engines were tried out on the Wenford Branch services and the sharp curves on the Quay, these 2-4-0WTs survived until 1962. Until 1908 the new timber-built shed was single-ended with access solely via

Top. Wadebridge East signal box was constructed in stone conforming to the central pillar style of LSWR boxes in the mid-1890s. After 1907 the frame held 43 levers (including eight spare). The signalman would issue Tyers single line Tablets to St. Kew Highway and Boscarne Junction. Double line Absolute Block signalling was in effect to Wadebridge West box. John Eyres, South Western Circle.

Left. Wadebridge station from the east in 1963. John Eyres, South Western Circle.

Below. The east end of Wadebridge goods yard in July 1964 showing the cattle pens, which by this time were virtually disused. Household coal at 'summer' prices account for the 16-ton wagon loads, though some may be for the locomotives. The amount of merchandise passing through the goods shed (left) had declined, and was finally concentrated by the Sundries Division of BR at Plymouth, with road delivery. The Station Masters house off the Guineaport Road is behind the lower trees. C.J.Knowles-Thomas.

Top. The weighbridge and entrance to the station in June 1963, with mobile crane behind. John Eyres, South Western Circle.

Left. On the down side was the extensive goods yard which handled all manner of merchandise with two mileage sidings enough for almost 40 wagons. There was a huge cattle trade with markets on the second Monday of each month. Pigs too were exported monthly whilst, wool, Padstow 'perishables' and other farm produce was shipped out in large numbers. John Eyres, South Western Circle.

Below. July 1960 and 45XX 2-6-2T waits to leave for Bodmin General whilst a pannier tank shunts some coaches. R.C.Riley, www.transporttreasury.co.uk

Two locomotives synonymous with the North Cornwall, July 1960. *Above*. Beattie Well Tank No. 30585 with crew and shed fitter right, T9 4-4-0 30729, a regular over the North Cornwall lines, parked alongside the coal stage. (See Chapter 10 for more details on the Beattie Well tank locomotives). Both photographs R. C. Riley, www.transporttreasury.co.uk

Below. Wadebridge in the early 1930s showing a Drummond L11 4-4-0 on a Padstow to Okehampton train and an O2 0-4-4T on a Bodmin train in the up loop. On the right is an ex-LBSCR brake van for the Wenford Branch workings, and wagons of engine coal, some of which was shipped through Highbridge S&DJR.

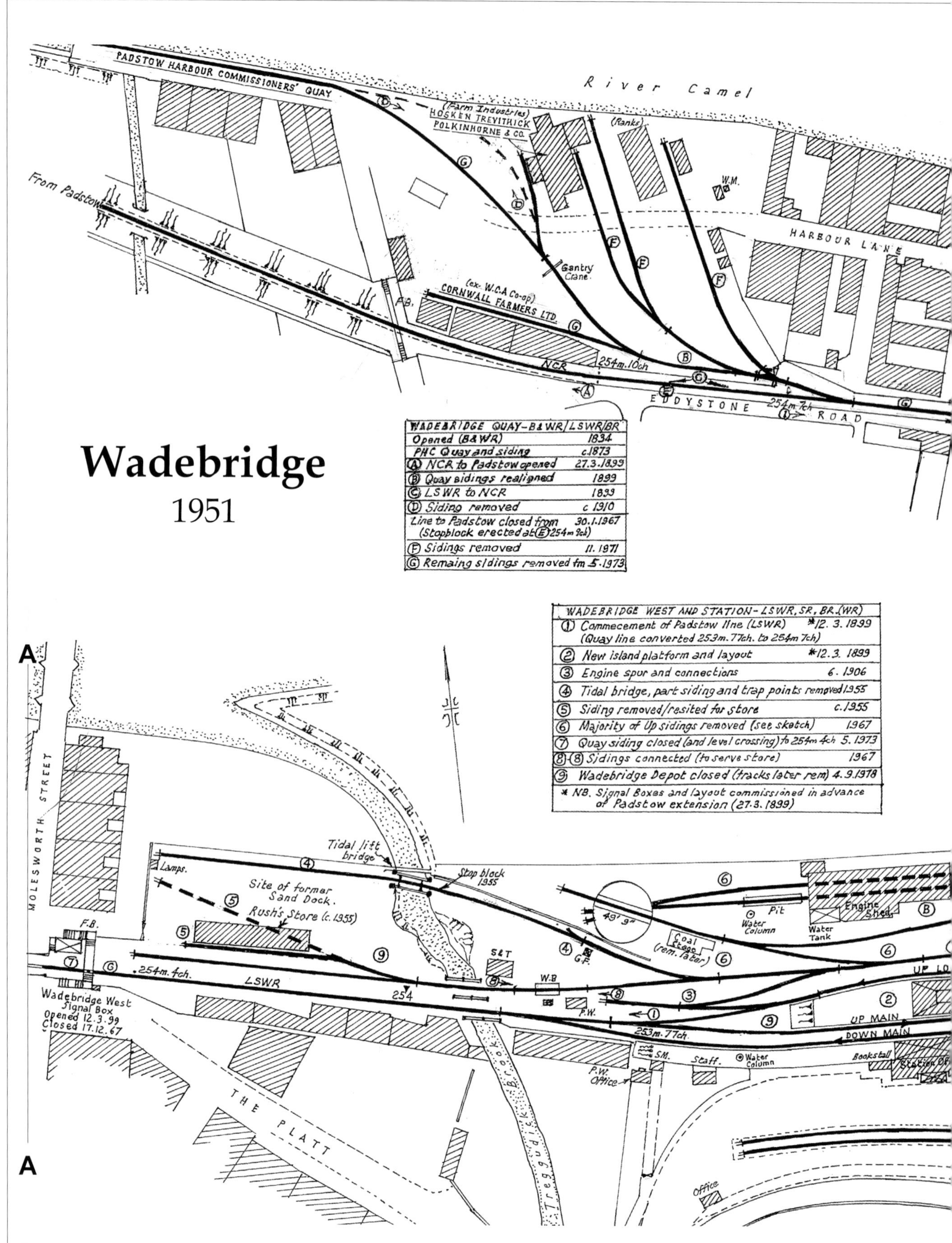

the turntable. Introduction of steam railcars saw an extension on the east side, making it a 'through' shed with sidings joining the Up line. Over the years Wadebridge shed retained a small complement of 'Jubilee' 0-4-2s and various 4-4-0s for the Okehampton line and '415' 4-4-2Ts and 'O2' 0-4-4Ts for Bodmin workings, latterly given over to ex-GWR pannier tanks and Ivatt 2-6-2Ts. The long-serving Beattie tanks were replaced by ex-GWR '1366' 0-6-0PTs. Always to be found on shed were visiting Okehampton or Exmouth Junction 0-6-0s and 'N' class 2-6-0s (from 1925) off goods work. The 4-4-0s and the new light Pacifics were mainly used on passenger turns but shared the goods working as required. In the final years of steam the 'Ns' were undertaking both roles.

The unpretentious station at Wadebridge dated from 1888, though the dressed stone and slate roof were handsome enough in comparison with the concrete blocks of the adjoining goods shed extension. The booking office held both LSWR and GWR 'positions' until 1915. The rear of the bookstall (left) was a Southern national bus timetable overprinted BUS STOP. Wadebridge station was the railhead for a number of services to the north side and St. Columb, Newquay and Truro. C. J. Knowle-Thomas.

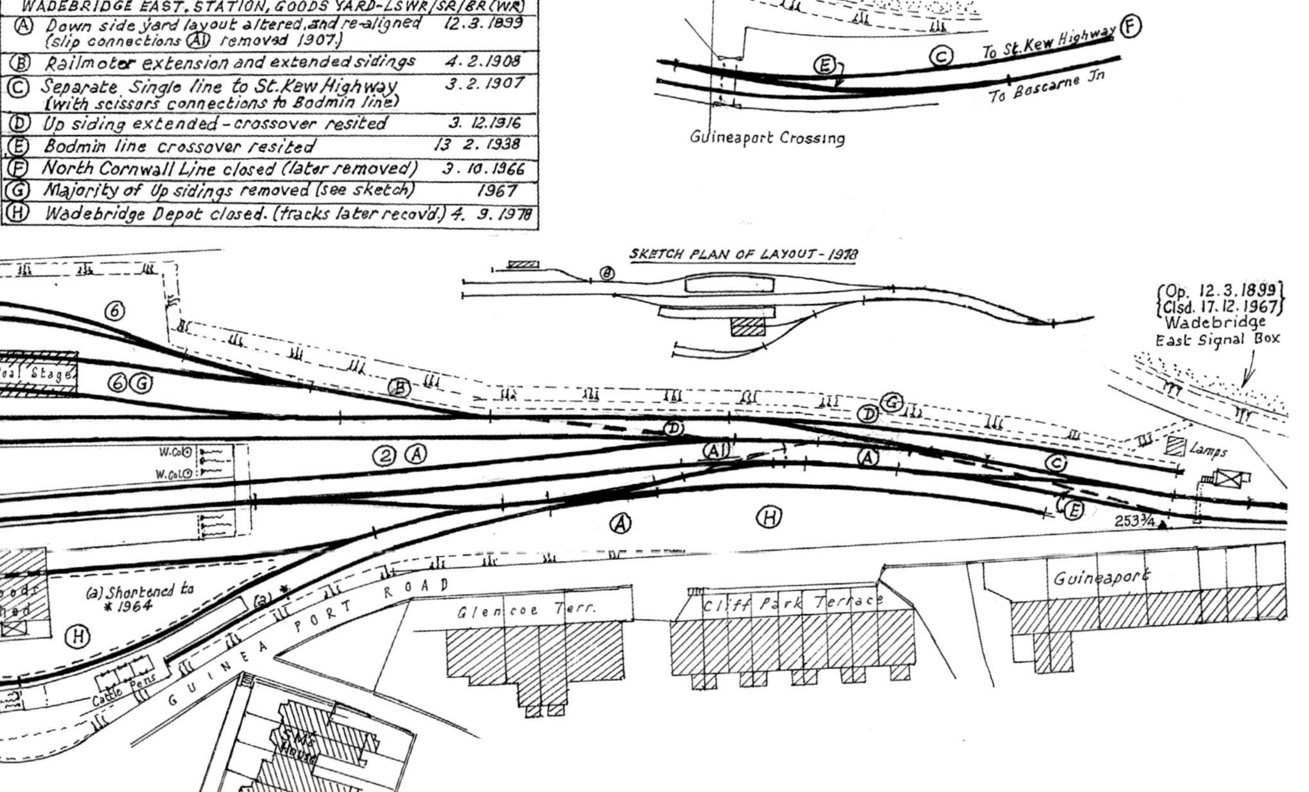

WADEBRIDGE EAST. STATION, GOODS YARD-LSWR/SR/BR(WR)	
(A) Down side yard layout altered, and re-aligned (slip connections (A1) removed 1907.)	12.3.1899
(B) Railmotor extension and extended sidings	4.2.1908
(C) Separate Single line to St. Kew Highway (with scissors connections to Bodmin line)	3.2.1907
(D) Up siding extended - crossover resited	3.12.1916
(E) Bodmin line crossover resited	13 2.1938
(F) North Cornwall Line closed (later removed)	3.10.1966
(G) Majority of Up sidings removed (see sketch)	1967
(H) Wadebridge Depot closed. (tracks later recov'd.)	4.9.1978

Isolated from the Exmouth Junction parent by 115 winding miles, Wadebridge men were required to be self-sufficient. There was a lifting crane and the fitting work that went with it, boiler washing out facilities, sand store and so on – far beyond what might otherwise be expected at a little shed like this. The staff of around forty included enginemen, cleaners, fitters and night men, all under a Foreman. True to type the drivers and firemen held their own self-taught locomotive instruction classes and first aid courses. They, like all railwaymen, knew that their work could be dangerous and ambulance and first aid practice were strongly pursued. Under Mr Brown, the Foreman in the last decade, 13 sets of enginemen worked in six 'links' taking in Wenford (1 set), North Cornwall (6), Bodmin (2),

Top. An unusual view of Wadebridge engine shed across the Camel River in 1964. Situated some 90 miles from Exmouth Junction, the parent shed, Wadebridge literally became self sufficient carrying out most of its own repair work and minor overhauls. John Eyres, South Western Circle.

Middle. N 2-6-0 No.31407 is framed beneath the engine hoist at the east end of the shed yard. In the post-war era thirty sets of men worked at the shed divided into six links. Wenford, North Cornwall, Bodmin. Rest Day Relief, Yard Pilot and Spare links. John Eyres, South Western Circle.

Below. Another view across the river showing the shed and station buildings beyond. John Eyres, South Western Circle.

Rest Day Relief (1), Yard Pilot (2) and one spare. The Western Region's take-over in the BR years (Wadebridge then coming under St Blazey) followed by the diesels, widened the field of transfer and promotion, though since the Southern Railway was formed in 1923 men had come west from London and Kent.

In the summer season and for the fish specials, firemen from Exeter would work from Wadebridge, lodging in the town before the last war. A dormitory coach was provided for Exeter crews working in on Friday evenings and out on Saturday mornings. Following its closure in January 1967, five men transferred from Wadebridge to Newton Abbot and four to St Blazey. Roy Wilce of Plymouth Laira, who learnt his calling on the footplate of a Wadebridge 'T9', later drove an InterCity HST on the former GWR main line, but 'Art' Ferret and Norman Wills ended their service here, as did the fitter

Top. **The wooden frame and cladding are evident in this interior view of Wadebridge shed in 1963. 1906 heralded the arrival of the steam railcars for services around Wadebridge, mostly to Bodmin. Their quick demise was unforseen by the LSWR as they ordered, and carried out, an extension to the building in 1907 'to accommodate steam motor carriages'. John Eyres, South Western Circle.**

Right. **The 'grand' new coal stage, and much welcome we understand, in 1963. Coal however, was still flung from wagons although assistance eventually arrived in the shape of a motorised conveyor belt.**

The sympathetic extension, at the far end, embodying the style of the original building nearest the camera. N class 2-6-0 No. 1854 was a long time servant of the North Cornwall still working the line long after this photograph was taken in 1933. W. A. Camwell.

Walter Harper and shedman Arthur Rush.

The layout at Wadebridge from 1899 remained largely constant until closure in 1966. The points and crossings at the East signal box required to be altered for the separation of the Bodmin and North Cornwall lines as from 3 February 1907, the number of levers in the frame increasing from the original 29. Direct facing crossovers, forming a 'scissors' pattern, encompassed all movements in and out of the Main platforms (1 and 2) and the two-end-worked Up loop (No.3). From 13 February 1938 these crossovers were separated and the Bodmin line was sited to the east of the occupation crossing. At the same time the Down outer home signals were removed and the inners moved towards St Kew by 30 yards to become 'home' signals. Wadebridge East box (from 1907) held 43 levers (ten spare) to work the switches and facing point locks. Shunting movements in and out of the down side goods yard and the engine shed/up sidings were controlled by the signalman. His Tablet machines were No.6 for the St Kew Highway and Boscarne single lines, while Preece 3-wire instruments operated the double 'open' block to Wadebridge West.

Railways first came to Wadebridge in 1834 and ended in 1978. The Bodmin and Wadebridge station stands where the furthest wagons are and Rush's Stone occupied the site of the former sand dock. Box vans of cattle feed and fertiliser came via the North Cornwall but from 7th September 1964 were diverted via Bodmin Road until final closure of Wadebridge as a 'full load' depot in 1978. John Eyres, South Western Circle.

Over a quarter of a mile towards Padstow, Wadebridge West signal box stood adjacent to Moleswoth Street level crossing – its gates folding against themselves to rail, and operated by a wheel. The box held 29 levers (seven spare) and, apart from the crossing and single line block to Padstow (No.6 returnable Tablet), controlled the western edge of Wadebridge station and the Quay sidings entrance points. One peculiar ancillary was an Annett's key kept in the signal box, to unlock a one-lever frame. This worked a protective catchpoint against false moves to a lift bridge over the Treguddick River. The bridge was left free to float clear on extra high tides and depended on a

Wadebridge, like many of these early sheds, suffered from a primitive layout which didn't always best serve the job it was designed to do. All movements in and out of the shed building were via the 50ft turntable which in the event of breakdown would isolate the locos inside and render the shed useless. The rebuilding and extensions carried out in 1907 took steps to remedy this problem putting in a run-round loop and resiting the coal stage to a more convenient position. The turntable was of course inadequate for the larger Bulleid Pacifics which arrived in 1947 but this too was remedied by the installation of a new 70ft unit at Padstow. John Eyres, South Western Circle.

counterbalance system. Before any movement was made over it to the sand siding the foreman had to ensure securing bolts were in position. The siding fronted a miniature tidal dock dating from B&WR days, wherein barges of sand from the estuary were off loaded into wagons for eventual distribution to the Bodmin sand drops and inland farms.

Although the new west layout was commissioned on opening to Padstow in March 1899, a further engine spur was laid in and a facility for starting Down trains from the Up loop became operable from June 1906. It appears to have coincided with the introduction of railmotor trains to Bodmin, with the occasional trip to Padstow. The No.1 Up siding terminated for a time in a weighbridge (replacing a B&WR one on

Top. **The North Cornwall starts the last leg of its journey to Padstow and literally squeezes between the panel and wire boundary fences to cross Molesworth Street in the distance. John Eyres, South Western Circle.**

Middle and below. **A general view towards Wadebridge station showing the original offices of the Bodmin and Wadebridge railway. On the right are the Company's original engine shed and carriage shed. John Eyres, South Western Circle.**

The 1834 Bodmin and Wadebridge carriage and workshops lasted until 1962. The freehold, from here as far as the end-on junction with the North Cornwall's Padstow extension, remained with the LSWR until 1923, when all passed to the Southern Railway. Remaining traces of the railway here were swept away in the 1980s to make way for a supermarket and car park.

its quay line). The 1899 alterations were quite sweeping to accommodate the new island platform. Enough land had been acquired by the LSWR before 1895 in anticipation of the NCR's arrival, although some reclamation was necessary by the river. Adjacent to the sand dock were a couple of sidings initially used by Currys as a base for constructing the Padstow extension. From May 1899 the No.1 siding was extended from the weighbridge, paralleling the Up loop to the East box; No.2 siding was outside and another beyond, both serving a re-sited coaling bank. Another change occurred here in February 1908, when the engine shed was extended to the east to house the railmotors; the sidings within connected with the No.1 Up siding, under East box control. In 1916 the Up siding was extended and the crossover to the loop moved east, to join the Up main close to the East box. In the far corner between the sand dock and Molesworth Street, a siding was extended westward at the same time, down to the footbridge with another across the old B&W sand dock. The former in the 1950s held an ex-LNWR sleeping car (No DM 198932) as the enginemen's dormitory. The latter siding was realigned in the same decade to serve a new store for Levers (cattle feeds). The sand dock had gradually silted up and was filled and levelled and a concrete hard standing provided. The tidal bridge, catchpoint and siding beyond were removed in 1955.

On the Down side the extensive goods yard, provided in 1888, included a goods shed siding and two mileage sidings for about 40 wagons. These, with hard standing, skirted the new station forecourt. A large cattle pen dock was formed and from 1899 a second short siding appeared on its flank. The cattle trade out of Wadebridge Market (then on the second Monday, monthly) grew very quickly once the North Cornwall opened, with large shipments to Exeter, Chichester and, by 1914, eastern England. Wadebridge Market on its latest site became weekly, when the yard filled with cattle, the drovers and station staff struggling to herd them through the pens into the wagons. The old practice of driving cattle through the streets was ended in the 1940s, by hiring lorries instead. All day the station pilot kept busy, marshalling and placing wagons in the docks.

Cattle specials were timetabled out of Wadebridge as normal events, and empty trains or wagons supplied to suit. The Station Master and agent had to be well briefed on likely requirements, and a Cattle Inspector would be on hand to see that rules and regulations were observed. Allied to cattle farming was the fresh meat trade; this had begun quite early on, to Nine Elms and Smithfield Market, using ventilated box wagons at first and, in due course, demountable containers. There was a weekly export of pigs, up to three or four wagons from farm collections by Lloyd Maunder and Blewitt (Trelill). Wool went in bales to Bradford and sheepskins to Buckfastleigh and Yeovil. Needless to say there was a large forwarding of rabbits: George Robinson & Sons and Tonkins maintained depots and the 3.15pm Padstow 'Perishables' (with its Medway and Midlands connections) was the favourite train for these. The latter carried small consignments of primroses and violets in season, and a considerable egg trade was conducted in containers, by the Cornish Egg Depot, Robinsons (Treguddick) and Tonkins. Wadebridge farmers could also find a profitable business in new potatoes to Covent Garden and Brentford Markets; inwards, loads of seed potatoes arrived from Scotland, latterly delivered over a wide area by Hammett of St Issey. Sugar beet went to Kidderminster and Ely. Rustic slate from Trebarwith loaded in open

Wadebridge West signal box and level crossing over Molesworth Street in August 1960, with footbridge behind. John Eyres, South Western Circle.

containers, granite headstones and curbs from Wenford by road, transhipped by the goods shed 1 ton 17 cwt crane, were typical freight in latter years, alongside ice cream going to Newquay! Out in the yard china clay in sheeted wagons and bagged in box wagons for Staffordshire, together with granite slabs on open or flat wagons from De Lank and Hentergantick, also containerised Royal Navy stores, were marshalled from the Wenford branch for Up North Cornwall goods trains. Wagon loads of bulk paper in rolls from Sittingbourne were routed to the 'Cornish Guardian' at Bodmin. Wadebridge was the railhead for St Eval (RAF) and St Merryn (RNAS) airfields and enormous quantities of stores passed during the Second World War and after – for St Mawgan too, after Newquay goods yard closed. The Royal Cornwall Show, held at Wadebridge in 1895, 1924, 1927 and 1957, found a permanent home at Wadebridge from 1960. Invariably farm implements and exhibitors' wares came by rail. When the Household Cavalry took part in the 1960s a whole train of green BR horse boxes transported its mounts from Knightsbridge via Kensington Olympia. Occasionally, unseen and secure, surplus coins and notes went by container to the Royal Mint from local banks, especially in the summer season. If one saw a petrol wagon or a banana van on the inward goods, they were bound for Bodmin (Esso) and for Rowes (the fruit ripened by steam heat just in time for sale).

The goods shed was enlarged in 1939, filling the gap up to the station buildings. This was a response to the rising quantity of household items from all manner of firms, sundry consignments from grocery wholesalers and so on. The Nine Elms road box (from the overnight 'Tavvy' to Plymouth) came in at 12.30pm but the Exeter and Friday vans, behind the Waterloo news van was earlier, at 9.15am. The return workings were on the 11.35am and 5.00pm goods. The tonnage through the shed increased from 3,767 in 1927 to 10,906 in 1944, while out in the yard (and at the Quay) about 10,000 wagons were forwarded and received – and 17,000 transferred – from one goods service to another. One could not say that the Wadebridge layout was cramped. There was enough room to handle the average 80 to 85 wagons a day these numbers suggest, for local traders or services from and to Padstow, Wenford, Bodmin, Bodmin Road, Exmouth Junction and the east. As we have seen the Wadebridge foreman would ask Delabole to keep wagons back. The increase in block fertiliser workings (mostly from Avonmouth) in the 1960s caused problems, with every foot of sidings in use at station and Quay.

The movement of china clay from Wenford was interesting. In the 1920s the Beattie 2-4-0WTs brought down wagons which then went direct to Padstow. After World War II Fowey and Par became the destination, requiring reverses at Boscarne, Bodmin General and Bodmin Road. A daily tonnage of North Devon Clay Co ball clay was routed through Halwill for Fowey. Wagons came in on the afternoon goods and the empties went back on the 5pm up service. The sundries business declined in the 1960s while the cattle traffic was lost to the roads; the end of freight traffic on the North Cornwall from 7 September 1964 left Wadebridge with the remaining 'wagon load' business routed through Bodmin General and Boscarne Junction.

Having squeezed through lower Wadebridge on the converted B&WR's route and across Molesworth Street with its attendant shunting problems, the points for the Quay lay immediately beyond, leading to the physical junction between the LSWR and NCR. The crossing problems were never resolved of course and an unwritten law forbidding obstruction exceeding two minutes was often broken, bringing renewed complaints. Some Quay shunts had to be conducted over the crossing. A Beattie tank would commence at 6.20am, and with the Padstow trains passing, plus trips into Wadebridge, hold-ups were inevitable. Nothing has changed – today's motorists are frustrated here by traffic lights!

Very few trains passed Wadebridge without stopping – even fish specials from Padstow. One that did trundle through was the Armoured Train on patrol in 1940/41. Manned by Polish troops, its role was to defend the Camel estuary, though it also went up to Port Isaac Road on occasion. Those wartime years put a great strain on Wadebridge. Peacetime holiday trains terminated at Padstow of course but evacuees and prisoners of war, in specials, came to Wadebridge. The evacuations from London took place in 1939, 1940 (when 580 mothers and children arrived) and in 1944 when the V weapon campaign was under way. The prisoners of war, Italian and German, were housed in a camp where the present Sports Complex is sited. All this time the normal passenger service was well patronised. The number of tickets issued doubled from 42,571 in 1938 to 92,471 in 1944. Coal came entirely by rail, the tonnage rising from 7,000 to 13,000 by 1944, but china clay exports to Europe had disappeared of course. Diversions from the GWR in 1941 (and 1963, see later) meant that the long Penzance trains needed dividing to get them up to Delabole and from Launceston to Meldon Junction. The 'N' 2-6-0s took eight corridors. The equivalent load for diverted goods trains was 29 wagons and two brake vans. Both operations required marshalling space at Wadebridge and the shed had to service the GWR engines (43XX 2-6-0s and 51XX 2-6-2Ts) which brought the trains in from Bodmin Road.

The ordinary Bodmin Road passenger trains numbered about three a day, using the running powers acquired by the GWR to Wadebridge in 1886. After nationalisation in 1948 some trains were extended from Bodmin Road to Padstow, at 7.50am, 10.05am, 6.15pm and 9.15pm and from Padstow at 9.03am and 10.55am. Shorter WR workings continued to and from

Eddystone Road runs alongside the line to Padstow in this 1963 view from the footbridge. The West Cornwall Agricultural Cooperative Association store is in the background along with a footbridge carrying a public footpath to the river. John Eyres, South Western Circle.

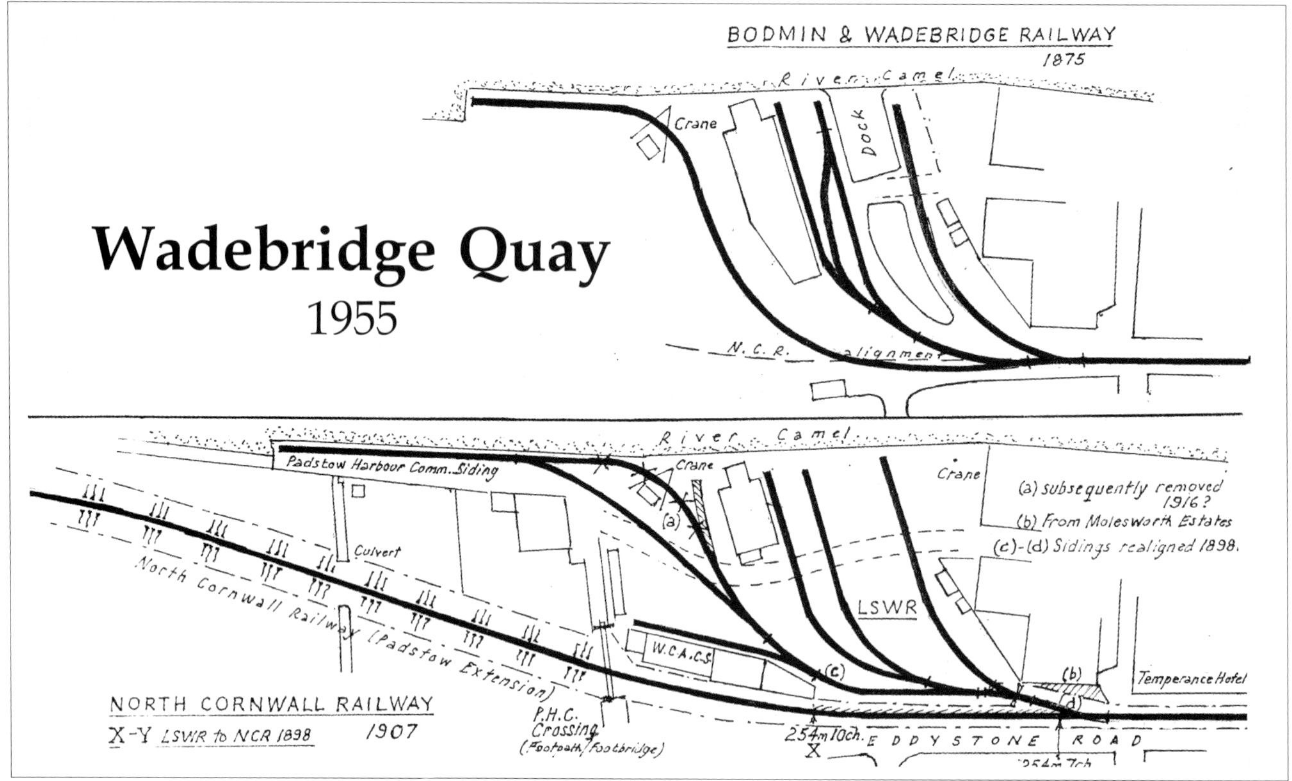

Wadebridge (some connecting for Padstow) for both Bodmin stations, with a two-hourly SR Service Wadebridge/ Bodmin North. From 1964 the Western Region operated a diesel railcar from Bodmin Road to Padstow, and Boscarne Junction (new platforms) to Bodmin North. A goods service had been instituted from 1888, some GWR trains being 'mixed' from Bodmin General to Wadebridge. Most wagon transfer took place at Wadebridge but a certain amount was made at Boscarne Junction sidings, mainly concerning the clay traffic. Cattle wagons from Otterham to Truro have already been noted; amongst other transfers, travelling funfair owners used the railway to take road trailers from one site to the next. Anderton & Rowlands, the St Austell proprietors, sent trailers from St Columb to Bude, via Wadebridge.

During 1971 considerable numbers of wagons still inhabited the Wadebridge yard, mostly fertiliser (290 from Severnside ICI and 162 from Cattewater out of a total of 633), basic slag from Scunthorpe and Corby and imported artificial fertiliser via Barry and Kings Lynn. Seed potatoes, in small tonnages from Aberdeen and Montrose, completed the list of inward loads. Only slate dust, coming by road from Delabole went out, in former salt 'Presflo' wagons, the majority to Tonbridge and the remainder in Derby and Sunderland. BR declared that working these wagons was becoming unprofitable, through wagons being shunted and marshalled several time en route. The last vestige of 'full load' – Speedlink – has long ceased, and all bulk traffic now comes into Cornwall in large lorries on expensively widened roads.

The 5-ton gantry crane and Farm Industries (successor to Hoskins, Polkinhorne and Trevithick) store in August 1964. John Eyres, South Western Circle.

The main station layout remained unchanged while the Bodmin Road to Padstow diesel cars maintained a seven-a-day return service. On this service being withdrawn from 30 January 1967 and a stop block erected west of Molesworth Street, the existing signalling and boxes remained operational until 17 December. From that date the East and West boxes were closed. Wadebridge then existed at the end of a 'long siding' from Boscarne Junction, controlled by a wooden staff. At the closure of the signal boxes the majority of the Up side was clipped out of use and subsequently removed. A small diversion was initiated at the river bridge where the old engine spur was joined to Levers siding to give adequate length for the bulk-feed wagons. The Quay sidings closed in April 1973 and Molesworth Street gates finally shut across the rails (254m 4ch). All remaining points were now converted to hand levers, though the points at the Boscarne end were kept locked by a key attached to the staff.

The three ex-GWR 1366 0-6-0PTs which replaced the Beattie tanks on the Wenford service in 1962 were themselves ousted by a 204hp diesel shunter in 1965, though it was not very successful. Standard 350hp shunters had been tried but could not work the Quay curves. By 1976 they were deemed capable of working all remaining services; that is, Bodmin Road, Boscarne Junction, Wenford and Wadebridge. Wadebridge was closed from 4 September 1978 although a brake van rail tour went down there in the December. A headshunt was established at Boscarne towards Nanstallon to reverse the Wenford trains, but even these ceased to run in September 1983.

The North Cornwall extension joined the LSWR end-on just beyond the Wadebridge West up home signals for loop and main. On the left are the trader's stores, served on their flanks by the Quay sidings. C. J. Knowle-Thomas.

Holken, Polkinhorne and Trevithick Co. again in August 1963 along with a BR brake and box van. John Eyres, South Western Circle.

The trackbed all the way from Wenford to Padstow, except in Wadebridge, has been converted to a footpath and cycle way. Bodmin Road (now 'Parkway') to General has been revived by preservationists in recent years, but Wadebridge and Padstow are unlikely ever to see trains again.

Over the years the Wadebridge Station Master (it was a Class 3 post) led a busy life. At one time he had 140 staff to pay weekly, though not all of them were under his personal control. There were about 40 drivers, fireman and shed staff and 35 in the Permanent Way department as well as his 65 clerks, porters, goods yard men and motor drivers. Up to 1915 there were GWR staff as well, a legacy of the 1888-1895 period. After 1927 the staff at Bodmin SR and the branch halts came into the fold. The weekday services occupied his, or his foreman's attention, from 5am until 10pm. On Sundays, however, Wadebridge virtually shut down, only the occasional 'ballast' train working locally, or perhaps one of the single summer return excursions which ran from the late 1920s. Station Master in 1924 was Mr Brown, followed over the years by Messrs Brazier, Clark and Clapp until Mr J. Taylor in 1966.

WADEBRIDGE QUAY

The Bodmin and Wadebridge Railway started at the Quay. A fan of sidings was laid down, curving sharply round from behind the Temperance Hotel; one fronted the river, one served a manure store and two more ran each side of a wet dock. Although isolated from its main system until 1895, the LSWR improved trade out of here, finding better rolling stock to do so. Wenford's china clay and granite traffic was transhipped to sailing coasters, the latter bringing in corn (for flour milling) coal and timber. De Lank granite was in great demand for public works in Victorian times. At the Wenford end it was brought down a steep cable-worked incline to be loaded into LSWR open two-plank wagons; at the Quay it was handled with a large sheerlegs tripod. Messrs Hocken, Trevithick and Polkinhorne built a commodious provender store and flour mill, followed by the Western Counties Agriculture Co-operative Society premises for grain and coal (later taken over by Fulford Trumps).

The Padstow Harbour Commissioners constructed their own quay extension with siding, to the west, in the 1870s. Access required an occupation crossing over the Padstow Extension from 1899 with a bridge (1902) to preserve footpath rights to the foreshore. The river was dredged to allow berthing of deeper draught steamers; the SS 'Dunraven' traded in general merchandise into the 1900s, later the MV 'Florence' brought flour from Ranks at Avonmouth. Ranks own premises were acquired by M. Thomas of Plymouth, which became the largest of the west country slag distributors. Obtained from iron furnaces, it was much favoured by farmers as a grass fertiliser. F. & J. Martyn's interests in the yard were acquired by Cornwall Farmers Ltd (corn and seed) later known as Farm Industries Ltd, retailing farm machinery. Balers, combines, drills, ploughs, all came exclusively by rail, always noticeable in their bright colours.

The LSWR relaid and remodelled the Quay in 1916, the inside siding and its turnouts having already been re-sited in 1899 to make room for the Padstow extension. A 5 ton overhead gantry crane was substituted for the sheerlegs and the small wet dock filled in. Vessels could still use the Quay until about 1954 for occasional cargoes of coal, slag and grain (some grain was also exported) but the river silted badly thereafter. After the passenger closure in 1967 a stopblock was erected on the Padstow line short of the Commissioner's Crossing (254m 09c) and several sidings were removed in 1971. Access across Molesworth Street meant opening and shutting the gates by hand. The yard closed in April 1973, and very little remains of this once thriving and profitable corner of railway activity in Wadebridge.

Wadebridge to Padstow

The views for passengers along the Camel estuary were comparable with those of the Exe at Dawlish, or from Lelant and Hayle. The river gradually widened towards the Town Bar, opposite Padstow, where it was almost a mile across to Porthilly (Rock), though it narrowed again considerably beyond the Padstow to about half a mile. The

Top and left. The buildings again with an Austin A40 parked to the right and in the distance a Morris 1000, a Ford Anglia and what looks like an Austin A30 van. John Eyres, South Western Circle.

Below. Padstow Harbour Commissions' Quay and ancient Camel Road bridge. The hold-ups brought about by the level crossing on Molesworth Street were legendary and exacerbated by some Quay shunts which had to be conducted over the crossing. John Eyres, South Western Circle.

On the far side of the River Camel can be seen the sidings emerging between the houses, curving sharply to each side of the two docks and to the river frontage.

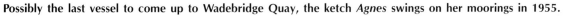

Possibly the last vessel to come up to Wadebridge Quay, the ketch *Agnes* swings on her moorings in 1955.

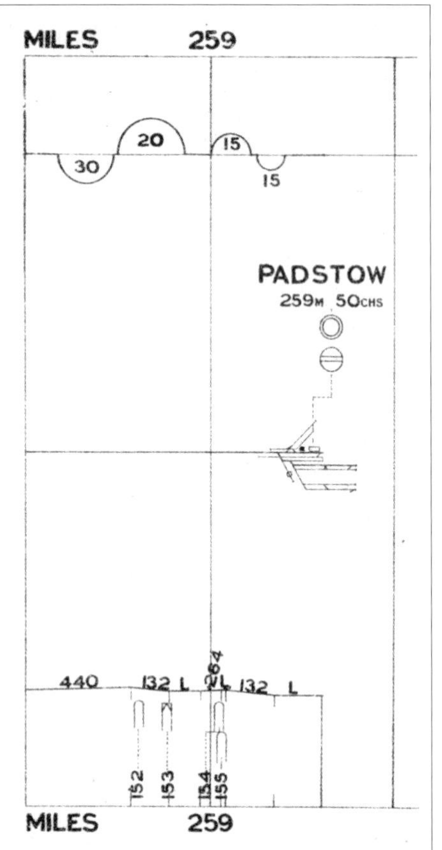

mud flats seen at low water at Wadebridge gave way to large expanses of sand banks beyond Whitehouse. The blue water, yellow dunes and green fields can still be enjoyed today from the same vantage points, on the trackbed.

After the long and straight embankment for the first mile out of Wadebridge, the NCR snaked along the foreshore on 40 chain reversing curves, over another short embankment where the streams came out of Polgammon Woods, and past the track from Tregunna to the shore, carried on the sole overbridge, a brick-faced masonry arch at 255m 74ch. There was another short embankment before the line rounded to the left before reaching the site of the Camel Quarries through an expanse of dumped waste material. Disused for some years before 1899, it nevertheless provided useful stone for pitching the embankments. The line then curved 30 chains to the right, damming the creek at Pinxton and cutting off the old quay within. To get round to the next creek, at Old Town (257m 57ch), a shelf had to be cut into the hillside and then a sharper 25 chain cutting (to the left) to pass through the corner of Ball Hill. A further curve took the line around under Tregonce, in St Issey Parish, to the wide inlet at Little Petherick.

The 200 yard embankment was first pierced by a small arch before taking its 20 chain curve to the right and over the well known, 400ft long viaduct. Then it eased to a 30 chain radius in a very deep cutting through the side of Dennis Hill. The monument above commemorates Queen Victoria's Jubilee of 1887. Just beyond was the last obstacle, Dennis Cove. The new embankment formed a lake but before the railway came there had been a shipyard here. It had seen one of the largest vessels (at 800 tons) ever launched from Padstow. Final curves of 15 chains bore the line right and left through another shallow cutting into the terminus.

PADSTOW (259m 43ch)
The sheltered inlet from the Camel had been a natural anchorage for ships from time immemorial, though the infamous Doom Bar further out into the estuary was what its name implied. Worthy of note is the Padstow Lifeboat, established in 1827, with its history of courage and tragedy. The recognisable port dates from the 1530s and it traded much with Ireland and Bristol in cloth, fish and tin, and coal from South Wales. In the 1850s it was even an emigrant departure port, mainly to Quebec. Not always called Padstow (it was 'Lodenek' in the 16th Century) it was briefly a borough in Elizabethan days. Since then it has rested under the semi-feudal care of the Lords of the Manor, the Prideaux-Brunes whose seat is Prideaux Place above the town. We have seen how Charles Gordon Prideaux-Brune was at the forefront in bringing the railway to the town and that Colonel C.R. Prideaux-Brune was one of the last directors of the NCR, in 1922.

In the 19th Century shipbuilding dominated, but wooden sailing vessels were ousted by steam, and the last was launched from the Higher Yard in 1889. It was during this period that the Padstow Harbour Commissioners were established, in 1844. The population of the town in the 1890s was about 1,700, rising slightly until World War 1 but falling again in the 1920s. High hopes had been placed on the new railway's contribution to Padstow as a

O2 class 0-4-4T No. 30193 with a Maunsell P set from Bodmin North approaching Padstow – the Denis Hill monument is beyond – on 14th August 1950.

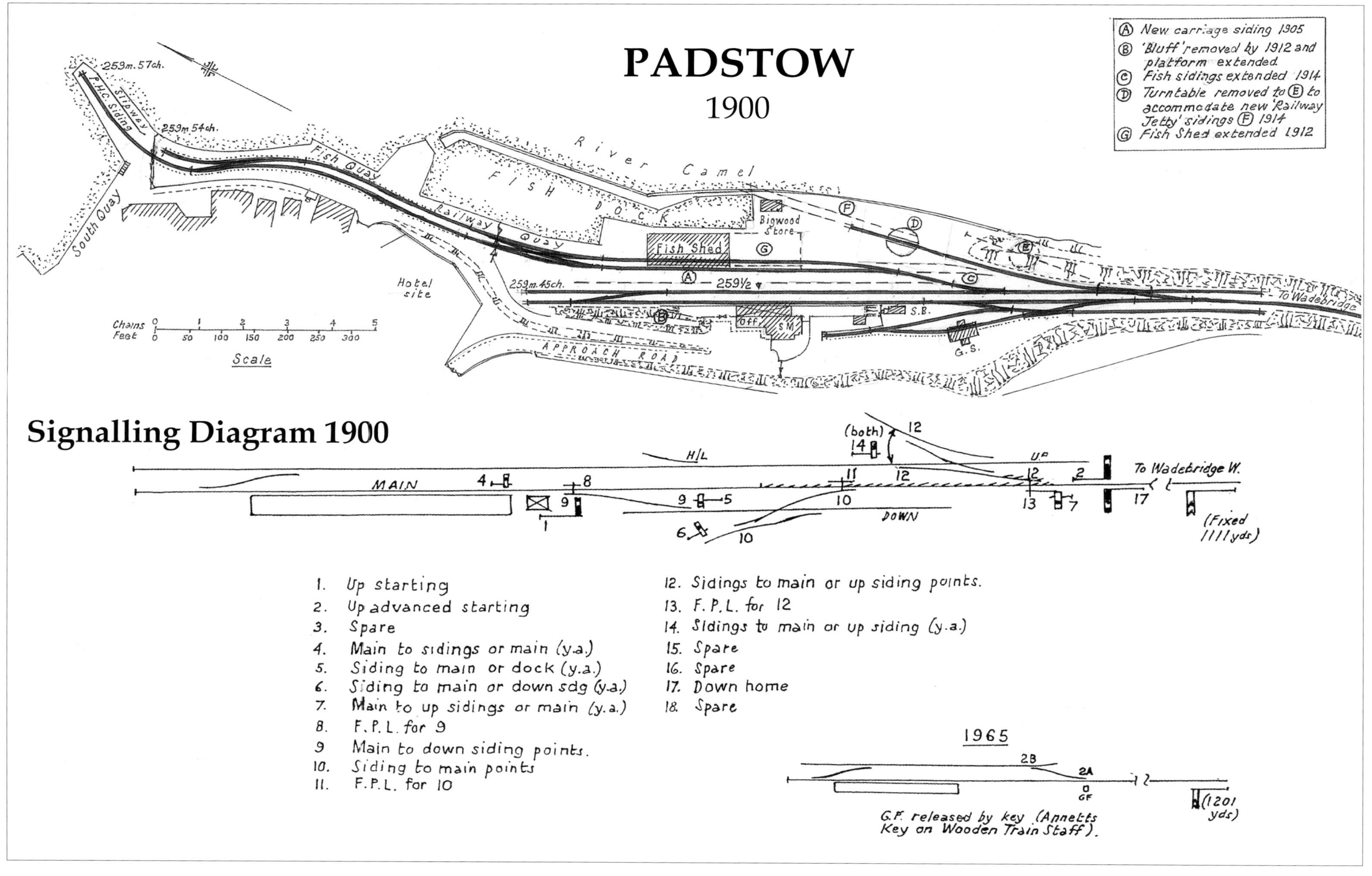
PADSTOW
1900
(A) New carriage siding 1905
(B) 'Bluff' removed by 1912 and platform extended
(C) Fish sidings extended 1914
(D) Turntable removed to (E) to accommodate new 'Railway Jetty' sidings (F) 1914
(G) Fish Shed extended 1912
259m.57ch.
P.H.C. Siding
Slipway
259m.54ch.
South Quay
Fish Quay
River Camel
Fish Dock
Railway Quay
Bigwood Store
Fish Shed
Hotel site
259m.45ch.
259½
To Wadebridge
S.B.
Off.
S.M.
G.S.
Approach Road
Chains 0 1 2 3 4 5
Feet 0 50 100 150 200 250 300
Scale
Signalling Diagram 1900
H/L
MAIN
UP
DOWN
(both)
To Wadebridge W.
(Fixed 1111 yds)
1. Up starting
2. Up advanced starting
3. Spare
4. Main to sidings or main (y.a.)
5. Siding to main or dock (y.a.)
6. Siding to main or down sdg (y.a.)
7. Main to up sidings or main (y.a.)
8. F.P.L. for 9
9 Main to down siding points.
10. Siding to main points
11. F.P.L. for 10
12. Sidings to main or up siding points.
13. F.P.L. for 12
14. Sidings to main or up siding (y.a.)
15. Spare
16. Spare
17. Down home
18. Spare
1965
2B
2A
GF
(1201 yds)
G.F. released by key (Annetts Key on Wooden Train Staff).

Above. As if heralding the end of an epic journey Little Petherick Creek was crossed on a magnificent three span wrought iron bridge. Seen from the cab of T9 4-4-0 No. 30719 in July 1960. R. C. Riley, www.transporttreasury.co.uk

Left and below. The views across the Camel estuary are well known and the photo from Denis Hill (below) demonstrates the spectacular nature of the river and rolling hills of the Cornish landscape.

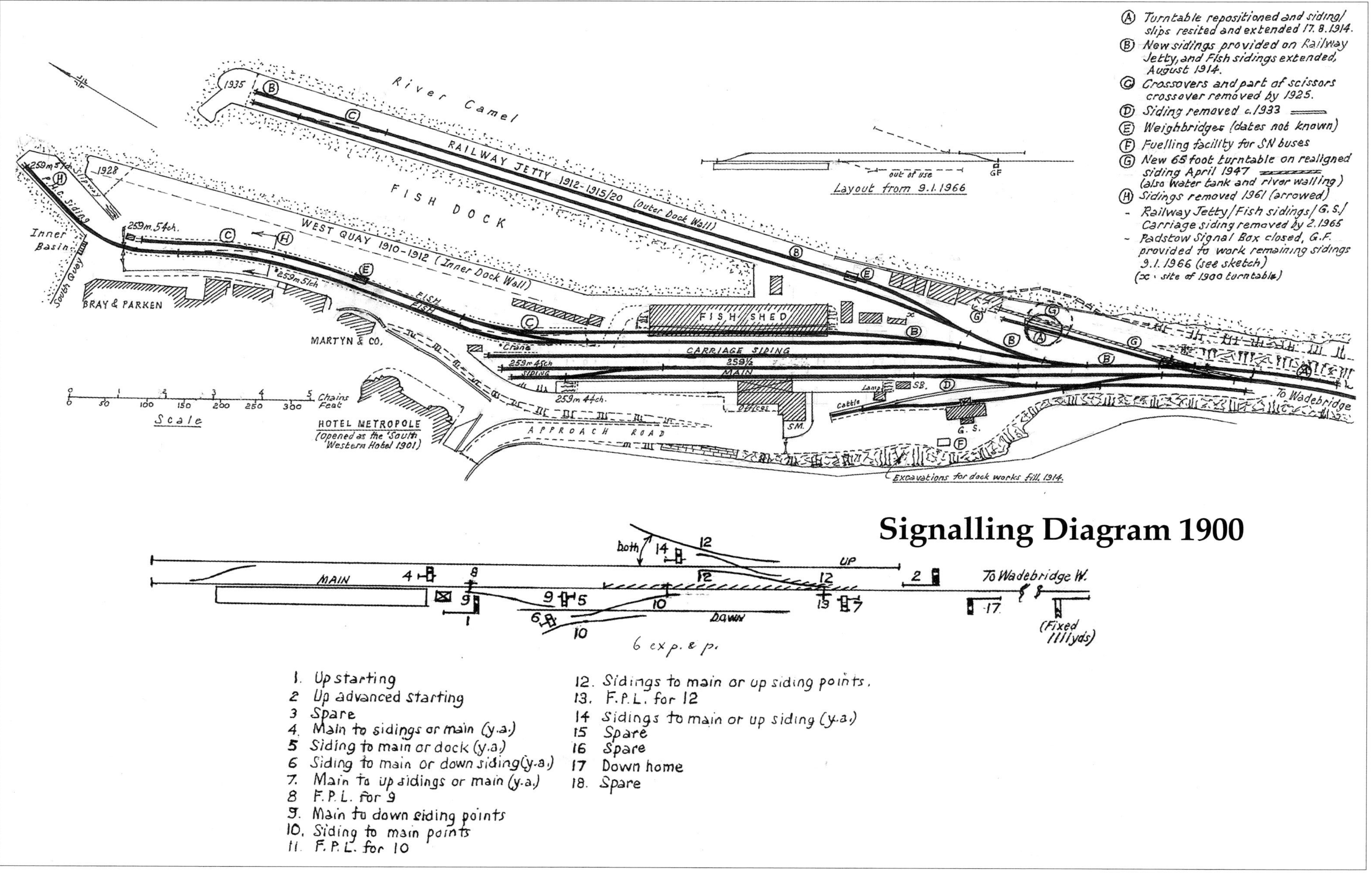
Ⓐ Turntable repositioned and siding/slips resited and extended 17.8.1914.
Ⓑ New sidings provided on Railway Jetty, and Fish sidings extended, August 1914.
Ⓒ Crossovers and part of scissors crossover removed by 1925.
Ⓓ Siding removed c.1933
Ⓔ Weighbridges (dates not known)
Ⓕ Fuelling facility for SN buses
Ⓖ New 65 foot turntable on realigned siding April 1947 (also water tank and river walling)
Ⓗ Sidings removed 1961 (arrowed)
- Railway Jetty/Fish sidings/G.S./Carriage siding removed by 2.1965
- Padstow Signal Box closed, G.F. provided to work remaining sidings 9.1.1966 (see sketch)
(x : site of 1900 turntable)
Layout from 9.1.1966
River Camel
RAILWAY JETTY 1912-1915/20 (Outer Dock Wall)
FISH DOCK
WEST QUAY 1910-1912 (Inner Dock Wall)
Inner Basin
South Quay
BRAY & PARKEN
MARTYN & CO.
HOTEL METROPOLE (Opened as the 'South Western Hotel 1901)
FISH SHED
CARRIAGE SIDING
MAIN
APPROACH ROAD
To Wadebridge
Excavations for dock works fill, 1914.
Scale
To Wadebridge W.
(Fixed 111yds)
6 exp. & p.
1. Up starting
2 Up advanced starting
3 Spare
4. Main to sidings or main (y.a.)
5 Siding to main or dock (y.a.)
6 Siding to main or down siding (y.a.)
7. Main to up sidings or main (y.a.)
8 F.P.L. for 9
9. Main to down siding points
10. Siding to main points
11. F.P.L. for 10
12. Sidings to main or up siding points.
13. F.P.L. for 12
14 Sidings to main or up siding (y.a.)
15 Spare
16 Spare
17 Down home
18. Spare

Signalling Diagram 1900

Above. T9 4-4-0 No.30338 shunting stock at Padstow on 4th June 1960.

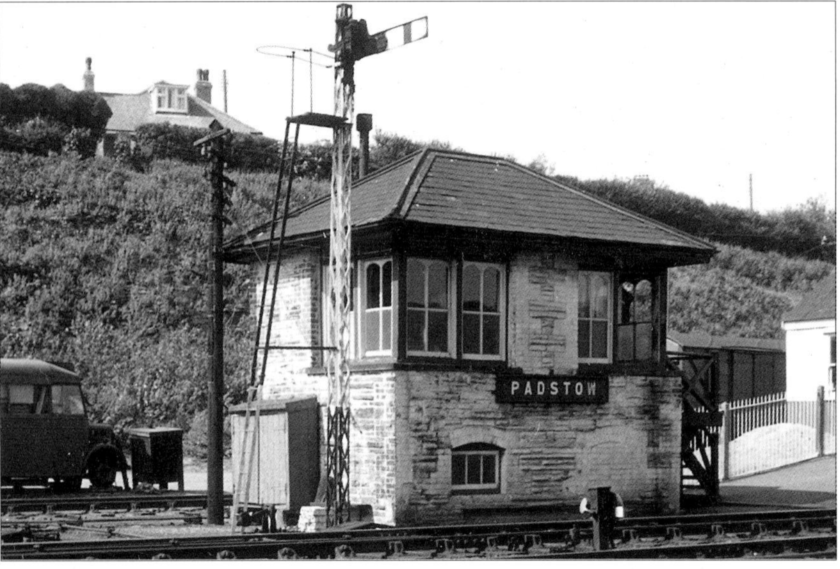

Left. Padstow signal box had opened on 12th March 1899 and was of the central brick pillared 1890s SW design. It closed in January 1966 leaving only a run-round loop (for operating the Bodmin school train) which was controlled by a two lever ground frame. John Eyres, South Western Circle.

Bottom. Approach to the goods shed in 1963 with loading dock and a box van. The corrugated iron hut was used to service station and signal lamps. John Eyres, South Western Circle.

holiday resort. The opening of the South Western, later Metropole Hotel in May 1901 as a draw for high class 'visitors' (as they are known in Cornwall) was successful but fine summer days brought influxes of day trippers from as far as Exeter. There is no promenade at Padstow but holiday makers were attracted to Trevone (within Padstow Parish and only two miles distant) or to Harlyn Bay, Treyarnon Bay and Portcothnan Bay, by horse vehicles and, later on, motor bus. Prominent in the transport field was William Pope, who was bringing visitors from Wadebridge by the North Cornwall coach at first, and by rail from 1895. He also ran buses from the new 1899 Padstow station, serving the coast towards Newquay. As Pope & Sons they were the LSWR's and SR's general cartage agents in the area, although by 1948 these were Bill

Top. **The little goods shed in August 1964. In comparison with Wadebridge, the commodities passing through the goods shed here could only be described as modest. Coal, fertiliser, building materials and timber all arrived and, up to 1936, china clay. Cattle and rabbits were the mainstay of the traffic out. John Eyres, South Western Circle.**

Left. **Padstow signal box had an 18 lever Steven's frame with one spare. The later ground frame was released by Annett's key attached to the wooden Train Staff. John Eyres, South Western Circle.**

Below. **The 70ft diameter turntable installed by the SR in 1947 for the Bulleid Pacifics. The Board of Trade had insisted that a turntable was installed at Padstow, a 50ft unit arriving in 1900. During yard and siding work realignments in 1914 it was repositioned. John Eyres, South Western Circle.**

Above and below. Padstow's Station Masters house and offices in August 1964. The building was constructed in local dressed stone and also featured the pronounced eaves of some of the other North Cornwall stations. John Eyres, South Western Circle.

Top. Padstow on 15th July 1960 with T9 4-4-0 No.30713 departing with the 12.55pm to Okehampton (the two rear coaches for Waterloo) and 30719 waiting to work the 3.13pm 'perishables' to Exeter Central. The train comprises 2 Maunsell 2-Set Ps. The first 2-Set P is likely to be either set 196 or 198 and after June 1960 these were made up from a Brake Third (Second) to Diagram 2113 and Brake Composite to Diagram 2401. Prior to this date the Brake Composite would have been a Diagram 2403 example but these were converted to Push-Pull driving trailers to replace older withdrawn Push-Pull sets. R. C. Riley, www.transporttreasury.co.uk

Cornish and Nick Reynolds. Reynolds and James commenced Brown's Bus Services in the 1920s with motor buses, plying as far as Bedruthan;, Hardy Colwill and the National Bus Co were also in the business. All these routes were in the Southern National Omnibus Co's system from 1935, one or two buses being stabled at Padstow Station.

Like Wadebridge, Padstow acquired Urban District Council status by 1900; it incorporated the expanding 'village' of Trevone, bringing the total population to something like 3,500 by 1939. Just over the river was Rock and Porthilly, part of St Minver and reached by a ferry. With a tourist trade growing quite rapidly and the development of the fishing port, the Station Master's position at Padstow was no sinecure. First to be appointed was Mr Buscombe, during the Great War came Mr Watkins then, in the 1930s, Messrs Portass and White, followed by Mr Penwarden in the 1940s. Many Padstonians remember, some with awe, Miss May Cavill, a booking clerk in the 1930s and 1940s. The number of staff necessary to run Padstow was large and although loading of fish trains was done by the traders' men, the railway goods checker had to be on hand. In comparison the amount of merchandise through the goods shed was much less than at Wadebridge, though coal, fertiliser, building materials and timber arrived in wagons for the local merchants, with outward cattle and Padstow's share of the rabbit trade. It has been noted that there were continuous shipments of china clay, brought by rail, up to 1936. With two signalmen, several passenger guards, porter, a carriage cleaner, the booking clerks and a goods clerk, by Nationalisation in 1948 (which subsequently added road lorry drivers) it was all pretty busy. The fish landings were, however, declining by this time; freight was passing to the roads in the 1960s and the rise of private motoring was taking a toll of the extra summer holiday trains. After the withdrawal of freight trains on 7 September 1964, nearly all the sidings were taken up in early 1965. The signal box was closed from 9 January 1966 leaving only the run-round loop (for operating the Bodmin school train) to be controlled by a two-lever ground frame unlocked by an Annetts Key on the wooden train staff, in use from Wadebridge West. In spite of much protest, the diesel railcar service from Bodmin Road was withdrawn from 30 January 1967, only a few months after the Okehampton/ Halwill closure.

The station layout stretched 400 yards from just inside the last cutting to the platform stop blocks at 259m 45ch, but the sidings ran towards the South Quay for another 200 yards to the end of the NCR's property. One was extended on to the PHC's pier itself. The goods yard was simplicity itself, just one siding skirting the goods shed, another to the cattle and end-loading dock, with

Top, middle and above**. The station in 1964. When first opened the layout comprised 100 yard platform, a run-round loop, the sidings to the harbour and some fish sheds. There was of course a small goods yard on the down side. The layout stretched some 400 yards from the cutting to the stop blocks at the end of the single platform and would really be the furthest point west a passenger could travel from Waterloo at 259m 45chains. However, the sidings ran towards the South Quay for a further 200 yards to the end of the North Cornwall property. The 1963 transfer to the Western Region heralded the end for Padstow and its through coaches to London. First to go was the goods traffic in 1964 followed some time after by through coaches. All through services ceased in September 1966. John Eyres, South Western Circle.**

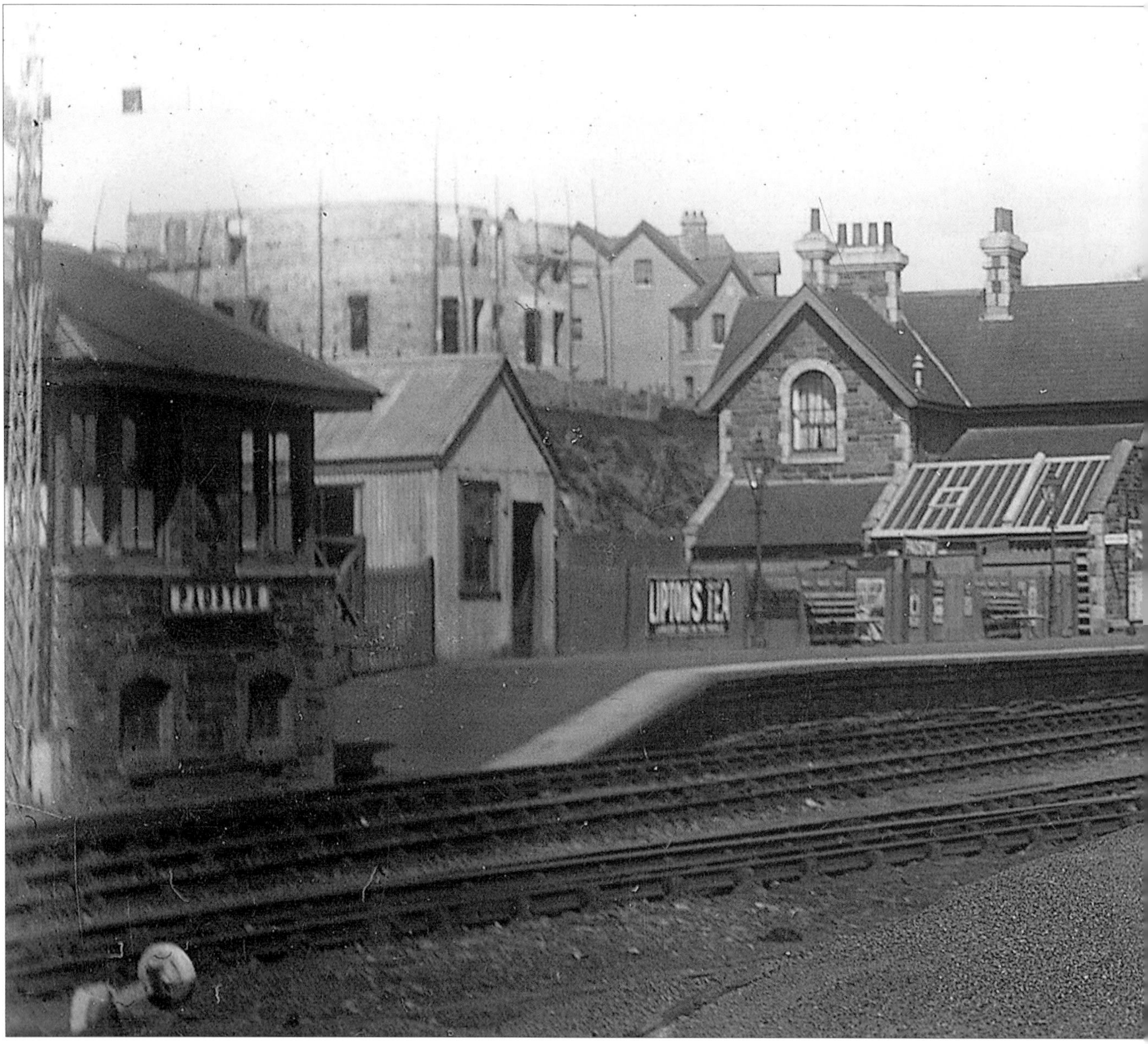

Fish dealers offices and corrugated iron storage shed in 1964. John Eyres, South Western Circle.

Padstow and the South Western Hotel in the 1900s. Work had begun on the Hotel in 1900 and was complete the following year. The Cardiff shipowner John Carey had completed it at a total cost of £12,000 including all the fittings. The name changed to The Metropole and saw a variety of visitors including MPs and the Prince of Wales in the 1930s, attracted by the local golf courses.

a short shunting neck to the east. The signal box controlled all movement this side. Part of this layout was even reduced in 1933, leaving one only siding by the goods shed to the dock.

The Up side and quayside sidings were much larger, totalling one and a half miles at its height in the 1920s. Alongside the platform was a run-round loop, but with long trains in the summer the engine would draw them right down to the stopblocks to enable at least eight coaches to be accommodated in the platform. After unloading the train would be pushed back, the engine released through a levered sprung points crossover. The platform had been lengthened 120 feet at the stop blocks end in 1912. A further carriage siding, joining the loop, was provided soon after opening. The original LSWR ground signals were replaced by SR discs and yellow arms, and the signal arms changed to upper quadrant, in the late 1930s. There were only three of the latter – the Down home, Up starting and Up advanced starting. The Down distant was fixed at caution and a long way out at Little Petherick, almost three quarters of a mile.

The development of the new quays and their sidings were described earlier. It would appear that Padstow initially would lack a turntable, for the LSWR was reluctant; there was after all already one at Wadebridge, and the subject was still under consideration in August 1899. The BoT insisted, however, and a 50ft table was installed in 1900, on the first of three sites. No other facilities were provided for engines at this time. The siding on the South Quay pier was under control of the PHC which complained in 1899 that rails were too near the edge. The LSWR was responsible, said the NCR, although only trucks went on the pier. A gate was installed here in tandem with one for the new road to the station. The narrow strip in front of the Custom House and the old Court House was formerly the quayside, the NCR fencing it off as far as St Edmunds Lane. An infill and a new quay face (West) was constructed here in 1899, paralleled by a siding making two (with a crossover between them) as far as the South Quay entrance. The shipyard itself had disappeared under Padstow's new station and fish sidings, but the narrow jetty enclosing the (fitting out?) basin was retained so giving some shelter to the vessels unloading to this new quay.

These two long sidings serving the fish shed, the West Quay and the one ending on the South Quay, survived until truncated at the far end in 1961. There was a certain amount of ship-to-rail traffic before 1914, and probably coal spasmodically until 1964 but the crossover (to the east of the siding gate here) was removed by 1925. The northernmost siding closely bounded the 1899 West Quay but new works from 1910 left a wider, 60ft, landing. Further development followed, including more offices for fish traders (one of them a quaint narrow two-storey wooden edifice) and a wagon weighbridge. The fish auction shed, specially built by the NCR, was 160ft by 50ft and incorporated a 20ft cantilever awning over the loading bank and siding. It still stands, with its timber stanchions and roof trusses clad in corrugated iron. The original layout was comparatively simple, the fish sidings joining the new run-round loop which continued to a dead end near the cutting. The turntable siding crossed it with double slips (No.12 points) leading to the single line. Movements towards the facing points in the single line were originally protected by treadle locks but the SR converted these to locking bars and inserted limited track circuiting.

The heavy works concerning the New or 'Railway' pier started in 1911 and the turntable had to be moved 50 yards to the east to accommodate pointwork for the two sidings laid to the pier. The existing fish shed sidings were lengthened at the same time. The new layout was in use from August 1914. The fish shed was lengthened by 100ft and a crossover was incorporated in the new pier sidings at the seaward end. Although the second station siding for cleaning and re-watering carriages was provided before 1905, there appeared

***Top.* South Jetty with one siding out of use. *Middle.* The Lower Basin. *Right.* P. H. C. sidings on South Quay and the end of the road some 259 miles 57chains from Waterloo. John Eyres, South Western Circle.**

South Jetty in August 1964 and a cargo of sand being unloaded. John Eyres, South Western Circle.

to be an embarrassing shortage of carriage sidings in earlier years, crowded out by the heavy fish traffic.

A lot of the fish was carried in sheeted open wagons before 1914, but ventilated vans (with vacuum pipes or through brake) tended to be used in the 1920s. The fish was packed in ice in boxes or barrels, and the whole trade was a cold, wet and smelly business. Naturally with such a perishable commodity speedy handling was essential, and the LSWR and SR were adept in supplying wagons, not only to get it away on the specials, but to ensure an adequate supply of boxes in return. When the East Coast fleet converted to steam in the 1920s a large quantity of coal arrived by rail (some by coastal vessels) to be stored on the West Quay. In a typical season over 700 wagons of coal would be required. Despite the contraction of the fishing fleets in 1914-18, the Lowestoft (and Ramsgate) vessels used Padstow the year round and the fish trains continued. The seasonal herring trade started again in 1919 and in 1922 over 500 crew and ancillary workers were quartered in the port, with 52 trawlers at sea. Pressure was intense to get several thousand tons of fish inland in the eleven week season from January to March. Estimating how much, and when, exercised the skills of the Station Master and his staff. In SR days the 3.15pm 'Perishables' could take some wagons but usually a special was laid on, a pathway being available at 4.40pm, into Okehampton at 7.26pm and Exeter 8.20, thence to Nine Elms for Billingsgate Market. As with all extra traffic, railway staff enjoyed overtime payments – the Padstow fish traffic was thus very popular.

The North Cornwall Ice & Cold Storage Co Ltd's factory of 1910 was owned by the Padstow Electric Supply Co, which also supplied current for lighting the quays and goods yard. It was extended in the 1920s. A further trade was kippers. A smoke shed employed Scottish girls and they lodged in the town during the season. The railway also carried a considerable quantity of boxes and barrels, sometimes up to 300 wagonloads in the season, to the quayside. The essential fish porterage, packing and loading was the concern of the traders who rented premises on the quay. In the late 1920s about twenty were listed, chief among them Hobson & Co (Lowestoft), The Lowestoft Fish Selling Co Ltd, Pawlyn Bros and Richard Thomas Ltd. The Great Grimsby Coal, Salt & Tanning Co Ltd dealt with ship's chandlery, while the Lowestoft Coaling Co Ltd's role was obvious. Around the corner on the South Quay timber and general merchants Bray & Parken received rail-borne traffic, unloaded on one of the long sidings, though they also imported coal by coastal vessel up to the 1940s.

Export of china clay from Padstow originated from the exploitation of large deposits on the west side of Bodmin Moor. As early as the 1880s a small amount was shipped from Wadebridge Quay brought down by B&W wagons from Wenfordbridge. It was not until 1906 that the North Cornwall China Clay Co opened Stannon Pit, six miles from Penpont on the Wenford branch. Clay slurry was piped to driers situated there, and by 1912 50,000 tons of clay were being produced, though most of this was exported through Fowey by rail via Boscarne Junction and Bodmin Road. The 1914 improvements at Padstow enabled the LSWR to expand clay shipments. Twenty-five flat wagons were built in 1914-15, each to carry eight hinged-side containers. There was a proposal for a special five ton travelling crane to handle the containers on the Railway Pier, but it is unlikely to have come to anything. They were actually handled at Padstow, interesting wagons that lasted only until 1923 when they were converted to side-opens. China clay exports slumped heavily from 1914 and were slow to pick up again, reaching only 3,000 tons by 1933. Padstow's facilities could not compare with those of the GWR at Fowey. The last known shipment from the Pier appears to have been in 1936, though there may have been some in World War Two. Any resumption of shipments from Padstow were thwarted by political considerations in 1946, which saw to it that all clay went through Fowey and Par, and not a 'non-registered' port like Padstow.

Right and far right. General views of West Quay fish dock in 1964. John Eyres, South Western Circle.

Below. T9 4-4-0 No.30717 and long time regular on of the North Cornwall lines, shunts stock in July 1960. The large building on the left is Pawlyn Bros. fish curing depot and store. R. C. Riley, www.transporttreasury.co.uk

Passing the east end of Meldon Quarry on 9th May 1961 is the 9.25am Okehampton to Padstow service behind T9 No. 30313, one of only nine to get the later style BR emblem. The leading vehicle is a Southern 4 wheel passenger brake 'Van C' (BY under BR) to Diagram 3092. The rear two Maunsell 2-coach P Set and XP van will be detached at Halwill for Bude. On the left is the abutment for a bridge which once took narrow gauge spoil trucks from the quarry to a tip. S. C. Nash.

The Ashwater signalman exchanges Tablets with the crew of No. 34066 *Spitfire* passing through on the 11.00am Padstow to Waterloo on 11th September 1964, the first three coaches formed from a BR Mark 1 3-coach set (BSK, CK, BSK). *Spitfire* was involved in the Lewisham disaster of 1956, but is seen here in the quiet valley of the Carey where it begins to narrow towards the south. R. A. Lumber.

Chapter Four
THE RISE AND FALL OF SERVICES ON THE NORTH CORNWALL

with additional information by Chris Tooth

The chapters so far have covered how the LSWR arrived in Devon and Cornwall; the hurdles the company overcame in order to build a line to Padstow and the physical features of the line and its stations. This chapter looks at how the train services on the North Cornwall changed over time between opening of a station in Halwill in 1879 and closure in 1967. An additional section has been added to give a basic overview of how the NCR was operated.

An overview to operating the NCR

It should be understood that the North Cornwall Railway was not operated simply by running trains from Exeter to Padstow, turning the loco round at the terminus and then sending the whole lot east again. It was certainly a lot more complex than that! This will become clear when we look at each of the main stations on the route.

Okehampton. This station was on the main line between Exeter and Plymouth. A few miles to the west, past Meldon Quarry and the viaduct, was Meldon Junction where the lines to Padstow and Bude peeled off to the north. This effectively made Okehampton a junction station. Here through coaches to/from Padstow and Bude would be detached/attached to services to/from Plymouth. Additionally, many local services to and from Bude, Launceston, Wadebridge and Padstow would terminate here. Adding to the passenger services were those carrying goods and they would have been shunted at Okehampton to ensure loads were forwarded to their correct destinations. In short, in the age of steam, Okehampton was an Mecca from those interested in shunting and the complex forming and reforming of trains.

Halwill Junction. Having left the Plymouth main line the next operational centre was Halwill Junction. At its northern end the line split three ways with routes going to Padstow, Bude and Torrington. From the time the NCR opened to Launceston the lines to Bude and, later Torrington, were considered the branches. The Halwill to Torrington passenger services were operated as a simple up-down shuttle service and had no interaction with those from Padstow or Bude. The main interest, however, was the dividing and joining of through coaches to and from Bude from services to and from Padstow. Down trains arriving at Halwill would have the Padstow portion next to the locomotive and the rear portion to Bude would be uncoupled. The Padstow service would depart leaving the Bude portion to be taken on by a second locomotive. On the return leg the Bude service would normally arrive first, the loco would run round its train and then pull the whole lot clear of the Padstow line junction. The Padstow service would then arrive and the Bude portion would be propelled on to the rear. The Bude loco would stay at Halwill. A similar set of moves were enacted for freight services.

Launceston. This was one of the few major population centres encountered by the NCR and was also served by the GWR line from Lydford. As such it should come as no surprise that it generated much traffic in terms of passengers and freight from the outlying areas. Launceston was a stop for long distance services but also a terminus for some local services to the west (Padstow and Wadebridge) and east (Okehampton and Exeter). In terms of freight Launceston was long associated with cattle markets and on market days special trains would be run to collect and return the beasts. It was also effectively a location where wagons from the smaller stations arrived in pick-up goods trains for sorting and onwards dispatch. The number and destination of trains terminating here varied over the years.

Wadebridge. After its initial low key beginnings Wadebridge became the junction of the NCR with the line from Wenford and Bodmin. It had a motive power department, a sub shed of Exmouth Junction, and facilities to sort and store both wagons and coaches. The main operational interest here was the interaction between services (both SR and GWR) to/from the Bodmin stations and those on the main NCR line. Some Bodmin services continued on to Padstow, either in their own right or as attached to through services. Not all Up services to Launceston and beyond started at Padstow, and Wadebridge provided the locomotives and stock for these. The engine shed at Wadebridge also serviced locomotives arriving from the east to Wadebridge and Padstow and, as such, there were light engine movements to and from Padstow.

Padstow. This was the end of the line for the North Cornwall! Despite this it will be clear by now that not all services along the line reached the terminus and that, other than a 70' turntable, Padstow had few facilities to prepare locomotives for their return trips. It also only had the one platform but this was made up by a number of long sidings that could be pressed into service for carriage storage between services or overnight. General goods facilities were sparse but the LSWR had built up quay-side facilities to serve the fishing industry. At the height of the fishing season it could generate large amounts of freight traffic.

The above is very much a simplification of operations at the key stations. It can be seen, however, that operations on the NCR were a complex overlap of through and local passenger services and that freight was collected en-route for sorting and onward dispatch from key centres such as Wadebridge, Launceston, Halwill and Okehampton. So far we have only looked at the routing of services but the operation was more complex still, as we shall see.

As far as passengers were concerned they only needed to know what time their train arrived at, and in which coach to get a seat. The train time information was published as the timetables that we are all familiar with but working timetables give us interesting operating details including the locations where up

On a warm afternoon in 1956 a Launceston family return home from Tower Hill whilst the driver of the U Class 2-6-0 No. 31610 is about to exchange single line Tablets with the signalman. 31610 was the first of the true U class, numbers 31790-31809, rebuilds of the ill fated K Class 'River' 2-6-4 tanks. It was allocated to Yeovil from October 1954 to January 1960 and was probably 'borrowed' by Exmouth Junction to deputise for a failed loco. The train appears to consist of a Maunsell 2-Set P. Brian Tunbridge.

and down trains crossed (station loops). The WWT also contained the actual times trains were due to arrive and depart – the departure times on the public timetable were slightly in advance to encourage early arrival!

The next layer of information was found in the Carriage Working Notices (CWN). These instructed staff how many coaches and of what type were used in each service, where they were to be added/detached and where they were to be stored when not in service. These are complex but interesting documents and detail the weekly ballet involved in ensuring that all stock returned to the correct location for the start of the next weeks services. To simplify complying with the CWN requirements was one reason why the LSWR, SR and BR(S) used their coaches in fixed, numbered 'sets'. Some special items of coaching stock, such as restaurant cars, were given duty numbers. For instance in 1959 duty number 24, covered a two-car buffet and trailer set, which travelled to Padstow on Friday for return to Waterloo on Saturday.

The final pieces in the operational jigsaw were the Engine Working manuals. These were used by staff at motive power depots to ensure that the correct engine staffed by the correct depot's crews were on the right service. The main point here is that, for instance, a single passenger service from Padstow to Waterloo would not have had the same loco all the way. An example was the 1.00pm departure from Padstow in 1959. A T9 4-4-0 (Duty 599) took the train as far as Wadebridge (this saved a light engine movement) where it was replaced by an N Class (Duty 593) which took the train as far as Okehampton. Here three coaches from the Padstow train were added to the Plymouth to Exeter service hauled by another T9 (Duty 578). The Engine Workings logged the actual motive power and the varying turns each loco was used for. These were called 'Duties' and each was given a reference number. To illustrate the complexities of this system the example of Duty 593 is given in full later in this Chapter. Pulling together the interaction between timetabled services, locomotive duty numbers and the stock used the three flowcharts *(opposite)* each looks at a separate summer Saturday service in 1959 and they cover:

- 12.25am departure from Waterloo, arriving Padstow at 7.26am and the following 8.30am return to Waterloo.
- 1.25am departure from Waterloo, arriving Padstow at 9.27am and the following 1.00pm return to Waterloo.
- 11.15am departure from Waterloo, arriving Padstow at 6.22pm.

Now we've completed the overview we continue to look at the initial development, rise and then fall of services on the NCR.

Initial growth of services

From the chapters so far it will be apparent that the North Cornwall line was in no real rush to reach Padstow. Indeed it took the 20 years from 1879 to 1899 to build the four sections, totalling 49 miles, between Halwill and Padstow. The milestones of railway development in the region were:

- 1834 Bodmin to Wadebridge
- 1879 Meldon Junction to Holsworthy via Halwill
- 1886 Halwill to Launceston (NCR 1st Section)
- 1893 Launceston to Delabole (NCR 2nd Section)
- 1895 Delabole to Wadebridge (NCR 3rd Section)
- 1898 Holsworthy extension to Bude
- 1899 Wadebridge to Padstow (NCR 4th Section)
- 1923 Halwill to Torrington

NCR to Launceston 1886

The opening of the line to Launceston on 21 July 1886 had a number of operational impacts. The most obvious was that the station at Halwill was promoted to 'junction' status. Less obvious was the demotion of the Halwill to Holsworthy line to a branch. This meant that through passenger trains from Okehampton now ran to the new station at Launceston. Holsworthy was served by a shuttle service from Halwill.

By the time the NCR reached Launceston the GWR had been

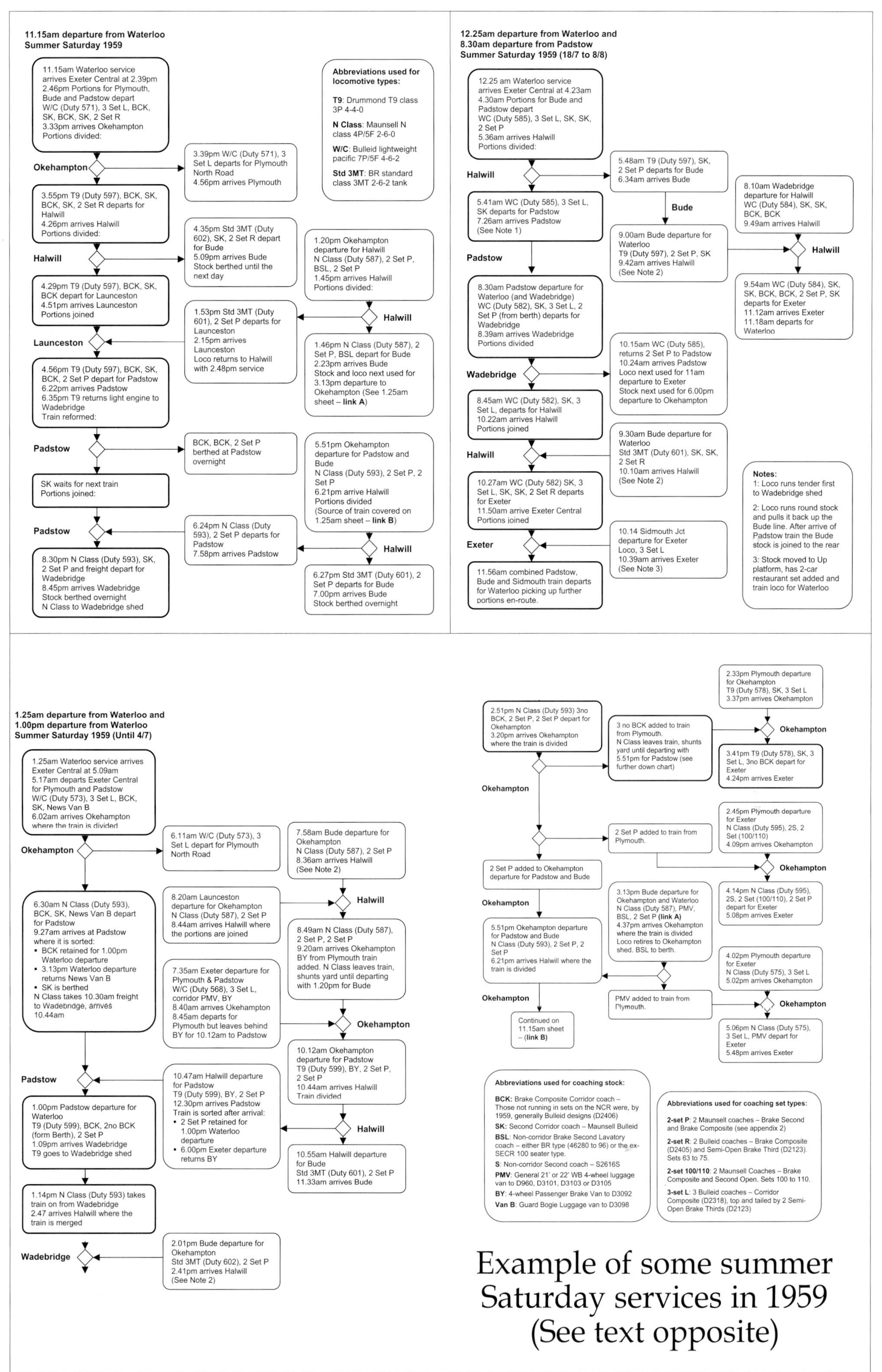
11.15am departure from Waterloo
Summer Saturday 1959
11.15am Waterloo service arrives Exeter Central at 2.39pm 2.46pm Portions for Plymouth, Bude and Padstow depart W/C (Duty 571), 3 Set L, BCK, SK, BCK, SK, 2 Set R 3.33pm arrives Okehampton Portions divided:
Okehampton
3.39pm W/C (Duty 571), 3 Set L departs for Plymouth North Road 4.56pm arrives Plymouth
3.55pm T9 (Duty 597), BCK, SK, BCK, SK, 2 Set R departs for Halwill 4.26pm arrives Halwill Portions divided:
Halwill
4.35pm Std 3MT (Duty 602), SK, 2 Set R depart for Bude 5.09pm arrives Bude Stock berthed until the next day
4.29pm T9 (Duty 597), BCK, SK, BCK depart for Launceston 4.51pm arrives Launceston Portions joined
1.53pm Std 3MT (Duty 601), 2 Set P departs for Launceston 2.15pm arrives Launceston Loco returns to Halwill with 2.48pm service
Launceston
4.56pm T9 (Duty 597), BCK, SK, BCK, 2 Set P depart for Padstow 6.22pm arrives Padstow 6.35pm T9 returns light engine to Wadebridge Train reformed:
Padstow
BCK, BCK, 2 Set P berthed at Padstow overnight
SK waits for next train Portions joined:
Padstow
6.24pm N Class (Duty 593), 2 Set P departs for Padstow 7.58pm arrives Padstow
8.30pm N Class (Duty 593), SK, 2 Set P and freight depart for Wadebridge 8.45pm arrives Wadebridge Stock berthed overnight N Class to Wadebridge shed
Abbreviations used for locomotive types:
T9: Drummond T9 class 3P 4-4-0
N Class: Maunsell N class 4P/5F 2-6-0
W/C: Bulleid lightweight pacific 7P/5F 4-6-2
Std 3MT: BR standard class 3MT 2-6-2 tank
1.20pm Okehampton departure for Halwill N Class (Duty 587), 2 Set P, BSL, 2 Set P 1.45pm arrives Halwill Portions divided:
Halwill
1.46pm N Class (Duty 587), 2 Set P, BSL depart for Bude 2.23pm arrives Bude Stock and loco next used for 3.13pm departure to Okehampton (See 1.25am sheet – link A)
5.51pm Okehampton departure for Padstow and Bude N Class (Duty 593), 2 Set P, 2 Set P 6.21pm arrive Halwill Portions divided (Source of train covered on 1.25am sheet – link B)
Halwill
6.27pm Std 3MT (Duty 601), 2 Set P departs for Bude 7.00pm arrives Bude Stock berthed overnight
12.25am departure from Waterloo and 8.30am departure from Padstow
Summer Saturday 1959 (18/7 to 8/8)
12.25 am Waterloo service arrives Exeter Central at 4.23am 4.30am Portions for Bude and Padstow depart WC (Duty 585), 3 Set L, SK, SK, 2 Set P 5.36am arrives Halwill Portions divided:
Halwill
5.48am T9 (Duty 597), SK, 2 Set P departs for Bude 6.34am arrives Bude
5.41am WC (Duty 585), 3 Set L, SK departs for Padstow 7.26am arrives Padstow (See Note 1)
Bude
9.00am Bude departure for Waterloo T9 (Duty 597), 2 Set P, SK 9.42am arrives Halwill (See Note 2)
8.10am Wadebridge departure for Halwill WC (Duty 584), SK, SK, BCK, BCK 9.49am arrives Halwill
Halwill
9.54am WC (Duty 584), SK, SK, BCK, BCK, 2 Set P, SK departs for Exeter 11.12am arrives Exeter 11.18am departs for Waterloo
Padstow
8.30am Padstow departure for Waterloo (and Wadebridge) WC (Duty 582), SK, 3 Set L, 2 Set P (from berth) departs for Wadebridge 8.39am arrives Wadebridge Portions divided
10.15am WC (Duty 585), returns 2 Set P to Padstow 10.24am arrives Padstow Loco next used for 11am departure to Exeter Stock next used for 6.00pm departure to Okehampton
Wadebridge
8.45am WC (Duty 582), SK, 3 Set L, departs for Halwill 10.22am arrives Halwill Portions joined
9.30am Bude departure for Waterloo Std 3MT (Duty 601), SK, SK, 2 Set R 10.10am arrives Halwill (See Note 2)
Halwill
10.27am WC (Duty 582) SK, 3 Set L, SK, SK, 2 Set R departs for Exeter 11.50am arrives Exeter Central Portions joined
10.14 Sidmouth Jct departure for Exeter Loco, 3 Set L 10.39am arrives Exeter (See Note 3)
Exeter
11.56am combined Padstow, Bude and Sidmouth train departs for Waterloo picking up further portions en-route.
Notes:
1: Loco runs tender first to Wadebridge shed
2: Loco runs round stock and pulls it back up the Bude line. After arrive of Padstow train the Bude stock is joined to the rear
3: Stock moved to Up platform, has 2-car restaurant set added and train loco for Waterloo
1.25am departure from Waterloo and 1.00pm departure from Waterloo
Summer Saturday 1959 (Until 4/7)
1.25am Waterloo service arrives Exeter Central at 5.09am 5.17am departs Exeter Central for Plymouth and Padstow W/C (Duty 573), 3 Set L, BCK, SK, News Van B 6.02am arrives Okehampton where the train is divided
Okehampton
6.11am W/C (Duty 573), 3 Set L depart for Plymouth North Road
7.58am Bude departure for Okehampton N Class (Duty 587), 2 Set P 8.36am arrives Halwill (See Note 2)
Halwill
6.30am N Class (Duty 593), BCK, SK, News Van B depart for Padstow 9.27am arrives at Padstow where it is sorted:
• BCK retained for 1.00pm Waterloo departure
• 3.13pm Waterloo departure returns News Van B
• SK is berthed
N Class takes 10.30am freight to Wadebridge, arrives 10.44am
8.20am Launceston departure for Okehampton N Class (Duty 587), 2 Set P 8.44am arrives Halwill where the portions are joined
8.49am N Class (Duty 587), 2 Set P, 2 Set P 9.20am arrives Okehampton BY from Plymouth train added. N Class leaves train, shunts yard until departing with 1.20pm for Bude
7.35am Exeter departure for Plymouth & Padstow W/C (Duty 568), 3 Set L, corridor PMV, BY 8.40am arrives Okehampton 8.45am departs for Plymouth but leaves behind BY for 10.12am to Padstow
Okehampton
10.12am Okehampton departure for Padstow T9 (Duty 599), BY, 2 Set P, 2 Set P 10.44am arrives Halwill Train divided
Padstow
10.47am Halwill departure for Padstow T9 (Duty 599), BY, 2 Set P 12.30pm arrives Padstow Train is sorted after arrival:
• 2 Set P retained for 1.00pm Waterloo departure
• 6.00pm Exeter departure returns BY
Halwill
1.00pm Padstow departure for Waterloo T9 (Duty 599), BCK, 2no BCK (form Berth), 2 Set P 1.09pm arrives Wadebridge T9 goes to Wadebridge shed
10.55am Halwill departure for Bude Std 3MT (Duty 601), 2 Set P 11.33am arrives Bude
1.14pm N Class (Duty 593) takes train on from Wadebridge 2.47 arrives Halwill where the train is merged
Wadebridge
2.01pm Bude departure for Okehampton Std 3MT (Duty 602), 2 Set P 2.41pm arrives Halwill (See Note 2)
2.51pm N Class (Duty 593) 3no BCK, 2 Set P, 2 Set P depart for Okehampton 3.20pm arrives Okehampton where the train is divided
3 no BCK added to train from Plymouth. N Class leaves train, shunts yard until departing with 5.51pm for Padstow (see further down chart)
2.33pm Plymouth departure for Okehampton T9 (Duty 578), SK, 3 Set L 3.37pm arrives Okehampton
Okehampton
3.41pm T9 (Duty 578), SK, 3 Set L, 3no BCK depart for Exeter 4.24pm arrives Exeter
Okehampton
2.45pm Plymouth departure for Exeter N Class (Duty 595), 2S, 2 Set (100/110) 4.09pm arrives Okehampton
2 Set P added to train from Plymouth.
2 Set P added to Okehampton departure for Padstow and Bude
Okehampton
Okehampton
3.13pm Bude departure for Okehampton and Waterloo N Class (Duty 587), PMV, BSL, 2 Set P (link A) 4.37pm arrives Okehampton where the train is divided Loco retires to Okehampton shed. BSL to berth.
4.14pm N Class (Duty 595), 2S, 2 Set (100/110), 2 Set P depart for Exeter 5.08pm arrives Exeter
5.51pm Okehampton departure for Padstow and Bude N Class (Duty 593), 2 Set P, 2 Set P 6.21pm arrives Halwill where the train is divided
4.02pm Plymouth departure for Exeter N Class (Duty 575), 3 Set L 5.02pm arrives Okehampton
Okehampton
PMV added to train from Plymouth.
Okehampton
Continued on 11.15am sheet – (link B)
5.06pm N Class (Duty 575), 3 Set L, PMV depart for Exeter 5.48pm arrives Exeter
Abbreviations used for coaching stock:
BCK: Brake Composite Corridor coach – Those not running in sets on the NCR were, by 1959, generally Bulleid designs (D2406)
SK: Second Corridor coach – Maunsell Bulleid
BSL: Non-corridor Brake Second Lavatory coach – either BR type (46280 to 96) or the ex-SECR 100 seater type.
S: Non-corridor Second coach – S2616S
PMV: General 21' or 22' WB 4-wheel luggage van to D960, D3101, D3103 or D3105
BY: 4-wheel Passenger Brake Van to D3092
Van B: Guard Bogie Luggage van to D3098
Abbreviations used for coaching set types:
2-set P: 2 Maunsell coaches – Brake Second and Brake Composite (see appendix 2)
2-set R: 2 Bulleid coaches – Brake Composite (D2405) and Semi-Open Brake Third (D2123). Sets 63 to 75.
2-set 100/110: 2 Maunsell Coaches – Brake Composite and Second Open. Sets 100 to 110.
3-set L: 3 Bulleid coaches – Corridor Composite (D2318), top and tailed by 2 Semi-Open Brake Thirds (D2123)

Example of some summer Saturday services in 1959 (See text opposite)

West Country Class No. 34030 Watersmeet drifts down from Meldon under bridge No. 610 and onto Okehampton with duty 582 from Wadebridge. The train comprises two Maunsell 2-set Ps - one from Bude and one from Padstow. Photo is pre-August 1961 as the tender has not yet been cut-down. R. C. Riley, www.transporttreasury.co.uk

established in the town for 21 years. The GWR broad gauge line between Plymouth and Tavistock had opened in 1859 and this had been extended to Launceston, via Lydford, by 1865. The extension of the LSWR's own line from Exeter to Okehampton reached Lydford in 1874 and it was a further 16 years before the LSWR had its own dedicated line into Plymouth. This meant that between 1874 and 1890 LSWR standard gauge trains continued their journey from Lydford to Plymouth (Devonport) via the now dual-gauge GWR line. Of the Devonport–Waterloo trains only two, the 10.20am and 2.55pm, were reasonably fast. Downwards, the 11.00am and 2.30pm reached Okehampton in five hours and, via connecting trains along the NCR, brought Launceston to about seven hours from the capital.

Five trains ran in each direction between Okehampton and Launceston, but Holsworthy did have one departing at 12 noon (Waterloo arr. 7.55) and from Okehampton (off the 5.50am Waterloo) arriving at 2.03pm. The 8.24am Okehampton originally ran only on the last Wednesday in each month for Launceston Cattle Market, but reverted to a goods train until 1890. The 9.00am from Waterloo caught up a 6.25am slow train at Crediton and exchanged portions. The 9.00 went on to Devonport and the 6.25 to Torrington. This fulfilled the 'Parliamentary' requirement of an all stations service for Third Class passengers at 1d per mile. Cheap fares were sold for Launceston Pannier Market on Saturdays (5/- from Exeter, 2/3d from Holsworthy and 1/0d from Ashwater). It was 5/- to Exeter for the Friday market. Third Class ordinary fares from Waterloo were 36/7d and First Class 70/3d.

Of consequence for the future of the North Cornwall was the horse coach which left Padstow (The Ship Hotel) at 8.25am and ran via Camelford (11.20am) to connect with the 1.50pm train from Launceston. Downwards a coach was waiting at Launceston station for passengers from the 9.00am Waterloo at 4.00pm, leaving for Padstow at 4.15pm. From 1875 the 'Vivid' coach had run from Launceston GWR to St Columb, but from 1881 the North Cornwall Coach Co's 'Pioneer' took over. As the North Cornwall Railway steadily extended westward the NCC Co's connections retreated until they ran only from Wadebridge to Haloon (St Columb Road GWR) and to Newquay, Atlantic Hotel. The LSWR opened a receiving office in Broad Street, Launceston in 1885. The GWR was running a horse bus from Bodmin Road to Padstow in the early 1880s. Hidden in the timetables were useful changes at Halwill and Okehampton which, in time, stimulated local communication across Devon, particularly to the Markets. Special rates were available to the 'Regrators' or 'higglers' who collected dairy products such as butter from outlying farms, to sell at the market. In 1888 a local train actually ran through from Holsworthy at 1.15pm, arriving at Launceston at 2.30pm.

The pattern of ordinary services established in the late 1880s lasted until the 1966 closures, except for connections from the early morning Waterloo trains, which no longer applied post-1914; there was also a better spread of the afternoon trains from the capital at 1.00pm and 3.00pm, with consequent changes in the west.

Principal passenger services : 1886							
		am	am	pm	pm	pm	
Launceston	Dep	7.50	10.30	1.50	2.50	6.45	
Okehampton	Arr	8.54	11.32	2.45	3.56	7.51	
Exeter	*Arr*	*9.59*	*12.32*	*4.21*	*5.10*	*9.23*	
Waterloo	*Arr*	*2.34*	*5.20*	*10.09*	*10.09*	*-*	
		am	am	am	am	am	pm
Waterloo	*Dep*	-	-	-	*9.00*	*11.00*	*2.30*
Exeter	*Dep*	*7.15*	*8.50*	-	*1.48*	*3.20*	*6.50*
Okehampton	Dep	8.24	10.02	11.50	2.54	4.25	8.30
Launceston	Arr	9.26	11.09	1.01	4.00	5.25	9.35

Extension to Delabole 1893

As described in Chapter 2 the Launceston extension to Delabole opened in three relatively closely timed stages; Tresmeer (28 July 1892), Camelford (14 August 1893) and Delabole (18 October 1893). Delabole thus became the western terminus of the North Cornwall until mid 1895. To permit the '395' 0-6-0s and the new 'Jubilee' 0-4-2s to run the right way round to Launceston and Okehampton it was provided with a turntable.

There were still five trains each way weekdays and, from 1893, one on Sunday evenings starting from Camelford at 5.40pm, also carrying mail. Most Okehampton connections were reasonably smart, but passengers off the 3.00pm Waterloo were subjected to a 35 minute wait. At first the 3.00pm train went to Delabole (arrive 10.43pm) but it was cut back to Tresmeer in 1894, and then only on Fridays for the Regrators, the coaches going back empty to Launceston. Holsworthy continued to have branch trains from Halwill Junction. Due to the unconsolidated track, trains at first were restricted to 25mph Launceston/ Tresmeer and 20mph Tresmeer/ Delabole.

In the summer period of 1894 the 8.25am from Okehampton, which had reverted to a goods train until 1890, was run as a passenger (mixed if required) running to Delabole. Turning round between 10.26 and 11.45am, it arrived back at 3.14pm. With variations, this purely local service appeared to be dictated by the needs of Launceston Market. There had been a gratifying increase in passenger traffic since 1890, with Launceston's receipts especially good. Another evening train was put on from Okehampton at 6.00pm, to connect with the re-timed 1.00pm from Waterloo. After arriving at Delabole 7.55pm, it too returned, this time running through to Exeter Queen Street to arrive at 11.20pm.

In addition to these extra services, the summer 1894 timetable contained the germ of the future holiday expresses. The 4.07pm from Okehampton off the 11.00am ('Alexandra') from Waterloo, missed out Ashbury, Ashwater, Tower Hill and Egloskerry, arriving at Delabole at 5.46pm compared with 6.25pm the previous winter. This missing out of stations improved the London to Delabole time from 7 hours 25 minutes to 6 hours 46 minutes. Hardly an 'express' at an average speed of 30mph, it of course had to slow down at the 'missed' stations to exchange single line staffs. A similar up train left Delabole at 1.45pm connecting to Waterloo (8.16pm).

To Wadebridge 1895

Wadebridge had been host to trains arriving from Bodmin (later named Bodmin North) since 4th July 1834. At first these were run by the Bodmin and Wadebridge Railway Company but in 1847 the LSWR took control of the line. This line remained detached from any other until 3rd September 1888 when the Great Western extended its standard gauge branch from Bodmin (later named Bodmin General) to connect to the Bodmin and Wadebridge at Boscarne Junction. By 1894 seven trains each way, including two mixed, were plying from the stations at Bodmin to Wadebridge.

North Cornwall extension to Wadebridge opened formally on the 1st June 1895 and finally the LSWR could promote direct services to Exeter and on to London. Upon opening the basic five trains each way service was extended from the previous Delabole terminus through to Wadebridge. Another down train was put on, leaving Launceston at 8.23am. It also carried the mails off the early goods train from Okehampton. Many years later it actually fitted the end timings of the 1.30am Waterloo Newspaper train.

The Waterloo 11.00am connection, the 4.07pm from Okehampton, now continued during the winter of 1895/ 96 to miss out some of the wayside stations, but passengers from east of Okehampton could be set down at Ashbury, Ashwater and Otterham. The 1.20pm from Wadebridge called only at Port Isaac Road, Delabole, Camelford, Launceston and Halwill Junction. It would take up London passengers at St Kew, and for Exeter and beyond at Otterham. Holsworthy continued to be served by branch trains from Halwill Junction, but the 6.06pm from Okehampton (off the 1.00pm Waterloo) had portions for both Wadebridge and Holsworthy. The mail was taken upwards on the 2.40pm from Wadebridge and the evening train from

The multi-portioned ACE running late past Ashbury in May 1962 behind Pacific No. 34065 *Hurricane*. L. R. Freeman, www.transporttreasury.co.uk

Launceston. The latter also ran on Sundays, but still from Camelford. The down mail on Sundays came on a goods train leaving Okehampton at 4.38am.

Noteworthy, in view of the eventual importance of meat traffic, was a statement in the 'Working Book' that the 6.05pm from Wadebridge 'will have a vacuum meat van attached for conveyance on the London goods'. Wadebridge, in 1895, was quite inadequate for the new service, the GWR trains from Bodmin, and from that year the restored service from Bodmin LSWR. As we have seen in Chapter 2, it was not until 1899 that the single platform was supplemented by a new island platform.

Passenger Services : November 1895								
		am	am	am	am	am	pm	pm
Waterloo	*Dep*	-	-	*5.50*	*9.00*	*11.00*	*1.00*	*3.00*
Exeter (Q St)	*Dep*	-	*9.05*	*10.48*	*1.45*	*3.10*	*5.15*	*6.38*
Okehampton	Dep	-	10.19	12.13	3.03	4.07	6.06	8.34
Launceston	Dep	8.23	11.22	1.12	4.03	4.56	7.17	9.35(a)
Wadebridge	Arr	9.41	12.37	2.32	5.22	5.59	8.36	
		am	am	am	pm	pm	pm	
Wadebridge	Dep	7.05	9.18	10.20	1.20	2.40	6.05	
Launceston	Dep	8.25	10.43	11.45	2.25	4.02	7.20	
Okehampton	Dep	9.41	12.02	1.05	3.29	5.14	8.30	
Exeter (Q St)	*Dep*	*10.25*	*12.45*	*2.10*	*4.15*	*6.00*	*9.28*	
Waterloo	*Arr*	*2.33*	*5.00*	*7.52*	*8.14*	*10.15*	-	

a: Extended to Tresmeer (arr 9.54pm) on Fridays b: Starts from Camelford 5.59pm

To Padstow 1899

Unlike Bude, opened the year before, the facilities at Padstow were simple. Engines were provided and serviced at the engine shed at Wadebridge. Padstow was effectively an outpost of Wadebridge and this resulted in light engine running between the two stations and loose coupled wagons and a brake van being tacked on to passenger vehicles to form 'mixed' trains. With trains extended off the North Cornwall line, and one of two locals from and to Bodmin, up to a dozen movements a day traversed the 5¾ mile extension. The mixed trains were restricted to 25mph and spent 15 minutes on their journey compared with 10 for normal passenger trains. Since the 1889 Regulating Act there were fewer 'mixed' workings to be found, and those apparently mixed trains seen with additional vehicles on the North Cornwall proper (and elsewhere) might be through vacuum braked stock with some of them, at least, 'piped'.

There were seven down North Cornwall trains terminating at Padstow in the summer of 1899, the usual 'stoppers' but one limited to calls only at Halwill Junction, Ashwater, Launceston, Camelford, St Kew Highway and Wadebridge. Again, the previous 4.07pm off Okehampton, connecting from the 11.00am Waterloo, with arrival at Padstow at 6.20pm, would stop specially at Ashbury for passengers off the 11.00am express, and at Tresmeer on Saturdays. In this season the last train no longer ran beyond Launceston (arrive 9.28pm). The balancing up limited-stop train – it could hardly be called an express – was the 1.04pm from Padstow. Port Isaac Road had a stop, but St Kew's for London passengers only. Camelford, Launceston, Ashwater and Halwill followed but only on Saturdays for Otterham and Tresmeer. With the change at Okehampton, total time elapsed was 7 hours 15 minutes. Compare this with the 10.25 am SO 'ACE' Padstow to Waterloo through train in 1938, which took 6 hours 17 minutes including a run non-stop from Launceston to Exeter St Davids.

For many years national newspapers, which then had limited circulation in the west country, were loaded on the 6.10am Weymouth and Exeter train, delivered some time during the afternoon. The widely read 'Western Morning News' printed in Plymouth, travelled by goods train at first. Later the LSWR ran a special to Exeter in the night hours, transferring bundles at Okehampton (later at Yeoford or Bow) to the first down goods to Launceston.

The first through coach was arranged by Superintendent of the Line Sam Fay (afterwards the Great Central General Manager; Sir Sam from 1912) to run in the 1.00pm Waterloo in the winter of 1901/2. Probably one of the 1898 tri-composites with lavatory accommodation, it returned on the

O2 0-4-4T No. 30236 waits at Wadebridge with a 2-Set P number 29 comprising a Maunsell Brake Second 2788 and Brake Composite 6567 for Bodmin North, in August 1958. A. E. Bennett, www.transporttreasury.co.uk

8.54am from Padstow (Waterloo 5.20pm). Then it was taken off, but with pressure from the North Cornwall Board was restored in September 1904, this time in the 11.00am from Waterloo, as an 'experiment' until Christmas. The success of the tourist traffic induced the LSWR to provide not just through coaches but, from 1900, a complete through train, Waterloo to Bude and Padstow; from 1907 it had a restaurant car. These were the forerunners of the 'Atlantic Coast Express' which is covered in Chapter 5.

Meanwhile the stopping trains plodded across Devon and Cornwall taking two hours for the 62¼ miles from Okehampton to Padstow. Nearly all the trains were, by 1905, dividing and attaching a Bude portion at Halwill Junction. Although this operation could take up to twelve minutes in the up direction, uncoupling for Bude and attaching the local tank did not take as long. Okehampton was always under criticism – the platforms were 'too low' and up connections took too long. Provision of an up bay was refused by the LSWR. Right up until 1964, passengers had to hang about while their empty North Cornwall train was shunted out the way of the up Plymouth arrival. Although there was a down bay there never was but the barest shelter on that side.

The then fashionable railmotor made its appearance at Wadebridge in 1906. Two were allocated to the Bodmin – Wadebridge services, though in 1909 three of these were extended through to Padstow during the day. Apart from delivery and overhaul journeys their lack of power meant there was no question of them running on the steep gradients of the North Cornwall to Halwill!

In summer the 1.00pm Waterloo included a through coach each for Padstow and Bude, as did the 8.20am from Padstow (Bude 9.26am). Reasonable connections were available at Halwill Junction, morning and evening, between Bude/Padstow trains right up to 1914. Several locals ran to and from Bude specially for this in July and August, and an 8.00pm from Padstow train connected at Okehampton for the Plymouth line. Thus in the summer of 1914 seven trains crossed North Cornwall each way, though the last down train terminated at Launceston. The Sunday service continued to be out of balance, there being only the evening mail train from Camelford in 1909 (but from Launceston in 1914) to Okehampton, thence to Exeter Queen Street.

So far we have looked mainly at the development of the passenger train services, with occasional mention made of the goods and mixed trains. It is useful therefore to include a summary of the winter 1911/12 working timetable to see how all the separate services interacted. Further working timetables for other periods are included within the Appendices. Note that the summary misses out many of the intermediate station stops.

The War Years

The period up to the First World War had seen the North Cornwall line built and train services established and grown. On the 4 August 1914 Britain declared war on Germany and the Great War began. Despite the remoteness of Cornwall we shall see that the war had an impact on the North Cornwall and LSWR which lasted beyond the end of the conflict on 11 November 1918. Alas 'the war to end all wars' didn't and, from 3 September 1939, the Southern Railway was to see its early hopes of long term recovery and growth in tourism dashed. The Second World War also had a great effect on the railways in the region. By the end of the war on the 8 May 1945 even the West of England lines were run down and exhausted. The dramatic impact of two wars in close succession on the railways was a significant factor in seeing them nationalised on 1 January 1948.

Local Services in World War One

When war was declared trains continued to run in 1915 as they had in 1914, apart from cancellations due to troop movements. In 1916 and 1917 withdrawal of engines for Government service and provision for extra cattle trains put paid to the summer extras and some locals on the Bude branch. Still, a basic five trains each way plied between Okehampton and Padstow, the last only to Launceston. The railmotors at Wadebridge were withdrawn leaving only three extra passenger trains and two mixed, each way to Padstow in April 1917. The limited Sunday service ceased from January 1917. Further reductions in May 1918 included the 1.12pm from Okehampton (from the 5.50am Waterloo) and some much later arrivals ensued at Waterloo for up trains from the west. In June 1919, for example, the 2.15pm Padstow passengers, having arrived at

Passenger Services : Summer 1899 – Weekdays

		am	am	am	am	am	am	pm	pm
Waterloo	*Dep*	-	-	-	*5.50*	*9.15*	*11.00*	*1.00*	*3.00*
Okehampton	Dep	-	8.15	10.19	12.13	2.43	4.07	6.10	8.37
Launceston	Dep	7.48	9.21	11.17	1.08	3.38	4.56	7.19	9.28
Padstow	Arr	9.31	10.55	12.44	2.45	5.07	6.20	8.43	-
NB The Sunday up mail train continued to start from Camelford									
		am	am	am	pm	pm	pm		
Padstow	Dep	6.50	8.54	10.20	1.04	2.1	5.40		
Launceston	Dep	8.25	10.42	11.53	2.25	4.02	7.20		
Okehampton	Arr	9.21	11.38	12.47	3.13	4.57	8.14		
Waterloo	*Arr*	*2.33*	*4.40*	*7.52*	*8.16*	*10.15*	-		

		am	am	pm	pm	pm
Okehampton	dep	-	10.04	1.08	3.47	7.45
Launceston	arr	7.45(d)	11.02	2.05	4.51	8.38
Padstow	arr	9.01	12.22	-	6.06	9.55
Padstow	dep	8.35	12.38	2.20	3.00	5.22
Launceston	dep	10.06	2.06	3.52	4.30	6.55
Okehampton	arr	11.08	3.04	5.11	5.26	7.56

Working Timetable Winter Down 1911/12		am	am	am	am	am (MX)	am	am	am # @	am	am (as req)
Waterloo	Dep	-	-	-	-	-	-	-	-	-	-
Exeter (Queen St)	Dep	-	-	12.35	-	-	-	-	5.27	-	5.50
Okehampton	Dep	-	-	3.15	-	6.00	-	-	7.00	-	9.00
Launceston	Dep	-	-	5.58	-	7.57	8.17	-	9.47	-	10.04
Wadebridge	Dep	6.10	7.15	7.44	8.40	-	9.26	9.32	12.54	11.40	-
Padstow	Arr	6.19	7.24	-	8.52	-	-	9.46	-	11.52	-
Type		Light Engine	Pass + Mail	Mail + Goods	Rail motor	Goods	Pass	Mixed	Goods	Rail motor	Cattle (Empty)

Mondays excepted this goods service originated in Exeter at 5.27 and stopped at all stations, with the exception of Ashbury, en-route to Wadebridge. The Mondays only service included an additional pickup at Ashbury but made up the time by reaching Egloskerry.
@ Fridays only an additional engine and brakevan left Launceston at 8.27 and arrived in Otterham at 8.56.

Down 1911/12: Cont		am	am	pm	pm	pm	am	pm	pm	pm (FO)	pm (SuO)
Waterloo	Dep	-	6.10	-	-	-	11.00	1.00	3.30	-	-
Exeter (Queen St)	Dep	8.48	10.17	-	-	-	2.36	5.18	7.00	-	-
Okehampton	Dep	10.10	11.07	-	-	-	3.47	6.12	8.40	-	4.55
Launceston	Dep	11.05	12.10	-	-	-	4.48	7.10	9.32	9.37	6.50
Tresmeer	Arr									9.54	
Camelford	Arr										7.33
Wadebridge	Dep	12.12	1.24	2.40	3.35	4.57	6.01	8.16	-	-	-
Padstow	Arr	12.21	1.33	2.54	3.47	5.06	6.10	8.25	-	-	-
Type		Pass	Pass	Mixed	Rail motor	Pass	Pass	Pass	Pass	Pass	Mail + Goods

Working Timetable Winter Up 1911/12		am	am (FO)#	am	am	am (MX)	am	am	am	pm	pm (as req)
Padstow	Dep	6.48		8.20	9.12		10.30		11.58	12.50	
Wadebridge	Dep	6.59		8.36	9.24		10.44	11.20	12.10	1.03	
Otterham	Dep		9.01								
Launceston	Dep	8.10	9.27	9.46		10.10		4.13		2.14	2.30
Okehampton	Dep	9.34		10.56		1.37		6.18		3.31	4.29
Exeter (Queen St)	Dep	10.17		12.00				8.39		4.15	5.23
Waterloo	Arr	1.47		3.15						8.07	
Type		Pass	Vans	Pass	Rail motor	Goods	Mixed	Goods	Rail motor	Pass	Cattle

Loco and brake van provided by the Friday only 8.27am from Launceston. The vans were then attached at Launceston to the 8.20am from Padstow

Up 1911/12: Cont		pm	pm (as req)	pm	pm	pm @	pm	pm	pm	pm (FO)	pm (SuO)
Padstow	Dep	2.25		3.20	3.55		5.50	8.00	8.50		
Wadebridge	Dep	2.42	3.00	3.34	4.07	4.25	6.02	8.09	8.59		
Camelford	Dep										6.30
Tresmeer	Dep									10.00	
Launceston	Dep	3.52	4.47			6.30	7.13			10.15	7.09
Okehampton	Dep	5.13				7.49	8.31				8.30
Exeter (Queen St)	Dep	6.02					9.27				9.28
Waterloo	Arr	10.34									
Type		Pass	Cattle	Mixed	Rail motor	Goods	Pass	Pass	Light Engine	Empty Pass	Pass + Mail

@ load not to exceed 20 vehicles between Wadebridge and Camelford and 23 beyond. A heavy brakevan was provided at the rear.

A light load for N Class No. 31855 approaching Maddaford Moor Halt over the high ground at East Bowerland on Saturday 11th July 1964 with the 5.51pm Okehampton to Wadebridge. In 1960 an additional 2-Set R was made up (76) with the first of the loose Bulleid Brake Composite (6713) to Diagram 2406 and a Semi Open Brake Third to Diagram 2125 from a former BRCW 3-set (4282). R. A. Lumber.

Okehampton at 4.47pm, had to wait until the Plymouth train came in at 5.21, eventually getting to Waterloo at 11.24pm - a nine hour journey, some two hours longer than pre-war! Of local interest, the 7.38am from Launceston stopped at the one coach platform at Meldon Quarry to 'take up wives of company servants gong to Okehampton'. The 3.00pm from Waterloo made connection at Yeoford Junction rather than Okehampton in 1918 and 1919, and its Bude connection from Halwill ceased to run. It was the summer of 1921 before restorations could be made, but the rather lavish service the LSWR had provided for its rural passengers and purely local tourism to 1914, never really returned.

Between the Wars 1919-1939

Thinner fare greeted locals in North Cornwall for the summer of 1919, a minimal service in fact; from Padstow at 8.10am, 12.30pm, 2.15 and 5.30pm, from Okehampton at 10.10am, 4.08pm and 6.38pm. The 8.08am from Launceston was mixed from Wadebridge to Padstow and took nearly two hours for the 36 mile journey. Launceston retained its early morning (Up) and late evening (Down) trains to Okehampton. They were in the hands of aging locos, Beattie 4-4-0s and Adams '460' class bearing the main burden.

By the summer of 1924 the through holiday trains were back, the new Southern Railway steadily restoring them as engine power and rolling stock permitted. Locally, the midday (Exeter) Okehampton to Launceston/Bude train was running again. This became important by the end of the decade as it also included vans for return loading. From 1927 the trains ran separately. The 2.45pm from Padstow was also a 'Perishable', as it was termed, and now ran through to Exeter Queen St where some vans were transferred to the 7.30pm fast goods train to Nine Elms, others going via Templecombe to the Midlands. As the herring business picked up again at Padstow, the 2.45pm could become heavily loaded at times. The summer of 1924 saw a through Brake Composite (1st/3rd Class) in the 3.00pm from Waterloo going through to Padstow, the Okehampton local train being extended beyond Launceston for this purpose. It is likely to have returned on the 8.20am from Padstow, the next morning. These extra summer period through coaches which graced local services were typical of LSWR and SR concern for passengers, and inconceivable in today's fixed train formations.

Since the demise of the railmotors in 1917, locals from Wadebridge to Padstow were in the hands of the surviving Adams 4-4-2Ts, some running to and from Bodmin, as before. There were four of these supplementing the North Cornwall trains with one mixed, and thus likely to take cattle to and from Wadebridge Market. Most cattle wagons were vacuum braked, and in those days a train did have to be officially designated 'mixed' to convey them. Passengers would have to wait at a rural stop, like Tresmeer, while the engine trundled off to the cattle dock to fetch and attach a wagon deemed to be urgent.

While the 3.00pm from Waterloo gave a connection right through to Padstow in 1927, the 1.00pm connection from Okehampton served only Bude. No through coaches were included, as before, but the 8.35am from Padstow (9.42am Bude) and the 11.00am from Waterloo (both named the 'Atlantic Coast Express' the previous year) now had them summer and winter. When the through train ran in the summer the name was transferred to it. In 1928 the North Cornwall saw its first Sunday train since 1917 but it was an excursion from Padstow to Exeter; 'well filled' with passengers, as the local newspaper put it. Even if a Sunday train service had been instituted in the 1920s it would have been unsustainable. No shops or places of entertainment were open, after all. In the eyes of the predominantly Methodist population, travelling on the Sabbath was not to be encouraged in any event. However, times were changing as the above report shows. World War Two brought Launceston a regular timetable service (it was even extended to Delabole for one summer in 1953) but it would have still been unremunerative to run trains in the thinly populated areas between Launceston and Wadebridge.

While the five basic services underlaid the North Cornwall's passenger service all through the 1930s, they were modified in the summer months in timings, loads and even destinations, by the presence of the through trains from and to Waterloo. This was especially so on Saturdays when this long, attenuated route could be close to capacity. Although crossing loops were reasonably well placed, any out of course running spelt trouble. Southern signalmen knew their trade and the phones would be hot as, for instance, they regulated late runners past the local goods and 'Perishables' patiently waiting at the starting signals. The Padstow station master not only had his Waterloos and locals, but fish trains as well to contend with from September. The Wadebridge shed foreman had to provide the 4-4-0s, some in pairs, and take care of Exmouth Junction engines and his own at the end of the day, while the Halwill staff put the through trains together, or divided them for Bude and Padstow. Extracts from the 1933 summer Working Timetable are included in Appendix 3.

The 10.00am from Okehampton was one of the trains with limited loading to keep it on time through North Cornwall as the holiday trains passed it at Halwill, Launceston, Delabole and St Kew. The 2.20 up from Padstow was crossing the down trains at St Kew, Port Isaac Road, Otterham, Launceston and Halwill. On Saturdays the last down train was extended to Delabole, Waterloo passengers changing at Halwill from a through coach to Bude. The stopping trains which normally took the 'Atlantic Coast Express' through coaches to Padstow only served up to Okehampton on Saturdays. With a mixture of holiday trains and local trains, some with through coaches attached, local passengers had to be aware of missed stops, like Egloskerry or Tower Hill. Luckily for them the station staff were adept at calling out such detail, loudly and in dialect perhaps, but at least the natives could understand, even if the poor Londoners might not!

Local Passenger Services in World War Two

As August 1939 wore on the unsettling imminence of war crept over the country. The winter timetable due to commence on 25 September would have lasted until 30 May 1940. During August a through excursion from Padstow (dep. 9.45am) to Bude (12 noon), returning to Padstow quite late at 10.56pm, ran each Sunday. The Bude line was now getting three services each way on Sundays in each summer (until 10 September that year). The situation became unreal as people cancelled holidays. Reservists were being recalled to their depots and barracks and Government plans to evacuate Britain's big cities were being activated. Not waiting for a reply to the ultimatum to Hitler over the invasion of Poland, the evacuation of school children started from London on 31 August and was completed by the day War started on 3 September. Many main line services and summer extras were cancelled, the stock diverted to evacuation specials. Waterloo was avoided as it was regarded as inevitable that air attacks would ensue, the subsequent congestion in central London making it impossible to use the station. The children (and teachers) were instead brought by bus and Underground to Vauxhall and Wimbledon. Destinations in North Cornwall were Bude, Launceston, Camelford and Wadebridge and Southern National and local operators' coaches distributed the evacuees to the country areas. The expected bombing did not materialise then, as it turned out, but it did in 1940 and 1941, and again in 1944.

The SR continued the summer timetable until 10 September, but with many cancellations. A drastically curtailed and decelerated service was then instituted but, under pressure, the company restored many trains on Monday 18th. Another timetable was issued from 16 October, termed 'Emergency Passenger Services'; it was given more publicity but revised again twelve days later on the 28th! The 1.00pm Waterloo ceased but its connection (the 5.50pm to Padstow/

On 28th August 1960 the 1pm from Padstow is arriving with a Brake composite, a Bulleid vehicle to D2406, through to Waterloo and a local Maunsell 2-Set P for Okehampton. The Set from the 2.01pm Bude has drawn back to await attachment. Drinking water for Dunsland Cross station is likely to be the contents of the churns. The mogul, 31841, has a BR chimney but is without general front end renewal. R. A. Lumber.

Just north of Port Isaac Road is the location in May 1957 as lined-black T9 No. 30717 saunters by with local Set No. 27 comprising a Manusell Brake Second 3775 and Brake Composite 6603 in contrasting 'blood and custurd', probably the 10.00am Okehampton to Padstow. Rail Archive Stephenson.

Bude) continued to run. The 10.35am departure provided through coaches to Bude arriving at 5.09pm, Launceston 4.44pm and Padstow at 6.19pm. There was a revised, but now nameless 'Atlantic Coast Express'. The up coaches now left at 11.28am (Bude) and 10.05am (Padstow) combining at Exeter Central with the 12.25pm Torrington, leaving at 2.30pm. The 1.05pm Padstow arriving at Exeter at 5.03pm, gave passengers a long wait there, not getting them to Waterloo until 10.30pm! The 3.00pm Waterloo, re-timed to 2.35pm, connected to Launceston (9.09pm) and Bude (9.26pm). The early morning trains from these towns, departing at 8.22am and 8.02am respectively, were retained with a connection to Waterloo (arr. 2.35pm). A 60mph limit on the main line, and additional stops, dictated the longer service times. On 1 January 1940 the Waterloo departures were eased to 10.50am and 2.50pm, and Up West of England arrival times to 2.35pm, 6.35pm and 10.08pm, but journeys remained between 8½ and 9 hours to and from far-off Padstow. By 1944 the through coaches ran weekdays from Padstow (8.30am) and Bude (9.35am) and arrived back at 5.09pm and 6.19pm. On the local scene the two afternoon up 'Perishables' from Padstow to Templecombe and Bude to Okehampton still ran, as essential food supplies to the big towns.

The 1.25am London newspaper train, another essential (together with the overnight 'Tavvy' fast goods) remained intact throughout the War. For years the newspaper vans had been transferred to the 6.0am goods at Okehampton, reaching Bude about 8.50am (7.15 in 1938) and Padstow at around 9.0am. Although through coaches were running to Plymouth in the 1930s, there had been inexplicable gaps, sometimes unadvertised. An early morning train from Launceston had taken on the Padstow news van at about 8.30am (7.44 in 1938) but it seems a local two-coach set was running unadvertised from Halwill, and probably Okehampton, from 1940. Bowing to pressure from servicemen on leave, mothers visiting evacuee children, etc, an advertised connection was made from Okehampton from 5 October 1942. The (now) 6.42am goods became 'mixed' and the 8.34am from Launceston took the 2-set on to Padstow arriving at 9.52pm. In 1944 this train was also 'mixed' between Launceston and Wadebridge. A connection to Bude arrived at 7.55am but no longer with a bogie news van, the papers being transferred at Halwill.

Most of these services were hauled by 4-4-0s, mainly 'T9s' of which twenty were now allocated to Exmouth Junction and the western sheds. The M7 and O2 0-4-4Ts remained on the Bude and Bodmin locals. The four-each-way North Cornwall trains at this period compared favourably with those in the 1938 timetable and, as elsewhere in Britain, were well used in the War years. There were nine (two mixed) services to Wadebridge/Bodmin SR and Padstow. GWR locals from Bodmin continued to ply from Bodmin Road to Wadebridge behind their 2-6-2Ts. This was a most useful link in wartime Cornwall, which would come into its own during the Plymouth 'Blitz', as we shall see.

The 'Phoney War', as it was known, lasted about nine months, many evacuees returning to London but with the invasion of the Low Countries and France in May 1940, the situation changed dramatically. The SR soon found itself at full stretch with the Dunkirk evacuation. Troop trains had already arrived in the west in 1939, and many more were to follow.

In spite of restrictions, cancellations and the famous exhortation 'Is Your Journey Really Necessary?' Rail travel actually burgeoned. There was little alternative, after all. Surprisingly, the 10.50am Waterloo actually included a Dining Car set through to Padstow daily, from February 1941 to January 1942. If traffic was heavy the set was included in a 10.59am relief, which also had four coaches to Plymouth and Brake Composites for Sidmouth, Exmouth and Bude. The return journey was in the 8.30am from Padstow, the erstwhile 'ACE' pathway now restored but slower. By October 1944 the 10.50am Waterloo and 8.25am Padstow were shown to have a 3-coach corridor set indicating a continuing demand west of Exeter. The journey times of eight hours and more were a natural outcome of the 60mph limit, additional stops and difficult manoeuvres with long trains at Waterloo. During the bombing in 1940 and 1941 Waterloo and Clapham Junction carriage sidings were repeatedly hit and Wimbledon was resorted to as a terminus on many occasions. In the winter of 1944/45 the last train into Launceston (9.35pm Okehampton) was extended on Fridays to Otterham for Servicemen stationed at Davidstow airfield.

Interestingly, from the mid-1930s, the Meldon Quarry staff and their wives were accommodated by the 1.20pm Okehampton to Bude/Launceston which stopped at the Quarry Halt. This train was piloted by an M7 tank (off the front of the 11.37 Exeter Central) on Saturdays. From Halwill, the 'M7' took the rear portion to Launceston, returning light engine, taking up duty as the 'new' engine for the Bude branch. The 'old' Bude M7 went light from Halwill to Okehampton and thence to Exeter as leading engine on the 2.35pm to Plymouth.

The London 'Blitz' in 1940 and 1941 brought further evacuation and specials. In June 1940 nearly 600 people arrived at Wadebridge, nearly 300 at Camelford and over 500 at Launceston. Many others came away to escape, or were actually bombed-out. Again, the V1' Doodlebug' menace in 1944 resulted in more evacuations, including specials from the Kent coast. The Southern Railway handled all this and the various troop trains, ammunition trains and, after the Invasion of Normandy in 1944, an influx of POW trains. The latter terminated at Holsworthy, Launceston and Wadebridge. The North Cornwall line escaped direct bombing and no incidents are known though late, very late, running often occurred as a result of actions in London and Exeter (1941), Plymouth Friary station suffered quite severe bomb damage too.

The Slow Decline to Closure

Rail travel remained paramount in the years after World War Two; petrol rationing persisted until the 1950s though bus services increased quite considerably. The latter were not a serious threat to the North Cornwall as few roads paralleled it. The Bude/Holsworthy to Launceston-Plymouth routes creamed off some traffic but as we have seen, the Southern National's Bude to Wadebridge route actually co-ordinated with rail at Camelford. More serious were Blake's services from Delabole to Plymouth, though the firm was bought out by the Southern National in 1952. The Southern Railway's holding in the National Co was 'nationalised' from 1 January 1948. The other portion, owned by Thomas Tilling Ltd, was bought by the British Transport Commission soon after. Little change ensued in the following 18 years until the railway closed, but the Southern National (now Western National) abandoned its depots at Bude and Delabole in 1971. The successor to the North Cornwall Coach Company horse route from Wadebridge via St Columb Major to Newquay existed into the 1950s. Southern National was then running a near-hourly service from Padstow station forecourt for Treyarnon, Constantine, Harlyn and Trevone (sometimes extended to Newquay) which annexed the territory claimed by the North Cornwall directors as theirs 60 years before. On the train-free Sundays the Southern National ran three buses each way from Padstow to Wadebridge, Bodmin and Bodmin Road. Extracts from the 1947 and 1952 summer Working Timetables are included in Appendix 3.

To work trains along the North Cornwall required quite a complicated roster of locomotive 'duties', with engines and men from Exmouth Junction, Okehampton, Launceston and Wadebridge sheds. Typical of these was Exmouth Junction duty No.593 of 1960, the workings of which are explained in the separate box. It can be seen that although only one engine was involved over a 15-hour period, it needed servicing and turning several times, with eight men involved. In the background were the traffic staff, the guards, signalmen, station staff, permanent way and signal and telegraph men, let alone night men in the engine sheds. At the turn of the 1960s, of all the trains hauled by the 'N' on duty 593, probably only the overnight Waterloo to Padstow train earned its keep by virtue of the high-value newspapers and merchandise it carried and the fares passengers might pay for a journey of up to 260 miles.

British Railways was already making an operational loss by this time and such a long straggling rural line as the North Cornwall, still with signal boxes at each of its ten stations, could not now be profitable. Nevertheless a reasonable passenger service was still on offer, the 1960/61 winter timetable showing that Launceston and Camelford enjoyed public transport barely thinkable in a rural area today.

While the 1.10am Waterloo passed down into Cornwall behind the 'N' 2-6-0, as we have already seen, at Launceston the first up train started away at 8.20am behind another 'N' going through to Okehampton. At Halwill a local 'P' set of two coaches from Bude was added, both portions affording a good connection to the first up Plymouth to Waterloo fast train. Meanwhile at Padstow the 8.30am 'Atlantic Coast Express' three-coach set left behind a light 4-6-2, an all stations train to Okehampton in the winter months. At Halwill a Brake Composite coach was placed on the rear by the Bude engine (a 2-6-2T) as its contribution to the eventual 7-part train which arrived at Waterloo in mid-afternoon. Following all the activity at Halwill, the 9.56am from Okehampton trundled in behind a 'T9' 4-4-0 with a bogie van and two 'P' sets, the rear one for Bude. It called at all stations in the tradition of North Cornwall 'stoppers', taking 2¼ hours, an average of 27mph. Even in the short reign of the diesel cars, the average was not above 33mph and they had little to obstruct their passage in 1966. On the rising gradients from Wadebridge to St Kew the latter only managed 30mph, though this rose to 42-45mph down the opening valley from Tower Hill to Launceston. The slow progress of these stopping trains,

Exmouth Junction duty No.593

This was a duty for one of Exmouth Junctions Maunsell 'N' class moguls outstationed at Okehampton. It left Okehampton shed at 6.00am and attached to the overnight Waterloo to Padstow coaches and newspaper van, 'road boxes' and a number of goods wagons and brake van. Exmouth Junction men who had travelled as passengers on the train from Exeter relieved the Okehampton pair at 6.05. The train left at 6.20 for Launceston where the Exmouth Junction men were relieved by Launceston's early shift at 7.55am. The latter then drove the 'N' through to Padstow, the Waterloo train being shunted into the middle sidings, and the engine turned. Wagons were assembled for a 10.10am goods to Wadebridge where more shunting took place before this engine was taken to shed at 11.30 for ash cleaning and servicing. Coming off at 12.49 the Launceston men exchanged their 'Woolworth' for the 'T9' now detaching from the 12.58pm Padstow to Okehampton. However, at Launceston the early shift men were relieved by the local second shift at 2.15 (who had booked in at 2pm). The train terminated at Okehampton up platform, but the through coach to Waterloo in the 1950s was dealt with by the station pilot, attaching it to the up Plymouth train. The 'N' went on shed from 3.18 to 4.00pm for turning and any other attention it might require, emerging at 4.05 to attach to the 4.24 local passenger to Bude in the bay. At Bude between 5.28 and 6.00 any necessary shunting was done and the engine turned again (6.05 to 6.50pm) before going into the bay to attach to the 7.05pm passenger (and mail) to Halwill. At the latter the Launceston men now handed the 'N' over to an Okehampton crew at 8.30pm. Then it was time for it to make the final haul by piloting the 5.00pm goods from Wadebridge on to Okehampton where the engine went on shed at 9.06 for the night.

In August 1939 the 10.40pm (SO) Waterloo to Padstow through train is arriving at Wadebridge at 4.45pm. T9 No. 703 would have had assistance from Exeter to Camelford or Delabole with the ten coach train which included a four-car dining set. On the right are several vans strung out from the goods shed, viz: LSWR ventilated, SR ventilated and an insulated (SR or LMS) probably to load meat, and (furthest) a GWR fitted van.

the circuitous route and lack of population near stations, had become an anachronism by 1965 in view of the rise in private motoring. In the climate of the 1980s, with a more sympathetic public view of rail travel, a speedier 'Sprinter' might make a more attractive proposition, but a large subsidy would have to be forthcoming.

There were no trains from Padstow to Okehampton after the 8.30am 'ACE' departure until the 12.58pm. A 'T9' off the 9.56am Okehampton took the later to Wadebridge (changing for an 'N' on Duty 593), consisting of a through brake composite for Waterloo, and a 'P' set. The mid-day mails from Launceston (and from Bude at 1.55pm) were loaded into the guards/luggage ends en route for Exeter. The Bude coaches were attached, as usual, at Halwill and the train was into Okehampton at 3.13pm. The Brake Composite was attached to the rear of the afternoon Plymouth train (Waterloo 8.00pm).

Every weekday afternoon the two up passenger and 'Perishables' left Bude and Padstow soon after 3.00pm. In their heyday both were hauled by 'T9' 4-4-0s and reference has been made to them already. Operating independently, the Bude train terminated at Okehampton where its van was attached to the following 3.13pm Padstow, bound for Exeter Central. Containers of meat from both lines (Holsworthy/Launceston/ Halwill) were transferred to the 4.15pm Bideford Goods to Nine Elms, leaving Exeter Central at 7.30pm. The express road van from Padstow was forwarded by this train or the following 5.25pm semi-fitted goods from Torrington to Nine Elms (10.40pm from Exmouth Junction). The number of meat containers had grown considerably by this time and, after the demise of the 'T9s' in 1961, this duty (Okehampton No.599) was taken over by 2-6-0s, well able to take the six or more wagons on the tail. This train also conveyed the empty news van to Exeter, en route to Clapham Junction. Both engines on these 'Perishables' carried the Okehampton/Padstow headcodes. It seems that any 'T9' or 'N' working out of Okehampton kept the codes up all day regardless of branch, which was a little confusing for photographers at Halwill, but not to the local signalmen. Passengers took (and take) little notice of headcodes anyway!

The 6.00pm from Padstow was a similarly heavy load for its Wadebridge 'T9', with the evening North Cornwall mails in a bogie van and another from Bude at Halwill. Three or more vacuum-braked box wagons – the returning road boxes for Exeter and Bristol (and Plymouth) – completed the train (a single 'P' set) from the Junction to Okehampton where the vans and wagons were transferred to the 7.20pm Plymouth-Exeter Central. This last up Padstow train passed the last down train, the 5.51pm from Okehampton with another 'T9' at Tresmeer, a cameo which hardly changed in 60 years. Imagine a drizzly wet winter's evening. Dim oil lamps on the platforms, local people back from Launceston market ready to walk a mile or so to Tresmeer village or towards Warbstow, some lucky to be fetched in a pony and trap or (later) a motor car. Parcels to be dropped off, Cornish voices in the dark, the single line Tablets handed to the drivers. Then with a toot of the whistle one 'T9' sets off with a resounding bark up and around to Otterham, while the other drifts off down the hill to Egloskerry. Signal restored with a clank of levers, final bell codes as the lines clear and Tresmeer shuts down for the night.

This was not the last down train to Launceston though. A connection was made off the 3.00pm Waterloo to Plymouth leaving Okehampton at 7.45pm. An 'N' class this time with a 2-set for Launceston and one for Bude. It left Halwill at 8.20 and terminated at Launceston at 8.42pm. At Halwill itself the passenger services may have started at 7.00am but the early signalman was on duty at 5 for the goods and mails. After eight o'clock in the evening the 5.00pm Wadebridge up goods was still shunting about the yard in the last hour, before leaving for Yeoford about 8.30pm.

The Sunday service for a 1960s summer was much the same as from 1940 onward, except that in these post-war years a through Brake Composite ran to Bude from the 11.00am Waterloo (and back at 9.45am) with connections for Launceston passengers (5.17pm arrive, 9.50am depart). In 1953 attempts were made to serve the Camelford/Tintagel areas by extending the service to Delabole. Launceston should have had a BR Standard 3 2-6-2T for this work but in the event WR 2-6-2T No.4583 was borrowed, though No.82013 was known to have been on the duty on 9 August and 6 September 1953. On 26 July, off shed at 9.30am, 4583 did a morning stint from Launceston to Bude, back to Halwill then on a 11.30am departure right down to Delabole where it ran round its 2 set between 1.33 and 1.52pm (buses connected to and from Camelford to Tintagel and Boscastle). There was little profit on these extensions to Delabole and they were not continued in 1954. A bus service, Southern National Route 418 Delabole - Camelford - Tintagel - Boscastle - Otterham Station - Launceston ran on the five Sundays in August 1954 taking two hours each way to connect at Launceston (arr. 2.30pm, dep. 5.25pm).

Looking forward into the final years, Bude and Launceston continued to have a train service in the summer periods until September 1965. For Bude only, a single return bus by Southern National (No.129) ran to and from Okehampton in the winters of 1963, 1964 and 1965. From summer 1965 five DMUs made four return trips between Exeter Central and Bude, with Launceston served from Halwill by dividing or attaching at Halwill.

The Change to Diesel Railcars 1965-66

The Western Region took control of the route west of Salisbury from 1 January 1963, though Southern Region rolling stock continued to penetrate on both express and local workings, even to Padstow. Exmouth Junction engine shed and its allocation became WR (83D) but for the first year little difference could be noticed. A newly-created Plymouth Division of the WR began to find its feet during 1963 and plans were made to integrate the former SR into the Paddington-Penzance services. In the background, nonetheless, Dr Beeching was calling for statistics of British Railways operations in just such places as Devon and Cornwall and this same year his 'Report' was published. There was to be little hope that the North Cornwall line would survive. Traffic was in serious decline. April 1964 saw the posting of closure notices for Okehampton to Bude and Wadebridge passenger trains. (Freight closure was announced in June to take effect from 7 September). The summer 1964 timetable, to take effect from 15 June, was to be the last 'Southern' one, with NC local trains connecting to and from Waterloo. The Monday to Friday basic five up trains from Padstow at 8.48am to Exeter Central, 9.35am to Waterloo, 1.00pm to Okehampton (no longer including a through coach to Waterloo), 3.10pm 'Perishables' to Exeter and 6.20pm to Okehampton, were augmented by the early 7.55am from Launceston. down, the 1.10am Waterloo 'news' no longer conveyed TCs for Padstow (though the newspaper van in the 6.25am Okehampton continued). The 10.00am Okehampton, 3.32pm (following the 'ACE' coaches at 3.08pm) and the 5.55pm still ran, the last two terminating at Wadebridge, at 5.25pm and 7.48pm. The last train (8.20pm Halwill, connecting through Okehampton from the 3.00pm Waterloo) terminated, as of yore, at Launceston. Bude local portions continued to be taken from Okehampton/Padstow trains (and vice versa) but the Monday to Friday 'ACE' Bude coach had ceased to run after September 1963.

The decline in use of North Cornwall local trains was borne out by the figures put forward by BR in its closure proposals. Few walked nowadays to Tower Hill or Port Isaac Road, the latter so isolated that it was probably unknown to a younger generation. Rising car ownership disregarded the railway as an anachronism, its fares 'expensive' but useful perhaps in an emergency! Yet many local people, particularly school children and shop workers in Launceston, Holsworthy, Bude and Okehampton, relied on it even in 1964. The handful of Maunsell 2-car 'P' sets, now reaching 40 years of service, were supplemented by later 1940s Bulleid coaches, a smattering of BR (Mark 1s) and some ex-GWR stock, to keep the service going until the onset of diesel railcars or, perhaps, closure. The 10.00am, 1.30pm (Bude) from Okehampton and the 1.00pm and 3.10pm from Padstow still conveyed parcel vans but more and more of the goods business was going by road.

With the cessation of freight services from 7 September 1964 the local scene changed considerably. Although there was still some semblance of the previous four/five trains, they were now integrated with the Paddington/Penzance main line, rather than Waterloo. Local steam working had to continue, however, until the required diesel railcars could be organised by the WR. The first conversion was the Exmouth branch from September 1963. On the SR main line only the 1.10am Waterloo news and passenger and the through Brighton/Plymouth trains came through Okehampton and showed any signs of 'express' running. A two-hourly service Waterloo-St Davids with limited stops east of Salisbury was supplemented by an all stations Salisbury/Plymouth or Ilfracombe service of WR three-car diesel sets. The latter were timed to connect at St Davids with the Paddington trains, further providing Okehampton connections for Padstow/Bude by steam-hauled trains, in a timetable cast for the proposed diesel railcars. Although locomotive haulage of freight had been largely separate from passenger until September 1964, quite a drastic change in engine duties was instituted. For the most part, the Okehampton, Padstow and Bude workings became self-contained, worked by BR 2-6-4Ts and the SR 'N' 2-6-0s. The Class 3 2-6-2Ts hitherto confined to the Bude branch appeared on North Cornwall workings as did some BR Class 4 4-6-0s by December. The latter were unable to turn at Launceston or Bude owing to their length. Betraying some recognition of the Padstow line's existence, a 1.19pm through train from Exeter Central connected off the 10.30am Paddington to Penzance at St Davids, and an 8.48am from Padstow ran through to Central, connecting to the 3.10pm arrival at Paddington. It was 'no missed stops' on the North Cornwall from now on, but the down train was swifter by calling only at North Tawton after St Davids, producing a respectable 5 hour, 39 minute journey to Padstow. On the last day of steam haulage (3 January 1965) the 1.19pm left St Davids with 82039, three coaches and a van. Eric Youldon of Exeter relates that 82039 was sadly in poor condition, with a stop at Bow to raise steam and again at North Tawton. How far 82039 went with its special headboard 'LAST REGULAR STEAM PASSENGER TRAIN EXETER TO PADSTOW' is not known. Sister engine 82040 was on the Halwill/Bude connections. The 2.40pm Bude to Okehampton was passed at Dunsland Cross by 4-6-0 75025 (tender first). On his return from Bude, Eric changed at Halwill into the 3.45pm from Padstow behind yet another Class 3, 82042. For the record his train to Exeter (5.15pm Plymouth to Eastleigh) was in the charge of 'Hymek' diesel D7099, a hint at what was afoot for the following Monday. It was also at this date that the WR insisted on the 24-hour clock timings.

From 4 January 1965 the 'steamers' lay cold in the sidings at Exmouth Junction and the diesel railcars took over. Based at Newton Abbot, the service was now required to start and finish at the Exeter end, only the 18.55 Okehampton to Wadebridge and its return trip, the 08.48 Padstow next morning, stabling overnight (a three car unit). The 06.15 Okehampton

A holiday extra train in the 1960s hauled by N Class No. 31843, climbing away from Tresmeer and crossing the high embankment at Treneglos on the way to Otterham. The embankment was substituted for a viaduct proposed here in 1893. The first two Bulleid coaches are 2-Set R set 70 formed from Brake Composite 6707 to Diagram 2405 and Semi-Open Brake Third 4378 to Diagram 2123. The third coach is a Bulleid 'loose' Brake Composite to Diagram 2406 (number series 6713-6752). The fourth and fifth coaches are probably a Maunsell 2-Set P.

(connections still from the 01.10 Waterloo to Plymouth newspaper train) came empty from Newton. At Halwill a single railcar was detached to form the 06.50 to Bude and at Launceston another single car was detached to go forward at 07.55 to Padstow. The 'main' train (a two or three car set) returned to Okehampton as the 07.52 from Launceston. The timetable remained generally similar to that of September 1964, except for minor adjustments. Bude/Halwill trains were now 'shuttles', but during the afternoon some were running separately to Okehampton and back. The 15.45 Padstow to Okehampton was altered to 15.15 and the 16.35 Bude to 16.05. Bude did quite well, getting two evening up services at 17.47 and 20.25 hours, making seven up and eight down trains per weekday, at least for Halwill. Samples of units employed in March 1965 were: 15.15 ex-Padstow; single car; 13.19 ex-Exeter Central; 3 car 'suburban' unit; 16.30 ex-Okehampton (to Bude); three car 'suburban'; 09.40 Bude to Halwill; single car. Day tickets were offered from Padstow (70 shillings), Launceston (54/6), and from all North Cornwall stations to London. The return for later travellers was the 01.10 Waterloo overnight train.

Not all the services were diesel car workings. Until April 1965 the afternoon Okehampton (12.10) and the return 14.40 from Bude 'Perishables' employed diesel locomotives (a Hymek or NBL D63XX) and coaches/vans. Steam reappeared on Sunday 5 September 1965, a special organised by the Great Western Society to celebrate the Centenary of the GWR Launceston branch arriving from Exeter at Launceston (via Lydford and Lifton) behind Ivatt 2-6-2T 41283. After terminating in the GWR station 41283 propelled the train back into Launceston (ex-SR). After running-round its train in the down loop, the tank left for Halwill and proceeded to Bude, before returning to Exeter.

The first casualty under 'Beeching' was the Torrington-Halwill passenger service. This light railway of 1925 never aspired to show in the Southern Railway's comprehensive Waterloo to the West of England timetable, but then it was hardly attractive to passengers, with its mixed trains and slow progress. Nonetheless there was always a connection at Halwill with the up 'ACE' and the 1.00pm Waterloo. The service would dieselise for its last winter of 1964/65, a single car working from Barnstaple Junction to Halwill mid-morning and late afternoon. The mixed trains trailing wagons of pit props and china clay into Halwill had ceased from 7 September 1964 and the line closed altogether south of Meeth after the 18.20 left Halwill on the evening of 27 February 1965. A brief re-opening occurred on 27 March for an enthusiasts' railtour – 'The Exmoor Ranger'.

From 1 March the early morning DMU combination was advanced to 06.25 from Okehampton but kept the same timings beyond Halwill. In spite of uncertainty over closure proposals, the Okehampton/Bude line service remained quite generous, and Launceston shared this to a degree. For the summer timetable, starting on 14 June 1965, a Sunday service was restored from Exeter Central to Bude, four trains each way with Launceston getting a single car twice from Halwill (turning round at 10.27/11.07 and in the evening at 18.56/19.15). The surprising inclusion of a Saturday holiday train from and to Paddington serving Bude (and Ilfracombe) resulted in several diesel locomotive-hauled workings. Coaches came in from Newton Abbott arriving at Bude at 09.04 and the down Paddington stock returned as a public train at 16.54.

The North Cornwall line, beginning to look woebegone (Otterham had lost its crossing loop already) was less fortunate. The service was reduced to three down trains, at 06.25 and 10.05 from Okehampton and at 15.35 from Halwill (also Halwill to Launceston at 18.18 and 19.08 hours) and three up, from Wadebridge at 08.57, 13.50 and 17.30 (Launceston extras at 07.52 and 19.50). The outlook was not inspiring. There was no connection to the Bude/Paddington train and passengers on the 13.50 had to wait at Halwill from 15.20 to 16.01 for the Bude-Exeter Central car to appear! It was small wonder that long distance passengers were deterred and local users discouraged by fewer trains and continual re-timings. During the winter of 1965/66 the lone Sunday service Bude/Okehampton reverted to a Southern National bus. The weekday 15.35 from Halwill with Wadebridge was altered to 14.35, but did at least connect with the 13.20 from Exeter St Davids to Bude with its fast running to Okehampton (less the call at North Tawton).

North Cornwall and Bude services were not expected to last beyond March 1966, some prospective upcountry passengers actually being told they had actually ceased! Even the Plymouth Divisional Office was under threat of closure. Until Ministerial consent for closure, the trains had to run, however. From 18 April 1966 an 'Emergency Timetable' was introduced; by this time consent *had* been given, and a termination date of 3 October was included, last trains to run on Saturday 1 October. North Cornwall simply got a morning, afternoon and evening train each way, but Bude continued to enjoy eight return services (five connecting at Okehampton). Three single (or twin) cars were sufficient to cover workings, none completely confined to either route. The flexibility of diesel units is illustrated by the 06.25 Okehampton (empty stock from Newton Abbot) which dropped a single car at Halwill for Bude and another at Launceston (to return at 07.48) before proceeding to Wadebridge. The car, arriving at Launceston at 19.21, was attached to the 18.40 from Wadebridge and in turn to the 19.25 from Bude, all going through to Exeter St Davids (the only train advertised to do so) thence empty to Newton Abbot.

By this time only Ashbury, Halwill, Launceston, Egloskerry and Camelford retained their loops, even though Halwill only had booked crossings. It was all very sad as the weeks melted away. Enthusiasts and locals decided to join the dwindling band of regular travellers paying for day returns – Okehampton to Bude: 10/-, Halwill to Launceston: 4/8d, Delabole to Wadebridge: 3/6d or even Wadebridge to Paddington for £4/12/0d. Meanwhile the substitute bus timetables were under preparation for October, but some places like Tresmeer and Port Isaac Road would never again enjoy six-days-a-week, four or five-services-a-day public transport.

Diesel locomotives had first invaded Wadebridge in 1961. NBL D63XX (later Class 22) based at St Blazey had replaced the 45XX 2-6-2Ts on the Bodmin Road trains but pannier tanks, successors to the 'O2s' continued on the former SR services to Bodmin North. On 7 September 1964 the WR set up a revised pattern which left Bodmin North with a 'shuttle' to and from a new short platform at Boscarne Junction and a longer one opposite, on the General line. Single unit diesel rail cars called at the latter on a Bodmin Road, Bodmin General, Boscarne, Wadebridge and Padstow service. (Grogley and Nanstallon Halts now got a call by every train). The single cars returned to St Blazey nightly but the AC 4-wheel railbus for Bodmin arrived on Mondays and stabled at Wadebridge until Saturday. A set of coaches, kept at Padstow, was retained for school traffic. For many years Bodmin Harleigh School pupils had used the train from Wadebridge to Bodmin SR, but from May 1948 the 'O2' and SR stock were diverted to Bodmin General. In 1957 a new school opened in Wadebridge and numbers increased, coming from both directions. 45XX 2-6-2Ts worked the afternoon service, but Padstow extensions were not always advertised to the public. 'O2s' worked the Bodmin Road service in latter years, replaced by WR 57XX 0-6-0PTs and then, in 1962, by Ivatt 2MT 2-6-2Ts.

Although the shadow of 'Beeching' crept across these branches as well as the North Cornwall, it is surprising to note the extent of the service. Sundays

The second down morning train from Okehampton (9.56am) calling at Delabole in 1961comprising Southern 4 wheel passenger brake 'Van C' (BY) to Diagram 3092, a Bulleid Open Saloon Third to Diagram 2017 (number series 1462-1506) and an unidentified Maunsell Corridor Coach. The driver and fireman of T9 No. 30719 have just exchanged with another crew and the engine shows signs of hard work on its lower smoke box door. In later years the station house had received a cladding of slate. R. C. Riley, www.transporttreasury.co.uk

Wadebridge and Bodmin trains strengthened the service to Padstow and were, for many years, in the hands of Adams O2 Class 0-4-4Ts. On 3rd September 1954 No. 30203 leaves Wadebridge for Bodmin North with a two coach Maunsell P Set, several wagons and a goods brake van. The B&WR original alignment was on the extreme left. The reverse curves dated from 1888 and Wadebridge East signal box from 1899. R. C. Riley, www.transporttreasury.co.uk

had a bus service, though it was not provided by BR. During the summer of 1965 the AC railbus took one return trip to Wadebridge and was used on 'guided tours' Padstow/Bodmin North in the summer of 1965 and 1966.

From 4 January 1965 the few North Cornwall DMUs mingled with the Bodmin/Padstow services, but from 7 June these were cut back to Wadebridge, except on Saturdays. There were not many connections to Padstow and in the last timetable (1966) they had been reduced to the 08.41 and 18.46 arrival and 08.45 departure services. Passengers from Padstow and Wadebridge, it would seem, were also directed towards Bodmin Road and Paddington, though even here connections were indifferent. Padstow was reduced to a single run-round loop and siding, signalled by a train staff and key, in 1965. This combined service from Bodmin Road lasted four months beyond the North Cornwall's closure. The last day of service was 28 January 1967, the farewell crowds accommodated in a three-coach train hauled by NBL No D6309.

Post Closure Passenger Transport

The stay of execution for the railway in 1966 enabled British Railways to arrange for some, if not the entire, coverage of the North Cornwall route by bus. The South Western Traffic Commissioners were asked to invite applications from local operators. There was to be a subsidy from BR (in reality paid by the National Bus Company) for a limited period. It was not difficult to attract offers for Okehampton/Bude and three were considered. W.J.O. Jennings of Queen St Bude, established for many years in the Kilhampton area and now operating tours from Bude, put forward an 'express' service of six return journeys (weekdays). D & M Perrie of Halwill was another contender, also Okeridge Motors of Okehampton. Perrie's proposals had more stops than the trains, including Stratton. The eastern end included stops at Halwill Junction, Ashbury Cross, Maddaford (Thorndon Cross). The Southern National Company did not apply and the winner was Jennings, through the firm's better fleet, it seems, and reliable garaging, at the right end. This firm initially ran the six return journeys (there was an extra in the summer) from Okehampton station (now the railhead) and Bude (Strand). The Sunday service, hitherto run by Southern National, was transferred to Jennings and would run year-round. Until 1980 the Exeter/Okehampton leg was provided by Devon General. The coaches still operate, modified in timings and number of journeys, after 25 years. Following closure of Okehampton in June 1972 they were extended to Exeter St Davids and into the city. The service remains essentially an 'express' in spite of additional stops.

It was a very different story from Halwill to Wadebridge. Bus substitution for the entire route was never considered, though a considerable but not very parallel length was covered for a few years in a limited form between Okehampton and Delabole. Southern National applied for a three-a-day return service, operating from its Delabole garage, and this was granted. It went nowhere near Halwill, going directly from Okehampton by the A30, through Lifton, to Launceston Square. It avoided Egloskerry, Tresmeer and Otterham. A local school bus proprietor took pains to point out in 1967 that he went through Egloskerry and Tresmeer (village) in term-time to Launceston. In 1969 there were only two Okehampton departures, at 11.35 (Delabole arr. 13.36) and 16.25 (Delabole 18.26). From Delabole there were departures at 09.20 (Okehampton 11.30) and 14.05 (16.15). This service (No.406, later 366) was discontinued on 31 December 1969. Existing Southern National Services in this area were never very competitive with the railway, except the cross-countries (with Western National) from Bude and Bideford through Launceston and Tavistock to Plymouth. Perrie applied for and was granted a licence to run a weekday service from Halwill through Ashwater village and Tower Hill to Launceston, one each way morning and evening, but this lasted only a year or so.

The 'coastal' service, Southern National No.122, continued to operate as it had prior to October 1966; that is, between Bude, Boscastle, Tintagel, Camelford, Delabole (and St Kew Highway) and Wadebridge. There were minor modifications to connections at Camelford and Delabole with Okehampton buses, and with the railway at Wadebridge. Noteworthy was the extension of the last bus (in 1967) from Okehampton to beyond Delabole on summer Saturdays. Journey time throughout to Wadebridge was two and a half hours for a fare of 7s 6d. In the south-west corner the Port Isaac/Port Isaac Road Station/ Wadebridge Station daily services (Southern National No.133) of two journeys each way continued in 1967. There were also services from Polzeath to Wadebridge. The Southern National routes were amalgamated with Western National in 1968, but on the precipitate closures of Bude and Delabole garages on 31 July 1971, these parts of North Cornwall became bereft of public transport except for some limited services taken up by Frys of Tintagel and Prouts of Port Isaac.

Wadebridge remained a railhead until the withdrawal of the Bodmin Road to Padstow diesel car service from 30 January 1967. A bus service was thereupon substituted between these points, initially with eight weekday journeys each way, the existing Sunday road service continuing until 1980. This route (Western National No.55) is still maintained with a not unreasonable frequency.

It may be surmised from the above that after 25 years the route of the North Cornwall is poorly served by public transport, especially toward Exeter and London. Only Bude, Halwill and Okehampton and Wadebridge to Padstow retain daily and connecting services to the BR system at St Davids and Bodmin Road (now Parkway) respectively. Launceston has been especially unlucky since 1969 for transport direct to the centre of Exeter and even the Royal Blue coaches have deserted it for Plymouth and the A38 road.

The last summer of the North Cornwall line, and on Saturday 2nd July 1966 the 16.50 Okehampton to Wadebridge, made up of Two Gloucester-built single car units, has some passengers at Camelford. In the distance are three rows of cottages built by the LSWR for its empoyees. On the right are Rush's agricultural stores in the goods yard. The upper quadrant SR signal arm is mounted on a pair of second-hand rails, typifying the economic re-use of materials by the old companies. R. A. Lumber.

R. E. Vincent records a busy scene at Okehampton in September 1953 as a Maunsell Brake Composite and Bulleid SK are propelled on to the rear of Bulleid 2-set R number 66. The various portions of the up ACE are being assembled ready for their journey eastwards to Exeter. In the bay is West Country Pacific No. 34031 *Torrington* whilst the down main line is occupied by a rake of cattle wagons. www.transporttreasury.co.uk

Still more shunting activity at Okehampton on the same day in September 1953. A goods train is in the distance whilst a T9 4-4-0 is on station pilot duties, moving a 2-Set P number 180 made up of a Maunsell Brake Second 3733 and Brake Composite 6674 on the up line. R. E. Vincent, www.transporttreasury.co.uk

Chapter Five

THE LURE OF THE NORTH CORNISH COAST

Additional information by Chris Tooth and Glen Woods

This Chapter looks specifically at passenger traffic on the North Cornwall and the role the development of the tourist trade had on the region and the holiday services on the North Cornwall Railway. The dramatic scenery and sandy coves were the consistent draw, and still are, and it was initially horse drawn coaches that took the well-heeled to these places. The arrival of the North Cornwall Railway meant the joys of the region were soon opened up to the more and more people and, with the coming of the five-day week and paid holiday leave, this gradually turned into a mass exodus from the cities every summer. Prior to World War II the vast majority of these holidays would have been by rail. The role the railways in general played in developing this traffic should not be under-estimated. The Southern Railway exploited the 'history' of the area, including King Arthur and Tintagel, and promoted new locally-named locomotives, the King Arthur and West Country classes. But the genius moment came with the naming of the 11am departure from Waterloo to the West Country the 'Atlantic Coast Express'. The lure was complete and the rest is history!

Early tourism

Tourist traffic was already quite heavy along the coastal road (today's A39) in the summer months of the early 1890s. Mention has been made of the North Cornwall Coach Co's successive connections from Launceston and finally Wadebridge. Operating to the north were Brendon's coaches, based at Bude and from 1895 both firms were offering an integrated two-day tourist service Ilfracombe/Newquay, actually using the new railway from Camelford and Wadebridge, from July to September and out of Clovelly. About 8,000 passengers were sampling this system every summer in the 1890s, lured by 'fifty miles of Coaching through the romantic scenery of the North Coast of Devon and Cornwall,

A local passenger train, comprising a 4-wheel passenger luggage van (BR code PMV) and a Maunsell 2-set P, hurries towards the North Cornwall Line over Meldon Viaduct in 1963. R. C. Riley, www.transporttreasury.co.uk

North Cornwall Coach Co., Ltd.

In conjunction with the

LONDON & SOUTH WESTERN RAILWAY COMPANY

— A Two or — Three Days' Tour

Including

50 miles of Coaching through the most Romantic Scenery of North Cornwall, and Hotel Accommodation

——— EVERY WEEK-DAY ———

from early in June, until middle of September

CHEAP THROUGH RAIL AND HOTEL COUPON TICKETS (3rd Class Rail) will be issued from Newquay for a Circular Trip to Boscastle, returning via Tintagel.

TWO DAYS' TOUR

Inclusive Fare - - 21/- (Saturdays excepted).

Passengers taking the above Tickets on arrival at Boscastle on the first day, will be provided with Luncheon, Table d'Hote Dinner, a specially reserved Bedroom and attendance at the Wellington Hotel; and on the second day, Breakfast and conveyance from Boscastle to Tintagel, Luncheon at the Wharncliffe Arms Hotel, Tintagel, and conveyance Tintagel to Camelford Station.

THREE DAYS' TOUR

Inclusive Fare - - 30/- (Fridays excepted).

Passengers taking the above Tickets will, on arrival at Boscastle on the first day be provided with Luncheon, Table d'Hote Dinner, a specially reserved Bedroom and attendance at the Wellington Hotel.

SECOND DAY—Breakfast, Luncheon, and attendance at the Wellington Hotel, leaving Boscastle at 1.15 p.m., for the Wharncliffe Arms Hotel, Tintagel, arriving there 2.0 p.m. Table d'Hote Dinner and specially reserved Bedroom.

THIRD DAY.—Breakfast, Luncheon and attendance at the Wharncliffe Arms Hotel and conveyance from Tintagel to Camelford Station.

THE TOUR WILL BE WORKED TO THE FOLLOWING TIME TABLE.

FORWARD JOURNEY.

		FIRST DAY.
		a.m.
NEWQUAY Headland Hotel	dep.	9 15
Atlantic Hotel	,,	9 25
Central Square	,,	9 35
Hotel Victoria	,,	9 45
Wadebridge Station	,,	1 0
Camelford	arr.	1 36
,, (By 'Bus or Brake)	dep.	1 45
BOSCASTLE (Wellington Hotel) ...	arr. about	2 45

RETURN JOURNEY.

TWO DAYS' TOUR.

		SECOND DAY.	
		a.m.	a.m.
BOSCASTLE (Wellington Hotel) by 'Bus or Brake)	dep.	10 0	10 0
TINTAGEL (Wharncliffe Arms Hotel)	arr.	10 45	10 45
		p.m.	p.m.
	dep.	4 15	3 15
Camelford	arr.	5 15	4 15
,, (Rail)	dep.	5 28	4 30
Wadebridge	arr.	5 57	4 52
,, (by Coach)	dep.	6 5	5 0
NEWQUAY Hotel Victoria	arr.	8 10	7 5
Atlantic Hotel	,,	8 20	7 15
Headland Hotel	,,	8 35	7 30

THREE DAYS' TOUR.

		SECOND DAY.	
		p.m.	p.m.
BOSCASTLE (Wellington Hotel, by 'Bus or Brake)	dep.	1 15	1 15
TINTAGEL (Wharncliffe Arms Hotel)	arr.	2 0	2 0
		THIRD DAY.	
		p.m.	p.m.
	dep.	4 15	3 15
Camelford	arr.	5 15	4 15
,, (Rail)	dep.	5 28	4 30
Wadebridge	arr.	5 57	4 52
,, (by Coach)	dep.	6 5	5 0
NEWQUAY Hotel Victoria	arr.	8 10	7 5
Atlantic Hotel	,,	8 20	7 15
Headland Hotel	,,	8 35	7 30

N.B.—The times shown above are only given as a guide to the usual time en route, and intending passengers should consult current announcements before travelling.

in direct communication with Through Fast Trains over the London & South Western Railway'. Arrangements were much the same in 1913, but the 'season' ran only from 2 June to 30 September (to 20 September north of Bude). This horse-coach tourism lasted until the early 1920s. Through rail and coach tickets were issued only for the northern leg from Waterloo and Exeter and so on to and from Bude. In 1913 the single through fare from Bude to Newquay was 13/9d (1st Class) and the Boscastle/Tintagel to Camelford local fare was 1/6d single. Earlier and later timed horse buses were connecting these places with Camelford trains, as well as between Padstow (up to 1899) and Newquay with Wadebridge. Horse brakes could be hired from Port Isaac Road by giving notice.

Excursions at Weekends and Bank Holidays

While the coastal tourist business expanded, the LSWR ran weekend excursions to and from the West of England, on Fridays, Saturdays and Mondays in July, August and September. As the NCR progressed steadily westwards between 1886 and 1899 special trains arrived at whichever railhead was currently open, though it was 1899 on the opening to Padstow before coaches ran through, obviating changes at Okehampton. Excursion tickets were available on the 9.00am from Waterloo in 1886 to Launceston for Wadebridge and Newquay. Returning from Padstow, the excursionist had to be up early for the 5.10am 'conveyance', to be in Waterloo at 5.15pm!

From 1899 through special weekend excursion trains definitely started running to and from Padstow. Leaving Waterloo at 7.40am, Exeter Queen Street was reached at 1.03pm in 5½ hours compared with 3½ hours by the best expresses! At Halwill the down service divided for Bude, with an arrival at 4.40pm for Padstow. Up departures were from Padstow at 7.40am, Bude 9.00am and Exeter 11.35am, giving a 4.37pm arrival at Waterloo – these on Mondays and Saturdays. Overnight Saturday excursion trains were also run at the height of the season before 1914, and it would appear that a connecting passenger coach was attached to the Sunday 4.33am goods and mail from Okehampton (and one from Halwill to Bude). Being a goods train, the passengers would have had to wait at Meldon Junction while wagons were attached – unthinkable today! While usually terminating at Camelford (though later back at Launceston) the train would continued with the coach to Delabole (arriving 6.18am) if required.

It is not certain what types of carriages were employed on these excursions. Almost certainly they were bogie stock, but non-lavatory and no refreshments either. The lengthy timings indicate this with stops at Andover, Salisbury and so on. Nevertheless excursions were obviously popular. As today, many Cornish people (and Devonians) had migrated to work in London, so at Easter and Christmas the LSWR pushed itself to the limit to provide extra trains, and special excursions. In 1910 on both 23rd and 24th December the normal 11.00am was formed into two 'Divisions'. The second left at 11.05am for Plymouth and Padstow only. The latter portion was reformed as an express at Exeter Queen Street leaving at 2.30pm arriving at Padstow at 5.21pm. On Christmas morning at 12.45am an excursion left Waterloo for Padstow and Bude, with a Plymouth portion on the rear. The arrivals at the resorts were for 9.01 and 7.56am respectively.

The following Easter on the Tuesday and Wednesday before the holiday, an 11.05am from Waterloo served Padstow,

The Atlantic Coast Express headboard, on Bulleid Pacific No. 34110 66 *Squadron* approaching Maddaford Moor Halt, was mounted at Exeter Central, this particular engine working through to Padstow and returning next morning. The first coach appears to be a Maunsell Corridor Third, possibly the 1935 variety to Diagram 2008. The second and third coaches are Bulleid 'loose' Brake Composites to Diagram 2406 (number series 6713-6752). On 12th May 1961 the (winter) formation was two for Padstow and a brake composite for Bude. S. C. Nash

Bude, Exmouth and Sidmouth only. It called at Salisbury, Otterham, Camelford, Port Isaac Road and Wadebridge. On Thursday 13 April an 11.30am excursion left for Plymouth, Padstow and Bude – all stations from Exeter but omitting Ashbury, Tower Hill and Egloskerry, and the 1.00pm carried through coaches, one for Padstow, one for Bude. During the evening a special 7.00pm took coaches for Padstow, Plymouth and Torrington. Arrival at Padstow was at the unearthly hour of 4.00am! This next day, Good Friday, saw yet another excursion leaving Waterloo, at 12.30pm, for Plymouth, Padstow and Bude. In 1912 a dining saloon was included in the 11.05am Second Division on 23 December working all the way to Padstow. As it was needed again for the next morning's 11.05 Waterloo, it was worked empty all the way back to Clapham Junction, leaving Padstow at 6.20pm. Arriving on Christmas Eve it spent Christmas Day (along with the crew, presumably) at Padstow and was then taken empty to Exeter on the 27th, en route to Bournemouth for use on the 28th. There is less evidence of this sort of working in the 1920s and 1930s, though the timetables indicate overnight excursion trains, especially Fridays/Saturdays. Christmas and Easter holidays had lengthened somewhat. Trains always ran on Christmas Day, but only for early-hour arrivals in North Cornwall.

Motor Buses and Charabancs Compete in the 1920s

Brendon's horse-coach excursions ceased in 1922 but the direct competition from the motor charabancs didn't begin to appear until after after World War One. The co-ordination with the LSWR at Bideford, Bude and Camelford also ended. A serious motor bus contender was the Hardy-Colwill Company of Bideford. By 1925 its red and white buses were operating along the coast as far as Newquay. To the south the Devon Motor Transport Co had established themselves in Okehampton, but their Launceston local route failed to compete with the railway. The Southern Railway showed more concern when, in 1927, the National Omnibus & Transport Co, already in Somerset, acquired Hardy-Colwill. Moves were already afoot by all four main line railway companies to obtain an interest in the omnibus field. Parliamentary powers obtained in 1928 enabled the SR to buy into the National Co and as from 1929 the Southern National Co was formed, with an office in Exeter, to operate buses in the Southern Railway's territory, the latter owning 51% of the capital. There was a similar arrangement between the Western National Co and the GWR, which had run buses on its own account for many years. A successor to the coastal horse and coach route appeared in the 1930s when an Ilfracombe-Newquay ('Cornish Riviera') service commenced. Both ways it stopped over at Bude for about an hour for lunch and called at Camelford and Wadebridge stations. The Southern Railway did not influence the National Co's operations and there was little or no conflict along the North Cornwall line. Indeed, a Bude-Wadebridge service connected at Camelford station for Camelford, Tintagel and Boscastle, as we have seen, and there was even a service by Prouts from Port Isaac to Port Isaac Road, a successor to wagonettes. Through bookings were available to Boscastle, Tintagel and (via Padstow) to Bedruthan and Trevone; also Wadebridge to St Columb Major. Inter-availability between train and bus (though a supplementary charge was payable by those returning by train) was permitted between Padstow and Wadebridge, St Kew Highway, Delabole and Port Isaac Road to Wadebridge, and Wadebridge to Camelford. Long distance travel from London by coach became possible post-World War II when the Royal Blue

The Southern National Omnibus Company tied its No. 122 coastal stage route Bude/Wadebridge to rail services at Camelford station for Camelford town, Tintagel and Boscastle. In June 1957 a single decker is leaving Boscastle on the 'new' road – necessarily keeping to the right hand to negotiate the hairpin bend. David Wroe.

The King Arthur Castle Hotel at Tintagel, built by Sir Robert Hardy and managed by a Mr. Taylor in the early years, opened at the turn of the century. It reflected the desire to accommodate high class visitors to the Atlantic coast following the opening of the railway to Camelford in 1893. Much of the material and furnishings were brought by John Fry's wagons from Camelford goods yard. David Wroe.

LONDON AND SOUTH WESTERN RAILWAY.

COACHING ARRANGEMENTS BETWEEN

BIDEFORD, CLOVELLY AND BUDE

(In connection with Trains to and from BIDEFORD STATION), also between

BUDE, BOSCASTLE, TINTAGEL & CAMELFORD STATION

CONNECTING at CAMELFORD STATION with trains to and from WADEBRIDGE, in connection with Coaches between WADEBRIDGE, ST. COLUMB and NEWQUAY.

Commencing SATURDAY, 7th JUNE, and until SATURDAY, 20th SEPTEMBER, 1913, inclusive, Fast Four-horse Coaches or other Conveyances will run on EVERY WEEK-DAY, between Bideford Railway Station and Clovelly, in connection with Fast Trains to and from Bideford: also between Clovelly, Hartland Cross (for Hartland), Kilkhampton, Stratton and Bude as shown below.

During the same period, Fast Four-horse Coaches will also run between Bude, Boscastle and Camelford Station, and between Tintagel and Camelford Station on EVERY WEEK-DAY as shown below. The Coaches will connect at Camelford Station with trains to and from Wadebridge, in connection with which the North Cornwall Company's Coach runs between Wadebridge, St. Columb and Newquay, *thus providing Seventy miles of Coaching through the romantic scenery of the North Coast of Devon and Cornwall*, in direct communication with Through Fast Trains over the London and South Western Railway.

Tourists will find this one of the most delightful trips in England, the Coach Drive is through the most beautiful scenery of North Devon and Cornwall, with an almost uninterrupted sea view for the entire journey.

TIME TABLE—2nd JUNE TO 30th SEPTEMBER, 1913.

DOWN JOURNEY.		BREAK or other Conveyance from Bideford to Clovelly every Week-Day.	COACH from Clovelly to Bude every Week-Day 7th June to 20th Sept.	COACH from Bideford to Clovelly every Week-Day 7th June to 20th Sept.	COACH from Bude to Camelford every Week-Day, 7th June to 20th Sept., and from Wadebridge to Newquay every Week-Day. Commencing July 18th.	Until July 17th inclusive.	
		a.m.	p.m.	a.m.			
LONDON (Waterloo)	dep.	...	...	11F0			...
				p.m.			
EXETER (Queen Street)	"	8 40	...	2 29			...
ILFRACOMBE	"	9 10	...	1 37			...
Barnstaple Junction	"	10 14	...	3 38			...
BIDEFORD	arr.	10 39	...	3 59			...
BIDEFORD	dep.	10 45	...	4 10			...
		p.m.					
CLOVELLY	arr.	12 35	C	5 55			...
CLOVELLY	dep.	...	4 0	C			...
BUDE (Falcon Hotel)	arr.	...	7 0				...
					a.m.	a.m.	
Bude (Falcon Hotel)	dep.	...	...	...	9 0	9 0	...
					noon.	noon.	
BOSCASTLE (Wellington Hotel)	arr.	...	...	See Note A	12 0	12 0	...
					p.m.	p.m.	
BOSCASTLE (Wellington Hotel)	dep.	Bus	...		3 15	4 15	...
Camelford Station	arr.	Bus	...	...	4 15	5 15	...
Camelford Station (Bus)	dep.	...	...	...	4 40	5 35	...
Tintagel (Wharncliffe Hotel)	arr.	...	...	...	5 40	6 35	...
Tintagel (Wharncliffe Hotel)(Bus)	dep.	...	...	...	3 15	4 15	...
Camelford Station	arr.	...	...	...	4 15	5 15	...
Camelford Station (by Rail)	dep.	...	...	...	4 30	5 25	...
Wadebridge Station	arr.	...	...	...	4 52	5 57	...
Wadebridge	dep.	...	...	...	5 0	6 5	...
St. Columb (Red Lion Hotel)	arr.	...	...	...	6 10	7 15	...
NEWQUAY (Hotel Victoria)	"	...	...	...	7 5	8 10	...
NEWQUAY (Atlantic Hotel)	"	...	...	...	7 15	8 20	...
NEWQUAY (Headland Hotel)	"	...	...	...	7 30	8 35	...

UP JOURNEY.		COACH from Newquay to Wadebridge every Week-Day and from Camelford to Bude every Week-Day 7th June to 20th Sept.	COACH from Clovelly to Bideford every Week-Day 7th June to 20th Sept.	COACH from Bude to Clovelly every Week-Day 7th June to 20th Sept.	BREAK or other Conveyance from Clovelly to Bideford every Week-Day.
		a.m.		a.m.	
NEWQUAY (Headland Hotel)	dep.	9 15	...	...	...
NEWQUAY (Atlantic Hotel)	"	9 25	...	...	...
NEWQUAY (Hotel Victoria)	"	9 45	...	...	...
St. Columb (Red Lion Hotel)	"	11 5	...	...	...
		p.m.			
Wadebridge Station	arr.	12 40	...	...	...
Wadebridge (by Rail)	dep.	1 3	...	...	...
Camelford Station	arr.	1 39	...	...	...
Tintagel (Wharncliffe Hotel)(Bus)	dep.	12 30	...	...	...
Camelford Station	arr.	1 30	...	...	...
Camelford Station (Bus)	dep.	1 50	...	...	...
Tintagel (Wharncliffe Hotel)	arr.	2 50	...	...	...
Camelford Station	dep.	(Bus) 1 50	...	...	...
BOSCASTLE (Wellington Hotel)	arr.	(Bus) 2 50	See Note A	...	...
BOSCASTLE (Wellington Hotel)	dep.	4 0		...	...
Bude (Falcon Hotel)	arr.	7 0		...	...
BUDE (Falcon Hotel)	dep.	...		9 0	...
			a.m.		p.m.
CLOVELLY	arr.	...		12 0	
CLOVELLY	dep.	...	9 10	D	4 0
BIDEFORD	arr.	...	10 55		6 0
BIDEFORD (by Rail)	dep.	...	[illegible]	...	[illegible]
Barnstaple Junction	arr.	...	11 32	...	6 51
			p.m.		
ILFRACOMBE	"	...	12 24	...	7 42
EXETER (Queen Street)	"	...	12 48	...	10B4
LONDON (Waterloo)	"	...	4G38	...	...

A—A break or other conveyance will run from Boscastle to Tintagel after arrival of the Coach from Bude, leaving Boscastle 1.15 p.m., arriving Tintagel 2.0 p.m. It will return from Tintagel at 3.15 p.m., arriving Boscastle 3.55 p.m. in connection with the Coach leaving Boscastle for Bude at 4.0 p.m. A Conveyance will also leave Boscastle at 10.0 a.m., arriving Tintagel 10.45 a.m. for Passengers stopping at the Wellington Hotel who may wish to proceed to Tintagel earlier than by the 1.15 p.m. conveyance. B—Leave Bideford 8.7 p.m. C—Passengers with Through Rail and Coach Tickets from London or any other Station for Bude, arriving at Clovelly the previous day, or by the Morning Coach the same day, can proceed by the 4.0 p.m. Coach from Clovelly to Bude. (See also Note E.) D—Passengers holding Through Coach and Rail Tickets for Stations beyond Bideford by the 9.0 a.m. Coach from Bude can stop at Clovelly the night, and go on by the Morning Coach to Bideford, and any Train from there the next day or join the 4.0 p.m. Coach from Clovelly the same day, and stay the night at Bideford, Barnstaple or Exeter, and proceed by any Train the next day. (See also Note E.) E—Passengers to or from Bude or North Cornwall will be allowed to break their journey at Clovelly and proceed by either Coach within one week. F—Leave London (Waterloo) 11.10 a.m. commencing 1st July. G—During June arrive London (Waterloo) 4.48 p.m.

Through Tickets for Clovelly and Bude are issued at Waterloo Station, London; Queen Street and St. David's Stations, Exeter; the Ilfracombe, Lynton and Lynmouth, and Barnstaple Stations; the London & South Western Railway Office, High Street, Ilfracombe; and Through Tickets may also be had at the London & South Western Railway Station, Bude. Tickets are also to be obtained of Messrs. H. Ascott & Son, New Inn Family Hotel, Bideford, the Railway Station, Bideford, or at the New Inn or Post Office in Clovelly.

THROUGH ORDINARY AND TOURIST FARES BY RAIL AND COACH.

FROM	To CLOVELLY. Single Journey. Ordinary. 1 s.	d.	2 s.	d.	3 s.	d.	To CLOVELLY. Return Journey. Ordinary. 1 s.	d.	2 s.	d.	3 s.	d.	To BUDE, Via Bideford. See Note A. Single Journey. Ordinary. 1 s.	d.	2 s.	d.	3 s.	d.
LONDON (Waterloo Station)	37	4	23	6	19	5	64	6	40	0	36	10	43	4	28	6	24	5
EXETER (Queen St. & St. David's)	12	6	8	0	7	0	21	0	12	9	12	0	18	6	13	0	11	0
ILFRACOMBE or MORTEHOE	8	6	5	6	5	0	14	0	8	6	7	11	14	6	10	6	9	10
LYNTON and LYNMOUTH (See Note B.)	9	4	7	4	5	4½	14	3	10	7	8	9	15	4	12	4	10	4½
BARNSTAPLE JUNCTION	6	0	4	0	3	9	9	3	5	7	5	6	12	0	9	0	8	9

Tourist Tickets to CLOVELLY and Back.

	1st Cl. s.	d.	2nd Cl. s.	d.	3rd Cl. s.	d.
From LONDON (Waterloo) To CLOVELLY (via Bideford)	62	0	40	0	34	6

For Tourist fares from London to Bude see Tourist Programme.

Through fares Bude and Newquay (via Camelford). Single Journey, 1st Class, 13s. 0d., 2nd Class, 12s. 11d., 3rd Class, 12s. 7½d. Return Journey, 1st Class, 22s. 0d., 2nd Class, 20s. 6d., 3rd Class, 20s. 3d.

A.—Similar tickets are issued from Bude. B.—Second Class Passengers with Through Tickets travel First Class over the Lynton and Barnstaple Railway.

Through ordinary Return and Tourist Tickets issued to or from Bude or Clovelly (via Bideford) will not be available for the Coach Journey after 20th September, as the Coaches will not run after that date.

LOCAL COACH FARES:—BETWEEN BIDEFORD and CLOVELLY.—Single journey, 4s. 6d. inside, 3s. outside; Double journey, 7s. inside, 4s. outside. CLOVELLY and BUDE.—Single journey, 7s. inside, 6s. outside. BIDEFORD and BUDE.—Single journey, 10s. 6d. inside, 8s. outside: Double journey, 17s. inside, 12s. outside. BOSCASTLE and TINTAGEL; BOSCASTLE and CAMELFORD STATION or TINTAGEL and CAMELFORD STATION, Single journey, 1s. 6d., Double journey, 3s.; BOSCASTLE and CAMELFORD STATION (via Tintagel), Single journey, 3s. Double journey, 10s. inside, 8s. outside. BUDE and BOSCASTLE.—Single journey 7s. inside, 6s. outside: Double journey, 9s. 6d. inside, 8s. outside.

Mrs. Berriman, of the "New Inn," Clovelly, will deliver all Luggage to and from the Coaches at reasonable charges.

Further information can be obtained of Mr. HENRY HOLMES, Superintendent of the Line, Waterloo; Mr. A. H. HOYLE, District Superintendent, Queen Street Station, Exeter; Messrs. H. ASCOTT & SON, New Inn Family Hotel, Bideford; Mr. G. BRENDON, Falcon Hotel, Bude; Mr. W. J. FRY, Wellington Hotel, Boscastle; or at the Stations.

The Proprietors will use their best endeavours to keep the time, but will not be responsible for unavoidable delay.

H. A. WALKER, General Manager.

S. O.
T. T.

Waterlow and Sons Limited, Printers, London Wall, London.

(owned, ironically, by the two National companies!) started serving Polzeath, Camelford, Wadebridge and Padstow in the summer months. In the end the rise of private motoring in the 1960s really killed holidays-by-rail. People in cars became the new 'tourists' in North Cornwall. Their intrepid forebears, slowly traversing the Atlantic coast in the coach-and-fours, lodging in style at the Falcon at Bude or the Wellington Hotel at Boscastle, gave way to a more restless generation, staying in overnight accommodation or parking their caravans at approved sites. For those who do not motor, only Bude, Padstow and Wadebridge are effectively served by substitute bus services from rail heads; 'package' coach tours have taken care of the rest.

Though charabancs multiplied in the west country in the 1830s, infiltrating the coastal resorts formerly the preserve of the railways, the latter did not merely sit back. Reference has been made to the opening of the North Cornwall line for an excursion in 1928. It must have proved fairly successful as it was repeated in the following summers, though the only ones booked in 1932 were from Bodmin to Paignton and Exmouth to Padstow. A so-called Half Day Excursion left Padstow at 10.10am and returned at 11.02pm. Presumably the half day was the time spent at Paignton between 2 and 7pm, on that Sunday 28 August. While the branch signal boxes were open the Exmouth train came down into Padstow at 2.16pm. Again, the evening signalmen saw this train away at 7.25pm. The Wadebridge engine crews exchanged footplates at Okehampton in the morning and Ashbury at 9.15pm that night. It is interesting to note that the Okehampton-Bude line was open on most 1930s summer Sundays in August and September, handling a variety of excursions from as far away as Bournemouth and Bristol. Bude got its first regular Sunday services in the summer of 1937, and Launceston from 1941.

Summer Holiday Trains and 'The North Cornwall & Bude Express'

The 'Atlantic Coast Express' antecedents date back to 1900 when the LSWR began running a 'North Cornwall Express' from July until the following September. It left Waterloo on Mondays to Saturdays at 11.10am, called at Okehampton at 4.10pm and, after shedding a portion for Bude at Halwill, arrived Padstow at 6.40pm. It called beyond Okehampton to set down London passengers at Ashbury; then Halwill, Ashwater, Tower Hill (special arrangement 'by signal when required to take up passengers for Wadebridge and Bodmin'), Launceston, Tresmeer (Saturdays only), Otterham (London passengers set down), Camelford and the rest of the stations to Padstow. It shared the train to Exeter Queen St with a Sidmouth coach and a portion for Plymouth leaving Queen St ten minutes later at 2.35pm. In the opposite direction portions left Padstow at 12.45pm and Bude at 1.48pm, with provisos to stop at St Kew Highway ('by signal to take up for London passengers only'). Otterham ('for Exeter and east'). Otherwise stops were made at all stations to Okehampton though only on Saturdays at Tresmeer and Egloskerry. It was hardly an express west of Exeter, but with a four hour timing it was not very fast between there and Waterloo either. In the winter of 1900/01 the 10.50am from Waterloo was advertised as the 'Plymouth and North Cornwall Express' but a change was needed at Okehampton (3.24/3.40pm) with a Padstow arrival at 6.10pm. Already

Waterloo, or Okehampton passengers, had not been required to change at Halwill for the most part. Holiday trains or locals would consist of North Cornwall and Bude portions divided or combined at this junction. In the last summer of steam, on the morning of Saturday 22nd August 1964, the 8.30am Atlantic Coast Express from Padstow arrives behind N Class No. 31846, while a portion from Bude waits to be attached by Standard Class 4 2-6-4T No. 80039. Both trains comprise Bulleid 3-set Ls. Set 781 (4323, 5762, 4324) from Bude comprises the earlier (1947) build coaches which had 10¼" deep sliding window ventilators, whilst set 838 (3987, 5856, 3988) from Padstow is of the later (1950) series which had the ventilators deepened to 15 inches.P. W. Gray.

from 1896, as we have seen, the connections from the 11.00am Waterloo and the 1.20pm from Wadebridge were making limited stops (some to take up and set down as described above) thus recognising the tourist potential in North Cornwall.

Consider the situation with the line open all the way to Padstow from 1899. The LSWR management having subsidised the completion of the North Cornwall and to Bude (1898), wanted to maximise revenue, for tourism had grown considerably and the horse-and-coaches along the coast were carrying several thousands in the summer period. This was the era of the 'Grand' hotels. In due course there would open the 'Grenville' at Bude, the 'King Arthur's Castle' at Tintagel and the 'Metropole' (originally the 'South Western') at Padstow. Large houses were constructed with many rooms, suitable for letting for long periods in the summer. The well-off Edwardians on holiday with large families, sometimes 'Colonials' on leave, would travel with servants and quite a mountain of luggage, though rolling stock in use at the turn of the century was not really adequate, especially for the long distance to Padstow – 260 miles from Waterloo. The GWR had already

The Western Region provided a final through service to Bude, but from Paddington, not Waterloo, in 1965. Part of this went to Ilfracombe. D6342 hauls BR Standard and ex-LMS corridors forming the Exeter Central to Bude portion on 21st August 1965. The diesel unit in the bay is a Swindon Cross-Country 3-car set possibly running as a two-car set without the centre coach. It is connecting to Wadebridge, the goods yard beyond having not seen any traffic since the previous September. R. A. Lumber.

improved its running to Newquay and Ilfracombe and a start was made in 1900 in building bogie corridors for the Exeter line. By 1907 complete new sets with dining saloons, some from 'Eagle' trains, were available for the 'North Cornwall and Bude Express'. Until 1908 there were no gangways at the ends of the Padstow six-coach (two dining saloons) and the Bude four coaches. Presumably the latter's passengers made do with luncheon and tea baskets.

The 'express' end of the journey was improved. Drummond 'T9' 4-4-0s were coming into use from 1899 and the 11.00am Waterloo was arriving in Exeter at 2.57pm in under four hours. From 1906 the Exeter arrival was 2.36pm and in the 1909 summer 2.15pm. By dint of non-stop running from Exeter St Davids to Halwill Junction (to detach the Bude portion) Padstow was now reached at 5.02pm. Calls were made only at Launceston, Camelford and Port Isaac Road to Wadebridge. The up train left Padstow at 11.00am calling additionally at Otterham and also at Okehampton, reached Waterloo at 5.12pm. To and from Exeter reliance was placed on Adams '460' 4-4-0s but the weight of the new rolling stock forced larger engines to be used in North Cornwall. From the 1906 season Drummond S11s Nos.397 and 398 were stationed at Wadebridge for this work. Apart from the summer expresses, it was usual to include through coaches on the 1.00pm Waterloo and the 8.20am Padstow, but pre-1926 there was no real equivalent of the regular weekday 'Atlantic Coast Express' with its collection of through carriages for many destinations. For the next years the 'NC & BE' ran each summer (extending into October to a certain extent). Restaurant (or 'Dining') cars were invariably included in the Padstow portions. The 'North Cornwall & Bude Express' with its Padstow and Bude portions was timed thus in 1914, with non-stop running Exeter St David/ Halwill Junction and stops only at Launceston, Otterham, Camelford and Port Isaac Road.

Outside the period from 18 July to 29 September the 11.00 had some resemblance to the future ACE with its Ilfracombe and Plymouth portions. Padstow and Bude coaches called at all stations below Okehampton, Padstow being reached at 6.14pm. In the up

The 9.30am from Bude arrives at Halwill at 10.10am. The engine ran round the 3-coach Set No. 781, then drew back onto the Bude line. After the 8.30am Padstow had gone into the up loop, No. 80039 then propelled the Set onto its rear. All the coaches (including Set No. 838 and a corridor third) from Padstow were Bulleid stock, even the single brake composite in the foreground. This was the 8.52am from Torrington which had arrived at 10.18am behind Ivatt Class 2 No. 41283. In the bay is another Class 4 tank No. 80038, the second Bude engine which would work down to Launceston and back during the afternoon. P. W Gray.

North Coast of Cornwall.

THE

MOLESWORTH ARMS HOTEL

WADEBRIDGE.

S. POLLARD, JUNR., PROPRIETOR.

Posting in all its branches. Families comfortably accommodated.

WADEBRIDGE is the most convenient centre for some of the romantic scenery of Cornwall. Visitors would do well to halt here a night *en route* to Tintagel, Boscastle, St. Knighton's Kieve, Delabole Slate Quarries, Padstow, Valley of Lanherne, Bedruthan Steps, and Newquay. Any of these places can be seen in a day. Fly Fishing in the Camel. A Pack of Fox Hounds, and a Pack of Harriers in the neighbourhood.

'BUSES FROM PADSTOW AND BODMIN ROAD DAILY.

Wholesale and Retail Wine and Spirit Merchant.

TINTAGEL.

Wharncliffe Arms Hotel,

(Recently enlarged and improved,) replete with every accommodation.

POSTING IN ITS VARIOUS BRANCHES.

John Walter, Proprietor.

This Hotel is situated near the Sea, and within Five Minutes Walk of the Celebrated

KING ARTHUR'S CASTLE.

And the Finest and most Romantic Coast Scenery in England.

Families at per Week if desired.

THE

"COMMERCIAL"

Family and Posting Hotel,

WADEBRIDGE.

SAMUEL M. LEE,

PROPRIETOR.

Good Bedrooms & Private Sitting Rooms

Increased Stabling and Coach House Accommodation.

A large Hall attached to the Hotel, 60 feet by 20 feet, suitable for Concerts and Public Dinners. Booking Office for "Pioneer" Coach and L. and S. W. Rly.

Masonic Hall attached. Cyclist's Head Quarters, by appointment.

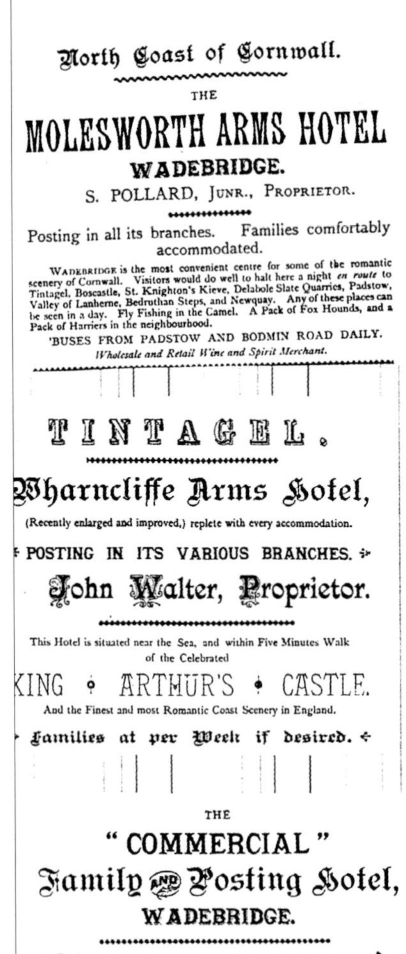

direction it left Padstow at 8.20am, into Waterloo at 3.17pm. During the summer the 1.00pm Waterloo also carried through carriages for Bude and Padstow on a daily basis (weekdays). It is not clear when these coaches returned, possibly on the 12.47pm from Padstow (1.48pm from Bude), though ECS working was not uncommon on the LSWR.

The Great War did not seriously affect the services until 1917, and it appears that summer extras ran in 1915 and 1916. Drastic economies from 1 January 1917 left the local services in North Cornwall slower and thinner and more cuts in May 1918 reduced London connections to three (including the Launceston short workings) each way. The most serious was the 1.12pm Okehampton to Padstow and the 6.40am Wadebridge (below Launceston). A good deal of LSWR main line stock was on the Continent in 1919, including some Dining Cars in leave trains from/to Bari (Italy) to Calais.

In July 1920 a 10.00am from Waterloo was put on, with a 'Luncheon and Tea Car' to Padstow (arr. 5.06pm) and a portion for Bude (arr. 4.08pm). After Okehampton it called only at Halwill Junction, Launceston, Otterham, Camelford and Port Isaac Road to Wadebridge. The Up train with similar stops left Padstow at 9.10am (Bude 10.05am) and arrived Waterloo at 4.30pm. The 11.00am Waterloo (and the 8.15am Padstow) did not appear to include through coaches at this time. From 1921 the 'West of England' trains were timed out of Waterloo at 9.00am, 11.00am, 3.00pm and 6.00pm. The 11.00am commenced a Saturday-only combination that year to include Brake Composites (LSWR) for Padstow, Bude and Torrington. 1922 and 1923 saw the 10.00am running once more and the 11.00am, with Brake Composites again on Saturdays. There was also a 10.55am through train to Bude on August Saturdays in 1923.

1924 saw the Luncheon Car terminating at Exeter Queen Street, with stops as in 1920; Okehampton was being passed in both directions. The 1.00pm and the 3.00pm Waterloo conveyed through coaches to Bude and to Padstow, the latter arriving on the coast at 9.42pm.

The Atlantic Coast Express from 1926

The formation of the Southern Railway in 1923 was followed by a co-ordinated attempt to allay criticism, particularly by London commuters. The Southern's punctuality and their outdated facilities were publicly lampooned by writers of

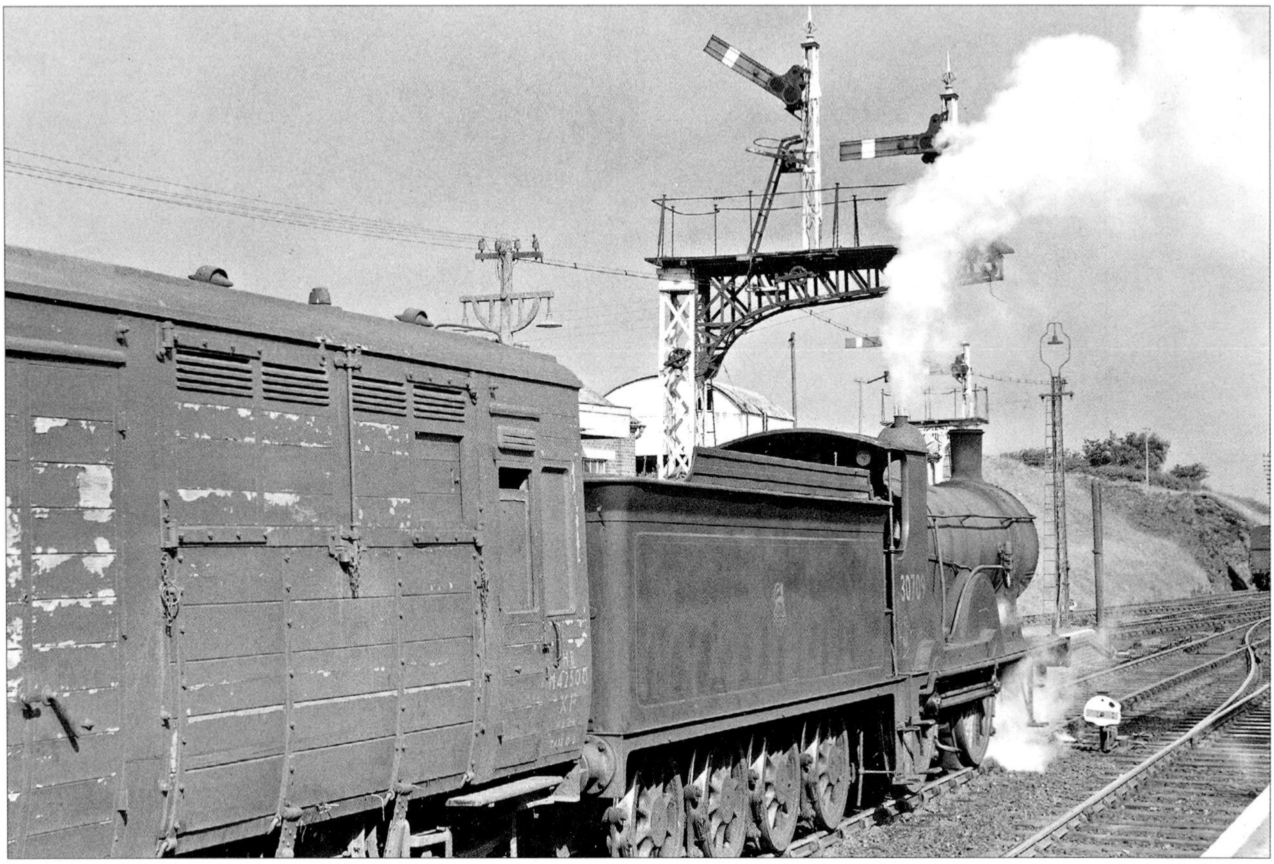

On a warm August morning in 1960, the 9.56am Okehampton to Padstow has the road to Ashwater en route to Padstow. Dubs-built T9 No. 30709 leads an ex-LMS horse box with its groom's compartment. Such vehicles were usually conveyed in passenger trains. The down main and bay starting signal pairs on their brackets dated from 1934 when the heights of the arms were altered. Up on the embankment is the large water tank for locomotive supply and cattle washing points. R. A. Lumber.

SOUTHERN RAILWAY

TOUR NORTH DEVON & NORTH CORNWALL

WITH A

7-DAY "HOLIDAY" SEASON

10/6 3rd CLASS each area.

15/- 1st CLASS each area.

FOR AREAS Nos. 10, 14 & 22 SEE OVER

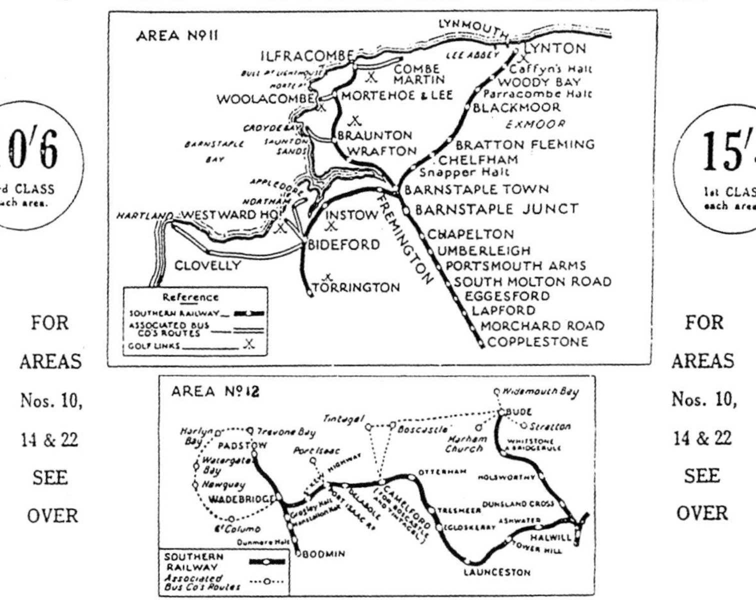

The Cheapest Way to Explore the Beauties of North Devon and North Cornwall

is by using a local 7-DAY "HOLIDAY" SEASON, issued DAILY from March 29th until October 31st, 1934, at ANY S.R. STATION shown on the above maps.

The Tickets are available by ANY TRAIN at ANY S.R. STATION in the area, for 7 days, including date of issue.

Fares do not include cost of Road Travel. No allowance or extension of date can be granted on these tickets in consequence of there being no Sunday Service of Trains in certain areas.

CHILDREN UNDER 14—HALF PRICE

Travel WHEN - -
WHERE - -
and AS OFTEN as you like

Local 7-Day "Holiday" Season Tickets may also be obtained in advance at S.R. London Termini and Agents. Season Tickets for Dogs and Bicycles accompanying Passengers holding 7-Day "Holiday" Season Tickets are issued at the following charges:—Dog 2/6 per week. Bicycle 5/- per week. For details of 7-Day "Holiday" Seasons covering other areas, get handbills at the Local S.R. Stations and Offices.

Waterloo Station, S.E. 1. March, 1934.

H. A. WALKER, General Manager.

C.X. 459/—

the time including J K Jerome. The solution, innovative for its time was to engage a Public Relations and Advertising Assistant and former cavalryman and journalist, J B Elliot was appointed. Elliot saw that their direct competition on the London – Plymouth route, the GWR, had been using positive publicity for 20 years and had invented the 'Cornish Riviera'. He looked around for a similar positive image and found it in Tintagel Castle. The castle itself is thought to have been built as a '12th Century' tourist attraction after Geoffrey of Monmouth had used the location in his King Arthur story. In his book, 'Portrait of the Atlantic Coast Express', Stephen Austin suggests that the more recent tourist exploitation can be traced back to the Rev R B Kinsman, Vicar between 1851 and 1891, who it seems fully embraced the 'creative' Victorian attitude to history to aid the bank balance! Neither of these points seems to have overly bothered Elliot and by 1924 he had proposed that the next batch of Southern express engines should carry names from the Arthurian legend. And so the 'King Arthur' class was born.

Naming the Urie Class N15 4-6-0s had caught the public's imagination and so Elliot is next credited with looking for a name for the train they pulled. The services in question, the 11.00am Waterloo and the returning 12.30pm from Exeter with its North Devon and North Cornwall feeding services, were about to receive new SR corridor coaches and were to be the Southern's flagship. The 'Southern Railway Magazine' for July 1925 therefore duly set out a competition for the title. Guard F Rowland of Woking, who was about to move to Torrington, suggested the 'Atlantic Coast Express' and his winning submission earned him three guineas. Sadly, just six years later he became the only person to be killed on the North Devon & Cornwall Junction Railway after being knocked down in a shunting accident.

For those that have grown up with the 'modern' railway, where whole trains travel from A to B and passengers change between services to reach their destination, the concept of a multi-portioned train like the Atlantic Coast Express (or ACE) will seem quite strange. For these readers it is worth spending a paragraph explaining how the ACE worked, albeit in very simplified terms, as the season and day changed the number of trains, their destinations served and the number of coaches involved. In the age of the ACE, passengers got on to a specific coach on a train and that coach carried them and their mountain of luggage all the way through to their final destination. The ACE leaving Waterloo dropped coaches off at Axminster (for forwarding to Lyme Regis), Seaton Junction (for Seaton), Sidmouth Junction (for Sidmouth and Exmouth) before reaching Exeter. After Exeter the train was divided still further with eventual destinations for portions being Ilfracombe, Torrington (via Barnstaple), Plymouth, Bude and Padstow. It can be imagined like a tree, with the base of its trunk grounded in London and the resorts being the tips of ever divergent branches. On the up return leg to London separate trains had to be timed to leave the resorts, make their separate ways down various branches, so as to be ready to be joined to the main train. This was truly a masterpiece of timetabling and logistical planning.

The inaugural train left Waterloo on 19 July 1926 at 11.00am behind E779 'Sir Colgrevance' for Plymouth and Ilfracombe. At 11.10am the Padstow/Bude train departed behind E776 'Sir Galagars'. At Exeter the Dining Car pair detached, then between Exeter St Davids and Halwill this ACE ran non-stop behind an S11 4-4-0. The Bude portion was detached (arrive 4.42pm) while the main train ran on to Launceston, Otterham, Camelford, Delabole, Port Isaac Road, Wadebridge and arrived at Padstow at 5.41pm. The up train left Padstow at 8.35am and Bude at 9.45am and eventually arrived at Waterloo at 3.39pm. These were the Monday to Friday trains. On Saturdays a Dining car was in the Bude portion (dep. 11.00am) and this combined with the Padstow (10.00am) portion at

In August 1963 the 8.30am Padstow arrives at Halwill behind No. 34083 *605 Squadron*. The leading vehicle is a Southern 4-wheel utility van 'Van U' (CCT under BR) to Diagram 3101 whilst behind is a P Set. A local set from Bude waits to be attached at the rear. The engine of the 9.00am from Torrington has propelled its coach away from the platform (right) to the distant run-round loop. Peter Paye.

Halwill, to run non-stop to Exeter St Davids. It left Queen St at 1.10pm, called at Salisbury, and arrived at 4.29pm.

Whilst the Atlantic Coast Express name undoubtedly gave travellers the right mental picture, looking at a map will reveal it was not factually that apt a title. Stephen Austin points out that only one of the termini that the train served was actually on the Atlantic coast and that over half the mileage was covered at speeds averaging around 30pmh – hardly an express! The Southern partly addressed the geography issue as coaches bound for the East Devon resorts, Seaton, Sidmouth and Exmouth would carry roof boards 'Waterloo West of England' and ACE boards were reserved for the Padstow, Bude and Ilfracombe vehicles. Only one train carried the title in each direction. Whilst the ACE lived up to its 'express' title between Waterloo and Exeter, the exhilarating running to Salisbury and on Honiton bank could hardly be matched west of Exeter. Despite some fast running being possible between Coleford Junction and Okehampton, the 38 miles between Exeter St Davids and Halwill would be covered at a leisurely 60 minutes by non-stop holiday trains. By 1960 the upper limit was 85mph but slowings were necessary at Crediton (45mph), Coleford Junction (40mph), Okehampton (45mph) and down to 10mph for taking the Tablet at Meldon Junction (after 20 over the viaduct). Official speed limit for taking the Tablets at the subsequent passing loops was 10mph, though this was often honoured in the breach with some deft swapping and sore arms from catching the hoops. The maximum permitted speed on the North Cornwall itself was 55mph, though it is known to have been exceeded on several occasions in late running. The line was improved considerably in the 1930s by introducing better transitions off the curves and raised canting (super elevation), up to five inches in places.

From 1928 the through (Mondays to Fridays) Waterloo to Padstow/Bude

Tower Hill was the quietest of the Devon Stations, the nearest habitations being St. Giles and Broadwoodwidger. Included in this train bound for Launceston on 19th August 1957, behind T9 No. 30712, is an ex-LNER vehicle (second) converted to a Cafeteria car. 'Loose' coaches such as this, and the Maunsell 3rd corridor (leading), were probably going to Padstow for weekend holiday train formations, the usual local 'P' Set bringing up the rear. K. J. Rea collection.

train ran each summer at 10.40am (10.35 from 1932). The usual starting times from Padstow were 9.40am and 10.38am from Bude. Dining cars were included from 1933, now in the Padstow portion, and the typical formation of the 9.40am from Padstow was (in 1930); LSWR corridor brake 3rd, SR corridor 3rd, two SR corridor Brake Composites. At Halwill the Bude portion, one SR corridor Brake Composite, SR corridor 3rd, LSWR corridor Brake Composite, SR corridor 3rd, was attached to the rear. A SR Dining Car and Open 3rd were attached at Exeter Queen St.

While it can be seen that LSWR corridors were still in evidence (and continued to be employed until the mid-1940s) most coaching stock was by now of Southern Railway design. The Brake Composites which figured so often in the ACE formations dated from Maunsell's 1926 and 1930 designs. Other corridors, not in sets, were formed from a growing fleet of 'loose' vehicles and marshalled at Clapham Junction yard to an annual summer programme. New SR dining cars appeared in 1934, paired with 'open' third saloons. All this new stock was equipped with Pullman gangways and buckeye couplings.

By 1932 holiday travel from Waterloo was sufficient to warrant separate trains to and from Padstow and Bude on Saturdays. The 10.45am Waterloo left St Davids at 2.16pm, running non-stop to Launceston (3.33pm) then only Otterham, Camelford, Delabole and Port Isaac Road to Wadebridge, arriving Padstow at 4.57pm. The Bude trains were: Waterloo 11.00am, detached from a Plymouth portion at Okehampton and running non-stop to Holsworthy and an Up train following the same pattern in reverse after leaving Bude at 10.40am. The Saturday afternoon trains from Waterloo would also include through coaches to Padstow and Bude. From 23 July to 10 September (the dates for the foregoing) there was an extra at 12 noon on Fridays (Padstow 7.03pm), a 2.00pm (SO) to Plymouth connecting to Padstow (8.36pm) and a 3.10pm (SO) relief to the 3.00pm which included through coaches to Bude, the usual Okehampton to Launceston 2-set being extended to Delabole (9.24pm).

The new ACE was not confined to the summer months. In the winter of 1926/27 the 11.00am Waterloo commenced its well-known role as a provider of through coaches to many destinations in Devon and Cornwall. The ten 59-foot Brake Composites appearing in August and September 1926 were just sufficient to serve Seaton, Exmouth, Torrington, Padstow and Bude each way daily. They contained four third, two first and a guard/luggage compartment. After detachment from the Plymouth portion at Okehampton at 3.42pm, the (all stations) Padstow coach arrived at 5.59pm (and the Bude coach at 4.57pm). The Up departures were at 8.35am and 9.45am respectively. It is not clear whether these coaches ran during the winter of 1927/28. With only ten Brake Composites there may have been problems, but another 50 were constructed in 1930 (with large windows on the corridor side) and from July they were utilised in the ACE portions. Usually one Brake Composite was sufficient for Padstow in the winters of 1930/31 to 1938/39, but occasionally there were two, as traffic required. In 1935 six two-car sets were formed for West of England and Swanage services. The usual formation leaving Okehampton was a local (LSWR) 2-set and one or two Brake Composites for 2-set (as above) and the Bude Brake Composite.

In the final pre-war summers of 1937-1939 the Saturday ACE 10.40am Waterloo/9.40am, 10.40am Padstow/Bude were running from early June to mid-September. Holiday travel was reaching new heights and it is worth seeing how the SR coped with the demand in the 1938 summer timetable. Many Britons now enjoyed holidays with pay, and visitors descended in large numbers on Ilfracombe and Newquay. Bude had also become very popular, so much so that the SR improved the layout there in 1939 to accommodate trains of up to 16 coaches. The Wadebridge East crossovers were moved eastward in 1938, and signalling simplified, to improve operations. The

Exmouth Junction Inspector Smith and crew on the footplate of T9 No. 30719 at Tower Hill in July 1960 with the Padstow 'Perishables'. R. C. Riley, www.transporttreasury.co.uk

N Class No. 31837 pauses for water at Launceston in May 1961 with a train bound for Okehampton. Coach S6664S is a Maunsell Brake Composite and, along with Brake Third S2777S, belonged to set 172. The rear shot of 31837 is interesting in that it clearly shows the outside steam pipes that some of the N Class received when the front ends were strengthened. R. C. Riley, www.transporttreasury.co.uk

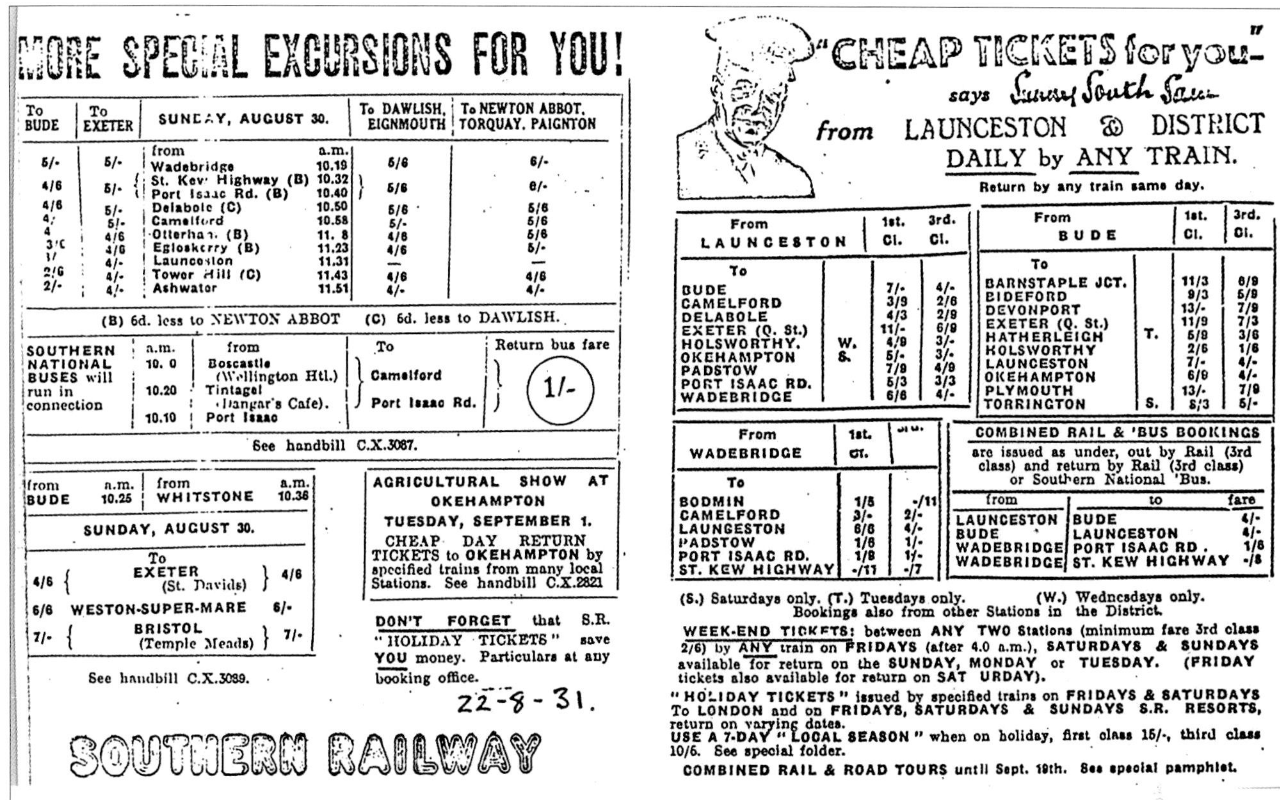

MORE SPECIAL EXCURSIONS FOR YOU!

To BUDE	To EXETER	SUNDAY, AUGUST 30. from	a.m.	To DAWLISH, EIGNMOUTH	To NEWTON ABBOT, TORQUAY, PAIGNTON
5/-	5/-	Wadebridge	10.19	5/6	6/-
4/6	5/-	St. Kew Highway (B)	10.32	5/6	6/-
		Port Isaac Rd. (B)	10.40		
4/6	5/-	Delabole (C)	10.50	5/6	5/6
4/	5/-	Camelford	10.58	5/-	5/6
4	4/6	Otterham (B)	11. 8	4/6	5/6
3/6	4/6	Egloskerry (B)	11.23	4/6	5/-
[illegible]	4/-	Launceston	11.31	—	—
2/6	4/-	Tower Hill (C)	11.43	4/6	4/6
2/-	4/-	Ashwater	11.51	4/-	4/-

(B) 6d. less to NEWTON ABBOT (C) 6d. less to DAWLISH.

SOUTHERN NATIONAL BUSES will run in connection	a.m.	from	To	Return bus fare
	10. 0	Boscastle (Wellington Htl.)	Camelford / Port Isaac Rd.	1/-
	10.20	Tintagel (Dangar's Cafe).		
	10.10	Port Isaac		

See handbill C.X.3087.

from BUDE	a.m. 10.25	from WHITSTONE	a.m. 10.36

SUNDAY, AUGUST 30.

	To	
4/6	EXETER (St. Davids)	4/6
6/6	WESTON-SUPER-MARE	6/-
7/-	BRISTOL (Temple Meads)	7/-

See handbill C.X.3089.

AGRICULTURAL SHOW AT OKEHAMPTON

TUESDAY, SEPTEMBER 1.

CHEAP DAY RETURN TICKETS to OKEHAMPTON by specified trains from many local Stations. See handbill C.X.2821

DON'T FORGET that S.R. "HOLIDAY TICKETS" save YOU money. Particulars at any booking office.

22-8-31.

SOUTHERN RAILWAY

"CHEAP TICKETS for you"

says Sunny South Sam

from LAUNCESTON & DISTRICT

DAILY by ANY TRAIN.

Return by any train same day.

From LAUNCESTON To		1st. Cl.	3rd. Cl.
BUDE		7/-	4/-
CAMELFORD		3/9	2/6
DELABOLE		4/3	2/9
EXETER (Q. St.)		11/-	6/9
HOLSWORTHY.	W.	4/9	3/-
OKEHAMPTON	S.	5/-	3/-
PADSTOW		7/9	4/9
PORT ISAAC RD.		5/3	3/3
WADEBRIDGE		6/6	4/-

From BUDE To		1st. Cl.	3rd. Cl.
BARNSTAPLE JCT.		11/3	6/9
BIDEFORD		9/3	5/9
DEVONPORT		13/-	7/9
EXETER (Q. St.)		11/9	7/3
HATHERLEIGH	T.	5/9	3/6
HOLSWORTHY		2/6	1/6
LAUNCESTON		7/-	4/-
OKEHAMPTON		6/9	4/-
PLYMOUTH		13/-	7/9
TORRINGTON	S.	8/3	5/-

From WADEBRIDGE To	1st. Cl.	3rd. Cl.
BODMIN	1/5	-/11
CAMELFORD	3/-	2/-
LAUNCESTON	6/6	4/-
PADSTOW	1/6	1/-
PORT ISAAC RD.	1/8	1/-
ST. KEW HIGHWAY	-/11	-/7

COMBINED RAIL & 'BUS BOOKINGS

are issued as under, out by Rail (3rd class) and return by Rail (3rd class) or Southern National 'Bus.

from	to	fare
LAUNCESTON	BUDE	4/-
BUDE	LAUNCESTON	4/-
WADEBRIDGE	PORT ISAAC RD.	1/6
WADEBRIDGE	ST. KEW HIGHWAY	-/8

(S.) Saturdays only. (T.) Tuesdays only. (W.) Wednesdays only.
Bookings also from other Stations in the District.

WEEK-END TICKETS: between ANY TWO Stations (minimum fare 3rd class 2/6) by ANY train on FRIDAYS (after 4.0 a.m.), SATURDAYS & SUNDAYS available for return on the SUNDAY, MONDAY or TUESDAY. (FRIDAY tickets also available for return on SATURDAY).

"HOLIDAY TICKETS" issued by specified trains on FRIDAYS & SATURDAYS To LONDON and on FRIDAYS, SATURDAYS & SUNDAYS S.R. RESORTS, return on varying dates.
USE A 7-DAY "LOCAL SEASON" when on holiday, first class 15/-, third class 10/6. See special folder.

COMBINED RAIL & ROAD TOURS until Sept. 19th. See special pamphlet.

coves and beaches facing the Atlantic from Crackington Haven and Polzeath to Harlyn Bay and Constantine also attracted the discerning and they used Otterham, Camelford, Wadebridge and Padstow as railheads.

The 1938 summer timetable extended from 3 July to 24 September (Sundays). Overnight travel was rare in these parts, but a down train had run on Friday nights/Saturday mornings for many years, with inducement fares, as an 'excursion'. The debut of Monthly Return tickets, widely available, had replaced the latter by 1938. There was only one nocturnal train that summer. On Friday 29 July, an 11.00pm Waterloo to Plymouth train detached a portion for Bude to arrive there at 5.16 the next morning.

From Monday to Friday the ACE departed Waterloo for North Devon and North Cornwall at 10.35am with a Dining car bound for Padstow (arrive 4.24pm). The 5 hour 49 minute journey was helped by non-stop running from Exeter St Davids to Halwill; after that the train called only at Launceston, Otterham, Camelford, Delabole and Port Isaac Road to Wadebridge. From Exeter Central the Corridor 3rd and Dining Car pair for Padstow, also the Corridor 3rd and Corridor Brake Composite for Bude (detached at Halwill at 2.47pm) were headed by a pair of 'T9' 4-4-0s. The equivalent Up train left Padstow at 9.40am and Bude at 10.40am, combined at Okehampton with a Plymouth portion and arrived Exeter Central at 12.40pm then, in due course, at Waterloo 4.12pm. Although the 11.00am Waterloo to Plymouth only connected to Padstow (5.36pm) and Bude (4.54pm) from Okehampton, the 1.00pm Waterloo included a Brake Composite for Padstow. The Plymouth portion detached this at Okehampton for the 5.50pm stopping train to Padstow and Bude. On Saturdays this service was much expanded, the ACE running as a 10.35am to Ilfracombe and Torrington, 10.38am to Padstow, 10.40am to Bude and 11.00am to Plymouth (Padstow and Bude). The afternoon departures were also enhanced.

The formation of the 10.38 to Padstow included a 4-car Dining Car set in a formation of ten coaches and was worked forward from Exeter by two 4-4-0s, one of which was detached at Camelford or Delabole. Beyond Launceston, as on the other weekdays, Egloskerry, Tresmeer and St Kew were passed by, limited to 10mph for Tablet exchanging. The 11.00am passengers changed into the local ex-LSWR two coach sets for Padstow and Bude, but the 1.00pm Waterloo detaching five Corridors at Exeter, two for Plymouth, a Corridor 3rd and Brake Composite for Padstow and a Corridor Brake Composite to Bude, appears to have gained another local Set from Exeter through to Bude on Saturdays, as well as one attached at Okehampton for Padstow. The 2.00pm Waterloo had yet another North Devon and Plymouth extra, with a Corridor 3rd coming off at Okehampton for Padstow, again attached to the local sets for there and Bude. Illustrating the pressure that extended into mid-afternoon, the 3.00pm Waterloo was run in two parts, if necessary, during August. At 3.06 a three-coach Corridor Composite set (Plymouth), two Corridor 3rds (Bude), a Brake Composite and Dining Car (Exeter) as well as three coaches for Exmouth, followed the 3.0pm in (publicly) the same timings. The local Sets were attached to the Waterloo-Bude coaches, with division again at Halwill. On these Saturdays, whether in the 3.00 or 3.06 timings, the usual Launceston local Set was extended to Delabole, arriving at 9.25pm (thence empty stock back to Launceston).

Just as the last hopefuls departed for the Atlantic coast, happy (and bronzed?) holiday makers were arriving back at Waterloo. The ACE Up line series on these 1938 Saturdays started with the 10.10am from Ilfracombe, 10.22am Torrington, 10.25am Padstow and 10.30am Ilfracombe, ending with the 10.40am Bude (and Plymouth) all, except the last, with Dining Cars from the coast. Many passengers did use the early morning Launceston and Bude train; in those days the strict Saturday changeover system in hotels and boarding houses dictated prompt vacation of rooms, often by 10.00am. The Southern National buses were co-ordinated to connect from (and to) Tintagel and Harlyn Bay etc (carrying luggage on the roof in those days) and taxis crowded the forecourts at Padstow, Bude and Wadebridge. The all stations 8.40am from Padstow and Bude (9.40am) with non-corridor local sets to Okehampton (connecting to Waterloo) accommodated those returning from St Kew Highway, Tresmeer, Egloskerry and the other stations missed out by the following ACE services beyond Launceston and Holsworthy. The 10.25am and 10.40am (Bude) were again

The original awning over the up platform at Camelford's 1893 station was replaced by a more substantial version by 1900, Camelford being regarded as the railhead for Tintagel and Boscastle and thus uniquely endowed for a wayside station. No further luxuries were provided and passengers had to use the adjacent road bridge or (unofficially) the foot crossing at the platform ends, lit at night by oil lamps. 31836 waits with the 11.26am goods from Okehampton in the down loop at Camelford on 24th August 1960. R. A. Lumber.

hauled by pairs of 4-4-0s, usually 'T9s' but 'L11s' and 'S11' as available. The 'N' 2-6-0s (and the 'U1s drafted in from 1937) monopolised the Plymouth and Ilfracombe trains. The 12.30pm Padstow through coaches were reinforced by a local Set to Okehampton joined by a portion from Bude (also with a local Set) at Okehampton.

The Halwill staff were kept pretty busy on these Saturdays, and well into the evenings! LSWR Corridor gangways were now equipped with adapters to fit the 'Pullman' versions on SR Stock, but coupling and uncoupling the SR 'buckeyes' and hooking screw couplings off local Sets into them was time consuming. Okehampton was hard-pressed at times, especially for supplying and disposing of engines. At Padstow and Bude the preparation and assembling (re-watering and cleaning) of up trains and restocking of the Dining Cars – then contracted to Frederick Hotels – brought overtime for staff there. Down trains required berthing and the motive power foremen needed to ensure the engines were to hand and disposed of at the right time. To cover all turns, firemen from Exmouth Junction would lodge overnight at Bude, Wadebridge and Launceston.

Although Sunday travel was not universal in the 1930s as it is today, by

Maunsell N Class 31836 with a motley collection of stock incluing a Maunsell Brake Composite (Diagram 2403), Bulleid Open Saloon Third (Diagram 2017), Bulleid Brake Composite (Diagram 2406), Bogie Luggage Van 'B' (Diagram 3093) with newspaper roof boards, three 'XP' rated vans and a Southern 4-wheel passenger brake 'Van C' (BY under BR) to Diagram 3092. The 1.30am ex-Waterloo is snaking its way across country near Port Issac Road in May 1956. Rail Archive Stephenson.

1937 both the Padstow and Bude lines were regularly open in the summer months for excursions. Starting that year, three trains each way were advertised (July to September) between Okehampton and Bude. The 3.35pm from Okehampton connected from the 11.00am and the 9.15pm from the 4.00pm Waterloo. Passengers from the 10.10am Bude could arrive at Waterloo at 3.50pm, and from the 2.05pm at 8.22pm (with a long wait at Okehampton for the Plymouth train to appear). The 1939 summer timetable was similar, but it was 1941 before Sunday trains including Launceston, re-appeared and they were extended into the winter periods. Christmas and Boxing Day attracted a Sunday service and, looking ahead somewhat, on 26 and 27 December 1954, the North Cornwall line actually gained a connection from the 4.00pm Waterloo, terminating Padstow at 11.44pm – the latest known!

The Last Twenty Years 1945-1965

In comparison with the First World War, when extra services continued to run in the summer of 1915, the 1940 timetable showed none. The local passenger service from Okehampton, left largely intact, had to cater for those who came to Cornwall for holidays (there were quite a few) and a much increased demand due to petrol rationing, evacuation and servicemen's travel. The SR restored through coaches and trains to meet demand up to 1945, as noted earlier.

When peace came in 1945 the SR was not nearly as short of resources as was the LSWR in 1918, but demand almost outstripped its ageing coaching fleet. Long queues formed at Waterloo for down trains on Saturdays in 1946 (they were a mile-long at Paddington) to meet a pent-up demand for seaside holidays once again. Many ex-servicemen brought their families to show them the scenes of their wartime postings. The weekday 10.50am Waterloo had already regained its Brake Composites to Padstow and Bude, with the former returning at 8.25am, making an eight hour journey to the capital in 1946. During the summer of 1947 a 12.20am Saturday relief train to Padstow and Bude could be laid on to ease the pressure on the 1.25am Newspaper train, which had gained through coaches to Padstow since 1942. The 10.50am Waterloo was relieved by a 10.20am on Saturdays. Well patronised, it was reported running on 10 July as a thirteen-coach train (ten, including Buffet-Restaurant pair for Padstow and three for Bude). The 12.20 ran non-stop from Halwill to Launceston and again to Otterham. The 10.20am omitted Okehampton and minor stations. Over the years these were usually Maddaford Moor Halt, Ashwater, Tower Hill, Egloskerry and (sometimes) St Kew Highway. Roof boards were officially restored from September 1947, new Bulleid stock and the employment of the 'West Country' 4-6-2s giving the 'Atlantic Coast Express' a new look, to use the contemporary term. The 'West Countries' could now turn, following the enlargement of Okehampton and Padstow turntables in 1947.

As in pre-Second World War days the weekday ACE was multi-portioned again, though with differences. In 1948/49 winter timings and formations were: Waterloo dep. 10.50am, Salisbury dep. 12.36pm, Sidmouth Junction 2.11pm, Exeter Central arrive 2.29pm. At Seaton Junction a coach was detached for Seaton and at Sidmouth Junction, further coaches were left for Sidmouth and Exmouth (via Budleigh). At Exeter the Restaurant car pair was removed and the train divided. After the Torrington and Ilfracombe coaches left at 2.34pm, the Plymouth, Padstow and Bude coaches (2+2+1) departed at 2.42pm. There were calls at St Davids and North Tawton to Okehampton where the Plymouth through coaches were detached. It was then: 3.55pm all stations to Padstow (including Halwill to detach the Bude Brake Composite), Launceston 4.52pm, Wadebridge 6.01pm and Padstow 6.22pm. Upwards, the Padstow departure at 8.25am was followed by the Launceston call at 9.54am. Bude passengers endured a rather lengthy shunting process at Halwill whereby their through coach (on the front) and local Set were run-round by the 'M7' tank, then drawn back well clear of the up platform. This allowed the Padstow ACE coaches (one Third Corridor and a Brake Composite) behind their 'West Country' to sweep round the curve from Ashwater and enter at 10.22am. Nine minutes were then taken up to attaching the Bude Brake Composite, and local set (through to Okehampton). The buckeye couplings required a resounding clash to engage after an agonising slow approach! At this time there was no up Plymouth portion, so after a call at Okehampton (10.59/11.01am) and in contrast to the down journey, it was now all stations (except Newton St Cyres) for an arrival at Exeter Central for 12 noon. The North Devon portion arrived at 12.28 and the combined train, with a Restaurant/Buffet set, went forward at 12.35pm to reach Waterloo at 4.36pm. From 1952 a Plymouth portion (dep. Friary 9.59am) became the main train from Okehampton. It was now necessary for the station pilot to draw the North Cornwall coaches back into the Military sidings. The attachment process, as at Halwill, was repeated, all this occupying 22 minutes with much making and unmaking of the vacuum brakes, and attendant testing by the crew and guard. No wonder passengers felt they were not getting very far and slowly at that!

In the Down direction it was a much simpler task to divide the ACE at Sidmouth Junction, Exeter, Okehampton and Halwill – the forwarding engine just backing on to the coaches left by the main train in the down platforms.

The Mondays to Fridays 'express' was restored in the summer of 1949 as the 10.35am from Waterloo (including a Restaurant/Buffet to Padstow on Fridays). With calls omitted at the stations mentioned before, Bude arrival (two coaches) was 4.20pm, Padstow's four coaches terminating at 5.17pm. The Restaurant Car was detached at Exeter (except Fridays) and a Plymouth portion at Okehampton. The up version of this ACE left Padstow at 9.52am, Bude 10.58am, Exeter 12.50pm (Restaurant/Buffet) and arrived at Waterloo at 4.36pm. On Saturdays a 7.36am Waterloo to Padstow and Bude was running (with a Restaurant Car) in 1950-53.

During the winter of 1949/50 the midday local train from Padstow, conveying the returning Newsvan and parcels van(s) was timed at 12.50pm for

PADSTOW

AS A SUMMER RESORT.

Tourists, Artists, Invalids,

And others, who desire to spend their

Summer Holidays

Pleasantly, should visit Padstow, on the estuary of the Camel, near which they will find the finest North Cornwall COAST SCENERY, and have

Bedruthan Steps, Lanherne Valley, Trevose Head,

St. MINVER SANDS, and the bold promontory of PENTIRE within easy access.

There are ten miles of River Scenery, smooth and sheltered Beaches (with bathing houses), and good Sea and River Fishing. Safe and convenient Boats can be hired at low rates. Respectable Private Lodgings, good and cheap Hotel Accommodation, and Posting Establishments. Daily communicati with Launceston by North Cornwall Coach. 'Buses daily to Railway Station and two Mail deliveries.

Particulars respecting Lodgings, Trains, Buses, &c., may be obtained on application to the undersigned,

WILLIAM H. POPE.

Padstow, 1884.

T9 No. 30338 with the 9.56am Okehampton to Padstow train prepares to leave Wadebridge on 4th June 1960. L. R. Freeman, www.transporttreasury.co.uk

departure, and now included two coaches (returning from the overnight Newspaper train) for Waterloo. These went forward on the 4.30pm from Exeter. At this time of the year the through coaches on the ACE and the 'News' were essentially 'local' west of Okehampton, hence a preponderance of all-stations calls (including Maddaford Moor). The consequential inconvenience of retimings on local trains at this end was, however, contributing to the loss of working people to buses and cars from the mid-1950s. There seemed to be little effort to study its effect and the transfers of control from and to the Southern and Western Regions in 1950 and 1958 hardly helped. The Southern re-cast the ACEs' point-to-point timings for the summer of 1952 and introduced its first 60mph schedule between Waterloo and Salisbury. The 10.50am departure was restored to the familiar 11.00am. Padstow was reached at 4.54pm (vice 5.19pm) and the 8.30am up ACE portion, though still leaving in the 12.30pm combination from Exeter, now arrived Waterloo at 3.40pm instead of 4.20pm.

The ACE now adhered to 11.00am for its Waterloo departure on Mondays to Fridays in the summer months, until 1964. From 1959 there was a (at first unadvertised) separation, in July and August, when the Ilfracombe/ Torrington service departed at 11.05am. In the up direction the Padstow/Bude separate train would run only on Mondays and Fridays (except during the height of the season). Padstow departure was generally at 9.30am and from Bude at 10.20am. In both directions local stations, as previously mentioned, were omitted. Generally no Restaurant/Buffet services were included, except on Fridays, when the 11.00am took (an unadvertised) pair through to Padstow convenient for a return on the busier Saturdays. Noticeably, on summer Sundays, though not named the ACE, a through Brake Composite served Bude (arrive 5.23pm) and departed at 9.45am. Launceston benefited by connections at Halwill. The missed stops by the weekday schedules were catered for by the earlier 8.30am from Padstow, and a Down local from Okehampton varying from departures at 4.36pm in 1949 to 3.32pm in 1964.

The early 1950s were boom years for the ACE and holiday trains, especially on Saturdays. The Western Region ran so many extras, funnelling them from the north and London through Taunton, Exeter and Newton Abbot, that it found itself in quite a fix on occasions. The Southern, coming 'the other way' through Exeter, was required to thread through the Western between St Davids and Cowley Bridge Junction – a potential source of delay. No evidence has been found of advertised through coaches or trains from the Midlands or north to the Okehampton line. This would have meant reversal in St Davids, and the LSWR/SR were there only by sufferance. Changes of train there, especially on busy Saturdays, were discouraged, thus the Atlantic Coast stretching from Westward Ho! to Harlyn Bay tended to become largely a London and Home Counties holiday preserve.

Rakes of LMS and LNER coaches did arrive in troop trains during World War Two and after, especially to Bude, where the Army continued to maintain an anti-aircraft gun practice camp for Territorials. Up to sixteen coaches worked in that direction, assisted by the 1939 signalling alterations at Bude, whereas the North Cornwall could handle but twelve, rarely more than ten and usually eight coaches or less, in its loops. Ironically the Western Region's crack express, the 'Cornish Riviera' was diverted over the North Cornwall when the line was blocked at Wivelscombe. It was Wadebridge's role to divide it (and other Penzance services) into portions capable of 'N' class haulage over the summits at Otterham and Meldon Junction. Short platforms, short loops (such as Launceston), restrictive signalling particularly where electrical release on starting signal was coupled to the (non-returnable) No.3 Tablets and infrequent water columns mitigated against long trains. In 1938 the pilot

West Country pacific No. 34017 *Ilfracombe*, crosses Molesworth Street, Wadebridge, in July 1951 with the Padstow portion of the Atlantic Coast Express. B. A. Butt.

4-4-0 (usually one of two 'T9s') on ten-coach Down trains was detached at Camelford or Delabole, and at Meldon Junction or Okehampton from Up trains. Post-war light Pacifics needed no assistance with up to eight coaches, but two 'N' 2-6-0s were booked for eight or more. Tablet exchangers were unknown on the LSWR and SR. Consequently some deft hand exchanges took place at the lesser stations like Egloskerry – not always at the regulation 10mph! With some relaxation of restrictions on Meldon Viaduct in 1949 two 'Ns' were seen at Exeter on the 10.35am Waterloo in 1953, Nos.31846 and 31841. Similarly 31836 and 31838 were on the nine coach 10.45am Padstow while 31833 took the 11.45am Bude through to Exeter. By this time the fleet of 'T9s' was dwindling and the 'L11s' and 'S11s' were going fast. From 1957 more use was being made of Pacifics on these services.

The Southern Region continued to provide a fairly generous summer timetable as of yore, contemplating even in the early 1960s faster schedules and introducing new BR coaching stock, but the 'Beeching' threat loomed and control by the Western Region came in 1963. The new mobility of long distance motorists, aided by an expanding 'bed-and-breakfast' trade, would soon eclipse train travel. Even 'Luggage in Advance' carted by the railway to and from home and away addresses, through coaches, connection buses, ready-waiting taxis, came to be regarded as cumbersome. Not that the motor car could travel much faster to the coast. The notorious Exeter Bypass and the narrow A30 through Honiton and Okehampton were headline news. After the 1952 accelerations Padstow, with the 3 hour 5 minute Waterloo-Exeter 'sprint' and an hour to Okehampton together with the omitted local stops, was still over six hours from Waterloo. This was rarely bettered, though remarkably in the winter of 1964/5 a 5 hour 40 minute journey was possible off the 10.30am Paddington, by a change at Exeter St Davids.

This period also saw the demise of restaurant cars in the Padstow service. Times were changing and the post-war bucket and spade hoards were quite happy to make do with sandwiches and flasks on their journey. Certainly by the summer of 1959 the only Padstow service to see a restaurant set was the Saturdays only 11.00am departure. The restaurant set arrived at Padstow on the previous Friday having been run unstaffed from Exeter as part of the 3.48pm Exeter to Okehampton and the 5.51pm Okehampton to Padstow. In the late 1950s until 1962 the restaurant set would more than likely comprise one

By 1950 the fish trade at Padstow was moribund and rail freight declining. The line of 16 ton wagons on the jetty would be household coal at summer prices, which was sustaining traffic at this end of the system. N Class No. 31837 is attached to the coaches for the 12.55pm to Okahampton and Waterloo and comprises Bulleid 2-Set R of a Brake Composite (Diagram 2405) and a Semi-Open Brake Third (Diagram 2123) with a Maunsell Open Saloon Third (Diagram 2007). The single coach is indeed a ex-LSWR 'Ironclad', formerly a 6 Compartment Brake Third (Diagram 137). Of these only 4046 and 4047 were converted to departmental use. T. Gough.

At first glance it would appear that T9 30719 is shunting Set 236 but this is not so as the second coach is a Bulleid. During the summer months a number of vehicles were 'borrowed' from other sets, and loose stock, in order to maintain the service at peak times. It would appear that a BSK, from set 236, was one such vehicle in this summer of 1960. Later in the season Maunsell Brake Second 2797, from set 236, was noted working with Bulleid Brake Composite 6742 as a make-do local 2-set. Despite this the Maunsell Brake is clearly shown attached to a Bulleid all Second - interestingly this means the train has no first class accommodation. R. C. Riley, www.transporttreasury.co.uk

of the infamous Bulleid Tavern Car sets, albeit in non-pub rebuilt form. Coaches 7899 and 7834 were recorded as a regular pairing used in 1960 and 1961. In 1962 it was recorded that BR MK 1 RKBs 1552 and 1553 had replaced the Bulleid buffets but that these still ran with their predecessor's trailers. The final year for the inclusion of restaurant (buffet) facilities on the Saturday 11am departure for Waterloo was 1963. After years of using Bulleid and then modern BR MK 1 vehicles, the final services used Maunsell coaches dating from 1927/30. Two coaches were allocated to share the service, numbers 7957 and 7869, (workings 44 and 45 respectively). Both had started their lives as Kitchen/ Dining Firsts but in 1954 were converted by BR to Buffet Cars to D2666. This was to be their swansong as both vehicles were withdrawn from service at the end of 1963.

In 1963, timed at 11.00am from Waterloo, the through summer Mondays to Fridays train shed the Restaurant/Buffet set at Exeter Central. Calling only at St Davids, North Tawton, Okehampton and Halwill it then omitted the usual minor stations to Wadebridge, arriving Padstow at 5.00pm. The Up service left Padstow at 9.33am with a similar pattern of stops and timings. BR figures compiled in support of closure proposals throw interesting light on the 11.00am on Saturday 13 July 1963; there were. 87 passengers in the train at Halwill (or joined it), twelve alighted at Launceston, twenty-six at Camelford, thirty-six at Wadebridge and twenty-six at Padstow. Only two joined at Launceston, but fifteen at Wadebridge. The 9.33am took on sixteen from Padstow, twelve joined at Wadebridge, five at Camelford, five at Launceston, twenty-eight at Halwill (eighteen from the 10.20am Bude connection) and there were sixty-seven continuing (or alighting) at Okehampton. Very few people (if any) used the other stops. The Mon/Fri numbers averaged thirty going through in comparison, even the 12.30am Waterloo Saturday morning bringing only sixteen (a party?) for Port Isaac Road, six for Wadebridge and nineteen for Padstow. The all-stations 8.30am Padstow (and 9.30am Bude) produced one 198 at Okehampton on the Saturday, all going forward in the through coaches. The 7.28am Waterloo to Padstow only had 32 people on board at Halwill, nearly all bound for Camelford and Wadebridge.

This, the penultimate summer service from/to Waterloo, showed only too well the deterioration of usage compared with only ten years earlier. Small wonder the WR calculated there would be little hardship if summer holiday trains were curtailed, though nearly 200 passengers with their suitcases would be an embarrassment at Okehampton. It came as no surprise when, from June 1963, the Bude, Torrington and Plymouth through ACE carriages were withdrawn except on summer Saturdays.

The 1964 summer service retained most of the extras, the period lasting from 15 June to 6 September. The 11.05am Waterloo ACE ran Mondays to Fridays, as before, also the 10.35am (SO) to Padstow (still running non-stop from St Davids to Halwill). Through coaches had ceased to serve Bude from June 1963 (also Torrington and Plymouth) on Mondays to Fridays. The Southern Region was still providing the stock for the three through trains (or portions) each way, happily in familiar green livery and by now, there had been an influx of BR Mark 1 coaches in three car sets. The 11.00 or 11.05 Waterloo to Padstow ACE, also the 10.35am on Saturdays, consisted of a mixture of these and odd Bulleid coaches on these summer Saturdays (usually two or three) but there were no more separate trains. Light Pacifics were in charge, while a BR 2-6-4T and some 'Ns' worked Halwill/Bude.

The last ACE running to the fast 60mph-plus schedule from Waterloo to Exeter ran on Friday 4 September 1964. It left Waterloo at precisely 11am with driver Sibley of Salisbury at the controls of 35022 *Holland America Line*. Upon reaching Exeter the Padstow portion, comprising of mixed MK1 and Bulleid coaches in set 565, was headed by 34015 Exmouth. On the final Saturday, 5 September, 35022 was again in charge of the head of the 13-coach Waterloo to Exeter train. The final 11.00am Padstow ACE left with six BR Mark 1 coaches behind 34023 *Blackmore Vale*. A BR Class 3 tank brought up two coaches from Bude and attached them at Okehampton. In a pleasant link with the past, the train beyond Exeter was hauled by 73085 which carried the name of one of the original King Arthurs *Melisande*. The 'Atlantic Coast Express' had lasted thirty-eight years and the old 'North Cornwall Express' had started in 1900. The halcyon years had been the late 1930s when Padstow and Bude both would have 'Refreshment' car trains,

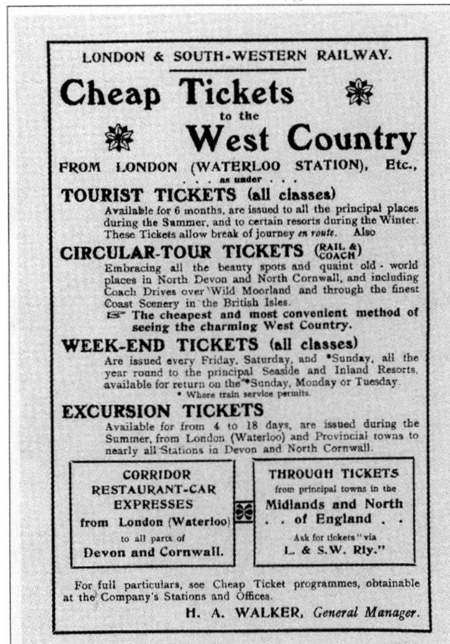

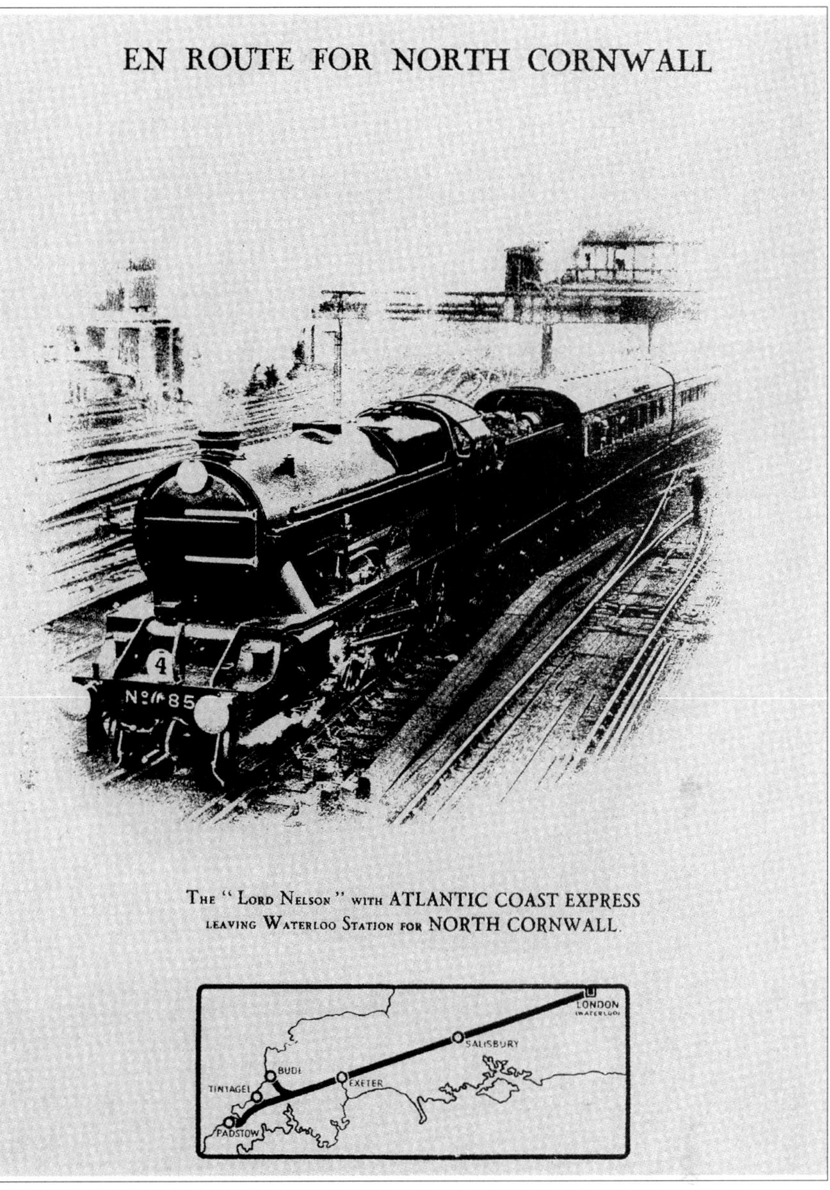

with down trains arriving late into Saturday evenings, while the attractions of Bude were such that a Waterloo, Salisbury to Exeter train then ran non-stop to Holsworthy!

The through coach rather lost its identity west of Okehampton on the regular ACE, as it pottered through Tower Hill and St Kew, yet it was only five hours or so since it left the sight of 'Big Ben' and the tenements of Lambeth. It would leave a London fog and enter a different, soaking wet one, covering the high ground at Otterham. But the 'Southern' was always associated with sunshine and the ACE between capital and seaside promised the joys of paddling in rock pools, giant sand castles or a walk along the cliffs. This intimate link has gone forever.

This was not quite the end of holiday trains, however. Recognising, perhaps, that a few hundred passengers presenting themselves and their luggage at Okehampton and Exeter St Davids would present problems, the WR instituted a summer Saturdays through train to Ilfracombe and Bude. This was part of an 11.05 Paddington and ran each Saturday from 19 June to 4 September 1965. Routed via Westbury, Yeovil and Exeter Central, it arrived at Bude at 16.11. Upwards it left Bude at 1.055 and the five-coaches and the Ilfracombe portion duly arrived at Paddington at 16.10, by the same route. Engine power in the west was either an NBL Type 2 or Hymek Type 3. The Bude through train had no North Cornwall connection, but a Saturday London connection with a change at Exeter St Davids, otherwise London connections from Paddington involved one change, at Exeter St Davids.

In 1966 there were no through trains in the 'emergency' timetable, except that Bude gained a 14.15 from Exeter Central, and an 11.10 up train to Exeter on Saturdays 18 June to 3 September. Fast running St Davids/Okehampton and omission of Maddaford Moor and Ashbury stops by these railcar connections were the last vestige of any concern for holiday passengers to North Cornwall. Ironically neither gave nor received connections to or from the Padstow line!

Selling the Public the Cornish Holiday Dream

As already recounted earlier in this chapter the fledgling Southern Railway had accepted it was losing the public relations battle and so John Elliot was appointed to turn the matter around. The art used in the Southern's promotional and advertising media was a strange mix. It ranged from the uninspiring traditional (almost Victorian), with slogans including one proclaiming North Devon the "Fairyland of the West", through to more striking, modern art deco work.

The first major campaign to improve its image appeared in 1925 under the heading 'The Truth about the Southern'. It also emphasised its 'investment programme' including suburban electrification, the building of new steam locomotives, and gave information on how carriages were cleaned and the challenges of dealing with rush-hour traffic. Examples relevant to the NCR and the ACE included:

- 'Steam': Announcing the arrival of the King Arthur class for the West of England expresses with "91 of the most powerful engines are being delivered to the Southern Railway this summer costing over £600,000"
- 'Rolling Stock': Stating that "850 coaches are being built for the Southern Railway's £8,000,000 electrification scheme - 120 new main line corridor coaches are nearing completion". Within the 120 corridor coaches were some 3-coach sets, restaurant pairs and brake composites for West Country services.

The single most effective and memorable Southern Railway tourism poster has to be the one showing a small boy with a suitcase speaking to a driver leaning out of his locomotive. The original photograph was taken in 1924 by commercial photographer Charles E Brown at the end of one of the platforms at Waterloo Station. Various posters using the original snapshot were produced, including some in French

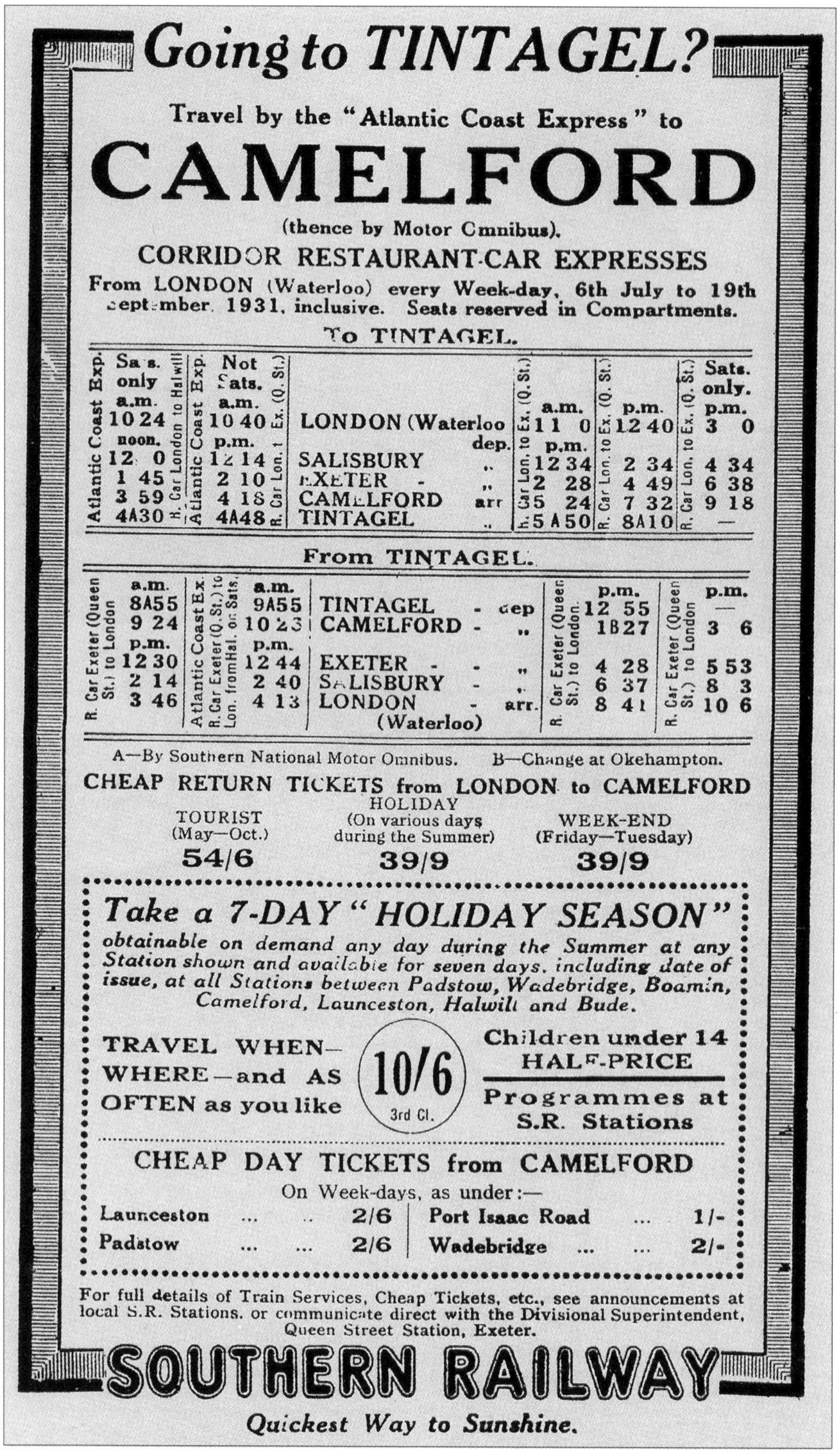

Going to TINTAGEL?

Travel by the "Atlantic Coast Express" to

CAMELFORD

(thence by Motor Cmnibus).

CORRIDOR RESTAURANT-CAR EXPRESSES

From LONDON (Waterloo) every Week-day, 6th July to 19th September 1931, inclusive. Seats reserved in Compartments.

To TINTAGEL.

Atlantic Coast Exp. Sats. only	R. Car London to Halwill / Atlantic Coast Exp. Not Sats.	R. Car Lon. to Ex. (Q. St.)		R. Car Lon. to Ex. (Q. St.)	R. Car Lon. to Ex. (Q. St.)	Sats. only.
a.m.	a.m.			a.m.	p.m.	p.m.
10 24	10 40		LONDON (Waterloo dep.	11 0	12 40	3 0
noon.	p.m.			p.m.		
12 0	12 14		SALISBURY ..	12 34	2 34	4 34
1 45	2 10		EXETER - ..	2 28	4 49	6 38
3 59	4 18		CAMELFORD arr	35 24	7 32	9 18
4A30	4A48		TINTAGEL ..	5 A 50	8A10	—

From TINTAGEL.

R. Car Exeter (Queen St.) to London	Atlantic Coast Ex. R. Car Exeter (Q. St.) to Lon. fromHal. on Sats.		R. Car Exeter (Queen St.) to London	R. Car Exeter (Queen St.) to London
a.m.	a.m.		p.m.	p.m.
8A55	9A55	TINTAGEL - dep	12 55	—
9 24	10 23	CAMELFORD - ..	1B27	3 6
p.m.	p.m.			
12 30	12 44	EXETER - - ..	4 28	5 53
2 14	2 40	SALISBURY - ..	6 37	8 3
3 46	4 13	LONDON - arr. (Waterloo)	8 41	10 6

A—By Southern National Motor Omnibus. B—Change at Okehampton.

CHEAP RETURN TICKETS from LONDON to CAMELFORD

TOURIST (May—Oct.)	HOLIDAY (On various days during the Summer)	WEEK-END (Friday—Tuesday)
54/6	39/9	39/9

Take a 7-DAY "HOLIDAY SEASON"

obtainable on demand any day during the Summer at any Station shown and available for seven days, including date of issue, at all Stations between Padstow, Wadebridge, Bodmin, Camelford, Launceston, Halwill and Bude.

TRAVEL WHEN— WHERE—and AS OFTEN as you like

10/6 3rd Cl.

Children under 14 HALF-PRICE

Programmes at S.R. Stations

CHEAP DAY TICKETS from CAMELFORD

On Week-days, as under:—

Launceston	2/6	Port Isaac Road ...	1/-
Padstow	2/6	Wadebridge	2/-

For full details of Train Services, Cheap Tickets, etc., see announcements at local S.R. Stations, or communicate direct with the Divisional Superintendent, Queen Street Station, Exeter.

SOUTHERN RAILWAY

Quickest Way to Sunshine.

Pleasant Trips to — King Arthur's Land.

Rocky Valley (Tintagel).

"Along the thundering shores of Bude and Bos . . . . to dark Tintagel by the Cornish Sea" and from the latter spot westward to Padstow is a coastline which for rugged grandeur and sublime beauty defies comparison.

During the Summer Months

5/- RAIL AND COACH TRIPS

leave Exeter and Plymouth every week-day for the

NORTH CORNWALL COAST.

These tours afford a splendid opportunity of visiting the pretty village of Boscastle, with its curious harbour and the more noted Tintagel for King Arthur's Castle and Rocky Valley, allowing ample time at each place for exploring the principal places of interest. The drives are through lovely scenery, and magnificent views of the Channel and coast are obtainable throughout.

On Mondays, Wednesdays and Saturdays circular tickets, at the same fare, are issued to Otterham including

COACH DRIVE OF ABOUT 20 MILES TO & FROM TREBARWITH SANDS

affording fine views of the surrounding country from Rough Tor to Hartland Point, and from the Bodmin Monument to the Dartmoor Hills.

BY THE CORNISH SEA

NORTH CORNWALL TOURS.—continued.

Another attractive tour from Plymouth (7/-) and Okehampton (5/6) on Mondays, Wednesdays and Saturdays is

TO BUDE AND DRIVE TO CLOVELLY.

The drive of 18 miles is through Kilkhampton, Crimp (for Morwenstowe) affording almost an uninterrupted sea view. (Lundy Island in the distance). This trip allows of over three hours stay in Clovelly, world-renowned for the cobble-stepped High Street and donkey carriers and famous Hobby Drive.

In addition to the foregoing

—— CHEAP DAY EXCURSIONS ——

run on certain days from Exeter to Padstow (4/6), Port Isaac Road for Port Isaac and Port Gavern (4/3), Camelford for Boscastle and Tintagel (4/-), and Bude (4/-).

There are also bookings in connection with these trips from other stations in Devon. Full particulars of which are given in programmes.

Kingsley's Country and Land of the Doones.

Numerous popular Excursions to these parts from Exeter, Plymouth and surrounding stations. See pamphlets.

On the route of the
ATLANTIC COAST EXPRESS
Read the charmingly written and brilliantly illustrated book

ACE

an account of what is seen from the compartment window, by S. P. B. Mais, illustrated by Anna Zinkeisen.

Published by the Southern Railway.

On Sale at Bookstalls, etc., price 2/6.

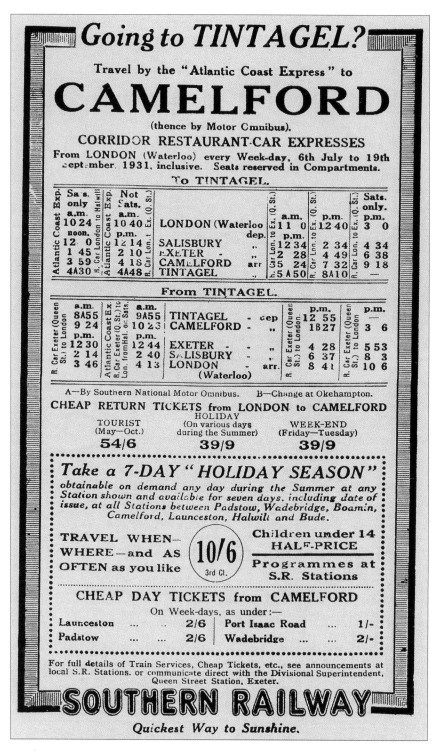

and German but it was the 1936 edition that was the most inspired. In a flash of brilliance, that has timeless appeal, a caption in child's writing was added to the foot of the photograph saying "I'm taking an early holiday cos I know summer comes soonest in the south". Interestingly British Rail revisited this idea in 1978 with a similarly posed shot of a small child (in jeans) talking to the driver of a HST!

In 1937 the Southern engaged the writing talents of the grandly titled Mr Stuart Petre Brodie Mais and the combined them with art deco illustrations from Miss Anna Zinkeisen. Together they produced an 'out of the carriage window' guide to the ACE journey from London to destinations in the West. The chief purpose of the book was to 'bring to life the towns, country and counties you will pass through'. It certainly does this with rose-tinted glasses firmly applied and in doing so reflects the inter-war optimism, albeit from the viewpoint of city folk looking down upon the charming activities of their rural cousins. Priced at 2/6d it was available from all station bookstalls.

In 1946 the theme was modernised for a post-war Britain by S N Pike in the publication entitled 'Travelling on the Southern Railway – the Journey Mile by Mile – What to see every mile of the journey – rivers, roads, junctions, viaducts, tunnels, cuttings, embankments, gradients, speeds and times'. On its cover was a distinctive Southern lower quadrant home signal set at 'clear'.

The post-war period saw the Southern engaged in promoting summer travel back to pre-war levels. In 1946 the Southern was able to publicise its new West Country Pacifics and their intended use on West of England services. Interestingly this 'First in the Field' poster carried the slogan "Southern Railway – getting into its stride again" as a footer. In 1947 a series of picture style posters was produced covering such destinations as Bude, Ilfracombe and Plymouth. Two in this series covered the NCR, specifically the Padstow area. The first, almost a picture postcard, showed a seascape and the rocky headland form of Pentire Head with the caption 'North Cornwall by Southern Railway'. The second carried the caption 'See the West Country from the train by Southern

Battle of Britain 4-6-2 No. 34069 *Hawkinge*, on the 8.30am Atlantic Coast Express from Padstow, passing T9 No. 30709 heading the 9.56am from Okehampton on 29th August 1960. The cross rails to the down line cess (right) and the pedestal in the four foot were for manoeuvring the Tower Hill motorised permanent way trolleys. R. A. Lumber.

Railway' and included a 'cartoonised' image of the railway crossing Little Petherick Creek. By 1948 the Southern had ceased to be and the dearth of posters from the period may indicate that little advertising attention was paid by British Railways to the North Cornwall and Devon destinations in the 1950s. The period was all about the Modernisation Plan and progress – neither of these images fitted the NCR well! Surprisingly there were at least two posters produced in the early 1960s with the ACE as a theme. They proclaimed 'Atlantic Coast Express – to the West of England from London (Waterloo) every weekday at 11am'. Both included the travel durations to Exeter (3hrs), Ilfracombe (5hrs approx), Bude (5¼hrs), Plymouth (5½hrs) and Padstow (6hrs). Each used cartoon style images, one of a young girl with rock pool net sitting on a pile of suitcases; the other a young girl in bikini, spade in hand, paddling around a Cornwall shaped sandcastle. Alas this seems to have been the final flurry as the next posters looking at the NCR concerned its closure.

Southern-inspired Ramblings

In an inspired piece of Southern Railway cross-selling Mr S P B Mais in the introduction to the ACE booklet also says "On your journey by the ACE you, no doubt, often wished that you could have lingered a while to explore the country you were passing through. Mr S P B Mais did; and has recorded the result of his ramblings in a booklet entitled 'Let's get out here'. It contains a full description, with maps and photographs, of 26 walks that can be made from different points on the route of the ACE. The price is only 6d, and it is on sale at all station bookstalls."

The 'Let's get out here' book predated the ACE guide by about a year and, of its 26 walks, four started and ended at locations on the North Cornwall line. The walks were "For lovers of the rugged granite sea-cliffs and sandy coves of North Cornwall, the lonely high granite tors of Bodmin Moor, the tall grey churches and staunch grey windswept farms of the Atlantic Coast".

Arriving in Padstow Mais states that "if you arrived in Padstow, as I did by the Atlantic Coast Express, you will not be able to resist the temptation to explore the immediate neighbourhood at once". Thus emboldened he then describes the five-mile walk number 23 which starts in Padstow and heads north along the western flank of the Camel estuary, past the War Memorial to the pre-historic St George's Well. Turning inland he passes through Tregirls before passing "the battlemented, rather gaunt, grey mansion of Prideaux Place". The walk returns to Padstow which he thought "retained more of its accident individuality and beauty than any other Cornish port". It would be interesting indeed to see what Mais would have made of the current 'celebrity chef' restaurants! From his writings it was clear that Mais loved the sea and 14 mile long walk number 24 takes in a significant stretch of the coastline between Gunver Head and Porthcothan. Not known for sitting on the fence, he proclaims that "There are many excellent cliff walks along the coast of North Cornwall, but for colour, constant surprise, and general beauty, this walk is not, I think, to be eclipsed". Starting again from Padstow the walk proceeds past Prideaux Place and through Crugmeer to Gunver Head. Here Mais delighted in the "jolly sight of red-beaked puffins, shrilly piping and relentlessly flitting from ledge to ledge of the magenta-coloured cliffs". He then continued along the coast past Trevone Bay to Harlyn Bay where he cuts across the Trevose headland, through Constantine, to rejoin the coast at Treyarnon Point. From here the coast was again reached at Treyarnon and followed south to Porthcothan. From here to Porthcothan Mais commented that "Each cove seemed to have its own hidden history of old wreckers and smugglers". The return to Padstow through St Merryn was along what is now the B3276 – presumably this leg of the walk saw very few cars in 1936 compared with today.

Concerned that "the average visitor to Cornwall concentrates solely on the seacoast" Mais's next walk, number 25 at 14 miles, aimed to ensure that "every visitor should make a point of conquering Cornwall's only two high

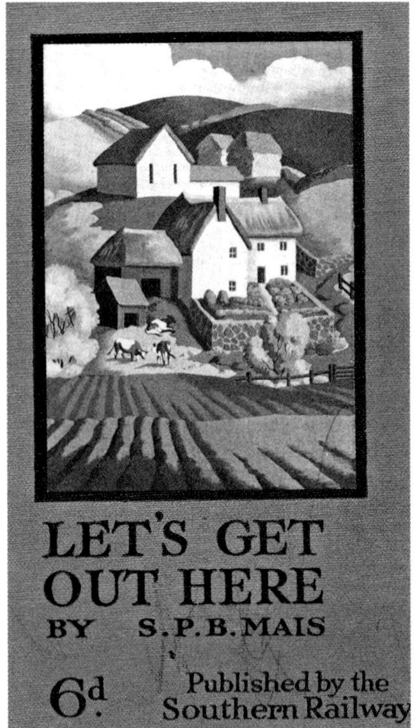

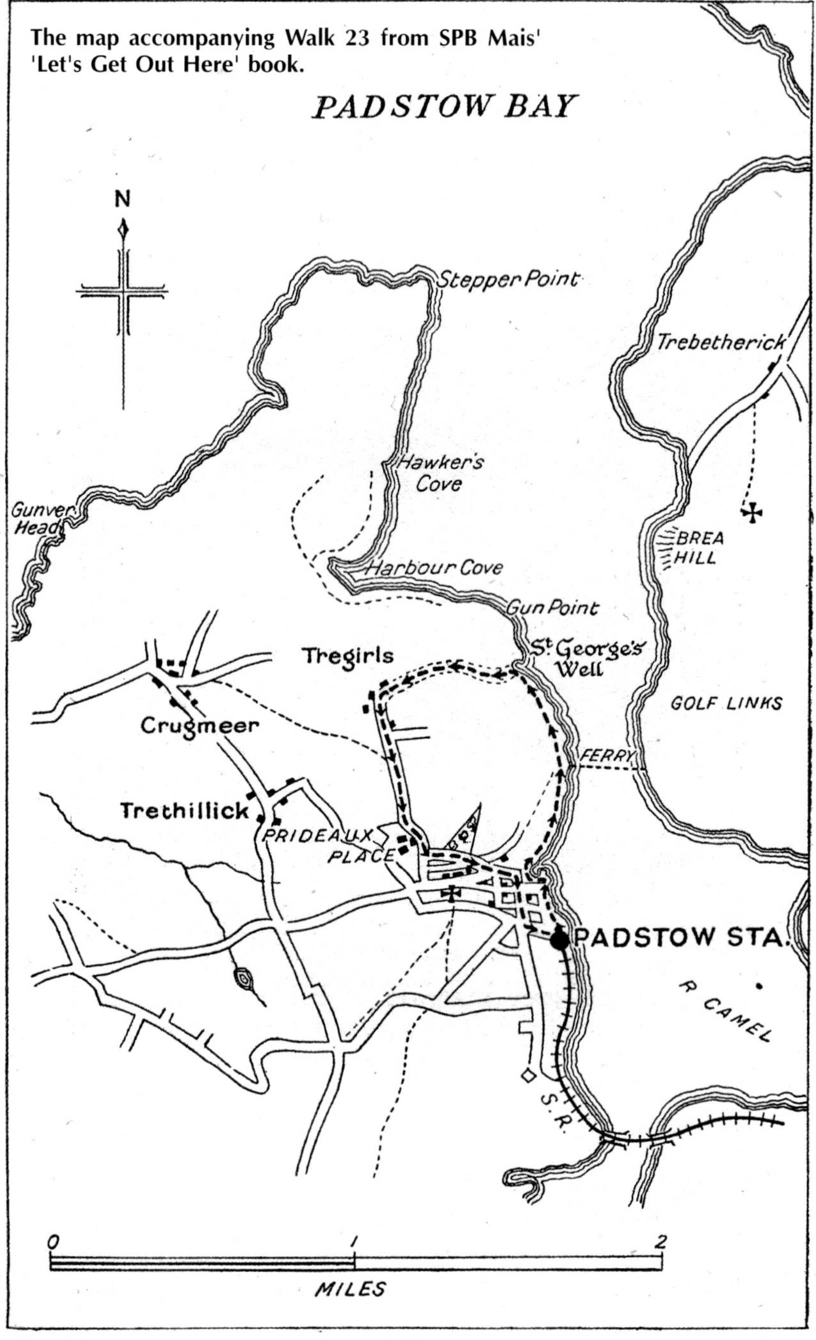

The map accompanying Walk 23 from SPB Mais' 'Let's Get Out Here' book.

hills, Brown Willy and Rough Tor". As a change from the previous two walks this one required a train ride along the NCR to Port Isaac Road station. From here it heads east, crossing the River Allen near Penvose and the River Camel at Tucking Mill. At the foot of Candra Hill he writes that "the dark crags of Rough Tor lay straight ahead... Larks sang above the heather and peat in scores, curlew rose from the marshes on all sides, there were the small black cattle of Angus and the black-faced sheep and a few ponies grazing". From the summit he saw "almost from the northern sea to the southern sea". The return was to Camelford Station passing Slaughter Bridge, the "supposed site of the battle in which King Arthur received his death wound".

The final walk, number 26 at 10 miles, starts from Padstow in a different fashion and involves a ferry crossing of the River Camel estuary to Rock. The first part of the walk is inland past the "little church of St Enodoc" to the coast at Polzeath. Here Mais was disturbed to be "confronted by an unhappy growth of ugly bungalows, the first suburb of Polzeath". With this in mind I doubt he would be too pleased with the further development that has occurred in this area! Next Mais records that he took off his "shoes and stockings, crossed the sands to Pentire-glaze and then began an unforgettable walk all round the extreme edge of the grand promontory of Pentire Point". At pentire he "enjoyed a rich cream tea and had to milk my own cow for the milk". On his return he cut across Hayle Bay at low tide and made his way back to the Rock ferry via the Greenway and Trebetherick Point. He ends the final walk in the Padstow area by stating that it was "one of the most enjoyable cliff walks that I can remember".

Reading the above it will be clear that S. P. B. Mais did his very best to sell the virtues of the North Cornwall area served by the Southern. Imagine being stuck in drab London in the late 1930s and reading his rose-tinted accounts. You too would wish to be travelling by train to the enchanting land he described in the guide, and that was the intended result - to generate traffic. The book was so successful that it was followed in 1938 by a companion volume by Mais 'Walks in North Devon' which was "an account of 10 walks in the North Devon district served by The Atlantic Coast Express". It can be seen that the pre-war Southern Railway provided the whole package; the advertising at home, the trains to get there, entertainment along the way and many ideas for activities once you were there. It is no wonder therefore that summer Saturdays saw Waterloo packed with holiday makers heading west and the main lines choked with trains.

Welcome to 'Betjeman Land'

The stretch of coast near Padstow from Pentire Point to Polzeath was well known to (Sir) John Betjeman, the late Poet Laureate. He was apparently happiest of all in North Cornwall, from his first steps on the beach at Trebetherick until his peaceful end in May 1984 in a bedroom on Daymer Lane. He fondly recalls in his 1960 autobiographical work 'Summoned By Bells' how they would journey all day from Waterloo on the train eventually arriving at Wadebridge station to be met by a horse-drawn brake. Alas those

Some six hours on from Waterloo, Battle of Britain Pacific, No. 34081 *92 Squadron* drifts into Wadebridge on 19th August 1958 with the Padstow portion of the Atlantic Coast Express. A. E. Bennett, www.transporttreasury.co.uk

wishing to physically retrace his steps can now only travel by train as far as Yeoford.

Reliving the ACE on the line to Padstow

Whilst the track on the NCR has been lifted, its stations closed and the ACE no longer visits Padstow, it is still possible to take a trip along the line in your mind's eye. It is through reproducing the words within the Okehampton – Padstow section of the 1937 S. P. B. Mais ACE booklet that we are once again able to travel along the NCR. So sit back and enjoy the journey……

'ACE. It has often been said by authorities on England's countryside that the best way of seeing the country is by train. This is largely because the windows of a railway carriage, except in cuttings, are higher than the fences which guard the lines. On the other hand, long stretches of the roads of England are confined by houses or by high hedges in such a way as to prevent the country beyond them being seen.

Frequently the Southern Railway have been asked whether they provide books which tell the traveller what can be seen from the carriage window.

As it was thought that there was more need for this on long journeys through the less inhabited parts of the country, a first attempt has been made for the route covered by the Southern Railway's famous train, the 'Atlantic Coast Express', which journeys between Waterloo and the West of England.

'Mr S P B Mais and Miss Anna Zinkeisen have therefore collaborated to tell you by word and picture some of the history of the countryside which you will see from the carriage window."

'Okehampton – Padstow. Soon after we leave the Plymouth line the railway runs north and at Maddaford Moor Halt we get a superb view of the tors of Dartmoor, the church on Brentor, and the Cornish tors of Rough Tor and Brown Willy; while north over the rich fields of Devon we can also see the thin long line of Exmoor. I put this view as one of the most extensive and colourful in the whole of England.

'Then comes Ashbury for North Lew. This is a land of little fields full of pigs and plover with wide views on every side. The roofs of Hatherleigh can be seen above the Torridge as we draw into Halwill, the junction for Bude, a grand stretch of sands on the Atlantic that attracts more and more visitors every year. The way to Bude lies through Holsworthy, famous for its Peter's Fair for horses, over the Tamar, and alongside a canal that is only navigable for a mile and cost £100,000. But our line turns sharply westwards down a gentle valley where we are joined by a wayward stream and knolls covered with trees. This brings us through Ashwater down the winding valley with its ghostly woods and gentle stream (which is one of the tributaries of the Tamar) to Tower hill, the last village in Devon, with a typical whitewashed farm and outhouses standing just above the south side of the station.

'We then cross the Tamar itself, with a large country house on its banks away to the north, and enter Cornwall at the fascinating town of Launceston, which stands high on a rock above the station with a round, ivy-covered castle higher even than the rocky town. Launceston was a stronghold in Saxon times. Its gatehouse dates from Henry VIII's reign, and the Keep looks impregnable as it has a tower within a tower, but it was surrendered three times in the Civil War. As the walls are twelve feet thick the cause can only have been starvation. The church is richly decorated with figures and shields.

'There is a figure of Mary Magdalene on the eastern front of the church, and it is believed that anyone who can lodge a stone on her back will have good luck for a year. The stream that accompanies us after Launceston is running the opposite way from the previous stream. It also is on its way to join the Tamar.

'We start to climb into a very different land through Egloskerry and Tresmeer, hamlets with two typically magic Cornish names, and rhododendrons growing on the station platforms. Then come many cuttings of shale and slate, with peeps of gaunt square granite farms protected from the gales by trees, with white gates, stone balls on the gate-posts, and long drives leading up to the houses. We are now upon the open moor again, and at Otterham, which is 800 feet above sea-level, we get a wide view of the open Atlantic beyond the treeless downs and cliffs. We can, on a clear day, see the sea-cliffs of Crackington and Bude.

'But this is the only view of the Atlantic we get from the train in this wild country, for the stations lie just out of sight of the coast resorts they serve.

No. 34078 *222 Squadron* with the 8.30am Padstow Atlantic Coast Express leaves Launceston on 25th July 1964. The train appears to be a Bulleid 3-set L - and one of the 1950/1 batches with deeper 15inch window ventilators. The fourth coach is a BR MK 1 Second corridor or open, the final coach being a Bulleid Brake Composite. Even as late as the 1960s, loading was still quite heavy in the summer months, mainly from Padstow, Wadebridge, Camelford and Otterham. The train would take on two or three through coaches from Bude, also a very popular resort, at Halwill.

Lonely wind-swept trees stand on the field banks. This is very unlike rich Devon. This is nearer the Ireland of Connemara. Everywhere humps in the ground betray the burial-grounds of pre-historic men. Down in the south over the bogs rise the eerie rocky tors of Brown Willy and Rough Tor, and while we are still looking at them we pass close by Slaughter Bridge where King Arthur is said to have fought his last fight and been killed in AD542.

'This is just outside Camelford, which is the station for the quaint harbour of Boscastle and the romantic castle of Tintagel, one of the most magic places in the world. And while our eyes are still glued on those southern tors, we pass, still on the southern side, the vast abyss of five hundred feet from which is quarried the famous Delabole slate. It has employed 400 men for 400 years, and 10,000 tons of slate are quarried here every year and despatched by rail from this tiny station. This is a quaint mining village, but you cannot see the beauty over the hill where the sea rocks rise above Trebarwith Strand, nor can you see very well the comfortable little villages full of trees just below you, but you can see, and cannot help admiring, the number and grandeur of the tall church towers of St Teath, Michaelstow, and St Tudy on the south, or St. Endellion and St Minver on the north, as you come to the lonely little station of Port Isaac Road standing among the upland fields.

'The rugged coastal rocks and grey fishing villages of Port Isaac, Portquin, and Portgaverne lie three miles or so over the hills out of sight, but the wildness of the countryside is well seen from these uplands. Southwards rise the hump of King Arthur's Downs, all the bare expanse of Bodmin moors with the eerie pyramids of china clay rising like white ships on a grey, undulating ocean, and tiny granite towers of little lonely churches lost in the heart of the distant hills. It is amazing to think that every year at least 100,000 tons of this china clay are conveyed out of the Duchy by the Southern Railway. This keeps everybody pretty busy right through the year.

'The line falls steeply now with the unexpectedly gentle valley of the Allen Water just below on the south through the station of St Kew Highway, where we look across the valley to the upland hamlet of St Mabyn with its glorious high church tower standing 85 feet above the ground, a landmark for many miles. And suddenly we are down on sea-level joining the tidal Camel and the line from Bodmin, the second oldest railway line in England, among the fields of Egloshayle, the church and churchyard wall of which reach almost down to the waterfront.

'A white rabbit haunts this churchyard wall together with the headless ghost of the man who, disbelieving in the rabbit's existence, tried to shoot it some two hundred years ago. You can tell the man's age by the clothes he still wears. Just beyond stands the fine seventeen-arched fifteenth-century granite bridge of

LEAVING THE FERRY AT ROCK.

Wadebridge set on bags of wool, the approach to which is exactly like the approach to Barnstaple. The bridge is 320 feet long. Here are the same green fields, the same tidal river with vast expanse of sands when the water is low on which you will see flocks of gulls, herons, curlew, sandpipers. oyster-catchers and cormorants.

'On the downs of St. Breoc above Wadebridge are ancient stone circles and long barrows, the tiniest being a circle of nine maidens who were turned into stone for dancing on the Sabbath. The line runs along the west bank of the estuary, where the fields are bounded by rectangular slabs of slate instead of hedges. On the opposite bank you will see a perfect example of the lichen-covered roofs of a Cornish farm, standing above a creek on the hill-side below a ruined windmill. Then you will see the white, handsome houses of the village of Rock and behind it Alpine-like sand-slopes, quite steep enough and high enough for sand ski-running. Here lie a church almost buried in the sand and one of the best golf courses in the West Country.

'And now, as we round another bend, we can see at last the white waves breaking over the Doom Bar raised by a mermaid who threw a handful of sand into the water with a curse, as a vengeance on a young man who tried to shoot her with an arrow, and the open Atlantic with the vast rock of Newland in the mouth of the bay, the rock of Pentire Point on the north and the smooth green slopes leading to Stepper Point on the south. Tens of thousands of tons of silting sand are removed from the estuary every year.

'And, nestling cosily among woods under the green slopes, facing the sun and protected against the west wind, lies our destination, Padstow, the terminus of the ACE and the threshold of our Cornish adventure. It is an ancient place of narrow, crooked alleys and palm trees and fuchsias growing in every garden, the landing-place of St. Petroc, who sailed to Rome in a silver bowl and lived for seven years on the miraculous diet of one fish which he ate every day. He came back to Padstow to find a wolf guarding the robe he left on the beach. Anyone baptised in the ancient font of this church is said to be immune from hanging, but one Eliot, who robbed the mails, found the tradition to be false. The ivy-covered battlemented house on the top of the town, once a monastery, is now the seat of the Prideaux family. Padstow is a tremendously alive harbour, as you will find as you watch the trawl fish being loaded into the railway vans. They call it a poor season when they do not send away a thousand tons.

'Every May morning the Padstow people parade a 'Horse' and a man, each wearing a devil's mask, and sing the Padstow May-songs to commemorate the 'Hobby Horse' who stood on Stepper Point during the siege of Calais and made the French believe he was the Devil. One look of Padstow from the railway station will be enough to convince you that here is your ideal holiday centre if your hobbies are sailing, bathing or walking. The walks inland over the upland pixy-haunted moors or seaward along the menacing cliffs are infinitely various and at all times enchanting. We have reached the Atlantic. The nearest land is in another hemisphere, three thousand miles away.'

Below. The very last 'official' run of the down Atlantic Coast Express, on 4th September 1964. The ACE had made its inaugural run on 19th July 1926 behind King Arthur No. E779 _Sir Colgrevance_ with the standard formation over the Salisbury to Exeter route becoming, generally, eleven coaches, a twelfth being detached at Salisbury for the Seaton branch. Coaches were detached systematically from the train at various points along the route to make the ACE the most multi-portioned train in the country. West Country Pacific No. 34015 _Exmouth_ has come to a stand at Padstow. S. C. Nash.

The 1.15pm goods from Bude having arrived at Halwill (in the distance) at 4.52pm had there awaited the 12.10pm goods from Wadebridge. Cattle wagons and the more urgent traffic from both lines are now behind N Class No. 31846 on the Bude train, photographed soon after departure at 6pm on 4th August 1964. These front wagons, including the cattle, would be transferred at Yeoford to the 12.45 Torrington to Feltham Yard, the remainder continuing to Exmouth Junction sidings. P. W. Gray.

Chapter Six
LIVESTOCK AND MERCHANDISE BY TRAIN
Additional information by Chris Tooth

This Chapter reviews the evolution of freight services on the North Cornwall Railway. Initially we look at how the services in general grew over the first 40 years, were affected by the war years and then declined due to road competition. Following this we look at the development of the Road Box System and then at some of the other more important traffics including livestock, sand, clay, slate and granite.

The First 40 years

During the 1880s the LSWR was dispatching 'fast' goods trains from Nine Elms depot every night, including a 10.30pm to Exeter. Wagons from the latter were put on to a 5.30am to Devonport, again 'fast' though in reality limited-stop – calling at Okehampton at 6.18am. In turn for Holsworthy and the new 1886 Launceston branch, wagons were formed into a 6.43am goods train. This meant more shunts at Halwill, performed by the Launceston engine (having come up at 6.40) but enabled wagons to arrive at Launceston at 9.30am. Even before this activity Halwill was already alive with the noise of buffers as a 2.45am from Devonport was sorting. It had brought mail from Yeoford (transferred at Okehampton) coal and merchandise from Plymouth and a transferred road box from Exeter. In 1886 and 1887 it apparently ran as a 'mixed' train on the last Wednesday of the month from Okehampton to Launceston.

The 1889 Railway Regulation Act severely curtailed the running of mixed trains. Up to then a passenger coach might well be at the rear of a line of loose coupled wagons. After 1889 the coach had to be behind the engine and equipped with automatic brakes. All mixed trains then had to be listed in the Working Timetable (WTT). Several trains were mixed between Wadebridge and Padstow, in due course, and in 1914 the 5.20am goods from Halwill to Wadebridge could convey a passenger coach on most Mondays. There is a distinction between mixed trains as regulated and those 'apparently mixed', which include goods wagons with vacuum brakes or a through pipe. Even the latter have to comply with regulations on the number of axles allowed.

The opening in October 1893 of the North Cornwall extension from Launceston to Delabole brought a necessary reorganisation to the goods service. An additional five stations were now served and the length of the line from Halwill more than doubled.

The mainstay of the goods traffic to Wadebridge in the final years was fertiliser in sacks from Avonmouth. The line of wagons on the quay in July 1964 shows how heavily it had developed. The end of the Quay was owned by the Padstow Harbour Commissioners. The stores on the right were erected about 1899. C. J. Knowles-Thomas

About to pass under Delabole Barton bridge in June 1957 is 34033 *Chard* working the 11.15am Wadebridge to Okehampton goods. Use of the light Pacifics on goods workings was not uncommon on the North Cornwall line.

Therefore, from December 1893, a through train commenced running from Exeter Queen St leaving at 1.00am, seven days a week. It conveyed mail, road boxes and urgent traffic and was limited to 25 wagons from Yeoford to Camelford where it terminated at 6.50am. A supplementary train left Okehampton at 7.38am taking 'ordinaries', arriving at Delabole at 11.17am. Upwards, road boxes returning to London, Exeter and Plymouth left Delabole at 1.00pm and at Okehampton were held from 6.40pm until 8.00pm for transfer to the Plymouth-Nine Elms overnight goods (arriving 3.53am). A second goods left Delabole at 6.55pm and worked its way up to Okehampton dealing with purely local traffic until 10.55pm. Okehampton engine shed was under enlargement and able to cope with increased workings to Holsworthy/Delabole. Adams '395' 0-6-0s and a handful of Beyer Peacock single-framed 0-6-0s hauled these goods trains up and down the 1 in 73 gradients with the assistance of one (sometimes two) 10 ton brake vans.

Goods guards and travelling shunters staffed most trains, their expertise tested to the full in controlling long trains of loose-coupled wagons when descending the North Cornwall's long banks which contained gradients of up to 1in73. The most testing stretches were Ashbury to Halwill, Halwill to Ashwater, Otterham to Launceston and Delabole to St Kew Highway. Wagon hand brakes would be 'pinned down' as required to prevent a train actually pushing its engine out of control and a guard, often called a brakesman, would ever be at his wheel to avoid snatching of couplings. A coupling breaking under strain was usually the cause of divided trains. In spite of regulation, or through carelessness, wagon runaways did occur at Halwill and Otterham, as recounted elsewhere. In February 1905 a goods train became divided in the section between Ashbury and Halwill Junction. The rear half, after a while, gained momentum and crashed into the front half on the level crossing at Halwill, causing damage and destruction to 22 wagons. The engine was thrust the length of the platform and the fireman sustained serious injuries.

The Devonport (Plymouth) goods by 1896 worked into Launceston and turned around there between 7.30 and 9.00am. Then it meandered its way back to Devonport taking nearly twelve hours in the process. This cross-country train appeared in the WTT up to the First War, though by 1914 it ran only if required. Meldon Junction was an important staging place in those years, though there were only two long sidings, one on each up side of the junction points to Halwill. Most trains stopped to exchange wagons. The nocturnal 1.00am from Exeter spent from 3.40 to 4.50am there in 1899 taking on wagons from the Plymouth line. What it must have been like up there, nearly 1,000 feet above sea level on the edge of Dartmoor, in bad weather and in darkness, is beyond conjecture. The reason for its existence would seem to have been the need to avoid taking trains into and out of Okehampton. Certain down trains were booked for banking assistance up the 1 in 77 from Okehampton. Meldon Junction sidings ceased to figure in the 1920s (though they were retained as refuges for goods trains) probably after the arrival of the more powerful 'N' engines and 25 ton brake vans, and with more use made of Okehampton.

When at last the North Cornwall line opened into Wadebridge in June 1895, the LSWR could establish a suitable terminal for goods operation – a sizeable engine shed with turntable, some new sidings and use of the existing B&W Quay sidings. The lines from Bodmin, Wenford Bridge, Ruthern Bridge and the exchange point at Boscarne Junction (although GWR goods trains ran into Wadebridge), also offered potential inward merchandise, coal, manure, cattle and, at this stage, limited china clay traffic. Adams 'Jubilee' 0-4-2 mixed traffic engines were sent to Wadebridge to assist the existing '395' 0-6-0s. The 'Jubilees' were equipped with steam sanding gear, much appreciated on the steep hills up to Otterham and Halwill Junction.

Two down morning, and two up goods set a general pattern on the North Cornwall for the rest of its existence. Based on Exeter Queen Street (later Exmouth Junction sidings) Okehampton and Wadebridge., these trains exchanged wagons into the Nine Elms 'fast' services with the North Devon line at Crediton (later at Yeoford), at Okehampton/Meldon Junction with the Plymouth line, and locally for Bude at Halwill Junction. Although traffic passed to the GWR at Exeter, the LSWR would primarily route wagons for Midlands via Templecombe and the S&DJR. Otherwise Basingstoke served for the GWR and from the 1920s wagons went via Woking and the new Feltham yard (instead of Willesden LNWR) to the northern and eastern lines. Padstow was served locally from Wadebridge, but the Bude line had its own services to and from Okehampton and Exeter.

Goods Services between the Wars 1920-1939

In the mid-1920s the Goods and Mail train left Exeter Queen Street at 12.05am (it still called briefly at Meldon Junction in 1924) and got into Launceston at 5.55am. The second goods, with transferred Nine Elms, Plymouth and Exeter road boxes, left Okehampton at 5.55am arriving at Wadebridge at 1.53pm. There was some re-organisation of services from 1925 when the new 'N' Moguls were introduced, and Exmouth Junction sidings to the east of Exeter became the focal point for London and west of England exchanges. The up morning goods, formerly Launceston to Devonport, and later Wadebridge to Exeter, ceased to run, replaced by an afternoon service. The main Up services from Bude and Wadebridge were timed to exchange wagons at Halwill Junction. The importance of these trains should be seen in the context of the road box system, shortly to be described. Upwards, there was livestock for the Midlands (via Templecombe), Salisbury, Basingstoke, Woking and Maiden Lane (LMSR), market produce for Nine Elms, fresh meat (Launceston and Halwill) to Nine Elms, with 'ordinary' wagons transferred at Crediton. The Halwill loops were filled as rafts of wagons were taken from the Wadebridge train and placed on the back of the 12.55pm Bude. This went on six days a week, year in, year out, until the end of freight working in 1964, though most 'perishable' traffic and two primary Nine Elms road boxes were speeded up from the 1930s by attachment to the two mid-afternoon passenger trains from Padstow and Bude.

The down London newspaper traffic expanded in the 1930s concurrent with a 'circulation war'. Although passenger-rated, specially allocated bogie vans served Bude and the North Cornwall stations. The 5.55am Okehampton goods attached these vans from the 1.30am Waterloo to Plymouth News. Together with the Nine Elms and Friary for stations to St Kew and Wadebridge Road Boxes and a limit tail of wagons, it was smartly timed down to Launceston, in 25 minutes from Halwill. Ashwater's tablet to Launceston was left in a special box and signals lowered the night before by departing signalmen – an uncommon arrangement. The news van was transferred to the 7.45am Launceston to Padstow (arrive 9.03am). Otherwise in 1938, apart from the time-honoured early down (and the afternoon up) trains with their 'vacuum' wagons, a 10.15am goods ran from Okehampton and a 5.00pm back from Wadebridge. Both meandered through north Cornwall and west Devon picking up and setting down 'ordinary' wagons, reminding us of the very local nature of rail transit in these times. A truckload of hay might go only from St Kew to Launceston, or a load of bricks from Whitstone (on the Bude Branch) to Otterham, and there were always the 'empties' for return to a distant colliery or – by 1938 – a tank wagon to a petrol distributor.

Wartime Pressures

No part of Britain really escaped the Second World War. The North Cornwall in 1940 lay well within the range of German airfields in Brittany and a number of raids occurred as well as numerous 'alerts'. Bodmin was hit but the local lines escaped. The 1941 Blitz on Plymouth, however, had a direct reaction on Wadebridge and the NCR's useful alternative way round the destruction. It happened in April and the GWR was severely blocked. For a

The signal box at Ashwater on the down platform was of the fully glazed pattern adopted by the LSWR in the 1880s. N Class 2-6-0 No. 31845 arrives with the up afternoon goods from Wadebridge in the 1960s. R. K. Blencowe.

N Class No. 31830 propelling wagons over the down loop at Launceston en route to service Troods and the Gas Works sidings beyond the bridges. Troods (later Fulfords) used rail extensively for its general buildings' supplies, agricultural products and coal business, opening new premises at Newport in 1894.

total of eleven days, in five periods, passenger and goods trains were diverted off the Cornwall main line at Bodmin Road, reversals taking place there, at Bodmin GWR, at Wadebridge and, eventually, at Exeter St Davids. GWR engines could not work on the North Cornwall (until 1943) as their footsteps and outside cylinders fouled the loading gauge (platform edges). The ubiquitous 'N' 2-6-0s therefore stood in. Wadebridge bore the brunt of these operations as the GWR 2-6-2Ts and 0-6-0PTs, having brought their trains over the hilltop at Bodmin, were replaced by the 'Ns' or SR 4-4-0s with the necessary re-arrangement of goods trains. The prolonged 1 in 75 gradients up to Delabole – 650 feet to be climbed in ten miles – proscribed loads in excess of 29 wagons and brake van.

Even in 1939 building materials and Government stores started to arrive at Wadebridge and Padstow for an Anti-Aircraft Practice Camp established at St Eval, later an RAF Coastal Command base. St Merryn airfield, above Padstow, and a gunnery range at Treligga (Delabole) followed. In 1942 runways were laid on Davidstow Moor, rail-served from Otterham. Most wagons were sent by normal goods services, but the smaller NCR stations yards were sorely tried. The stockpiling of ammunition and stores for the US Army, which was preparing for the Normandy invasion in June 1944, led to goods facilities being expanded at two locations. Tower Hill came to life again, regaining its loop and two new gated sidings and by 1943 eight additional sidings, with a capacity of 220 wagons, were laid at Halwill. Once again the 'Ns' shouldered the burden. The spur between the two Launceston stations, also opened in 1943, was for these trains to pass from Tower Hill (and Halwill) to Tavistock Junction yard and Plymouth. The 'Ns' would take them into Launceston SR, a pair of GWR 45XX 2-6-2Ts then attaching to the rear to take the spur directly towards Lifton.

Livestock traffic continued, and increased until by 1944 it was double that of 1939 with many more sheep, even the difficult pigs. Their delicate feelings were sacrificed to the war effort. Ironically, fresh meat was being sent into the west, such was the slaughtering policy and food rationing system. Coal was diverted by rail and none arrived by sea at Padstow or Wadebridge after 1940. As a precaution a large coal dump was laid down at Delabole; there was plenty of room in the yard and demand for roofing slate rose as a result of bomb damage in England. Normal exchange traffic between the companies was prohibited at Launceston, only special traffic as above, but the situation altered after Nationalisation in 1948, as detailed elsewhere. It is recounted that one evening there were three trains to be brought into Launceston from Tower Hill. The SR driver said he would bring the last two down as one, providing Launceston was clear. This done, two pairs of 2-6-2Ts took the wagons on to Plymouth.

Interestingly St Teath, between Port Isaac Road and Delabole, was the site of a major accident involving the 6.37am freight train from Okehampton to Padstow. This occurred just after noon on the 22nd July 1947 and was covered on the following Saturday by the 'Cornish and Devon Post' which reported that: 'Passenger traffic became disorganised. At Port Isaac Road and Delabole stations intending passengers were conveyed by 'bus to and from these places. Several wagons became total wrecks and the contents considerably damaged. At Launceston a coach from the Great Western Railway was taken to Delabole to bring the passengers who would normally have arrived in Launceston at 2pm. It is understood there were no personal injuries.'

Road Transport Triumphs

Freight traffic remained quite heavy into the 1950s, in fact bulk commodities – coal, grain (maize) and animal feeds – actually increased. Outwards a flow of sugar beet started to East Anglia and Kidderminster, a trade unknown in pre-war days. With farm subsidies, especially for those fields on poorer land as might be found in the semi-moorlands, bagged artificial fertilisers came by the trainload. The number of wagons on hand sometimes reached embarrassing levels, but this was very seasonal. All this time, however, such staples as building materials and general merchandise gradually seeped away to road transport. Easing of restrictive long distance 'A' licensing and abolition of 'C' licensed short-haul road transport operations from the 1950s with its unassailable door to door flexibility, was bound to have an effect. In 1938 the four big railway companies had campaigned for the relaxation of their Common Carrier requirement, that is carriage (without refusal) of many classes of goods and at published rates. It was too easy for a road haulier to study these rates and undercut them. The Common Carrier legislation was only replaced in 1963.

The two goods services in the down direction continued until cessation in September 1964. The twelve midnight Goods and Mail from Exmouth Junction with its main calls at Yeoford, Okehampton and Halwill, still terminated at Launceston but in the 1960s was later by an hour, at 7am. Letter mail, Exeter and Plymouth road boxes, the 'Western Morning News' (ex-Plymouth) and calf traffic dictated timings. The 1.30am Waterloo Newspaper train (5.55am off Okehampton) now had through coaches to Padstow, and a collection of vacuum and loose goods vehicles to Launceston. The second goods train was more ordinary and worked all day on the North Cornwall line, finally arriving Wadebridge at 7pm.

Upwards, the 11.35am from Wadebridge, noted over the years for its 'meet' at Halwill Junction with its counterpart from Bude between 5 and 6pm, continued in the post-1945 period to forward North Cornwall livestock exports to London and eastern England. As mentioned elsewhere, fresh meat was regarded now as passenger-rated insofar as the vans were taken by the respective 3.15pm Perishable and Passenger trains from Padstow and Bude. The vans were away from Exeter at 7.30pm to Templecombe and Nine Elms, whereas

Although of poor quality these two rare photos of the St. Teath accident, which occurred on 22nd July 1947 involving the 6.37am freight train from Okehampton to Padstow, were kindly supplied by Rod Keat. To see more of the North Cornwall Railway and the area around St. Teath go to www.stteath.co.uk

The engine shed and goods yard at Okehampton in July 1961. The goods yard is full of a variety of cattle wagons, box vans with fertiliser and animal foodstuffs and even an oil tanker. The yard on the down side saw an almost continual transfer and exchange of wagons for Plymouth, Bude and the North Cornwall Lines. Up to 200 wagon transfers were made in an average day with rakes of wagons and even whole trains being made up here. R. C. Riley, www.transporttreasury.co.uk

On 5th May 1964 the combined effort of two N Class moguls, 31849 (front) and 31840 (rear) was required to haul the loaded clay wagons from Boscarne Junction to Bodmin General. The majority of this 2½ mile long bank was at gradients of between 1 in 49 to 1 in 37 and clearly required great effort on the part of crews and their locomotives. The clay and their wagons were destined for the docks at Lostwithiel and Fowey and would have been taken beyond Bodmin General by former GWR locomotives. Whilst all of the open wagons appear to have the white staining characteristic of the Weford china clay, around this time wagons containing the creamy white Marland ball clay were also being routed to Fowey via Wadebridge and would have been added to Wenford wagons at Boscarne Junction. S. C. Nash.

cattle wagons went on to the 12.45am Torrington at Crediton. Latterly Feltham Yard received them, via Woking, being the main sorting yard on the Southern for north and eastern England. Alas, here too the traffic declined, accelerated by the footplatemen's strike in 1955, and had all but ceased by 1964. Meat vans were succeeded by demountable containers soon after the war and by 1960 the abattoirs at Launceston, Wadebridge, Halwill and Holsworthy were producing a sizeable tonnage for rail transit. The development of specialised refrigerated road transport of meat sealed the fate of the insulated containers and they ceased running from the west in 1965.

Blocks of wagons of fertiliser from Avonmouth would appear in season on the down morning goods trains, and there was a rise in coal carryings in the 1960s around July and August, the NCB offering 'summer prices'. The empties from these trundled back on the 5.00pm goods from Wadebridge, reaching Okehampton about 9pm. This train terminated at Exmouth Junction and later Salisbury.

Matters at Launceston were complicated. From 31 December 1962 WR passenger services Plymouth-Launceston had ceased to run. At first the portion from Tavistock South to Lifton was retained for milk traffic (including the Ambrosia firm) henceforward being served from the SR main line via the wartime connection at Lydford. The Lifton-Launceston (North Goods) track was retained, though closed. A bizarre situation now arose whereby the Launceston engine (now an Ivatt 2-6-2T) ran light to Meldon Junction, reversed to Lydford to work the Tavistock South Goods and ran thence to Lifton to collect milk tanks for Plymouth.

The value of diversionary routes was proved again in 1963 following a landslip at Wiveliscombe between St Germans and Saltash. GWR goods trains were again sent via the North Cornwall line to Exeter.

Consternation at proposals by the Western Region to withdraw all freight services from the North Cornwall and Bude lines from September 1964 brought protest visits by Launceston and Holsworthy traders to Paddington. Launceston's goods facilities would be retained, but the locals were concerned at the loss of Ashwater and Camelford. Launceston could be reconnected to Lydford, as will be seen, and Wadebridge was still linked to Cornwall via Boscarne Junction. The Western Region was adamant on closure. The bulk traffic which loomed so large in the 1960s was obtained by BR at a below cost contract. Total losses per month were running at £6,000. Worse, local road hauliers, aware of the prices, were undercutting even at a loss to themselves. For bulk agricultural feeds and fertilisers, eight-ton lorries were stationed at Launceston and Wadebridge to deliver to existing warehouses along the line, or direct to farms. The Sundries traffic had ceased in the 1960s, victim again of road transport.

Freight from Exmouth Junction ceased to run west of Okehampton from 9 September 1964 (and to Tavistock South from 26 September). However, as Launceston was to be retained as a railhead for wagonload traffic, the Lifton-Launceston line re-opened to serve it. Wagons were brought from Tavistock Junction, on the outskirts of Plymouth, via Beer Alton and across at Lydford. By this time trains were in the hands of the NBL D6300 diesels. This service lasted until 28 February 1966, the North (ex-GWR) sidings being clipped out immediately. The South (ex-SR) yard was taken out of use in the following July. Both places (and the Launceston passenger stations) have been obliterated by spreading industrial premises.

Wadebridge retained full load facilities until 17 December 1978, served by a daily train from St Blazey which also handled the china clay from Wenford Bridge. A Class 08 diesel shutter was employed on this, the clay traffic lasting until September 1983. This brings to a close our account of the rise and fall of freight services and now we turn our attention to traffics that were particularly important to the North Cornwall.

The Road Box System

Road box is a description that could conjure up all manner of mental

A mixed goods train comprising box van, three clay wagons from Wenford, a coal wagon and a goods van are being marshalled by Beattie Well tank No. 30587 at Wadebridge yard in the late 50s. www.transporttreasury.co.uk

Railways first came to Wadebridge in 1834 and they ended there in 1978. The Bodmin & Wadebridge 'station' once stood near the furthest wagon, and Lever's/Rush's store is on the site of the old sand dock. In July 1964 box vans of cattle feed and fertilisers came via the North Cornwall, but from 7th September were diverted via Bodmin Road until final closure of Wadebridge as a 'full load' depot in 1978. On the right are the ex-LNWR dormitory coach, a bogie 'Queen Mary' brake van and an ex-GWR breakdown van. C. J. Knowles-Thomas.

pictures and, without further explanation, could lead to some confusion. The LSWR 'road boxes' or 'road vans' were essentially goods carrying brake vans, similar to those employed by most railway companies around this time. They had a single veranda at one end and, unusually to 'modern' eyes, had large double side doors giving access to the guard's compartment. These doors allowed the guard to quickly load and unload 'smalls', meaning sundry small consignments such as groceries and perishable goods of an urgent or semi-urgent nature, at station stops.

There was a complex network of numbered road box destinations which enabled smalls traffic to be sent from and to virtually all places on the LSWR system (and beyond) in 24 hours. In effect it was a very early version of what we might now refer to in the age of road traffic deliveries as logistics. The first Adams vans were constructed between 1880 and 1885 and photographs exist of them in use on the Bodmin line c1890. Further batches (including Diagrams 1541 and 1544) were built up to 1911 but from 1915 onwards the LSWR started constructing what we would recognise as typical brake vans with twin verandas, side duckets and no side doors (Diagrams 1543 and 1547). Despite the size and weight of the road vans steadily increasing, from the initial 10-ton rating up to the final 20-ton designs, they were killed off in the 1920s by increased business resulting in the need for a heavier brake-force on goods trains. During this period 24-ton brake vans, referred to as 'New', were put on to certain North Cornwall line trains, concurrently with heavier loadings enabled by the Maunsell N Class 2-6-0s. They were followed in the late 1920s by the familiar SR 25-ton 'Pill-Box' brakes termed 'New Heavy' vans. The midnight Exeter-Launceston Goods and Mail was an example, using a 'New Heavy' on Nos.4 and 5 services and returning on the 5.00pm up Goods from Wadebridge. From the 1920s LSWR designed box vans, fitted with vacuum brake and oil-filled axle boxes (i.e. not grease) took on the role of the road boxes for carrying the 'smalls'. With ventilators they were suitable for market produce and, with modification, meat carcasses. By the 1930s SR versions had largely replaced the earlier wagons in the 'road box system'. Some of the original road vans were converted for use by the Mechanical Engineer's Department as mobile stores vans and were stripped of their brake gear. Additionally it is notable that 10-ton road van 54663 was allocated to work only between Bodmin, Wadebridge and Padstow from 1939 through to about 1961.

Many of the road boxes left Nine Elms in the fast overnight freights to Dorset and the West of England. In 1930 the down 'Tavvy', the 9.32pm (8.33pm SO) from Nine Elms, included road boxes for stations Launceston to St Kew Highway (No.26), Ashbury/Halwill (No.27), Okehampton and stations to Bude (No.28). Arriving at Okehampton at 4.53am, No.26 working, a box from Exeter for Launceston and all stations to Wadebridge (No.242) and a box from Plymouth Friary (No.288) were made up into a 5.55am departure. It called only at Halwill and Launceston, then all stations to Wadebridge, except Tresmeer. The latter station was served by Egloskerry. A road box (No.209) from Templecombe (3.52pm) was transferred in the early hours to the Launceston goods and Mail at Okehampton leaving at 4.00am, thence from Launceston on the 8.38am to Wadebridge. In this case it was a non-vacuum van. Lastly the 3.26am from Exmouth Junction to Bude left Okehampton at 7.38am taking No.27, the London-Halwill box with goods for Ashbury, Ashwater, Tower Hill and the stations on the Torrington branch; No.28 was London-Bude; No.243 Exeter-Bude and No.286 Plymouth-Bude.

A similar system operated in the up direction, the principal trains being the 11.15am from Wadebridge, the 12.53pm from Bude and the 7.27pm from

Crediton to Nine Elms. An interesting road box working (No.275) concerned a through van from Bude (6.57am dep.) to Bristol LMS. It spent a long time getting there, lingering at Exmouth Junction and Honiton between transfers, and arriving at Bristol about 48 hours later!

Livestock

From the beginning of the century long distance movement of cattle from west Devon and North Cornwall increased considerably. The Exeter dealer William Harris began buying in livestock from the existing markets at Holsworthy, Launceston, Camelford and Wadebridge. This was encouraged by the LSWR and, in due course, Mr Harris was taking store cattle to eastern England (private sales) and to Chichester market. Fat cattle were destined for Maiden Lane LNWR where the London (Smithfield) abattoirs were located. In 1909, special-notice empty wagons were sent down from Exeter at 5.50am (Launceston 10.09 arrival). At 2.30pm a special worked through to Crediton and Exeter (arrive 5.23pm) where wagons were put on a Monday night special leaving at 6.15pm for Fratton LSWR, to be taken on by the LBSCR to Chichester fortnightly market. A second 3.00pm left Wadebridge with Exeter-bound cattle, clearing ordinary goods wagons as far as Halwill, thence Crediton, for the Midlands and London, the engine returning light to Wadebridge. These special arrangements still applied in 1914 and into World War One – vitally in 1917, for the German submarine menace was seriously threatening Britain's food supplies in that year. Both a 2.40pm Launceston and a 2.55pm Wadebridge Special were augmenting the regular goods services, as well as trains from the Bude line. By 1919 only one 'special notice' running survived, a 2.00pm relief from Wadebridge to Launceston only. After 1921 cattle sales declined considerably, and were not to revive until the early 1930s.

Although livestock forwardings had declined in the 1920s this later recovered due to a rising demand for fresh meat in the cities. The Southern Railway speeded up overnight delivery to the markets from 1927. A new service at 7.30pm from Exeter Queen Street Goods Yard was in to Nine Elms at 12.51am, two hours earlier than the 12.45pm Torrington, the principal carrier west of Exeter. The exchange of vehicles at Halwill around 5.00pm continued, whereby Bude and Wadebridge/ Launceston market vans were in due course forwarded for attachment to the Torrington train at Crediton (7.29pm). However a number of vans, mostly of meat but some carrying flowers and horticultural products, were now put on the rear of the 3.06pm Padstow passenger and 'perishables' at Halwill. This train left at 5.17pm arriving at Exeter Queen Street at 6.32pm in time for the above-mentioned 7.30pm fast goods. The 11.35am Wadebridge in fact had road boxes or vans for Nine Elms, Plymouth Friary and Exeter, continuing to Okehampton. The Exeter boxes, also from Bude and a Bude to Bristol (LMS), went forward on the 10.10pm from Okehampton (the 5.00pm Wadebridge to Salisbury, calling at Templecombe). All these operations were subject to prompt despatch by local staff, with the added element of some smart shunting. The SR published summaries of wagon formations in the WTT.

Cattle, or livestock as the Southern Railway termed it (to cover sheep/ lambs and horses for slaughter as well as cows) began moving again in quantity from about 1932 as indicated by a Special Notice pathway on Tuesdays (Launceston Market) at 2.36pm, to relieve the 11.35am Wadebridge and to run to Exeter if necessary. This was in the summer of 1938, with the 11.35 itself re-timed on Saturdays to leave at 10.50am. These amendments, and those on the Bude line, below Halwill, were to accommodate the extra holiday trains from Waterloo to Padstow/Bude in the afternoons. Pigs, not good travellers, were rarer and in any case were more likely to be killed locally on farms and their carcasses sent by rail. There was a steady trade of 'baconers' to the Harris

An interesting variety of pre-Grouping stock in the bay at Halwill in the 1930s. Behind the rebuilt LBSCR E1R class No. 2096, which worked the Torrington Line from 1928 until 1953, is an SR cattle wagon built to an earlier SECR design (diagram 1515). The coach (diagram 415) was rebuilt from LSWR H13 Railmotor, the work to remove the cab, boiler and steam bogie being undertaken around 1919. Thus we have a representative of all three Southern Railway constituent companies.

Halwill saw many attaching and detaching moves over the years demonstrated here in the late 1950. The heavily loaded Bude goods has already arrived behind N Class No. 31835 with the 11.30am from Wadebridge standing on the curve in the background. 31835 is assumed to have already detached some of its wagons to the train from Bude as a Delabole Presflo is already in place just behind the locomotives tender. D. Wroe

factory at Calne, Wiltshire. The carriage of horses for slaughter was spasmodic. They were strictly regulated (as to numbers per wagon) and were never a popular loading task for station staff.

Best horses, the pride of the gentry, went by special horse boxes to the numerous shows. It is said that owners wouldn't let them walk far on these occasions and a box would be taken merely from Egloskerry into Launceston. Most horse box wagons were attached to passenger trains, but for big events such as Launceston Horse Show, the Holsworthy and Stratton Agricultural Show, or the prestigious Royal Cornwall (then movable year-to-year) there would be much rail activity. The LSWR and SR provided 'Prize' or special cattle wagons (with owner's compartments) from all over the place, not just locally, as well as demonstration agricultural machinery on flat wagons. If the Royal Cornwall was at Launceston or Wadebridge, extra shunting power came from Exmouth Junction (often a 'K10' 4-4-0). The normal cattle market aftermath is described in the stations chapter. Again, an extra shunting engine would be needed for the constant marshalling into the cattle pens and making up specials. Pathways for the livestock specials rarely now showed in the WTT, for they were timed by Special Notice. During World War Two the Ministry of Food was the sole buyer of livestock and slaughtering was permitted only in selected inland centres. Consequently the number of livestock specials increased at the expense of fresh meat forwardings. The late afternoon goods would take as many wagons as possible, even the 3.15pm Padstow Perishables and Passenger would take some (within the limit of the 'T9s' capability) from Launceston to Halwill. Otherwise a special would run, headed by a 'K10' or 'L11' through to Exeter. Empty wagons were held at Yeoford for distributions as required.

Post-1945, cattle were despatched to Boston (for sea transport to Europe) and Easingwold (Yorkshire). Ministry controls eased in 1954 and local slaughtering was again permitted. A new enlarged slaughterhouse opened at Halwill and Jaspers of North Petherwin started loading at Launceston for London (Smithfield). Demountable rail/road containers (road boxes) appeared in the late 1930s, but it was from the 1950s that exclusive use was made of them for fresh meat traffic. The 3.15pm from Padstow would take some (as did the similar 3.13pm from Bude). The locomotivemen's strike in 1955 caused the first dent in this lucrative traffic, though it remained buoyant into the 1960s. With the freeing of road licensing restrictions and the withering of rail freight traffic generally, culminating with withdrawal of services in September 1964, road traffic took over. Today, the meat trade is quite different, being concentrated on only a few large abattoirs in the west of England, and wholly dependent on road transport.

Fish

Five fish vans were involved in the Tresmeer accident in November 1898 and, significantly, their attachment at Port Isaac Road had delayed the Up goods. The previous year, in October, 150 tons of herrings brought up from Port Isaac quay in carts and wagons by local farmers had been despatched, in some fifteen wagons. As recounted in the 'Padstow Harbour Developments' section in Chapter 2, the coming of the NCR to Padstow in 1899 meant that the powerful East Coast herring fleets could now fish from there and place their catches directly on trains to London and the rest of the country. The harbour became filled with trawlers from Lowestoft, and a boom in the herring fishery took place. Ice and packing facilities were gradually built up on the quays to meet this demand but the First World War caused the trawlers to desert the town never again to return in such numbers. During the fishing boom both

Port Isaac and Padstow were well served by the LSWR and SR, taking this highly perishable trade to Exeter, London and the Midlands. Pre-grouping photographs of the Padstow Quays show that the fish was ice-packed in wooden crates and barrels. The wagons used in this period seem primarily to be LSWR 5-plank opens with curved ends, although smaller quantities of vans are also present. Although there were undoubtedly fish 'specials' before 1927, not until this year did the timetable show conditional train times. Empties from Exeter arrived at Padstow at 10.25am and were loaded for despatch at 4.40pm, passing Okehampton at 7.27pm. The up train was re-engined at Exmouth Junction (in 1932 this apparently took only nine minutes between 8.13 and 8.22pm). The decline was however setting in. By 1923 the value of the catch landed at Padstow was less than £66,000 and this shrank to £34,000 by 1936. Perhaps reflecting the reduction in trade 1938 timetable shows no fish special times. The herring seasons declined but Lowestoft and Grimsby trawlers were still producing smaller scale catches of white fish for auction in Padstow Fish Shed up to the early 1940s. A mid-afternoon passenger train ran for many years from Padstow and Bude, but from 1924 the portions were separated into two trains, available to take rail traffic of a perishable nature. Both ran through to Exeter Queen Street behind 4-4-0s. As far as goods traffic was concerned, any attached vans were 'passenger' rated (referred to as 'XP') so that fish vans from Padstow, rabbit vans serving almost all North Cornwall stations, and some meat vans, mainly from Wadebridge, Launceston and Halwill, were accorded a faster and guaranteed run to Exeter for the overnight fast goods services.

Sand, Granite, Clay and Slate

The North Cornwall region had a number of economically viable workings, including sand, granite, clay and slate. Through the life of the NCR all these generated traffic for the railway.

Sand dredged from the Camel estuary was used as an early, natural, fertiliser to improve the poor farmland in the Bodmin and Wadebridge areas. It was the need to transport this stuff inland that resulted in the creation of the Bodmin and Wadebridge Railway Company and its lines to Ruthen Bridge and Wenford Bridge in 1834. Transport was via one of the company's 40 open wagons and the sand traffic, rather than passengers, initially generated the majority of the B&WRC's income. Amazingly farmers adjacent to the line could arrange for the sand to be unloaded from wagons directly into fields at any point along the lines. The discovery of alternative fertilisers and soil improvers resulted in a decline of the sand trade and was partly the reason for the B&WRC's directors seeking to sell the company to the LSWR. The LSWR took control of the lines in 1847 and absorbed them in 1886 but they were not connected to the NCR until 1895 when the line reached Wadebridge. By this time, estuary sand had all but ceased to be a commodity. The Wenford Bridge line had, at its terminus, a link to T W Ward & Son's De Lank granite quarry. This was a rope worked incline that between the 1890s and 1940s generated traffic in the form of large granite blocks. These were conveyed by the LSWR and SR in open 10 to 15 ton capacity wagons which had 1, 3 or 4 plank high sides. From 1895 onwards, in common with other traffic to and from the Bodmin area, the granite could be conveyed eastwards to London either via the Wadebridge/NCR (Southern) route or the Bodmin Road (Great Western) alternative.

Apart from the De Lank works and the Delabole Slate quarry, the only other rail linked mineral working on the North Cornwall was the blue stone quarry of Messrs. Tom Bros. Known locally as (Betty &) Tom's siding, the rail link to the quarry's stone crusher opened in 1922 and remained operational until 1964. The sidings were about ¼ mile to the north of Port Isaac

The fireman of Beattie Well tank No. 30585 exchanges some pleasantries with the driver as they marshal a goods train at Wadebridge in July 1960. R. C. Riley, www.transporttreasury.co.uk

A variety of wagons and vans are being assembled at Wadebridge Yard in June 1962. R. C. Riley, www.transporttreasury.co.uk

Road and were unusual in that they were the only private sidings on the North Cornwall not located at a station. For more information on the resultant trip workings refer to Chapter 3 [pages 135 to 138].

Clay is a natural product from the breakdown of rocks including shale and granite. Looking at the geology of the region it is not surprising that it could be found in many locations in Cornwall. In the Meeth/Petrockstow area, on the Halwill to Torrington line, 'ball clays' were dug at the Marland site and normally transported 'as dug' in blocks or balls - hence the name. The ball clay from Marland was a very distinctive creamy colour and one use was the production of unusual cream coloured bricks, much sought after in the Devon coastal resort building boom between 1880 and 1900. Around Bodmin Moor, served by the Wenford Bridge to Wadebridge line, white china clay (or kaolin) is normally extracted using water jets and then dried in kilns to a fine white powder. This powder is used in the manufacture of fine porcelain, electrical insulators and other white ceramics. Despite these works being rail linked surprisingly little tonnage of the clays went to the east by rail, with shipment by sea being the preferred long-distance transport method. Commencing in 1862 most of the china clay output from Stannon Pit (piped to the driers at Wenford) was initially taken by rail to the wharves at Wadebridge and, by 1899, Padstow. These ports were inadequate for this traffic as they could only be used by small coastal vessels. Despite co-operation and encouragement from the LSWR, transhipments never rose above a weekly shipload or so. This co-operation included the building in 1914/15 of 25 special china clay wagons for the Cornwall China Clay Company. Each wagon could carry eight containers which could be lifted and tipped into a berthed vessel at Wadebridge or Padstow. By 1922 these wagons had fallen out of use and they were all rebuilt as 25-ton brake vans to Diagram 1547. (see Plates 108-110, Volume 1, *An Illustrated Guide to Southern Wagons*). The fly in the LSWR's ointment was the extension of the GWR line from Bodmin to Boscarne Junction in 1888. This gave access to the more attractive, deeper water, port at Fowey and drew the traffic away from Wadebridge and Padstow. The last china clay working from Wenford was on 26th September 1983, many years after the closure of the NCR.

Oddly enough, in the 1960s, a considerable tonnage of ball clay was traversing the whole length of the North Cornwall on the way from Meath, in North Devon to Lostwithel and Fowey Docks. This traffic was re-routed from Fremington Quay near Barnstaple and resulted in small numbers of clay wagons being added at Halwill to the Wadebridge bound freights. Consulting a rail map will show that the routing involved the train being reversed no less than four times at Halwill, Wadebridge, Bodmin General and Bodmin Road in order to reach its destination. Interestingly the clay traffic from Marland was often combined with that from Wenford at Boscarne Junction and the resulting load required the combined effort of two N Class moguls to get up the bank to Bodmin General. (see picture on page 232) Obviously this traffic ceased with the closure of the NCR between Halwill and Wadebridge in 1966. Both types of clay were generally transported in open wagons, covered by tarpaulins when loaded. The ball clay used a variety of wooden or steel open wagons and was unloaded using crane grabs at docks. The china clay, being a powder, could be end-tipped from special wagons directly into ships. During this operation the powder coated the wagon giving the characteristic ghostly appearance seen in many photographs. As well as the china clay container wagons mentioned above, GWR wagons to the O12/O13 design were used and, from 1955, wagons to BR Diagram 1/051 were introduced. To close the section on clay traffic there are three further aspects regarding china clay that should be remembered. First, at this time, steel bodied wagons were not used for china clay as it contaminated the load. Second, that the blue 'clay hood' type sheets did not come into use until the 1970s - long after the demise of the NCR. Lastly, that china clay could also be bagged at the clay dries and could therefore also be loaded into 12T vans.

Delabole Slate has been used as a building material for well over 600 years, and has been quarried continuously since the early 17th century. During the reign of Elizabeth I, the five quarries that existed within the vicinity of the present pit assumed considerable importance, delivering slate 'throughout the realm, and even exporting it by sea to Brittany and the Netherlands'. In 1841, the five quarries formed themselves into a single controlled unit, and the Old Delabole Slate Company was formed. Working the slate was a very labour intensive undertaking and by 1859 it employed around 1000 'men', a good proportion of which would have been boys by today's standards, who raised an average of 120 tons of slate per day.

Before the arrival of the railway, the slate was cut and hauled six miles to Port Gaverne where it would be loaded onto vessels moored in the harbour area. It would take thirty wagons, pulled by over a hundred horses to load a sixty ton ship and as late as 1890, women still assisted with the stowing of slates. It is easy to see, therefore, why the slate company supplied land free of charge to the NCR! In 1893 the NCR arrived on the scene and by the late 1930s over 10,000 tons of slate per year were forwarded from Delabole station. The slate blocks and roofing slates would have been shipped by rail in open wagons. As mentioned in Chapter 3 slate dust was at first an unwanted by-product of the quarrying and finishing process. By about 1930 a use for the waste had been found as a filler and this was marketed as 'Delafila'. At first the dust was sent away in bags but later on bulk handling was trialled using a BR Diagram 1/210 Covhop. For whatever reason this was not successful and alternatives were sought.

The first successful wagon used was the Diagram 1/272 Presflo. It is thought that five were branded for use with slate powder, including one from the 1961 B87334x batch. These had bauxite bodies and carried white lettering within the body-side ribs PRESFLO, DELAFILA, SLATE POWDER IN BULK. Observations made in 1964 indicate that there was usually one Presflo wagon in each Up North Cornwall goods. This would have reaching Halwill by late afternoon and its final destination would have been Tonbridge. In 1957/8 BR produced 20 wagons to a revised design of Diagram 1/272 Presflo for ICI Salt. These had a pair of silos, instead of just one on the 'normal' Presflo wagon, and could be distinguished by duplication on the discharge pipes and valves, and a different bottom to the hopper. At some time during the 1960s they transferred to other traffic including Delafilla and slate powder. An example, B888183, photographed in 1968 shows this carried simplified lettering BULK, DELAFILA.

The Old Delabole Slate Company had a long and chequered history before finally being liquidated in 1977. Happily, after a short lived 'corporate' period, a management buy-out in June 1999 returned the quarry to local ownership. The Delabole Slate Company Ltd is now, once again, a private Cornish company. The quarry itself is about half a mile long, a quarter of a mile across and 400 feet deep and has outlived the historical blip that was the North Cornwall Railway.

A goods train from Bodmin Road running into Wadebridge on 14th July 1964 behind NBL No. D6348. After withdrawal of freight services on the North Cornwall in the following September, the remaining traffic at Wadebridge continued to be routed this way, until the latter's closure in 1978. C. J. Knowles-Thomas

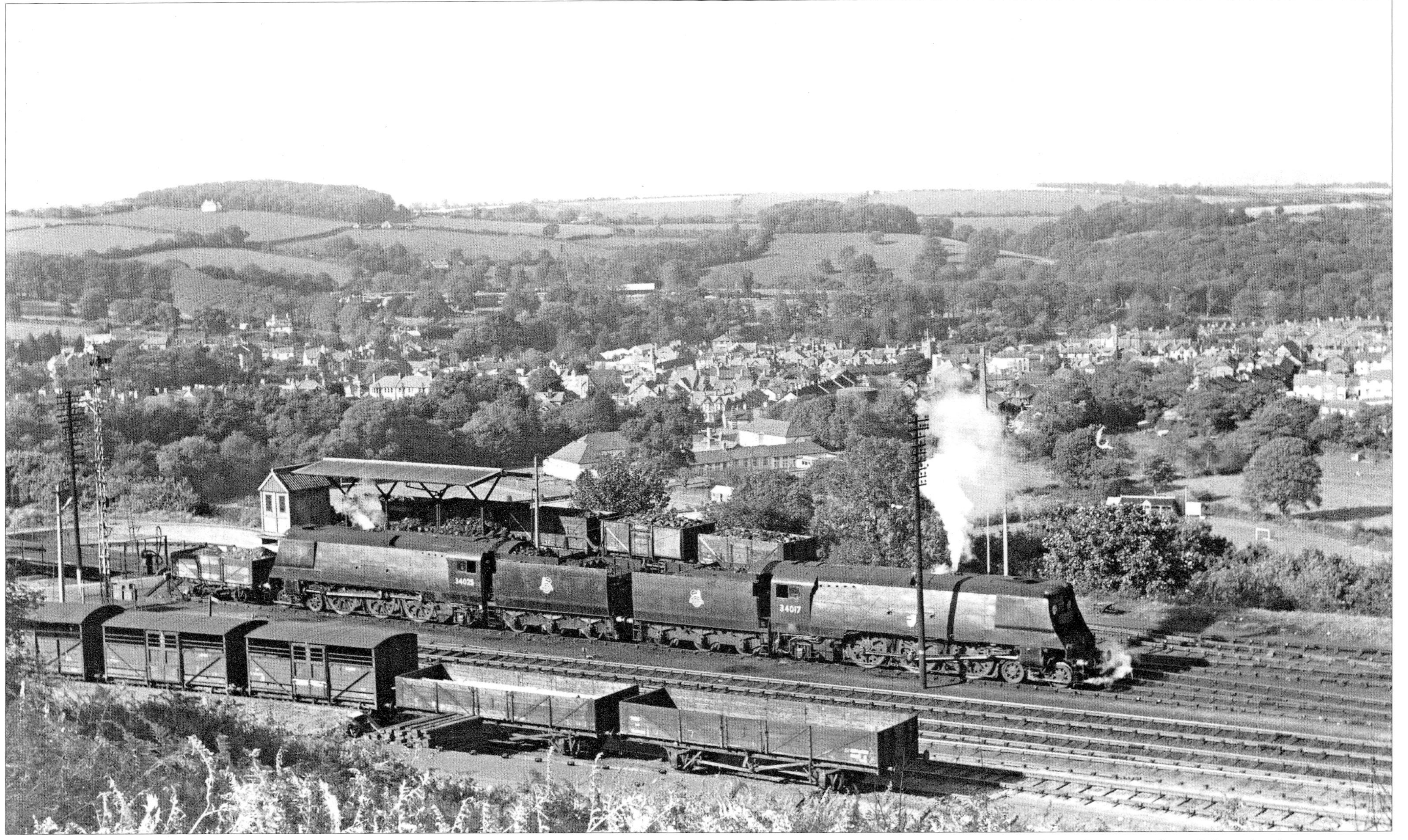

Whimple No.34025 (left) and 34017 *Ilfracombe* (right) outside the shed at Okehampton in October 1953. *Ilfracombe* is awaiting the arrival of the Padstow portion of the Atlantic Coast Express and will take the train forward to Exeter. R.E. Vincent, www.transporttreasury.co.uk

Chapter Seven

MOTIVE POWER ON THE NORTH CORNWALL

Additional information by Chris Tooth

If asked about the motive power on the North Cornwall Railway enthusiasts will straight away name the Beattie Well Tanks, the Drummond T9s, Maunsell N Class and Bulleid light Pacifics as the signature classes of the line. Interestingly the first and last on this list represent locomotive designs separated by over 70 years. The fact that both ran side-by-side at Wadebridge for many years sheds some light on the particular problems faced by the LSWR, Southern and BR in providing engines suited to the restrictions of the line. The North Cornwall was relatively lightly constructed, had steep gradients and tight curves and this is reflected in the long list of locomotive types discussed in the following pages that were tried and found wanting in some way or other.

In the early pre-grouping period it was the sheer length of the North Cornwall (from Okehampton) that dictated a tender engine policy. Until closure, water was available only at Halwill, Launceston, Delabole and Wadebridge and the coal capacity of the earlier tank engines was very limited. As time progressed it was the 4-4-0s and 2-6-0s that were generally the most successful on passenger services but these were found to be deficient in power to match the ever lengthening trains of the 1930s. The breakthrough in terms of haulage capacity came with the Bulleid Pacifics. These were light enough to run on the line but packed enough punch to pull the longest trains unaided.

When looking at motive power one cannot escape the fact that the shed at Exmouth Junction (72A), east of Exeter Central, provided the majority of locos running on the line. It stocked sub-sheds at Bude and Okehampton and supported Wadebridge (72F). Building on the excellent work by David Wroe this chapter has therefore been expanded to include the Exmouth Junction locomotives that ran on the line. This is especially true for the later periods, for it is a sad fact that far more reliable data exists for the last 40 years than the first 20. Readers must not lose sight, however, that 'foreign' motive power 'borrowed' from sheds such as Plymouth, Yeovil and Salisbury also ran on the line from time to time. As part of the BR boundary changes Exmouth was eventually handed over to the Western Region and was recoded 83D in December 1962. From this point there

Adams Class 415 4-4-2T No. 125 at Okehampton on 14th July 1924. At this time, the 415s were working the Bude branch as the headcode denotes. H. C. Casserley, courtesy R. M. Casserley.

Drummond 700 Class 0-6-0s occasionally worked on the North Cornwall line. Here at Okehampton on 14th July 1924 No.694, rebuilt with an Eastleigh type superheater in 1922, awaits its next duty. H. C. Casserley, courtesy R. M. Casserley.

was a gradual run-down of steam, until June 1965, when Exmouth Junction was closed to steam.

The pre-grouping Locomotives

Initially goods trains on the Okehampton to Holsworthy branch were in the hands of Beattie 0-6-0s. The turntable at the terminus being only 42ft in diameter restricted the use of longer wheelbase locomotives. William Adams had provided three new Class '46' 4-4-0 tank engines at Okehampton in 1879 to work passenger trains, but these were replaced by Beyer Peacock 4-4-0Ts soon after. On the opening to Launceston in 1886 a 50ft turntable was installed there, matched by another at Halwill Junction. One of the first engines to try it out was a newish Adams '445' Class 4-4-0, No.448. It hauled the Directors train and was obviously a show piece for the day, as its 7′ 1″ driving wheels were unsuited for general work locally. In the photograph of this event what looks like one of the Beattie 2-4-0s rebuilt as a tender locomotive, possibly No.195, stands in the yard. One of this class, No.215, was stationed at Launceston in 1887 with No.185 at Okehampton. In their original 2-4-0 well tank configuration, three of these Beattie engines were destined for remarkably long lives at Wadebridge as described separately in Chapter 10.

Until the arrival of the Adams 'Jubilee' 0-4-2s the motive power supplied by the LSWR was somewhat elderly. For goods work there were a few Adams '395' 0-6-0s but, more often during the early 1890s, Beattie 0-6-0s (both the double and single framed Beyer Peacocks) and even lightweight 'Ilfracombe' goods engines, toiled up the long slopes and were serviced at the little sheds at Delabole and Launceston. A '395' could head a passenger train if required (after 1889 most LSWR engines had the vacuum brake) and, in the mixed traffic role, shared duties with the Beyer Peacock 4-4-0s coming on the scene about 1893.

A Beyer-Peacock 0-6-0 No. 394 at Wadebridge c.1900. One of the Ilfracombe Goods Class dating from 1880, she was eventually sold in 1918 to the East Kent Railway and, that line's No. 3, lasted until the 1930s at Shepherdswell.

One of the legendary Beattie well tanks beside the cattle pens at Wadebridge in 1961. More details of this class can be found in Chapter 10. H. F. Andrews, www.transporttreasury.co.uk

These '380' Class – the 'Steamrollers' nicknamed for their disc bogie wheels or, it is said, for their propensity to flatten out curves – and the Adams '460s' were the regulars through the later 1890s, and up to 1914. The 'Jubilees' and Drummond's newer breeds of 4-4-0s, the 'K10s' and 'L11s' could also be noted on North Cornwall trains in this next decade.

Of the '380s', Nos.386, 390 and 391 were sent to Wadebridge in 1895, and there were five others at Exeter. No.386 was involved in the Tresmeer collision on 19 November 1895. The 'Steamrollers' soldiered on, their lives prolonged by the 1914-18 war, and two were still at Okehampton in the early 1920s. The Adams '460s' became the passenger workhorses for many years. The new shed at Wadebridge received a couple on opening, capable of working the lengthier summer trains emerging at the end of the century. Nos.474 and 526 were there in 1914 and 0464, 0469, 0471 and 526 in 1924. By that time they were relegated to the ordinary stopping passenger trains, and the Padstow fish specials as required, to Okehampton. At Halwill they would pass a '460' from Barnstaple after the Torrington line was opened in 1925.

Whatever tank engines were employed on the Holsworthy (late Bude) branch services, few of them went on to the North Cornwall line. Over the years, until the 1950s, 'O2', 'T1' and finally 'M7' 0-4-4Ts (as well as, for a period, '415' 4-4-2Ts), attached or detached Bude coaches at Halwill from Okehampton/Padstow trains. The '460s' from Barnstaple were replaced by 'Brighton' rebuilds (the 'E1/R' 0-6-2Ts) from 1928. The latter never ventured onto the North Cornwall, but over the years a Bude 'M7' would work into Launceston on Saturdays and regularly on Sundays in the 1940s. The South Western end of the North Cornwall was tank territory again, principally Wadebridge to Bodmin/Wenford and, to a certain extent, Padstow. After the realignment works on the Bodmin branch the 'O2' 0-4-4Ts were permitted to work it, Nos.182 and 219 being present from 1896. On and off there were always a couple of 'O2s' at Wadebridge until their demise in the 1950s. The railmotor (1906-1918) and the '415' periods (1918-1926) were exceptions. Apart for a brief push pull interlude in 1918 the 'O2s' always ran round their trains at Bodmin, Wadebridge and Padstow. The 'M7s' and 'T1s' were not permitted between Wadebridge and Bodmin owing to axleweight restrictions (as were most of

The aftermath of the Tresmeer accident of 1895 in which 'Steamroller' 380 Class No. 386 was involved.

The Adams 0415 Class 4-4-2Ts, displaced from London by the M7s, arrived at Wadebridge in late 1919 although they had been familiar locomotives at Halwill from the early 1900s, working some of the Okehampton-Bude services. Here regular locos Nos.E050 and 169 are on shed at Wadebridge in 1926 and 1922 respectively. Note that E050, built by Stephenson in 1883, has rectangular spectacles plates whilst 169, from Dubs & Co in 1884, has round ones.

the 4-4-0s) though in the very last years 'N' 2-6-0s and light Pacifics were allowed. Thus the very light 'O2s' persisted alongside the antique Beattie well tanks. Goods working to Wenford Bridge called for the latter's services (severe curvature was the problem here).

The story of the Beattie tanks is well known, and they were continually photographed in their various guises. Suffice to say that the first one was shipped into Wadebridge from Southampton in May 1893 (No.248) and the last (No.30587) left in September 1962. As far back as 1900 their replacement was mooted. A local 'O2' (No.228) and 'Ilfracombe Goods' No.301 were tried out, as was an SECR 'P' Class 0-6-0T and PD & SWJ 0-6-0T 'A S Harris' in 1929, but the curves defeated them. The well tanks were noted as station pilots at Wadebridge and chuntered along to Padstow and back, often on the 'mixed' trains.

The not unduly steep gradients of the Bodmin-Wadebridge-Padstow lines prompted the LSWR to introduce railcars, or railmotors, i.e. single carriages powered by steam and two of the later Drummond H13 Class, Nos.13 and 14, commenced running on 1 June 1906. An extension at Wadebridge engine shed housed them overnight. They were expected to provide an economical service in this somewhat rural area. In 1914 nine return trips were made to Bodmin between 5.50am (ex-Wadebridge) until the 9.29pm from Bodmin. None then appeared to be running to Padstow, compared with several in 1909. The surviving three LSWR cars, 3, 4 and 10, carried on until March 1918 when they were replaced, only for a while, by 'O2s' equipped for motor train control. The 4-4-2Ts were not seen at Wadebridge until about 1919, but they were familiar sights at Halwill at the turn of the century working from Okehampton and Bude. Displaced by 'M7s' and electrification in London and its suburbs, these elderly tanks (1883-85) decanted to the Bodmin/Padstow local workings, Nos.050, 054, 0169 and 0522 being there at Grouping in 1923. They also reappeared on the Bude branch. All had gone by 1927, their Bodmin duties once again in the hands of the 'O2's while the Bude-Halwill shuttle had firstly 'T1's and then 'M7's from 1926. Other tank engines entering Wadebridge from the east, but then going no further, were on GWR trains from Bodmin Road. The one-time 0-6-0 saddle tanks eventually gave away to Churchward 2-6-2Ts shedded at St Blazey. Some seven return (one 'mixed') passenger services were recorded in 1932.

Mention of the Drummond 4-4-0s underlines the fact that during the summers up to 1914 the Waterloo/Padstow through train, and some of the locals with attached through coaches, presented some haulage problems on the 1 in 73 grades. Keeping time and crossing at loops in the right order was quite a task. The 'K10's were adequate for the local three-coach trains of the period, (up to five including through coaches) that they shared with the '460's and the 'Jubilees', but the eight-coach 'North Cornwall Express' was a different proposition. In 1906 two mixed traffic 'S11' Class 4-4-0s (of 1903) were stationed at Wadebridge for this express. After superheating in the early 1920s two were sent to Exmouth Junction and one, No.401, to Wadebridge for similar duties, though they could work goods trains when required. The 'K10's at Exmouth Junction in 1903 were Nos.152, 153, 383, 383 and 389 along with ten 'A12's and four '460' Class; any of them could be outstationed at Okehampton for working the North Cornwall line. Wadebridge always had two 'A12's until the 'N' 2-6-0s arrived in 1924. Very popular engines, especially with their steam sanding gear, these 0-4-2Ts could be seen on anything from a passenger train to a fish special.

By the 1930s the '395' 0-6-0s were rarely seen farther west than Okehampton. If so it was probably on a ballast working. No.29, then 029, then 3029 in SR days and finally BR No 30564, was a familiar example for many years. It usually served as the Okehampton pilot but had been seen on the Bodmin branch in the 1920s. The Drummond 4-4-0 type, the 'Large Hoppers' of his 'L11' Class, started working on the North Cornwall when new from 1904-07. The usual stud at Exmouth Junction until the 1920s was about six to eight. The 'K10's and 'L11's were never superheated like

Adams X6 Class No. E662 at Wadebridge in August 1928. Although not a regular class on the North Cornwall these robust locomotives were used on goods trains from Exeter where a number were allocated.

A12 Class 0-4-2 No. E645 at Wadebridge in August 1928. The 'Jubilees' replaced the elderly LSWR locos on the North Cornwall when they arrived in the mid-1900s. They were ideally suited to the line, their Holt & Gresham steam sanding gear proving particularly useful in the weather experienced in some of the more exposed parts of the North Cornwall. E645 was finally withdrawn in 1933.

(eventually) the 'S11's and the 'T9s, so they were to be found principally on goods.

Double heading on the LSWR and SR was not commonplace, though the Bude branch was an exception, probably because of the steep rise from sea level to 660 feet at Halwill (and nearly 600 feet at Meldon) in 19 miles. There were also operational problems at Bude which called for piloting in the down direction. Sixteen-coach trains were not unusual in World War Two and after! Not that double-heading was unknown on the North Cornwall line, though weight restrictions over Meldon Viaduct prohibited two 2-6-0s or a 4-4-0 and a 2-6-0 coupled together. As the Padstow summer expresses became heavier in the 1930s it was the custom to schedule two 4-4-0s all the way to Okehampton or Exeter. This is where the 'K10's and 'L11's came in useful as pilots, though a pair of 'T9s was usual. On Saturdays, even before World War One, non-stop running from Exeter St Davids to Launceston was timetabled. In the reverse direction a stop at Okehampton was inserted, probably to release the pilot engine. In this respect the eight-wheeled Drummond 'water cart' tenders on the 'T9s were more than welcome in the 1930s. Some of the remaining Adams 'X6' 4-4-0s were pressed into service in the 1920s on local passengers or as pilots, though the Bude-Halwill portions of the summer 'Atlantic Coast Express' was usually their concern.

Steam 'Railmotors', in vogue on some railways in the period before the 1914 War, appeared at Wadebridge in 1906. They were employed on services to Bodmin as well as occasional trips to Padstow, where No. 10 is seen illustrated that year. The LSWR withdrew the last ones from Wadebridge (Nos.3, 4 and 10) in March 1918.

Top left. **S11 Class No.404 awaits departure to Exeter in August 1945. She was one of ten in the Class and had lately been loaned to the LMS (1941-1944). Two S11s were allocated to Wadebridge pre-1914 and again in the 1920s to work the heavier trains from and to Exeter, and were to be seen on the Bude and Padstow 'Perishables' in the 1930s. H. C. Casserley.**

Middle. **Many miles from the parent shed at Exmouth Junction, Wadebridge fitters carried out all manor of repairs and here O2 No.30193 receives attention to its axleboxes. There was always a couple of O2s stationed at Wadebridge, heavily employed on the Bodmin services until their demise in the 1950s.**

Drummond 700 Class 0-6-0

The LSWR ordered 30 0-6-0s from Dubs & Co, Glasgow, for delivery in 1897. They shared many parts with the M7 0-4-4T and indeed the motion, boilers and cylinders were interchangeable between classes. Nicknamed the "Black Motors" they were relatively uncommon west of Okehampton, though they occasionally shared goods duties with the 'Jubilee' 0-4-2Ts on the North Cornwall or worked Sunday engineers trains at the Halwill end. There was usually one at Okehampton on station pilot or local Plymouth line goods turns in the week. There was even a report that 30691 hauled the 3.13pm Padstow 'Perishables' in October 1960. Those allocated to Exmouth Junction included 30315, 30317, 30327, 30689, 30691, 30697 and 30700. All were withdrawn between 1961 and 1962.

The ubiquitous North Cornwall T9s were long associated with the line. Their versatility contributed to their longevity; No. 289 is on a local stopping train from Okehampton to Padstow. They were equally at home hauling heavy summer holiday trains as well as lengthy goods trains to Exeter.

T9 No. 30719, on station pilot duties between turns, shunts the Military Sidings at Okehampton in 1961.

return, piloting the Atlantic Coast Express. Return was on a passenger to Wadebridge. Launceston's No.732 worked Padstow-Okehampton passenger turns. Okehampton itself had No.723, which worked to Bude, Exeter and Plymouth. Exmouth Junction had six engines and these were more widely used, available for a Saturday duty to Padstow and Bude amongst others. Piloting the summer through trains has been mentioned. By 1939 ten coach trains were in vogue, hauled by 'U1' 2-6-0s allocated to Exmouth Junction from 1937, though double-heading by 4-4-0s persisted. On the outbreak of war in 1939 the number of 'T9s' increased by eight (three retaining six-wheel tenders after transfer from the Eastern Section). Long passenger trains continued during the war, firstly evacuation specials and then troop trains. The 'Ns' took some share in this, whereas it was uncommon for one to be on passenger duties in pre-war days.

T9 30717 was a Wadebridge engine in 1948 and was used regularly over the North Cornwall and Bude lines. By the time this photo was taken in 1961 the loco had but a few weeks before withdrawal, its duties passing initially to U1Moguls.

Drummond T9 Class 4-4-0

The Drummond 'T9' 4-4-0s will always be associated with the North Cornwall line, yet they were quite late on the scene. When built in 1899/1901 they were the LSWR's principal express engines and remained so until displaced, partially by Drummond's 4-6-0s before World War One, and completely by Urie and Maunsell 4-6-0s from the 1920s. Even then a number were transferred to the Eastern and Central Sections of the SR. However, they could be seen at Okehampton working on the Plymouth main line from 1901. All the sixty-six engines received superheated boilers in the 1922-29 period, and during this time the first regular workings to Padstow occurred as the Adams 4-4-0s were withdrawn. There were ten at Exmouth Junction in 1932, seven of them 'Dubs' engines built in Glasgow in 1899/1900. Wadebridge received its first one soon after and in 1939, according to Bradley, Nos.703 and 710 worked a daily duty to Okehampton and return together with, on Saturdays, a job to Exeter and The T9s took on goods duties, and the mixed trains (Bude/Holsworthy and Launceston/Wadebridge/Padstow) mainly in response to the increase in cattle traffic. The introduction of Pacifics curbed their activities somewhat from 1945, but as troop trains continued on the Bude line (not suitable for Pacifics, as explained later) the seven T9s at Exmouth Junction had plenty to do.

Nearly all the stopping passenger trains Okehampton/Padstow were now 'T9' turns worked by Okehampton using Wadebridge engines (Nos.703 and

717 in 1948). Until 1961 the enthusiasts were busy photographing them hauling their usual pair of coaches or perhaps the up 'Perishable' and its tail of vans and meat containers. By 1959 the eight at Exmouth Junction (including three outstationed at Okehampton and one each at Launceston and Wadebridge) were virtually the only ones left running on the Southern, but the end was nigh. 30313, 30709, 30715 and 30717 were at Okehampton until July 1961 when they were finally withdrawn, latterly working the 1.00pm Okehampton to Bude, returning at 3.15pm. The Bude and Padstow 'Perishables' then passed to the 'N' Moguls.

Maunsell Locomotives

Three classes of Maunsell mogul including the Ns ran over the line. The 'N' Class became one of the North Cornwall's 'signature' classes and both the 'U' and 'U1' Classes were seen occasionally.

Maunsell N Class 2-6-0

There was quite a sensation so far as the locomotive scene was concerned in 1924 when a 2-6-0 tender engine arrived for trials, initially to Ilfracombe, and later on to Wadebridge and Bude. The SR had been looking for a more powerful type than the 'Jubilees' and 4-4-0s, especially for goods working to Bude and North Cornwall, and for passenger working to Ilfracombe and Plymouth, able at the same time to use the 50ft turntables.

As it happened the Government was anxious to dispose of a quantity of their SECR-designed 2-6-0 tender engines manufactured at Woolwich Arsenal for the Ministry of Munitions, post-1918. Because of the bargain price, as whole or in parts, they became popularly known as 'Woolworths'. Compared to the T9s, their smaller driving wheels (5'6" vs 6'7") and higher tractive effort (26,000 vs 17,670) made them eminently suitable for goods workings.

After some troubles with hot axleboxes on the tenders they were

Drafted in to replace the ageing and underpowered 'Jubilees', the N 2-6-0s were ideal for the North Cornwall and Bude lines and were able to turn on the 50ft turntables on the line. Although primarily needed for heavy goods workings over the steeply graded line, the Ns performed equally well on the heavy summer holiday trains from Exeter. *Top*. The 12.58pm Padstow – Waterloo train at Wadebridge on 27th May 1961 hauled by No.31847. L. R. Freeman, www.transporttreasury.co.uk *Below*. 31849 at Okehampton in August 1959. Ken Fairey.

Number	Exmouth Junct. Allocated	Comments
31406	2/62-9/64	Slope-sided 4000gal tender. New frames, cylinders and Std 4 chimney Jan 1960.
31407	<5/49-1/51	Slope-sided 4000gal tender. Left hand drive
31408	<5/49-1/51	Left-hand drive and slope-sided 4000gal tender. New frames, cylinders and Std 4 chimney Apr 1957.
31409	<5/49-1/50, 10/61-11/62	Left-hand drive and slope-sided 4000gal tender.
31812	8/63-7/64	From original 1920/23 SECR batch.
31818	1/62-9/63	From original 1920/23 SECR batch.
31821	8/63-7/64	From original 1920/23 SECR batch.
31828	<5/49-6/51	Std 4 chimney fitted late 50s, early 60's
31829	8/50-6/51	New frames, cylinders Oct 1960.
31830	8/50-10/62	New frames, cylinders Oct 1955.
31831	<5/49-10/62	New frames, cylinders and Std 4 chimney Aug 1960.
31832	<5/49-10/62	
31833	<5/49-10/62	New frames, cylinders and Std 4 chimney Jun 1959.
31834	<5/49-9/64	Std 4 chimney fitted late 50s, early 60's
31835	<5/49-9/64	New frames, cylinders and Std 4 chimney May 1957.
31836	10/50-1/64	BR Std 4 chimney
31837	<5/49-11/52, 1/53-9/64	New frames, cylinders and Std 4 chimney Feb 1961.
31838	<5/49-2/64	New frames, cylinders and Std 4 chimney Jun 1957.
31839	<5/49-12/63	Std 4 chimney fitted late 50s, early 60's
31840	<5/49-6/52, 9/52-9/64	New frames, cylinders and Std 4 chimney Jan 1957.
31841	<5/49-6/52, 9/52-3/64	BR Std 4 chimney
31842	5/51-6/52, 11/52-6/54, 2/55-6/55, 11/56-7/64	New frames, cylinders and Std 4 chimney Dec 1957.
31843	1/51-11/52, 11/56-9/64	New frames, cylinders and Std 4 chimney Aug 1958.
31844	1/51-8/52, 9/53-12/63	
31845	<5/49-7/53, 9/53-9/64	New frames, cylinders and Std 4 chimney Mar 1960.
31846	10/50-9/64	New frames, cylinders May 1959.
31847	<5/49-9/63	Std 4 chimney fitted late 50s, early 60's
31848	4/51-10/55, 10/61-2/64	New frames, cylinders Oct 1955.
31849	4/51-7/64	
31850	5/59-1/64	
31851	4/51-9/51, 7/53-1/55, 5/59-11/59	BR Std 4 chimney
31852	4/51-9/51, 5/59-11/59	
31853	<5/49-9/51, 5/59-9/64	New frames, cylinders and Std 4 chimney Jul 1960.
31854	8/63-7/64	New frames, cylinders and Std 4 chimney Aug 1957.
31855	<5/49-9/51, 1/61-9/64	New frames, cylinders Nov 1955.
31856	<5/49-9/51, 1/61-7/64	
31857	1/61-10/62	
31859	8/63-9/64	
31860	5/59-10/63	
31866	10/50-4/51	BR Std 4 chimney
31867	10/50-4/51	Std 4 chimney fitted late 50s, early 60's
31869	<5/49-4/51	New frames, cylinders and Std 4 chimney Feb 1958.
31874	<5/49-11/50, 1/61-3/64	New frames, cylinders and Std 4 chimney May 1957.
31875	<5/49-11/50, 1/61-8/64	Std 4 chimney fitted late 50s, early 60's

accepted by local crews and went on to be firm favourites. Put on North Cornwall goods workings straight away, those involved were from the A826-A860 series (from 1931 onwards numbered 1826 to 1860). They began by working the midnight Exmouth Junction to Launceston Goods, the 6.00am and 10.00am Okehampton to Wadebridge and the 11.30am and 5.00pm from Wadebridge. One always worked to Bude, leaving Exmouth Junction at 3.30am and arriving back at 9.00pm that night. With a (mandatory) heavy 25-ton brake van, a maximum of 40 loaded wagons was allowed for the Ns. This was, however, tempered by length restrictions imposed by passing loops and the steep gradients. Between Wadebridge and Delabole, for instance, trains were limited to 34 wagons.

The war starting in 1939 soon drew the 'Ns' away from the North Cornwall and to the South East to assist with increasing wartime traffic. They were to return in numbers again by 1945. In 1946 they were pressed on to passenger trains

Number	Exmouth Junct. Allocated
(3)1890*	Autumn 1937 to Autumn 1939
(3)1891	Autumn 1937 to Autumn 1939
(3)1892	Autumn 1937 to Autumn 1939
(3)1893	Mid 1937 to Autumn 1939
(3)1894	Mid 1937 to Autumn 1939
(3)1895	Mid 1937 to Autumn 1939
(3)1896	Autumn 1937 to Autumn 1939
(3)1897	Autumn 1937 to Autumn 1939
(3)1898	Mid 1937 to Autumn 1939
(3)1899	Mid 1937 to Autumn 1939
(3)1900	February 1937 to Autumn 1937

* Rebuilt from River 2-6-4T

Number	Exmouth Junct. allocated
31626	9/58-2/59
31634	1/51-6/51
31635	1/51-6/51,6/56-1/57
31636	1/51-6/51
31790*	9/58-5/59
31791*	9/58-5/59
31804*	6/56-1/57
* Rebuilt from the ill-fated 'River' class 2-6-4Ts from 1928	

more often, particularly to Bude on the heavy summer trains, and single handed at that! One heavy load for a 'Woolworth' by this time was the 5.55am from Okehampton. It was now a 'mixed' train of sorts, that is, passenger coaches and a Newspaper bogie van off the 1.30am Waterloo and anything up to twenty goods vehicles plus a brake van.

The complex post-1950 allocations to Exmouth Junction are detailed in the table and it will be seen that no less than 44 of the class, at some time, worked in the area. As a consequence of distortion cracks, and starting with 31848 in October 1955, 29 of the Ns underwent frame rebuilding. No doubt the curves on the North Cornwall had something to do with this as the majority of those receiving this attention had worked the line. The new frames lengthened the front of the engine by 4½" and modified engines can be distinguished by the curved, rather than triangular, shape of the frames above the buffer beam. New cylinders, with outside steam pipes, were also included in the package of rebuilding work. There was a chimney modification too, which was also applied to some non-rebuilt locomotives. Details of which engines received the various modifications are given in the allocation table on the previous page.†

After 1961 they took over all the T9 turns, including the two 'Perishables', but the light Pacifics were also involved (except to Bude) as we shall see. From December 1962 the Western Region, took control and acquired 'Woolworths' 31834-31849, 31853, 31855, 31856, 31860, 31874 and 31875 as well as ex-SECR 'N' 31818 and SR No.31406. During 1963 31812 and 31821 (ex-SECR) and 31854 and 31859 arrived at Exmouth Junction. Only a small number were withdrawn by the start of 1964, with 21 remaining there in this last year of freight services west of Okehampton. All had gone by September, the remaining duties covered by Standard 2-6-4Ts and 4-6-0s. No.1874 survives, the only true 'Woolworth', preserved on the Mid Hants Railway.

The wrestle between the ever increasing power requirements of the summer timetables and the axle loading limitations imposed by the bridges and platforms was always a problem for the

†*For more information and a comprehensive article see February 2008 issue of* British Railways Illustrated.

34014 *Budleigh Salterton* backs down along the island platform at Wadebridge to run into the shed and await its next turn of duty. The Southern Railway intended to use more powerful locomotives on the lines west of Exeter from the 1940s. Up to 1939 pairs of 4-4-0s hauled the heaviest holiday trains on the North Cornwall and Bude lines, but after 1945 these Bulleid light axle-weight Pacifics could handle up to eight coaches with ease on the Cornish and Devon gradients. R. E. Vincent, www.transporttreasury.co.uk

North Cornwall. Over time this led to various locomotive types being tried out, including the 3-cylinder 'U1' Class. Although the tractive effort was marginally lower than the 2-cylinder 'N' Class (25,387lb vs 26,000lb) it was hoped that their larger wheels (6' vs 5'6") and quicker acceleration would improve the service West of Exeter and reduce the need for double-heading. Between 1937 and 1939 eleven of the class were allocated to Exmouth Junction (see table). They were used on services to Padstow and Plymouth.

The trial was not a success. The engines were heavy on coal and water, which enginemen can forgive if the engine is willing, but the 3-cylinders were found to quickly drain the boiler on the heavily graded North Cornwall banks. Mechanically their leading driving wheels suffered excessive flange wear due to the continually curving nature of the line. By autumn 1939 all had been transferred to Guildford and Redhill to work the heavy wartime traffic. They were replaced by members of the 'T9' Class.

The 'U1s' were not seen in the West again until 1961 when, as potential replacements for the aging T9s, 31901-31904 were allocated to Exmouth Junction. They were used mainly on passenger services, including the 10.12am and 5.51pm Okehampton to Padstow workings, the 3.13pm Padstow to Okehampton. Presumably the same issues raised with the class in the 1930s cropped up again and they only stayed from May to September. Despite their short stay they were often captured on film.

Despite seven of them being allocated to Exmouth Junction from time to time, the Us were rare visitors to the North Cornwall line. Perhaps the legacy of their 3-cyclinder sisters, the 'U1s', dissuaded their regular use. Photographic evidence does exist that Exmouth Junction occasionally 'borrowed' locomotives, including the 'U' Class, from as far away as Yeovil Town. 31610 (1956 and 1958) and 31802 (c1960) are examples of this.

Bulleid Locomotives

The only Bulleid locos to run on the line were his original light Pacifics. The later rebuilds of the class were too heavy for the line's permanent way.

Bulleid Light Pacifics

Replacement of the 4-4-0s in the West Country had been foreseen in pre-World War Two days. In April 1941 twenty passenger engines had actually been ordered, and a 3-cylinder 2-6-0 design drawn up. After progressing through a 2-6-2 it became a 4-6-2. Perhaps the growing burden of the summer through trains had been in mind, though at the time (1943) the only lengthy trains were troop specials. Whatever decisions were made by Bulleid and the Southern Railway management as to their use in the west, and by now on the Eastern Section as well, the Bulleid light Pacifics were born. A further ten, to make the order to 30, were ordered in September 1944. A second order subsequently increased this to 45 in 1945.

As the engines had been designed to meet the requirements in the West of England the Southern's General Manager, Sir Eustace Missenden, recommended that they be known as the West Country class. A number of the new locomotives were named after local places on or near the North Cornwall line, including: 21C106 *Bude*, 21C107 *Wadebridge*, 21C108 *Padstow*, 21C112 *Launceston*, 21C113 *Okehampton*, 21C116 *Bodmin*, 21C121 *Dartmoor*, 21C124 *Tamar Valley*, 21C125 *Rough Tor* (*Whimple* after May 1948) 21C126 *Yes Tor*, 21C131 *Torrington*, 21C132 *Camelford* and 21C139 *Boscastle*. To maximise positive publicity in the post-war period, official naming ceremonies were held at the stations of the towns after which the locomotives were named. Part of the ceremony included the presentation of a coffee table inlaid with the appropriate coat of arms to the local dignitary christening the engine.

The first 'West Countries' to be seen west of Okehampton were 21C107 and 21C108 arriving on 31 October 1945 to be named *Wadebridge* and *Padstow* by the respective Urban District Council Chairmen. The following day 211C112 was named *Launceston* by the Mayor. The local turntables were not long enough, so they worked back tender first with their trains of saloon, a Pullman Car (the first seen in North Cornwall?) and a borrowed LNER sleeping car. 21C106 *Bude* was also named on 1 November. 21C116 *Bodmin* was allowed to run specially down the branch for naming on 26 August 1946, still not 'turnable'.

When it became apparent that the 4-6-2s would work on the Eastern Section it was decided that members of

New West Country 4-6-2 No. 21C112 *Launceston* being named there on 1st November 1945. For the Southern Railway's Directors and Officers the train (in the up loop) was formed of saloons and a borrowed LNER sleeping car.

More Bulleid Pacifics at Okehampton in 1953 but this time Battle of Britain Class No. 34062 *17 Squadron*. The introduction of these powerful 7P/6F locos revolutionised running over the line on both passenger and goods workings. Behind is a North Cornwall regular, T9 No.30712 on station pilot duties. R. E. Vincent, www.transporttreasury.co.uk

the class would carry the names of squadrons, airfields and personalities linked with the Battle of Britain. Light Pacifics carrying such names were thereafter referred to as the Battle of Britain class despite their being no mechanical difference between the two. Three additional orders were eventually placed and the final locomotive, 34110, entered traffic in February 1951. These final batches included local North Cornwall names 34096 *Trevone* and 34097 *Holsworthy*, neither of which was officially named. Locomotives from 34071 onwards had wider 9ft cabs and larger capacity 5500 gallon tenders.

These unusual engines, with their 'air-smoothed' casings and 'boxpok' wheels, their original bright malachite green (with yellow lining) livery and dark green from mid-1949, together with their multiple-jet exhaust, became well known on the sun-drenched (or rain-swept!) hillsides at Otterham, or shunting in Launceston yard on occasion. They were not popular on these latter duties, inclined as they were to slip, or in the shed at Wadebridge with their obscured 'innards' as the Cornish would put it. Nevertheless, when it came to hauling the six-coach through trains up the 1 in 73 gradients, their 31,000lb tractive effort and superb steam producing boilers meant they were in their element. A maximum of ten coaches could be taken, but there were difficulties in the loops, especially at Launceston and Egloskerry, in passing other trains. Initially turning such large tender engines was not possible on the North Cornwall. The 50ft turntables at Okehampton, Bude, Wadebridge and Padstow were too short for their 57ft 6in wheelbase. From April 1947 the class could be turned at Padstow through the provision of a 70ft 'table and by October 1947 Okehampton's had been upgraded to 70ft. The lack of suitable turning capacity at Bude was never addressed and occasional visits by the class to the line resulted in tender-first running on the return trip. The West Countries were however, designed for this. It proved useful during the 1947 enlargement of Okehampton's turntable when they were used in place of the usual T9s. Wadebridge was considered close enough to Padstow for locos to be turned there. Timetabled workings resulted again in some tender-first running between Padstow and Wadebridge.

They were, of course, designated mixed traffic engines (7P6F latterly) and once the Padstow turntable was in commission they would haul North Cornwall goods or passenger trains. Initially the newcomers worked the up 'Atlantic Coast Express' – only two or three coaches in winter – the 8.30am from Padstow, the engine coming down on the 10.10am goods from Okehampton, staying overnight at Wadebridge. In later years the class was rostered to work the 8:30 and 11:00 morning departures from Padstow and the afternoon arrivals of the 10:35 and 11:15 services from Waterloo.

Over the twenty years of their active existence a great number of the class could be noted running on the North Cornwall. During 1947, for instance, 21C107, 21C108, 21C111 and 21C120 were regular visitors. The light pacific duties were performed by Exmouth Junction allocated engines and the occasional loco 'borrowed' from other sheds. The table details the known allocations of the class to Exmouth Junction and photographic evidence indicates that the majority of these would, at some time, have travelled along the North Cornwall to Padstow.

From 1957, however, British Railways decided to rebuild the class in a more conventional form. This included removing the air-smoothed casing replacing the chain-drive valve gear and associated oil bath with Walschaerts valve gear and cutting down the 'raves' on the tenders. The work increased their driving wheel axle weights from 18 tons 15cwt to over 20 tons and resulted in the rebuilt engines being banned from working from Meldon Junction into North Cornwall. The weak underbridges (of old rails) between there and Launceston are understood to have been the reason. Whilst 'local' engines *Boscastle*, *Bodmin*, *Trevone* and *Camelford* were all so treated the rebuilding programme was halted in 1961 after 60 of the 110 locos had been

Number	Exmouth Junct. allocated	Number	Exmouth Junct. allocated
34001	6/45-10/57	34046	11/46-5/51
34002	6/45-9/64	34047	11/46-5/51
34003	6/45-4/48, 5/50-6/50, 9/50-9/57	34048	1/49-2/51
34004	6/45-2/58	34049	4/51-5/51
34005	7/45-4/51	34050	4/51-6/51
34006	8/45-4/51	34051	4/51-6/51
34007	9/45-4/51	34052	4/51-6/51
34008	9/45-4/51	34053	4/51-6/51
34009	9/45-4/51	34054	4/51-6/52, 11/63-9/64
34010	9/45-4/51	34055	4/51-6/52
34011	10/45-4/48, 3/59-11/63	34056#	4/51-11/54, 12/54-11/60
34012	10/45-4/48, 12/50-2/51, 3/51-4/51	34057	4/51-5/51, 5/52-11/54, 12/54-11/60
34013	10/45-4/48, 5/51-9/57	34058#	4/51-9/60
34014	11/45-2/58	34059*	4/51-10/55
34015	11/45-2/51, 3/51-9/64	34060#	5/51-10/60
34016	11/45-2/58	34061	6/51-11/60, 11/63-6/64
34017	12/45-3/54	34062#	6/51-1/59
34018	12/45-4/51	34063	3/59-5/63
34019	12/45-4/48, 12/48-4/51	34064	6/59-5/62
34020	12/45-4/51, 5/62-9/64	34065	6/59-4/64
34021	7/47-4/48, 12/50-1/58	34066	2/61-9/64
34022	5/51-1/58	34069	3/54-11/63
34023	5/51-9/64	34070	11/61-9/64
34024#	7/47-8/49, 8/49-12/60	34072	2/58-7/64
34025	7/47-10/57	34074	2/58-6/63
34026	10/47-2/58	34075	10/57-4/64
34027	2/48-10/57	34076	10/57-9/64
34028#	2/48-2/51, 3/51-6/58	34078	2/61-9/64
34029#	2/48-10/58	34079	2/58-9/64
34030	12/48-9/64	34080	1/58-9/64
34031#	12/49-12/50, 10/51-10/58	34081	10/57-7/64
34032#	3/50-9/50, 5/51-8/60	34083	11/61-8/64
34033	1/50-3/50, 5/51-10/51, 12/51-9/64	34084	11/60-5/63, 11/63-9/64
34034#	10/50-12/50, 3/52-6/60	34086	10/57-2/58, 5/61-9/64
34035	1/58-6/63	34096#	1/58-2/61
34036#	1/58-6/60	34097#	11/60-1/61
34037	1/58-2/58	34098#	11/60-1/61
34038	1/58-11/60	34104#	2/58-3/61
34041	9/49-1/50	34106	2/58-9/64
34042	10/46-4/48	34107	6/59-9/64
34043	10/46-2/50	34108#	2/58 2/61
34044	10/46-5/51	34109#	2/58-1/61
34045	10/46-5/51	34110	3/59-11/63

Key: # Also allocated to Exmouth junction after rebuilding by BR.

rebuilt. For clarity, the dates the rebuilt locos were allocated to Exmouth Junction are not included in the list.

Rebuilding also impacted on the original engines. In many cases those with larger 5500 gallon tenders found them transferred to the rebuilt locos and replaced by the narrower 4500 gallon variety.

Of the class known to have run on the North Cornwall a few are of particular interest. From 1948 34006 ran with extended smoke deflectors, a souvenir from the locomotive exchanges of that year. 34064 was fitted with a Giesl oblong ejector in September 1962. Visibly this altered the chimney from the large hole as designed by Bulleid to a long thin shape but reduced spark throwing and increased power, some say, up to that of a Merchant Navy. The tenders running with 34069, 34072, 34074, 34075 and 34078 were never 'cut-down' and retained their high-sided 'raves' right to the end. For more detail on this fascinating but complicated class the reader is recommended to refer to *The Book of the West Country and Battle of Britain Pacifics* by Richard Derry and also published by Irwell Press.

27 of the original engines were transferred to the WR at Exmouth Junction from 1 January 1963. The WR withdrew freight services in September 1964 beyond Meldon Junction, and steam haulage generally from 3 January 1965, leaving Exmouth Junction with a rapidly declining allocation. The last 'West Countries' at Padstow were 34015

On the sunny morning of 25th August 1960 the 6.30am from Okehampton (with coaches and newspaper van from the 1.30am Waterloo) has reached Wadebridge at 9.15am behind N Class No.31847. After Nationalisation in 1948 several Bodmin Road trains were extended to Padstow. Former GWR 2-6-2T No.4565 (St. Blazey) with a B Set is on a return working calling at Wadebridge at 9.20am. R. A. Lumber.

on the down 'ACE' (4 September 1964) and 34023 on the final up train.

Many Bulleid light Pacifics, in original and re-built forms, escaped the scrapyards. It is pleasing to note that 'local' engine 34016 *Bodmin* is preserved as rebuilt on the Mid-Hants Railway, although is currently out of steam, and that 34007 *Wadebridge* re-steamed in 2007.

WR Visitors

GWR 45XX 2-6-2Ts could be found at Wadebridge (working the Bodmin to Wadebridge/Padstow services) and also at Launceston. The Laira engines kept very much to the Western side at Launceston until 1951 but then, with the closure of the ex-GW station in June 1952, they used the ex-SR station (but not the SR shed as yet). A reported shortage of tank engines for an extended Sunday service to Delabole brought quite a surprise in 1953. In the spring a 45XX was given clearance tests from Okehampton to Bude and Delabole. On 26 July No 4583, sub-shedded at Launceston, set off on that Sunday morning at 9.50am to Halwill. From there she took the 10.29 to Bude, returning to Halwill at 11.51am. At 12.19 she arrived back at Launceston, then went on to Delabole. After running round (and taking water) 4583 simmered at Delabole before taking the 12.55pm back to Launceston, going on shed at 2.40. 4583 was back again on 20 September doing the whole turn Launceston-Bude-Halwill-Delabole-Launceston between 9.15am and 2.45pm. The steps had to be cut back and the ATC shoe clipped up to operate on the SR lines.

On the Bodmin branch in 1961 two ex-GWR pannier tanks, 4666 and 4694, were substituted for the 'O2' tanks. At that time under Southern Region control, they were not quite 'at home' in Wadebridge shed. Further ex-GWR engines arrived in 1962. The Beattie well tanks, showing their extreme age, were withdrawn. To hand were displaced Weymouth Quay 0-6-0 pannier tanks Nos1367-1369; although six-coupled, the short wheelbases enabled them to work on the Wenford branch. Meanwhile the Churchward 45XX 2-6-2Ts soldiered on from Bodmin to Wadebridge/Padstow.

LMR Visitors

The Region contributed two classes to the workings in the area.

Ex-GWR 45XX tank No.4552 and B set arrive at Wadebridge with the 1.23pm Padstow-Bodmin Road passenger train. L.R. Freeman, www.transporttreasury.co.uk

One of the two ex-GWR pannier tanks sent to replace the ageing O2 tanks on the Bodmin branch turns. 4694 is at Wadebridge with the 12.25pm, made up of an SR 2-set, train for Bodmin North in May 1961. L. R. Freeman, www.transporttreasury.co.uk

Fairburn 4MT 2-6-4T

In 1951 the shed pits at Bude were repaired preventing access to the turntable for tender locos. Additionally the M7s required these pits for servicing their inside gear which of course, with their outside gear, the 2-6-4Ts didn't. For the duration of the repairs, so as to prevent tender-first running, four Fairburn tanks were drafted in from the Central Section (see table). During their stay of around four months they were used in place of T9s on the afternoon Okehampton/Bude passenger service. The apparent success of the class on the line may have been one of the prompts for the introduction of the BR Class 3 tanks on the Bude line. The Fairburns can be seen as the forerunners of the BR Class 4 tanks which arrived ten years later in 1962.

Ivatt 2MT 2-6-2T

The Ivatts were allocated to Bude from time to time but the line's gradients meant they were found wanting in power for any more than the two coach sets. It was more usual to see a BR 82XXX tank on the Bude services. They were, however, perfectly at home on the Torrington/Halwill lightweights, where they replaced the 'E1/R' 0-6-2Ts. Here they would be regularly seen with a Bulleid brake composite coach and a few vans in tow. Replacing the 'O2' 0-4-4Ts and the succeeding WR pannier tanks the Ivatts found a niche on the Bodmin branch between 1962 and 1964. Those involved were taken from Exmouth Junction's allocation and locos including 41270, 41272, 41275 and 41320 could thus be seen on Wadebridge shed. The restrictions on six-coupled engines were eased to Bodmin North from Boscarne Junction in the 1950s. The circuitous trips for a Launceston-based Ivatt tank in 1962/63 is described elsewhere. 41272 was the 7000th engine built at Crewe works and carried a brass plaque on its tank sides to record the fact. Ivatt tank 41321 held the dubious honour of being the last steam engine to be withdrawn from Exmouth Junction in July 1965.

One of the three replacements for the withdrawn Beattie Well Tanks, pannier tank No.1369 had been displaced from its Weymouth Quay duties along with 1367 and 1368 in 1962.

The BR Standards

Despite the introduction of the BR Standard types there was no quick and wholesale eradication of older pre-

Number	Exmouth Junct. Allocated
42099	9/51-1/52
42102	11/51-1/52
42103	9/51-1/52
42105	9/51-1/52

departed Exmouth Junction in June 1956. This was not the end of the 75XXXs on the North Cornwall as four re-appeared in 1964 (see table). The later arrivals differed from the first by having BR2 3,500 gallon tenders which were inset at the top to give a better look out, but crews were still not impressed. Not obvious in the black and white photos of the period is that all four wore the lined BR Green livery favoured by the WR. All bar 75025 had double blastpipes and chimney. They were employed on passenger workings to Wadebridge, the Bude to Okehampton afternoon service, Meldon Quarry workings and freights to Okehampton and Plymouth. The last inhabitant of Launceston shed was one of these, working the North Cornwall in December 1964. With the closure of Exmouth Junction to steam in May 1965 all four were transferred to Worcester.

The Ivatt 2-6-2Ts had been drafted in from Exmouth Junction to succeed the O2s and pannier tanks on the Bodmin branch services. 41272 is at Wadebridge on 26th June 1962; it was accompanied by sister locos Nos.41270, 41275 and 41320. R. C. Riley, www.transporttreasury.co.uk

grouping designs. The Beattie Well tanks still pottered between Wadebridge and Wenford and the T9s continued to haul passenger trains as they had done for decades. There were casualities in the area however, and from 1952 the Bude branch lost its 'M7' tanks which were pushed aside by the Ivatt Class 2 2-6-2Ts and BR Class 3 tanks. The North Cornwall, on the other hand, rarely saw 'Standards' until the introduction of the Class 4 2-6-4Ts in 1962.

BR 75XXX Standard Class 4 4-6-0

In September 1955 ten BR Class 4 4-6-0s (75070-75079) were allocated to Exmouth Junction. Unfortunately their 51ft long wheelbase was too long for the 50ft turntables at Launceston and Bude, meaning that they could not be turned. Whilst their BR1B, 4,725 gallon, high-sided tenders were suitable for reverse running, this sort of working was unpopular with crews. There must have been little suitable work for the new engines as upon arrival 75079 was quickly 'loaned' to Yeovil Town. All ten

BR 80XXX Standard Class 4MT 2-6-4T

In 1962 twelve Class 4 tanks, redundant from Tonbridge and elsewhere, went to Exmouth Junction to augment the lacklustre Class 3s (see table). The BR 2-6-4Ts were doing the much reduced 'Perishables' duties from Okehampton in 1964 and on the Halwill/Bude (from 1962) in place of the Class 3s. They were also involved in goods working with the Ns and Pacifics, but were principally to be found on the 10.12am and 5.50pm from Okehampton and the 3.13pm and 6.00pm from Padstow. It is interesting to note they were turned at Padstow to give 'collar' to the uphill return journey. Those not withdrawn were transferred to Yeovil Town, Templecombe, Bath and Bristol, before and after the end of steam working in early January 1965.

BR 82XXX Standard Class 3MT 2-6-2T

The first batch of 82XXX (82010-82019) tanks arrived new at Exmouth Junction in the summer of 1952 (see table). 82012/14-16 were quickly spirited away to Eastleigh within eight months of arrival. The remaining engines replaced some M7s on their previous haunts. A reported shortage of tank engines for an extended Sunday service to Delabole in August 1953 resulted in 82013 being 'borrowed' from the Bude branch to take the afternoon working to Okehampton from Launceston, going

Number	Exmouth Junct. allocated
75005	3/64-5/65
75008	9/64-5/65
75022	4/64-2/65 and 3/65-5/65
75025	3/64-5/65

Displaced by electrification in Kent and Sussex, BR 4MT 2-6-4Ts reigned supreme on the Bude branch in the early 1960s, though the North Cornwall, previously a tender engine preserve, shared their services. 80041 is preparing to depart from a frosty Launceston station for Okehampton on 15th December 1964. Courtesy R. Joanes.

Number	Exmouth Junct. allocated
80035	5/62-9/64,1/65-2/65
80036	5/62-11/64 wdn
80037	6/62-1/65,3/65-5/65
80038	6/62-7/63,9/63-9/64 wdn
80039	6/62-1/65,3/65-5/65
80040	6/62-7/64 wdn
80041	6/62-5/65
80042	6/62-2/65 wdn
80043	6/62-9/64
80059	6/62-9/64
80064	6/62-5/65
80067	5/62-9/64

on at 4.15pm to Delabole (6.06pm) before going back to Launceston. A second batch (82022-82025) arrived in 1954 and then the Exmouth Junction allocation remained fairly static until the early 1960s. All these early arrivals carried the standard lined black livery. With the arrival of the more powerful BR Class 4 tanks in 1962, all ten remaining 3MTs departed for Nine Elms.

As services were scaled back in Cornwall and loads got lighter there was again a need for the 3MTs and eight stayed for various lengths of time between April 1963 and the end of steam. WR influences resulted in 82001, 82002, 82030 82039, 82042 carrying the lined BR green livery and 82035 and 82040 being finished in unlined green. Whilst it was rare for a Standard 3 tank to be seen working the North Cornwall line they did occasionally deputise for the 4MT tanks. Notably 82042 appeared at Wadebridge on the last day of steam, 2 January 1965.

Dieselisation and DMUs

The Modernisation Plan brought not only the elimination of steam to the North Cornwall but also its replacement by diesel locomotives and multiple units. The Western Region NBL diesel-hydraulic Type 2s were first to arrive on the scene in 1961 when they infiltrated Wadebridge on WR Bodmin trains. From 1964 they were also used

The smaller Standard Class 3 82XXX 2-6-2Ts were also to be seen on the North Cornwall although they were something of a rarity. 82042 seen here at Padstow in October 1964 appeared at Wadebridge on the last day of steam on 2nd January 1965. Courtesy R. Joanes.

Number	Exmouth Junct allocation
82001	4/63-12/63
82002	4/63-2/64
82010	6/52-9/62
82011	8/52-9/62
82012	8/52-1/53
82013	8/52-9/62
82017	8/52-9/62
82018	9/52-9/62
82019	9/52-9/62
82022	10/54-9/62
82023	10/54-9/62
82024	8/54-9/62
82025	8/54-9/62
82030	6/64-5/65
82035	3/64-9/64
82039	3/64-5/65
82040	10/63-5/65
82042	6/64-5/65
82044	6/64-5/65

on the Okehampton-Bude afternoon workings. Among those noted were Plymouth Laira-based D6309, D6342 and D6348. As with other NBL classes, the D63XXs were plagued by chronic engine problems which blighted the class from their introduction. Indeed many locomotives hardly saw ten years of service before being scrapped.

By 1965 all steam had been banished from the line and passenger services were covered by DMUs and single car units. DMUs included the Derby-built suburban 3-car 'heavyweight' units, the suburban 3-car units built by BRC&W and the Swindon cross-country 3-car units. Photographic evidence suggests that the centre cars were removed from time to time leaving the DMUs running as 2-car units. Two types of 'bubble car' were also noted on the North Cornwall, the Pressed Steel single-car unit and the Gloucester single-car unit. The two types can be differentiated by the roof mounted, 4-digit, headcode box carried by the Pressed Steel vehicles, with the destination blinds located at the top of each central cab window. Interestingly an early nickname for the Gloucester style cars was 'coffin nails', as most of the routes on which they were used became victims of the "Beeching Axe" with closure usually soon after introduction!

Both the DMUs and single-car units were significantly more reliable in service than the NBL locomotives. Had they been introduced to the line sooner maybe the reduced operating costs would have stayed closure for a few more years. Perhaps the last fee-earning locomotive to run on a section of the North Cornwall was 25080. This worked 'The Wadebridge Wanderer' railtour on the 30th September 1978, of which part of the route was from Bodmin General to Boscarne Junction and Wadebridge. A final special, comprising two DMUs from Bodmin Road, ran on 17th December 1978.

A rare flurry of activity at Halwill as passengers change from the DMU Bude train on the right to the Wadebridge bound train in the Bay.

A foul wet winter day at Padstow in 1967. The single-car unit was built by the Gloucester Railway Carriage & Wagon Company (GRCW) from 1958. It carries the usual two-character route indicator for the line 'C2'. As built the units had green ends with 'speed whiskers' but by the time they were in service on the NCR the whiskers had been replaced by the small yellow warning panel as shown here. Courtesy R. Joanes.

Approaching Launceston on 5th January 1965, this Derby-built 'Heavyweight' suburban sets was one of the later 1958 batch that had a two-figure route indicator panel fitted from new. Again it carries the C2 route code and has the later small yellow warning panel in place of the earlier speed whiskers. R. L. Goodman.

The Southern Railway introduced a 25-ton goods brake van in the late 1920s. Several were soon allocated to Exmouth Junction yard for North Cornwall trains, their movements specified in the working timetables. Use of the new N 2-6-0s from 1925 enabled haulage of up to 40 unbraked wagons, the long and steep gradients calling for careful control by engine crews and guards. In some places, such as Otterham to Launceston, wagon standing brakes were also pinned down to aid matters.

The parcels van carrying tin cans cases to the Ambrosia Creamery at Lifton managed to get derailed one afternoon after a rough shunt, which also pushed a cattle wagon over the top of the stopblocks. The logging business beyond was part of Bartlett's, long a user of the railway at Launceston. The locomotive, N Class No.31835, was allocated to Exmouth Junction from May 1949 through to its withdrawal in September 1964. This therefore dates the scene prior to May 1957 as the loco received a major overhaul including new cylinders, with outside steam pipes, a Standard Class 4 Chimney and completely new frames. R. L. Goodman collection.

Chapter Eight

TRAINS, STRUCTURES, PERMANENT WAY AND SIGNALLING

Additional information from Chris Osment

In 1879 a passenger for Okehampton would have climbed aboard a four or six-wheel coach at the Holsworthy terminus. At the head of the train would be a 4-4-0T and three vehicles or so, one of which was solely for the guard and his parcels. This last vehicle had a large caboose raised above the roof and from here the guard could observe the engine and apply his handbrake as necessary, as these were the days before the automatic vacuum through brake. There was communication of a sort if Clark's patent cord system was present. At night oil lamps were let into the roofs of the coaches but there was no heating unless 'footwarmers' were available (possibly not at Holsworthy!). The old LSWR varnished teak or dark green

Two views of the ex-LNWR 12-wheeler coach, DM 198932 in July 1960. The coach fulfilled two important functions throughout its life at Wadebridge. It was a venue for a Rules instruction class at the locomotive depot (the code MP on the side denotes this) but more importantly, it provided accommodation for the men on lodging turns. It had a kitchen, saloon and sleeping compartments - all additions since its reputed former life as part of the LNWR Royal train.

Above. The austere and earlier lineage of Ashbury station is apparent in comparison to that of the North Cornwall examples. Single story with none of the grand gables of say, Ashwater or Padstow, the station had opened with the line to Bude in 1879.

Left. Camelford station in July 1964. The station acted as railhead for both Tintagel and Boscastle and warranted, in the view of the directors, a canopy, the only one at a wayside station. The Atlantic gales meant the Station Masters house was slate clad. C. J. Knowles Thomas.

Bottom. Otterham in 1958 could easily be mistaken for some leafy London suburb. Most of the stations along the North Cornwall were constructed in dressed stone although two, Tresmeer and Egloskerry, were in red brick. Note the lean of the trees on the right of the photograph! A. Harding.

London South Western Railway Co.
North Cornwall Railway Station Buildings

The drawings represent the basic design and measurements of the North Cornwall station buildings, waiting shelters and goods sheds but there were some detail differences at each location.

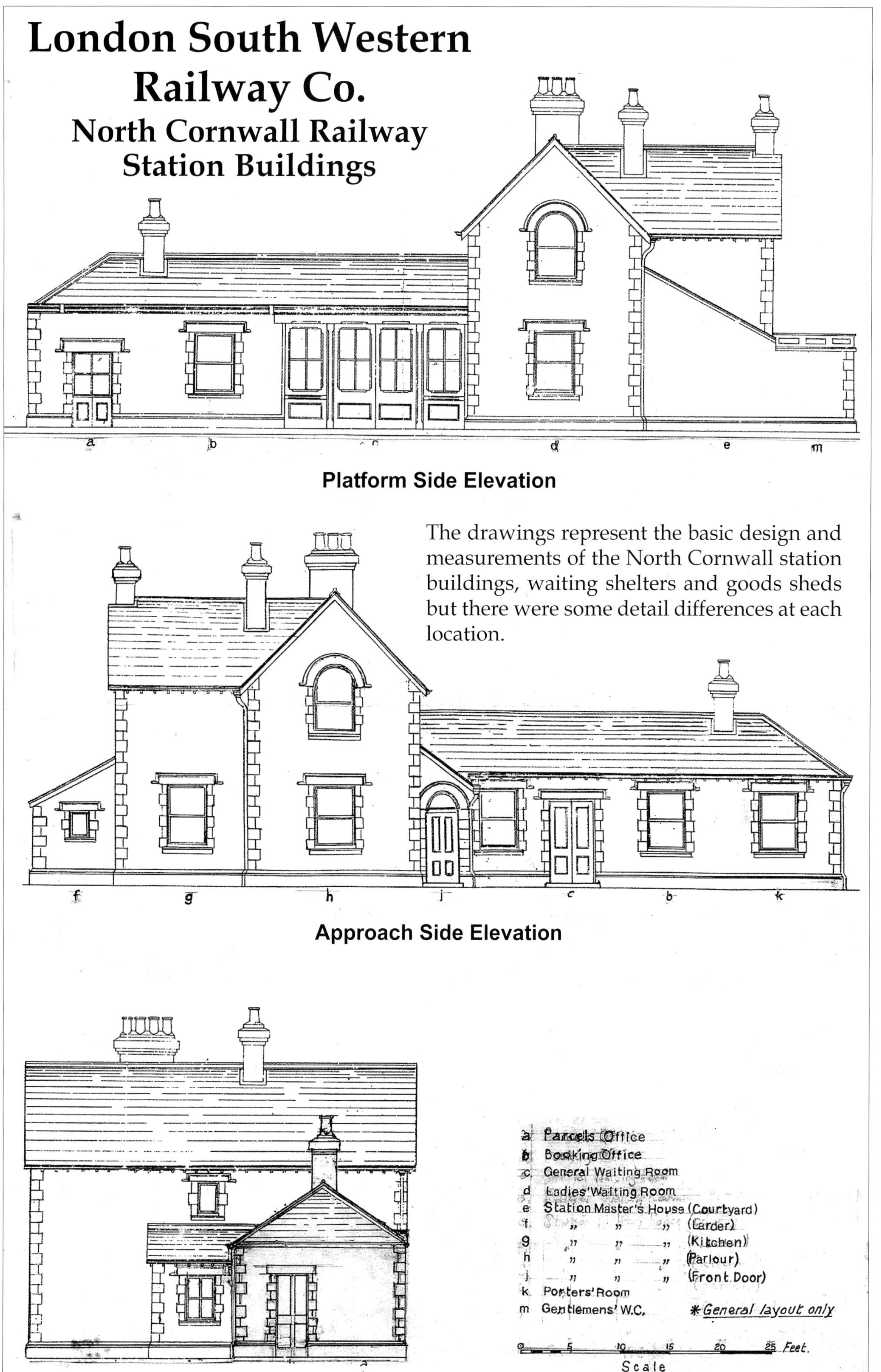

Above. Constructed in 1888 Wadebridge, like Launceston, did not have an integral Station Masters house, this was located a short distance away in Guinea Port Road.

Left. A 1960s view of the terminus at Padstow. Although of a later period, the unmistakable pattern of North Cornwall stations is clear. A canopy was deemed necessary at this seaside location.

Bottom. Launceston signal box is included here because of its unique construction. Although built to the LSWR's 1880s style, an extension at the rear of the building, carried out in 1916, accommodated the GWR signalman, locking frame, levers and Electric Token to Lifton.

livery was about to be replaced by the unusual 'salmon pink' and brown. Platform heights were being increased to 2ft 6ins and the new branch was built to this standard, though by 1900 heights were set at 3ft (e.g. Padstow).

These collections of 4 and 6 wheelers, 24, 25 and 28-foot long and dating from the 1870s, gave way to bogie stock about 1895. The North Cornwall appeared to be re-quipped with 42-foot Thirds and 42 or 46-foot Tri-composites ($1^{st}/2^{nd}/3^{rd}$ Class) dating from the 1880s, but some of the older 6-wheel 30-foot Guards Brake Vans were retained, supplemented by new 44-foot bogie vans. These were formed into more or less permanent 'sets' and were the last

***Top.* John Wildith, transferred from the SR's Eastern Section, stands outside Camelford signal box in 1928 accompanied by his niece Sophie. Like St. Kew Highway underneath, they typified many of the boxes on the North Cornwall Railway, built in a style favoured by the LSWR in the 1880s. St. Kew was one of the last to be constructed to this pattern and was equipped with a Tyers Single line Tablet apparatus.**

of the Victorian low arc-roofed coaches, though they lasted locally until about 1910. At this time the LSWR dropped the use of the separate vans and formed two-coach sets with inclusive brake/ luggage compartments. Identifying Set numbers were now applied to the coach ends and generally speaking, those traversing the North Cornwall and Bude lines were within the 186 to 229 series. Each set now consisted of a 42-foot Brake Third (1890-94) rebuilt from an all-Third and a 45-foot Brake Composite (1892-93) rebuilt from a Tri-composite. After 1923 the SR renumbered these sets in the series 34 to 55.

In the 1930s there was another minor 'cascading' of LSWR elliptical-roofed stock to local services and after 1936 SR Sets 7 to 21, 42 to 46, 51 to 54 and 56 might be noted west of Meldon Junction. Carriage workings took them to Honiton and also to Plymouth in the course of a week. The sets most used on Padstow and Bude trains were Nos.7 to 21, originally consisting of a 48-foot Brake Third (ex-1896 Tri-composites) and 56-foot Brake Composite (1st/3rd Class) dating from 1912. In 1936 the 48-foot coaches were rebuilt and lengthened to 58-foot, and these non-corridors equipped with lavatories in some compartments (from their main line days) lasted another twenty years on the local scene. Each set would seat about 100 Third and 10 First Class passengers together with fairly liberal guard/luggage/parcels compartments for the large amount of personal luggage in those days (commercial travellers' 'samples' for instance) as well as rabbits, calves, boxes of fish, even seaweed destined for medical use.

Some of the old 6-wheel carriages and many guards vans were sold off to become chalets, some surviving to be rescued by the preservationists – at least the bodywork! The Southern Railway introduced wooden-bodied vans, long wheelbase with two axles, and bogie vehicles. Best known, and still to be seen today relegated to tool and mess vans for the engineers, were the 'Utility' Parcels and Mail vans (PMVs). Very common on the North Cornwall and the western lines generally, especially during the years of the lucrative rabbit trade, these too had scheduled duties laid down in the working books. Guards compartments with hand brakes (and periscopes to observe signals) were provided in a number of these vans, particularly the bogie vans carrying the newspapers from London which actually had roof boards lettered NEWSPAPER TRAFFIC. In due course BR 4 and 8-wheel vans appeared, along with the odd ex-LMS, LNE or GW examples. No complete parcels trains ran on the North Cornwall. 'Tail' traffic sufficed, often lengthy in nature, behind 2-sets. Such a 'tail' would consist of the various van types, returning Road Vans (latterly branded 'XP') and meat

Camelford up platform viewed from a passing train. The canopy, signalbox, station masters house and platform details are all clearly visible in this July 1961 photograph. The station is now the home of the British Cycling Museum. John Ayres, South Western Circle.

containers on flat wagons – making quite formidable loads for the 'S11's and 'T9's.

The GWR stock working into Wadebridge in the 1890s was made up of four wheelers; the LSWR's inherited Bodmin & Wadebridge open 'trucks' being discarded after 1888 (though one survives at York). The re-opened LSWR Bodmin services in 1895 utilised similar coaching to the North Cornwall, until the advent of the Railmotors in 1906. After 1918 the latter were converted into pure carriage stock and coupled to suitably equipped 'motor' tank engines. Thus 'O2' 0-4-4Ts could be seen at Wadebridge with their 'push and pull' trains, but only for a while. It would seem that they and the '415' 4-4-2Ts involved with mixed trains, and thus shunting, were inconvenienced by the LSWR's complicated rod and wire system. Trains reverted to engine run-rounds each time at Bodmin, Wadebridge and Padstow. The converted Railmotors figured in 3-coach workings until the late 1940s, sharing with the 2-sets, single LSWR non-corridors and even the odd SR corridor (from a London working) pressed into use.

While the Bodmin local service had variety, the North Cornwall locals were almost exclusively 2-sets until the end of steam. The only extra coach working to be seen was the Meldon Quarrymen's daily shuttle from Okehampton and the single example to Launceston on Saturday afternoons. In the 1930s it was an ex-SECR all third bogie, but usually an LSWR vehicle – S2611S in BR crimson livery in 1958, for instance. The ND & CJLR's single coach from Torrington appeared at Halwill three times a day, twice on mixed trains.

The SR (and the LSWR) kept much of their coaching stock in sets and numbered. The LSWR salmon pink and

The lamp room on the down platform at Camelford, clad in the modish corrugated iron of the late Victorian period, was a vital part of station working. It stored paraffin for the signal lamps and, until 1966, the platform, offices and house lighting. C. J. Knowles-Thomas.

St. Kew Highway waiting shed on the down side platform, together with oil lamps. The platform copings were slate slabs from Delabole – some of these may be seen at Waterloo to this day. C. J. Knowles-Thomas.

brown, abandoned in the First World War, had given way to dark green, perpetuated by the SR until Nationalisation. Lining out and numbering was applied in yellow or gilt.

In the period before the Night Newspaper train from Waterloo included through corridor coaches to Padstow, there was accommodation (of a sort) for those in the know. In 1938 a 2-set went down on the 5.21am (MO) goods from Halwill, and from Okehampton at 4.00am goods on other weekdays. This early morning train started as the 12.01am Goods and Mail from Exmouth Junction (to Launceston). At Launceston the 2-set became an advertised train at 7.44am on to Padstow. It returned with vans as the 2.55pm 'Perishables' through to Exeter. On summer Saturdays in 1938 its duties were quite different. As with other sets it had to fit in with through Waterloo/ North Cornwall workings. On these Saturdays it left Okehampton at the back of the 11.00am Waterloo through

LSWR North Cornwall Railway - Waiting Shed

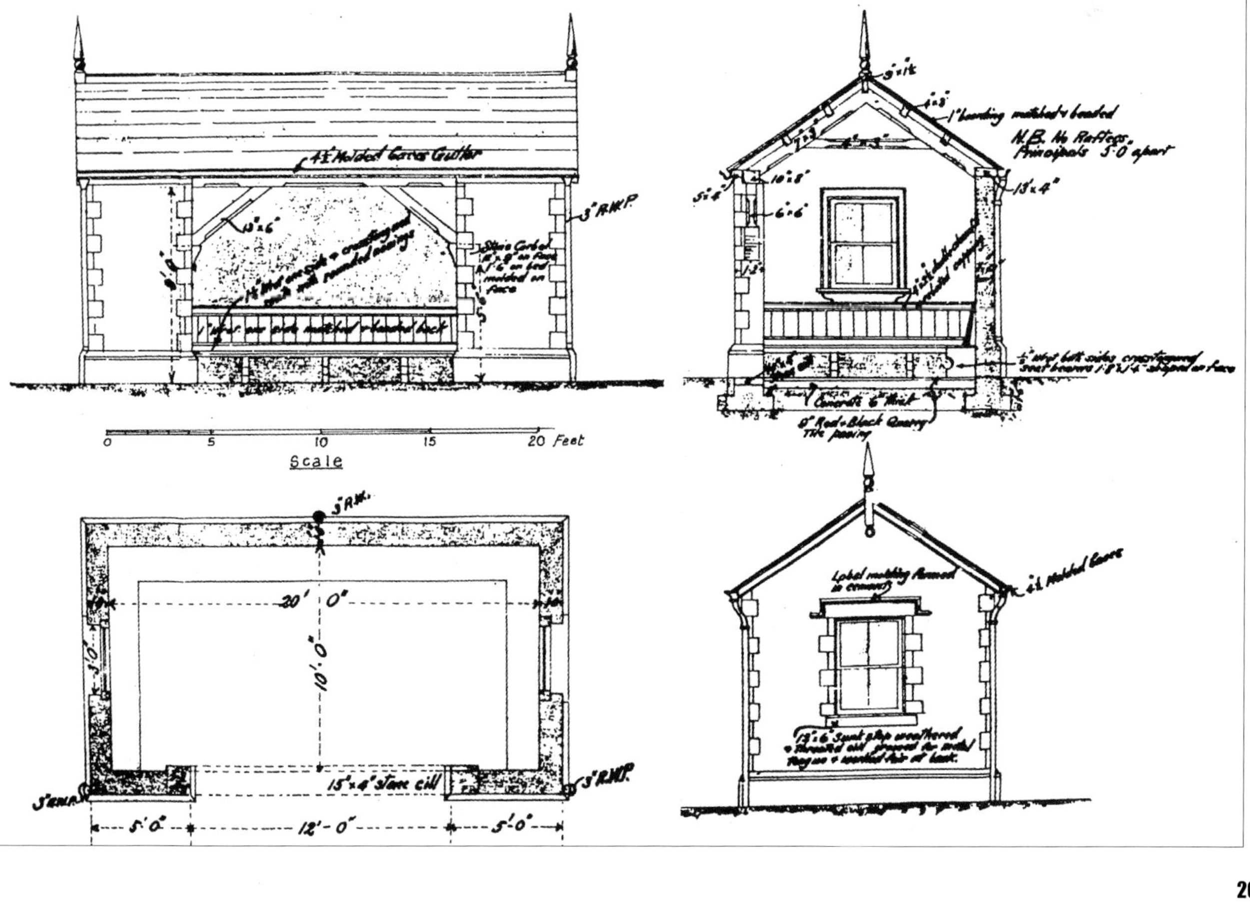

The LSWR blue and white enamel signs have by this time given way to the Exmouth Junction concrete versions which initially had green backgrounds and white lettering, giving way in turn to the Western Region brown backgrounds in the early 1950s. C. J. Knowles-Thomas.

coaches to Bude at 3.30pm, eventually gaining Exeter Central on the 7.12pm local from Bude. On Sundays it worked to and from Honiton/Exeter Central.

Although through Monday to Friday six sets were employed part of their day on the North Cornwall and Bude lines on ten local services, their diagrams became quite complicated on summer Saturdays. In 1938 several Waterloo/ Plymouth extras shed portions, to Bude particularly. From the 1.00pm and 3.06pm Waterloo train, 2-sets were added at Okehampton, keeping the station pilot busy. The 3.06 (Okehampton 7.47pm) had one to Delabole arriving at 9.25pm, returning ECS to Launceston. The workings of these 2-sets were not confined to Cornwall. Some went to Plymouth and Diagram 173 was a working to Sidmouth from Exeter Central before arriving at Okehampton to form the 1.00pm to Padstow. Only Bude was getting a Sunday service in 1938 involving a set, but on several August Sundays a berthed 'overnighter' at Padstow was used on an excursion to Exeter. The decanting of main line stock to local passenger services is noted above when the LSWR 2-sets arrived in the 1890s. The same thing happened in the 1940s when Maunsells' SR main line coaches were relegated.

There seems no doubt that excursions from London (see Chapter 2 on the Wadebridge opening page 39) ran through to North Cornwall in the 1890s, particularly at Christmas and Easter. Patrons probably had to make do with whatever stock was available, and timings appeared to be very liberal to allow for personal needs at stations en route! The 1890s non-corridors did have limited lavatory accommodation and these possibly figured as the experimental single through coaches of 1902 and 1904 and again 1905, when regular services started. In 1907 the first purpose-built through brake tri-composites (1st/2nd/3rd) appeared, 56ft long, with corridors and now gangways (see below). They even had steam heating. The luggage compartment was generous as well, reflecting the amount Edwardian travellers took with them. The 11.00am Waterloo (and 8.54am return next day) included one for Padstow along with others for Sidmouth, Exmouth, Torrington and Bude. In these pre-1914 summers the 1.00pm Waterloo also included one each for Bude and Padstow.

For the 'North Cornwall and Bude Express' of 1907 the LSWR converted the 1892 'Eagle' boat train saloons. The six for Padstow (including a dining car pair) and the four for Bude had central vestibules and gangways within each set. The lack of connections at the ends deprived Bude passengers of access to the dining cars! This was rectified in 1908. These and their 56-foot corridor successors were a heavy load for a '460' in the Up direction, non-stop from Halwill to Exeter St Davids by 1914. LSWR corridors were still appearing in holiday trains just after 1945.

New Corridor Stock from 1926

For the 'Atlantic Coast Express' that year ten Brake Composites were built at Eastleigh in 1926, Nos.6565-6574. They were 59ft over ends and 9ft wide ('Restriction 1') with four Third and two 1st Class compartments seating 32 and 12 respectively. An end-lavatory and a guard/luggage compartment (14ft 9ins) completed the accommodation. These coaches had with Pullman gangways and buckeye automatic couplers. From this date the shunters at Okehampton and Halwill and so on had to be conversant with coupling them from the existing screw hooks of older stock, retracting buffers and using gangway adapters where necessary. While they were designed for the individual services of the ACE formation at this date, other Maunsell 59ft stock was appearing in through trains. The summer 1930 10.24am (SO) Waterloo to Bude was all new SR stock except for one LSW corridor brake third at each end. None of these coaches were in 'Sets' and the formations were from 'loose' vehicles generally formed up each summer season. Interestingly, the 10.24 included a new Maunsell kitchen dining saloon and open saloon for Bude, as did the Up 10.45am SO from Bude, arriving empty the previous day. The Padstow portions were no more than four coaches out of ten. As the decade progressed the Restaurant Cars were diverted to the North Cornwall line, with new SR three and six-coach sets.

Top. **The original aqueduct carrying the mill leat at Newport, Launceston in 1991. The narrow gauge track was laid on the North Cornwall formation in 1983 by the Launceston Steam Railway and takes its trains several miles out to New Churches. David Wroe.**

Middle. **The restricted headroom over the A39 trunk road became untenable in the new motor age. After the railway closure in 1966 the road was straightened (to the right) but the bridge remains today in a cul-de-sac. Unusually at this end of the line, the arch is of dressed stone. The signal is St. Kew Highway's down home. C. J. Knowles-Thomas.**

Bottom. **This handsome bridge at Otterham station carried the A39 coast road over the railway at the Camelford end of the layout.**

One of the new dining cars, No.8000, was displayed at Wadebridge for the Bodmin & Wadebridge Centenary exhibition in September 1934. Increasing traffic on Saturdays prompted the SR to run separate trains to Bude and Padstow, let alone Ilfracombe and East Devon resorts. A further 40 brake composites were built in 1930 as well as the new Kitchen/ Dining Saloons. All these were part of a large number of corridor coaches ordered by the SR at that time, and included three car 'P' Sets and 'loose' vehicles, many of which appeared in the North Cornwall summer through trains in the 1930s and will into the 1950s.

A Waterloo wartime working of October 1941 surprisingly served Padstow by a through three-car Restaurant Set. The 10.59am (SO) had a 3rd brake for Plymouth and a brake composite each for Sidmouth, Exmouth

Wadebridge in June 1955. The concrete footbridge had replaced an aging wooden affair in the mid-1920s and was similar to hundreds found all over the Southern system. 45XX tank No. 4565 heads a two coach B Set to Bodmin General. E. Vincent, www.transporttreasury.co.uk

The magnificent Meldon Viaduct in 1963. Concerns over the safety of the structure led to singling of the track, and speed restrictions, on 24th April 1966 between Meldon Junction and Meldon Quarry signal boxes, with traffic regulated by Western Region key token instrument. R. C. Riley, www.transporttreasury.co.uk

The Wadebridge goods shed was obviously deemed insufficient having received a concrete block extension at some time. At the wayside stations, and Padstow, two main types of goods shed were constructed, aptly named Goods Shed No.1 North Cornwall Railway and Goods Shed No.2 North Cornwall Railway. No. 1 was constructed on a red splayed brick plinth with red brick dressed windows and housed a 6cwt crane with a 12ft radius. A valance boarded screen sheltered the main track-side door whilst on the road-side a small awning was added. No. 2 was similar in size but did not have windows on the sides of the building but, strangely, had a larger radius crane of 13ft. Most were constructed in local stone with red brick dressings but oddly Ashwater's shed was in corrugated iron.

and Bude. A brake composite detached at Salisbury worked all stations to Exeter. Even wartime circumstances did not prevent the daily 'ACE' coaches arriving off the 10.50am Waterloo, and the provision of Saturday trains such as the one above. By May 1946 the 'ACE' was a very heavy train, comprised of three-car sets for Ilfracombe and Plymouth. Padstow had two Brake Composites while Seaton, Sidmouth, Exmouth, Bude and Torrington had one each. A Dining car twin set was detached at Exeter. At this time the 1.35am Waterloo Newspaper train detached a news van and two corridor thirds for Padstow from the Plymouth main train at Okehampton. The Southern Railway embarked on new coach building after 1945, with Bulleid, better known for his 4-6-2s, responsible for the overall design. His Brake Composites, following the traditions of the through Waterloo/Atlantic Coast workings, appeared in 1948 under BR guise but retained the SR malachite green livery. Nos.6713-6752 followed the earlier Maunsell layout except the lavatory compartment was in mid-coach, between the 1st and 3rd accommodation. An adjacent cross vestibule largely accounted for a longer length of 64ft 6ins. These comfortable coaches, with curved sides and windows, were three inches wider inside than the Maunsells (though still at an overall 9ft) and saw out steam haulage, until 1964. There were also two and three coach sets, 'R' and 'L' to be seen on Padstow summer trains, though it is doubtful if Bulleid Restaurant cars infiltrated west of Exeter. As BR Mark 1 corridor stock became available in the 1950s, the last of the 'ACE' workings acquired them, usually in three car formations. In spite of the predilection for set working, 'loose' corridor vehicles often made up the summer Saturday Up trains, and local trains would include one or more en route for Bude or Padstow.

Local 'P' Two Coach Sets from 1948

The LSWR two coach sets were phased out in 1948 in favour of demoted Maunsell corridors – none other than erstwhile 'ACE' through Brake Composites coupled to other brake thirds. Eight of these, Nos.22 to 29, fulfilled the duties required by the five or so each-way services, Okehampton/ Padstow/Bude. They lasted until the early 1960s, all but one (No.28) passing to WR control in January 1963. Already in 1958 a further eleven sets ('W') were put together and numbered 100 to 110. The difference from the 'P' Sets was the substitution of the Brake Seconds by open saloons. Only Nos.102, 103 and 110 passed to the WR. There were yet more local sets; two in 1962, Nos.30 and 31, conformed to the earlier 'P' sets, and another nine were original 1936 main line pairs, demoted in 1960/61. These nine, Nos.168, 172, 178-180, 196 and 198-200, were not confined to this area but also worked on the east Devon and Callington branches. Six of these passed to the WR as well as over 40 Bulleid Composite Brakes (1st/2nd and 3rd). All third class accommodation was renamed second in 1956. After January 1963 many of the Maunsell coaches were withdrawn and Bulleid Composites substituted, so that by the end of steam working few of the original SR sets were recognisable. There was increased use of three-coach sets on the North Cornwall line at that time – the SR 'R' sets and their BR equivalent Mark 1s. Finally, Torrington trains into Halwill employed every sort of coach from LSWR Corridors, ex-railmotor 'gate' stock, Maunsell, Corridors to Bulleid Composites, usually one only – two sets were never seen.

'Foreign' coaching stock was fairly rare on the North Cornwall, the Bude branch seeing more because of the AA establishment at Cleave (Morwenstowe) and the Second World

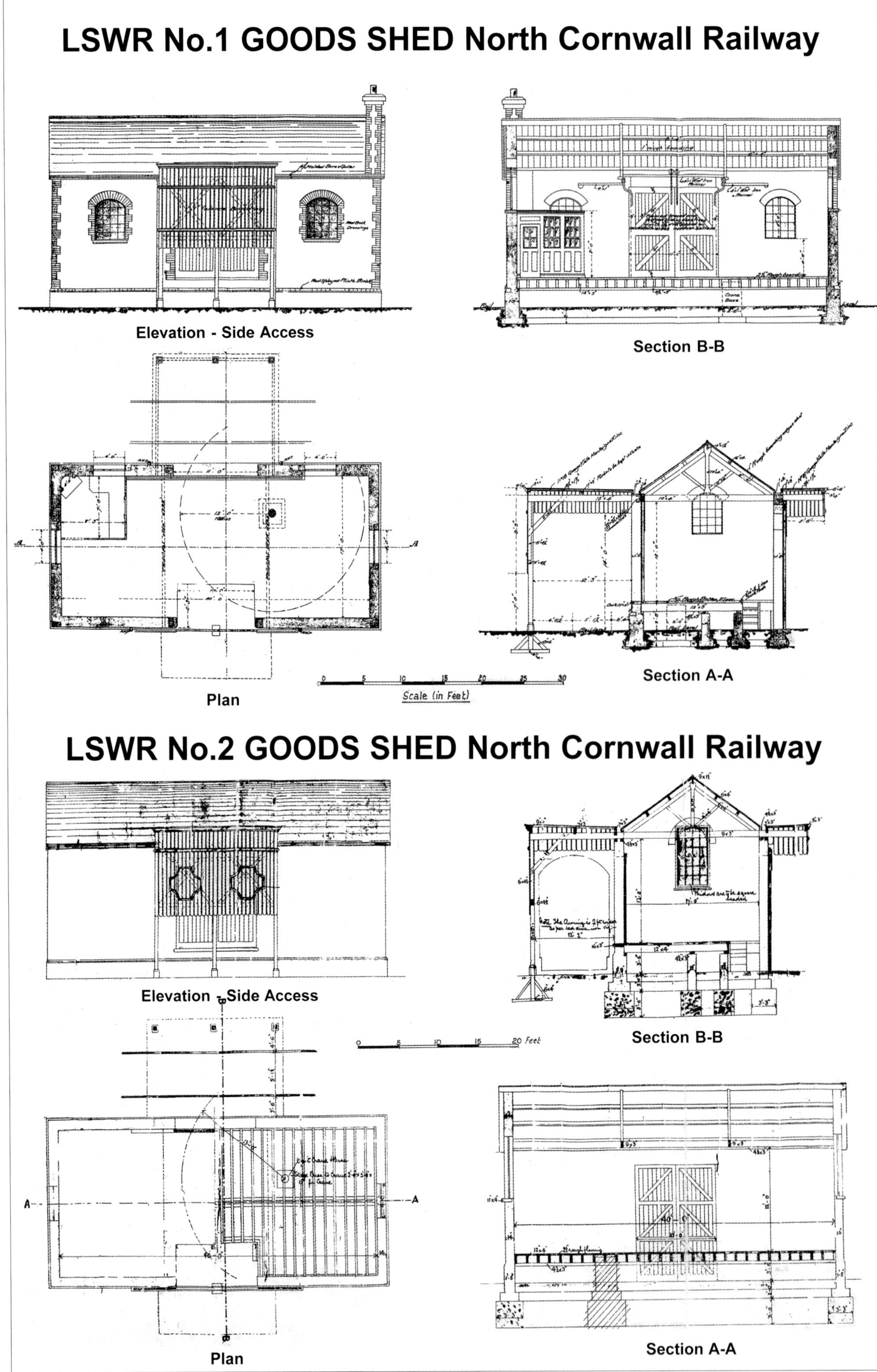
LSWR No.1 GOODS SHED North Cornwall Railway
Elevation - Side Access
Section B-B
Plan
Section A-A
Scale (in Feet)
0
5
10
15
20
25
30
LSWR No.2 GOODS SHED North Cornwall Railway
Elevation - Side Access
Section B-B
0
5
10
15
20 Feet
Plan
Section A-A

After the First World War there were five turntables (all 50ft) that locos working over the North Cornwall could call upon, Okehampton, Halwill Junction, Launceston, Wadebridge and Padstow. After 1952, and the closure of Launceston GWR station, the turntable there continued in use although SR engines required extension ramps. The introduction of the Bulleid Pacifics over the line after the War saw two 70ft units installed, one at Okehampton the other at Padstow. *Left.* In July 1949 one of the Drummond T9 4-4-0s sits well within the 70ft diameter of the turntable at Padstow with the vacuum connected to the turning mechanism. *Below.* 45XX tank No. 5541 on the Launceston turntable in May 1961. In the background is the GW shed, accessed via a loop at the up end of the station layout. H. C. Casserley, courtesy R. M. Casserley and R. C. Riley, www.transporttreasury.co.uk

War movement of firstly British, and then US personnel. Troop trains were frequent in the summer for the AA camp until the 1950s, trains of LNER, LMS and GWR stock (but never their engines) appearing at weekends. The terminus at Bude was uniquely able to handle up to sixteen coaches. Such lengths were virtually unknown on the North Cornwall due to the many loops to be negotiated. There were, however, numerous Prisoner of War specials to Launceston and Wadebridge, and it is known that an Ambulance train was at Delabole, though whether it was hauled by the usual ex-GER 'B12' 4-6-0 cannot be confirmed. The greatest occasion occurred on 9 May 1956 when the Royal train of eleven heavy coaches left Launceston in charge of 'N's 31830 and 31845. It had previously worked empty stock from Plymouth (via Meldon Junction). The LNWR examples in this train were not the first seen on the North Cornwall, as one was parked at Wadebridge and one at Launceston, serving as enginemen's dormitories in the 1950s. On the change from WR steam to diesel locomotives in mid-Cornwall the 45XX 2-6-2Ts and NBL D6300s invariably came into Wadebridge from Bodmin Road with a two-coach ex-GWR 'B' set – similarly Launceston 'South' after 1951, though the 45XX and their Plymouth trains were more likely to consist of a pair of ex-GWR corridors.

R. Wilson, www.transporttreasury.co.uk

Both pages. The sheds of the Wadebridge 'district' comprised Launceston and Delabole with a turntable at Padstow. Okehampton worked independently under the auspices of the Western District headquarters at Exmouth Junction. Delabole had a small corrugated iron shed, similar in appearance to Launceston shed. Indeed an LSW minute had ordered that the Launceston shed be refixed at Delabole but it looks like this was never carried out and a new structure erected instead. A 48ft turntable had also been supplied, the work in these early years for the shed confined to duties surrounding the nearby quarry. The shed did not last long and had been converted into a store by the mid-1900s. Launceston had opened with the station in 1886 and was to eventually serve the nearby Great Western locomotives when their station closed in 1952. That was the intention, but some GW locos still returned to 'their' shed for turning and watering. Launceston also had a 48ft turntable which remained in use until

R. E. Vincent, www.transporttreasury.co.uk

W. A. Camwell.

the end even though the shed lay in partial ruins. There were ten men at Launceston in 1943, two crews for each company with two Southern cleaners. Relationships were most amicable – so much so that each 'group' would cover the other in case of sickness! Wadebridge was an outpost at the very edge of the Southern's system and lay some 80 miles from Exmouth Junction, the District headquarters. Thus a certain amount of independence was enjoyed, the staff carrying out repairs only a shed like Exmouth Junction normally would. With the arrival of the North Cornwall in 1895 the original two road Bodmin & Wadebridge shed was abandoned in favour of a wooden two road building with brick built water tower, turntable and coal stage. This shed was enlarged and rearranged into a more convenient layout in 1907.

Goods Rolling Stock

The four-wheel wagon with its short wheelbase has disappeared from the BR scene, but a century ago thousands upon thousands were on the move, or sitting in sidings (some for days on end) throughout Britain. The LSWR could not compare with its northern neighbours as a major freight career, yet almost all its stations had a yard and goods shed. The classification of certain box wagons as 'Express Passenger' (dating from the 1930s) has been noted. They were equipped with the vacuum brake (and oil axle boxes) for inclusion in passenger trains and fast running. Many cattle wagons, all container flats and all horse boxes were similarly treated. Other box wagons with the vacuum brake (or 'piped' to run with these) were the staple of the overnight Nine Elms/Exeter/Plymouth fast freights. Carrying mostly household merchandise and foodstuffs, on detachment (e.g. at Okehampton) they would be shunted to the front of local goods trains, providing added brake force for the usual collection of loose wagons. None of these refinements graced the earlier Beattie or Adams wagons, almost four-square in shape, though spring buffers and a hand brake were provided. These brakes served not only for the obvious purpose of parking, but would be 'pinned down' by the guard to assist the driver in controlling a heavy train down a gradient such as Otterham to Launceston.

The rise in cattle forwarding to the east of England very much concerned the North Cornwall line and resulted in the LSWR producing a standard type of 10-ton wagon with vacuum brake (or 'piped' for vacuum). No less than 430 of Diagram 1506 were taken over by the SR in 1923 and the company continued to reinforce the fleet until Nationalisation. Allied to the cattle trade, the meat carcass traffic developed by the LSWR and SR was carried in ventilated vans, again equipped for a fast running. After 1945 this meat was taken in containers (insulated) on flat wagons. Readers are referred to the 'History of Southern Wagons, Vol. 1' (Oxford Publishing Co 1984) for a comprehensive coverage of LSWR wagons. Fuller details of china clay, granite, fish and ballast wagons (and brake vans) may be studied therein. Other company's wagons were, of course, commonly seen on the North Cornwall and British Railways new stock from 1951 figured largely in the block fertiliser trains of the 1960s. During this decade the slate dust from Delabole was being carried in ex-'Presflo' wagons, latterly from Wadebridge. No trace has been found regarding coal wagons owned by local merchants, though the china clay firms' vehicles occasionally, earlier on, travelled east from Wenford and colliery wagons (e.g. Stephenson Clarke) were familiar up until World War Two. Roadstone from Hoare Bros of Wilminstone, and possibly by Betty & Toms in their own wagons from Port Isaac Road, occasionally appeared in local goods trains, as did oil tank wagons from Regent, Esso or Royal Daylight.

Signalling & Telegraph

The LSWR was already installing the Block Telegraph system on its lines when the Meldon Junction to Holsworthy branch opened in 1879. Signalling was still comparatively primitive even then, and the four single line sections were equipped with Train Staffs and Tickets, albeit under Block Telegraph control. Semaphore signals for the drivers were not universal (the Inspecting Officer asked for them to be placed at the loop entrances on the branch, rather than ground signals). The principle of the Block Telegraph was to prevent two trains being in a section at the same time, the adjacent signalmen using bell codes and visual instruments to notify the approach, passage and exit of each train. This was in addition to the Train Staff already used for many years. A staff was allocated to each section between signal boxes, each differing by shape and colour to reduce the risk of a driver proceeding with the wrong one. Between Meldon Junction and Ashbury the Staff was blue and diamond-shaped for Ashbury to Halwill whilst Beaworthy was red and circular. An obvious inflexibility of one Staff per section was overcome by the issue of 'Train Tickets'. If two (or more) trains were to follow in the same direction a separate Train Ticket was obtained form a special box in the signal cabin. This was given to the driver of the first train and the Train Staff shown to him. The Staff was given to the driver of the second (or last) train. As the North Cornwall progressed Block Telegraph and Staffs were provided for each section:

Halwill Junction and Ashwater	Green
Ashwater and Tower Hill	Yellow
Tower Hill and Launceston	Blue
Launceston and Egloskerry	Green
Egloskerry and Tresmeer	Red
Tresmeer and Otterham	Yellow
Otterham and Camelford	Blue
Camelford and Delabole	Not Known

It was essential to keep trains in the right order under this system. Hence the heading notes in the working timetables of this period. 'Train No ... to pass Train No ...' as the appropriate passing loop. Indeed the LSWR stipulated that where drivers should exchange Staffs, and which should have Tickets. Surprisingly, in the event of late running, where the all-important Staff was at the wrong end of a section, adjacent Station Masters could agree over the telegraph to permit a driver of a train to proceed without it, but in possession of a 'Train Order'. The continuing development of electrical communication led to the invention by Edward Tyer of his Electric Train Tablet system in 1878. Instead of a Staff, the authority to proceed was a small circular metal tablet with distinguishing holes and the section signal box names inscribed. Adjacent boxes housed machines capable of holding 30 Tablets for each direction. Only one cold be released at a time, an action co-ordinated by the two signalmen using bell codes and the Block Telegraph apparatus. Thus a succession of trains could be passed in one direction providing the Tablets were restored correctly in the machine in advance. Should all the Tablets (or too many) end up in the advance box, only the Signal Lineman could retrieve them and carry them back to the box in the rear. It was not uncommon for this to happen on the North Cornwall, especially in the summer season.

In 1893 the LSWR authorised the replacement of the Staffs between Meldon Junction and Holsworthy/Delabole by Tyers No.3 Tablets. It is not known how quickly this was done, though it is believed the Ashbury-Halwill Staff survived into the 1900s. All that the passenger might notice was a wire hoop, passing to and from signalmen and engine crews, which carried a small pocket for the Tablet. The four sections, Delabole to Port Isaac Road, Port Isaac Road to St Kew Highway, St Kew Highway to Wadebridge Junction and Wadebridge Junction to Wadebridge, had Tyers No.3 Tablets from opening in 1895. The drawback of the No.3 Tablet was that it could not be returned to the issuing machine but had to be carried through to the next. The Tyers No.6 system ('Returnable' and patented in 1892) allowed restoration to the issuing machine. Tyers No.6 was provided between Wadebridge West and Padstow on opening in 1899. At this date the new Wadebridge West and East signal boxes communicated by Preece 3-wire double line instruments. Following the closure of Wadebridge Junction in 1907 the St Kew Highway to Wadebridge East section was re-equipped with No.6 Tablets. They also eased the working between Camelford and Delabole and Delabole and Port Isaac Road as from November 1923. The latter enabled the siding at Tom's Quarry to be operated by a ground frame, released by the Tablet and the train allowed to return to Port Isaac Road. It is not known which types were provided in the new Maddaford Loop Box in 1899 but on closure in 1919, a No.6 safeguarded the restored Meldon Junction to Ashbury section. The closure of Tower Hill between 1920 and 1943 extended the No.3 Tablet between Ashwater and Launceston, but on its re-opening in 1943, No.6 Tablets were installed for each direction.

Already the Electric Key Token was making its appearance. In 1943 Ashbury to Halwill was converted, in this case to ease the situation at Halwill ground frame 'C' where trains could be 'shut in' to the new lower yard by restoration of the Key Token in an auxiliary machine.

The Block Telegraph was separate to the other station-to-station communication – the Single Needle Telegraph operated by booking clerks. Before the advent of speaking instruments (the telephone) messages were tapped out in Morse code adapted for railway use, though the system was visual to an extent, using a deflecting needle. Like the telephone which replaced it, the circuits were organised into 'omnibus' systems. Consequently all and sundry could eavesdrop; no wonder news travelled fast on the railway! Resulting from these instruments were miles of telegraph wires supported on poles about 55 yards apart. The maintenance and repair of these lines was never ending on the North Cornwall, particularly on the high ground from Otterham to Delabole open to the salty ocean gales and rain. The LSWR and SR employed a lineman and a mate at Okehampton, Launceston and Wadebridge for all the signal and telegraph work. Their Inspector was at one time in the District Engineer's department, but by the time of SR renewals in the 1930s the 'S&T' had its own.

Chris Osment has very kindly supplied the following chronology, in part based on information which has become available since 1995, after the original book was published. Even so the listing is not entirley complete, and probably never can be; 'grey' areas will surely remain. See Key *right* for abbreviations.

1886 Sections Halwill Junction-Ashwater-Tower Hill-Launceston opened with TS&T.

1892 Sections Launceston-Egloskerry-Tresmeer opened with TS&T.

1893 Sections Tresmeer-Otterham-Camelford-Delabole opened with TS&T.

After the subsequent introduction of ETT working the LSWR replaced all the TS&T sections with ETT3 at unknown dates from 1893 onwards. The last replacement seems to have been Ashbury-Halwill Junction, posibly in the early 1900s.

1895 Sections Delabole-Port Isaac Road-St Kew Highway-Wadebridge Junction-Wadebridge opened with ETT3.

Subsequently Wadebridge station was rebuilt and Wadebridge Signal Box replaced by new Wadebridge East and Wadebridge West boxes, in 1899. After this the section from Wadebridge Junction was to Wadebridge East. It is assumed that the existing ETT3 was re-used for this new section.

1899 Wadebridge West-Padstow opened with ETT6. The Signalling Record Society 'Box Register' gives 12th March as opening date for both new Wadebridge boxes and also Padstow box. This was the first use of ETT6 on the North Cornwall south of Halwill Junction. By now ETT6 was being used by the LSWR for all new work, and had already been employed west from Holsworthy to Bude in 1898 and again in 1899 at Maddaford Moor (see below).

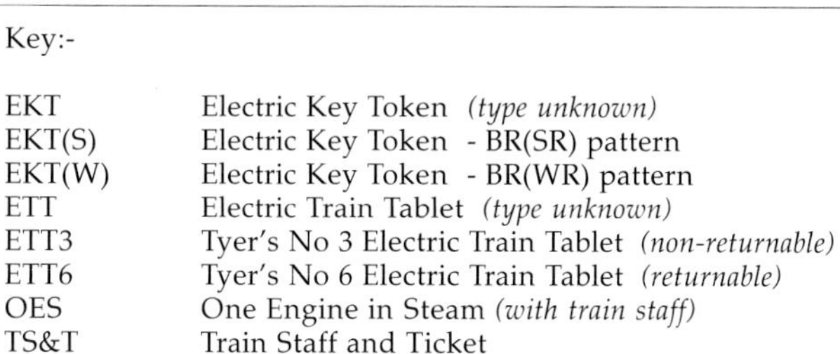

Key:-

EKT	Electric Key Token *(type unknown)*
EKT(S)	Electric Key Token - BR(SR) pattern
EKT(W)	Electric Key Token - BR(WR) pattern
ETT	Electric Train Tablet *(type unknown)*
ETT3	Tyer's No 3 Electric Train Tablet *(non-returnable)*
ETT6	Tyer's No 6 Electric Train Tablet *(returnable)*
OES	One Engine in Steam *(with train staff)*
TS&T	Train Staff and Ticket

1899 Maddaford Moor loop and signal box opened, splitting the Meldon Junction-Ashbury section into two. It was not clear when David Wroe was writing what type of ETT was used, but LSWR records for 1911 show that Meldon Junction-Maddaford Moor was ETT6, whilst Maddaford Moor-Ashbury was ETT3.

It is assumed that TS&T on the Meldon Junction-Ashbury section had been replaced by ETT3 prior to then and that this ETT set was re-used.

1907 Wadebridge Junction Signal Box closed on 3rd February and the section became St Kew Highway-Wadebridge East, as ETT3. David Wroe believed the section to have been worked by ETT6, but LSWR records for both 1911 and 1923, now available, reveal it to have been ETT3. As this closure resulted in a surplus of equipment (rather than needing extra as was the case at Maddaford Moor) then it would have been more economical just to have re-used one of the sets of ETT3.

1919 Maddaford Signal Box closed and section became Meldon Junction-Ashwater using ETT6. There is a reference in the Signalling Record Society 'Cullum Index' to 'closure of signal-box' there in August 1919 while the society's 'Box Register' gives closure as April 1919. David Wroe in his original writings implies 3rd May that year. An LSWR 'Signal Instruction' of October 1921 refers to 'removal of signal-box, signals etc'. It is assumed that the ETT working was altered when the box closed in 1919.

1920 Tower Hill loop and box closed and the section became Ashwater-Launceston using ETT3. The Signalling Record Society 'Box Register' gives date of closure as 15th June.

1923 Camelford-Delabole-Port Isaac Road sections changed from ETT3 to ETT6. This was probably to ease shunting at Delabole and also to permit 'trip' working from Port Isaac Road to Betty & Toms siding.

An SR 'Signal Instruction' of 21 of 1923 records the changes on both the Camelford-Delabole and Delabole-

South Western Staff at Wadebridge in 1910, goods shed behind.

Launceston's Station Master Walter Greenslade with his SR and GWR joint staff in 1937. Front row: Hugh Godbear, signalman; Horace Martin, shunter; Harry Bishop, porter; Fred Manning, goods clerk; Francis Parkhouse, goods clerk; Walter Greenslade, Claude Sowdon, booking clerks; Monty Phillips, booking clerk with 'Tiny'; Sidney Mitchell, parcels clerk; Charlie Bradford, goods checker; Wesley Sleep, porter. Back row: Jim Walters, District Inspector; Oscar Kitts, GWR passenger guard; Sidney Webber, GWR passenger guard; Jack Osborne, parcels porter; Jack Endacott, Clerk (Chaplins); Albert Vodden, goods guard; Bill Manning, relief signalman; Ted Andrews, goods checker; Fred Wright, porter; Jack Chilcott, goods guard; Mr Passmore, W. H. Smith & Sons Manager; Mr Palk, District Cattle Inspector. R. L. Goodman collection, courtesy C. Barrett.

Port Isaac Road sections as 29th November, though there is an earlier reference, in an LSWR 'Signal Instruction' of January 1922, to a change on the Delabole-Port Isaac Road section. So it is not entirely clear exactly what happened here; I am assuming both changes took place at the same date.

1943 Tower Hill loop and box re-opened on 28th March 1943, according toan SR 'Signal Instruction' later that year. The sections were now Ashwater-Tower Hill-Launceston as ETT. David Wroe claims both sections were ETT6 and is almost certainly correct, given that this was the case in BR days.

1943 Ashbury-Halwill Junction was converted to ETT on 26th September 1943 and, given the date, this must surely have been SR-pattern EKT. It is curious to note that this occurred in the same year as ETT6 was used at Tower Hill, but probably EKT was necesary to 'shut in' at Halwill Junction Ground Frame 'C'.

By about 1950 the sections, equipment and tablet/token configurations are believed to have been as in the table *right*.

The following changes are known: 1954 St Key Highway-Wadebridge East section changed from ETT to EKT(W) configuration 'A' on 25th July. This is the only known use of the WR-pattern EKT on the North Cornwall (south of Halwill Junction, as it also appeared on the Bude Branch).

1960
Launceston-Egloskerry section changed from ETT3 to ETT6 on 26th June.

Egloskerry-Tresmeer section changed from ETT3 to ETT6 on 3rd July.

Tresmeer-Otterham section changed from ETT3 to ETT6 on 10th July.

1961
Halwill Junction-Ashwater changed from ETT3 to EKT(S) configuration 'C' on 27th August.

Port Isaac Road-St Kew Highway section changed from ETT3 to EKT(S) configuration 'B' on 24th September. Otterham-Camelford changed from ETT3 to EKT(S) configuration 'A' on 17th December.

1965
Otterham loop and box closed on 7th February and section then became Tresmeer-Camelford (equipment and configuration unknown).

Ashwater and Tower Hill loops and SBs closed on 7th November and section then Halwill Junction-Launceston with EKT(S) configuration 'C'.

Tresmeer loop and box closed on 14th November and section then Egloskerry-Camelford with EKT(S) configuration 'A'.

St Kew Highway loop and box closed 21st November and section then Port Isaac Road-Wadebridge East with EKT(S) configuration 'B'.

1966
Padstow Signal Box was closed on January 9th and replaced by a ground frame. Wadebridge West-Padstow section changed from ETT6 to OES with round, red staff with 'A'

From	To	Equipment	Configuration
Meldon Jcn	Ashbury	ETT6	A
Ashbury	Halwill Jcn	EKT	B
Halwill Jcn	Ashwater	ETT3	n/k
Ashwater	Tower Hill	ETT6	B
Tower Hill	Launceston	ETT6	A
Launceston	Egloskerry	ETT3	B
Egloskerry	Tresmeer	ETT3	A
Tresmeer	Otterham	ETT3	B
Otterham	Camelford	ETT3	A
Camelford	Delabole	ETT6	B
Delabole	Port Isaac Road	ETT6	A
Port Isaac Road	St Kew Highway	ETT3	B
St Kew Highway	Wadebridge East	ETT	n/k
Wadebridge East	Wadebridge West	Preece 3-wire	
Wadebridge West	Padstow	ETT6	A

The location of these platelayers cannot be identified with certainty, but they are perhaps in the Higher Shipyard area at Padstow and may show contractor's temporary way under removal. Protection for the men seems to be under the watchful eye of a traffic department handsignalman (right). H. Hambly collection.

configuration Annett's key to unlock the Ground Frame at Padstow. At Wadebridge the working between the East and West boxes was controlled by Preece 3-wire equipment, with (presumably) one set for the Up and Down main lines and another set for the Loop. At some unknown date prior to closure the main lines set was replaced by BR(WR) commutator block instruments, but the loop retained Preece 3-wire.

David Wroe makes a number of references to ETT6 at Wadebridge East. The section to St Kew Highway was listed by the SR in 1930 as ETT3 and the section to Boscarne Junction was still ETT3 at closure. The section to St Kew Highway may have changed at some time, as it is unclear what existed immediately prior to the change to EKT(W), though it would seem odd if BR(WR) targeted an ETT6 section for change in preference to ETT3. But then, they left an ETT3 section alone on the Bude line, and any change might have been linked simply to some equipment failure.

At the time of closure in 1966 the sections and equipment were as noted in the table below.

The Structures and Permanent Way

Mention of 'standard' North Cornwall station building should in reality refer to LSWR architecture from the 1870s. The same applies to the supply of signalling equipment and permanent way. The NCR had little to say in these matters as Galbraith and Church were the LSWR Consulting Engineers and the LSWR would 'work' the line by agreement. This also applied to the Devon & Cornwall Railway. On the latter, although Okehampton and Holsworthy stations generally followed (with detail changes) the LSWR standard, Ashbury, Halwill and Dunsland Cross housed the station master and staff in unadorned single storey edifices. The NCR rural stations (only Tower Hill was demolished after 1966) were strictly utilitarian. The circular lintel of the upper storey windows and the grey and brown stone give them a rather sombre look. Portland stone quoining cheered things up and none of them ever became blackened – the rain, sun and clean air from the Atlantic saw to that. Nearly all were constructed in local dressed blocks, varying from brown sandstone at Ashwater to grey/blue slate stone at Port Isaac Road. Egloskerry and Tresmeer, however, were built of brick. There appeared to be a shortage of stone in this area and the proposed Treneglos viaduct was not built for this reason, an embankment being substituted. The SM residences were quite commodious, though without bathrooms, and the WCs were in the back yard. The size was deceptive, as the ladies waiting and cloakroom occupied one of the ground floor rooms. The general waiting area was within the booking hall in the single storey end, the remainder housing the booking office, parcels office and porters' rooms. The SM also had an office. Launceston and Wadebridge were not NCR stations and were quite different, though somewhat similar in appearance and layout, the Station Masters having in separate accommodation. Awnings were attached to these station buildings and also at Padstow and Camelford. Camelford was intended as the railhead for the gentry and visitors to the coast, recognising at the same time the rainfall here is one of the highest in Cornwall! All platforms were constructed in local stone with various edge copings. Slate slabs were used at Delabole and Port Isaac Road.

Goods shed, where provided, followed LSWR country style and with similar stonework to the stations. Okehampton, Launceston and Wadebridge goods sheds were larger, and differed according to the LSWR's contemporary designs. This principle also applied to signalboxes though all,

From	To	Equipment	Configuration
Meldon Jcn	Ashbury	ETT6	A
Ashbury	Halwill Jcn	EKT	B
Halwill Jcn	Launceston	EKT	C
Launceston	Egloskerry	ETT6	B
Egloskerry	Camelford	EKT(S)	A
Camelford	Delabole	ETT6	B
Delabole	Port Isaac Road	ETT6	A
Port Isaac Road	Wadebridge East	EKT(S)	B
Wadebridge East	Wadebridge West	Main – WR Commutator	Loop – Preece 3-wire
Wadebridge West	Padstow	OES	Round Red+ 'A' key

P. W. staff pause at Bridge No. 54, New Mill Bridge, in the 1950s.

from Ashwater to St Kew, had the mid-1880s 'glasshouse' appearance. Many terraces of three or six houses were erected by the LSWR for PW staff and are readily noticeable near most stations to the present day. Brick also appeared in the arches of the mainly dressed stone bridges west of Launceston. Wrought iron girders were employed on the wider river crossings and for some roads but apart from the skew span over the GWR at Launceston, none approached the size of the Little Petherick Viaduct at Padstow. The restrictions on locomotives passing over Meldon Viaduct have been mentioned, but other insignificant underbridges contributed to the ban on rebuilt 4-6-2s from Meldon Junction westwards.

The LSWR developed a works at Exmouth Junction for concrete products, everything from mileposts and fencing to footbridges. It was enlarged and extended by the SR from 1923 to supply the whole system from Kent to Cornwall. Every possible form of wayside structure emerged, and soon appeared on the NCR, starting with station name boards. Concrete fencing panels hardly enhance the scenery and the utilitarian slabs of the new Wadebridge footbridge compared poorly with the original timber structure with its graceful finials. One thing is certain, if all else disappears, Exmouth Junction concrete fencing posts will be found in the undergrowth along the NCR.

Concrete sleepers in the track were first installed in the 1930s, not like the sophisticated ties seen today in our main lines but simply reinforced for use with bull head rails in the lower speed range. In the 1880s the 'permanent way' by contrast was comparatively complicated. The rails were double-headed and laid in cast iron chairs, then wedged tight by oak or elm 'keys'. The chairs, in turn, were spiked to the wood sleepers by wood 'treenails' (or 'trenails' – the spelling varies), 'hollow treenails' and iron spikes. The Holsworthy line through Halwill had been laid with 75lb to the yard wrought iron rails, only 18ft long under 2ft 8ins sleeper centres. The fishplated rail joints were 'suspended', a form adopted by the LSWR only since 1860. For the opening to Launceston in 1886, new 82lb/yd double-head steel rails in 24ft lengths were stipulated by the LSWR. The same sort of material, only second-hand, was laid on the Padstow extension in 1899. It was not long (1908) before new 90lb/yd bull head 45ft rails were laid here! Nearly all the North Cornwall had been re-laid by 1910, though the earlier (1879) line through Ashbury had been re-laid with 87lb/yd double head 45ft lengths in the mid-1890s.

To maintain the length from Halwill Junction to Padstow (the contractor handed over after twelve months following each opening) were nineteen gangs, each of five men for approximately 2½ miles of route. From 1895 the existing Wadebridge gang looked after the stretch from the new junction to the end of the embankment at Polgammon, including several miles of sidings in the yard and quay. Between Meldon Junction and Halwill were four gangs, and two between Wadebridge and Padstow. Most of the men taken on were local, probably learning their skills with the contractor beforehand. It was attractive work, paying better than agriculture rates, and many were favoured with housing at reasonable rents. In the 1920s Ganger Trewin, based at Otterham, maintained the exposed section over the 860ft summit, while Ganger Lawry's length, down through the damp Tilleslow woods at Ashwater, was always at risk from washouts from the adjacent River Carey.

These small gangs lasted until the 1930s. The four main line companies were adopting motorised trolleys on single lines for 'economic maintenance' and the gangs from Meldon Junction to Padstow were re-grouped to consist of Ganger, Sub-Ganger, Trolley Driver, Patrolman and two or three Lengthmen. The original trolleys were simple, belt-driven from a JP motor, open to the elements but with front screens. They could be turned and run off to the cess by an under lift-jack. In BR days replacements came in the form of Wickham trolleys of higher power and capable of towing a trolley. Except from between Ashwater and Launceston up to 1943, no facilities for side-tracking were provided and the tablets were required to be carried as a normal train between signal boxes.

A relaying gang was based at Launceston in the 1930s when much renewal was undertaken; in the 1950s its ten men would prepare the 'road' for renewal by throwing out the old ballast to the sides. This took place during the week, followed on Saturday nights/Sundays by removal of the rails and sleepers and replacement by new material. All this work was by hand, even to the loading of spent ballast – though new ballast would be run out from hopper wagons. If points and crossings were involved, a crane would come from Exeter, and some mechanisation crept in finally, principally to handle heavy concrete sleepers.

Although traffic volume was relatively light, the advent of the six-coupled 'N's and later the Pacifics increased the wear and tear on the rails. The 50mph limit (later 55mph) was achieved over the 30 and 40 chains radius curves by superelevating the higher rail. Most curves were uprated in the 1930s to a maximum five inches in conjunction with the extensive renewals. New 45ft rails of 95lb/yd, with resleepering, replaced the old LSWR material. Many sidings were re-laid with the best of the latter. Some American 39lb bullhead rail was laid in below Delabole in the last war, and after Nationalisation new BR 'flat-bottom' rails (98lb) were put in at Halwill, Halwill-Ashwater, Tower Hill, Launceston, and Wadebridge. There was always a good supply of ballast hereabouts, either from Meldon Quarry, Hingston Down (Callington branch) or from Tom's Quarry at Port Isaac Road.

Two Permanent Way Inspectors directed track maintenance in this area, Halwill's extending from Meldon Junction to Delabole (in BR days to Otterham), also the Bude branch and four miles of the Torrington-Halwill line. The remainder came under Wadebridge (taking in the Bodmin and Wenford branches). In 1966 Mr Bill Geach was the Halwill Inspector, and until 1963, Mr Charles Mitchell at Wadebridge.

Notes

Track plans are based on LSWR, SR and BR originals. Derived scales in chains/feet are appended to most of these and it should be noted that the statute mile and chain (80 to the mile) are valid today. The chain measurement, although now declared obsolete, is still regarded as a useful division by BR's engineers and the provision of mile and quarter mile posts remain requirements of the 1845 Consolidation Act.

Opening, closing and alteration dates have been verified as far as possible, but the reader should be aware that official published versions could be postponed, or facilities even used in advance! Attention is drawn, particularly to when trains 'last ran' and 'on and from' closure dates. In the case of Meldon Junction to Bude and Wadebridge the track remained in situ, even used (to store wagons for example) for varying periods after 3 October 1966 before lifting.

Above. **The iron viaduct at Little Petherick Creek, Padstow, in 1899. Three pairs of N-trussed girders supported wrought iron cross members and rail bearers, the latter carrying the sleepers of the lightly ballasted track. Curry & Reeves' platelayers are completing this ballasting while carpenters (right) are finishing the walkways.**

Left. **Lunch break at Little Petherick Creek. Pasties galore, the odd bottle of beer and even a flask!**

Okehampton looking west from the North Cornwall/ Bude bay. 34065 *Hurricane* has just left with the 8.41am Exeter to Plymouth train, whilst T9 4-4-0 No. 30313 waits for clearance to proceed to Meldon Junction and onwards with the 9.56am Okehampton - Padstow train.

Between duties T9 30338 acts as station pilot at Okehampton.

Chapter Nine

FREEMAN'S FORAYS

Leslie Freeman made many journeys over the railway system in this country, carefully recording in his diaries, times, locations and locomotives encountered on his travels. Here are two such trips he made over the North Cornwall line in 1960 and 1961, presented courtesy of The Transport Treasury. All photographs L. R. Freeman.

Okehampton to Holsworthy and return – Thursday 2 June 1960

The next stage of our journey was over the Bude branch as far as Holsworthy by the 1.18pm ex-Okehampton which was in the bay, a parcel van, two corridors and another van headed by T9 30718. This locomotive we had seen earlier working the Plymouth Portion of the up Atlantic Coast Express and earlier still at Bere Ferrers working the 7am ex-Okehampton. We had only a 6-minute interval at Okehampton but this did not really seem to impress itself on the writer who not only decided to buy himself an ice-cream in the refreshment room, but then wandered down to the platform end to photograph T9 30338 standing by the shed coaling stage.

West Country class No. 34032 *Camelford* has just arrived from Exeter with the down ACE and waits for the Plymouth coaches to be detached at the rear to continue its journey on to Padstow and Bude. The ACE still had four years to run at this time although the weekday Plymouth portion ceased in 1962.

Having just arrived with the 12.58pm Padstow-Waterloo train (Exmouth Junction duty 593), N class 31842 proceeds to the turntable at Okehampton shed to prepare for more turns to Bude and Halwill later in the day.

When he turned round T9 30718 was just drawing out with my pal Jim leaning out of the window waving his arms and shouting that there was somebody coming! The porter looked at Jim, then at the guard; the guard looked at Jim, then at the porter; still 30718 drew on, then suddenly the brakes were applied and the train ground to a stop with one coach still in the platform. By this time the 'lost' soul was in full pursuit down the up platform, over the footbridge and so to the down side bay, where, hot and out of breath, he regained the train. Jim's caustic comments regarding the episode are best left unrecorded but it took the writer a long time to live down 'The Okehampton Incident'.

After this interruption, 30718 made a good climb to Meldon Junction and

Right. **T9 4-4-0 No. 30718 arrives at Halwill with the 1.18pm Okehampton-Bude service.**

Below. **BR Class 3 2-6-2Ts came to the west as early as 1952 to work the Bude services. Here 82011 is parked in the up platform at Halwill while a North Cornwall train gets the all clear to depart for Wadebridge.**

then ran very fast over the branch to Halwill and on to Holsworthy where we arrived punctually at 1.58pm. I have called the Halwill line a branch because it is single track from Meldon Junction to both Padstow and Bude but it is of course a main line in effect. After Halwill, Dunsland Cross is the first station reached on the Bude line. It has a crossing loop and the offices are in an unimpressive single-storey building on the down platform with a small shelter and the signal box on the up side. A small yard is attached.

Holsworthy is a much more impressive station. Again there is a

***Right.* The fireman of N 31839 gets coal forward for the onward journey from Halwill to Okehampton having just arrived with the 12.58pm Padstow train. Behind are a Bulleid corridor coach with two Maunsell coaches including a brake third.**

***Below.* 30313 pauses at Halwill with the 9.56am Okehampton-Padstow train to exchange tablets for the onward journey to Ashwater.**

crossing loop and on the up side a large cream coloured station house and office. A small waiting room and the signal box adorn the down platform. Like Dunsland Cross, Holsworthy has a small yard. We had nearly twenty minutes here before travelling back to Okehampton on the 1.55pm ex-Bude which crossed our train out from Okehampton at Whitstone. As expected, the regular Bude engine was on the train, Standard 2-6-2T 82011. The load was four corridors, quite well filled, which 82011 worked vigorously up the hills to Halwill, where she ran round and pulled them out of the

Right. **Ivatt 2-6-2T No. 41314 is about to leave from the North Devon and Cornwall Junction platform at Halwill with the 10.38am Torrington train and its solitary Bulleid coach. Two fresh meat wagons stand outside the slaughter house on the right. The place received ice from Bude on a daily basis.**

Below. **T9 30313 all clear to proceed from Halwill with the 9.56am Okehampton to Padstow train.**

Leslie Freeman has left the train and has raced up Station Road to St. Thomas' Road bridge in time for No. 34032 *Camelford*, departing for Egloskerry with the down ACE.

platform to await the arrival of the Padstow portion. This, the 12.58pm ex-Padstow, arrived consisting of N 31839 and three corridors. 82011 duly added her train and then, two minutes late at 2.46pm, the N drew out with her now five-coach train.

It soon became clear that 31839 was not in tip-top condition. She had to be worked very hard up the banks and she made heavy weather of the start from Ashbury. However, the N ran fast downhill and did not lose any more time to Okehampton where she came off and T9 30338 drew the train back into the sidings to await the Plymouth portion, not due until 3.29pm. Meanwhile, Jim and I returned to the down platform and travelled back to Halwill by the down 'Atlantic Coast Express'.

We made our way to the down platform at Okehampton in order to travel to Halwill by the down Atlantic Coast Express.

Due out of Okehampton at 3.12pm, it was running eleven minutes late, five corridors headed by West Country class 34032 'Camelford'. It soon became clear that the lateness was no fault of the

N class No. 31836 shunts a goods train at Launceston made up of Presflo wagon, three cattle wagons, a fertiliser van, a meat van and a covered wagon.

locomotive. Some very fast running was made to Halwill where the last two coaches were detached to be worked forward to Bude by 82011. 3 ½ minutes had been recovered from Okehampton and now with only three coaches left the running between stations was fully up to main-line standards.

The five miles to Ashwater was covered in 6 ½ minutes start to stop, a gain of 2 ½ minutes. Ashwater has a

Right. **Churchward 45XX class 2-6-2Ts worked into Launceston from Lifton along their own branch but used the SR station after 1952. Here No. 5569 arrives with the 3.05pm from Plymouth, a pair of ex-GWR corridor coaches.**

Below. **The 3.13pm from Padstow makes ready to depart for Okehampton. No. 30709 was on the North Cornwall for many years, finally departing for the scrap yard in July 1961.**

loop with the main stone-built house on the up side. On the down platform is a shelter and the signal box. There is a small yard on the up side at the north end of the station. From Ashwater the fast running continued with speeds of over 60mph so that by Tower Hill a further minute had been recovered. This station has a similar layout to Ashwater. Another minute was recovered between Tower Hill and Launceston and we arrived at the latter station three minutes late at 4.8pm.

Right. **A flurry of activity at Launceston as Leslie Freeman photographs No. 5569 again, from the footbridge. The 3.13pm, a two coach P set, a van and a fertiliser van, departs for Okehampton.**

Below. **5569 has now shunted across to the down platform at Launceston and gets the right of way with the 5.40pm return to Plymouth. GWR trains were able to run into the SR station via a war-time loop.**

Okehampton to Wadebridge-Saturday 27 May 1961

Whilst I waited at Okehampton, two trains came through, 34066 *Spitfire* eight minutes late with the 8.41am ex-Exeter Central and 34030 *Watersmeet* with the up troop train whose passengers were assembling when I left Tavistock earlier. *Spitfire* left a van behind when she left for Plymouth; this was removed to the yard by T9 30709 which then coupled up to a van and four corridors in the down bay. This was the 9.56am to Padstow. Due to the late running it was 10.8am before we set off.

The start up the 1 in 77 to Meldon Junction was good and the climbing steady, producing a maxima of 28mph at Meldon Quarry. The junction was passed in 8½ minutes, after which the T9, although eased, fairly flew down the more favourable grade to Maddaford Moor Halt, speed rising to 56mph, so that we stopped at the latter halt in 11 minutes 28 seconds, a few seconds inside the schedule. After a very brief stop we attained 39mph on the 1 in 78 to MP205 and so covered the four miles to Ashbury, mainly up hill, in 7 ¼ minutes against the schedule of 8 minutes. Thus our arrival at 10.27am was eleven minutes late, a pretty good

T9 4-4-0 No 30709 on station pilot duty at Okehampton in 1961. These long time stalwart of the North Cornwall had but a short time before withdrawal.

34023 *Blackmore Vale* arrives at Halwill with the down portion of the Atlantic Coast Express.

Blackmore Vale has now left and BR class 3 No. 82011 prepares to depart with the Bude portion of the ACE.

Having finished its duties as station pilot at Okehampton 30709 is now heading the 5.51pm Okehampton-Wadebridge train over the level-crossing at Halwill Junction.

Left. An Ivatt 2-6-2T sits in the ND&CJ bay at Halwill with its solitary coach which formed the 6.30pm Torrington train.

Below, and right. 30709 has arrived at Launceston and awaits clearance to continue on to Wadebridge with the 5.51pm, after a train of meat vans pulls to a stop in the up platform. In 1960 Exmouth Junction had eight, 30313, 30138, 30709, 30715, 30717, 30718, 30719 and 30729 for the duties out of Okehampton but by 1961 N class 2-6-0s were taking over the duties especially as faults were detected in the fireboxes of 30338, 30718, 30719 and 30729. All failed boiler examinations in April 1961. 30120 was drafted in to Okehampton to give temporary assistance until the summer when 30120, 30313, 30709, 30715 and 30717 were all called to Eastleigh for scrapping.

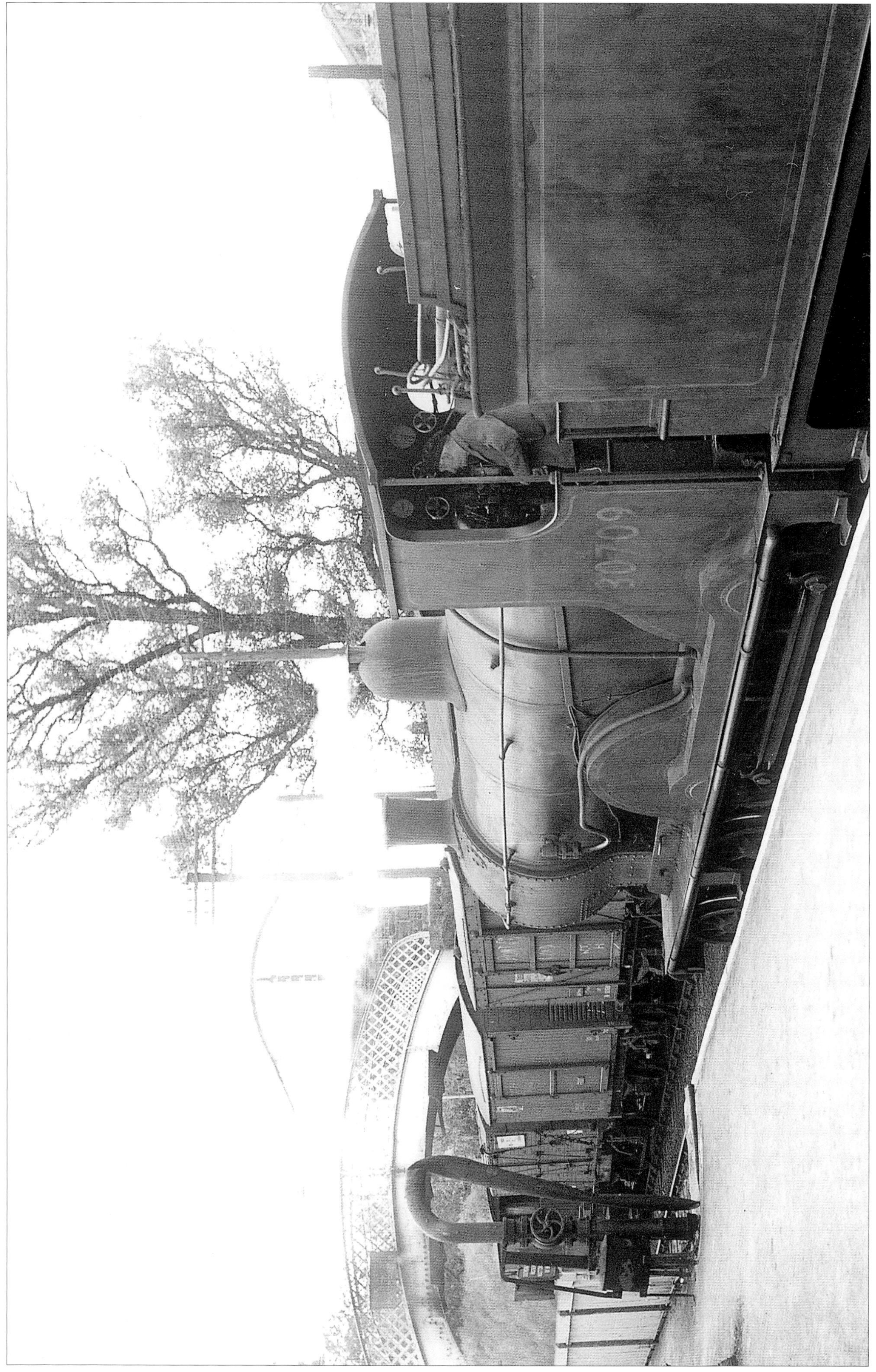

start by the old engine. Now, however, we ran into trouble. At Halwill the 9.56am is booked to pass the up Atlantic Coast Express but as we were late, they decided to hold us at Ashbury so as to avoid delaying the latter train. Thus we spent nine minutes simmering before 34065 *Hurricane* arrived, running in fact a minute early. Guards were exchanged and we departed 10.37¾ am, a few seconds after 'Hurricane' and 21¾ minutes late.

It is only 3 ¼ miles to Halwill, mostly downhill, nevertheless to cover the distance in 5 minutes and 12 seconds with a maxima of 52mph was good, especially since the schedule is 7 minutes. Arrival at Halwill at 10.43am was thus exactly twenty minutes late. Here five minutes were allowed for detaching the rear two Bude coaches, but smart work by the staff got us away in 3¾ minutes. Standard 2-6-2T 82011 was waiting to work the two Bude coaches forward; N 31853 was in the up loop, waiting to run light to Okehampton and Ivatt 2-6-2T 41313 was standing in the North Devon platform with the 10.38am to Torrington.

From Halwill 30709 continued her merry progress and as it was very much her swansong I give the remainder of the run in some detail below. The load was now a featherweight of a van and two corridors. Nevertheless, 30709 was in very run-down condition and only a

Miles	Time	Schedule	Actual
210	Halwill depart	10.28	10.46.45
	Fast downhill after the junction, maxima 57mph at MP214		
215	Ashwater arrive	10.37	10.53.45
	Ashwater depart		10.54.25
	Speed rose to 50mph on the descent to MP217 after which steam was shut off and we drifted to		
219	Tower Hill arrive	10.44	11.00.00
	Tower Hill depart		11.00.48
	Very fast running indeed with 68mph at MP222 5 miles in 6 minutes 12 seconds		
224	Launceston arrive	10.52	11.07
	Launceston depart		11.08.25
	38mph attained on the climb out of Launceston and then ran easily till signal stop 11.17.40 – 11.18 outside Egloskerry for gates to be opened.		
228.25	Egloskerry arrive	11.03	11.19
	Egloskerry depart		11.19.25
	Good start up 1in120, steepening to 1in78 and 1in74 before Tresmeer. The final 1in74 was tackled at 35mph.		
231.75	Tresmeer arrive	11.11	11.25.55
	Tresmeer depart		11.27.10
	Again steeply uphill, 1in74, 1in73 to MP234. Very vigorously attacked and breasted at 42mph. Speed rose to 48mph on easier grades after the summit and this was maintained on the final 1in75 to		
236.75	Otterham arrive	11.22	11.35.5
	Otterham depart		11.35.10
	The start is at 1in73, the 1in100 before the line begins its descent to Wadebridge. 30709 was worked hard on the up grade but was eased on the later falling grade. Maxima 59mph at MP239.5.		
241	Camelford arrive	11.30	11.42.18
	Camelford depart		11.43
	Over 50mph on falling grades		
243.5	Delabole arrive	11.37	11.47
	Delabole depart		11.47.24
	Down 1in80, 1in74. Very fast running round curves, maxima 67mph at MP246		
247.5	Port Isaac Road arrive	11.44	11.52.10
	Port Isaac Road depart		11.52.30
	59mph was reached by MP249		
250	St Kew Highway arrive	11.49	11.56.12
	St Kew Highway depart		11.56.40
	Fast finish produced 63mph at MP253.		
254	Wadebridge arrive	11.56	12.02.5

fortnight later, her career on the North Cornwall line came to an end with the influx of Moguls displaced by the Kentish electrification.

The actual start from Halwill was gentle, negotiation of the sharply curved junction necessitated this, but afterwards the T9 was really set to work. Thus from Ashbury 15¼ minutes had been recovered, 14 minutes of it by the engine and crew. A fine performance by the old Drummond and the fact that they ran her at speeds well over 60mph on a far from straight secondary line suggests her riding qualities even in run down condition were good. I left the train at Wadebridge, where the four minutes allowed for station work was cut to two so that 30709 stormed away to Padstow 4½ minutes late! I guess her final arrival was not much more than 3 minutes down.

After this stirring performance and listening to her fading exhaust I had a look round the station. Not that there was much moving. N 31846 was in the

Right. **30709 pauses briefly at Egloskerry for the few passengers to alight and to pick up the Egloskerry-Tresmeer tablet.**

Below. **Padstow and the end of the journey for Leslie Freeman; the return to Okehampton beckons behind T9 4-4-0 No. 30338.**

shed yard and another, 31833, followed 30709 in with a down goods, probably one of two we passed at St Kew Highway. Station pilot was 2-4-0WT 30587, simmering gently outside the goods shed whilst the picture was completed by 0-6-0PT 4694 waiting with the 12.25pm to Bodmin North.

After a trip to Bodmin Road, I returned to Wadebridge and at Wadebridge shed some shunting disclosed, briefly, 2-4-0WT 30585, N 31831 and 0-6-0PT 4668. I now boarded the 3.13pm to travel back as far as Launceston, there to continue to Plymouth via the northern part of the Western branch. It was, as will be apparent, the return working of the 9.56am which I caught earlier at Okehampton, and was my last journey behind a T9 in regular service. 30709 left Wadebridge a minute late at 3.31pm and took things a bit too easily at first so that by Delabole, where we passed N 31853 in the yard, we were three minutes late. The crew decided that they had better do something about this, with the result we roared up the bank to Camelford at 40mph and reduced our lateness to one minute. 47mph was attained beyond Camelford as we swung inland, catching a last glimpse of the Atlantic as the descent through Otterham to Launceston began. Otterham we left nearly two minutes early, but even so 60mph was attained down the hill to Tresmeer, where we

Above. **30709 at Egloskerry. The train was meant to pass the down ACE at Tresmeer but due to late running proceeded to Egloskerry which allowed Leslie Freeman to wander around this lonely outpost, awaiting the principal express of the day.**

Below. **30709 arrives at Launceston. Leslie Freeman left the train here to return to Plymouth along the GWR branch.**

arrived and left five minutes early! I hope no one missed it - they would have rather a long wait if they did, until 7.6pm! Despite this we carried on our merry way with an acceleration to 56mph to bring us into Egloskerry at 4.25pm, nine minutes early! Stop to stop timings from Delabole were:

Delabole - Camelford
4 minutes 50 seconds

Camelford - Otterham
7 minutes 32 seconds

Otterham - Tresmeer
6 minutes 35 seconds

Tresmeer - Egloskerry
5 minutes 40 seconds

Now our progess came to a temporary halt. At Tresmeer we were supposed to pass the down Atlantic Coast Express but as it was late (and we early) the T9 was allowed on to Egloskerry. There we waited, not that one could complain about that considering our earliness. In fact, 34023 *Blackmore Vale* soon arrived with the Atlantic Coast Express and we set off again at 4.34pm, still a minute early. Six minutes and 20 seconds was the time taken to Launceston, with a maxima again of 56mph. Arrival at Launceston station at 4.40pm was four minutes early and so ended my last run in regular service behind a Drummond express engine. This train is not booked to leave Launceston until 4.51pm, water being taken and on this occasion, the Launceston branch engine, 2-6-2T 5569, added another coach and a van. Punctually, 30709 departed and disappeared slowly out of sight. 5569 then collected her two coaches and took the T9's place in the up platform as the 5.40pm to Plymouth.

Above. **5569 shunts stock around Launceston for the journey to Plymouth.**

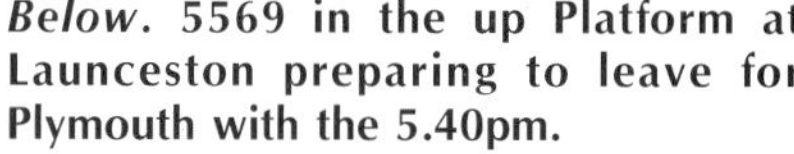

Below. **5569 in the up Platform at Launceston preparing to leave for Plymouth with the 5.40pm.**

Proud men and proud machines – the shed staff at Wadebridge pose by the trio of veteran Beattie Well Tanks on 21June 1962. This was the last summer for the Well Tanks; their replacements – ex-GWR '1366' class Pannier Tanks – had already arrived at Wadebridge and the Well Tanks were to be withdrawn at the end of the year. R. C. Riley; www.transporttreasury.co.uk

A smashing picture of 0314 (later 30585) in the late 1920s. Note the stovepipe chimney, the 'wheel' for the steam-driven pump for the feed-water heating system (removed in 1931), the 'E' prefix on the splasher instead of above the number, and the generally impressive black goods livery. When built in the 1860s and '70s the Well Tanks had had open footplates with only a front weatherboard for protection, though some later acquired rear weatherboards; the only ones to be fitted with full cabs were those which went to Wadebridge. www.transporttreasury.co.uk

Chapter Ten

BEATTIE WELL TANKS

By Martin Smith

For no less than 69 years Wadebridge shed had an allocation of Joseph Beattie's famous little 2-4-0 Well Tanks, but although their principal – and certainly best-known – duties were on the Wenford Bridge mineral branch rather than on the North Cornwall line, their close and lengthy association with Wadebridge justifies their being mentioned in this book.

The L&SWR took over the Bodmin & Wadebridge Railway in 1846 but it was 1886 before the absorption was legalised by an Act of Parliament. The inheritance from the B&W included the mineral line from Boscarne Junction to Wenford Bridge which, because of its lightly-laid track and sharp curves, had to be worked by lightweight, short-wheelbase locomotives. In the early 1890s the L&SWR considered that the two locos it had inherited from the Bodmin & Wadebridge company needed to be replaced, but the lightweight nature of the Wenford Bridge line severely restricted the types of locomotives which could be used. One of the very few types were the Beattie Well Tanks. Eighty-five of these locos had been built for the L&SWR between 1862 and 1875 – three at Nine Elms Works and the remainder by Beyer Peacock – and although they were originally used on the L&SWR's extensive London suburban services, by the early 1890s they had been displaced from those duties by modern, more powerful types.

The first Well Tank arrived at Wadebridge in May 1893, No.248 being brought in by sea from Southampton. (As the North Cornwall line did not reach Wadebridge until 1895 the L&SWR had no rail access to the town, hence the need to send the loco by sea.) In June 1895 No.248 was replaced at Wadebridge by No.298, and it was subsequently joined there by Nos.44 and 266. In 1898 Nos.266 and 298 were replaced by Nos.314 and 329, the latter, incidentally, having been the very last of the Beattie Well Tanks to have been built. By the end of the year all the other eighty-two Beattie Well Tanks had been withdrawn and, as the Wadebridge trio were themselves in poor condition, the L&SWR earmarked them for withdrawal as well. Adams O2 0-4-4Ts were selected as possible replacements and one was sent for trials on the Wenford Bridge line, but it was found to be unsuitable. As there were no suitable alternatives it was decided to give the Well Tanks major overhauls and keep them on the line. As withdrawal had been expected, the three locos had been placed on the Duplicate List and were renumbered 0298, 0314 and 0329.

30585 passes the signal box (and also passes 30586) at the east end of Wadebridge station on 6 July 1955. R. C. Riley; www.transporttreasury.co.uk

30585 is jacked up at Wadebridge shed on 10 May 1958. Clearly, the removal of the connecting and coupling rods was deemed superfluous. Above the loco's number is a '0P' power classification; presumably a remote assessor had thought that a loco with 5ft 7in wheels was bound to be employed on passenger work. R. Wilson, www.transporttreasury.co.uk

As noted in the text, 30586 had had its tank filler cap raised and could not, therefore, easily take on water at Pencarrow on the Wenford Bridge branch, so this loco usually worked at Wadebridge. Here, it is on the Yard Pilot duty (duty 604) on 10 May 1958. R. Wilson, www.transporttreasury.co.uk

30586 on the Yard Pilot duty on 10 May 1958. Interestingly, five of the eight coal wagons are wooden-bodied. R. Wilson, www.transporttreasury.co.uk

Although the Wenford Bridge line was the *raison d'être* for their presence at Wadebridge, the locos had other duties as well. Indeed, around the turn of the century (the previous century, of course) the china clay trains to and from Wenford Bridge ran only on Tuesdays, Thursdays and Saturdays, so the locos were also used on passenger trains to Padstow and Bodmin, local carriage piloting and shunting. The passenger work came to an end in the early 1900s when O2s took over the local services to Padstow and Bodmin.

In the early 1920s all three Well Tanks were fitted with new boilers which had necessarily been constructed specially. After the Grouping they were routinely given the 'E' prefix. The 'E' stood for Eastleigh, the 'home workshops' of ex-L&SWR locos; similarly, ex-LB&SC locos were prefixed 'B' Brighton and ex-SE&CR locos prefixed 'A' Ashford. In 1929 No.0329 was condemned and was replaced at Wadebridge by a 'P' class 0-6-0T, but the longer wheelbase of the 'P' damaged the track on the Wenford Bridge line so No.0329 was reprieved, overhauled and returned to traffic. In 1931 No.0314 was found to have cracked frames and worn-out cylinders – considering that it was 57 years old and had run almost 1,100,000 miles this was somewhat forgivable – and had to be fitted with new front-end framing and springing and new cylinders. While having the work done at Eastleigh it was also fitted with a Drummond chimney and new injectors, and had its wooden buffer beam replaced by a steel one with standard buffers. The other two Well Tanks later received similar modifications.

The Southern Railway's renumbering scheme of 1933 allotted the 3000 number block to duplicated locos, so the three locos were duly renumbered 3298, 3314 and 3329. In the latter half of the 1930s all three were painted plain black instead of lined black. Shortly after nationalisation they became 30585 (ex-3314), 30586 (ex-3329) and 30587 (ex-3298). 30586 had its new number and lettering in the Bulleid style (it also had its 'British Railways' wording on the side of the tank), whereas the other two had standard BR numerals and lettering. In the fullness of time all three acquired the first BR emblem and, eventually, the second one.

By BR days the usual division of duties for the Well Tanks was for one of the three to be on the Wenford Bridge line, another shunting and carriage piloting at Wadebridge, and the third spare. The Wadebridge shunting and piloting was usually undertaken by 30586, as that loco was now unsuited to the Wenford Bridge line. To explain… in 1948 the filler hose on the much-photographed water tank at Pencarrow Woods had been lowered, and as 30586 had had its bunker water cap raised to prevent small coal falling into the tank, it could no longer take water there, hence its subsequent use on the Wenford Bridge line only in an emergency.

Much to the delight of enthusiasts, in the autumn of 1953 the Well Tanks were once again seen on ordinary passenger services. The Saturdays Only 11.50am Padstow-Wadebridge, a special train run in connection with sporting fixtures, was worked as part of Duty 607 by one of the Well Tanks. A correspondent in one of the contemporary journals excitedly remarked: 'Although these still-sprightly ancients have, in emergencies, appeared on the Bodmin passenger services on not a few occasions, it must surely be several years since one has been *diagrammed* for a passenger train!' But there was even more to come…

At the start of the following year's summer timetable the Well Tanks acquired a daily passenger working, the Wadebridge Yard Pilot (Duty 604) now being booked to include the 11.40am (SX), 11.46am (SO) Wadebridge-Padstow and the 11.55am (SX), 12.10 (SO) Padstow-Wadebridge. These were through trains from Bodmin North; the use of the Well Tanks on the

It's 21 June 1960, and 30586 still looks very smart after its heavy overhaul and repaint four months earlier. It is thought that this was the first steam loco to have diesel-type numerals applied. www.transporttreasury.co.uk

A splendid view of 30586's rear while piloting at Wadebridge on 12 July 1960. Compare this picture to those of 30585 and 30687 and it will be evident that, unlike that pair, 30586 had rectangular splashers for the leading coupled wheels and a panel extending forwards from the cab side sheet. R.C.Riley, www.transporttreasury.co.uk

Wadebridge-Padstow section enabled the O2 (which had brought the train in from Bodmin) to visit Wadebridge shed for coaling. A visitor to Wadebridge in early July (1954) reported that, during the week ending 3 July, 30586 was employed on Duty 604 (except on 1 July when O2 30203 deputised), and '...with a train of two corridor coaches, some surprisingly high speeds were attained by this 80-year-old locomotive'. During that same week 30585 was the regular engine on the Wenford goods (Duty 607).

All three Well Tanks received general overhauls in 1960. The first to be dealt with was 30586 which went to Eastleigh in February; during its works visit its number was applied in BR diesel-type numerals – it was thought that it was the first steam loco to have this style of numerals.

A visitor to Wadebridge on 7 September 1960 arranged a trip with 30587 on the Wenford Bridge branch. His report of the trip appeared in the *Railway Observer:* 'The trip proved very interesting as traffic from the China Clay Co's sidings at Wenford Bridge was very heavy. The load for 30587 from Wadebridge to Boscarne Junction where the lines to Bodmin General and Bodmin North diverge was nine wagons. Twenty-three china clay empties were attached at the junction and four containers which we had brought from Wadebridge were put off. As wagons are left for loading on the running line at the China Clay Co's siding, several complicated shunts are necessary, including propelling loaded box wagons of bagged clay and pulling the rest of the train for the last few yards to Wenford Bridge. On the return journey, departure from the sidings with nineteen loaded 10-ton clays and thirteen others, excluding the van, proved a heavy task for the veteran tank, but was managed with comparative ease. The nineteen clays were detached at Boscarne Junction...Arrival back at Wadebridge with the rest of the train of thirteen wagons, which included some containers of bagged clay for the Potteries, was slightly delayed by the complicated manoeuvres required at Boscarne Junction where some shunting by gravity is necessary, owing to restricted siding space. Incidentally, on this day the bag of the ancient water "column" at Penhargard (*Pencarrow Woods),* where water is brought by pipe across a field, was renewed and a siding at the Wenford terminus was being relaid. At Wadebridge, sister Beattie 30586 was shunting in the yard and 30585 was away at Eastleigh'.

Sadly, but somewhat inevitably, by that time the days of the Well Tanks were numbered. By the early 1960s they were by far the oldest working locomotives in BR stock (the youngest, 30586, had its 85th birthday in November 1960!) and each had run more than 1¼ million miles but, of course, the task of replacing them was far from simple as the Wenford Bridge branch – which was still doing good business – was out of bounds to almost all other types of locomotives. As we have seen, various other types had been unsuccessfully tried on that line, so when ex-GWR '1366' class 0-6-0PT 1368 was dispatched from Weymouth to Wadebridge for trials on the branch in April 1962, in certain quarters it was felt that the Pannier Tank would also be doomed to failure. But not so. Apart from a problem with the water tank at Pencarrow Woods being too low for 1368 to take on water, the locomotive itself performed satisfactorily on the line.

Consequently, two other '1366s' – 1367 and 1369 – were sent from Weymouth to Wadebridge in June, and after the water tank at Pencarrow was heightened they took over from the Well Tanks. And so, after almost seventy years, Wadebridge lost its three hugely

30586 on Wadebridge piloting duties in July 1960. R.C.Riley, www.transporttreasury.co.uk

30587 pulls off the turntable at the west end of Wadebridge shed yard on 19 June 1962. This loco had had the 'diesel-type' numerals and the second style of BR totem applied during its major overhaul in June/July 1960, but compare the positioning to that of 30586 – the latter had the number on the bunker side sheet and the totem on the panel in front of the cab, which is the opposite way round to what we see here. Another point to note is that 30587 had smaller buffer heads than the other two. R. C. Riley, www.transporttreasury.co.uk

30587
TARE
23 TONS

popular veterans. They were withdrawn in December 1962 but, fortunately, 30585 and 30587 were saved for preservation. 30585 was acquired by the London Railway Preservation Society (which later became the Buckinghamshire Railway Society, based at Quainton Road) and was returned to steam on 22 March 1970. In 1999 work was started on a major overhaul, and the loco returned to action on 7 October 2006. A week later she left for the Bodmin & Wenford Railway where she met her sister engine 30587 which, after a stint as a static exhibit at Buckfastleigh on the South Devon Railway, had been acquired for the National Railway Museum's collection and had also been restored to full working condition. This was the first time the two locos had operated together since an enthusiasts' special in 1962. 30585 returned from Bodmin to Quainton in January 2007, while 30587 has been a very popular guest on various preserved lines around the country.

Although the Wadebridge Yard Pilot job was usually undertaken by 30586 – and we've provided plenty of pictorial proof – there were, of course, occasions when that loco was unavailable and one of the other Well Tanks had to deputise. Here, 30587 is standing in for 30586 on the pilot job on 16 May 1958. Alec Swain, www.transporttreasury.co.uk

Alongside the coal stack at Wadebridge shed, July 1962. Mr.Heard, www.transporttreasury.co.uk

30585 and 30586 at Wadebridge, 22 June 1962. R.C.Riley, www.transporttreasury.co.uk

The displacer and the soon-to-be-displaced – the date is 22 June 1962, and 30585, which had performed sterling service at Wadebridge since 1898, stands alongside incomer 1368 which, with sisters 1367 and 1369, was soon to take over the Wenford Bridge duties. R.C.Riley www.transporttreasury.co.uk

Above. A wet day at Okehampton in 2008 but hopefully a brighter future.

Below. 'A view from the footbridge'...

Chapter Eleven

THE NORTH CORNWALL RAILWAY TODAY

Words and photographs by Ian Barnes

The North Cornwall Railway closed some forty three years ago and has gradually succumbed to the elements. Many of the station buildings survive in private use today and permission was sought by the author to gain access to the station sites. Here then is Ian Barnes story of the railway today and how he, and his colleague Nikki Barton, tackled the task of recording this West Country byway.

My journey started with the chance discovery of the original North Cornwall Railway book at my local library. Leafing through it I was fascinated by the station buildings and living in the area was aware how most had survived since the closure of the railway in the 1960s. As a youngster, in the 1970s, I had lived in a house which overlooked the station at Padstow. I worked too in North Cornwall and on my travels was intrigued by the many old station buildings still surviving. I was fascinated at the way the buildings had been standardised, based on the same basic plan yet varied by the use of local stone or brick. Indeed it was amazing that many were in such excellent condition.

***Above.* The beautifully restored departures board at Okehampton in 2008 and the home of the Dartmoor Railway.**
***Below.* Gradient post survivor at Halwill Junction in 2007**

A chance call to George Reeve at Irwell Press, about the availability of the original book, led to a conversation about photographing the buildings and railway today for inclusion in a updated and expanded version of the original book. I joined forces with researcher Nikki Barton and set out to record, and research, the station buildings today.

First stop was Okehampton station which has been carefully restored to its former glory. On Sundays, it is possible to catch a steam train up the steep gradient to the end of the restored Meldon Viaduct, which now serves as a link in the local/national cycle way network. Alternatively, on some Sundays in the summer it is possible to catch a train to Exeter St Davids.

Unfortunately as we go to press the railway has been closed by its owners ECT whose interim General Manager Nick Francis said "We could not afford to put any more money into the railway and so the business is to be sold as a going concern." There have been some offers submitted which may see the line open once again.

Ashbury

The first stop was Ashbury Station a few miles from Oakhampton. On that day, we were unable to contact the residents of the buildings but from the bridge on the public highway, we could see plenty of evidence of a well cared for station building, which had been converted into a number of dwellings. The sweeping approach road reminded us of the halcyon days of the railway. This building, like Halwill, was of course on the original section of line to Bude, a more austere and prosaic design to those found along the rest of the North Cornwall. From our viewpoint on the bridge, there were plenty of Southern Railway concrete features to be seen such as the fence gate and signposts surviving along with the tubular handrail still painted green. At the rear the goods shed appears to be converted to a dwelling but sympathetically, retaining its character. On closer examination of the photos, we spotted some railway track and ballast in the background.

Halwill Junction

We arrived at Halwill Junction where sadly most evidence of the railway has long gone. However, a call at the Junction Inn produced a number of splendid old photographs of the place in its heyday and an excellent Sunday lunch! Looking out from the inn all evidence of the level crossing has gone, but the odd SR concrete fence panel is a subtle reminder of the railway past. At the crossroads is a fine old road sign with Halwill Junction proudly cast on the vertical post and distances to most of the stations in the area. Walking along the appropriately named Beeching Close, revealed a new housing estate on the site of the station and yard but a pleasant stroll can be had along the old track bed, which is now a wildlife sanctuary. Just a few hundred yards along the trackbed to Bude the branch off to Launceston is quite clear while a further few hundred yards on is the branch to Torrington.

Ashwater

Ashwater, a few miles on, is truly a splendid sight where the station buildings still retain much of their original character, with plenty of SR paint still around! Talking to the current owner, who moved here a number of years ago with her husband, we learnt about his love of the railway and how he used to create model railways in the old entrance hall of the station. We were treated to a tour of the ticket office and hall and enjoyed seeing the original hatch for the sale of tickets. It was not hard to imagine the tickets being sold here many years ago. Back outside, the original concrete Ashwater sign is still in place. Our journey continued towards Launceston and brought us to Tower Hill, sadly a complete contrast to our visit to Ashwater. Very little remains of the railway apart from the line of cottages and the road bridge.

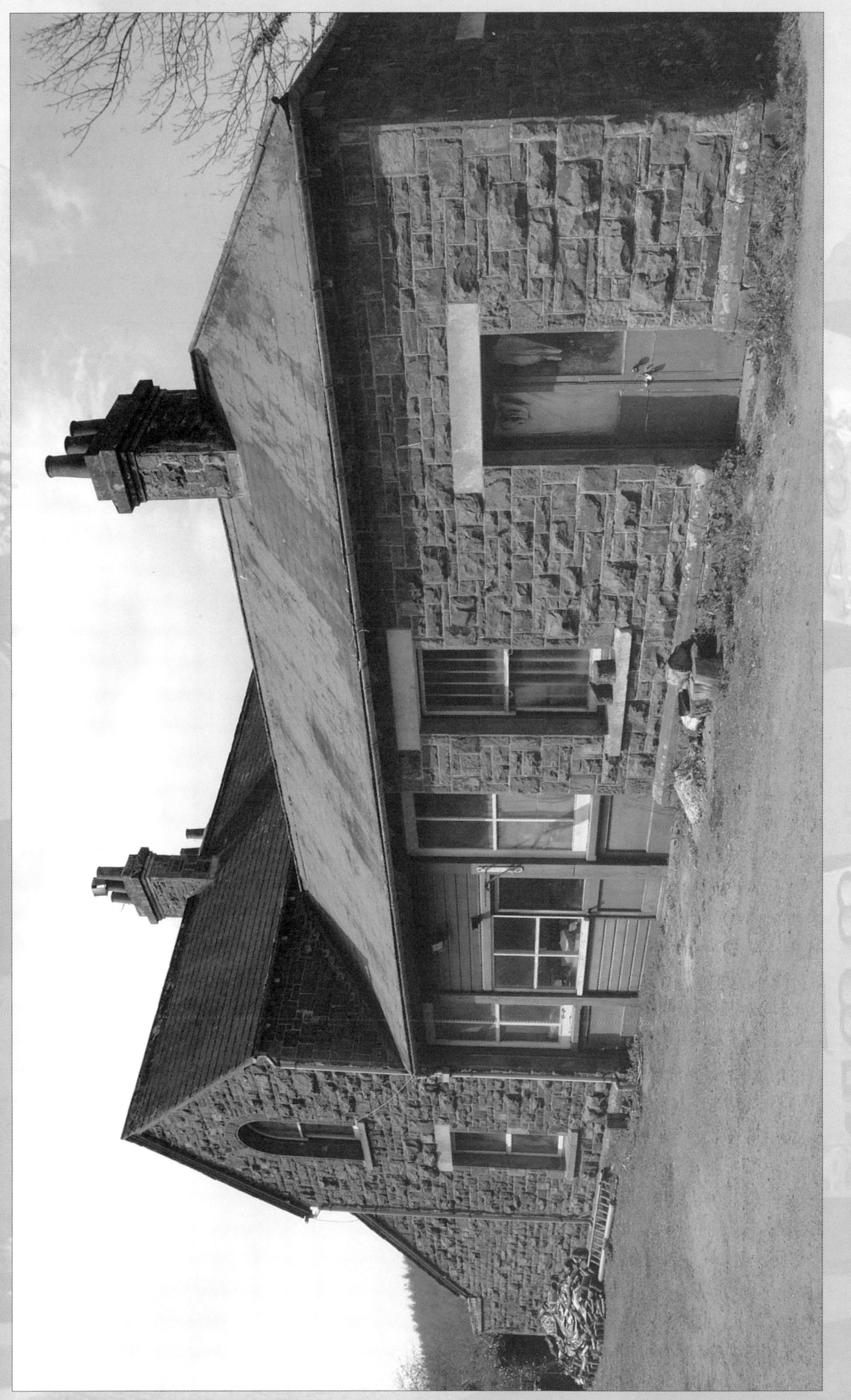

Launceston and the Launceston

It's hard to imagine that forty years after closure of the line visitors to Launceston can still enjoy a journey along the North Cornwall Railway behind a steam locomotive. The Launceston Steam Railway links the historic town of Launceston with the hamlet of Newmills. The line runs for two and a half miles through the glorious Kensey Valley along the trackbed of the North Cornwall Railway.

In 1965, owner and inspiration behind the railway, Nigel Bowman, purchased the locomotive *Lilian* from the Penrhyn Slate Quarry in North Wales. Although on a teacher training course, he set up a workshop and foundry at his parents' home where *Lilian* was rebuilt. In 1968, she returned to steam and was occasionally used on a short length of track owned by a friend.

With a locomotive, Nigel Bowman started looking for somewhere to run it on his own railway. He decided to abandon his career in teaching to build a railway to run *Lilian* on. However, with land prices in Surrey rocketing, and unsympathetic planners, it was decided to look elsewhere. By 1971, after looking at various sites, Nigel had identified Launceston as a possibility. With old school friend Jim Stone, an approach was made to Launceston Council, with proposals to lay a narrow gauge railway. This was supported from the outset by the council, and the task of purchasing the trackbed started. Much of the twelve years between the initial idea and opening was taken up by legal wrangles for odd parcels of land which had become the target of property developers. For example, the site of the current Launceston Station at one time was to become a housing development. However, the property boom quietened by the mid-1970s, allowing the purchase of the land.

The first ½ mile of track opened on Boxing Day 1983. Since then successive extensions have been made, the latest to Newmills opening in 1995.

The car park at Launceston is on the site of the LSWR station, while the new station occupies the old gas works. The café and booking office were built in 1919 for the first Ideal Home Exhibition, and were erected as a 3-bedroom bungalow in Surrey. The canopy is from Tavistock North, and was erected in 1986/1987. The workshop and museum buildings were originally used by the Launceston Gas Company.

Your train is hauled by narrow gauge (2' 0") locomotives built in Queen Victoria's reign, and you can ride in open or closed carriages depending on the weather; whatever you choose, you are assured of a marvellous view. A seat in the front of the train is as good as being on the footplate.

Tickets are "Day Rovers" so you can ride the trains as often as you wish, or you can break your journey for a picnic, to explore the footpaths around the Kensey Valley or visit the Newmills Farm Park.

With a train every 50 minutes or so, many passengers choose a picnic or a walk in the valley, and return on a later service. The guard will stop the train, on request, at Hunt's Crossing.

Above and below. **Nigel and Kay Bowman on the railway in 2007.**

am Railway

Egloskerry

Short extract from Sir John Betjeman's autobiography

Summoned by Bells

Attend the long express from Waterloo
That takes us down to Cornwall. Tea Time shows
The small fields waiting, every blackthorn hedge
Straining inland before the south-west gale.
The emptying train, wind in the ventilators,
Puffs out of Egloskerry to Tresmeer
Through minty meadows, under bearded trees
And hills upon whose sides the clinging farms
Hold Bible Christians. Can it really be
That this same carriage came from Waterloo?

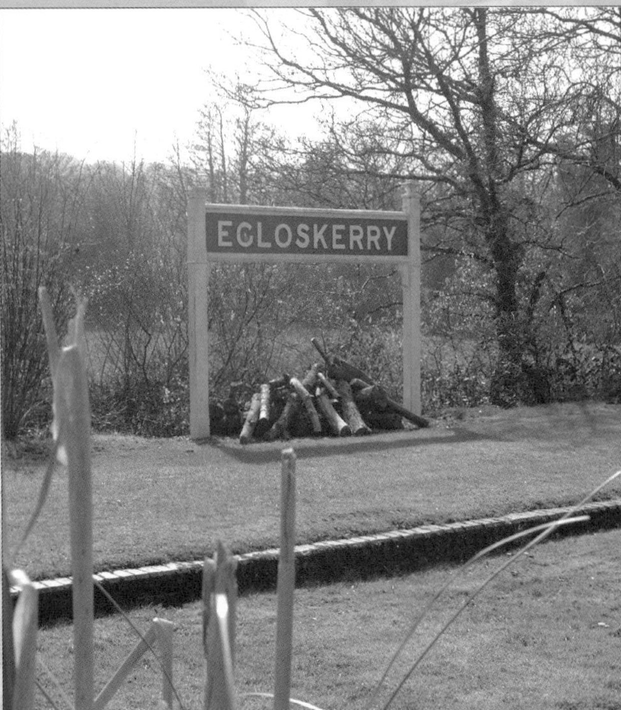

On arrival at Egloskerry, one is initially drawn to the most striking feature of this station, a full sized parcels van on a short length of track. It has been wonderfully restored and sits as if waiting for the next train. Looking across the platform is the station building which is now a private dwelling in beautiful condition. It has been sympathetically extended and modernised using red brick to match the original construction. A number of signs, streetlights and railings enhance the authentic feel of this quiet rural station.

WAY OUT

EGLOSKERRY
GENTLEMEN

Tresmeer

Tresmeer is the next stop which can easily be viewed from the road at the end of the platform. The trackbed had been partially filled to create a pleasant garden terrace between the platforms. The old Tresmeer sign nestles in the rhododendrons whilst the foundations of the signal box have been converted into a garden shed. Just a few yards away is the old goods shed and store, still used by local businesses.

Otterham

A few miles on through the beautiful Cornish countryside, we arrived at Otterham Station. Here the station building has recently (reluctantly) been sold after many years as a family home. The design remains essentially the same but it is in local stone rather than brick. Although the materials are standing the test of time the outgoing owner commented that it still takes a lot to maintain the building.

Camelford

Another success story for a former North Cornwall Station. Camelford has been lovingly restored by John and Sue Middleton to house the nation's foremost museum of cycling history.

The Old Station, Camelford,
PL32 9TZ Cornwall
TELEPHONE (01840) 212811

OVER 400 EXAMPLES OF CYCLES
OLD CYCLE REPAIR WORKSHOP
OVER 1000 CYCLING MEDALS,
FOBS AND BADGES FROM 1881
EXTENSIVE LIBRARY OF BOOKS
THE FIRST CYCLE OIL LAMP
WINDOW DISPLAYS OF GAS, CANDLE,
BATTERY AND OIL LIGHTING
GALLERY OF FRAMED CYCLING PICTURES
DISPLAYS OF CERAMIC CYCLING ITEMS
MODELS OF CYCLES
A HISTORY OF CYCLING FROM 1818
OPEN SUNDAYS TO THURSDAYS 10 am-5 pm ALL YEAR

Private Parties at other times by appointment
ONE MILE NORTH OF CAMELFORD
ON THE BOSCASTLE ROAD

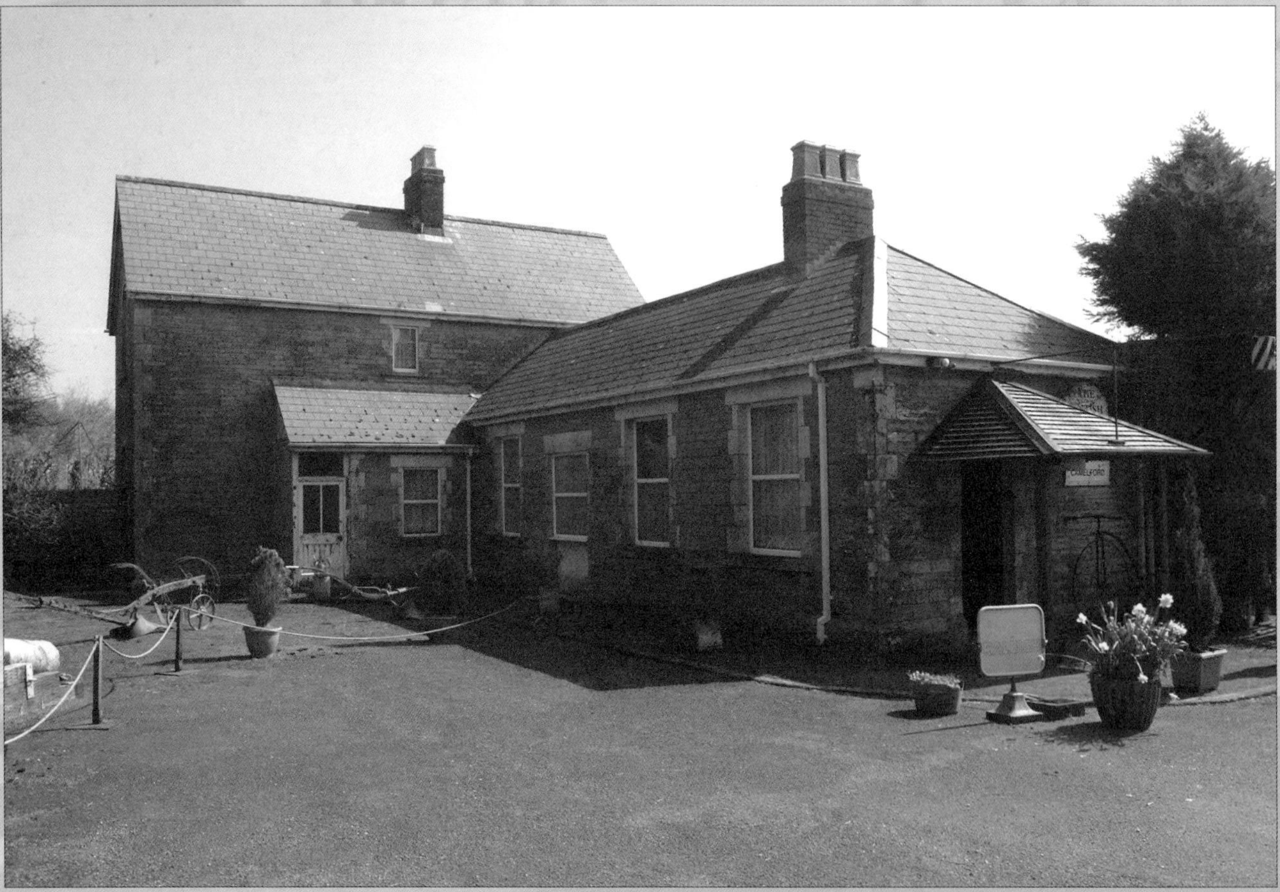

OPEN
THE
BRITIS
CYCLING
MUSEUM
THE OLD STATION
CAMELFORD

Delabole

Delabole station is next to the old slate quarry and again has been turned into a family home. Bizarrely it sits alongside newer houses in a much needed local housing estate with the cavernous quarry just a few yards away. It is possible to visit the offices of the Delabole slate company and see the ancient Simplex narrow gauge engine on display.

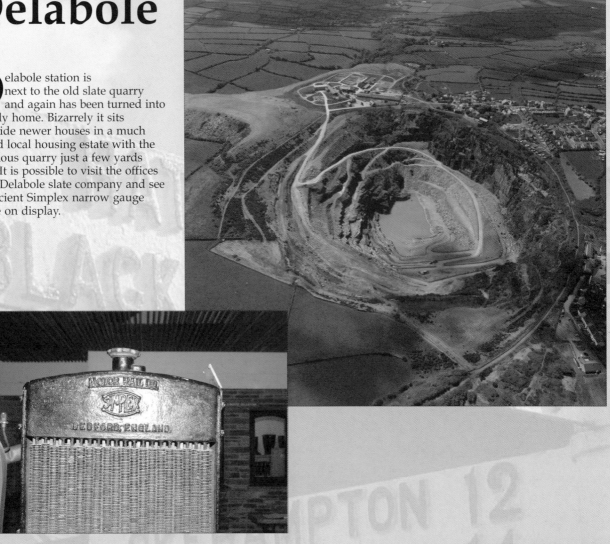

Port Isaac Road

Nestled away in the North Cornish countryside is Port Issac Road, as remote today as it was in the 1800s. Now a home and small business premises, this was probably our favourite station on the journey to Padstow. Many of the original features survive and it has remained little altered from opening in 1894.

PETHERICK

St. Kew Highway

St. Kew Station boasts the only surviving platform shelter on the line. There is even a fine fishpond in the track bed. This is truly a wonderful home and currently owned by 'Aunt Avice' who bakes superb Cornish Pasties at the nearby St. Kew Garage.

Sir John Betjeman, Wadebridge

The John Betjeman Centre is in the main station building at Wadebridge and was refurbished through the generous voluntary contributions of many who raised over £300,000. The two phase refurbishment, and additional building, took six years to complete and was officially opened by Viscountess Falmouth on the 29th May 1991. There is a memorabilia room dedicated to Sir John Betjeman with many of his personal effects on display.

A variety of books, videos, post cards and mementos are on sale and although the Centre doesn't have a curator a member of staff will give a short talk explaining Sir John's work and his association with North Cornwall.

The John Betjeman Centre
Telephone: 01208 812392

Continuing down the Allen Valley and on to the Camel flood plain we come to Wadebridge station. Most evidence of its past has long disappeared under housing although the old station and goods shed still remain. The main station building has been converted into the John Betjeman Centre, a venue for the town's senior citizens and the goods shed into a community centre and youth club. At the goods yard and car park end of the site, a new library has been built with good access to the town.

The end of the line, after the beautiful trip along the Camel Trail, is Padstow Station. The building survives under the ownership of Padstow Town Council and is put to good use as administrative offices and

dstow and the Camel Trail

The Camel Trail was made on the trackbed between Wadebridge and Padstow about 15 years ago and of course is almost level for the seven mile journey. The trail is principally used by cyclists and is best tackled during the summer months as some parts of it can turn muddy.

If you haven't got a bike they can be hired at a very reasonable price. The wonderful views over and along the Camel estuary, once savoured by holiday makers on the last leg of their journey from Waterloo, can again be enjoyed on the ride, which will take about an hour.

Padstow is a wonderful, picturesque, fishing harbour and has gained fame recently with Rick Stein and his Fish Restaurant near the harbour. Always worth a visit.

the council chamber. Hopefully under the guardianship of the council its future is secure for many years to come.

Many artefacts still exist no doubt encouraged and cared for by sympathetic owners. Without exception, all of the owners were very helpful in providing access but it must be emphasised that most of stations are in private ownership and **DO NOT** offer public access without permission which we always sought in advance. Please respect everyone's privacy and remember that most stations can be viewed from the public highway.

N 2-6-0 No.31833 passes under North Lew Road Bridge No. 12 at Ashbury Station with the 4.24pm Okehampton to Bude train on 25th May 1961. L. R. Freeman, The Transport Treasury.

Appendix 1

L&SWR NORTH CORNWALL RAILWAY

Numbered Bridges & Culverts

Meldon Junction, Halwill Junction and Whitstone

L. & S. W. Rly.—NUMBERED BRIDGES, &c., BETWEEN MELDON JUNCTION AND WHITS

No.	Known as	Locality: M. Chs.	Locality: Stations between	Public or Private	Crossing (under Railway)	Carrying (over Railway)	Type of Construction	No. of Spans	Dimensions of Spans: On Square Ft.	On Square Ins.	On Skew Ft.	On Skew Ins.	Minimu Ground To under of Gird Ft.
1	Tavistock Road Bridge	200 27	Meldon Jct. and Ashbury	Public	Road	...	Brick arch and abutments	1	20	0	29	0	...
2	Hatherleigh Road Bridge	200 53½	" " "	"	...	Road	Brick arches, piers and abutments	3	30	0	...		...
3	Bowerlands Bridge	201 9	" " "	Private	...	"	Brick arch and abutments	1	28	0	...		...
4	Ridgson Bridge	201 65	" " "	"	...	"	" " "	1	28	0	...		...
5	Okehampton Road Bridge	202 4	" " "	Public	...	"	" " "	1	28	0	34	0	...
5A	Tablet Bridge	202 20	" " "	...	...	...	Rolled steel girder and stanchions	1	33	0	...		14
6	Blagdon Bridge	202 47	" " "	Private	Road	...	Brick arch and abutments	1	10	0	...		...
7	Weeks-in-the-Moor Bridge	202 79	" " "	"	...	Road	Masonry arch and abutments	1	28	0	...		...
8	Manstage Bridge	204 39½	" " "	"	Road	...	" " "	1	13	0	14	9	...
9	Melbury Bridge	205 0	" " "	"	...	Road	" " "	1	28	0	...		...
10	Cockswell Bridge	205 36	" " "	"	Road	...	" " "	1	10	0	...		...
11	Burden Bridge	205 44	" " "	"	...	Road	" " "	1	28	0	...		...
12	North Lew Bridge	205 72½	" " "	Public	...	"	" " "	1	28	0	28	7	...
13	Beamsworthy Bridge	206 60	Ashbury and Halwill Jct.	Private	...	"	" " "	1	28	3	...		...
14	Patchacott Bridge	207 13½	" "	Public	...	"	" " "	1	28	0	...		...
14A	Culvert	207 41	" "	...	Stream	...	Masonry arch and walls	1	4	0	...		...
15	Beaworthy Rectory Bridge	207 64	" "	Private	Road	...	Masonry arch and abutments	1	12	0	...		...
16	Hall Bridge	208 4½	" "	Public	...	Road	" " "	1	28	0	30	0	...
16A	Culvert	208 20	" "	...	Stream	...	Masonry arch and walls	1	4	0	...		...
17	Madworthy Bridge	208 22½	" "	Public	Road	...	Masonry arch and abutments	1	15	0	22	0	...
17A	Culvert	208 47	" "	...	Stream	...	Masonry arch and walls	1	3	1	3	8	...
18	Madworthy Farm Bridge	208 55	" "	Private	Road	...	Masonry arch and abutments	1	10	0	...		...
19	Beaworthy Road Bridge	209 25	" "	Public	Road	...	W.I. girders, W.I. and timber decking, masonry abutments	1	15	0	...		14
20	Whiteley Bridge	211 72½	Halwill Jct. and Dunsland Cross	Private	...	Road	Masonry arch and abutments	1	28	0	...		...
20A	Culvert	212 4½	" "	...	Stream	...	Masonry arch, walls and invert	1	3	0	...		...
21	Morcombe Bridge	212 30	" "	Private	...	Road	Masonry arch and abutments	1	28	0	...		...
22	Cansmoor Bridge	212 71	" "	"	Road	...	" " "	1	10	0	...		...
23	Dunsland Cross Bridge	213 31	Dunsland Cross and Holsworthy	Public	"	...	" " "	1	15	0	21	6	...
24	Week Moor Bridge	214 33½	" " "	Private	"	...	" " "	1	10	0	...		...
25	Sellick Bridge	214 61½	" " "	"	...	Road	" " "	1	28	0	...		...
26	Hollacombe Bridge	215 12½	" " "	Public	...	"	" " "	1	30	0	31	6	...
26A	Culvert	215 27	" " "	...	Stream	...	Masonry arch, walls and invert	1	3	1	...		...
26B	"	215 39	" " "	...	"	...	" " " "	1	3	2	...		...
27	Anvil Corner Bridge	215 60	" " "	Public	...	Road	Masonry arch and abutments	1	28	0	...		...
28	Simson Cattle Creep	216 12	" " "	Private	Road	...	Old rail and timber girders, timber decking, masonry abutments	1	8	0	...		6
29	Simson Farm Bridge	216 49	" " "	"	"	...	Masonry arch and abutments	1	11	0	...		...
30	Cross Park Bridge	216 72	" " "	"	"	...	Old rail and timber girders, timber decking, masonry abutments	1	8	0	...		7
31	Holsworthy Road Bridge	217 32	" " "	Public	"	...	Masonry arch and abutments	1	15	0	22	0	...
32	Holsworthy Viaduct	217 40	" " "	...	Stream	...	Masonry arches, piers and abutments	8	50	0	...		...
33	Holsworthy Station Bridge	217 48	" " "	Public	Road	...	Masonry arch and abutments	1	20	0	...		...
34	Holsworthy Road Bridge	217 69	Holsworthy and Whitstone	"	"	...	Trough decking, brick abutments	1	15	0	...		15
35	Darraton Viaduct	217 74	" "	...	River	...	Concrete arches, piers and abutments	9	50	0	...		...
36	Darraton Farm Bridge	218 7	" "	Private	...	Road	Brick arch and abutments	1	28	0	...		...

Halwill Junction to Launceston

L. & S.W. Rly.—NUMBERED BRIDGES, &c., BETWEEN HALWILL JUNCTION AND LAUNC

No.	Known as	LOCALITY. M. Chs.	LOCALITY. Stations between.	Public or Private.	Crossing (under Railway).	Carrying (over Railway).	Type of Construction.	No. of Spans.	DIMENSIONS OF SPANS. On Square. Ft.	On Square. Ins.	On Skew. Ft.	On Skew. Ins.	Mini Grou To und of G Ft.
1	Lane End Bridge	210 48	Halwill Junction and Ashwater	Public	...	Road	Masonry arch and abutments	1	28	0	32	6	...
2	Brendon Farm Bridge	211 23½	" " " "	Private	...	"	" " " "	1	28	0	...		...
3	Cary River Bridge	211 58	" " " "	...	River	...	Masonry barrel	1	5	0	diam.		...
4	Blagaton Bridge	212 15	" " " "	Public	Road	...	W.I. girders and timber decking, masonry abutments	1	15	0	15	4	14
5	Blagaton Cattle Creep	212 41½	" " " "	Private	"	...	" " " " " "	1	9	10	...		12
6	" " "	212 60	" " " "	"	"	...	" " " " " "	1	6	0	...		5
7	" " "	212 79	" " " "	"	"	...	" " " " " "	1	6	0	...		5
8	Cary River Bridge	213 8	" " " "	...	River	...	Masonry arch and abutments	1	18	3	20	4	...
8A	Culvert	213 19	" " " "	...	Stream	...	Masonry arch and walls	1	3	0	3	6	...
9	Beckett Farm Bridge	213 53½	" " " "	Private	Road	...	W.I. girders, timber decking, masonry abutments	1	8	0	...		7
10	Thorn Farm Bridge	214 25	" " " "	"	"	...	Masonry arch and abutments	1	8	0	...		...
10A	Culvert	214 28	" " " "	...	Stream	...	Masonry arch and walls	1	3	0	...		...
11	Ashwater Mill Weir Bridge	214 32½	" " " "	...	River	...	Masonry arches, pier and abutments	2	15	6	17	0	...
11A	Culvert	214 41	" " " "	...	Stream	...	Masonry arch and walls	1	3	0	3	6	...
12	Cary River Bridge	214 45	" " " "	...	River	...	Masonry arches, pier and abutments	2	15	0	18	0	...
13	Thorndon Farm Bridge	214 46½	" " " "	Public	Road	...	W.I. girders and decking, masonry abutments	1	14	10	...		15
14	Ashwater Bridge	214 64	" " " "	"	...	Road	Masonry arch and abutments	1	28	0	...		...
14A	Culvert	214 79	Ashwater and Tower Hill	...	Stream	...	Masonry arch, walls and invert	1	3	0	...		...
15	Bradaford Farm Bridge	215 13	" " " "	Private	Road	...	W.I. girders, timber decking, masonry abutments	1	8	0	...		6
15A	Culvert	216 4	" " " "	...	Stream	...	Masonry arch, walls and invert	1	3	0	...		...
16	Tillislow Farm Bridge	216 56½	" " " "	Private	Road	...	W.I. girders, timber decking, masonry abutments	1	8	0	...		7
17	Virgin Stow Bridge	217 1	" " " "	Public	...	Road	Masonry arch and abutments	1	28	2	...		...
17A	Culvert	217 24	" " " "	...	Stream	...	Masonry arch, walls and invert	1	3	0	...		...
18	Scotland Farm Bridge	217 26	" " " "	Private	Road	...	W.I. girders, timber decking, masonry abutments	1	8	0	...		8
19	Scotland Cattle Creep	217 69	" " " "	"	"	...	" " " " "	1	8	0	...		6
20	Tower Hill Farm Bridge	218 14	" " " "	"	"	...	" " " " "	1	8	0	...		6
21	Tower Hill Bridge	218 33	" " " "	Public	...	Road	Masonry arch and abutments	1	28	0	...		...
21A	Culvert	...	" " " "	(Carrying accommodation road over stream)			" " " "	1	6	0	...		...
22	Station Culvert	218 36½	Tower Hill Station	...	Stream	...	" " " "	1	6	0	6	5	...
23	Downacary Bridge	218 57½	Tower Hill and Launceston	...	"	...	W.I. girders, timber decking, masonry abutments	1	6	0	...		6
23A	Coombe Mill Leat	218 79	" " " "	...	"	...	Masonry arch and abutments	1	6	0	7	0	...
23B	Coombe Mill Culvert	219 14	" " " "	...	"	...	" " " "	1	4	0	4	6	...
24	Cary River Bridge	219 20½	" " " "	...	River	...	W.I. girders, timber decking, masonry piers and abutments	3	10	0	18	0	11
25	Hawkadon Cattle Creep	219 34	" " " "	Private	Road	...	" " " " " " "	1	8	0	...		5
26	Hawkadon Farm Bridge	219 51	" " " "	"	...	Road	Masonry arch and abutments	1	28	4	...		...
27	Hawkadon Cattle Creep	219 65	" " " "	"	Road	...	W.I. girders, timber decking, masonry abutments	1	6	0	...		6
28	Boldford Bridge	219 69½	" " " "	Public	...	Road	Masonry arch and abutments	1	28	0	32	3	...
29	Jay's Farm Bridge	220 24	" " " "	Private	...	"	" " " "	1	28	0	...		...
30	Jay's Pond Bridge	220 28	" " " "	...	Waterway	...	W.I. girders, timber decking, masonry abutments	1	8	0	...		4
31	Coleman Cattle Creep	220 71½	" " " "	Private	Road	...	W.I. girders, timber decking, masonry abutments	1	5	10	...		6
32	Coleman Bridge	220 78½	" " " "	"	"	...	Masonry arch and abutments	1	10	0	...		...
32A	Tettridge Mill Leat	221 0½	" " " "	...	Stream	...	Masonry arch and walls	1	4	0	4	9	...
33	Hale Bridge	221 8	" " " "	Public	Road and River	...	Over Road.—W.I. girders and plate decking Over River.—Masonry arches, piers and abutments	3	15	0	...		14

Launceston to Tresmeer

L. & S.W. Rly.—NUMBERED BRIDGES, &c., BETWEEN TOWER HILL AND TRESM

No.	Known as	LOCALITY. M. Chs.	LOCALITY. Stations between.	Public or Private.	Crossing (under Railway).	Carrying (over Railway).	Type of Construction.	No. of Spans.	DIMENSIONS OF SPANS. On Square. Ft.	On Square. Ins.	On Skew. Ft.	On Skew. Ins.	MINIMUM GROUND To unders of Girde Ft.	In
34	Hale Farm Bridge	221 18	Tower Hill and Launceston ...	Private ...	Road ...	...	Masonry arch and abutments	1	9	10	...		...	
35	Nethercott Bridge	221 52	„ „ „ „ ...	„ ...	...	Road ...	„ „ „ „	1	28	2	...		...	
36	Flood Bridge	221 74	„ „ „ „ ...	„ ...	Road and Waterway	...	W.I. girders, trough decking, masonry abutments	1	35	6	...		8	6
37	Tamar River Bridge	222 9	„ „ „ „ ...	...	River ...	...	W.I. girders, timber decking, masonry piers and abutments	3	30	4	32	0	18	3
38	Colbay Bridge	222 17	„ „ „ „ ...	Public	...	Road ...	Masonry arch and abutments	1	28	0	30	0	...	
39	Ridge Grove Farm Bridge ...	222 60	„ „ „ „ ...	Private	Road ...	...	„ „ „ „	1	12	0	...		...	
40	Kensey River Bridge	222 66	„ „ „ „ ...	...	River ...	...	Masonry arches, piers and abutments	3	28	0	...		...	
41	G.W.R. Bridge	222 75	„ „ „ „ ...	Private ...	Railway ...	...	W.I. girders, timber decking, masonry abutments	1	31	0	73	0	15	6
42	Ridge Grove Bridge	223 $5\frac{1}{2}$	„ „ „ „ ...	Public ...	...	Road ...	Masonry arch and abutments	1	28	0	38	0	...	
43	Footbridge	223 $37\frac{1}{2}$	Launceston Station	Public ...	Footpath ...	...	W.I. girders, timber decking, masonry abutments	1	28	0	...		14	11
44	St. Thomas' Bridge	223 $41\frac{1}{2}$	Launceston and Egloskerry ...	„ ...	...	Road ...	Masonry arch and abutments	1	28	0	29	4	...	
45	Mill Bridge	223 59	„ „ „ ...	„ ...	...	„ ...	„ „ „ „	1	28	0	32	5	...	
46	Mill Leat Aqueduct	223 63	„ „ „ ...	...	...	Stream...	Brick arch and C.I. girders and plates	1	37	0	42	6	14	0
47	Kensey River Bridge	223 69	„ „ „ ...	...	River ...	...	Masonry arches, pier and abutments	2	14	9	...		...	
48	New Church Farm Bridge ...	224 $0\frac{1}{2}$	„ „ „ ...	Private ...	Road ...	...	Trough decking, masonry abutments	1	9	0	...		11	9
49	„ „ „ „ ...	224 24	„ „ „ ...	„ ...	„ ...	...	Masonry arch and abutments	1	8	0	...		...	
50	„ „ „ „ ...	224 37	„ „ „ ...	„ ...	„ ...	...	„ „ „ „	1	8	0	...		...	
51	„ „ „ „ ...	224 52	„ „ „ ...	„ ...	„ ...	...	„ „ „ „	1	8	0	...		...	
52	„ „ „ „ ...	224 62	„ „ „ ...	„ ...	„ ...	...	Trough decking, masonry abutments	1	8	0	...		5	9
53	Canney Park Cattle Creep ...	225 6	„ „ „ ...	„ ...	„ ...	...	„ „ „ „	1	8	0	...		6	6
54	New Mill Bridge	225 43	„ „ „ ...	Public	...	Road ...	Masonry arch and abutments	1	28	0	...		...	
54A	New Mill Leat Bridge ...	...	„ „ „ ...	(Carrying Public Road over stream) ...			„ „ „ „	1	6	0	6	9	...	
55	Trewethick Farm Bridge ...	226 0	„ „ „ ...	Private ...	Road ...	...	Trough decking, masonry abutments	1	8	0	...		6	6
56	Curnick Farm Bridge	226 $9\frac{1}{2}$	„ „ „ ...	Public ...	...	Footpath	Masonry arch and abutments	1	28	0	...		...	
57	Kensey River Bridge	226 79	„ „ „ ...	...	River ...	...	Masonry arches, pier and abutments	2	10	0	10	5	...	
58	„ „ „	227 26	„ „ „ ...	Private ...	Road and River	...	„ „ „ „ „	2	10	0	10	6	...	
59	Cleaver Bridge...	227 $37\frac{1}{2}$	„ „ „ ...	Private ...	...	Road ...	Masonry arch and abutments	1	28	2	...		...	
60	Skinnish Bridge	227 47	„ „ „ ...	„ ...	Road ...	...	Trough decking, masonry abutments	1	8	0	...		7	3
61	Skinnish Wood Bridge ...	228 0	Egloskerry and Tresmeer ...	„ ...	„ ...	...	„ „ „ „	1	6	0	...		5	3
62	Killycoff Bridge	228 $17\frac{1}{2}$	„ „ „ ...	„ ...	„ ...	...	„ „ „ „	1	8	0	...		6	3
63	Treborrow Cattle Creep ...	228 45	„ „ „ ...	„ ...	„ ...	...	„ „ „ „	1	8	0	...		6	0
64	Kensey River Bridge	228 56	„ „ „ ...	...	River ...	...	Brick arches, masonry pier and abutments	2	8	0	9	4	...	
65	Treborrow Bridge	228 56	„ „ „ ...	Public ...	...	Road ...	Masonry arch and abutments	1	28	0	...		...	
66	Lanzion Bridge	229 $19\frac{1}{2}$	„ „ „ ...	Private ...	Road ...	...	„ „ „ „	1	10	0	...		...	
67	Kensey River Bridge	229 $25\frac{1}{2}$	„ „ „ ...	...	River ...	...	Masonry arches, pier and abutments	2	6	6	...		...	
68	Lanzion Farm Bridge	229 30	„ „ „ ...	Private ...	Road ...	...	Brick arch, masonry abutments	1	10	0	...		...	
69	Lanzion Bridge	229 47	„ „ „ ...	Public ...	...	Road ...	Masonry arch and abutments	1	28	3	35	6	...	
70	Danakerry Bridge	230 $3\frac{1}{2}$	„ „ „ ...	„ ...	...	„ ...	Masonry arch, natural rock foundations	1	54	0	55	0	...	
70A	Culvert	230 33	„ „ „ ...	...	Stream ...	...	Masonry arch, walls and invert	1	3	0	3	3	...	
71	Westcott Bridge	230 $57\frac{1}{2}$	„ „ „ ...	Public ...	...	Road ...	Masonry arch and abutments	1	28	0	29	8	...	
72	Bates' Bridge	231 $7\frac{1}{2}$	„ „ „ ...	Private ...	...	„ ...	„ „ „ „	1	28	0	...		...	
73	Station Road Bridge	231 28	„ „ „ ...	Public ...	...	„ ...	„ „ „ „	1	36	0	...		...	

Tresmeer to Port Isaac Road

L. & S.W. Rly.—NUMBERED BRIDGES, &c., BETWEEN TRESMEER AND PORT ISAAC ROAD.

No.	Known as	Locality: M. Chs.	Locality: Stations between.	Public or Private.	Crossing (under Railway).	Carrying (over Railway).	Type of Construction.	No. of Spans.	Dimensions of Spans: On Square Ft.	Ins.	On Skew Ft.	Ins.	Minimum Ground To under of Girders Ft.	Ins.
73A	Culvert	231 55	Tresmeer and Otterham	...	Stream	...	Masonry arch and walls	1	3	0	...		...	
74	Roose Bridge	231 76½	" " "	Public	...	Road	Masonry arch and abutments	1	28	0	...		...	
75	Treneglos Cattle Creep	232 14½	" " "	Private	Road	...	" " " "	1	8	0	...		...	
76	Treneglos Bridge	232 30	" " "	Public	...	Road	Masonry arch, natural rock foundations	1	57	0	...		...	
76A	Culvert	232 43	" " "	...	Stream	...	Masonry arch and walls	1	5	0	...		...	
77	Trescassick Road Bridge	232 52½	" " "	Public	...	Road	Masonry arch, natural rock foundations	1	55	0	58	0	...	
78	Trewonard Bridge	233 7	" " "	"	...	"	Masonry arch and abutments	1	28	0	...		...	
78A	Culvert	233 27½	" " "	...	Stream	...	Masonry arch and walls	1	3	4	...		...	
79	Treskellow Bridge	233 40	" " "	Private	...	Road	Masonry arch and abutments	1	28	2	...		...	
80	Beathel Bridge	234 5	" " "	Public	...	"	Masonry arch, natural rock foundations	1	55	0	...		...	
81	Tregeya Bridge	234 39	" " "	Private	...	"	Masonry arch and abutments	1	28	3	...		...	
82	Culvert	234 54½	" " "	...	Stream	...	" " " "	1	6	6	...		...	
83	Greylake Bridge	234 60	" " "	Public	Road	...	" " " "	1	15	0	17	6	...	
84	East Roose Cattle Creep	234 74	" " "	Private	"	...	Trough decking, masonry abutments	1	8	0	...		7	9
85	West Roose Bridge	235 32	" " "	"	"	...	" " " "	1	10	0	...		12	0
86	Halgarden Bridge	235 67	" " "	"	"	...	Masonry arch and abutments	1	12	0	...		...	
87	Otterham Bridge	236 21	Otterham and Camelford	Public	...	Road	" " " "	1	36	0	...		...	
88	Helsett Farm Bridge	236 47	" " "	Private	Road	...	" " " "	1	8	0	...		...	
89	Trewenion Bridge	237 8	" " "	Public	...	Road	" " " "	1	28	0	...		...	
90	Penvellick Bridge	237 50	" " "	Private	...	"	" " " "	1	28	0	...		...	
90A	Culvert	237 61	" " "	...	Stream	...	Masonry arch, walls and invert	1	3	0	...		...	
91	Treslay Bridge	237 76	" " "	Private	...	Road	Masonry arch and abutments	1	28	0	...		...	
92	Halwell Farm Bridge	238 16½	" " "	"	...	"	" " " "	1	28	0	...		...	
93	Halwell Road Bridge	238 32	" " "	Public	Road	...	" " " "	1	20	0	20	9	...	
94	Halwell Cattle Creep	238 44½	" " "	Private	"	...	" " " "	1	8	0	...		...	
94A	Culvert	238 75	" " "	...	Stream	...	Masonry arch, walls and invert	1	3	0	...		...	
95	Hallott's Cattle Creep	239 0	" " "	Private	Road	...	Masonry arch and abutments	1	8	0	...		...	
96	Treekeek Cattle Creep	239 33½	" " "	"	"	...	" " " "	1	8	0	...		...	
97	Treekeek Bridge	239 49	" " "	Public	"	...	" " " "	1	15	0	...		..	
97A	Culvert	239 50	" " "	...	Stream	...	Masonry arch, walls and invert	1	3	0	...		...	
98	Hendraweather Bridge	239 54	" " "	Private	Road	...	Masonry arch and abutments	1	8	0	...		...	
99	Worthyvale Cattle Creep	240 7½	" " "	"	"	...	Trough decking, masonry abutments	1	8	0	...		5	6
100	Worthyvale Road Bridge	240 15	" " "	Private	Road	...	Masonry arch and abutments	1	12	0	...		...	
100A	Culvert	240 19½	" " "	...	Stream	...	Masonry arch, walls and invert	1	3	0	...		...	
101	Horragutter Bridge	240 34½	" " "	Private	...	Road	Masonry arch and abutments	1	28	0	...		...	
102	Camelford Station Bridge	240 61	Camelford and Delabole	Public	...	"	" " " "	1	28	0	...		...	
103	Trethern Bridge	241 33	" " "	Private	Road	...	" " " "	1	10	0	11	6	...	
104	Trethern Road Bridge	241 57½	" " "	"	...	Road	" " " "	1	28	5	...		...	
105	Delhi Farm Bridge	242 0	" " "	"	Road	...	" " " "	1	10	0	...		...	
106	Delabole Barton Bridge	242 31½	" " "	Public	...	Road	Brick arch, masonry abutments	1	28	0	51	0	...	
107	Delabole Quarry Footbridge	242 64	" " "	Private	...	Footpath	Rolled steel girders, timber decking, masonry abutments	1	28	1	...		14	2
108	Delabole Road Bridge	243 14	Delabole and Port Isaac Road	Public	...	Road	Masonry arch and abutments	1	28	5	...		...	

Delabole to Wadebridge

L. & S.W. Rly.—NUMBERED BRIDGES, &c., BETWEEN DELABOLE AND PADSTOW.

No.	Known as	Locality: M. Chs.	Locality: Stations between.	Public or Private.	Crossing (under Railway).	Carrying (over Railway).	Type of Construction.	No. of Spans.	Dimensions of Spans: On Square Ft.	On Square Ins.	On Skew Ft.	On Skew Ins.	Minimum Ground To underside of Girder Ft.	In.
109	Delemere Bridge	243 64	Delabole and Port Isaac Road ...	Private	Road	...	Masonry arch and abutments	1	10	0	...		...	
110	Newel Lane Bridge	244 24	,, ,, ,, ,, ,, ...	Public	,,	...	,, ,, ,, ,, ...	1	15	0	15	2	...	
111	Vicarage Farm Bridge ...	244 28	,, ,, ,, ,, ,, ...	Private	,,	...	Trough decking, masonry abutments	1	8	0	...		11	6
112	St. Teath Road Bridge ...	244 50	,, ,, ,, ,, ,, ...	Public	...	Road	Masonry arch and abutments	1	28	0	39	0	...	
113	Trewinan Farm Bridge ...	244 73	,, ,, ,, ,, ,, ...	Private	Road	...	,, ,, ,, ,, ...	1	10	0	...		...	
114	Treosiel Bridge...	245 8½	,, ,, ,, ,, ,, ...	,,	...	Road	,, ,, ,, ,, ...	1	28	0	29	0	...	
115	,, ,, ...	245 17	,, ,, ,, ,, ,, ...	Public	Road	...	Trough decking, masonry abutments	1	15	0	16	9	14	[illegible]
116	St. Fenton Farm Bridge ...	245 27½	,, ,, ,, ,, ,, ...	Private	,,	...	Masonry arch and abutments	1	8	0	...		...	
117	Key Road Bridge	246 1½	,, ,, ,, ,, ,, ...	Public	...	Road	,, ,, ,, ,, ...	1	28	0	...		...	
118	Key Cattle Creep	246 16	,, ,, ,, ,, ,, ...	Private	Road	...	,, ,, ,, ,, ...	1	6	0	...		...	
119	Trewicket Farm Bridge ...	246 37	,, ,, ,, ,, ,, ...	,,	,,	...	,, ,, ,, ,, ...	1	10	0	...		...	
120	No Man's Land Bridge ...	246 55	,, ,, ,, ,, ,, ...	Public	...	Road	,, ,, ,, ,, ...	1	28	3	33	0	...	
121	Redford Cattle Creep	246 68	,, ,, ,, ,, ,, ...	Private	Road	...	,, ,, ,, ,, ...	1	6	0	...		...	
122	Port Isaac Bridge	247 3½	,, ,, ,, ,, ,, ...	Public	,,	...	,, ,, ,, ,, ...	1	15	0	16	9	...	
123	Trewarne Road Bridge ...	247 28½	Port Isaac Rd. & St. Kew Highway	,,	...	Road	,, ,, ,, ,, ...	1	28	0	45	0	...	
124	Trelill Bridge	247 54½	,, ,, ,, ,, ,, ,,	,,	...	,,	,, ,, ,, ,, ...	1	28	0	37	0	...	
125	Trelill Tunnel	247 60 TO 247 77	,, ,, ,, ,, ,, ,,	,,	...	,,	Masonry arch	1	16	0	...		...	
126	Bokelly Cattle Creep	248 13	,, ,, ,, ,, ,, ,,	Private	Road	...	Trough decking, masonry abutments	1	6	0	6	11	6	10
127	Bokelly Farm Bridge	248 37½	,, ,, ,, ,, ,, ,,	,,	...	Road	Masonry arch and abutments	1	28	0	...		...	
128	Trequite Road Bridge... ...	248 51	,, ,, ,, ,, ,, ,,	Public	Road	...	,, ,, ,, ,, ...	1	15	0	16	8	...	
129	Trequite Bridge	248 74	,, ,, ,, ,, ,, ,,	,,	...	Footpath	,, ,, ,, ,, ...	1	28	0	...		...	
130	St. Kew Bridge	249 36½	,, ,, ,, ,, ,, ,,	,,	Road	...	,, ,, ,, ,, ...	1	15	0	16	6	...	
131	St. Kew Highway Bridge ...	249 58½	,, ,, ,, ,, ,, ,,	,,	,,	...	,, ,, ,, ,, ...	1	20	3	34	0	...	
132	Benbole Bridge	250 1½	St. Kew Highway & Wadebridge	Private	...	Road	,, ,, ,, ,, ...	1	28	0	...		...	
133	Benbole Cattle Creep	250 15	,, ,, ,, ,, ,,	,,	Road	...	,, ,, ,, ,, ...	1	7	0	...		...	
134	Demansbridge Road Bridge ...	250 34½	,, ,, ,, ,, ,,	Public	...	Road	,, ,, ,, ,, ...	1	28	0	...		...	
135	Rocksy Bridge...	250 58½	,, ,, ,, ,, ,,	,,	...	,,	,, ,, ,, ,, ...	1	28	0	...		...	
136	Rocksy Cattle Creep	250 69	,, ,, ,, ,, ,,	Private	Road	...	Trough decking, masonry abutments	1	8	0	...		9	10
137	Higher Lamail Cattle Creep ...	251 5½	,, ,, ,, ,, ,,	,,	,,	...	Masonry arch and abutments	1	6	0	...		...	
138	Lamail Bridge	251 34½	,, ,, ,, ,, ,,	Public	...	Road	,, ,, ,, ,, ...	1	28	0	...		...	
139	Ingan Mill Bridge	251 50	,, ,, ,, ,, ,,	,,	...	,,	,, ,, ,, ,, ...	1	28	0	31	0	...	
140	Trewardor Cattle Creep ...	252 12	,, ,, ,, ,, ,,	Private	Road	...	,, ,, ,, ,, ...	1	10	0	15	0	...	
141	Slade's Bridge	252 56	,, ,, ,, ,, ,,	Public	,,	...	,, ,, ,, ,, ...	1	25	6	33	9	...	
142	River Bridge	252 67	,, ,, ,, ,, ,,	...	River	...	,, ,, ,, ,, ...	1	20	0	25	9	...	
143	Pendavey Bridge	252 71	,, ,, ,, ,, ,,	Public	Road	...	,, ,, ,, ,, ...	1	28	0	29	9	...	
144	Camel River Bridge	252 78	,, ,, ,, ,, ,,	...	River	...	W.I. girders, trough decking, masonry pier and abutments ...	2	30 9	0 0	31 9	0 6	16	0
145	Treraven Cattle Creep... ...	253 9½	,, ,, ,, ,, ,,	Private	Road	...	Trough decking, masonry abutments	1	6	0	...		6	3
145A	Treraven Bridge	253 47	,, ,, ,, ,, ,,	,,	...	Road	Cast iron and old rail girders and concrete, masonry abutments	1	26	0	...		13	8
145B	Culvert	253 52½	,, ,, ,, ,, ,,	...	Stream	...	Masonry arch and walls	1	3	0	...		...	
145C	Station Footbridge	253 72½	Wadebridge Station ...	Private ...	...	...	Timber girders, decking and trestles	1	39	0	...		14	8
146	Tregullick Bridge	253 79	Wadebridge and Padstow	...	River	...	Trough decking, masonry abutments	1	16	0	19	6	8	9
146A	Lift Bridge	253 79	,, ,, ,,	...	,,	...	Timber girders and decking, masonry abutments	1	18	0	21	6	7	0
147	Molesworth Street Bridge ...	254 4	,, ,, ,,	Public	...	Footpath	Steel girders, timber decking, masonry abutments ...	1	28	0	...		13	6

Lord Beaverbrook No. 34054 and the Atlantic Coast Express nears its final destination of Padstow as it passes over Little Petherick Creek and the magnificent Bridge No.153, 258 miles and 61 chains from Waterloo. Sid Nash.

Ashwater Station Road Bridge, No. 14, on 20th August 1958 with 34031 Torrington crossing an up Wadebridge passenger train hauled by T9 No. 30710. A. E. Bennett, www.transporttreasury.co.uk

Wadebridge to Padstow

L. & S.W. Rly.—NUMBERED BRIDGES, &c., BE[illegible] E AND PADSTOW. (Wadebridge & [illegible]

No.	Known as	Locality: M. Chs.	Locality: Stations between.	Public or Private.	Crossing (under Railway).	Carrying (over Railway).		No. of Spans.	Dimensions of Spans: On Square: Ft.	On Square: Ins.	On Skew: Ft.	On Skew: Ins.	Min. Gro[illegible]: To u[illegible] of [illegible] Ft.
147A	Commissioners Bridge ...	254 13	Wadebridge and Padstow ...	Public ...	...	Footpath	... ...	1	22	0	...		13
148	White House Bridge ...	255 74	" " " ...	" ...	...	Road	Ma[illegible]onry arch a[illegible]	1	28	0	28	4	
149	Camel Quarry Bridge ...	256 54½	" " " ...	Private ...	Road ...	...	" " "	1	12	0	12	10	
150	Pixton Bridge	257 22	" " " ...	...	Waterway ...	...	" " " "	1	15	0	17	6	
151	Old Town Bridge	257 57	" " " ...	Public ...	Road ...	...	" " " "	1	15	0	...		
151A	Culvert	257 60	" " " ...	...	Stream ...	...	Masonry arch and walls	1	3	0	...		
152	Tregonce Bridge	258 49	" " " ...	Public ...	Road ...	...	Masonry arch and abutments	1	12	0	...		
153	Little Petherick Bridge ...	258 61	" " " ...	...	River ...	...	W.I. girders, timber decking, C.I. piles, concrete and masonry abutments	3	130	0	...		32
154	Dennis Bridge	259 4	" " " ...	Public ...	Road ...	...	Masonry arch and abutments	1	12	0	12	3	
[illegible]5	Culvert	259 4½	" " " ...	...	Stream ...	...	Masonry arch and walls	1	3	6	...		
							BETWEEN WADEBRIDGE AND BODMIN.						
	[illegible]tle Creep	1 24	Wadebridge and Bodmin ...	Private ...	Road ...	...	Old rail decking, masonry abutments	1	4	9	...		6
	[illegible]avy Bridge	1 27	" " " ...	...	River ...	...	W.I. girders, trough decking, masonry pier and abutments...	2	25	3	31	6	14
	[illegible] Creep	1 28	" " " ...	Private ...	Road ...	...	Old rail decking, masonry abutments	1	4	9	...		6
	[illegible]ock Bridge	2 40	" " " ...	Public ...	...	Road ...	Brick arch and al[illegible]	1	16	2	...		..
	[illegible]rock Culvert	2 49½	" " " ...	...	Stream ...	...	Brick arch, concrete walls and invert...	1	4	6	...		..
	Cattle Creep	3 69½	" " " ...	Private ...	Road ...	...	Old rail decking, masonry abutments	1	6	0	...		6
5A	Boscarne Culvert	5 18	" " " ...	...	Stream ...	...	Masonry arch and abutments	1	6	3	6	6	..
6	Dunmere Bridge	5 22½	" " " ...	...	River ...	...	W.I. girders, trough decking, masonry abutments	1	40	0	53	0	35
6A	Dunmere Footbridge	5 22½	" " " ...	(Public footpath over river)		... ...	W.I. girders, timber joists and decking, masonry abutments	1	40	0	42	0	31
6B	Dunmere Junction Footbridge	5 27	" " " ...	Public ...	...	Footpath	Timber girders, decking and trestles	1	22	6	...		14
7	Dunmere Road Bridge ...	5 40	" " " ...	" ...	...	Road ...	Brick arch, masonry abutments	1	28	0	29	9	..
7A	Culvert	5 45	" " " ...	...	Stream ...	...	Brick arch, masonry walls, concrete invert	1	3	9	...		..
7B	Culvert	...	" " " ...	(Stream under site of old railway)		...	Masonry arch and walls	1	4	6	...		..
7C	Culvert	6 14	" " " ...	...	Stream ...	...	Flat granite top, masonry walls	1	3	0	...		3
8	Berrycombe Bridge	6 27	" " " ...	Public ...	...	Road ...	W.I. girders, trough decking, masonry abutments	1	26	0	...		14
8A	Culvert	...	" " " ...	(Stream under public road)		... ...	Brick arch, masonry walls	1	4	6	5	3	..
9	Bore Lane Bridge	6 50	" " " ...	Public ...	...	Road ...	W.I. girders, trough decking, masonry abutments	1	26	0	...		14
10	Culvert	...	" " " ...	(Stream under public road)		... ...	Brick arch and wall[illegible]crete invert	1	3	6	4	0	..
11	Culvert	...	" " " ...	(Stream under cottages, &c.)		... ...	Masonry ar[illegible]	1	4	9	...		..
			Situated at				**RUTHE[illegible]ANCH.**						
1	Grogley Bridge...	3 15	Grogley	...	River ...	...	Timber girde[illegible]ng, masonry pier and abutments ...	2	25	3	26	0	15
2	Grogley Culvert	3 18	"	...	Stream ...	...	Masonry arch and [illegible]	1	4	0	...		..
			Situated between				**WENFORD BRANCH.**						
1	Dunmere Culvert	5 44	Dunmere and Helland	...	Stream ...	...	Masonry arch and abutments	1	4	0	...		..
2	Outland Culvert	6 24½	" " "	...	" ...	...	" " " "	1	8	0	9	6	..
[illegible]	Stockbridge Bridge	10 3½	Helland and Tresarrett... ...	...	" ...	...	C.I. girders, timber decking, masonry abutments	1	9	0	11	0	8
	[illegible]rrett Bridge	10 42	" " "	...	" ...	...	Masonry arch and abutments	1	6	0	6	2	..
	.. ..	10 44	" " "	...	" ...	...	Masonry arch and walls	1	3	5	...		..
	... ...	10 74	Tresarrett and Wenford ...	...	River ...	...	Masonry arch and [illegible]	1	17	0	18	0	..
	Creep	11 63	" " " ...	Private ...	Road ...	...	Old rail and gra[illegible]g, dry stone walls... ...	1	3	3	...		5

Appendix 2

Maunsell '2-set P' Compositions

By Chris Tooth

Chapter eight briefly described the Maunsell two-coach local sets that were the mainstay of local services on the Padstow, Bude and Bodmin branches. The sets normally consisted of a six-compartment brake third paired with a six compartment brake composite. Both coaches were to Maunsell designs and, being brakes, were easily distinguished from the later Bulleid and BR MK1 coaches by the guard's compartments being inset and slab-sided. Maunsell coaching stock was built from 1926 to 1936 and over this time the style and treatment of the doors and windows varied resulting in four distinct body styles or 'patterns'. A knock-on effect was that three diagram numbers were used for the brake thirds (D2102, D2110 and D2113) and two for the composite brakes (D2401 and D2403). The Southern Railways Group has established descriptions for each of these distinct patterns and the text that follows is based on their wording.

Pattern 1: In 1925, the SR placed orders for new carriages for West of England and Central Section services to London. The body (which was in essence a 'bow-ended' design with a basic length of 59' along the coach centreline) included passenger compartments each with an external door and corridors with 'low' main windows (lights). The windows were fitted into a wooden frame arranged such that the glass was noticeably recessed into the body side. The maximum width over the body sheeting was 9'-0" (Route Restriction 4) and there was a marked tumblehome. The luggage and guard's compartments had vertical sides (8'-7" wide with a small tumblehome at the base) and steel duckets. All coaches built to this pattern had single, large vent hoods above the lavatory window. The doors on the corridor side were directly opposite the compartment side doors. The most significant distinguishing feature was that the top of the corridor side windows was level with the top of the door droplights.

Pattern 2: The first or 'low' pattern of Maunsell bodyside, remained in production until 1933 for certain types of carriage but in 1929, a second 'pattern' was introduced which featured 'High corridor windows. The majority of windows on the corridor side now extended almost to the underside of the roofline. Since the change was only cosmetic the diagram numbers used for the pattern 1 coaches were not changed. The doors on the corridor side were still directly opposite the compartment side doors. The pattern 2 coaches started off being built with single, large vent hoods above the lavatory window but from order E633 onwards this feature was replaced by two smaller vents which all subsequent coaches had.

Pattern 3. The next major change in design occurred in 1935. The windows were virtually flush with the body sides and the larger windows (lights) had large radius corners. The body was marked by numerous screw heads where the steel sheeting was fixed to the wooden framing. Droplights were frameless. The 'double' battery boxes used on previous batches were dispensed with and two single boxes, each offset to the left of the coach centreline when viewed on each side were fitted. The doors on the corridor side were re-positioned to midway between compartment side doors. The associated adjustment of window locations resulting in a different look to the corridor side.

Pattern 4. The final pattern appeared in 1936, with the fixed windows (small radius corners) mounted in a neat frame, giving the appearance of a moulding on the body side. Droplights were frameless except on the Open Third design where frames were again used. The numerous screw heads disappeared giving a flush finished side. The doors on the corridor side remained in the pattern 3 locations but the two-large, one-small arrangement of windows between doors was revised to delete the previous 'fake' door windows and the large windows got larger. The end result was probably the most attractive of Maunsell's carriage designs.

The table that follows includes some of the longer term coach formations for the 2-set Ps. Photographic evidence and other records suggests that there were additional shorter-term set make ups as individual coaches were stopped for repairs or servicing. As such the data below should be taken as a general guide.

			Maunsell Brake Third			Maunsell Brake Composite		
Set No	Date From	Date To	Pattern 2 D2102 1 lav vent	Pattern 2 D2110 2 lav vents	Pattern 3 D2113 2 lav vents	Pattern 1 D2401 1 lav vent	Pattern 2 D2401 1 lav vent	Pattern 3 D2403 2 lav vents
22	01/1948	06/1960			2790			6691
	06/1960	09/1960			2790		6589	
	09/1960	11/1960			2790		6648	
	11/1961	12/1964			2790		6669	
23	01/1948	12./1959			2792		6575	
	09/1960	11/1960			2792		6646	
	11/1961	12/1962			2792		6652	
24	01/1948	07/1964			2832		6602	
25	01/1948	06/1962		3780			6665	
	06/1963	07/1964		3780			6648	
26	01/1948	12/1961			2831		6586	
	06/1962	12/1962			2831		6593	
27	01/1948	12/1962		3775			6603	
28	01/1948	12/1961			2787	6569		
	06/1962	12/1962			2787		6591	
29	01/1948	12/1959			2788	6567		
	09/1960	04/1961			2788		6643	
	04/1961	12/1962			2788		6653	
30	02/1962	12/1962		3788			6668	
31	02/1962	11/1964			2838		6662	
168	10/1935	06/1960			2776			6695
	06/1960	09/1960			-	6655	6654	
	09/1960	11/1960			2776		6655	
	11/1960	01/1963			2776		6659	
172	01/1935	06/1960			2777			6696
	06/1960	11/1964			2777		6664	
178	01/1935	06/1960			2836			6690
	06/1960	11/1962			2836		6666	
179	09/1930	02/1961	3732				6673	
		01/1962	3732				6658	
	02/1962	12/1962			2837		6658	
180	01/1935	07/1961	3733				6674	
	09/1961	12/1962	3733				6650	
196	01/1935	06/1960			2778			6697
	06/1960	12/1964			2778		6667	
197	01/1935	01/1941			2779			6698
198	01/1935	06/1960			2780			6699
	06/1960	12/1962			2780		6670	
199	01/1930	08/1961	3736				6657	
	09/1961	12/1962			2833		6657	
200	07/1930	11/1962	3737				6588	

Note: All the Diagram 2403 coaches were removed from the P-Sets in 1960 and converted to Push-Pull coaches with a driving cab at the guards end.

Readers wanting to research the topic of Maunsell Coaches further should consult the standard texts on the subject: 'An Illustrated History of Southern Coaches' by Mike King and 'Maunsell's SR Steam Carriage Stock' by David Gould.

Appendix 3

Working Timetables

Supplied by Roger Merry Price

1933

B

PASSENGER TRAIN LOADS.

The loads of passenger trains running between London and Exeter must be limited as under, and in no circumstances must these loads be exceeded unless specially authorised.

LONDON AND EXETER.

Down Trains FROM WATERLOO		Maximum Load.		Up Trains FROM EXETER			Maximum Load.
8 40 a.m.	...	11 Bogies.	B	7 20 a.m.	...	as from Templecombe	11 Bogies.
8 44 a.m. SO	...	13 "		9 35 a.m. MO	...	... ...	11 "
9 0 a.m. SO	...	11 "		10 0 a.m. SO	...	... ...	13 "
10 35 a.m.	...	12 "		10 30 a.m.	...	as from Templecombe	11 "
10 45 a.m. SO	...	13 "		11 25 a.m. SO	...	... ...	13 "
11 0 a.m.	...	13 "		12 10 p.m. SO	...	... ...	13 "
11 10 a.m. SO	...	13 "		12 30 p.m. SO	...	... ...	13 "
11 45 a.m. SO	...	13 "		12 32 p.m. NS	...	... ...	13 "
12 0 noon FSO	...	12 "		12 34 p.m.	...	... ...	13 "
12 40 p.m.	...	12 "	C	12 46 p.m. NS	...	... ...	13 "
2 0 p.m. SO	...	13 "		12 46 p.m. SO	...	... ...	13 "
3 0 p.m.	...	11 "		1 24 p.m. SO	...	... ...	12 "
3 10 p.m. SO	...	13 "		1 35 p.m. SO	...	... ...	13 "
6 0 p.m.	...	11 "		2 11 p.m. SO	...	... ...	11 "
				2 26 p.m.	...	... ...	13 "
				2 26 p.m. NS	...	... ...	12 "
				3 12 p.m. SO	...	... ...	13 "
				4 15 p.m. FSO	...	... ...	13 "
				4 30 p.m.	...	... ...	11 "
				5 55 p.m.	...	... ...	12 "

B—On Saturdays, 22nd July to 9th September, the load of this train not to exceed 9 Bogies from Waterloo and be made up to not more than 13 Bogies from Salisbury with coaches arriving by 8.44 a.m. from Portsmouth Harbour. C—Will be made up to 13 Bogies from Salisbury if necessary.

EXPLANATION OF REFERENCES AND GENERAL INSTRUCTIONS.

The figures with a line between thus | arr. 10 | dep. 50 | arr. dep. 10/50 | indicate the time at which a Train that does not stop should pass the Station or Junction opposite which such time may appear.

A place marked thus, ● indicates where a Train is to pass, or be passed by another.

A place marked thus, ——— indicates that the Train does not proceed farther on the same Line.

× Indicates crosses another Train on the Single Line.

● Indicates shunts for or passes another Train.

A Train marked thus "✻" at the top of a column or at any Station, indicates that a special instruction applies to it, for particulars of which see Freight Train Working notes on pages B, H, I, J, K, L, M and N.

†—Empty Coaches.
‖—Light Engine.
MFSO—Mondays, Fridays and Saturdays only.
MThO—Mondays and Thursdays only.
MO—Mondays only.
MWFO—Mondays, Wednesdays and Fridays only.
MOQ—Mondays only when required.
NM—Not Mondays.
NMM—Not Monday mornings.
TuO—Tuesdays only.
TuThO—Tuesdays and Thursdays only.
TuThSO—Tuesdays, Thursdays and Saturdays only.
WO—Wednesdays only.
WFO—Wednesdays and Fridays only.
WSO—Wednesdays and Saturdays only.
NFS—Not Fridays and Saturdays.
NWS—Not Wednesdays and Saturdays.
WThSO—Wednesdays, Thursdays and Saturdays only.
ThO—Thursdays only.
FO—Fridays only.
FSO—Fridays and Saturdays only.
NF—Not Fridays.
SO—Saturdays only.
NS—Not Saturdays.
Q—Runs when required.

¶ ¶¶ Improved Running Schedules for Passenger Trains. See page D for particulars.

ADVERTISED DEPARTURE TIMES FROM STATIONS.

The departure times of all steam trains from intermediate stations advertised to the public, are slightly in advance of the actual service times.

In quoting particulars to members of the public, the times shown on the public announcements must be given.

At stations where the lines are single the arrival times of all trains are advertised to the public as the departure time. This will allow of a train proceeding to the next station, when required, without waiting for the service book departure time.

WORKING AND PUBLIC TIME BOOKS, TIME BILLS, &c.

For Instructions see page 221 of the Appendix to the Book of Rules and Regulations and Working Time Tables dated 25th July, 1921.

DISCONTINUANCE OF, OR ALTERATION TO, ORDINARY PASSENGER TRAINS.

For Instructions see page 221 of the Appendix to the Book of Rules and Regulations and Working Time Tables dated 25th July, 1921.

HORSE, CARRIAGE, &c., TRAFFIC.

Horse Boxes and Carriage Trucks must only be conveyed by the trains specified on Week-days and not by any ordinary train without the consent of the Divisional Superintendent being first obtained.

WATERLOO AND CITY RAILWAY.

For particulars of the train service, etc., on the Waterloo and City Railway, see Public Time Table.

ARRANGEMENTS FOR SUPPLYING COAL AND STORES TO INTERMEDIATE SIGNAL BOXES, &c.

Station from which Goods are sent.	Signal Box or Crossing.	Means of Conveyance.	Station from which Goods are sent.	Signal Box or Crossing.	Means of Conveyance.
Tisbury...	Quarry Crossing ...	4.20 a.m. Freight from Yeovil Junction.	Crediton ...	Salmon Pool Gates ...	By Porter.
" ...	Tisbury Gates ...	7. 0 a.m. Freight from Salisbury.	Yeoford ...	Coleford Junction ...	6.0 a.m. Freight from Exmouth Junction.
			Umberleigh ...	Umberleigh Gates ...	By Porter.
Sherborne ...	Lenthay Crossing	9.20 a.m. Freight from Templecombe.	Barnstaple Jc.	Westcott's Crossing ...	Fetched by Gateman.
"	Wyke Crossing		" Town	Pettington Levl Crosing	3.54 p.m. Freight from Barnstaple Junction.
Crewkerne ...	Hardington ...	10.15 p.m. Freight from Friary	" "	Pottington Signal Box	
" ...	Crewkerne Crsng Gates	9.50 a.m. " " Yeovil Jc.	" "	C'mercial Rd Crsng Gtes	Fetched by Gateman.
" ...	Hewish ...	9.50 a.m. " "	Wrafton ...	Duckpool Crossing	11.15 a.m. Freight from Ilfracombe.
Chard Junc. ...	Broom Crossing ...	8.15 a.m. " " Yeovil Jc.	Braunton ...	Vellator Crossing	
" " ...	Axe Gates ...	8.15 a.m. " " "	" ...	Georgeham Crossing	10.19 a.m. Freight from Barnstaple Junction.
Axminster ...	Axminster Gates ...	10.15 p.m. " " Friary.	" ...	Stoney Bridge Gates	
Honiton ...	Honiton Incline ...	10.15 a.m. " " Friary.	" ...	Heddon Mill ...	
			Okehampton	Meldon Quarry ...	By a suitable train.
			" ...	Meldon Junction ...	8.55 a.m. Freight from Yeof'd
Sidmouth Junc.	Gosford Gates ...	9.10 a.m. Freight from Sidmouth Jct.	Ashbury ...	Venn Down Gates ...	6.57 a.m. Freight from Bude.
Ottery St. Mary	Cadhay Gates ...	By Porter.	Bodmin ...	Nanstallon Gates ...	By a suitable train.
Broad Clyst ...	Crannaford Gates ...	9. 2 a.m. Freight from Exmth Junction Sidings.	" ...	Boscarne Junction ...	2.5 p.m. Mixed from Bodmin
			Friary ..	Cattewater Junction ...	2.45 p.m. Freight from Friary

PERMANENT SPEED RESTRICTIONS.—For particulars see separate announcements.

154247—A*

90

OKEHAMPTON, BUDE AND NORTH CORNWALL LINE.

Summer Service, 17th July to 9th September only.

Distance m.	c.	m.	c.	DOWN TRAINS. WEEK-DAYS.	11.59 p.m. Freight and Mail, Exmouth Jc. Sidings. A arr.	dep.	Freight and Mail. ★ arr.	dep.			Freight. ★ arr.	dep.	Pass. arr.	dep.	Pass. arr.	dep.	3.26 a.m. Freight Exmouth Jc. Sidings. arr.	dep.
					a.m.	a.m.	a.m.	a.m.			a.m.	a.m.	a.m.	a.m.	a.m.	a.m.	a.m.	a.m.
				Okehampton	3A10	4 0	...	4 32	...	...	...	6 2	...	...	...	...	6 40	7 20
2	52			Meldon Junction	4	14	4	46	...	...	6	16	...	...	...	...	7	34
4	70			Maddaford Moor H.	...	...	...	...	...	...	...	...	...	...	...	...	...	...
8	51			Ashbury	4	29	5	1	...	...	6	31	...	...	...	...	7x49	8 22
12	36			Halwill	4 37	...	5 9	...	...	...	6 40	...	...	...	...	...	8 32	...
...	...	...	...	Halwill	...	...	...	5 12	...	...	...	...	...	...	...	8 15	...	8 48
15	65	3	29	Dunsland Cross	...	...	5 21	5 22	...	...	...	...	...	...	8 21	8 22	8 58	9 10
20	30	7	74	Holsworthy	...	...	5 32	5 50	...	...	...	...	...	...	8x30	8 32	9x22	9 39
25	27	12	71	Whitstone and Bridgerule	...	...	6	1★	...	...	...	...	...	...	8 40	8 41	9 49	10x10
...	...	13	38	Whitstone Brick Siding	...	...	...	...	...	...	...	...	...	...	...	...	10 12	10 22
30	73	18	37	**Bude**	...	...	6 12	...	...	...	...	...	...	...	8 50	...	10 31	...
...	...			Halwill	...	5 21	...	...	...	...	...	6 50	...	...	...	...	...	...
17	41			Ashwater	5 31	5 34	...	...	...	...	6	59	...	...	...	...	...	...
21	18			Tower Hill	...	...	...	...	...	...	7	6	...	...	...	...	...	...
26	18			Launceston	5 50	...	...	...	...	...	7x15	8 38	...	7 45	...	...	...	...
30	36			Egloskerry	...	...	...	...	...	...	8★53	9 0	7 53	7 54	...	...	...	...
34	08			Tresmeer	...	...	...	...	...	...	9	13	8 2	8 3	...	...	...	...
38	78			Otterham	...	...	...	...	...	...	9 30	9x54	8 12	8 13	...	...	...	...
43	34			Camelford	...	...	...	...	...	...	10 x6	10 48	8 21	8 22	...	...	...	...
45	63			Delabole	...	...	...	...	...	...	10 ●54	12x18	8 27	8 28	...	...	...	...
49	44			Toms Siding	...	...	...	...	...	...	...	...	...	...	...	...	...	...
49	71			Port Isaac Road	...	...	...	...	...	...	12x28	12 45	8 35	8 36	...	...	...	...
52	42			St. Kew Highway	...	...	...	...	...	...	12 51	1 x5	8 40	8 41	...	...	...	...
56	51			**Wadebridge**	...	...	...	...	...	...	1 16	...	8 48	8x52	...	...	...	...
62	23			**Padstow**	...	...	...	...	...	...	...	...	9 1	...	...	...	...	...

DOWN TRAINS. WEEK-DAYS	S O Freight. arr.	dep.			N S Pass. ¶ arr.	dep.			S O Pass. arr.	dep.			Pass. B arr.	dep.	Freight. C arr.	dep.
	a.m.	a.m.			a.m.	a.m.			a.m.	a.m			a.m.	a.m.	a.m.	a.m.
Okehampton	...	...	...	...	...	10 0	...	...	...	10 0	...	...	...	...	...	10 10
Meldon Junction	...	...	...	...	10	9	...	...	10	9	...	...	...	...	10	24
Maddaford Moor H.	...	...	...	...	10 13	10 14	...	...	10 13	10 14	...	...	...	...	...	...
Ashbury	...	...	...	...	10 21	10 23	...	...	10 21	10 23	...	...	...	...	10x39	10 51
Halwill	...	...	...	...	10 29	...	...	...	10 29	...	...	...	...	...	11x 1	...
Halwill	...	...	...	...	...	...	...	...	...	...	...	...	...	10 39	...	...
Dunsland Cross	...	...	...	...	...	...	...	...	...	...	...	...	10 45	10 46	...	...
Holsworthy	...	...	...	...	...	...	...	...	...	...	...	...	10x54	10B57	...	...
Whitstone and Bridgerule	...	...	...	...	...	...	...	...	...	...	...	...	11 7	11B 8	...	...
Whitstone Brick Siding	...	...	...	...	...	...	...	...	...	...	...	...	...	...	...	...
Bude	...	...	...	...	...	...	...	...	...	...	...	...	11B17	...	...	...
Halwill	...	...	...	...	x	10 32	...	...	x	10 32	...	...	...	...	...	11 25
Ashwater	...	...	...	...	10 39	10 40	...	...	10 39	10 40	...	...	...	...	11 35	11C50
Tower Hill	...	...	...	...	10 46	10 47	...	...	10 46	10 47	...	...	...	...	12C 0	12 10
Launceston	...	...	...	...	10x55	10 58	...	...	10 55	11x 1	...	...	...	...	12C20	1 35
Egloskerry	...	...	...	...	11 5	11 6	...	...	11 8	11 9	...	...	...	...	1 ●47	2x26
Tresmeer	...	...	...	...	11 13	11 14	...	...	11 16	11 17	...	...	...	...	2 40	2x50
Otterham	...	...	...	...	11 23	11 24	...	...	11 26	11x30	...	...	...	...	3x 8	3 38
Camelford	...	...	...	...	11 31	11 32	...	...	11 37	11 38	...	...	...	...	3x50	4 ●30
Delabole	...	...	...	...	11 ●37	11 38	...	...	11 ●43	11 44	...	...	...	...	4 36	4 56
Toms Siding	...	11 32	...	...	...	...	...	...	...	...	...	...	...	...	...	...
Port Isaac Road	11 35	...	...	...	11 44	11 45	...	...	11 50	11 51	...	...	...	...	5x 6	5 25
St. Kew Highway			...	...	11x49	11 50	...	...	11x54	11 55	...	...	...	...	5 ●32	5 50
Wadebridge	...	...	...	...	11 56	12 0	...	...	12 1	12 5	...	...	...	...	6 2	...
Padstow	...	...	...	...	12 9	...	...	...	12 14	...	...	...	...	...	...	...

A—On Mondays start from Exmouth Jct. 12.38 a.m. and arrive Okehampton 3.20 a.m. B—Runs five minutes later from Holsworthy to Bude on Saturdays. C—On Saturdays, depart Ashwater 12.8 p.m. and run 18 minutes later than shown to Launceston.

51

OKEHAMPTON, BUDE AND NORTH CORNWALL LINE.

Summer Service, 17th July to 9th September only.

DOWN TRAINS. WEEK-DAYS.	NS		NS				NS		SO				SO		NS	
	Pass.		Freight.		Pass. ¶		Pass.		Pass.				10.45 a.m. Pass. Waterloo.		10.35 a.m. Pass Waterloo.	
	arr.	dep.	arr.	dep.	arr.	dep.	arr.	dep.	arr.	dep.			arr.	dep.	arr.	dep.
	p.m.	noon	p.m.	p.m.	p.m.	p.m.	p.m.	p.m.	p.m.	p.m.			p.m.	p.m.	p.m.	p.m.
Okehampton ...	...	...	...	...	...	1 0	...	...	...	1 14	...	...	...	...	...	...
Meldon Junction...	...	...	...	...	1	9	...	...	1	23	...	...	2 58	3 1	2 58	3 1
Maddaford Moor H	...	...	...	...	1 13	1 14	...	...	1 27	1 28	...	...	...	...	...	...
Ashbury	...	...	...	...	1x21	1 22	...	...	1x36	1 37	...	...	3	9	X 3	9
Halwill	...	...	...	...	1 28	...	...	...	1 44	...	...	...	3	15	3 15	...
Halwill ...	...	12 0	...	...	...	...	...	1 32	...	1 45	...	...	...	...	...	3 25
Dunsland Cross	12 6	12 7	...	...	...	...	1 38	1 39	1 51	1 52	...	...	...	...	3	30
Holsworthy	12 15	12 17	...	...	...	...	1 47	1 48	2x 0	2 6	...	...	...	...	3x36	3 38
Whitstone and Bridgerule ...	12 25	12 26	...	...	...	...	1x56	1 57	2x14	2 15	...	...	...	...	3 46	3 47
Bude	12 35	...	...	...	...	...	2 6	...	2 24	...	...	...	...	...	3 56	...
Halwill	...	...	...	...	...	1 36	...	...	...	...	...	...	...	...	...	3 20
Ashwater	...	...	...	...	1 43	1 44	...	...	...	...	...	...	3	22	3	28
Tower Hill	...	...	...	...	1 50	1 51	...	...	...	...	...	...	3	26½	3	32½
Launceston	...	...	...	...	1 59	2x 1	...	...	...	...	...	...	3x33	3 39	3 39	3x41
Egloskerry	...	...	...	...	2 ●9	2 10	...	...	...	...	...	...	3	46½	3	48½
Tresmeer	...	...	...	...	2x17	2 18	...	...	...	...	...	...	3	53½	3	55½
Otterham	...	...	...	...	2 27	2 28	...	...	...	...	...	...	4 3	4 5	4x 5	4 11
Camelford...	...	...	...	...	2 35	2 36	...	...	...	...	...	...	4 13	4 17	4 ●18	4 22
Delabole	...	...	...	...	2 41	2 42	...	...	...	...	...	...	4 22	4 23	4 27	4 29
Toms Siding.........	...	...	...	2 13	...	...	...	...	...	...	...	...	...	...	...	...
Port Isaac Road ...	...	...	2 16	2 30	2x49	2 51	...	...	...	...	...	...	4 30	4 32	4 36	4 37
St. Kew Highway	...	...	2x37	2 42	2 55	2 56	...	...	...	...	...	...	4	36	4	41
Wadebridge ...	...	...	2 52	...	3x 3	3 17	...	...	...	...	...	...	4 44	4 48	4 47	4 51
Padstow...........	...	...			3 31	...	...	...	...	...	...	...	4 57	...	5 0	...

DOWN TRAINS. WEEK-DAYS.	SO				NS		SO		NS				SO		Th. & SO	
	11.0 a.m. Pass. Waterloo.		11.0 a.m. Pass. Waterloo.		Pass.		Pass.		3.0 p.m. Pass. Waterloo.				3.0 p.m. Pass. Waterloo.		Pass.	
	arr.	dep.	arr.	dep.	arr.	dep.	arr.	dep.	arr.	dep.			arr.	dep.	arr.	dep.
	p.m.	p.m.	p.m.	p.m.	p.m.	p.m.	p.m.	p.m.	p.m.	p.m.			p.m.	p.m.	p.m.	p.m.
Okehampton ...	...	3 17	...	3 43	...	5 52	...	6 27	...	7 40	...	...	...	7 47	...	...
Meldon Junction...	3	26	3	52	6	1	6	36	7	49	...	...	7	56	...	...
Maddaford Moor H	...	...	3 56	3 57	6 5	6 6	...	...	7 53	7 54	...	...	8 0	8 1	...	...
Ashbury	3	34	4 4	4 5	6X13	6 14	6x45	6 46	8x 2	8 3	...	...	8x 9	8 10	...	...
Halwill	3	40	4x11	...	6 20	...	6 52	...	8 10	...	...	...	8 17	...	...	...
Halwill	...	...	...	4 21	...	6 30	...	6 56	...	8 17	...	...	...	8 24	...	...
Dunsland Cross	x 3	44	4x27	4 28	6 36	6 36½	7 2	7 3	8 23	8 24	...	...	8 30	8 31	...	...
Holsworthy	3x50	3 52	4x36	4 38	6 44½	6 45½	7 11	7 12	8 32	8 33	...	...	8 39	8 40	...	9 37
Whitstone and Bridgerule ...	4 0	4 1	4 46	4 47	6 53½	6 54	7x20	7 21	8 41	8 42	...	...	8 48	8 49	9 45	9 46
Bude	4 10	...	4 56	...	7 3	...	7 30	...	8 51	...	...	...	8 58	...	9 55	...
Halwill	...	...	...	4 16	...	6 25	...	7 0	...	8 13	...	...	...	8 20	...	...
Ashwater	...	...	4x23	4 24	6x33	6 34	7 8	7 8½	8x21	8 22	...	...	8x28	8 29	...	...
Tower Hill	...	...	4 30	4 31	6 40	6 41	7 14½	7 15	8 28	8 29	...	...	8 35	8 36	...	...
Launceston	...	...	4x39	4 45	6 49	6 52	7x23	7 24	8 37	...	...	...	8 44	8 46	...	...
Egloskerry	...	...	4 53	4 54	7x 0	7 6	7x32	7 33	...	...	...	...	8 54	8 55	...	...
Tresmeer	...	...	5 1	5 2	7x13	7 14	7 40	7 41	...	...	...	...	9 2	9 3	...	...
Otterham	...	...	5 11	5 12	7 23	7 24	7 50	7 51	...	...	...	...	9 12	9 13	...	...
Camelford...........	...	...	5 19	5 20	7 31	7 32	7 58	7 59	...	...	...	...	9 20	9 21	...	...
Delabole	...	...	5x25	5 26	7 37	7 38	8 4	8 5	...	...	...	...	9 26	...	...	...
Toms Siding.........	...	...	...	...	...	...	...	...	...	...	...	...			...	...
Port Isaac Road ...	...	...	5x33	5 34	7 45	7 46	8 12	8 13	...	...	...	...	...	...	...	...
St. Kew Highway	...	...	5 ●38	5 39	7 50	7 51	8 17	8 18	...	...	...	...	...	...	...	...
Wadebridge	...	...	5 46	6x 0	7 58	8 0	8 25	8 27	...	...	...	...	...	...	...	...
Padstow	...	...	6 9	...	8 9	...	8 36	...	...	...	...	...	...	...	...	...

DOWN TRAINS. WEEK-DAYS.				Q						SO	NS			NS	SO	
	Engine.	7.27 a.m. Pass. Bodmin.	7.45 a.m. Pass. Launceston.	Empty.	Mixed.	10.0 a.m. Pass. Okehampton.	Mixed.	2.5 p.m. Pass. Bodmin.	1.0 p.m. Okehampton Mixed.	10.45 a.m. Pass. Waterloo.	10.35 a.m. Pass. Waterloo.	11.0 a.m. Pass. Waterloo.	6.37 p.m. Pass. Bodmin.	5.52 p.m. Pass. Okehampton.	6.27 p.m. Pass. Okehampton.	8.45 p.m. Pass. Bodmin.
	B			D		C										
	a.m.	a.m.	a.m.	a.m.	a.m.	noon.	p.m.	p.m.	p.m.	p.m.	p.m.	p.m.	p.m.	p.m.	p.m.	p.m.
Wadebridge dep.	7 36	7 48	8 52	9 20	9 50	12 0	1 40	2 30	3 22	4 48	4 51	6 0	7 0	8 0	8 27	9 9
Padstow ... arr.	7 45	7 57	9 1	9 30	10 4	12 9	1 54	2 39	3 36	4 57	5 0	6 9	7 9	8 9	8 36	9 18

B—Engine for 8.35 a.m. from Padstow. C—On Saturdays only, run 5 minutes later. D—Runs on second and fourth Mondays monthly, and Cattle Sale days at Wadebridge. Wadebridge and Padstow to arrange.

52

NORTH CORNWALL, BUDE AND OKEHAMPTON LINE.

Summer Service, 17th July to 9th September only.

Distance.		UP TRAINS. WEEK-DAYS.									NS				SO			
			Freight.		Pass.		Pass.				Pass. Waterloo.				Pass. Waterloo.			
			A		B		C											
			arr.	dep.	arr.	dep.	arr.	dep.			arr.	dep.			arr.	dep.		
m	c.		a.m.	a.m.	a.m.	a.m.	a.m.	a.m.			a.m.	a.m.			a.m.	a.m.		
...	...	**Padstow**	...	...	...	...	...	8 35	...	...	...	9 40	...	...	...	...	...	...
5	52	**Wadebridge**......	...	...	...	...	8x44	8 49	...	...	9 49	9 53	...	...	...	...	...	...
9	61	St. Kew Highway	...	...	...	...	8 57	8 58	...	...	10	0	...	...	...	...	...	...
12	32	Port Isaac Road ...	...	...	...	...	9 5	9 7	...	...	10 7	10 9	...	...	...	...	...	...
16	40	Delabole	...	...	...	...	9 16	9 18	...	...	10 18	10 19	...	...	...	...	...	...
18	69	Camelford..........	...	...	...	...	9 24	9 27	...	...	10x25	10 29	...	...	...	...	...	...
23	25	Otterham	...	...	...	...	9x35	9 37	...	...	10 37	10 39	...	...	...	...	...	...
28	15	Tresmeer	...	...	...	...	9 44	9 46	...	...	10	46	...	...	...	...	...	...
31	67	Egloskerry	...	...	...	...	9 52	9 53	...	...	10	51½	...	...	...	...	...	...
36	10	Launceston	...	...	...	7 39	10 0	10 4	...	...	10x58	11 0	...	...	...	...	...	...
41	10	Tower Hill	...	...	7 47	7 48	10 12	10 13	...	...	11	7	...	...	...	...	...	...
44	59	Ashwater	...	...	7 55	7 56	10 20	10 21	...	...	11	13	...	...	...	...	...	...
49	67	Halwill	...	...	8 6	...	10 31	...	...	...	11 22	...	...	...	...	...	...	...
...	...	m c. **Bude**	...	6 57	...	7 20	...	9 40	...	...	...	10 38	...	...	...	10 40	...	...
...	...	5 46 Whitstone ...	7	10	7 31	7 32	9x51	9 52	...	...	10	48	...	...	10	50	...	...
...	...	10 43 Holsworthy ...	7 x 20	11●10	7●41	7 48	10 ●1	10 3	...	...	10x56	10 ●58	...	...	10 58	11X 1	...	...
...	...	15 08 Dunsland Cross	11 24	11 47	7 52	7 53	10 12	10 13	...	...	11	5	...	...	11	8	...	...
...	...	18 37 Halwill	11 57	...	8 0	...	10 20	...	...	...	11 12	...	...	...	...	...	...	...
...	...	Halwill	...	12 30	...	8 9	x	10 39	...	...	x	11 28	...	...	11	15	...	...
53	52	Ashbury	12x46	1A33	8x18	8 19	10x48	10 50	...	...	...	...	...	...	...	...	...	...
57	38	Maddaford Moor H.	...	...	8 27	8 28	10 58	10 59	...	...	...	...	...	...	...	...	...	...
59	51	Meldon Junction...	1	50A	B 8	34	11	5	...	...	11	47	...	...	11	36	...	...
62	23	**Okehampton** ...	1A56	...	8B 38	...	11 9	C	...	...	11 51	11 56	...	...	11 40	11 56	...	...
...	...	**Waterloo**	...	...	2 9	...	3 46	...	...	...	4 14	...	...	...	4 21	...	...	...

UP TRAINS WEEK-DAYS.	SO		NS		SO						SO				NS	
	Pass. Waterloo.		Pass.		Freight.				Freight.		Pass.				Pass.	
									★E							
	arr.	dep.	arr.	dep.	arr	dep.			arr.	dep.	arr	dep.			arr.	dep.
	a.m.	a.m.	p.m.	p.m.	a.m.	a.m.			a.m.	a.m.	p.m.	p.m.			p.m.	p.m.
Padstow..........	...	10 25	...	...	...	...	...	...	...	...	...	...	...	...	...	...
Wadebridge......	10 34	10 39	...	...	...	...	...	...	...	11E35	...	...	...	...	...	...
St. Kew Highway	10	47	...	...	...	...	...	...	11E48	12 2	...	...	...	...	...	...
Port Isaac Road ...	10 55	10 57	...	...	...	11 15	...	...	12E12	12X30	...	...	...	...	...	...
Toms Siding.........	...	...	...	...	11 18	...	...	...	...	...	...	...	...	...	...	...
Delabole	11 x 6	11 8	...	...			...	...	12 44	1 0	...	...	...	...	...	...
Camelford...........	11 14	11 20	...	...	...	...	...	...	1 ●10	1 38	...	...	...	...	...	...
Otterham	11x28	11 32	...	...	...	...	...	...	1 49	2 5	...	...	...	...	...	...
Tresmeer	11	39	...	...	...	...	...	...	2X16	2 41	...	...	...	...	...	...
Egloskerry	11	44½	...	...	...	...	...	...	2 52	3 2	...	...	...	...	...	...
Launceston	11 51	11 54	...	...	...	...	...	...	3 ●14	3x53	...	...	...	...	...	...
Tower Hill	12	1	...	...	...	...	...	...	4 2	4 12	...	...	...	...	...	...
Ashwater	12	7	...	...	...	...	...	...	4x22	4 35	...	...	...	...	...	...
Halwill	...	...	...	...	...	...	...	...	4 50	...	...	...	...	...	...	...
Bude	...	...	...	12 40	...	...	...	...	...	...	...	1 40	...	...	...	1 44
Whitstone and Bridgerule ...	...	...	12x51	12 52	...	...	...	...	...	...	1 51	1 52	...	...	1x55	1 58
Holsworthy ...	...	...	1 1	1 2	...	...	...	...	...	...	2 1	2x 5	...	...	2 7	2 8
Dunsland Cross	...	...	1 11	1 12	...	...	...	...	...	...	2 14	2 15	...	...	2 17	2 18
Halwill	...	...	1 19	...	...	...	...	...	...	...	2 22	...	...	...	2 25	...
Halwill	12	15	...	...	...	...	...	...	...	6X21	...	2 24	...	...	...	...
Ashbury	...	...	...	...	...	...	...	...	6x 36	6 59	...	...	...	...	...	...
Maddaford Moor H.	...	...	...	...	...	...	...	...	...	...	...	...	...	...	...	...
Meldon Junction ...	12	34	...	...	...	...	...	...	7	16	2	43	...	...	...	...
Okehampton ...	12	37	...	...	...	...	...	...	7 22	...	2 47	3 26	...	...	...	...
Waterloo	4 38	...	...	...	...	...	...	...	...	...	7 30	...	...	...	...	...

A—On Saturdays run 5 minutes later from Ashbury to Okehampton. B—Call at Meldon platform on Saturdays to take up the wives of Company's servants proceeding to Okehampton. Arrive Okehampton 8.42 a.m. on Saturdays. On Saturdays only, arrival time at Waterloo 1.41 p.m. C—Mondays to Fridays only, 17th July to 8th September, depart Okehampton 11.14 a.m. for Exeter. E—On Saturdays only, depart Wadebridge 10.50 a.m., pass St. Kew Highway 11.2 a.m. and arrive Port Isaac Road 11.11 a.m. Thence as shown.

NORTH CORNWALL, BUDE AND OKEHAMPTON LINE.

Summer Service, 17th July to 9th September only.

UP TRAINS WEEK-DAYS.	Pass. A		N S Freight.		Freight to Exmouth Jct. Sdgs. F ★		S O Pass.		N S Pass.		Pass.		N S Perishable Temple-combe. B		N S Pass.	
	arr.	dep.	arr.	dep.	arr.	dep.	arr.	dep.	arr.	dep.	arr.	dep.	arr.	dep.	arr.	dep.
	p.m.	p.m.	p.m.	p.m.	p.m.	p.m.	p.m.	p.m.	p.m.	p.m.	p.m.	p.m.	p.m.	p.m.	p.m.	p.m.
Padstow	...	12 38	...	...	...	...	...	...	...	...	...	2 17	...	...	...	...
Wadebridge	12 47	12 52	...	1 20	...	...	...	...	...	...	2 26	2 31	...	3B24	...	...
St. Kew Highway	1 x0	1 1	1 30		...	...	...	...	...	...	2x39	2 41	3 32	3 33	...	...
Port Isaac Road	1 8	1 10	1 41	1 50	...	...	...	...	...	...	2X48	2 50	3 39	3 44	...	...
Toms Sidings	...	...	1 53	...	...	...	...	...	...	...	...	...	...	...	...	...
Delabole	1 19	1 20			...	...	...	...	...	...	2 59	3 0	3 52		...	...
Camelford	1●26	1 28	...	...	...	...	...	...	...	...	3 6	3 7	3X58	4 2	...	...
Otterham	1 36	1 37	...	...	...	...	...	...	...	...	3x15	3 16	4x10	4 14	...	...
Tresmeer	1 44	1 45	...	...	...	...	...	...	...	...	3 23	3 24	4 21	4 23	...	...
Egloskerry	1x51	1 52	...	...	...	...	...	...	...	...	3 30	3 31	4 29	4 30	...	...
Launceston	1x59	2 3	...	...	...	...	...	...	...	...	3x38	3●43	4x37	4 44	...	...
Tower Hill	2 11	2 12	...	...	...	...	...	...	...	...	3 51	3 52	...	...	...	...
Ashwater	2 19	2 20	...	...	...	...	...	...	...	...	3 59	4 0	4 56	4 58	...	...
Halwill	2 30	...	...	...	...	...	...	...	...	...	4 10	...	5 7	...	...	...
Bude	...	...	...	...	...	2F7	...	3 10	...	3 15	...	...	...	...	...	5 30
Whitstone and Bridgerule	...	...	...	...	2F22	2 50	3 21	3 22	3 26	3 27	...	...	...	...	5 41	5 42
Holsworthy	...	...	...	...	2x59	3●58	3●31	3 33	3X36	3●43	...	...	...	...	5 51	5 53
Dunsland Cross	...	...	...	...	4x11	4 32	3X42	3 45	3 52	3 54	...	...	...	...	6 2	6 3
Halwill	...	...	...	...	4 42	...	3 52	...	4 1	...	...	...	...	...	6 10	...
Halwill	...	2 34	...	...	...	5x55	...	...	...	...	x	4 15	...	5 17	...	...
Ashbury	2 43	2 44	...	...	6x10	6 15	...	...	...	...	4 24	4 25	...	...	...	...
Maddaford Moor H.	2 52	2 53	...	...	...	...	...	...	...	...	4 33	4 34	...	...	...	...
Meldon Junction	2 59		...	...	6 30		...	...	...	...	4 40		5 39		...	...
Okehampton	3 3	...	...	...	6 35		...	...	...	...	4 44	...	5 43	5 50	...	...
Waterloo	8A41	...	...	...	...	...	...	...	...	...	10 9	...	...	...	...	...

UP TRAINS. WEEK-DAYS.	S O Pass.		Freight Salisbury C		N S Pass.		S O Pass.		N S Pass. and Mail.		S O Pass. and Mail.		Th. S O Pass.		S O Empty.	
	arr.	dep.	arr.	dep.	arr.	dep.	arr.	dep.	arr.	dep.	arr.	dep.	arr.	dep.	arr.	dep.
	p.m.	p.m.	p.m.	p.m.	p.m.	p.m.	p.m.	p.m.	p.m.	p.m.	p.m.	p.m.	p.m.	p.m.	p.m.	p.m.
Padstow	...	...	...	...	...	...	...	...	...	5 48	...	5 48	...	...	...	...
Wadebridge	...	...	...	5 0	...	...	...	...	5x57	6 5	5x57	6 5	...	...	...	...
St. Kew Highway	...	...	5 11		...	...	...	...	6x13	6 15	6x13	6 15	...	...	...	...
Port Isaac Road	...	...	5x21	5 40	...	...	...	...	6 22	6 24	6 22	6 24	...	...	...	...
Toms Siding	...	...	...	...	...	...	...	...	...	...	...	...	...	...	...	...
Delabole	...	...	5 54	6 11	...	...	...	...	6x33	6 34	6x33	6 34	...	...	...	9 35
Camelford	...	...	x6 20		...	...	...	...	6 40	6 42	6 40	6 42	...	...	9 40	
Otterham	...	...	6●32	7 0	...	...	...	...	6●50	6 51	6●50	6 51	...	...	9 47	
Tresmeer	...	...	7 10	7 15	...	...	...	...	6 58	6 59	6 58	6 59	...	...	9 54	
Egloskerry	...	...	x7 24C		...	...	...	...	7 x 5	7 7	7x 5	7 7	...	...	10 0	
Launceston	...	...	7C35	7 54	...	...	...	...	7x14	7●20	7x14	7 25	...	...	10 7	...
Tower Hill	...	...	8 5	8 15	...	...	...	...	7 26	7 29	7 31	7 34	...	...		
Ashwater	...	...	8x25	8 35	...	...	...	...	7 36	7 38	7 41	7 43	...	...	...	...
Halwill	...	...	8 50	...	...	...	...	...	7 48	...	7 53	...	...	...	...	...
Bude	...	5 48	...	...	...	7 4	...	7 8	...	...	...	...	...	9 10	...	...
Whitstone and Bridgerule	5 59	6 0	...	...	7 15	7 16	7x19	7 22	...	...	...	...	9 21	9 22	...	...
Holsworthy	6 9	6 10	...	...	7 25	7 26	7 31	7 32	...	...	...	...	9 31	...	...	...
Dunsland Cross	6 19	6 20	...	...	7 35	7 36	7 41	7 42	...	...	...	...			...	...
Halwill	6 27	...	...	...	7 43	...	7 49	...	...	...	...	...	...	...	...	...
Halwill	...	...	...	9 5	...	...	...	...	...	7 52	...	7 57	...	...	...	...
Ashbury	...	...	9 20		...	...	...	...	8x 1	8 4	8x 6	8 11	...	...	...	...
Maddaford Moor H.	...	...	...	...	...	...	...	...	8 12	8 14	8 19	8 20	...	...	...	...
Meldon Junction	...	...	9 34		...	...	...	...	8 20		8 27		...	...	...	...
Okehampton	...	...	9 40	10 10	...	...	...	...	8 24	...	8 31	...	...	...	...	...
Waterloo	...	...	...	...	...	...	...	...	...	...	...	...	...	...	...	...

UP TRAINS. WEEK-DAYS.	Pass. Bodmin.	Pass. Okehampton.	Pass.	N S Pass. Waterloo.	Q Mixed. D	S O Pass. Waterloo.	Freight.		Pass. Okehampton.	Pass. Okehampton.	Pass. Bodmin. B	Pass. and Mail Okehampton.		Pass.	Pass. Bodmin.		Pass.	Pass.
	a.m.	a.m.	a.m.	a.m.	a.m.	a.m.	a.m.		p.m.	p.m.	p.m.	p.m.		p.m.	p.m.		p.m.	p.m.
Padstow ... dep.	8 2	8 35	9 12	9 40	10 20	10 25	11 20		12 38	2 17	2 52	5 48		6 32	7 47		8 40	9 30
Wadebridge arr.	8 11	8 44	9 21	9 49	10 34	10 34	11 34	...	12 47	2 26	3 1	5 57	...	6 41	7 56	...	8 49	9 39

A—On Fridays and Saturdays arrive Waterloo 7.30 p.m. B—Vehicles containing perishable traffic from Padstow will be attached to the 2.52 p.m. to Wadebridge, and there attached to the perishable train. C—On Saturdays arrive Egloskerry 7.25 p.m., depart 7.34 p.m., and arrive Launceston 7.45 p.m. D—Runs the second and fourth Mondays in each month and cattle sale days at Wadebridge only. Wadebridge and Padstow to arrange. F—On Saturdays depart Bude 1.55 p.m. and run 12 minutes earlier to Whitstone and Bridgerule.

OKEHAMPTON, BUDE AND NORTH CORNWALL LINE.

Winter Service, commencing 11th September.

Distance m.	Distance c.	DOWN TRAINS. WEEK-DAYS.	11.59 p.m. Freight and Mail, Exmouth Jc. Sidings. A		Freight and Mail. ★		N M Q 4.15 a.m. Fish Empties Exeter.		Freight. ★		Pass.		Pass.		3.25 a.m. Freight Exmouth Jc. Sidings.	
			arr.	dep.	arr.	dep.	arr.	dep.	arr.	dep.	arr.	dep.	arr.	dep.	arr.	dep.
			a.m.	a.m.	a.m.	a.m.	a.m.	a.m.	a.m.	a.m.	a.m.	a.m.	a.m.	a.m.	a.m.	a.m.
...	...	Okehampton	3A10	4 0	...	4 32	5 13	5 40	...	6 2	...	...	...	...	6 40	7 20
2	52	Meldon Junction	4 14		4 46		5 49		6 16		...	...	...	...	7 34	
4	70	Maddaford Moor H.	...	...	...	...	...	...	...	...	...	...	...	...	...	...
8	51	Ashbury	4 29		5 1		5 58		6 31		...	...	...	...	7X49	8 22
12	36	Halwill	4 37	...	5 9	...	...	...	6 40	...	...	...	...	...	8 32	...
...	...	(m. c.) ... ... Halwill	...	...	...	5 12	...	...	...	...	...	...	...	8 15	...	8 48
15	65	3 29 Dunsland Cross	...	...	5 21	5 22	...	...	...	...	...	...	8 21	8 22	8 58	9 10
20	30	7 74 Holsworthy	...	...	5 32	5 50	...	...	...	...	...	...	8X30	8 32	9X22	9 39
25	27	12 71 Whitstone and Bridgerule	...	...	6 1★		...	...	...	...	...	...	8 40	8 41	9 49	10X10
...	...	13 38 Whitstone Brick Siding	...	...	...	...	...	...	...	...	...	...	...	...	10 12	10 22
30	73	18 37 Bude	...	...	6 12	...	...	...	...	...	...	...	8 50	...	10 31	...
...	...	Halwill	...	5 21	...	...	6 5		...	6 50	...	...	...	...	...	...
17	44	Ashwater	5 31	5 34	...	...	6 15		6 59		...	...	...	...	...	...
21	18	Tower Hill	...	...	...	...	...	...	7 6		...	...	...	...	...	...
26	13	Launceston	5 50	...	...	...	6 28	6 40	7X15	8 38	...	7 45	...	...	...	...
30	36	Egloskerry			...	...	6 48		8★53	9 0	7 53	7 54	...	...	...	...
34	08	Tresmeer			...	...	6 55		9 13		8 2	8 3	...	...	...	...
38	78	Otterham	...	...	...	...	7 4		9 30	9X54	8 12	8 13	...	...	...	...
43	34	Camelford	...	...	...	...	7 11		10X 6	10 48	8 21	8 22	...	...	...	...
45	63	Delabole	...	...	...	...	7 16		10●54	12 18	8 27	8 28	...	...	...	...
49	44	Toms Siding	...	...	...	...	...	...	...	...	...	...	...	...	...	...
49	71	Port Isaac Road	...	...	...	...	7 23		12X28	12 45	8 35	8 36	...	...	...	...
52	42	St. Kew Highway	...	...	...	...	7 27		12 51	1X 5	8 40	8 41	...	...	...	...
56	51	Wadebridge	...	...	...	...	7 34	7 37	1 16	...	8 48	8X52	...	...	...	...
62	23	Padstow	...	...	...	...	7 46	...	...	...	9 1	...	...	...	...	...

DOWN TRAINS. WEEK-DAYS.	S O Freight.		Pass. C		Pass.		N S Freight.		Freight.		Pass.		11.0 a.m. Pass. Waterloo.		Pass.		3.0 p.m. Pass. Waterloo. B	
	arr.	dep.	arr.	dep.	arr.	dep.	arr.	dep.	arr.	dep.	arr.	dep.	arr.	dep.	arr.	dep.	arr.	dep.
	a.m.	a.m.	a.m.	a.m.	a.m.	a.m.	p.m.	p.m.	a.m.	a.m.	p.m.	p.m.	p.m.	p.m.	p.m.	p.m.	p.m.	p.m.
Okehampton	...	...	...	10 0	...	...	...	...	...	10 10	...	...	...	3 43	...	5 52	...	7 40
Meldon Junction	...	...	10 9		...	...	...	...	10 24		...	...	3 52		6 1		7 49	
Maddaford Moor H.	...	...	10 13	10 14	...	...	...	...	...	...	...	...	3 56	3 57	6 5	6 6	7 53	7 54
Ashbury	...	...	10 21	10 23	...	...	...	...	10X39	10 51	...	...	4 4	4 5	6X13	6 14	8X 2	8 3
Halwill	...	...	10 29	...	...	...	...	...	11 1	...	...	...	4 11	...	6 20	...	8 10	...
Halwill	...	...	...	...	...	10 39	...	...	...	...	...	2 35	...	4 21	...	6 30	...	8 17
Dunsland Cross	...	...	...	...	10 45	10 46	...	...	...	...	2 41	2 42	4X27	4 28	6 36	6 36½	8 23	8 24
Holsworthy	...	...	...	...	10X54	10 57	...	...	...	...	2 50	2 51	4 36	4 38	6 44½	6 45½	8 32	8 33
Whitstone and Bridgerule	...	...	...	...	11 7	11 8	...	...	...	...	2 59	3 0	4 46	4 47	6 53½	6 54	8 41	8 42
Whitstone Brick Siding	...	...	...	...	...	...	...	...	...	...	...	...	...	...	...	...	...	...
Bude	...	...	...	...	11 17	...	...	...	...	...	3 9	...	4 56	...	7 3	...	8 51	...
Halwill	...	...	X	10 32	...	...	...	...	...	11 25	...	...	...	4 16	...	6 25	...	8 13
Ashwater	...	...	10 39	10 40	...	...	...	...	10 35	10 50	...	...	4X23	4 24	6X33	6 34	8X21	8 22
Tower Hill	...	...	10 46	10 47	...	...	...	...	12 0	12 10	...	...	4 30	4 31	6 40	6 41	8 28	8 29
Launceston	...	...	10 55	10 58	...	...	...	...	12 20	1 35	...	...	4X39	4 45	6 49	6 52	8 37	8B39
Egloskerry	...	...	11 5	11 6	...	...	...	...	1●47	2X26	...	...	4 53	4 54	7X 0	7 6	8 47	8 48
Tresmeer	...	...	11 13	11 14	...	...	...	...	2 40	2X50	...	...	5 1	5 2	7X13	7 14	8 55	8 56
Otterham	...	...	11 23	11 24	...	...	...	...	3 8	3 38	...	...	5 11	5 12	7 23	7 24	9 6	9 6
Camelford	...	...	11 31	11 32	...	...	...	...	3X50	4●30	...	...	5 19	5 20	7 31	7 32	9 13	9 14
Delabole	...	...	11●37	11 38	...	...	...	...	4 36	4 56	...	...	5X25	5 26	7 37	7 38	9B19	...
Toms Siding	...	11 32	...	...	...	...	...	2 13	...	...	...	...	...	...	...	...		
Port Issac Road	11 35	...	11 44	11 45	...	...	2 16	2 30	5 6	5 25	...	...	5X33	5 34	7 45	7 46	...	...
St. Kew Highway			11X49	11 50	...	...	2 37	2 42	5 32	5 50	...	...	5●38	5 39	7 50	7 51	...	...
Wadebridge	...	...	11 56	12 0	...	...	2 52	...	6 2	...	...	...	5 46	6X 0	7 58	8 0	...	...
Padstow	...	...	12 9	...	...	...					...	...	6 9	...	8 9	...	...	...

DOWN TRAINS. WEEK-DAYS.	Q 4.15 a.m. Fish Empties Exeter.	Eng. C	7.27 a.m. Pass. Bodmin.	7.45 a.m. Pass. Launceston.	Q Empty. E	Mixed.	10.0 a.m. Pass. Okehampton.	Mixed.	2.5 p.m. Pass. Bodmin. D	4.23 p.m. Pass. Bodmin.	3.43 p.m. Pass. Okehampton.	6.37 p.m. Pass. Bodmin.	5.52 p.m. Pass. Okehampton.	8.45 p.m. from Bodmin.
	a.m.	a.m.	a.m.	a.m.	a.m.	a.m.	noon	p.m.	p.m.	p.m.	p.m.	p.m.	p.m.	p.m.
Wadebridge ...... dep.	7 37	7 36	7 48	8 52	9 30	9 50	12 0	1 40	2 30	4 44	6 0	7 0	8 0	9 9
Padstow ...... arr.	7 46	7 45	7 57	9 1	9 40	10 4	12 9	1 54	2 39	4 53	6 9	7 9	8 9	9 18

A—On Mondays start from Exmouth Jct. 12.38 a.m. and arrive Okehampton 3.20 a.m. B—Runs to Delabole on Saturdays only. C—Engine for the 8.35 a.m. from Padstow. Pilots Fish Empties when running. D—Commencing 11th September. E—Runs on second and fourth Mondays monthly, and Cattle Sale days at Wadebridge. Wadebridge and Padstow to arrange.

NORTH CORNWALL, BUDE AND OKEHAMPTON LINE.

Winter Service, commencing 11th September.

Distance. m.	c.	UP TRAINS. WEEK-DAYS.	Freight. arr.	Freight. dep.	Pass. A arr.	Pass. A dep.	Pass. arr.	Pass. dep.	S O Freight. arr.	S O Freight. dep.	Freight. ★ B arr.	Freight. ★ B dep.	Pass. arr.	Pass. dep.	Pass. arr.	Pass. dep.	N S Freight. arr.	N S Freight. dep.
			a.m.	a.m.	a.m.	a.m.	a.m.	a.m.	a.m.	a.m.	a.m.	a.m.	p.m.	p.m.	p.m.	p.m.	p.m.	p.m.
...	...	Padstow	...	...	...	...	...	8 35	...	...	...	...	...	...	...	12 38	...	...
5	52	Wadebridge	...	...	...	...	8X44	8 49	...	...	...	11B35	...	...	12 47	12 52	...	1 20
9	61	St. Kew Highway	...	...	...	...	8 57	8 58	...	...	11B48	12 2	...	...	1X0	1 1	1	30
12	32	Port Isaac Road	...	...	...	...	9 5	9 7	...	11 15	12B12	12X30	...	...	1 8	1 10	1 41	1 50
...	...	Toms Siding	...	...	...	...	...	...	11 18	...	...	...	...	...	...	...	1 53	...
16	40	Delabole	...	...	...	...	9 16	9 18			12 44	1 0	...	...	1 19	1 20		
18	69	Camelford	...	...	...	...	9 24	9 27	...	...	1●10	1 38	...	...	1●26	1 28	...	...
23	25	Otterham	...	...	...	...	9X35	9 37	...	...	1 49	2 5	...	...	1 36	1 37	...	...
28	15	Tresmeer	...	...	...	...	9 44	9 45	...	...	2X16	2 41	...	...	1 44	1 45	...	...
31	67	Egloskerry	...	...	...	...	9 52	9 53	...	...	2 52	3 2	...	...	1X51	1 52	...	...
36	10	Launceston	...	...	...	7 39	10 0	10 4	...	...	3●14	3 53	...	...	1X59	2 3	...	...
41	10	Tower Hill	...	...	7 47	7 48	10 12	10 13	...	...	4 2	4 12	...	...	2 11	2 12	...	...
44	59	Ashwater	...	...	7 55	7 56	10 20	10 21	...	...	4X22	4 35	...	...	2 19	2 20	...	...
49	67	Halwill	...	...	8 6	...	10 31	...	...	...	4 50	...	...	...	2 30	...	...	...
...	...	m. c. Bude	...	6 57	...	7 20	...	9 40	...	...	...	...	...	1 45	...	...	...	...
...	...	5 46 Whitstone	7	10	7 31	7 32	9X51	9 52	...	...	...	...	1X56	1 57	...	...	...	...
...	...	10 43 Holsworthy	7X20	11●10	7●41	7 43	10●1	10 3	...	...	...	...	2 6	2 8	...	...	...	...
...	...	15 08 Dunsland Cross	11 24	11 47	7 52	7 53	10 12	10 13	...	...	...	...	2 17	2 18	...	...	...	...
...	...	18 37 Halwill	11 57	...	8 0	...	10 20	...	...	...	...	...	2 25	...	...	...	...	...
...	...	Halwill	...	12 30	...	8 9	X	10 39	...	...	X	8 30	...	...	...	2 34	...	...
53	52	Ashbury	12 46	1 33	8X18	8 19	10X48	10 50	...	...	...	...	...	...	2 43	2 44	...	...
57	33	Maddaford Moor H.	...	...	8 27	8 28	10 58	10 59	...	...	...	...	...	...	2 52	2 53	...	...
59	51	Meldon Junction	1	50	A 8	34	11	5	...	...	8	59	...	...	2	59	...	...
62	23	Okehampton	1 56	...	8A38	...	11 9	...	...	...	9 5	...	...	...	3 3	...	...	...
...	...	Waterloo	...	...	2 9	...	4 0	...	...	...	...	...	...	...	8 41	...	...	...

UP TRAINS. WEEK-DAYS.	Freight to Exmouth Jct. Sdgs. ★ arr.	dep.	Pass. D arr.	dep.	N S Perishable and Pass. Templecombe. arr.	dep.	S O *Perishable and Pass. Okehampton.* arr.	dep.	Q *Fish.* arr.	dep.	Freight Salisbury. arr.	dep.	Pass. and Mail. arr.	dep.	Engine. arr.	dep.	S O *Empty.* arr.	dep.
	p.m.	p.m.	p.m.	p.m.	p.m.	p.m.	p.m.	p.m.	p.m.	p.m.	p.m.	p.m.	p.m.	p.m.	p.m.	p.m.	p.m.	p.m.
Padstow	...	...	...	...	...	2 55	...	2 55	...	4 30	...	...	...	5 48	...	...	...	...
Wadebridge	...	...	...	...	3 4	3 16	3 4	3 16	4 39	4 44	...	5 0	5X57	6 5	...	...	...	...
St. Kew Highway	...	...	...	...	3 25	3 26	3 25	3 26	4	53	5	11	6X13	6 15	...	...	...	...
Port Isaac Road	...	...	...	...	3 33	3 38	3 33	3 38	5X0	5 15	5X21	5 40	6 22	6 24	...	...	...	...
Toms Siding	...	...	...	...	...	...	...	...	...	...	...	...	...	...	...	...	...	...
Delabole	...	...	...	...	3 47	3 49	3 47	3 49	5X24	5●35	5 54	6 11	6X33	6 34	...	...	...	9 30
Camelford	...	...	...	...	3 55	3 59	3 55	3 59	5	41	X6	20	6 40	6 42	...	...	9	35
Otterham	...	...	...	...	4 7	4 12	4 7	4 12	5	48	6●32	7 0	6●50	6 51	...	...	9	42
Tresmeer	...	...	...	...	4 19	4 21	4 19	4 21	5	55	7 10	7 15	6 58	6 59	...	...	9	49
Egloskerry	...	...	...	...	4 27	4 28	4 27	4 28	6	5	X7	24	7X5	7 7	...	...	9	55
Launceston	...	...	...	...	4X35	4 41	4X35	4 41	6 12	6 14	7 35	7 54	7X14	7●20	...	...	10 2	...
Tower Hill	...	...	...	...	4 49	4 50	4 49	4 50	...	...	8 5	8 15	7 26	7 29	...	...		
Ashwater	...	...	...	...	4 57	4 59	4 57	4 59	6X28	6 35	8X25	8 35	7 36	7 38	...	...	...	...
Halwill	...	...	...	...	5 8	...	5 8	...	6	46	8 50	...	7 48	...	...	...	...	...
Bude	...	2 0	...	3 18	Conveys passengers between Padstow and Exeter only.		*Conveys passengers between Pastow and Okehampton*		...	...	...	...	...	7 4	...	7 30	...	...
Whitstone and Bridgerule	2 12	2 40	3 29	3 30					...	...	...	...	7 15	7 16	...	...	...	...
Holsworthy	2X49	3●58	3 39	3●46					...	...	...	...	7 25	7 26	...	...	...	...
Dunsland Cross	4X11	4 32	3 55	3 56					...	...	...	...	7 35	7 36	...	...	...	...
Halwill	4 42	...	4 3	...					...	...	...	...	7 43	...	8 8	...	...	...
Halwill	...	5X55	D	4X13	...	5 18	...	5 18	...	...	...	9 5	...	7 52	...	...	...	...
Ashbury	6X10	6 15	4 22	4 23	5 30	5 31	5 30	5 31	...	...	9	20	8X1	8 4	...	...	...	...
Maddaford Moor H.	...	...	4 31	4 32	...	...	...	...	...	...	...	...	8 12	8 14	...	...	...	...
Meldon Junction	6	30	4	38	5	42	5	42	7	5	9	34	8	20	...	...	...	...
Okehampton	6	35	4D42	...	5 46	5 50	5 46	...	7 9	7 26	9 40	10 10	8 24	...	...	...	...	...
Waterloo	...	...	10 9	...	...	...	...	...	...	...	...	...	...	...	...	...	...	...

UP TRAINS. WEEK-DAYS.	Pass. Bodmin.	Pass. Okehampton.	Pass.	Q *Mixed.* C	Freight.	Pass. Okehampton.	Perishable and Pass.	Q *Fish.*	Pass. Bodmin.	Pass. and Mail Okehampton.	Pass.	Pass. Bodmin.	Pass.	Pass.
	a.m.	a.m.	a.m.	a.m.	a.m.	p.m.	p.m.	p.m.	p.m.	p.m.	p.m.	p.m.	p.m.	p.m.
Padstow ... dep.	8 5	8 35	9 12	10 20	11 20	12 38	2 55	4 30	4 58	5 48	6 32	7 47	8 40	9 30
Wadebridge ... arr.	8 14	8 44	9 21	10 34	11 34	12 47	3 4	4 39	5 7	5 57	6 41	7 56	8 49	9 39

A—Call at Meldon platform on Saturdays to take up the wives of Company's servants proceeding to Okehampton. Arrive Okehampton 8.42 a.m. on Saturdays. B—On Saturdays only, depart Wadebridge 10.50 a.m., pass St. Kew Highway 11.2 a.m. and arrive Port Isaac Road 11.11 a.m. Thence as shown. C—Runs on the second and fourth Mondays in each month and cattle sale days at Wadebridge only. Wadebridge and Padstow to arrange. D—Conveys vacuum fitted vehicles containing Market traffic from Halwill to Okehampton.

56

OKEHAMPTON, BUDE AND NORTH CORNWALL LINE.

Timing No.	297		297				310		309		309		309		307	
DOWN TRAINS. SUNDAYS.	*Engine.*		*Half-Day Excursion Plymouth.*				*Half-Day Excursion Plymouth.*		*Engine.*		*9.30 a.m. Half-Day Excursion Yeovil.* A		*Half-Day Excursion Yeovil.*		*Half-Day Excursion Salisbury.*	
	arr.	dep.	arr.	dep.			arr.	dep.	arr.	dep.	arr.	dep.	arr.	dep.	arr.	dep.
	a.m.	a.m.	a.m.	a.m.			a.m.	a.m.	p.m.	noon	p.m.	p.m.	p.m.	p.m.	p.m.	p.m.
Okehampton	...	...	...	11 30	...	...	...	11 35	...	12 0	12A15	12 21	...	...	1 10	1 25
Meldon Junction	...	...	11	39	...	...	11	44	12	9	12	30	...	...	1	34
Maddaford Moor H.	...	...	...	...	...	...	...	...	...	...	...	...	...	...	...	...
Ashbury	...	...	11	47	...	...	11	52	12	17	12	38	...	...	1	42
Halwill	...	...	11 53	...	...	...	11 58	...	12 33	...	12 44	...	...	...	1 48	...
Halwill	...	...	...	11 55	...	...	...	12 0	...	...	...	...	12 44	12 50	...	1 50
Dunsland Cross	...	...	12	0	...	...	12	5	...	...	...	...	12	55	1	55
Holsworthy	...	...	12 6	12 8	...	...	12 11	12 13	...	...	...	...	1 1	1 3	2 1	2 3
Whitstone and Bridgerule	...	...	12	15	...	...	12	20	...	...	...	...	1	10	2	10
Bude	...	...	12 24	...	...	...	12 29	...	...	...	...	...	1 19	...	2 19	...
Halwill	...	10 45			...	...					...	12 46				
Ashwater	10	53			...	...					12	54				
Tower Hill	...	...			...	...					...	...				
Launceston	11 6	...			...	...					1 6	1 8				
Egloskerry					...	...					1	16				
Tresmeer					...	...					1	23				
Otterham					...	...					1	32				
Camelford					...	...					1 39	1 40				
Delabole					...	...					1 45	1 46				
Toms Siding					...	...					...	...				
Port Isaac Road					...	...					1 53	1 54				
St. Kew Highway					...	...					1	58				
Wadebridge					...	...					2 5	2 7				
Padstow					...	...					2 16	...				
	6th AUGUST and 3rd SEPTEMBER ONLY.		6th AUGUST and 3rd SEPTEMBER ONLY.				30th JULY, 27th AUGUST and 24th SEPTEMBER ONLY.		23rd JULY, 20th AUGUST and 17th SEPTEMBER ONLY.		23rd JULY, 20th AUGUST and 17th SEPTEMBER ONLY.		23rd JULY, 20th AUGUST and 17th SEPTEMBER ONLY.		16th JULY, 13th AUGUST and 10th SEPTEMBER ONLY.	

Timing No.	356		316 & 318		317 & 318				360		297				297	
DOWN TRAINS. SUNDAYS.	*Return Half-Day Excursion Paignton and Exeter.* B		*Return Half-Day Excursion from Paignton and Ilfracombe.*		*Return Half-Day Excursion Plymouth and Ilfracombe.*				*Return Half-Day Excursion Bristol.*		*Return Half-Day Excursion B'mouth.*				*Return Half-Day Excursion from B'mouth.*	
	arr.	dep.	arr.	dep.	arr.	dep.			arr.	dep.	arr.	dep.			arr.	dep.
	p.m.	p.m.	p.m.	p.m.	p.m.	p.m.			p.m.	p.m.	p.m.	p.m.			p.m.	p.m.
Okehampton	...	...	10 7	10 13	...	10 20	...	...	10 44	10 50	...	11 30	...	...	...	...
Meldon Junction	9	7	10	22	10	29	...	...	10	59	11	39	...	...	...	...
Maddford Moor H.	...	...	...	...	...	...	...	...	...	...	...	...	...	...	...	...
Ashbury	9X16	9B18	10 31	10 32	10 38	10 39	...	...	11 8	11 9	11 48	11 49	...	...	...	...
Halwill	9 25	...	10 39	...	10 46	...	...	...	11 16	...	11 56	...	...	...	...	...
Halwill	...	...	...	10 41	...	10 48	...	...	...	11 18	...	11 58	...	...	...	...
Dunsland Cross	...	...	10 47	10 48	10 54	10 55	...	...	11 24	11 25	12 4	12 5	...	...	...	...
Holsworthy	...	...	10 56	10 58	11 3	11 5	...	...	11 33	11 35	12 13	12 15	...	...	...	...
Whitstone and Bridgerule	...	...	11 6	11 7	11 13	11 14	...	...	11 43	11 44	12 23	12 24	...	...	...	...
Bude	...	...	11 16	...	11 23	...	...	...	11 53	...	12 33	...	...	...	...	...
Halwill	...	9 26					...	...					...	...	...	12 5
Ashwater	9 33	9 34					...	...					...	...	12 13	12 14
Tower Hill	9 40	9 41					...	...					...	...	12 20	12 21
Launceston	9 49	9 50					...	...					...	...	12 29	...
Egloskerry	9 58	9 59					...	...					...	...		
Tresmeer	10 6	10 7					...	...					...	...		
Otterham	10 16	10 17					...	...					...	...		
Camelford	10 24	10 25					...	...					...	...		
Delabole	10 30	10 31					...	...					...	...		
Toms Siding	...	...					...	...					...	...		
Port Isaac Road	10 38	10 39					...	...					...	...		
St. Kew Highway	10 43	10 44					...	...					...	...		
Wadebridge	10 51	10 53					...	...					...	...		
Padstow	11 2	...					...	...					...	...		
	23rd JULY, 20th AUGUST and 17th SEPTEMBER ONLY.		16th JULY, 13th AUGUST and 10th SEPTEMBER ONLY.		30th JULY, 27th AUGUST and 24th SEPTEMBER ONLY.				23rd JULY, 20th AUGUST and 17th SEPTEMBER ONLY.		6th AUGUST and 3rd SEPTEMBER ONLY.				6th AUGUST and 3rd SEPTEMBER ONLY.	

A—Change enginemen at Okehampton with men working 10.10 a.m. H.D. Excursion from Padstow, due 12.18 p.m.
B—Change enginemen at Ashbury with men working 7.25 p.m. Return H.D. Excursion from Padstow, due 9.12 p.m.

57

NORTH CORNWALL, BUDE AND OKEHAMPTON LINE.

Timing No.	297				317 & 318				316 & 318				360				356	
UP TRAINS. SUNDAYS.	*Half-Day Excursion to B'mouth.*				*Half-Day Excn. to Plymouth and Ilfracombe.*				*Half-Day Excn. to Paignton and Ilfracombe.*				*Half-Day Excursion to Bristol.*				*Half-Day Excn. to Paignton and Exeter.*	
	C				BC				C				C				A	
	6th AUGUST and 3rd SEPTEMBER ONLY.				30th JULY, 27th AUGUST and 24th SEPTEMBER ONLY.				16th JULY, 13th AUGUST and 10th SEPTEMBER ONLY.				23rd JULY, 20th AUGUST and 17th SEPTEMBER ONLY.				23rd JULY, 20th AUG. and 17th SEPT. ONLY.	
	arr.	dep.			arr.	dep.			arr.	dep.			arr.	dep.			arr.	dep.
	a.m.	a.m.			a.m.	a.m.			a.m.	a.m.			a.m.	a.m.			a.m.	a.m.
Padstow			...	...			...	...			...	...			...	...	...	10 10
Wadebridge			...	...			...	...			...	...			...	...	10 19	10 21
St. Kew Highway			...	...			...	...			...	...			...	...	10 30	10 31
Port Isaac Road			...	...			...	...			...	...			...	...	10 38	10 39
Toms Siding			...	...			...	...			...	...			...	...	...	...
Delabole			...	...			...	...			...	...			...	...	10 48	10 49
Camelford			...	...			...	...			...	...			...	...	10 55	10 56
Otterham			...	...			...	...			...	...			...	...	11 4	11 5
Tresmeer			...	...			...	...			...	...			...	...	11 12	11 13
Egloskerry			...	...			...	...			...	...			...	...	11 19	11 20
Launceston	...	10 5	...	...			...	...			...	...			...	...	11 27	11 28
Tower Hill	10 13	10 14	...	...			...	...			...	...			...	...	11 36	11 36½
Ashwater	10 21	10 22	...	...			...	...			...	...			...	...	11 43½	11 44
Halwill	10 32	...	...	...			...	...			...	...			...	...	11 54	...
Bude	...	10 0	...	...	...	10 0	...	...	...	10 0	...	...	...	10 0	...	...		
Whitstone and Bridgerule	10 11	10 12	...	...	10 11	10 12	...	...	10 11	10 12	...	...	10 11	10 12	...	...		
Holsworthy	10 21	10 23	...	...	10 21	10 23	...	...	10 21	10 23	...	...	10 21	10 23	...	...		
Dunsland Cross	10 32	10 33	...	...	10 32	10 33	...	...	10 32	10 33	...	...	10 32	10 33	...	...		
Halwill	10 40	...	...	...	10 40	...	...	...	10 40	...	...	...	10 40	...	...	...		
Halwill	...	10 43	...	...	...	10 43	...	...	...	10 43	...	...	...	10 43	...	...	...	11 55
Ashbury	10 52	10 54	...	...	10 52	10 54	...	...	10 52	10 54	...	...	10 52	10 54	...	...	...	...
Maddaford Moor Halt	...	...	...	...	...	...	...	...	...	...	...	...	...	...	...	...	...	...
Meldon Junction	11	7	...	...	11	7	...	...	11	7	...	...	11	7	...	...	12	14
Okehampton	11 11	...	...	...	11 11	B	...	...	11 11	11 16	...	...	11 11	11 16	...	...	12A18	12 21

Timing No.	297				307		310				309		309				297	
UP TRAINS. SUNDAYS.	*Return Half-Day Excursion to Plymouth.*				*Return Half-Day Excursion Bude to Salisbury.*		*Return Half-Day Excursion Bude to Plymouth.*				*Return Half-Day Excursion to Yeovil.*		*Engine.*				*Engine.*	
	—		—		—		—				D		—				—	
	6th AUGUST and 3rd SEPTEMBER ONLY.				16th JULY, 13th AUGUST and 10th SEPTEMBER ONLY.		30th JULY, 27th AUGUST, and 24th SEPTEMBER ONLY.				23rd JULY, 20th AUGUST and 17th SEPTEMBER ONLY.		23rd JULY, 20th AUGUST and 17th SEPTEMBER ONLY.				6th AUGUST and 3rd SEPTEMBER ONLY.	
	arr.	dep.			arr.	dep.	arr.	dep.			arr.	dep.	arr.	dep.			arr.	dep.
	p.m.	p.m.			p.m.	p.m.	p.m.	p.m.			p.m.	p.m.	p.m.	p.m.			p.m.	p.m.
Padstow			...	...					...	...	...	7 25			...	...		
Wadebridge			...	...					...	...	7 34	7 36			...	...		
St. Kew Highway			...	...					...	...	7	45			...	...		
Port Isaac Road			...	...					...	...	7 52	7 53			...	...		
Toms Siding			...	...					...	...	...	...			...	...		
Delabole			...	...					...	...	8 2	8 3			...	...		
Camelford			...	...					...	...	8 9	8 10			...	...		
Otterham			...	...					...	...	8	18			...	...		
Tresmeer			...	...					...	...	8	25			...	...		
Egloskerry			...	...					...	...	8	30½			...	...		
Launceston			...	...					...	...	8 37	8 39			...	...	...	11 30
Tower Hill			...	...					...	...	8	46			...	...	...	...
Ashwater			...	...					...	...	8	52			...	...	11	45
Halwill			...	...					...	...	9 1	...			...	...	11 55	...
Bude	...	7 20	...	...	...	7 25	...	8 20	...	...	...	8 10	*Works 10.50 p.m. from Okeh'mpton to Bude.*		...	...	*Works 12.5 Midn't. Halwill to Launceston.*	
Whitstone and Bridgerule	7 31	7 32	...	...	7 36	7 37	8 31	8 32	...	...	8 21	8 22			...	...		
Holsworthy	7 41	7 43	...	...	7 46	7 48	8 41	8 43	...	...	8 31	8 33			...	...		
Dunsland Cross	7 52	7 53	...	...	7 57	7 58	8 52	8 53	...	...	8 42	8 43			...	...		
Halwill	8 0	...	...	...	8 5	...	9 1	...	...	...	8 50	...			...	...		
Halwill	...	8 2	...	...	...	8 6	...	9 2	...	...	...	9 3	...	9 20	...	...	...	...
Ashbury	...	...	...	...	...	...	...	...	...	...	9X12	9D19	...	...	...	...	...	...
Maddaford Moor Halt	...	...	...	...	...	...	...	...	...	...	...	...	...	...	...	...	...	...
Meldon Junction	8	21	...	...	8	25	9	21	...	...	9	31	9	49	...	...	...	...
Okehampton	8 25	E	...	...	8 29	8 48	9 25	...	...	...	9 35	9 37	9 53	...	...	...	...	...

A—Stop at Okehampton not to be advertised. Change enginemen at Okehampton with men working 9.30 a.m. H.D. Excursion from Yeovil due 12.15 p.m.
B—Plymouth Line passengers go forward by 11.3 a.m. ordinary train from Yeoford.
C—Available for ordinary passengers to connect at Okehampton with 10.25 a.m. Plymouth to Waterloo, etc.
D—Change enginemen at Ashbury with men working Return H.D. Excursion from Exeter due 9.16 p.m.
E—Passengers to go forward by 7.26 p.m. ordinary from Exeter.

Working Timetable

supplied by Peter Richards

1947

2

INDEX.

REFERENCES.

X Indicates crosses another Train on the Single Line.

● Indicates shunts for, or passes another Train.

A Train marked thus "§" at the top of a column or at any Station, indicates that a special instruction applies to it, for particulars of which see Freight Train Working notes.

¶ / ¶¶ } Improved Running Schedules for Passenger Trains. See page 5 for particulars.

——→ For continuation, see subsequent column.

←—— Continued from a previous column.

CS—Stop when required.
MO—Mondays only.
MX—Mondays excepted.
MFO—Mondays and Fridays only.
MWO—Mondays and Wednesdays only.
MWX—Mondays and Wednesdays excepted.
MTFO—Mondays, Tuesdays and Fridays only.
TO—Tuesdays only.
TX—Tuesdays excepted.
TWThO—Tuesdays, Wednesdays & Thursdays only.
TThO—Tuesdays and Thursdays only.
TThX—Tuesdays and Thursdays excepted.
WO—Wednesdays only.
WX—Wednesdays excepted.
WSO—Wednesdays and Saturdays only.
WThSO—Wednesdays, Thursdays & Saturdays only.
WSX—Wednesdays and Saturdays excepted.
ThO—Thursdays only.
ThX—Thursdays excepted.
ThSO—Thursdays and Saturdays only.
FO—Fridays only.
FX—Fridays excepted.
FSO—Fridays and Saturdays only.
FSX—Fridays and Saturdays excepted.
SO—Saturdays only.
SX—Saturdays excepted.
†—Empty Train.
‖—Light Engine.
Q—Conditional train.
✖—Engines of trains marked thus will work through from Exeter Central to Waterloo.
◆—Worked by G.W. Company's engine.
★—Push and Pull train.

The timings shown on this page WILL NOT APPLY ON SATURDAYS, 21st June to 20th September, 1947.

OKEHAMPTON, BUDE AND NORTH CORNWALL LINE.

Distance m.	c.	DOWN TRAINS. WEEK-DAYS.	Mixed. arr.	Mixed. dep.	arr.	dep.	arr.	dep.	arr.	dep.	¶ arr.	¶ dep.
			a.m.	a.m.	a.m.	a.m.	a.m.	a.m.	a.m.	a.m.	a.m.	a.m.
...	...	**Okehampton**	...	6 37							...	9 56
2	52	Meldon Junction	6 51								10 4	
4	70	Maddaford Moor H.	...	...							10 8	10 9
8	51	Ashbury	7 6	7 6½							10 16	10 18
12	36	Halwill	7 16½	...							10X24	...
...	...	m. c. ... ... Halwill				7 25				8 53		10 39
15	65	3 29 Dunsland C.			7 31	7 31½			8 59	9 0	10 45	10 46
20	30	7 74 Holsworthy			7 38½	7 40			9 8	9 10	10X54	10 59
25	27	12 71 Whitstone & B.			7 48	7 49			9 18	9 19	11X 7	11 8
30	72	18 37 **Bude**			7 58				9 28		11 17	
...	...	Halwill	...	7 31½							...	10 30
17	44	Ashwater	7 41½	7 42							10 37	10 38
21	13	Tower Hill	7 52	7 53							10 44	10 45
26	13	Launceston	8 3					8 34			10X52	10 56
30	36	Egloskerry					8 42	8 43			11 3	11 4
34	08	Tresmeer					8 51	8 52			11X11	11 12
38	78	Otterham					9 1	9 3			11 21	11 24
43	34	Camelford					9X11	9 14			11 31	11 33
45	63	Delabole					9 19	9 20			11 38	11 39
49	71	Port Isaac Road					9 27	9 28			11 45	11 46
52	42	St. Kew Highway					9 32	9 33			11 50	11 51
56	51	**Wadebridge**					9X40	9 50			11 57	12 1
62	23	**Padstow**					10 4				12 10	...

DOWN TRAINS. WEEK-DAYS.	arr.	dep.	SO arr.	SO dep.	¶ arr.	¶ dep.	¶ arr.	¶ dep.	¶ arr.	¶ dep.
	p.m.	p.m.	p.m.	p.m.	p.m.	p.m.	p.m.	p.m.	p.m.	p.m.
Okehampton	...	1 20	...	...	...	3 55	...	5 51	...	8 14
Meldon Junction	1 29				4 4		5 59		8 22	
Maddaford Moor H.	1 33	1 33½			4 8	4 10	6 3	6 4	8 26	8 27
Ashbury	1 39½	1 40			4X17	4 20	6X11	6 15	8 34	8 35
Halwill	1 46	...			4 27	...	6 21	...	8 42	...
Halwill		1 48				4 35		6 27		8 50
Dunsland Cross	1 54	1 55			4 41	4 42	6 33	6 33½	8 56	8 57
Holsworthy	2X 3	2 5			4 50	4 51	6 41½	6 42½	9 5	9 6
Whitstone & B'rule	2X13	2 16			4 59	5 0	6 50½	6 51	9 14	9 15
Bude	2 25				5 9		7 0		9 24	
Halwill			...	*1 53*	...	4 30	...	6 24	...	8 45
Ashwater			*2 0*	*2 1*	4 37	4 38	6 31	6 32	8 52	8 53
Tower Hill			*2 7*	*2 8*	4 44	4 45	6 38	6 39	8 59	9 0
Launceston			*2 15*		4X52	4 56	6 46	6 49	9 7	
Egloskerry					5 3	5 4	6 56	6 57		
Tresmeer					5 11	5 12	7X 4	7 5		
Otterham					5 21	5 22	7 14	7 15		
Camelford					5 29	5 32	7 22	7 22½		
Delabole					5 37	5 39	7 27½	7 28		
Port Isaac Road					5 46	5 48	7 34	7 34½		
St. Kew Highway					5 52	5 54	7 38½	7 39		
Wadebridge					6X 1	6 12	7 45	7 47		
Padstow					6 21	...	7 56	...		

DOWN TRAINS. WEEK-DAYS.	Eng.	7.22 a.m. Bodmin.		8.34 a.m. Launceston. (Mixed from Wadebridge).	9.56 a.m. Okeh'ton.		Mixed.	2.0 p.m. Bodmin. (Mixed)		4.28 p.m. Bodmin.		3.55 p.m. Okeh'ton.	6.43 p.m. Bodmin (Mixed from Wadebridge.)	5.51 p.m. Okeh'ton.	8.50 p.m. Bodmin.
	a.m.	a.m.	a.m.	a.m.	p.m.		p.m.	p.m.		p.m.		p.m.	p.m.	p.m.	p.m.
Wadebridge ...... dep.	7‖20	7 43	8 50	9 50	12 1	...	1 46	2 31	...	4 44	...	6 12	7 5	7 47	9 11
Padstow ...... arr.	7‖29	7 52	8 59	10 4	12 10	.	1 59	2 40	.	4 53	.	6 21	7 19	7 56	9 20

The timings on this page WILL NOT APPLY ON SATURDAYS, 21st June to 20th September, 1947.

NORTH CORNWALL, BUDE AND OKEHAMPTON LINE.

Distance m	c.	UP TRAINS. WEEK-DAYS.	¶ A arr.	¶ A dep.	To Exeter Ctl. ¶ arr.	To Exeter Ctl. ¶ dep.	arr.	dep.	SO Engine. arr.	SO Engine. dep.
			a.m.	a.m.	a.m.	a.m.	p.m.	p.m.	p.m.	p.m.
...	...	**Padstow**	...	...	...	8 25	...	1 0	...	...
5	52	**Wadebridge**			8 34	8 40	1 9	1 14		
9	61	St Kew Highway			8 48	8 49	1X22	1 23		
12	32	Port Isaac Road			8 55	8 56	1 29	1 31		
16	40	Delabole			9 5	9 6	1 40	1 41		
18	69	Camelford			9X12	9 15	1 47	1 48		
23	25	Otterham			9 22	9 24	1 55	1 57		
28	15	Tresmeer			9 31	9 33	2 4	2 5		
31	67	Egloskerry			9 39	9 42	2X11	2 12		
36	10	Launceston		8 22	9 49	9 58	2 19	2 25		*2‖48*
41	10	Tower Hill	8 29	8 30	10 5	10 6	2 32	2 33		
44	59	Ashwater	8 36	8 37	10 12	10 13	2 39	2 40	*3 2*	
49	67	Halwill	8 46	...	10 22	...	2 49	...	*3 12*	...
.	.	m c. **Bude**		8 0		9 35		2 3	*Change with engine of 2.3 p.m. Bude.*	
...	...	5 46 Whitstone	8 11	8 12	9 46	9 47	2X14	2 15		
.	.	10 43 Holsworthy	8 21	8 22	9 56	9 58	2 24	2 26		
...	...	15 08 Dunsland C.	8 31	8 32	10 7	10 8	2 35	2 36		
.	.	18 37 Halwill	8 39		10 16		2 43			
...	...	Halwill	...	8 49	X	10 31	...	2 55	...	*3 25*
53	52	Ashbury	8 58	8 59	10 40	10 41	3 4	3 5	*3 34*	
57	33	Maddaford Moor H.	9 6	9 7	10 49	10 50	3 12	3 13	...	...
59	51	Meldon Junction	9 13A		10 58		3 20		*3 49*	
62	23	**Okehampton**	9A17	...	11 0	11 5	3 24	...	*3‖53*	...
.	.	**Waterloo**	3 29							

UP TRAINS. WEEK-DAYS.	C arr.	C dep.	SX Perishable and Pass. Templec'be arr.	SX Perishable and Pass. Templec'be dep.	SO *Perishable and Pass. Okeh'mpton* arr.	SO *Perishable and Pass. Okeh'mpton* dep.	arr.	dep.	¶ D arr.	¶ D dep.
	p.m.	p.m.	p.m.	p.m.	p.m.	p.m.	p.m.	p.m.	p.m.	p.m.
Padstow	...	...	...	2 55	...	*3 15*	...	...	...	6 0
Wadebridge			3 4	3 20	*3 24*	*3 30*			6X 9	6 13
St. Kew Highway			3X29	3 32	*3 38*	*3 39*			6 21	6 22
Port Isaac Road			3 39	3 43	*3 46*	*3 48*			6 28	6 29
Delabole			3 52	3 54	*3 57*	*3 58*			6 38	6 39
Camelford			4 0	4 6	*4 4*	*4 6*			6 45	6 47
Otterham			4 14	4 19	*4 14*	*4 19*			6 54	6 56
Tresmeer			4 26	4 27	*4 26*	*4 27*			7X 3	7 6
Egloskerry			4 33	4 37	*4 33*	*4 37*			7 12	7 13
Launceston			4X44	4 53	*4X44*	*4 53*			7 20	7 23
Tower Hill			5 0	5 1	*5 0*	*5 1*			7 31	7 32
Ashwater			5 8	5 10	*5 8*	*5 10*			7 39	7 40
Halwill			5 19	...	*5 19*	...			7 50	...
Bude		3C13	Conveys passengers between Padstow and Exeter only.					5 30		7 2
Whitstone & B'rule	3 24	3 25					5 41	5 42	7 13	7 13½
Holsworthy	3C34	3 42					5 51	5 53	7 22½	7 25½
Dunsland Cross	3 51	3 52					6 2	6 3	7 34½	7 35
Halwill	3 59						6 10		7 42	
Halwill	...	4C 9	...	5 27	...	*5 21*			...	7 54
Ashbury	4X18	4 19	5 38	5 39	*5 30*	*5 31*			8 3	8 4
Maddaford Moor H.	4 27	4 28	...	...	...	...			8 12	8 14
Meldon Junction	4 34		5 50		*5 42*				8 20D	
Okehampton	4C38	...	5 54	5 58	*5 46*	...			8D24	...
Waterloo	10 26									

UP TRAINS. WEEK-DAYS.	To Bodmin.	To Exeter Cent.				To Okehampton		SO *To Bodmin.*	SX Pass. and Perishable Templecombe.	SO *Pass. and Perishable. Okehampton.*	To Bodmin.	To Okehampton	Eng.	To Bodmin.	Mixed.	
	a.m.	a.m.	a.m.		a.m.	p.m.		p.m.	p.m.	p.m.	p.m.	p.m.	p.m.	p.m.	p.m.	p.m.
Padstow ...... dep.	7 57	8 25	9 10	...	11 5	1 0	...	*2 55*	2E55	*3 15*	4 58	6 0	6‖35	8 2	8 40	9 30
Wadebridge ...... arr.	8 6	8 34	9 19	.	11 14	1 9	.	*3 4*	3E 4	*3 24*	5 7	6 9	6‖44	8 11	8 54	9 39

A—Call at Quarry Signal Box to take up wives of Company's employees on Saturdays, and arrive Okehampton 9.20 a.m.
C—If necessary run as a Mixed train from Bude to Holsworthy, and convey vehicles containing market traffic, Halwill to Okehampton.
D—Mondays, Wednesdays and Fridays call at Quarry Signal Box, 8.21½ to 8.23 p.m. to take up workmen, and arrive Okehampton 8.27 p.m.
E—Conveys passengers between Padstow and Exeter Central only.

SATURDAYS ONLY. The timings on this page WILL APPLY ON SATURDAYS ONLY, 21st June to 20th September, 1947, inclusive.

68

OKEHAMPTON, BUDE AND NORTH CORNWALL LINE.

DOWN TRAINS.	Q 12.20 a.m. Waterloo. arr.	dep.	Mixed. arr.	dep.	arr.	dep.	arr.	dep.	arr.	dep.	¶ arr.	dep.
	a.m.	a.m.	a.m.	a.m.	a.m.	a.m.	a.m.	a.m.	a.m.	a.m.	a.m.	a.m.
Okehampton	5 23	5 30	...	6 37	...	...	...	...	...	...	...	9 56
Meldon Junction		5 39		6 51								10 4
Maddaford Moor H.	...	...	...	...	...	...	...	...	...	...	10 8	10 9
Ashbury		5 49	7 6	7 6½							10 16	10 18
Halwill	5 54	...	7 16½	...	...	...	...	...	...	...	10X24	...
Halwill		6 8				7 25				8 53		10 39
Dunsland Cross	6 14	6 16	...	...	7 31	7 31½	...	...	8 59	9 0	10 45	10 46
Holsworthy	6 24	6 29			7 38½	7 40			9 8	9 10	10X54	10 59
Whitstone & B'rule	6 37	6 40	...	...	7 48	7 49	...	...	9X18	9 19	11 7	11 8
Bude	6 49				7 58				9 28		11 17	
Halwill	...	5 58	...	7 31½	...	...	...	...	...	...	...	10 30
Ashwater		6 5	7 41½	7 42							10 37	10 38
Tower Hill		6 11	7 52	7 53	...	...	...	...	...	...	10 44	10 45
Launceston	6 18	6 24	8 3					8 34			10X52	10 56
Egloskerry		6 31	...	...	...	...	8 42	8 43	...	...	11 3	11 4
Tresmeer		6 38					8 51	8 52			11 11	11 12
Otterham	6 47	6 50	...	...	...	...	9 1	9 3	...	...	11 21	11 24
Camelford	6 57	7 1					9X11	9 14			11 31	11 33
Delabole	7 6	7 8	...	...	...	...	9 19	9 20	...	...	11 38	11 39
Port Isaac Road	7 15	7 16					9 27	9 28			11X45	11 46
St. Kew Highway		7 21	...	...	...	...	9 32	9 33	...	...	11 50	11 51
Wadebridge	7 28	7 33					9X40	9 50			11 57	12 1
Padstow	7 42	...	...	...	...	...	10 4	...	...	...	12 10	...

DOWN TRAINS.	¶ arr.	dep.	10.20 a.m. Waterloo. arr.	dep.	¶ arr.	dep.	¶ arr.	dep.	¶ arr.	dep.
	p.m.	p.m.	p.m.	p.m.	p.m.	p.m.	p.m.	p.m.	p.m.	p.m.
Okehampton	...	1 20	...	...	...	3 55	...	5 51	...	8 14
Meldon Junction		1 29		2 54		4 4		5 59		8 22
Maddaford Moor H.	1 33	1 33½	...	...	4 8	4 10	6 3	6 4	8 26	8 27
Ashbury	1 39½	1 40		3 3X	4X17	4 20	6X11	6 15	8 34	8 35
Halwill	1 46	...	3 9	...	4 27	...	6 21	...	8 42	...
Halwill		1 48		3 18		4 35		6 27		8 50
Dunsland Cross	1 54	1 55	3 23	3 24	4 41	4 42	6 33	6 33½	8 56	8 57
Holsworthy	2X 3	2 5	3X32	3 36	4 50	4 51	6 41½	6 42½	9 5	9 6
Whitstone & B.	2X13	2 16	3 44	3 46	4 59	5 0	6 50½	6 51	9 14	9 15
Bude	2 25		3 55		5 9		7 0		9 24	
Halwill	...	1 53	...	3 13	...	4 30	...	6 24	...	8 45
Ashwater	2 0	2 1		3 20	4 37	4 38	6 31	6 32	8 52	8 53
Tower Hill	2 7	2 8		3 26	4 44	4 45	6 38	6 39	8 59	9 0
Launceston	2 15		3X31	3 38	4 52	4X56	6 46	6 49	9 7	
Egloskerry	...	...		3 45½	5 3	5 4	6 56	6 57	...	...
Tresmeer			3 53	3 55	5 11	5 12	7X 4	7 5		
Otterham	...	...	4 4	4 7	5 21	5 22	7 14	7 15	...	...
Camelford			4X14	4 18	5 29	5 32	7 22	7 22½		
Delabole	...	...	4 23	4 25	5 37	5 39	7 27½	7 28	...	...
Port Isaac Road			4 32	4 35	5 46	5 48	7 34	7 34½		
St. Kew Highway	...	...		4 39	5 52	5 54	7 38½	7 39	...	...
Wadebridge			4 45	4 51	6X 1	6 12	7 45	7 47		
Padstow	...	...	5 0	...	6 21	...	7 56	...	...	...

DOWN TRAINS.	Eng.	Q 12.20 a.m. Waterloo.	7.22 a.m. Bodmin.		8.34 a.m. Launceston. (Mixed from Wadebridge.)		9.56 a.m. Okehampton.	Mixed.	2.0 p.m. Bodmin. (Mixed).	10.20 a.m. Waterloo.	3.55 p.m. Okehampton.		6.43 p.m. Bodmin. (Mixed from Wadebridge.)	5.51 p.m. Okehampton.	8.50 p.m. Bodmin.
	a.m.	a.m.	a.m.	a.m.	a.m.		p.m.	p.m.	p.m.	p.m.	p.m.		p.m.	p.m.	p.m.
Wadebridge	7‖20	7 33	7 43	8 50	9 50	...	12 1	1 45	2 31	4 51	6 12	...	7 5	7 47	9 11
Padstow	7‖29	7 42	7 52	8 59	10 4		12 10	1 59	2 40	5 0	6 21		7 19	7 56	9 20

SATURDAYS ONLY. The timings on this page WILL APPLY ON SATURDAYS ONLY, 21st June to 20th September, 1947, inclusive.

NORTH CORNWALL, BUDE AND OKEHAMPTON LINE.

69

UP TRAINS.	A arr.	dep.	Q To Waterloo. arr.	dep.	¶ To Waterloo. arr.	dep.	To Waterloo. arr.	dep.	Engine. arr.	dep.	¶ arr.	dep.
	a.m.	a.m.	a.m.	a.m.	a.m.	a.m.	a.m.	a.m.	p.m.	p.m.	p.m.	p.m.
Padstow	...	...	...	...	...	8 25	...	11 15	...	...	...	1 0
Wadebridge				8 15	8 34	8 40	11 24	11 29			1 9	1 14
St. Kew Highway	...	...		8 23	8 48	8 49		11 37	...	...	1X22	1 23
Port Isaac Road			8 29	8 31	8 55	8 56	11X44	11 47			1 29	1 31
Delabole	...	...	8 40	8 43	9 5	9 6	11 56	11 58	...	...	1 40	1 41
Camelford			8 49	8 53	9X12	9 15	12 4	12 7			1 47	1 48
Otterham	...	...	9X 0	9 5	9 22	9 24	12 15	12 17	...	...	1 55	1 57
Tresmeer				9 12	9 31	9 33		12 24			2 4	2 5
Egloskerry	...	...		9 18	9 39	9 42		12 29½	...	...	2X11	2 12
Launceston		8 22	9 25	9 32	9 49	9 58	12 36	12 42		2‖48	2 19	2 25
Tower Hill	8 29	8 30		9 40	10 5	10 6		12 49	...	...	2 32	2 33
Ashwater	8 36	8 37	9 46	9 49	10 12	10 13		12 55		3 2	2 39	2 40
Halwill	8 46	...	9 58	...	10 22	...	1 4	...	3 12	...	2 49	...
Bude		8 0		9 5		9 35		12 15	Change with engine of 2.3 p.m. Bude.			2 3
Whitstone & B'rule	8 11	8 12	9X17	9 20	9 46	9 47	12 26	12 27			2X14	2 15
Holsworthy	8 21	8 22	9 29	9 31	9 56	9 58	12 36	12 40			2 24	2 26
Dunsland Cross	8 31	8 32		9 39	10 7	10 8	12 49	12 50			2 35	2 36
Halwill	8 39		9 46		10 15		12 57				2 43	
Halwill	...	8 49	...	10 4	...	10X31	...	1 9	...	3 25	...	2 53
Ashbury	8 58	8 59	10X14	10 19	10 40	10 41		1 17		3 34	3X 2	3 5
Maddaford Moor H.	9 6	9 7	...	...	10 49	10 50	...	...	...	...	3 12	3 13
Meldon Junction		9 13A		10 33		10 56		1 28		3 49		3 20
Okehampton	9A20	...	10 37	10 42	11 0	11 7	1 32	1 37	3‖53	...	3 24	...
Waterloo	2 29		3 25				6 6				8 38	

UP TRAINS.	¶ arr.	dep.	arr.	dep.	arr.	dep.	¶ arr.	dep.
	p.m.	p.m.	p.m.	p.m.	p.m.	p.m.	p.m.	p.m.
Padstow	...	...	...	3 15	...	...	...	6 0
Wadebridge			3 24	3 34			6X 9	6 13
St. Kew Highway	...	...	3 42	3 44	...	...	6 21	6 22
Port Isaac Road			3 51	3 54			6 28	6 29
Delabole	...	...	4 3	4 6	...	...	6 38	6 39
Camelford			4X13	4 17			6 45	6 47
Otterham	...	...	4 25	4 27	...	...	6 54	6 56
Tresmeer			4 34	4 35			7X 3	7 6
Egloskerry	...	...	4 41	4 42	...	...	7 12	7 13
Launceston			4X49	4 53			7 20	7 23
Tower Hill	...	...	5 0	5 1	...	...	7 31	7 32
Ashwater			5 8	5 10			7 39	7 40
Halwill	...	...	5 17	...	...	...	7 50	...
Bude		3 13				5 30		7 2
W'stone & B'rule	3 24	3 25	...	...	5 41	5 42	7 13	7 13½
Holsworthy	3X34	3 42			5 51	5 53	7 22½	7 25½
Dunsland Cross	3 51	3 52	...	...	6 2	6 3	7 34½	7 35
Halwill	3 59				6 10		7 42	
Halwill	...	4 9	...	5 21	...	...	...	7 54
Ashbury	4X18	4 19	5 30	5 31			8 3	8 4
Maddaford Moor H.	4 27	4 28	...	...	...	...	8 12	8 14
Meldon Junction		4 34		5 42				8 20
Okehampton	4 38	...	5 46	...	...	...	8 24	...
Waterloo	10 26							

UP TRAINS.	To Bodmin.	To Waterloo.			To W'loo.		To Okehampton.		To Bodmin.	To Okehampton.	To Okehampton.	Eng.	To Bodmin.	Mixed.	
	a.m.	a.m.	a.m.	a.m.	a.m.		p.m.		p.m.	p.m.	p.m.	p.m.	p.m.	p.m.	p.m.
Padstow dep.	7 57	8 25	9 10	11 0	11 15	...	1 0	...	2 55	3 15	6 0	6‖35	8 2	8 40	9 30
Wadebridge arr.	8 6	8 34	9 19	11 9	11 24		1 9		3 4	3 24	6 9	6‖44	8 11	8 54	9 39

A—Call at Quarry Signal Box, 9.14 to 9.15 a.m. to take up wives of Company's employees.

70

OKEHAMPTON, BUDE AND NORTH CORNWALL LINE.

DOWN TRAINS. SUNDAYS.	arr. a.m.	dep. a.m.			arr. p.m.	dep. p.m.			arr. p.m	dep. p.m.			arr. p.m.	dep. p.m.			arr. p.m.	dep. p.m.	arr. p.m.	dep. p.m.
Okehampton		11 48								4 12								9 35		
Meldon Junction	11 56								4 20								9 43			
Maddaford Moor H.	12 0	12 1							4 24	4 25							9 47	9 48		
Ashbury	12 8	12 9							4 32	4 33							9 55	9 56		
Halwill	12 15								4 39								10 2			
Halwill		12 19								4 43								10 6		
Dunsland Cross	12 25	12 26							4 49	4 50							10 12	10 13		
Holsworthy	12 34	12 36							4 58	5 0							10 21	10 23		
W'stone & B'rule	12 44	12 45							5 8	5 9							10 31	10 32		
Bude	12 54								5 18								10 41			
Halwill						12 25								4 52						10 15
Ashwater					12 32	12 33							4 59	5 0					10 22	10 23
Tower Hill					12 39	12 40							5 6	5 7					10 29	10 30
Launceston					12 47								5 14						10 37	
Egloskerry																				
Tresmeer																				
Otterham	Until 21st Sept. only.																Until 21st Sept. only.			
Camelford					Until 21st Sept. only.															
Delabole																			Until 21st Sept. only.	
Port Isaac Rd.																				
St. Kew Highway																				
Wadebridge																				
Padstow																				

UP TRAINS. SUNDAYS.	arr. a.m.	dep. a.m.	arr. a.m.	dep. a.m.			arr. p.m.	dep. p.m.	arr. p.m.	dep. p.m.			arr. p.m.	dep. p.m.			arr. p.m.	dep. p.m.	arr. p.m.	dep. p.m.
Padstow																				
Wadebridge																				
St. Kew Highway																				
Port Isaac Rd.																				
Delabole																				
Camelford													Until 21st Sept. only.				Until 21st Sept. only.			
Otterham			Until 21st Sept. only.																	
Tresmeer																				
Egloskerry																				
Launceston		9 50						2 35						6 46						
Tower Hill	9 57	9 58					2 42	2 43					6 53	6 54						
Ashwater	10 4	10 5					2 49	2 50					7 0	7 1						
Halwill	10 14						2 59						7 10							
Bude				9 45						2 35								6 42		
W'stone & B'rule			9 56	9 57					2 46	2 47							6 53	6 54		
Holsworthy			10 6	10 9					2 56	2 59							7 3	7 6		
Dunsland Cross			10 18	10 19					3 8	3 9							7 15	7 16		
Halwill	Until 21st Sept. only.		10 26						3 16								7 23			
Halwill				10 29						3 19								7 26		
Ashbury			10 38	10 39					3 28	3 29							7 34	7 35		
Maddaford Moor Halt			10 46	10 47					3 36	3 37							7 42	7 43		
Meldon Junction			10 53						3 43								7 49			
Okehampton			10 57						3 47								7 53			

110

OKEHAMPTON, BUDE AND NORTH CORNWALL LINE.

FREIGHT.													SX		SX Q		Q			
DOWN TRAINS. WEEK-DAYS.	12.1 a.m. Freight and Mail Exmouth Jct. Sdgs. A		Freight and Mail.								3.30 a.m. Exmouth Jct. Sdgs. E								§	
	arr. a.m.	dep. a.m.	arr. a.m.	dep. a.m.			arr. a.m.	dep. a.m.			arr. a.m.	dep. a.m.	arr. p.m.	dep. p.m.	arr. p.m.	dep. p.m.	arr. a.m.	dep. a.m.	arr. a.m.	dep. a.m.
Okehampton	3A10	4 0		4 37							7 40	8 10								10 10
Meldon Junction	4 14			4 51								8 24							10	24
Maddaford Moor H.																				
Ashbury	4 29		5 6	5 6½							8 39	9X 0							10X39	11 2
Halwill	4 37		5 16½								9 10								11 12	
Halwill				5 19			(Formed of 6.37 a.m. Mixed Okehampton.)					9E40							Will not run on Saturdays, 21st June to 20th Sept.	
Dunsland Cross			5 28								9E50	10X9								
Holsworthy			5 37	5 55							10E20	11 10								
Whitstone and B.			X 6	6							11 20	11 40								
Whitstone Brick Siding											11 42	11 48								
Bude			6 17								11 57									
Halwill		5 31																		11 35
Ashwater	5 41	5 44																	11 45	11 57
Tower Hill	5 52																		12 7	12 17
Launceston	6 0							9 28											12 27	1 35
Egloskerry							9X40	9 48											1X47	2 25
Tresmeer							10	2							*Will not apply when 1.5 p.m. Delabole runs.*				2 39	2 50
Otterham							10 19	10 35											3X 8	3 38
Camelford							10 47	11 15											3X50	4●30
Delabole							11●21	12X36						1 5		*1 45*			4X36	5●50
Toms Siding																				
Port Isaac Road							12 46	1 3					1X15	1 35	*1 55*	*2 15*			6X 0	6 30
St. Kew Highway							1 9	1X29					1 41	1 46	*2 21*	*2 30*			6 37	7 0
Wadebridge							1 40						1 56		*2 40*			*4 15*	7 10	
Padstow																	*4 29*			

FREIGHT.					SX										Q					
WEEK-DAYS.	F		G						§ D				To Ex'mth Jct. Sdgs. §				To Salisbury. SX Exmouth Jct. Sdgs. SO §			
	arr. a.m.	dep. a.m.	arr. a.m.	dep. a.m.	arr. a.m.	dep. a.m.			arr. a.m.	dep. a.m.			arr. p.m.	dep. p.m.	arr. p.m.	dep. p.m.	arr. p.m.	dep. p.m.		
Padstow																*3 40*				
Wadebridge						10 50				11D35					*3 54*			4 30		
St. Kew Highway					11	0			11D48	12X 0							4	40		
Port Isaac Road					11	8			12D10	12 20							4	49		
Toms Siding																				
Delabole					11 22				12X34	1 4							5 3	5 17		
Camelford									1 14	1 32							5X27	5 35		
Otterham									1 43	2 15							5 47	6 7		
Tresmeer									2 26	2 40							6	17		
Egloskerry									2 51	2 56							6	26		
Launceston									3X 8	3●48							6●38	7X57		
Tower Hill									3X58	4 5							8	7		
Ashwater									4X15	4 40							8 17	8 27		
Halwill									4 55								8 42			
Bude		5 45		8 15										1 20			Will not run on Saturdays, 21st June to 20th Sept.			
Whitstone and B.	6X 0	6 8	8 28	8 53									1 33	1 51						
Holsworthy	6	18F	9X 3	11 35									2X 1	3 53						
Dunsland Cross	6	29F	11 49	12 10									4 6	4 22						
Halwill	6F37		12 20										4●32							
Halwill				1015					X	6 50				5 58				9X 5		
Ashbury			1028	1X44					7	5			6	13X			9	20		
Maddaford Moor H.																				
Meldon Junction			2	4					7	20			6	29			9	34		
Okehampton			2 12						7 30				6	34			9 44	10 20		

A—Mondays depart Exmouth Jct. 12.38 a.m. arrive Okehampton 3.25 a.m.
D—Saturdays only, depart Wadebridge 10.50 a.m., pass St. Kew Highway 11.2 a.m., arrive Port Isaac Road 11.11 a.m.
E—Run 8 minutes later from Halwill to Holsworthy when 9.5 a.m. **Q** Pass. from Bude runs.
F—Call at Holsworthy 6X18 to 6.26 a.m., Dunsland Cross pass 6/38, Halwill arr. 6.46 a.m., when 6.8 a.m. **Q** Pass. from Halwill runs.
G—On Saturdays, 21st June to 20th September, run 3 minutes later Halwill to Ashbury.

Working Timetables
Supplied by Roger Merry Price
1952

2

For other Services see :—
Section " A "—Main Lines. } London West District.
Section " B "—Suburban Services. } London West District.
Section " C "—Isle of Wight. } London West District.
Section " D "—Southern District.
Waterloo and City Line—See Separate Time Table.
West London and Widened Lines—See Separate Time Table.
Freight Time Table—London WEST District.
Freight Time Table—SOUTHERN District.
Freight Time Table—WESTERN District.
Somerset & Dorset—See Separate Time Table.

INDEX.

REFERENCES.

CS—Stop when required.
MO—Mondays only.
MX—Mondays excepted.
TO—Tuesdays only.
TX—Tuesdays excepted.
WO—Wednesdays only.
WX—Wednesdays excepted.
ThO—Thursdays only.
ThX—Thursdays excepted.
FO—Fridays only.
FX—Fridays excepted.

SO—Saturdays only.
SX—Saturdays excepted.
W—Engine take water.
†—Empty train.
‖—Light engine.
Q—Conditional train.
■—Engines of trains marked thus will **not** be changed at Salisbury.
▲—Engines of trains marked thus will **not** be changed at Exeter Central.
◆—Worked by Western Region engine.
★—Push and Pull train.

X Indicates crosses another train on the single line.
● Indicates shunts for, or passes another train.
——→ For continuation, see subsequent column.
←—— Continued from a previous column.
Timings within brackets thus :—(8.14), indicate the previous or subsequent working of the engine or train concerned.
¶ / ¶¶ } Improved Running Schedules for Passenger Trains. See below for particulars.

Trains running on more than one day will be described by the combined initial letters thus, **MSO**—Mondays and Saturdays only.

IMPROVED RUNNING SCHEDULES FOR PASSENGER TRAINS.

Trains marked as shown below have timings arranged for the loads indicated.
These loads must not be exceeded unless absolutely necessary.

Salisbury and Exeter Line.	North Devon Line.	North Cornwall Line.
Tons. ¶ = 150, ¶¶ = 250 } Stopping trains.	Tons. ¶ = 160 Stopping trains. = 226 Fast trains.	Tons. ¶ = 128 Okehampton to Halwill, = 96 Halwill to Padstow. } Stopping trains.

Exeter and Exmouth Line.—Timings arranged for load of 166 tons, except on Sundays in Winter, when the timings apply for load of 100 tons.

GENERAL INSTRUCTIONS

3

STARTING TIMES FROM INTERMEDIATE STATIONS.—The advertised starting time from Intermediate Stations is, as a rule, slightly earlier than the booked service time and must be used in all quotations to the public. The trains must also be started at the advertised time whenever practicable.

SINGLE LINES.

The system of working on each section of single line is indicated on the pages showing distances by means of the following symbols :—

(E) One engine in steam or two or more engines coupled together.

(IK) Intermediate Key Token post (non-block post where trains not conveying passengers can be shunted for other trains to pass).

(K) Electric Key Token block post.

(P) Line worked as siding under special Appendix instructions.

(S) Electric Staff block post.

(ST) Train Staff and Ticket block post, **staff and crossing station.**

(T) Electric Tablet block post (returnable).

[T] Electric Tablet block post (non-returnable).

(TS) Electric Tablet short-section block post. (Can be closed and long-section working operate between block posts on each side).

GUARDS' JOURNALS

The throughout Journals of the undermentioned trains, and trains run as relief thereto, must be sent to the Superintendent of Operation daily, immediately after completion of the journey, also to each of the District Traffic Superintendents concerned.

Guards to report on Journals as to loading of the Passenger Trains, the number of Passengers (1st and 3rd class separately) to be given.

Certain of the following trains are detached portions. It is essential that the original train should be shown in the space provided in the top left-hand corner of the Journal.

PASSENGER TRAINS—WEEKDAYS

Time.	From	To
a.m. 1 25 ...	Waterloo ...	**Plymouth Friary.**
1 35 SO	Waterloo ...	**Ilfracombe.**
3 30 ... }	Salisbury ...	**Yeovil.**
3 40 SO }	Salisbury ...	**Yeovil.**
8 45 SO	Waterloo ...	Ilfracombe.
9 0 SO (Summer)	Waterloo ...	Sidmouth.
9 0 ...	Waterloo ...	Plymouth Friary.
9 3 SO	Portsmouth & S.	Plymouth Friary.
10 54 SO	Waterloo ...	Ilfracombe.
11 0 SO (Summer)	Waterloo ...	Plymouth Friary.
11 0SX (Summer)	Waterloo ...	Padstow.
11 0 (Winter)	Waterloo ...	Ilfracombe.
11 5 SX	Waterloo ...	Plymouth Friary.
11 30 ...	Brighton ...	Plymouth Friary.
noon 12 0 FSO	Waterloo ...	Ilfracombe.
p.m. 12 15 SO	Portsmouth & S.	Ilfracombe.
1 0 ...	Waterloo ...	Plymouth Friary.
3 0 ...	Waterloo ...	Plymouth Friary.
5 0 ...	Waterloo ...	Exeter Ctl.
6 0 ...	Waterloo ...	Plymouth Friary.

Time.	From	To
a.m. 7 30 ...	Exeter Ctl. ...	Waterloo.
8 15 ...	Plymouth Friary...	Waterloo.
9 40 ...	Padstow ...	Waterloo.
9 50(SO)	Plymouth Friary	Portsmouth & S.
10 30 ...	Ilfracombe ...	Waterloo.
11 0 ...	Plymouth Friary	Brighton.
noon 12 0 MSO	Ilfracombe ...	Waterloo.
p.m. 12 20 ...	Ilfracombe ...	Waterloo.
12 35 SO	Ilfracombe ...	Waterloo.
2 20 ...	Ilfracombe ...	Waterloo.
2 25 SO	Plymouth Friary...	Waterloo.
3 50 ...	Plymouth Friary...	Waterloo.

PASSENGER TRAINS—SUNDAYS

Time.	From	To
a.m. 1 35 ...	Waterloo ...	Yeovil.
10 45 ...	Waterloo ...	Ilfracombe.
11 0 ...	Waterloo ...	Plymouth Friary.
11 5 ...	Waterloo ...	Ilfracombe.
11 40 ...	Portsmouth & S.	Plymouth Friary.
noon 12 0 ...	Waterloo ...	Ilfracombe.
p.m. 4 0 ...	Waterloo ...	Plymouth Friary.

Time.	From	To
a.m. 9 50 ...	Ilfracombe ...	Waterloo.
10 0...	Plymouth Friary	Waterloo and Ports. & S.
noon 12 0 ...	Ilfracombe ...	Waterloo.
p.m. 2 0 ...	Ilfracombe ...	Waterloo.
2 45 ...	Ilfracombe ...	Waterloo.
2 50 ...	Plymouth Friary	Waterloo.

WEEKDAYS AND SUNDAYS

All Newspaper, Mail, Milk Tank, Milk Van, Van, and Empty Churn Trains.

HORSE, CARRIAGE, &c., TRAFFIC

Horse Boxes and Carriage Trucks must only be conveyed by the trains specified on Weekdays and not by any ordinary train without the consent of the District Traffic Superintendent being first obtained.

MIXED TRAINS

Mixed trains will be run as shown in the following pages under the heading " Mixed " under the conditions shown on pages 2 and 3 of No. 2 Supplement to the General Appendix to the Working Time Table dated 14th October, 1935. Other trains which may be run as mixed trains will be advised from time to time as required.

301841—Western—1a.

The timings shown on this page WILL NOT APPLY ON SATURDAYS, 5th July to 13th September, 1952.

OKEHAMPTON, BUDE AND NORTH CORNWALL LINE.

Distance m.	c.	DOWN WEEK-DAYS.	Mixed. AC arr. a.m.	Mixed. AC dep. a.m.	arr. a.m.	dep. a.m.	7.55 a.m. Bodmin Road. ◆ arr. a.m.	dep. a.m.	Engine. D arr. a.m.	dep. a.m.	C arr. a.m.	dep. a.m.	arr. a.m.	dep. a.m.	¶ arr. a.m.	dep. a.m.	Mixed. arr. p.m.	dep. p.m.	2.0 p.m. Bodmin North (Mixed). arr. p.m.	dep. p.m.	arr. p.m.	dep. p.m.
...	...	Okehampton	...	6 27	...	...	...	...	...	...	...	...	...	...	...	9 56	...	...	...	...	...	1 18
2	52	Meldon Junction	6	41	.	.	.	.	.	.	.	.	.	.	10	4	.	.	.	.	1	27
4	70	Maddaford Moor H.	...	...	...	...	...	...	...	...	...	...	...	...	10 8	10 9	...	...	...	...	1 31	1 31½
8	51	Ashbury	6A56	656½	.	.	.	.	.	.	.	.	.	.	10 16	10 17	.	.	.	.	1X37½	1 38
12	36	Halwill	7 6½	...	...	...	...	...	...	...	...	...	...	...	10X23	...	...	...	...	...	1 44	...
...	...	m. c. ... ... Halwill	.	.	.	7 15	.	.	.	.	.	.	.	8 53	.	10 39	.	.	.	.	.	1 46
15	65	3 29 Dunsland C.	...	...	7 21	721½	...	...	...	...	...	...	8 50	8 59½	10 45	10 46	...	...	...	...	1 52	1 53
20	30	7 74 Holsworthy	.	.	728½	7 31	.	.	.	.	.	.	9X 6½	9 7½	10X54	10 59	.	.	.	.	2X 1	2 7
25	27	12 71 Whitstone & B.	...	...	7 39	7 40	...	...	...	...	...	...	9 15½	9 16	11 7	11 9	...	...	...	...	2X15	2 16
30	73	18 37 Bude	.	.	7 49	.	.	.	.	.	.	.	9 25	.	11 18	.	.	.	.	.	2 25	.
...	...	Halwill	...	718½	...	...	...	...	...	...	...	...	...	...	...	10 30	...	...	...	...	...	1SO57
17	44	Ashwater	728½	7 29	.	.	.	.	Until 12th Sept. only.		.	.	.	.	10 37	10 38	.	.	.	.	2 4	2SO 5
21	13	Tower Hill	7 39	7 40	7.22 a.m. Bodmin North.		...	...			...	...	...	...	10 44	10 45	...	...	...	...	2X11	2SO15
26	13	Launceston	7 50	.			.	.			.	8 5	.	.	10X52	10 56	.	.	.	.	2SO22	.
30	36	Egloskerry	...	...			...	...	...	...	8 13	8 14	...	...	11 3	11 4	...	...	...	...	4.23 p.m. Bodmin North.	
34	08	Tresmeer	.	.			.	.	.	.	8 22	8 23	.	.	11 11	11 12	.	.	.	.		
38	78	Otterham	...	...	arr. a.m.	dep. a.m.	...	...	...	...	8 32	8 34	...	...	11 21	11 23	...	...	...	...		
43	34	Camelford	.	.			.	.	.	.	8 42	8 45	.	.	11 30	11 32	.	.	.	.	E	
45	63	Delabole	...	...			...	...	...	...	8 50	8 51	...	...	11 37	11 38	...	...	...	...	arr. p.m.	dep. p.m.
49	71	Port Isaac Road	.	.	.	.	.	.	.	.	8X58	9 2	.	.	11X44	11 45	.	.	.	.		
52	42	St. Kew Highway	...	...	...	...	...	...	...	...	9 6	9 7	...	...	11 49	11 50	...	...	...	...		
56	51	Wadebridge	.	.	7 41	7 46	8 30	8X41	.	8‖55	9 14	9X18	.	.	11 56	12 1	.	1 45	2 23	2 28	4 42	4E44
62	23	Padstow	...	...	7 55	...	8 50	...	9‖ 4	D	9 27	...	...	...	12 10	...	1 59	...	2 37	...	4E53	...

DOWN WEEK-DAYS.	11.0 a.m. W'loo. (Until 12th September only.) arr. p.m.	dep. p.m.	2.19 p.m. Exeter Ctl. C (Commences 15th September.) arr. p.m.	dep. p.m.	arr. p.m.	dep. p.m.	¶ (Until 12th September only.) arr. p.m.	dep. p.m.	(Commences 15th September) arr. p.m.	dep. p.m.	6.43 p.m. Bodmin North. arr. p.m.	dep. p.m.			Engine. arr. p.m.	dep. p.m.	¶ arr. p.m.	dep. p.m.	arr. p.m.	dep. p.m.
Okehampton	...	...	3 8	3 12	...	...	...	3 55	...	4 27	...	...	...	...	...	...	...	5 51	...	7 47
Meldon Junction	3	0	3	20	.	.	4	4	4	35	.	.	.	.	.	.	5	59	7	55
Maddaford Moor H.	...	...	3 24	3 25	...	...	4 8	4 9	4 39	4 40	...	...	...	...	...	...	6 3	6 4	7 59	8 1
Ashbury	3	8	3X32	3 33	.	.	4X16	4 19	4 47	4 48	.	.	.	.	.	.	6X11	6 15	8X 8	8 11
Halwill	3 14	...	3 39	...	...	...	4 26	...	4 54	...	...	...	...	...	...	...	6 21	...	8 17	...
Halwill	.	3 22	.	3 47	.	.	.	4 35	.	4 57	.	.	.	.	.	6‖15	.	6 27	.	8 25
Dunsland Cross	3	27	3X53	3 54	...	...	4 41	4 42	5 3	5 3½	...	...	...	...	6	22	6 33	6 33½	8 31	8 32
Holsworthy	3 33	3X35	4X 2	4 3	.	.	4 50	4 51	5 11½	5 12½	.	.	.	.	6	30	6 41½	6 42½	8 40	8 42
Whitstone & B'rule	3	43	4 11	4 12	...	...	4 59	5 0	5 20½	5 21	...	...	...	...	6	38	6 50½	6 51	8 50	8 51
Bude	3 52	.	4 21	.	.	.	5 9	.	5 30	.	.	.	.	.	6‖46	.	7 0	.	9 0	.
Halwill	...	3 18	...	3 43	...	...	...	4 29	...	...	...	...	...	...	Work 7.8 p.m.		...	6 24	...	8 20
Ashwater	3	24	3 50	3 51	Until 12th Sept. only.		4X36	4 37	.	.	.	.	.	.			6 31	6 32	8X27	8 28
Tower Hill	3	20	3X57	3 58			4 43	4 44	...	...	...	...	...	...	...	...	6 38	6 39	8 34	8 35
Launceston	3X36	3 38	4 5	4 8			4X51	4 56	.	.	.	.	.	.	.	.	6X46	6 49	8 42	.
Egloskerry	3	45½	4 16	4 17	...	...	5 3	5 4	...	...	...	...	...	...	...	...	6 56	6 57	...	...
Tresmeer	3	52½	4X24	4 25	.	.	5 11	5 12	.	.	.	.	.	.	.	.	7X 4	7 5	9.5 p.m. Bodmin Road.	
Otterham	4 2	4 4	4 34	4 35	...	...	5 21	5 22	...	...	...	...	...	...	...	...	7 14	7 15		
Camelford	4 11	4X13	4 42	4 43	.	.	5 29	5 32			.	.	.	.	.	.	7 22	7 22½		
Delabole	4 18	4 19	4 48	4 49	...	...	5X37	5 39	arr. p.m.	dep. p.m.	...	...	...	...	...	...	7 27½	7 28	arr. p.m.	dep. p.m.
Port Isaac Road	4 20	4 27	4X56	4 56½	.	.	5 46	5 48			.	.	.	.	.	.	7 34	7 34½		
St. Kew Highway	4	31	5 0½	5 1	...	...	5 52	5 54			...	...	...	...	...	...	7 38½	7 39		
Wadebridge	4 38	4 45	5X 8	5 12	.	5 18	6X 1	6 13	.	6 13	7 2	7 8	.	.	.	.	7 45	7 47	9 40	9 42
Padstow	4 54	...	5 21	...	5 27	...	6 22	...	6 22	...	7 17	...	...	...	...	...	7 56	...	9 51	...

A—Advertised departure Ashbury 6.52 a.m.

C—Conveys through coaches from Waterloo.

D—Work 9.40 a.m. to Waterloo.

E—Terminate at Wadebridge until 12th September.

Western Region trains from Plymouth arrive Launceston at 8.43 a.m., 12.15 p.m. S.O., 1.52 p.m., 4.39 p.m., 7.55 p.m., and 9.54 p.m. S.O.

The timings shown on this page WILL NOT APPLY ON SATURDAYS, 5th July to 13th September, 1952.

NORTH CORNWALL, BUDE AND OKEHAMPTON LINE.

Distance m.	c.	UP WEEK-DAYS.	To Bodmin General. ¶ arr. a.m.	dep. a.m.	arr.	dep.	¶ C arr. a.m.	dep. a.m.	arr.	dep.	To Bodmin Road. ◆ arr. a.m.	dep. a.m.	To Waterloo D (Until 12th Sept. only.) arr. a.m.	dep. a.m.	arr.	dep.	E arr. p.m.	dep. p.m.	arr.	dep.	SO To Bodmin North. arr. p.m.	dep. p.m.
...	...	Padstow	...	8 10	...	...	...	8 30	...	...	...	9 8	...	9 40	...	...	...	1245	...	...	...	2 55
5	52	Wadebridge	8 19	8 32	.	.	8X39	8 45	.	.	9X17	9 20	9 49	9 51	.	.	1254	1259	.	.	3 4	3 12
9	61	St. Kew Highway			...	...	8 53	8 54	...	...	...	...	9	59	...	...	1 7	1 8	...	...	SO	
12	32	Port Isaac Road	arr. a.m.	dep. a.m.	.	.	9X 0	9 1	.	.	.	.	10 7	10 8	.	.	1 14	1 15	.	.	Engine.	
16	40	Delabole			...	...	9 10	9 11	...	...	...	...	10 17	1018	...	...	1 24	1 25	...	...		
18	69	Camelford	¶ A		.	.	9 17	9 19	.	.	.	.	10X24	1026	.	.	1 31	1 32	.	.	arr. p.m.	dep. p.m.
23	25	Otterham			...	...	9X26	9 28	...	...	...	...	10 34	1035	...	...	1 39	1 40	...	...		
28	15	Tresmeer			.	.	9 35	9 36	.	.	.	.	10	42	.	.	1 47	1 48	.	.		
31	67	Egloskerry	...	...	...	...	9 42	9 43	...	...	...	...	10	47½	...	...	1X54	1 55	...	...		
36	10	Launceston	.	8 20	.	.	9 50	9 58	.	.	.	.	10 54	11X0	.	.	2X 2	2 6	.	.	.	2‖48
41	10	Tower Hill	8 27	8 28	...	...	10 5	10 6	...	...	...	...	11	7	...	...	2X13	2 14	...	...	...	...
44	59	Ashwater	8 34	8 35	.	.	10 12	10 13	.	.	.	.	11	13	.	.	2 20	2 21	.	.	3	2
49	67	Halwill	8 44	...	...	...	10 22	...	...	...	...	...	11 22	...	...	...	2 30	...	...	...	3 12	...
.	.	m. c. Bude	.	7 58	.	.	.	9 30	.	.	...	...	...	1040	.	.	.	1 44	.	.	Change with engine of 1.44 p.m. Bude.	
...	...	5 46 Whitstone	8 9	8 9½	...	...	9 41	9 42	...	...	...	...	10	50	...	...	1 55	1 56	...	...		
.	.	10 48 Holsworthy	818½	8 19	.	.	9 51	9 53	.	.	.	.	10 58	11X0	.	.	2X 5	2 7	.	.		
...	...	15 08 Dunsland C.	828½	8 29	...	...	10X 2	10 3	...	...	...	...	11	7	...	...	2 16	2 17	...	...		
.	.	18 37 Halwill	8 36	.	.	.	10 10	.	.	.	.	.	11 14	.	.	.	2 24	.	.	.		
...	...	Halwill	...	8 49	...	...	X	10 30	...	...	...	...	...	1128	...	...	...	2 34	...	...	...	3 20
53	52	Ashbury	8X58	8 59	.	.	10X39	10 40	.	.	.	.	11	36X	.	.	2 43	2 44	.	.	3X29	3 34
57	33	Maddaford Moor H.	9 6	9 7	...	...	10 48	10 49	...	...	...	...	...	...	...	...	2 51	2 52	...	...	...	...
59	51	Meldon Junction	9	13A	.	.	10	55	.	.	.	.	11	47	.	.	2	58	.	.	3	49
62	23	Okehampton	9A17	...	...	...	10 59	...	...	...	...	...	11 51	1155	...	...	3 2	...	...	...	3‖53	...
.	.	Waterloo	2 15	.	.	.	3 40	.	.	.	.	.	4 13	.	.	.	8 25	.	.	.	.	.

UP WEEK-DAYS.	F arr. p.m.	dep. p.m.	SX Perishable and Pass. Templec'be (Commences 15th Sept.) arr. p.m.	dep. p.m.	Perishable and Pass. Templec'be (Until 12th Sept. only.) arr. p.m.	dep. p.m.	SO *Perishable and Pass. Okeh'mpton* arr. p.m.	dep. p.m.	arr. p.m.	dep. p.m.	To Bodmin North. arr. p.m.	dep. p.m.	Engine. K arr. p.m.	dep. p.m.			¶ G H arr. p.m.	dep. p.m.	Engine. arr. p.m.	dep. p.m.
Padstow	...	...	...	2 55	...	2 55	...	*3 15*	...	5 0	...	5 0	...	5‖30	...	...	...	6 0	...	...
Wadebridge	.	.	3 4	3 20	3 4	3 20	*3 24*	*3 30*	5 9	.	5X 9	5 11	5‖39	.	.	.	6X 9	6 14	.	.
St. Kew Highway	...	...	3 29	3 31	3 29	3 32	*3 38*	*3 39*	...	...	...	...	...	...	...	...	6 22	6 23	...	...
Port Isaac Road	.	.	3 38	3 41	3 39	3 43	*3 45*	*3 47*	.	.	.	.	.	.	.	.	6X29	6 30	.	.
Delabole	...	...	3 50	3 52	3 52	3 56	*3 56*	*3 57*	Until 12th Sept. only.		Commences 15th Sept.		...	...	...	...	6 39	6 40	...	...
Camelford	.	.	3 58	4 3	4 2	4X12	*4 3*	*4 5*					.	.	.	.	6 46	6 48	Commences 15th Sept.	
Otterham	...	...	4 11	4 16	4 20	4X22	*4 13*	*4 16*					...	...	...	...	6 55	6 56		
Tresmeer	.	.	4X23	4 29	4 29	4 31	*4X23*	*4 27*	.	.	.	.	.	.	.	.	7X 3	7 7		
Egloskerry	...	...	4 35	4 37	4 37	4 39	*4 33*	*4 37*	...	...	...	...	...	...	...	...	7 13	7 14	...	...
Launceston	.	.	4X44	4 54	4 46	4 54	*4X44*	*4 54*	.	.	.	.	.	.	.	.	7 21	7 29	.	.
Tower Hill	...	...	5 1	5 2	5 1	5 2	*5 1*	*5 2*	...	...			...	...	...	...	7 37	7 38	...	...
Ashwater	.	.	5 9	5 11	5 9	5X11	*5 9*	*5 11*	.	.	arr. p.m.	dep. p.m.	.	.	.	.	7 45	7 46	.	.
Halwill	...	...	5 20	...	5 20	...	*5 20*	...	...	...			...	...	...	...	7 56	...	...	...
Bude	.	3F13	Conveys passengers between Padstow and Exeter only.				.	.	.	.	.	5 32	.	.	.	.	.	7G 8	After working 7. 8 p.m. Bude.	
Whitstone & B'rule	3 24	3 25					...	...	...	...	5 43	5 44	...	...	...	...	7G19	7 19½		
Holsworthy	3F34	3X43					.	.	.	.	5 53	5 54	.	.	.	.	7 28½	7 31½		
Dunsland Cross	3X52	3 55					...	...	...	...	6 3	6 4	...	...	...	...	7 40½	7 41		
Halwill	4 2	.					.	.	.	.	6 11	.	.	.	.	.	7 48	.		
Halwill	...	4 8	...	5 28	...	5 28	...	*5 22*	...	...	...	...	...	...	...	...	...	8 0	...	8‖30
Ashbury	4X17	4 18	5 38	5 39	5 38	5 39	*5 31*	*5 32*	.	.	.	.	.	.	.	.	8X 9	8 10	8	40
Maddaford Moor H.	4 26	4 27	...	...	...	...	...	...	...	...	...	...	...	...	...	...	8 18	8 19	...	...
Meldon Junction	4	33	5	50	5	50	*5*	*43*	.	.	.	.	.	.	.	.	8	25H	8	54
Okehampton	4 37	...	5 54	5 58	5 54	5 58	*5 47*	...	...	...	...	...	...	...	...	...	8H29	...	9‖ 0	...
Waterloo	10 8	.	.	.	.	.	.	.	.	.	.	.	.	.	.	.	.	.	.	.

UP WEEK-DAYS.	Engine. L arr. p.m.	dep. p.m.	arr. p.m.	dep. p.m.	To Bodmin Road. arr. p.m.	dep. p.m.	Mixed. arr. p.m.	dep. p.m.	arr. p.m.	dep. p.m.
Padstow	...	6‖35	...	6 35	...	8 2	...	8 40	...	10 5
Wadebridge	6‖44	.	6 44	.	8 11	8 13	8 54	.	10 14	.
	Until 12th Sept. only.		Commences 15th Sept.							

A—On Saturdays call at Quarry Halt 9.14 to 9.15 a.m. to take up wives of Railway employees and arrive Okehampton 9.20 a.m.

C—Conveys through coach for Waterloo.

D—Terminate at Exeter Central on Tuesdays, Wednesdays and Thursdays, 1st to 31st July, also 2nd to 11th September.

E—Conveys through coach, Padstow to Waterloo.

F—If necessary run as a Mixed Train from Bude to Holsworthy.

G—Advertised departure Bude 7.2 p.m. and Whitstone and Bridge rule 7.16 p.m.

H—On Mondays and Fridays call at Quarry Halt 8.26½ to 8.28 p.m. to take up workmen and arrive Okehampton 8.32 p.m.

K—After working 11.0 a.m. Waterloo until 12th September and 2.19 p.m. Exeter Central commencing 15th September.

L—After working 3.55 p.m. Okehampton; empty train will run in this timing on Fridays.

Western Region trains leave Launceston for Plymouth at 7.10 a.m., 10.15 a.m., 12.50 p.m. S.O., 2.12, 5.40 and 8.25 p.m. S.O.

The timings on this page WILL APPLY ON SATURDAYS ONLY, 5th July to 13th September, 1952, inclusive. **SATURDAYS ONLY.**

OKEHAMPTON, BUDE AND NORTH CORNWALL LINE.

DOWN.	12.35 a.m. Waterloo.		7.22 a.m. Bodmin North.		Mixed.								Engine.				Mixed.		7.33 a.m. Waterloo.		2.0 p.m. Bodmin North. (Mixed.)	
					AC				C						¶							
	arr. a.m.	dep. a.m.	arr. a.m.	dep. a.m.	arr. a.m.	dep. a.m.	arr. a.m.	dep. a.m.	arr. a.m.	dep. a.m.	arr. a.m.	dep. a.m.	arr. a.m.	dep. a.m.	arr. a.m.	dep. a.m.	arr. p.m.	dep. p.m.	arr. p.m.	dep. p.m.	arr. p.m.	dep. p.m.
Okehampton	5 19	5 27	...	...	...	6 27	...	...	...	...	...	...	After working 9.0 a.m. Bude.		...	10 15	...	...	12 3	12 8	...	...
Meldon Junction	5	37	.	.	6	41	.	.	.	.	.	.			10	23	.	.	12	17	.	.
Maddaford Moor H.	...	...	...	...	...	...	...	...	...	...	...	...			10 27	10 28	...	...	...	...	.	...
Ashbury	5	48	.	.	6A56	656½	.	.	.	.	.	.			10X35	10 42	.	.	12 28	12 36	.	.
Halwill	5 53	...	...	...	7 6½	...	...	...	...	...	...	...			10 48	...	...	...	12X42	...	...	...
Halwill	.	6 8	.	.	.	.	.	7 15	.	.	.	8 53	.	10‖35	.	10 55	.	.	.	12 52	.	.
Dunsland Cross	6 14	6 16	...	...	...	...	7 21	7 21½	...	...	8 59	859½	10	41	11 1	11 2	...	...	12 58	12 59	...	...
Holsworthy	6X24	6 29	.	.	.	.	7 28½	7 31	.	.	9X6½	9 7½	10	49X	11X10	11 15	.	.	1 7	1 9	.	.
Whitstone & B'rule	6 37	6 40	...	...	...	...	7 39	7 40	...	...	915½	9X16	10	57	11 23	11 24	...	...	1 17	1 18	...	...
Bude	6 49	.	.	.	.	.	7 49	.	.	.	9 25	.	11‖6	.	11 33	.	.	.	1 27	.	.	.
Halwill	...	5 58	...	...	...	718½	...	...	...	...	...	...	...	...	...	10 51	...	...	...	12 47	...	...
Ashwater	6	5	.	.	728½	7 29	.	.	.	.	.	.	.	.	10 58	10 59	.	.	12	54	.	.
Tower Hill	6	11	...	...	7 39	7 40	...	...	...	...	...	...	11.20 a.m. Bodmin North.		11 5	11 6	...	...	1	0	...	...
Launceston	6 18	6 24	.	.	7 50	.	.	.	.	8 5	.	.			11 13	11 20	.	.	1 6	1 11	.	.
Egloskerry	6	31	...	...	7.55 a.m. Bod. Rd.		...	...	8 13	8 14	...	...			11 27	11 28	...	...	1	18½	...	...
Tresmeer	6	38	.	.			.	.	8 22	8 23	.	.			11 35	11 36	.	.	1 26	1 28	.	.
Otterham	6 47	6 50	...	...	◆		...	...	8 32	8 34	...	...			11X45	11 47	...	...	1X37	1 40	...	...
Camelford	6 57	7 1	.	.			.	.	8X42	8 45	.	.			11 54	11 56	.	.	1X47	1 50	.	.
Delabole	7 6	7 8	...	...	arr. a.m.	dep. a.m.	...	...	8 50	8 51	...	...	arr. a.m.	dep. a.m.	12X 1	12 2	...	...	1 55	1 57	...	...
Port Isaac Road	7 15	7 16	.	.			.	.	8X58	9 2	.	.			12 8	12 9	.	.	2 4	2 6	.	.
St. Kew Highway	7	21	...	...			...	...	9 6	9 7	...	...			12 13	12 14	...	...	2	9	...	...
Wadebridge	7 28	7 33	7 41	7 46	8X30	8 41	.	.	9X14	9 18	.	.	11X39	1146	12X20	12 25	.	1 45	2 15	2 17	2 23	2 33
Padstow	7 42	...	7 55	...	8 50	...	...	...	9 27	...	...	...	11 55	...	12 34	...	1 59	...	2 26	...	2 42	...

DOWN.			4.5 p.m. Bodmin North.		10.22 a.m. Waterloo.						6.43 p.m. Bodmin North.								9.5 p.m. Bodmin Road.	
	¶								¶ C				¶				¶			
	arr. p.m.	dep. p.m.	arr. p.m.	dep. p.m.	arr. p.m.	dep. p.m.			arr. p.m.	dep. p.m.	arr. p.m.	dep. p.m.	arr. p.m.	dep. p.m.			arr. p.m.	dep. p.m.	arr. p.m.	dep. p.m.
Okehampton	...	1 18	...	...	...	...	...	...	...	3 55	...	...	...	5 51	...	...	...	7 47	...	...
Meldon Junction	1	27	.	.	2	53	.	.	4	4	.	.	5	59	.	.	7	55	.	.
Maddaford Moor H.	1 31	1 31½	...	...	...	...	...	...	4 8	4 9	...	...	6 3	6 4	...	...	7 59	8 1	...	...
Ashbury	1X37½	1 38	.	.	3	1X	.	.	4X16	4 19	.	.	6X11	6 15	.	.	8 X8	8 11	.	.
Halwill	1 44	...	...	...	3 7	...	...	...	4 26	...	...	...	6 21	...	...	...	8 17	...	...	...
Halwill	.	1 46	.	.	.	3 16	.	.	.	4 35	.	.	.	6 27	.	.	.	8 25	.	.
Dunsland Cross	1 52	1 53	...	...	3 22	3 23	...	...	4 41	4 42	...	...	6 33	6 33½	...	...	8 31	8 32	...	...
Holsworthy	2 1	2 3	.	.	3X31	3 36	.	.	4 50	4 51	.	.	6 41½	6 42½	.	.	8 40	8 42	.	.
Whitstone & B.	2X11	2 14	...	...	3 44	3 45	...	...	4 59	5 0	...	...	6 50½	6 51	...	...	8 50	8 51	...	...
Bude	2 23	.	.	.	3 54	.	.	.	5 9	.	.	.	7 0	.	.	.	9 0	.	.	.
Halwill	...	1 53	...	...	...	3 11	...	...	...	4 29	...	...	...	6 24	...	...	...	8 20	...	...
Ashwater	2 0	2 1	.	.	3	18	.	.	4X36	4 37	.	.	6 31	6 32	.	.	8X27	8 28	.	.
Tower Hill	2 7	2 8	...	...	3	24	...	...	4 43	4 44	...	...	6 38	6 39	...	...	8 34	8 35	...	...
Launceston	2 15	.	.	.	3X29	3 39	.	.	4 51	4X56	.	.	6X46	6 49	.	.	8 42	.	.	.
Egloskerry	...	...	...	...	3	46½	...	...	5 3	5 4	...	...	6 56	6 57	...	...	...	...	...	...
Tresmeer	.	.	.	.	3 54	3 56	.	.	5 11	5 12	.	.	7X 4	7 5	.	.	.	.	.	.
Otterham	...	...	...	...	4 5	4 7	...	...	5 21	5 22	...	...	7 14	7 15	...	...	...	...	...	...
Camelford	.	.	.	.	4X14	4 18	.	.	5X29	5 32	.	.	7 22	7 22½	.	.	.	.	.	.
Delabole	...	...	...	...	4 23	4 25	...	...	5 37	5 39	...	...	7 27½	7 28	...	...	...	...	...	...
Port Isaac Road	.	.	.	.	4 32	4 35	.	.	5 46	5 48	.	.	7 34	7 34½	.	.	.	.	.	.
St. Kew Highway	...	...	...	...	4	39X	...	...	5 52	5 54	...	...	7 38½	7 39	...	...	...	...	...	...
Wadebridge	.	.	4 24	4 26	4X45	4 51	.	.	6X 1	6 13	7 2	7 8	7 45	7 47	.	.	.	.	9 40	9 42
Padstow	...	...	4 35	...	5 0	...	...	...	6 22	...	7 17	...	7 56	...	...	...	...	...	9 51	...

A—Advertised departure Ashbury 6.52 a.m.
C—Conveys through coach from Waterloo.

Western Region trains from Plymouth arrive Launceston at 8.43 a.m., 12.15, 1.57, 4.39, 7.55 and 9.54 p.m.

SATURDAYS ONLY. The timings on this page WILL APPLY ON SATURDAYS ONLY, 5th July to 13th September, 1952, inclusive.

NORTH CORNWALL, BUDE AND OKEHAMPTON LINE.

UP.			To Waterloo.		To Bodmin Road.		To Waterloo.		To Bodmin Road.		*To Waterloo.*		To Waterloo.		Mixed.		To Bodmin North.				Empty.	
	A						¶		◆		Q								¶ H			
	arr. a.m.	dep. a.m.	arr. a.m.	dep. a.m.	arr. a.m.	dep. a.m.	arr. a.m.	dep. a.m.	arr. a.m.	dep. a.m.	arr. p.m.	dep. p.m.	arr. a.m.	dep. a.m.	arr. a.m.	dep. a.m.	arr. p.m.	dep. p.m.	arr. p.m.	dep. p.m.	arr. p.m.	dep. p.m.
Padstow	...	...	...	...	...	8 10	...	8 30	...	9 8	...	...	...	10 45	...	1130	...	1210	...	1 0	...	...
Wadebridge	.	.	.	8 5	8X19	8 32	8 39	8 45	9X17	9 20	.	.	10 54	10 59	1144	.	12X19	1228	1 9	1 14	.	.
St. Kew Highway	...	...	8	13	...	...	8 53	8 54	...	...	...	...	11	7	...	...	...	...	1X22	1 23	...	...
Port Isaac Road	.	.	8 19	8 21	.	.	9X 0	9 1	.	.	.	.	11 13	11 16	.	.	.	.	1 29	1 31	.	.
Delabole	...	...	8 30	8 33	...	...	9 10	9 11	...	...	...	...	11X25	11 27	...	...	...	...	1 40	1 42	...	...
Camelford	.	.	8X39	8 44	.	.	9 17	9 19	.	.	.	.	11 33	11 36	.	.	.	.	1X48	1 49	.	.
Otterham	...	...	8 51	8 55	...	...	9 26	9 28	...	...	...	...	11X44	11 48	...	...	...	...	1 56	1 57	...	...
Tresmeer	.	.	9	2	.	.	9X35	9 36	.	.	.	.	11	54	.	.	.	.	2 4	2 5	.	.
Egloskerry	...	...	9	8X	...	...	9 42	9 43	...	...	...	...	11	59½	...	...	...	...	2X11	2 12	...	...
Launceston	.	8 20	9 15	9 22	.	.	9 50	9 58	.	.	.	.	12 6	12 12	.	.	.	.	2 19	2 23	.	2†48
Tower Hill	8 27	8 28	9	30	...	...	10 5	10 6	...	...	...	...	12	19	...	...	...	...	2 30	2 31	...	...
Ashwater	8 34	8 35	9 36	9 38	.	.	10 12	10 13	.	.	.	.	12	25X	.	.	.	.	2 37	2 38	3	0
Halwill	8 44	...	9 49	...	...	...	10 22	...	...	...	...	...	12X34	...	...	...	...	...	2 47	...	3 9	...
Bude	.	7 58	.	9 0	.	.	.	9 30	.	.	*Formed of 11.45 a.m. Bude.*		.	11 45	.	.	.	.	.	2 1	Change engines at Halwill.	
Whitstone & B'rule	8 9	8 9½	9X12	9 17	...	...	9 41	9 42	...	...			11X56	11 57	...	...	...	...	2X12	2 13		
Holsworthy	8 18½	8 19	9 26	9 28	.	.	9 51	9 53	.	.			12 6	12 8	.	.	.	.	2 22	2 24		
Dunsland Cross	8 28½	8 29	9	36	...	...	10X 2	10 3	...	...	...	...	12 17	12 18	...	...	...	...	2 33	2 34		
Halwill	8 36	.	9 42	.	.	.	10 10	.	.	.	.	.	12 25	.	.	.	.	.	2 41	.		
Halwill	...	8 49	...	9 54	...	...	...	10 31	...	...	...	*12 27*	...	12 44	...	...	...	...	...	2 51	...	3 25
Ashbury	8X58	8 59	.	.	.	.	10X40	10 41	.	.	*12*	*35X*	12	52	.	.	.	.	3X 0	3 2	3	34
Maddaford Moor H.	9 6	9 7	10 9	10 10	...	...	...	...	...	...	...	...	...	...	...	...	...	...	3 9	3 10	...	...
Meldon Junction	9	13A	10	16	.	.	10	55	.	.	*12*	*50*	1	3	.	.	.	.	3	16	3	49
Okehampton	9A20	...	10 20	10 23	...	...	10 59	11 5	...	...	*12 54*	*1 0*	1 7	1 11	...	...	...	...	3 20	...	3†53	...
Waterloo	2 26	.	3 4	.	.	.	3 23	.	.	.	*5 37*	.	5 42	.	.	.	.	.	8 25	.	.	.

UP.			To Bodmin North.				To Bodmin North.				Engine.					Engine.		To Bodmin Road.		Mixed.			
	¶										J		¶ C			K							
	arr. p.m.	dep. p.m.	arr. p.m.	dep. p.m.	arr. p.m.	dep. p.m.	arr. p.m.	dep. p.m.	arr. p.m.	dep. p.m.	arr. p.m.	dep. p.m.	arr. p.m.	dep. p.m.		arr. p.m.	dep. p.m.	arr. p.m.	dep. p.m.	arr. p.m.	dep. p.m.	arr. p.m.	dep. p.m.
Padstow	...	...	...	2 55	...	3 15	...	4 40	...	...	...	5‖20	...	6 0	...	...	6‖35	...	8 2	...	8 40	...	10 5
Wadebridge	.	.	3 4	3 12	3 24	3 34	4X49	5 11	.	.	5‖30	.	6X 9	6 14	.	6‖44	.	8 11	8 13	8 54	.	1014	.
St. Kew Highway	...	...	...	...	3 42	3 44	...	...	...	...	...	...	6 22	6 23	...	...	...	...	...	...	...	...	...
Port Isaac Road	.	.	.	.	3 51	3 54	.	.	.	.	.	.	6X29	6 30	.	.	.	.	.	.	.	.	.
Delabole	...	...	...	...	4 3	4 6	...	...	...	...	...	...	6 39	6 40	...	...	...	...	...	...	...	...	...
Camelford	.	.	.	.	4X12	4 17	.	.	.	.	.	.	6 46	6 48	.	.	.	.	.	.	.	.	.
Otterham	...	...	...	...	4X25	4 27	...	...	...	...	...	...	6 55	6 56	...	...	...	...	...	...	...	...	...
Tresmeer	.	.	.	.	4 34	4 35	.	.	.	.	.	.	7X 3	7 7	.	.	.	.	.	.	.	.	.
Egloskerry	...	...	...	...	4 41	4 42	...	...	...	...	...	...	7 13	7 14	...	...	...	...	...	...	...	...	...
Launceston	.	.	.	.	4X49	4 54	.	.	.	.	.	.	7 21	7 29	.	.	.	.	.	.	.	.	.
Tower Hill	...	...	...	...	5 1	5 2	...	...	...	...	...	...	7 37	7 38	...	...	...	...	...	...	...	...	...
Ashwater	.	.	.	.	5 9	5 11	.	.	.	.	.	.	7 45	7 46	.	.	.	.	.	.	.	.	.
Halwill	...	...	...	...	5 20	...	...	...	...	...	...	...	7 56	...	...	...	...	...	...	...	...	...	...
Bude	.	3 13	.	.	.	.	.	.	.	5 32	.	.	.	7C 8	.	.	.	.	.	.	.	.	.
W'stone & B'rule	3 24	3 25	...	...	...	...	...	...	5 43	5 44	...	...	7G19	7 19½	...	...	...	...	...	...	...	...	...
Holsworthy	3X34	3 42	.	.	.	.	.	.	5 53	5 54	.	.	7 28	7 31½	.	.	.	.	.	.	.	.	.
Dunsland Cross	3 51	3 52	...	...	...	...	...	...	6 3	6 4	...	...	7 40½	7 41	...	...	...	...	...	...	...	...	...
Halwill	3 59	.	.	.	.	.	.	.	6 11	.	.	.	7 48	.	.	.	.	.	.	.	.	.	.
Halwill	...	4 8	...	...	...	5 22	...	...	...	...	...	...	...	8 0	...	...	...	...	...	...	...	...	...
Ashbury	4X17	4 18	.	.	5 31	5 32	.	.	.	.	.	.	8X 9	8 10	.	.	.	.	.	.	.	.	.
Maddaford Moor H.	4 26	4 27	...	...	...	...	...	...	...	...	...	...	8 18	8 19	...	...	...	...	...	...	...	...	...
Meldon Junction	4	33	.	.	5	43	.	.	.	.	.	.	8	25	.	.	.	.	.	.	.	.	.
Okehampton	4 37	...	...	...	5 47	...	...	...	...	...	...	...	8 29	...	...	...	...	...	...	...	...	...	...
Waterloo	10 8	.	.	.	.	.	.	.	.	.	.	.	.	.	.	.	.	.	.	.	.	.	.

A—Call at Quarry Halt, 9.14 to 9.15 a.m. to take up wives of Railway employees.
C—Advertised departure Bude 7.2 p.m. and Whitstone and Bridgerule 7.16 p.m. H—Conveys through coaches Padstow to Waterloo.
J—After working 10.22 a.m. Waterloo. K—After working 3.55 p.m. Okehampton.

Western Region trains leave Launceston for Plymouth at 7.10 a.m., 10.15 a.m., 12.50, 2.12, 5.40 and 8.25 p.m.

67

OKEHAMPTON, BUDE AND NORTH CORNWALL LINE.

Train No.																				
DOWN. SUNDAYS.									A											
	arr. a.m.	dep. a.m.	arr. a.m.	dep. a.m.	arr. p.m.	dep. p.m.			arr. p.m.	dep. p.m.			arr. p.m.	dep. p.m.	arr. p.m.	dep. p.m.	arr. p.m.	dep. p.m.	arr. p.m.	dep. p.m.
Okehampton				11 50						4 [illegible]2								9 23		
Meldon Junction			11	58					4	20							9	31		
Maddaford Moor H.			12 2	12 3					4 24	4 25							9 35	9 36		
Ashbury			12 10	12 11					4 32	4 33							9 43	9 44		
Halwill			12 17						4 39								9 50			
Halwill		10 29		12 21						4 43								9 54		
Dunsland Cross	10 35	10 36	12 27	12 28					4 49	4 50							10 0	10 1		
Holsworthy	10 44	10 45	12 36	12 40					4 58	5 0							10 9	10 11		
W'stone & B'rule	10 53	10 54	12 48	12 49					5 8	5 9							10 19	10 20		
Bude	11 3		12 58						5 18								10 29			
Halwill						12 27								4 52		7 28				10 0
Ashwater					12 34	12 35							4 59	5 0	7 35	7 36			10 7	10 8
Tower Hill					12 41	12 42							5 6	5 7	7 42	7 43			10 14	10 15
Launceston					12 49								5 14		7 50				10 22	
Egloskerry																				
Tresmeer																				
Otterham	Until 14th Sept. only.		Until 14th Sept. only.												Until 14th Sept. only.		Until 14th Sept. only.			
Camelford					Until 14th Sept. only.															
Delabole																			Until 14th Sept. only.	
Port Isaac Rd																				
St. Kew Highway																				
Wadebridge																				
Padstow																				

Train No.																				
UP. SUNDAYS.			C																	
	arr. a.m.	dep. a.m.	arr. a.m.	dep. a.m.	arr. a.m.	dep. a.m.	arr. p.m.	dep. p.m.	arr. p.m.	dep. p.m.	arr. p.m.	dep. p.m.	arr. p.m.	dep. p.m.	arr. p.m.	dep. p.m.			arr. p.m.	dep. p.m.
Padstow																				
Wadebridge																				
St. Kew Highway																				
Port Isaac Rd.																				
Delabole													Until 14th Sept. only		Until 14th Sept. only.				Until 14th Sept. only.	
Camelford																				
Otterham	Until 14th Sept. only.		Until 14th Sept. only.		Until 14th Sept. only.		Commences 21st Sept.													
Tresmeer									Until 14th Sept. only.											
Egloskerry																				
Launceston		9 50						2 37		2 37				6 46						9 15
Tower Hill	9 57	9 58					2 44	2 44½	2 44	2 44½			6 53	6 54					9 22	9 23
Ashwater	10 4	10 5					2 50½	2 51	2 50½	2 5[illegible]			7 0	7 1					9 29	9 30
Halwill	10 14						3 0		3 0				7 10						9 39	
Bude				9 45		11 15						2 32				6 42				
W'stone & B'rule			9 56	9 57	11 26	11 27					2 43	2 44			6 53	6 54				
Holsworthy			10 6	10 9	11 36	11 37					2 53	2 56			7 3	7 6				
Dunsland Cross			10 18	10 19	11 46	11 47					3 5	3 6			7 15	7 16				
Halwill			10 26		11 54						3 13				7 23					
Halwill				10 29						3 [illegible]		3 16				7 25				
Ashbury			10 38	10 39					3 10	3 1[illegible]	3 25	3 26			7 34	7 35				
Maddaford Moor Halt			10 46	10 47							3 33	3 34			7 42	7 43				
Meldon Junction			10	53					3	23	3	40			7	49				
Okehampton			10 57						3 27		3 44				7 53					
Waterloo			4 9						9 12		9 12									

A—Conveys through coaches from Waterloo until 14th September.
C—Conveys through coaches to Waterloo.

SOUTHERN OPERATING AREA.

Western District

Working Time Tables

OF

FREIGHT TRAINS

30th JUNE, 1952, and until further notice

Every person supplied with a copy of these Tables is held responsible that he reads carefully and obeys all the Special Notices and Instructions contained therein so far as they concern him.

On Bank Holidays and special events, some of the ordinary Services will be withdrawn and Special Services run, particulars of which will be shown in Special Traffic Notice.

In order to avoid the trainmen's hours of duty exceeding the stipulated hours, it is essential that everything possible should be done by all concerned to assist in keeping the trains to their scheduled time. Attention is directed to Rule 142, Clause (*a*) which explains the circumstances under which Freight Trains may be allowed to run in advance of the scheduled times. A great deal can be done in this direction at stations by ascertaining the actual running of Passenger Trains, and calculating the time required by Freight Trains to do their work and clear the station in advance, and the co-operation of the staff generally is invited to this end.

IMPORTANT NOTICE

SPEED OF TRAINS

A maximum speed of 60 miles an hour must not be exceeded by trains at any point and all restrictions which impose a lower speed than 60 miles an hour must be strictly observed.

REFERENCES

CE ... Change Engines.
CS ... Stops when required.
E ... Calls for change of crews only.
EB ... Engine and Brake only.
FO ... Fridays only.
FX ... Fridays excepted.
MO ... Mondays only.
MSO ... Mondays and Saturdays only.
MX ... Mondays excepted.
MSX ... Mondays and Saturdays excepted.
MTFO ... Mondays, Tuesdays and Fridays only.
MWFO ... Mondays, Wednesdays and Fridays only.

Q ... Runs when required.
RR ... Run Round.
S ... Shunts for other trains to pass.
SF ... Semi-fitted.
SO ... Saturdays only.
SX ... Saturdays excepted.
TO ... Tuesdays only.
TX ... Tuesdays excepted.
ThO ... Thursdays only.
ThX ... Thursdays excepted.
V ... Calls for working purposes only, if running late stop not to be made.
W ... Calls for Water only.
WO ... Wednesdays only.

WX ... Wednesdays excepted.
X ... Crosses another train on a Single Line.
/ Between figures denotes passing time, e.g. 8/10.
‖ ... Light engine.
→ ... For continuation, see subsequent column.
← ... Continued from a previous column.
★ Special instruction applies to train, see pages 42 to 47.
◆ Worked by Western Region engine.
⌘ Engines of trains marked thus will not be changed at Salisbury.

Timings within brackets thus :—(8.14), indicate the previous or subsequent working of the engine or train concerned.

Waterlow & Sons Limited, London and Dunstable.

OKEHAMPTON, BUDE AND NORTH CORNWALL. 29

m.	c.	m.	c.	DOWN TRAINS. WEEK-DAYS.	12.1 a.m. MX 12.38 a.m. MO Freight and Mail Exmouth Jct. Sdgs. A arr. a.m.	dep. a.m.			Freight and Mail. arr. a.m.	dep. a.m.			Mixed. C arr. a.m.	dep. a.m.	arr. a.m.	dep. a.m.			SO arr. a.m.	dep. a.m.
—	—	—	—	Okehampton	3A10	4 0				4 37				6 27	(Formed of				(Formed of	
2	52	—	—	Meldon Junction		4 14				4 51				6 41	6.27 a.m.				6.27 a.m.	
8	51	—	—	Ashbury		4 29				5 6			6C56	6 56½	Mixed				Mixed	
12	36	—	—	Halwill	4 37				5 14				7 6½		Okehampton.)				Okehampton.)	
—	—	—	—	Halwill						5 17										
15	65	3	29	Dunsland Cross						5 26										
20	30	7	74	Holsworthy					5 35	5 53										
25	27	12	71	Whitstone and B.						6 3X										
25	76	13	40	Whitstone Brick Siding											Will not run on				Until	
30	73	18	37	Bude					6 14						Saturdays				13th Sept. only.	
—	—	—	—	Halwill		5 31								7 18½	5th July					
17	44	—	—	Ashwater	5 41	5 44							7 28½	7 29	to					
21	13	—	—	Tower Hill		5 52							7 39	7 40	13th Sept.					
26	13	—	—	Launceston	6 0								7 50			8 40				8 40
30	36	—	—	Egloskerry	G											8 52			8X53	9 9
34	08	—	—	Tresmeer												9 6			9X23	9 38
38	78	—	—	Otterham											9X23	9 40			9 56	10 10
43	34	—	—	Camelford	arr. a.m.	dep. a.m.									9X52	10 27			10 22	10 50
45	63	—	—	Delabole											10S33	11 46			10X56	11 30
49	44	—	—	Toms Siding																
49	71	—	—	Port Isaac Road											11X56	12 11			11X40	12 15
52	42	—	—	St. Kew Highway											12 17	12 27			12 21	12 31
56	51	—	—	Wadebridge		7 20									12 37				12 41	
62	23	—	—	Padstow	7 34															

DOWN. WEEKDAYS.	Mixed. arr. p.m.	dep. p.m.	3.30 a.m. Exmouth Jct. Sdgs. arr. a.m.	dep. a.m.			SO 3.30 a.m. Exmouth Jct. Sdgs. arr. a.m.	dep. a.m.	Q H arr. p.m.	dep. p.m.			★ arr. a.m.	dep. a.m.	SX ★ arr. a.m.	dep. a.m.			SO ★ arr. a.m.	dep. a.m.
Okehampton			7 44	8 10			7 44	8 10						10 8		10 44				10 44
Meldon Jc.				8 24				8 24						10 22		10 58				10 58
Ashbury			8X39	9 0			8X39	9 0					10X37	11 2	11X13	11 37			11 13	11 23
Halwill			9 10				9 10						11 12		11 47				11 33	
Halwill				9 40				9 48												
Dunsland Cross			9X50	10 9			9X58	10 17					Com-		Until				Until	
Holsworthy			10S20	11 10			10X28	11 30					mences		12th Sept.				13th Sept.	
Whitstone and B			11 20	11 40			11X40	12 0					15th Sept.		only.				only.	
Whitstone Brick Siding			11 42	11 48			12 2	12 8												
Bude			11 57				12 15													
Halwill							Until							11 35		12 9				11 55
Ashwater							13th Sept.						11 45	12 5	12 19	12 30			12X 5	12 28
Tower Hill							only.						12 15	12 25	12 49	12 59				12 38
Launceston			Will not										12X35	2 7	1X 9	2 35			12S48	1 45
Egloskerry			run on				D.F.						2 19	2 28	2X47	2 52			1X57	2 25
Tresmeer			Saturdays				2.0 p.m. Bodmin North. (Mixed).						2X42	2 52	3 6	3 10			2X39	2 50
Otterham			5th July										3 10	3 38	3X34	4S23			3S 8	4X28
Camelford			to										3X50	4S55	4 35	5 5			4 40	5 9
Delabole			13th Sept.										5X 1	5 50	5S11	5X50			5X15	5S53
Toms Siding							arr. p.m.	dep. p.m.												
Port Isaac Road													6X 0	6 31	6X 0	6 31			6X 3	6 34
St. Kew Highway													6 37	7 3	6 37	7 3			6 40	7 3
Wadebridge		1 45					2 23	2F28		4H15			7 13		7 13				7 13	
Padstow	1 59						2F37		4H29											

A—On Mondays arrive Okehampton 3.20 a.m.
C—Advertised departure Ashbury 6.52 a.m.
D—Not to convey wagons to and from Boscarne Jct
F—On Saturdays, 5th July to 13th September, depart Wadebridge 2.33 p.m. and arrive Padstow 2.42 p.m.
G—On Saturdays 5th July to 13th September, start at 7.5 a.m. and arrive Padstow 7.19 a.m.
H—When required on Saturdays 5th July to 13th September, start at 4.5 p.m. and arrive Padstow 4.19 p.m.

30 NORTH CORNWALL, BUDE AND OKEHAMPTON.

m.	c.	m.	c.	UP WEEKDAYS.	arr. a.m.	dep. a.m.	A★ arr. a.m.	dep. a.m.	arr. a.m.	dep. a.m.	SO ★ arr. a.m.	dep. a.m.			SO ★ arr. a.m.	dep. a.m.	SX ★ arr. a.m.	dep. a.m.	SX ★ arr. a.m.	dep. a.m.
—	—	—	—	Padstow						10 15										
5	52	—	—	Wadebridge					10 29			10 40				10 50		11 35		11 35
9	61	—	—	St. Kew Highway								10 52				11 2	11X48	12 0	11X48	12 0
12	32	—	—	Port Isaac Road							11S 1	11X46			11X11	11 57	12X10	12 20	12X10	12 20
12	59	—	—	Toms Siding																
16	40	—	—	Delabole							12X 0	12 54			12 11	1 4	12 34	1 4	12X34	1 4
18	69	—	—	Camelford					Will not		1 4	1 22			1 14	1 41	1S14	1 41	1S14	1 41
23	25	—	—	Otterham					run on		1X33	2S15			1 52	2 15	1 52	2 15	1 52	2 15
28	15	—	—	Tresmeer					Saturdays		2X26	2 40			2X26	2 43	2 26	2 35	2X26	2 43
31	67	—	—	Egloskerry					5th July		2 51	2 56			2 54	2 59	2X46	2 56	2 54	2 50
36	10	—	—	Launceston					to		3X 8	3 48			3 11	3 45	3X 8	4 2	3 11	3 45
41	10	—	—	Tower Hill					13th Sept.		3 58	4 5			3X55	4 5	4 12	4 17	3X55	4 5
44	59	—	—	Ashwater							4X15	4 40			4 15	4 32	4X27	4 40	4 15	4 32
49	67	—	—	Halwill							4 55				4 47		4 55		4 47	
—	—	—	—	Bude		5 45		9 45												
—	—	5	46	Whitstone and B.	5X58	6 17		9 56			Until				Commences		Until			
—	—	10	43	Holsworthy		6 27X	10X 7	12A10			13th Sept.				20th Sept.		12th Sept.		Commences	
—	—	15	08	Dunsland Cross		6 38	12A23	12 40			only.						only.		15th Sept.	
—	—	18	37	Halwill	6 46		12 50													
—	—	—	—	Halwill				1 22			X	6 50			X	6 50	X	8 23	X	6 50
53	52	22	22	Ashbury			1X35	1 44				7 5				7 5		8 38		7 5
59	51	28	21	Meldon Junction				2 4				7 20				7 20		8 53		7 20
62	23	30	73	Okehampton			2 14				7 30				7 30		9 3		7 30	

UP WEEKDAYS.	SO Mixed. arr. a.m.	dep. a.m.	To Exmouth Jct. Sdgs. ★ arr. p.m.	dep. p.m.	SO To Exmouth Jct. Sdgs. ★ arr. p.m.	dep. p.m.	SX To Exmouth Jc. Sdgs. ★ arr. p.m.	dep. p.m.	Q arr. p.m.	dep. p.m.	SO To Exmouth Jct. Sdgs. ★ arr. p.m.	dep. p.m.	To Salisbury. SX Exmouth Jct. Sdgs. SO ★ arr. p.m.	dep. p.m.	SX To Salisbury. ★ arr. p.m.	dep. p.m.	Mixed. arr. p.m.	dep. p.m.
Padstow		11 30								3 35								8 40
Wadebridge	11 44								3 49			4 22		4 30		4 45	8 54	
St. Kew Highway											4X35	4 40		4 40		4 55		
Port Isaac Road												4 49	4X51	4 58		5 4		
Toms Siding																		
Delabole	Until										5X 3	5 17	5X13	5 30	5X18	5 40		
Camelford	13th Sept.										5X27	5 35	5 40	5 50		5 50		
Otterham	only.				Until		Until				5 46	6 7	6 1	6 11	6 1	6 11		
Tresmeer			Commences		13th Sept.		12th Sept.		Engine.			6 17		6 21		6 21		
Egloskerry			15th Sept.		only.		only.					6 26		6 30		6 30		
Launceston									C		6X38	7S57	6S42	7X57	6S42	7X57		
Tower Hill												8 7		8 7		8 7		
Ashwater									arr. p.m.	dep. p.m.	8X17	8 29	8X17	8 29	8X17	8 29		
Halwill											8 44		8 44		8 44			
Bude				1 20		1 28		1 20	(7 0)	7‖20	Until		Commences		Until			
Whitstone and B.			1X33	2S20	1 41	1 50	1X33	2S20	7C31	7 50	13th Sept.		15th Sept.		12th Sept.			
Holsworthy			2X30	4S 4	2X 0	3S53	2S30	3 56		7 59	only.				only			
Dunsland Cross			4 17	4 33	4 6	4 22	4 9	4 22		8 8								
Halwill			4S43		4S32		4 32		8‖15	(8 25)								
Halwill				5 58		5 58		5 58	Will not			9 5		9 5		9 5		
Ashbury				6 13X		6 13X		6 13X	run on			9 20		9 20		9 20		
Meldon Junction				6 28		6 28		6 28	Saturdays			9 35		9 35		9 35		
Okehampton				6 34		6 34		6 34	5th July to 13th Sept.		9 45	10 20	9 45	10 20	9 45	10 20		

A—On Saturdays 5th July to 13th September depart Holsworthy 11.43 a.m. and arrive Dunsland Cross 11S56 a.m.

C—Perform freight shunting.

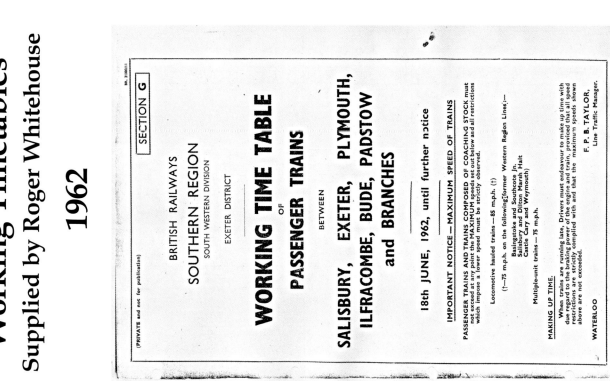

Working Timetables
Supplied by Roger Whitehouse
1962

(PRIVATE and not for publication)

BR. 31000/11

SECTION G

BRITISH RAILWAYS
SOUTHERN REGION
SOUTH WESTERN DIVISION
EXETER DISTRICT

WORKING TIME TABLE
OF
PASSENGER TRAINS
BETWEEN
SALISBURY, EXETER, PLYMOUTH, ILFRACOMBE, BUDE, PADSTOW and BRANCHES

18th JUNE, 1962, until further notice

IMPORTANT NOTICE—MAXIMUM SPEED OF TRAINS

PASSENGER TRAINS AND TRAINS COMPOSED OF COACHING STOCK must not exceed at any point the MAXIMUM speeds set out below and all restrictions which impose a lower speed must be strictly observed.

Locomotive hauled trains—85 m.p.h. (†)

(†—75 m.p.h. on the following former Western Region Lines:—
Basingstoke and Southcote Jn.
Salisbury and Dilton Marsh Halt
Castle Cary and Weymouth)

Multiple-unit trains—75 m.p.h.

MAKING UP TIME.

When trains are running late, Drivers must endeavour to make up time with due regard to the braking power of the engine and train, provided that all speed restrictions are strictly complied with and that the maximum speeds shown above are not exceeded.

WATERLOO

F. P. B. TAYLOR,
Line Traffic Manager.

G 64 WEEKDAYS Okehampton, Halwill, Bude, Bodmin, Padstow and Torrington Branch

DOWN (UP, Halwill to Torrington)

Mileage M	C	M	C	M	C	M	C	Station		No.	1.15 am Pass. and News Waterloo to Padstow		Mixed					1.15 am Pass. and News Waterloo	
											am	am	am		am	am	am	am	am
0	0							OKEHAMPTON	arr	1	5 57	..	..	..	..	..	..	..	..
									dep	2	6 30	..	..	..	..	..	..	..	..
2	52							Meldon Jn.	..	3	6 39	..	..	..	..	..	..	..	..
4	70							Maddaford Moor Halt		4	..	..	..	..	..	..	..	..	..
8	51							Ashbury	arr	5	6 50	..	..	..	..	..	..	..	..
									dep	6	6‡52	..	..	..	..	..	..	..	..
12	36	12	36	0	0			HALWILL	arr	7	6 58	..	..	..	..	..	..	..	..
									dep	8	7 16½	7 15	..	..	..	..	..	..	..
		15	65					Dunsland Cross	arr	9	..	7 21	..	..	..	..	..	..	..
									dep	10	..	7 21½	..	..	..	..	..	..	..
		20	30					Holsworthy	arr	11	..	7 28½	..	..	..	..	..	..	..
									dep	12	..	7 31	..	..	..	..	..	..	..
		25	27					Whitstone and	arr	13	..	7 39	..	..	..	..	..	..	..
								Bridgerule	dep	14	..	7 40	..	..	..	..	..	..	..
		30	73					BUDE	arr	15	..	7 49	..	..	..	..	..	..	..
				3	7			Hole	arr	16	..	..	..	..	..	..	..	..	..
									dep	17	..	..	..	..	..	..	..	..	..
				7	71			Hatherleigh	arr	18	..	..	..	..	..	..	..	..	..
									dep	19	..	..	..	..	..	..	..	..	..
				10	1			Meeth Halt	arr	20	..	..	..	..	..	..	..	..	..
									dep	21	..	..	..	..	..	..	..	..	..
				12	59			Petrockstow	arr	22	..	..	..	..	..	..	..	..	..
									dep	23	..	..	7 55	..	..	..	..	..	..
				14	78			Dunsbear Halt	arr	24	..	..	8 4	..	..	..	..	..	..
									dep	25	..	..	8 5	..	..	..	..	..	..
				16	5			Yarde Halt	arr	26	..	..	8 10	..	..	..	..	..	..
									dep	27	..	..	8 11	..	..	..	..	..	..
				18	69			Watergate Halt	arr	28	..	..	8 24	..	..	..	..	..	..
									dep	29	..	..	8 25	..	..	..	..	..	..
				20	47			TORRINGTON	arr	30	..	..	8 32	..	..	..	..	..	..
17	44							Ashwater	arr	31	7 26½	..	..	..	..	..	..	..	..
									dep	32	7 27	..	..	..	..	..	..	..	..
21	13							Tower Hill	arr	33	7 37	..	..	..	..	..	..	..	..
									dep	34	7 38	..	..	..	..	..	..	←	..
26	13							Launceston	arr	35	7 48	..	..	..	..	..	..	7 48	..
									dep	36	8 3	..	..	..	..	..	..	8 3	..
30	36							Egloskerry	arr	37	→	..	..	..	..	..	..	8 10	..
									dep	38	..	..	..	..	..	..	..	8 11	..
34	8							Tresmeer	arr	39	..	..	..	..	..	..	..	8 18	..
									dep	40	..	..	..	..	..	..	..	8 19	..
38	78							Otterham	arr	41	..	..	..	..	..	..	..	8 28	..
									dep	42	..	..	..	..	..	..	..	8 29	..
43	34							Camelford	arr	43	..	..	..	..	..	..	..	8 36	..
									dep	44	..	..	..	..	..	..	..	8 38	..
45	63							Delabole	arr	45	..	..	..	..	..	..	..	8 43	..
									dep	46	..	..	..	..	..	..	..	8 44	..
49	71							Port Isaac Road	arr	47	..	..	..	..	..	..	..	8 51	..
									dep	48	..	..	..	..	..	..	..	8 53	..
52	42							St. Kew Highway	arr	49	..	..	..	..	..	..	..	8X57	..
									dep	50	..	..	..	..	..	..	..	8 58	..
				0	0			BODMIN ROAD	dep	51	..	..	..	..	..	7 50	..	..	..
				3	43			BODMIN	arr	52	..	..	..	..	..	7 58	..	..	..
								GENERAL	dep	53	..	..	..	..	7 27	8 8	..	..	8 58
						0	0	BODMIN NORTH	dep	54	..	..	..	..	..	..	8 43	..	..
						1	31	Dunmere Halt	..	55	..	..	..	..	..	..	8 47	..	..
				6	9	1	69	Boscarne Jn.		56	..	..	..	..	7 33	8 14	8 48½	..	9 5
				6	38	2	18	Nanstallon Halt	..	57	..	..	..	..	7 34½	8 15½	8 50	..	..
				7	78	3	58	Grogley Halt		58	..	..	..	..	7 39	..	8 54½	..	..
56	51			10	70	6	50	WADEBRIDGE	arr	59	..	..	..	..	7 47½	8X27	9 2	9X 5	9 16
									dep	60	..	..	..	..	7 51	8 41	..	9 13	..
62	23			16	42	12	22	PADSTOW	arr	61	..	..	..	..	8 0	8 50	..	9 22	..

Okehampton, Halwill, Bude, [B]odmin, Padstow and Torrington Branch **WEEKDAYS** G 6

	7.10 am Plymouth North Road										Mixed		Mixed	10.40 am Plymouth North Road					Mixed
														SO					SO
	am	am		am	am	am	am	am	am	am	am	PM	PM	PM		PM		PM	PM
1																			
2							9 56		9 56									1 18	
3							10 4		10 4									1 26	
4							10a 9		10a 9									1 30	
5							10 16		10 16									1 36	
6							10 17		10 17									1 37	
7							10X23		10X23									1 43	
8		8 53					10 30	10 35	10 30	10 38	10 38							1 44	2 2
9		8 59						10 41		10X44								1 49½	
10		8 59½						10 42		10 50								1 50½	
11		9 6½						10X50		10X58								1 57½	
12		9 7½						10 53		11 1								1 59	
13		9 15½						11 1		11 9								2X 7	
14		9 16						11 2		11 10								2 9	
15		9 25						11 11		11 19								2 18	
16							Commencing 10th September	Commencing 10th September	Until 7th September inclusive	Until 7th September inclusive	10 47								
17											10 48								
18											11 5								
19											11 7								
20											11 16								
21											11 16½								
22											11X25½								
23											11 26½								
24											11 35½								
25											11 36								
26											11 41								
27											11 41½								
28											11 54½								
29											11 55								
30											12 2								
31					Until 7th September inclusive	Commences 10th September	10 37		10 37										2 12
32							10 38		10 38										2 13
33							10 44		10X44										2X23
34							10 45		10 49										2 27
35	8 43						10 52		10 56					12 15					2 37
36							10 56		11 0										
37							11 3		11 7										
38							11 4		11 8										
39							11 11		11 15										
40							11 13		11 16										
41							11 22		11 25										
42							11 23		11 26										
43							11 30		11 33										
44							11 32		11 34										
45							11 37		11 39										
46							11 38		11 40										
47							11 44		11 46										
48							11 45		11 47										
49							11X49		11X51										
50							11 50		11 52										
51				10 5								12 20							
52				10 13								12 28							
53				10 20								12 38							
54					11 20	11 20										2 0			
55					11 24	11 24										2 4			
56				10 26	11 25½	11 25½						12 44				2 5½			
57					11 27	11 27						12 45½				2 7			
58					11 31½	11 31½										2 11½			
59				10 37	11 39	11 39	11 56		11X58			12 57				2 19			
60				10 40	11 41		12 0		12 5				1 15			2 25			
61				10 49	11 50		12 9		12 14				1 29			2 34			

G 66 **WEEKDAYS** Okehampton, Halwill, Bude, Bodmin, Padstow [and] Torrington Branch

DOWN (UP, Halwill to Torrington)				Scholars	Scholars	LE			11.0 am or 11.5 am Waterloo				11.0 am Waterloo			3.5 pm Plymouth North Road	Mixed
				SX	SX	SO											SX
			PM	PM	PM	PM	PM	PM	PM	PM	PM	PM	PM	PM	PM	PM	PM
OKEHAMPTON	arr	1							3 2				3 2				
	dep	2							3 8				3 8		3 35		
Meldon Jn.		3							3 16				3 16		3 43		
Maddaford Moor Halt		4													3a48		
Ashbury	arr	5											3 26		3 55		
	dep	6							3 24				3 27		3 56		
HALWILL	arr	7							3 30				3 33		4X 2		
	dep	8							3 33	3 37			3 37	3 41	4 5		
Dunsland Cross	arr	9								3X43				3X47			
	dep	10								3 44				3 49			
Holsworthy	arr	11								3X52				3X57			
	dep	12								3 54				3 58			
Whitstone and Bridgerule	arr	13								4 2				4 6			
	dep	14								4 3				4 7			
BUDE	arr	15								4 12				4 16			
Hole	arr	16		Not advertised	Not advertised		Until 7th September inclusive	Commences 10th September	Until 7th September inclusive	Until 7th September inclusive	Until 7th September inclusive	Commences 10th September	Commences 10th September	Commences 10th September	Until 7th September inclusive		
	dep	17															
Hatherleigh	arr	18															
	dep	19															
Meeth Halt	arr	20															
	dep	21															
Petrockstow	arr	22															
	dep	23															4 37
Dunsbear Halt	arr	24															4 46
	dep	25															4 47
Yarde Halt	arr	26															4 52
	dep	27															4 53
Watergate Halt	arr	28															5 6
	dep	29															5 7
TORRINGTON	arr	30															5 14
Ashwater	arr	31		Runs during School terms only	Runs during School terms only ECS or LE will run in this timing when scholars train not required								3 44		4 12		Conveys workmen
	dep	32							3 39				3 45		4 13		
Tower Hill	arr	33											3 51		4X19		
	dep	34							3 44				3 52		4 20		
Launceston	arr	35							3 50				3 59		4 27	4 39	
	dep	36							3 53				4 4		4 30		
Egloskerry	arr	37											4 12		4X37		
	dep	38							4 0				4 13		4 41		
Tresmeer	arr	39											4X20		4 48		
	dep	40							4 7				4 24		4 49		
Otterham	arr	41							4X16				4 33		4 58		
	dep	42							4 17				4 34		4 59		
Camelford	arr	43							4 24				4 41		5 6		
	dep	44							4 25				4 42		5 7		
Delabole	arr	45							4 30				4 47		5 12		
	dep	46							4 31				4 48		5 13		
Port Isaac Road	arr	47							4 38				4X55		5X20		
	dep	48							4 39				4 55½		5 20½		
St. Kew Highway	arr	49											4 59½		5 24½		
	dep	50							4 43				5 0		5 25		
BODMIN ROAD	dep	51	2 30								4 35	4 35					
BODMIN GENERAL	arr	52	2 38								4 43	4 43					
	dep	53	2 48	4 8							4 50	4 50					
BODMIN NORTH	dep	54					4 23	4 23									
Dunmere Halt		55					4 27	4 27									
Boscarne Jn.		56	2 54	4 14			4 28½	4 28½			4 56	4 56					
Nanstallon Halt		57		4 15½			4 30	4 30			4 57½	4 57½					
Grogley Halt		58		4 20			4 34½	4 34½									
WADEBRIDGE	arr	59	3 5	4 27½			4 42	4 42	4 49		5 9	5 9	5X 7		5 31		
	dep	60			4 20	4‖20		4 46	4 51		5 10		5 12				
PADSTOW	arr	61			4 29	4‖29		4 55	5 0		5 19		5 21				

Okehampton, Halwill, Bude, Bodmin, Padstow and Torrington Branch — WEEKDAYS — G 67

No.										Mixed			6.20 pm Plymouth North Road						8.40 pm Plymouth North Road
	PM	PM	PM		PM		PM	PM		PM		PM	PM		PM	PM		PM	SO PM
1																			
2			4 24				5 51								7 45				
3			4 32				5 59								7 53				
4			4a37				6a 4								7c59				
5			4 45				6X11								8X 6				
6			4 46				6 15								8 11				
7			4 53				6 21								8 17				
8			4 54				6 24	6 27		6 30					8 20	8 25			
9			5 0					6 33								8 31			
10			5 1					6 33½								8 32			
11			5 9					6 41½								8 40			
12			5 10					6 42½								8 42			
13			5 18					6 50½								8 50			
14			5 19					6 51								8 51			
15			5 28					7 0								9 0			
16										6 29									
17										6 40									
18										6 57									
19										6 59									
20										7 8									
21										7 9									
22										7 18									
23										7 19									
24										7 28									
25										7 29									
26										7 34									
27										7 35									
28										7 48									
29										7 49									
30										7 56									
31							6 31								8 27				
32							6 32								8 28				
33							6 38								8 34				
34							6 39								8 35				
35							6X46						7 55		8 42				10 10
36							6 51												
37							6 58												
38							6 59												
39							7X 6												
40							7 7												
41							7 16												
42							7 17												
43							7 24												
44							7 25												
45							7 30												
46							7 30½												
47							7 36½												
48							7 37												
49							7 41												
50							7 41½												
51					6 17							8 0						9 42	
52					6X25							8X 8						9 50	
53					6 35							8 20						9 55	
54	5 44																		
55	5 48																		
56	5 49½				6 41							8 26½						10 1½	
57	5 51				6 42½							8 28						10 3	
58	5 55½				6 47							8 32½						10 7½	
59	6 3				6 54½		7 47½					8 40						10 15	
60		6 13			7 0		7 49											10 17	
61		6 22			7 9		7 58											10 26	

G 68 — SATURDAYS — Okehampton, Halwill, Bude, Bodmin, Padstow and Torrington Branch

DOWN (UP, Halwill to Torrington)		No.	LE	4.30 am Exeter Cent				LE	1.25 am Pass. and News Waterloo to Padstow			Mixed		1.25 am Pass. and News Waterloo	ECS	7.10 am Plymouth North Road	
			am	am	am		am	am	am	am	am	am	am	am	am	am	am
OKEHAMPTON	arr	1		5 20					6 2								
	dep	2	5‖17	5 26				5‖55	6 30								
Meldon Jn.		3	5 25	5 35				6j F10	6 39								
Maddaford Moor Halt		4															
Ashbury	arr	5						6 22	6 50								
	dep	6	5 34	5 45				6 F32	6‡52								
HALWILL	arr	7	5‖40	5 50				6‖39	6 58								
	dep	8		5 54	5 59				7 16½	7 15							8 53
Dunsland Cross	arr	9			6 5					7 21							8 59
	dep	10			6 6					7 21½							8 59½
Holsworthy	arr	11			6X14					7 28½							9 6½
	dep	12			6 16					7 31							9 7½
Whitstone and Bridgerule	arr	13			6 24					7 39							9X15½
	dep	14			6 25					7 40							9 16
BUDE	arr	15			6 34					7 49							9 25
Hole	arr	16															
	dep	17															
Hatherleigh	arr	18															
	dep	19															
Meeth Halt	arr	20															
	dep	21															
Petrockstow	arr	22															
	dep	23	From 21st July to 1st September inclusive	From 21st July to 1st September inclusive	From 21st July to 1st September inclusive			Until 14th July inclusive also 8th September				7 55					
Dunsbear Halt	arr	24										8 4					
	dep	25										8 5					
Yarde Halt	arr	26										8 10					
	dep	27										8 11					
Watergate Halt	arr	28										8 24					
	dep	29										8 25					
TORRINGTON	arr	30										8 32					
Ashwater	arr	31							7 26½								
	dep	32		6 0					7 27								
Tower Hill	arr	33							7 37								
	dep	34		6 6					7 38					←			
Launceston	arr	35		6 12					7 48					7 48		8 43	
	dep	36		6 16					8 5					8 5			
Egloskerry	arr	37							→					8 13			
	dep	38		6 23										8 14			
Tresmeer	arr	39												8 22			
	dep	40		6 30										8 23			
Otterham	arr	41		6 39										8 32			
	dep	42		6 41										8 34			
Camelford	arr	43		6 48										8X42			
	dep	44		6 50										8 45			
Delabole	arr	45		6 55										8 50			
	dep	46		6 56										8 51			
Port Isaac Road	arr	47		7 3										8X58			
	dep	48		7 4										9 2			
St. Kew Highway	arr	49												9 6			
	dep	50		7 8										9 7			
BODMIN ROAD	dep	51									7 50						
BODMIN	arr	52									7 58						
GENERAL	dep	53					7 27				8 8				8†59		
BODMIN NORTH	dep	54											8 43				
Dunmere Halt		55											8 47				
Boscarne Jn.		56					7 33				8 14		8 48½		9 5		
Nanstallon Halt		57					7 34½				8 15½		8 50				
Grogley Halt		58					7 39						8 54½				
WADEBRIDGE	arr	59		7 14			7 47½				8X27		9 2	9X14	9†16		
	dep	60		7 17			7 51				8 41			9 18			
PADSTOW	arr	61		7 26			8 0				8 50			9 27			

G 6 **SATURDAYS** Okehampton, Halwill, Bude, Bodmin, Padstow and Torrington Branch

DOWN
(UP, Halwill to Torrington)

Station		No.	PM (10.35 am Waterloo)	PM	PM	PM	PM (3.5 pm Plymouth North Road)	PM (11.15 am Waterloo)	PM		PM		PM	PM	PM (Mixed)	PM	PM (6.20 pm Plymouth North Road)
OKEHAMPTON	arr	1						3 33									
	dep	2						3 55					5 51				
Meldon Jn.		3	2 53					4 4					5 59				
Maddaford Moor Halt		4						4a 9					6a 4				
Ashbury	arr	5						4X17					6X11				
	dep	6	3X 1					4 19					6 15				
HALWILL	arr	7	3 7					4X26					6 21				
	dep	8	3 11	3 16				4 29	4 32				6 24	6 27	6 30		
Dunsland Cross	arr	9		3 22					4 38					6 33			
	dep	10		3 23					4 39					6 33½			
Holsworthy	arr	11		3X31					4 47					6 41½			
	dep	12		3 36					4 49					6 42½			
Whitstone and Bridgerule	arr	13		3 44					4 57					6 50½			
	dep	14		3 45					4 58					6 51			
BUDE	arr	15		3 54					5 7					7 0			
Hole	arr	16													6 39		
	dep	17													6 40		
Hatherleigh	arr	18													6 57		
	dep	19													6 59		
Meeth Halt	arr	20													7 8		
	dep	21													7 9		
Petrockstow	arr	22													7 18		
	dep	23													7 19		
Dunsbear Halt	arr	24													7 28		
	dep	25													7 29		
Yarde Halt	arr	26													7 34		
	dep	27													7 35		
Watergate Halt	arr	28													7 48		
	dep	29													7 49		
TORRINGTON	arr	30													7 56		
Ashwater	arr	31						4 36					6 31				
	dep	32	3 18					4 37					6 32				
Tower Hill	arr	33						4 43					6 38				
	dep	34	3 23					4 44					6 39				
Launceston	arr	35	3 29				4 39	4X51					6X46				7 55
	dep	36	3 36					4 56					6 51				
Egloskerry	arr	37						5 3					6 58				
	dep	38	3X43½					5 4					6 59				
Tresmeer	arr	39	3 51					5 11					7X 6				
	dep	40	3 53					5 12					7 7				
Otterham	arr	41	4 2					5 21					7 16				
	dep	42	4 4					5 22					7 17				
Camelford	arr	43	4X11					5X29					7 24				
	dep	44	4 15					5 32					7 25				
Delabole	arr	45	4 20					5 37					7 30				
	dep	46	4 22					5 39					7 30½				
Port Isaac Road	arr	47	4 29					5 46					7 36½				
	dep	48	4 32					5 48					7 37				
St. Kew Highway	arr	49						5 52					7 41				
	dep	50	4X36					5 54					7 41½				
BODMIN ROAD	dep	51			5 0						6 17					8 0	
BODMIN	arr	52			5 8						6X25					8 8	
GENERAL	dep	53			5 19						6 35					8X20	
BODMIN NORTH	dep	54				5 36											
Dunmere Halt		55				5 40											
Boscarne Jn.		56			5 26	5 41½					6 41					8 26½	
Nanstallon Halt		57			5 27½	5 43					6 42½					8 28	
Grogley Halt		58				5 47½					6 47					8 32½	
WADEBRIDGE	arr	59	4X42		5 39	5 55		6X 1			6 54½		7 47½			8 40	
	dep	60	4 51					6 13			7 0		7 49				
PADSTOW	arr	61	5 0					6 22			7 9		7 58				

Okehampton, Halwill, Bude, Bodmin, Padstow and Torrington Branch **SATURDAYS** G 6

No.	am	am	am	am	am	am (Mixed)	PM	PM (10.0 am Saltash)	PM (Mixed)	PM (7.30 am Waterloo)	PM		PM (12.14 pm Plymouth North Road)	PM	PM	PM	PM	PM (LE)	PM
1																			
2				10 12						12 1						1 20			
3				10 20						12 9						1 28			
4				10a25												1 32			
5				10X32												1 38			
6				10 38						12 17						1 38½			
7				10 44						12X23						1 44½			
8				10 47	10 50	10 52				12‡27	12 32					1 46½	1 53		
9					10 56						12 38					1 52			
10					10 57						12 39					1 53			
11					11X 5						12X47					2 1			
12					11 7					‡ 12.25 pm	12 49					2 3			
13					11 15						12X57					2X11			
14					11 16						12 58					2 14			
15					11 25						1 7					2 23			
16						11 1													
17						11 2													
18						11 19													
19						11 23													
20						11 32													
21						11 32½													
22						11X41½													
23						11 42½				From 30th June to 18th August inclusive	From 30th June to 18th August inclusive							Runs on 23rd June and again commencing 25th August	
24						11 51½													
25						11 52½													
26						11 57													
27						11 57½													
28						12 10½													
29						12 11													
30						12 18													
31				10 54						12X34							2 0		
32				10 55						12 37							2 1		
33				11 1													2 7		
34				11 2						12 43							2 8		
35				11 9				12 15		12 49			1 47				2 15		
36				11 13						12 53									
37				11 20															
38				11 21						1 0½									
39				11 28						1 8									
40				11 29						1 10									
41				11 38						1 19									
42				11 39						1 22									
43				11 46						1 29									
44				11X49						1 32									
45				11 54						1X37									
46				11 55						1 45									
47				12 1						1 51									
48				12 2						1 53									
49				12 6															
50				12 7						1 56									
51		10 10					12 43								2 30				
52		10 18					12 51								2 38				
53		10 35					12 56								2 48				
54			11 20											2 0					4 5
55			11 24											2 4					4 9
56		10 41	11 25½				1 2							2 5½	2 54				4 10½
57			11 27				1 3½							2 7					4 12
58			11 31½											2 11½					4 16½
59		10 52	11X39	12X13			1 15			2 2				2 19	3 5				4 24
60	10 15	11 15	11 46	12 21					1 20	2 5				2 25				3‖50	4 26
61	10 24	11 24	11 55	12 30					1 34	2 14				2 34				4‖0	4 35

G 72 WEEKDAYS Padstow, Bodmin, Bude, Halwill, Okehampton and Torrington Branch

UP (DOWN, Torrington to Halwill)

Mileage M	C	M	C	M	C	M	C	Station	No.	ECS	Mixed and ECS		To Plymouth North Road					Mixed
										am	am	am	am	am	am	am	am	am
0	0			0	0			PADSTOW dep	1						8 12			
5	52			5	52			WADEBRIDGE arr	2						8X21			
								dep	3			6 55		7 58	8‡30			
				8	44			Grogley Halt	4			7 3		8 6	8 38			
				10	4			Nanstallon Halt	5			7 7½		8 10½	8 42½			
				10	33	10	33	Boscarne Jn.	6			7 9		8 12	8 45			
				10	71			Dunmere Halt	7					8 14				
				12	22			BODMIN NORTH arr	8					8 18				
						12	79	BODMIN GENERAL arr	9			7 17			8 53			
								dep	10									
						16	42	BODMIN ROAD arr	11									
9	61							St. Kew Highway arr	12									
								dep	13									
12	32							Port Isaac Road arr	14									
								dep	15									
16	40							Delabole arr	16									
								dep	17									
18	69							Camelford arr	18									
								dep	19									
23	25							Otterham arr	20									
								dep	21									
28	15							Tresmeer arr	22									
								dep	23									
31	67							Egloskerry arr	24									
								dep	25									
36	10							Launceston arr	26									
								dep	27				7 5				8 20	
41	10							Tower Hill arr	28								8 27	
								dep	29								8 28	
44	59							Ashwater arr	30								8 34	
								dep	31								8 35	
				0	0			TORRINGTON dep	32		6 25							8 52
				1	58			Watergate Halt arr	33		6 32							8 59
								dep	34		6 33							9 0
				4	42			Yarde Halt arr	35		6 46							9 13
								dep	36		6 48							9 14
				5	49			Dunsbear Halt arr	37		6 52							9 18
								dep	38		6†55							9 19
				7	68			Petrockstow arr	39		7† 4							9 28
								dep	40									9 29
				10	46			Meeth Halt arr	41									9 38
								dep	42									9 39
				12	56			Hatherleigh arr	43									9 48
								dep	44									9 50
				17	40			Hole arr	45									10 8
								dep	46									10 9
		0	0					BUDE dep	47	6†20						7 58		
		5	46					Whitstone and Bridgerule arr	48							8 9		
								dep	49	6 30						8 9½		
		10	43					Holsworthy arr	50							8 18½		
								dep	51	6 38						8 19		
		15	8					Dunsland Cross arr	52							8X28½		
								dep	53	6 45						8 29		
49	67	18	37	20	47			HALWILL arr	54	6†52						8 36	8 44	10 18
								dep	55								8 49	
53	52							Ashbury arr	56								8 58	
								dep	57								8 59	
57	33							Maddaford Moor Halt	58								9a 7	
59	51							Meldon Jn.	59								9 13	
62	23							OKEHAMPTON arr	60								9 17	
								dep	61									
								Notes			When required, call at Marland Clay Coy's Siding to attach wagons, and arr. Petrockstow 7.17 am						On Saturdays stops at Quarry Halt 9a15 am to take up wives of Railway employees and arr. Okehampton 9.20 am.	

SATURDAYS Okehampton, Halwill, Bude, Bodmin, Padstow and Torrington Branch SUNDAYS G 7

No.	Sat.	Sat.	Sat.	Sat.	Sat. 8.40 pm Plymouth North Road	Sun.	Sun.	Sun.	Sun.	Sun.	Sun. 12.10 p.m. Exeter Central	Sun.	Sun.	Sun.	Sun.	Sun.	Sun.	Sun.	Sun.
	PM	PM		PM	PM		am		am	PM	PM		PM	PM		PM		PM	
1											1 0								
2	7 45								11 40		1 15		4 15					9 20	
3	7 53								11 48		1 23		4 23					9 28	
4	7c59								11a53		1 26½		4a28					9a33	
5	8X 6								12 0		1 32½		4 35					9 40	
6	8 11								12 1		1 33		4 36					9 41	
7	8 17								12 7		1 39		4 42					9 47	
8	8 20	8 25					10 29		12 11	12 18	1 40		4 46	4 50		7 30		9 51	
9		8 31					10 35		12 17				4 52					9 57	
10		8 32					10 35½		12 18				4 53					9 58	
11		8 40					10 43½		12 26				5 1					10 6	
12		8 42					10 44		12 30				5 5					10 8	
13		8 50					10 52		12 38				5 13					10 16	
14		8 51					10 52½		12 39				5 14					10 17	
15		9 0					11 1½		12 48				5 23					10 26	
16–30							Until 9th September inclusive		Until 9th September inclusive	Until 9th September inclusive	Commences 16th September		Through Coaches, Waterloo to Bude until 9th September inclusive	Until 9th September inclusive		Until 9th September inclusive		Until 9th September inclusive	
31	8X27									12 25	1 47			4 57		7 37			
32	8 28									12 26	1 47½			4 58		7 38			
33	8 34									12 32	1 53½			5 4		7 44			
34	8 35									12 33	1 54			5 5		7 45			
35	8 42				10 10					12 40	2 1			5 12		7 52			
36–50																			
51				9 42															
52				9 50															
53				9 55															
54																			
55																			
56				10 1½															
57				10 3															
58				10 7½															
59				10 15															
60				10 17															
61				10 26															

G 74 **WEEKDAYS** Padstow, Bodmin, Bude, Halwill, Okeha[mpton] and Torrington Branch

UP (DOWN, Torrington to Halwill)							To Exeter Ctl.	To Exeter Ctl. SX Okehampton SO		Mixed	Scholars	To Plymouth North Road					
											SX						
			PM		PM	PM	PM	PM	PM	PM	PM	PM	PM	PM	PM		PM
PADSTOW	dep	1	2 52	..	..	..	3 13	3 13	..	..	..	..	..	5 2	..	..	5 24
WADEBRIDGE	arr	2	3 1				3 22	3 22						5X11			5 33
	dep	3	3 9	..	..	..	3 32	3 32	3 24	..	4 43	..	5 12	5 12	..	..	5 34
Grogley Halt		4	3 17										5 20	5 20			
Nanstallon Halt		5	3 21½	..	..	..	..	..	..	..	4 54	..	5 24½	5 24½	..	..	5 46½
Boscarne Jn.		6	3 23						3 36		5h 0		5 26	5 26			5 48
Dunmere Halt		7	3 25	..	..	..	..	‡ 4.25 pm	..	..	..	..	5 28½	5 28	..	..	..
BODMIN NORTH	arr	8	3 29										5 32½	5 32			
BODMIN	arr	9	..	..	..	..	..		3 44	..	5 8	..	..	..	..	..	5 56
GENERAL	dep	10							3 54								6 1
BODMIN ROAD	arr	11	..	..	..	..	..		4 1	..	..	..	..	..	..	..	6 8
St. Kew Highway	arr	12			Until 7th September Inclusive	Commences 10th September	3 40	3 40	Mixed train from Bodmin General		Not advertised		Until 7th September inclusive	Commences 10th September			Mixed train from Bodmin General
	dep	13	..	..			3 41	3 41		..		..			..	..	
Port Isaac Road	arr	14					3 47	3 47									
	dep	15	..	..			3 48	3 48		..		..			..	..	
Delabole	arr	16					3 57	3 57									
	dep	17	..	..			3 59	3 58		..		..			..	..	
Camelford	arr	18					4 5	4 4									
	dep	19	..	..			4 7	4 5		..		..			..	..	
Otterham	arr	20					4X‡15	4 13									
	dep	21	..	..			4 21	4 15		..		..			..	..	
Tresmeer	arr	22					4 28	4X22									
	dep	23	..	..	..	..	4 29	4‡28	..	..		..	..	..	..	..	..
Egloskerry	arr	24					4 35	4 34									
	dep	25	..	..	..	..	4X40	4 37	..	..		..	..	..	..	..	..
Launceston	arr	26					4 47	4 44									
	dep	27	..	..	..	..	4 54	4 54	..	..		5 40	..	..	..	..	..
Tower Hill	arr	28					5 1	5 1									
	dep	29	..	..	..	..	5 2	5 2	..	..	..	..	..	..	..	..	..
Ashwater	arr	30					5 9	5X 9									
	dep	31	..	..	..	..	5 11	5 11	..	..	..	..	..	..	..	..	..
TORRINGTON	dep	32					Until 7th September Inclusive	Commences 10th September		4 0	Runs during School terms only						Until 7th September Inclusive
Watergate Halt	arr	33	..	..	..	..			..	4 7		..	..	..	..	..	
	dep	34								4 7½							
Yarde Halt	arr	35	..	..	..	..			..	4 20		..	..	..	..	..	
	dep	36								4 20½							
Dunsbear Halt	arr	37	..	..	..	..			..	4 24½		..	..	..	..	..	
	dep	38								4 25							
Petrockstow	arr	39	..	..	..	..			..	4X34		..	..	..	..	..	
	dep	40								4 35							
Meeth Halt	arr	41	..	..	..	..			..	4 44		..	..	..	..	..	
	dep	42								4 44½							
Hatherleigh	arr	43	..	..	..	..			..	4 53½		..	..	..	..	..	
	dep	44								4 55½							
Hole	arr	45	..	..	..	..			..	5 13		..	..	..	..	..	
	dep	46								5 14							..
BUDE	dep	47	..	..	3 9	3 11	MFO—Stops at Quarry Halt 5.52 pm to take up workmen and arr. Okehampton 5.55 pm	MFO—Stops at Quarry Halt 5.52 pm to take up workmen and arr. Okehampton 5.55 pm	..	..	..	..	..	..	5 32	..	..
Whitstone and	arr	48			3 20	3 22									5 43		
Bridgerule	dep	49	..	..	3 21	3 23			..	..	..	..	..	..	5 44	..	..
Holsworthy	arr	50			3 30	3 32									5 53		
	dep	51	..	..	3 33	3 36			..	..	..	..	..	..	5 54	..	..
Dunsland Cross	arr	52			3X42	3X45									6 3		
	dep	53	..	..	3 47	3 51			..	..	..	..	..	..	6 4	..	..
HALWILL	arr	54			3X54	3 58	5 20	5 20		5 23					6 11		
	dep	55	..	..	4 5	4 5	5 28	5 28	..	..	..	..	..	..	..	..	..
Ashbury	arr	56			4 14	4 14	5 38	5 38									
	dep	57	..	..	4 15	4 15	5 39	5 39	..	..	..	..	..	..	..	..	..
Maddaford Moor Halt		58			4a24	4a24											
Meldon Jn.		59	..	..	4 30	4 30	5 50	5 50	..	..	..	..	..	..	..	..	..
OKEHAMPTON	arr	60			4 34	4 34	5 54	5 54									
	dep	61	..	..	..	..	5 58	5 58	..	..	..	..	..	..	..	..	..

Padstow, Bodmin, Bude, H[alwill], Okehampton and Torrington Branch **WEEKDAYS** G [74]

		To Exeter Ctl.		To Waterloo	To Plymouth North Road			To Waterloo				To Plymouth North Road				To Okehampton		To Waterloo	
												SO							
	am	am		am	am	am	am	am	am		am	PM	am	PM		PM		PM	PM
1	..	8 30	..	8 30	..	9 3	..	9 33	..	..	10 57	..	11 55	..	..	..	..	12 58	..
2		8X39		8X39		9X12		9 42			11 6		12X 4					1 7	
3	..	8 46	..	8 46	..	9 18	..	9 44	9 50	..	11 9	..	12 25	12 25	..	..	..	1 14	1 25
4									9 58				12 33	12 33					1 33
5	..	..	..	..	..	9 30½	..	..	10 2½	..	11 21½	..	12 37½	12 37½	..	..	..	..	1 37½
6						9 32			10 4		11 23		12 39	12 39					1 39
7	..	..	..	..	..	..	..	..	10 6	..	..	..	12 41	12 41	..	..	..	..	..
8									10 10				12 45	12 45					
9	..	..	..	..	..	9 40	..	..	..	..	11 31	..	..	..	..	..	..	..	1 47
10						9 45					11 40								1 55
11	..	..	..	..	..	9 52	..	..	..	..	11 47	..	..	..	..	..	..	..	2 2
12		8X54		8X54														1 22	
13	..	8 59	..	8 59	..	..	..	9 50½	..	..	..	..	..	..	..	..	..	1 23	..
14		9 5		9 5				9 55										1 29	
15	..	9 6	..	9 6	..	..	..	9 56	..	..	..	..	..	..	..	..	..	1 30	..
16		9 15		9 15				10 4										1 38	
17	..	9 16	..	9 16	..	..	..	10 5	..	..	..	..	..	..	..	..	..	1 39	..
18		9 22		9 22				10X 9										1 44	
19	..	9 24	..	9 24	..	..	..	10 10	..	..	..	..	..	..	..	..	..	1 45	..
20		9X31		9X31				10 17										1 52	
21	..	9 32	..	9 32	..	..	..	10 18	..	..	..	..	..	..	..	..	..	1 53	..
22		9 39		9 39														2 0	
23	..	9 40	..	9 40	..	..	..	10 25	..	..	..	..	..	..	..	..	..	2 1	..
24		9 46		9 46														2 7	
25	..	9 47	..	9 47	..	..	..	10 30½	..	..	..	..	..	..	..	..	..	2 8	..
26		9 54		9 54				10 37										2 15	
27	..	9 58	..	9 58	10 15	..	..	10 41	..	..	..	12 40	..	..	..	..	..	2 18	..
28		10 5		10 5														2X25	
29	..	10 6	..	10 6	..	..	..	10X48	..	..	..	..	..	..	..	..	..	2 25½	..
30		10 12		10 12														2 31½	
31	..	10 13	..	10 13	..	..	..	10 54	..	..	..	..	..	..	..	..	..	2 32	..
32		Until 7th September inclusive		Commences 10th September			Until 7th September inclusive	Until 7th September inclusive					Until 7th September inclusive	Commences 10th September					
33	..		..		..	..			..	..	..	..			..	..	..	..	..
34																			
35	..		..		..	..			..	..	..	..			..	..	..	..	..
36																			
37	..		..		..	..			..	..	..	..			..	..	..	..	..
38																			
39	..		..		..	..			..	..	..	..			..	..	..	..	..
40																			
41	..		..		..	..			..	..	..	..			..	..	..	..	..
42																			
43	..		..		..	..			..	..	..	..			..	..	..	..	..
44																			
45	..		..		..	..			..	..	..	..			..	..	..	..	..
46																			
47	9 30	..	..	..	..	..	10 20	..	..	..	..	..	..	..	..	1 55	..	..	..
48	9 41															2X 6			
49	9 42	..	..	..	..	..	10X30	..	..	..	..	..	..	..	..	2 8	..	..	..
50	9X51						10 38									2 17			
51	9 53	..	..	..	..	..	10 40	..	..	..	..	..	..	..	..	2 18	..	..	..
52	10X 2															2 27			
53	10 3	..	..	..	..	..	10X47	..	..	..	..	..	..	..	..	2 28	..	..	..
54	10 10	10X22		10X22			10 54	11 2								2 35		2 41	
55		10 28	..	10 28	..	..		11 6	..	..	..	..	..	..	..		..	2 45	..
56		10 37		10 37														2 54	
57	..	10 38	..	10 38	..	..	..	11 14	..	..	..	..	..	..	..	..	..	2 55	..
58		10a47		10a47														3a 3	
59	..	10 53	..	10 53	..	..	..	11 23	..	..	..	..	..	..	..	..	..	3 9	..
60		10 57		10 57				11 27										3 13	
61	..	11 2	..	11 19	..	..	..	11 31	..	..	..	..	..	..	..	..	..	3 33	..

Padstow, Bodmin, Bude, Ha… Okehampton and Torrington Branch **WEEKDAYS** G

			LE	ECS				LE	LE	LE	To Plymouth North Road								
				FO							SO								
	PM		PM	PM	PM	PM	PM	PM	PM	PM	PM	PM		PM	PM	PM			
1			5‖35	5†45		6 0		6‖35				7 35		8 30		10 22			
2			5‖44	5†54		6 9		6‖44				7 44		8 39		10 31			
3	5 27					6 14	6 12					7 55			8 55				
4							6 20					8 3							
5	5 39½						6 24½					8 7½			9 7½				
6	5 41						6 26					8 9			9 9				
7																			
8																			
9	5 49						6X33					8 17			9 17				
10	5 54						6 43								9 25				
11	6 1						6 50								9 32				
12	Mixed train from Bodmin General		SX until 5th July inclusive, FSX from 9th July to 30th August and weekdays commencing 3rd September	From 6th July to 31st August inclusive		6 22													
13						6 23													
14						6X29													
15						6 30													
16						6 39													
17						6 40													
18						6 46													
19						6 48													
20						6 55													
21						6 56													
22						7X 3													
23						7 9													
24						7 15													
25						7 16													
26						7 23													
27						7 29					8 35								
28						7 37													
29						7 38													
30						7 45													
31						7 46													
32	Commences 10th September				‡ Bude 7.2 pm Whitstone and Bridgerule 7.13 pm			ECS train will run in this timing on Fridays until 7th September inclusive											
33																			
34																			
35																			
36																			
37																			
38																			
39																			
40																			
41																			
42																			
43																			
44																			
45																			
46																			
47					7‡ 5				7‖32										
48					7 16														
49					7‡16½				7 42										
50					7 25½														
51					7 28½				7 51										
52					7 37½														
53					7 38				8 0										
54					7 45	7 56			8‖ 8										
55						8 0				8‖25									
56						8X 9													
57						8 10				8 37									
58						8a19													
59						8 25				8 53									
60						8 29				8‖59									
61																			

The ti… s shown on this page …

G 76 **SATURDAYS** Padstow, Bodmin, Bude, Halwill, Okehamp… and Torrington Branch

UP (DOWN, Torrington to Halwill)		LE		Mixed and ECS		To Plymouth North Road						To Waterloo				Mixed
		am		am	am	am	am	am	am		am	am	am		am	am
PADSTOW dep	1												8 12			
WADEBRIDGE arr	2												8X21			
dep	3				6 55		7 58					8 10	8†30			
Grogley Halt	4				7 3		8 6						8 38			
Nanstallon Halt	5				7 7½		8 10½						8 42½			
Boscarne Jn.	6				7 9		8 12						8 45			
Dunmere Halt	7						8 14									
BODMIN NORTH arr	8						8 18									
BODMIN GENERAL arr	9				7 17								8 53			
dep	10															
BODMIN ROAD arr	11															
St. Kew Highway arr	12	From 21st July to 1st September inclusive														
dep	13											8 17				
Port Isaac Road arr	14											8 23				
dep	15											8 25				
Delabole arr	16											8 34				
dep	17											8 37				
Camelford arr	18											8X43				
dep	19											8 48				
Otterham arr	20											8 55				
dep	21											8 58				
Tresmeer arr	22															
dep	23											9 5				
Egloskerry arr	24															
dep	25											9X11				
Launceston arr	26											9 18				
dep	27					7 5			8 20			9 22				
Tower Hill arr	28								8 27							
dep	29								8 28			9 30				
Ashwater arr	30								8 34			9 36				
dep	31								8 35			9 38				
TORRINGTON dep	32			6 25					Stops at Quarry Halt 9a15 am to take up wives of Railway employees		From 21st July to 1st September inclusive	From 21st July to 1st September inclusive				8 52
Watergate Halt arr	33			6 32												8 59
dep	34			6 33												9 0
Yarde Halt arr	35			6 46												9 13
dep	36			6 48												9 14
Dunsbear Halt arr	37			6 52												9 18
dep	38			6†55												9 19
Petrockstow arr	39			7† 4												9 28
dep	40															9 29
Meeth Halt arr	41															9 38
dep	42															9 39
Hatherleigh arr	43															9 48
dep	44															9 50
Hole arr	45															10 8
dep	46															10 9
BUDE dep	47	5‖50		When required, call at Marland Clay Coy's Siding to attach wagons, and arr. Petrockstow 7.17 am				7 58			9 0				9 30	
Whitstone and Bridgerule arr	48	6X 1						8 9			9X12				9 41	
dep	49	6 4						8 9½			9 17				9 42	
Holsworthy arr	50	6X13						8 18½			9 26				9 51	
dep	51	6 20						8 19			9 28				9 53	
Dunsland Cross arr	52							8 28½							10X 2	
dep	53	6 29						8 29			9 36				10 3	
HALWILL arr	54	6‖37						8 36	8 44		9 42	9 49			10 10	10 18
dep	55								8 49			9 54			10 27	
Ashbury arr	56								8 58							
dep	57								8 59			10 2				
Maddaford Moor Halt	58								9a 7							
Meldon Jn.	59								9 13			10 13				
OKEHAMPTON arr	60								9 20			10 17				
dep	61											10 22				

G 78 **SATURDAYS** Padstow, Bodmin, Bude, Halwill, Okeham[...] and Torrington Branch

UP (DOWN, Torrington to Halwill)					Mixed			To Plymouth North Road	LE			–		LE		LE To Yeoford	To Plymouth North Road
			PM	PM	PM	PM	PM	PM	PM		PM	PM	PM	PM	PM	PM	PM
PADSTOW	dep	1	..	3 13	..	4 40	..	..	5‖20	..	..	6 0	..	6‖35	..	..	..
WADEBRIDGE	arr	2		3 22		4X49			5‖30			6X 9		6‖44			
	dep	3	3 24	3 34	..	5 11	..	..	..	..	..	6 14	6 12	..	7 0	..	..
Grogley Halt		4				5 19							6 20				
Nanstallon Halt		5	..	..	..	5 23½	..	..	..	..	..	..	6 24½	..	7 12½	..	..
Boscarne Jn.		6	3 36			5 25							6 26		7 14		
Dunmere Halt		7	..	‡ 4.10 pm	..	5 27	..	..	..	..	..	..	..	..	..	..	..
BODMIN NORTH	arr	8				5 31											
BODMIN	arr	9	3 44		..	..	..	..	..	..	..	..	6X33	..	7 21	..	..
GENERAL	dep	10	3 54										6 43				
BODMIN ROAD	arr	11	4 1		..	..	..	..	..	..	..	..	6 50	..	..	..	..
St. Kew Highway	arr	12		3 42								6 22					
	dep	13	..	3 44	..	..	..	..	..	..	..	6 23	..	..	..	..	..
Port Isaac Road	arr	14		3 51								6 29					
	dep	15	..	3 54	..	..	..	..	..	..	..	6 30	..	..	..	..	..
Delabole	arr	16		4 3								6 39					
	dep	17	..	4 4	..	..	..	..	..	..	..	6 40	..	..	..	..	..
Camelford	arr	18		4X10								6 46					
	dep	19	..	4‡17	..	..	..	..	..	..	..	6 48	..	..	..	..	..
Otterham	arr	20		4 25								6 55					
	dep	21	..	4 27	..	..	..	..	..	..	..	6 56	..	..	..	..	..
Tresmeer	arr	22		4 34								7X 3					
	dep	23	..	4 35	..	..	..	..	..	..	..	7 9	..	..	..	..	..
Egloskerry	arr	24		4 41								7 15					
	dep	25	..	4 42	..	..	..	..	..	..	..	7 16	..	..	..	..	..
Launceston	arr	26		4X49								7 23					
	dep	27	..	4 54	..	..	..	5 40	..	..	..	7 29	..	..	..	..	8 35
Tower Hill	arr	28		5 1								7 37					
	dep	29	..	5 2	..	..	..	..	..	..	..	7 38	..	..	..	..	..
Ashwater	arr	30		5 9								7 45					
	dep	31	..	5 11	..	..	..	..	..	..	..	7 46	..	..	..	..	..
TORRINGTON	dep	32			4 40						‡Bude 7.3 pm Whitstone and Bridgerule 7.13 pm						
Watergate Halt	arr	33	..	..	4 47	..	..	..	..	..		..	..	..	..	..	..
	dep	34			4 48												
Yarde Halt	arr	35	..	..	5 1	..	..	..	..	..		..	..	..	..	..	..
	dep	36			5 2												
Dunsbear Halt	arr	37	..	..	5 6	..	..	..	..	..		..	..	..	..	..	..
	dep	38			5 7												
Petrockstow	arr	39	..	..	5 16	..	..	..	..	..		..	..	..	..	..	..
	dep	40			5 17												
Meeth Halt	arr	41	..	..	5 26	..	..	..	..	..		..	..	..	..	..	..
	dep	42			5 27												
Hatherleigh	arr	43	..	..	5 36	..	..	..	..	..		..	..	..	..	..	..
	dep	44			5 38												
Hole	arr	45	..	..	5 56	..	..	..	..	..		..	..	..	..	..	..
	dep	46			5 57												
BUDE	dep	47	..	..	..	..	5 32	..	..	..	7‡ 5	..	..	..	..	7‖35	..
Whitstone and	arr	48					5 43				7 16						
Bridgerule	dep	49	..	..	..	..	5 44	..	..	..	7‡16½	..	..	..	..	7 46	..
Holsworthy	arr	50					5 53				7 25½						
	dep	51	..	..	..	..	5 54	..	..	..	7 28½	..	..	..	..	7 55	..
Dunsland Cross	arr	52					6 3				7 37½						
	dep	53	..	..	..	..	6 4	..	..	..	7 38	..	..	..	..	8 4	..
HALWILL	arr	54		5 20	6 6		6 11				7 45	7 56				8 11	
	dep	55	..	5 22	..	..	..	..	..	..	..	8 0	..	..	..	8 25	..
Ashbury	arr	56		5 31								BX 9					
	dep	57	..	5 32	..	..	..	..	..	..	..	8 10	..	..	..	8 37	..
Maddaford Moor Halt		58										8a19					
Meldon Jn.		59	..	5 43	..	..	..	..	..	..	..	8 25	..	..	..	8 53	..
OKEHAMPTON	arr	60		5 47								8 29				8 58	
	dep	61	..	..	..	..	..	..	..	..	..	..	..	..	..	9 6	..

Padstow, Bodmin, Bude, Hal[...] Okehampton and Torrington Branch **SATURDAYS** G 7

	To Waterloo	To Redruth			To Waterloo		To Waterloo		To Plymouth North Road		LE	To Plymouth North Road	To Okehampton	To Waterloo		LE		LE to Exmouth Jn.	
	am	am	am	am	am	am	am	am	PM	PM	PM	PM	PM	PM	PM	PM	PM	PM	PM
1	8 30	..	9 3	..	..	..	11 0	11 35	..	12 10	..	..	..	1 5	..	..	..	..	2 52
2	8 39		9X12				11 9	11 44		12X19				1 14					3 1
3	8 45	..	9 18	9 50	..	..	11 13	11 54	..	12 28	..	..	..	1 19	1 23	..	..	2‖54	3 9
4				9 58						12 36					1 31				3 17
5	..	..	9 30½	10 2½	..	..	..	12 6½	..	12 40½	..	..	..	..	1 35½	..	..	..	3 21½
6			9 32	10 4				12 8		12 42					1 37				3 23
7	..	..	..	10 6	..	..	..	..	..	12 44	..	..	..	..	..	..	..	..	3 25
8				10 10						12 48									3 29
9	..	..	9 40	..	..	..	..	12 15	..	..	..	..	..	..	1 45	..	..	..	..
10			9 45					12 23							1 50				
11	..	..	9 52	..	..	..	..	12 30	..	..	..	..	..	..	1‡57	..	..	..	..
12	8 53				‡12.26 pm	‡12.26 pm								1 27	‡ 2.0 p.m.				
13	8 54	..	..	..			11 21	..	..	..	..	..	..	1 28		..	..	3 1	..
14	9X 0						11 27							1 34					
15	9 1	..	..	..			11 30	..	..	..	..	..	..	1 35		..	..	3 7	..
16	9 10						11 39							1X43					
17	9 11	..	..	..			11 41	..	..	..	..	..	..	1 44		..	..	3 16	..
18	9 17						11 47							1 49					
19	9 19	..	..	..			11X50	..	..	..	..	..	..	1 50		..	..	3 22	..
20	9 26						11 58							1 57					
21	9 28	..	..	..			12 0	..	..	..	..	..	..	1 58		..	..	3 29	..
22	9X35													2 5					
23	9 36	..	..	..			12 4	..	..	..	..	..	..	2 6		..	..	3 36	..
24	9 42													2 12				3X42	
25	9 43	..	..	..			12 11½	..	..	..	..	..	..	2 13	..	..	..	3 45	..
26	9 50						12 18							2 20				3 52	
27	9 58	10 15	..	..			12 22	..	12 40	..	..	2 5	..	2 23	..	2‖48	..	3 55	..
28	10 5													2 30					
29	10 6	..	..	..			12 29	..	..	..	..	..	..	2 31	..	..	..	4 3	..
30	10 12													2 37					
31	10 13	..	..	..			12X35	..	..	..	..	..	..	2 38	..	3 0	..	4 9	..
32					Commences 14th July	Until 7th July Inclusive					Until 18th August Inclusive also 8th September							From 30th June to 18th August inclusive	
33	..	..	..	..			..	..	..	..		..	..	..	..	..	..		..
34																			
35	..	..	..	..			..	..	..	..		..	..	..	..	..	..		..
36																			
37	..	..	..	..			..	..	..	..		..	..	..	..	..	..		..
38																			
39	..	..	..	..			..	..	..	..		..	..	..	..	..	..		..
40																			
41	..	..	..	..			..	..	..	..		..	..	..	..	..	..		..
42																			
43	..	..	..	..			..	..	..	..		..	..	..	..	..	..		..
44																			
45	..	..	..	..			..	..	..	..		..	..	..	..	..	..		..
46																			
47	..	..	..	..	11 45	11 45	..	..	..	..	12‖40	..	2 1	..	..	..	3 13	..	..
48					11X56	11X56					12X52		2X12				3 24		
49	..	..	..	..	11 57	11 57	..	..	..	..	1 0	..	2 13	..	..	..	3 25	..	..
50					12 6	12 6							2 22				3X34		
51	..	..	..	..	12 8	12 8	..	..	..	..	1 9	..	2 24	..	..	..	3 42	..	..
52					12 17	12 17							2 33				3 51		
53	..	..	..	..	12 18	12 18	..	..	..	..	1 18	..	2 34	..	..	..	3 52	..	..
54	10 22				12‡X25	12‡X25	12 44				1‖25		2 41	2 47		3‖ 9	3 59	4X19	
55	10 27	..	..	..	12 28	12 28	12 45	..	..	..	..	..		2 51	..	..	4 6	4 30	..
56	10X36													3X 0			4X15		
57	10 37	..	..	..	12 36	12 36	12 53	..	..	..	..	..	..	3 2	..	..	4 18	4 39	..
58	10a47													3a10			4a27		
59	10 53	..	..	..	12 49	12 49	1 3	..	..	..	..	..	..	3 16	..	..	4 33	4 51	..
60	10 57				12 53	12 53	1 7							3 20			4 37	4 55	
61	11 0	..	..	..	12 59		1 11	..	..	..	..	..	..	3 41	..	..	..	5 20	..

Padstow, Bodmin, Bude, H[illegible] Okehampton and Torrington Branch — SUNDAYS — G

SATURDAYS

								To Waterloo											
		PM	PM	PM	PM	am		am		am		PM		PM		PM		PM	
1	..	7 35	8 30	..	10 5	..	..	..	..	..	..	..	..	..	..	..	..	..	..
2	..	7 44	8 39	..	10 14	..	..	..	..	..	..	..	..	..	..	..	..	..	..
3	..	7 55	..	8 55	..	..	..	..	..	..	..	..	..	..	..	..	..	..	..
4	..	8 3	..	..	..	..	..	..	..	..	..	..	..	..	..	..	..	..	..
5	..	8 7½	..	9 7½	..	..	..	..	..	..	..	..	..	..	..	..	..	..	..
6	..	8 9	..	9 9	..	..	..	..	..	..	..	..	..	..	..	..	..	..	..
7	..	..	..	..	..	..	..	..	..	..	..	..	..	..	..	..	..	..	..
8	..	..	..	..	..	..	..	..	..	..	..	..	..	..	..	..	..	..	..
9	..	8 17	..	9 17	..	..	..	..	..	..	..	..	..	..	..	..	..	..	..
10	..	..	..	9 25	..	..	..	..	..	..	..	..	..	..	..	..	..	..	..
11	..	..	..	9 32	..	..	..	..	..	..	..	..	..	..	..	..	..	..	..
12	..	..	..	..	..	..	..	..	..	..	..	..	..	..	..	..	..	..	..
13	..	..	..	..	..	..	..	..	..	..	..	..	..	..	..	..	..	..	..
14	..	..	..	..	..	..	..	..	..	..	..	..	..	..	..	..	..	..	..
15	..	..	..	..	..	..	..	..	..	..	..	..	..	..	..	..	..	..	..
16	..	..	..	..	..	..	..	..	..	..	..	..	..	..	..	..	..	..	..
17	..	..	..	..	..	..	..	..	..	..	..	..	..	..	..	..	..	..	..
18	..	..	..	..	..	..	..	..	..	..	..	..	..	..	..	..	..	..	..
19	..	..	..	..	..	..	..	..	..	..	..	..	..	..	..	..	..	..	..
20	..	..	..	..	..	..	..	..	..	..	..	..	..	..	..	..	..	..	..
21	..	..	..	..	..	..	..	..	..	..	..	..	..	..	..	..	..	..	..
22	..	..	..	..	..	..	..	..	..	..	..	..	..	..	..	..	..	..	..
23	..	..	..	..	..	..	..	..	..	..	..	..	..	..	..	..	..	..	..
24	..	..	..	..	..	..	..	..	..	..	..	..	..	..	..	..	..	..	..
25	..	..	..	..	..	..	..	..	..	..	..	..	..	..	..	..	..	..	..
26	..	..	..	..	..	..	..	..	..	..	..	..	..	..	..	..	..	..	..
27	..	..	..	..	..	9 50	..	..	..	..	..	2 32	..	..	..	6 50	..	..	..
28	..	..	..	..	..	9 57	..	..	..	..	..	2 39	..	..	..	6 57	..	..	..
29	..	..	..	..	..	9 58	..	..	..	..	..	2 39½	..	..	..	6 57½	..	..	..
30	..	..	..	..	..	10 4	..	..	..	..	..	2 45½	..	..	..	7 3½	..	..	..
31	..	..	..	..	..	10 5	..	..	..	..	..	2 46	..	..	..	7 4	..	..	..
32	..	..	..	..	..	Until 9th September inclusive	..	Until 9th September inclusive	..	Until 9th September inclusive	..	..	..	..	..	Until 9th September inclusive	..	Until 9th September inclusive	..
33	..	..	..	..	..		..		..		..	..	..	..	..		..		..
34	..	..	..	..	..		..		..		..	..	..	..	..		..		..
35	..	..	..	..	..		..		..		..	..	..	..	..		..		..
36	..	..	..	..	..		..		..		..	..	..	..	..		..		..
37	..	..	..	..	..		..		..		..	..	..	..	..		..		..
38	..	..	..	..	..		..		..		..	..	..	..	..		..		..
39	..	..	..	..	..		..		..		..	..	..	..	..		..		..
40	..	..	..	..	..		..		..		..	..	..	..	..		..		..
41	..	..	..	..	..		..		..		..	..	..	..	..		..		..
42	..	..	..	..	..		..		..		..	..	..	..	..		..		..
43	..	..	..	..	..		..		..		..	..	..	..	..		..		..
44	..	..	..	..	..		..		..		..	..	..	..	..		..		..
45	..	..	..	..	..		..		..		..	..	..	..	..		..		..
46	..	..	..	..	..		..		..		..	..	..	..	..		..		..
47	..	..	..	..	..	..	..	9 45	..	11 18	..	..	..	2 28	..	..	..	6 45	..
48	..	..	..	..	..	..	..	9 56	..	11 29	..	..	..	2 39	..	..	..	6 56	..
49	..	..	..	..	..	..	..	9 57	..	11 29	..	..	..	2 40	..	..	..	6 57	..
50	..	..	..	..	..	..	..	10 6	..	11 38	..	..	..	2 49	..	..	..	7 6	..
51	..	..	..	..	..	..	..	10 9	..	11 39	..	..	..	2 54	..	..	..	7 9	..
52	..	..	..	..	..	..	..	10 18	..	11 48	..	..	..	3 3	..	..	..	7 18	..
53	..	..	..	..	..	..	..	10 19	..	11 48	..	..	..	3 4	..	..	..	7 19	..
54	..	..	..	..	..	10 14	..	10 26	..	11 55	..	2 55	..	3 11	..	7 13	..	7 26	..
55	..	..	..	..	..	..	..	10 29	..	..	..	..	..	3 16	..	..	..	7 28	..
56	..	..	..	..	..	..	..	10 38	..	..	..	..	..	3 25	..	..	..	7 37	..
57	..	..	..	..	..	..	..	10 39	..	..	..	..	..	3 26	..	..	..	7 38	..
58	..	..	..	..	..	..	..	10a47	..	..	..	..	..	3a34	..	..	..	7a46	..
59	..	..	..	..	..	..	..	10 53	..	..	..	..	..	3 40	..	..	..	7 52	..
60	..	..	..	..	..	..	..	10 57	..	..	..	..	..	3 44	..	..	..	7 56	..
61	..	..	..	..	..	..	..	11 17	..	..	..	..	..	..	..	..	..	..	..

Working Timetable
1964/65

P2

EXPLANATION OF REFERENCES

M ... Monday — Th ... Thursday
T ... Tuesday — F ... Friday
W ... Wednesday — S ... Saturday

The addition of the letter "O" indicates that the train will run on that day or those days only. The letter "X" indicates that the train will not run on that day or those days

GL — Goods Line. ML — Main Line. RL — Relief Line.

AE — Stops only to attach or detach assisting engine.
C — Change trainmen, etc.
- C in both arrival and departure times — Change trainmen only.
- C in departure time — Change trainmen and work.
- TW in both arrival and departure times — Change trainmen and water.

D — Stops only to set down (passenger) or detach traffic (freight).
E — Stops for examination, etc.
- E in departure time only — Traffic and examination.
- E in both arrival and departure times — Examination only.
- E in arrival time and * in departure time — Examination and shunts for other trains to pass.
- WE in both arrival and departure times — Examination and water.
- EL in both arrival and departure times — Examination and change engine.
- EC in both arrival and departure times — Examination and change trainmen.

EBV — Engine and Brake van.
ECS, † — Empty coaching stock train.
L — Stops only to change engine.
LD, LE, ‖ — Light engine.
M — Mails delivered or received at line side apparatus.
P — Stops only to pin down or pick up wagon brakes. P in arrival, for pinning down, and in departure for picking up.
Q — Runs when required.
R — Stops when required.
U — Stops only to take up (passenger) or attach traffic (freight).
W — Stops for water, etc.
- W in both arrival and departure times — Water only.
- W* in both arrival and departure times — Water and shunts for other trains to pass.

X — Indicates points at which trains are booked to cross each other on a single line at a crossing place.
‡ — Advertised time in public time table.
* — Shunts for other trains to pass, etc.
- * in departure time — Traffic and shunts for other trains to pass.
- * in both arrival and departure times — Stops or shunts for other trains ahead or to pass only.

§ — Indicates that head code and/or number is changed en route.
→ — For continuation of train timings, see subsequent column.
← — Train timings continued from previous column.
a — Arrives ½ minute earlier. d — Arrives 2½ minutes earlier.
b — Arrives 1½ minutes earlier. e — Arrives 3 minutes earlier.
c — Arrives 2 minutes earlier. f — Arrives 3½ minutes earlier.
g — Arrives 4 minutes earlier.
★ — Denotes Local Passenger Trains worked by Steam Locomotive.
♦ — Denotes class of Diesel Locomotive and Load. (See Tables on pages P4 and P5).
▽ — Denotes Diesel Multiple Unit, including Single Diesel Unit, Drive-end Trailer and Parcels Diesel.
◇ — Denotes Diesel Hauled freight train at Diesel point-to-point timings (see table on page P6).
♠ — Not to convey vehicles of less than 15 foot wheelbase.
♠♠ — Not to convey 4 wheeled vehicles.

P66 WEEKDAYS OKEHAMPTON, HALWILL, BUDE AND PADSTOW

SINGLE LINE between Meldon Jn. and Bude and Padstow worked by Electric Token. Crossing places at all stations except Maddaford Moor Halt. MAXIMUM PERMISSIBLE SPEED—55 Miles per Hour (50 Miles per hour between Whitstone & Bridgerule and Bude).

Mileage M	C	DOWN		Ruling Gradient 1 in		6.0 am Bodmin Road Freight					LE	ECS	7.50 am Bodmin Road	Pass and News		10.10 am Bodmin Rd	
						9C38			2C77		0C26	3C62	2C62	2C69		2C62	
						am			am		SX am	am	▽ am	am		▽ am	
0	0	OKEHAMPTON	arr	—	1												
			dep		2									6 15			
2	52	Meldon Jn.		—	3									6 24			
4	70	Maddaford Moor Halt		78F	4												
8	51	Ashbury	arr	78R	5									6 35			
			dep		6									6 37			
12	36	HALWILL	arr	78F	7									6 43			
			dep		8				6 50					7 4			
15	65	Dunsland Cross	arr	88F	9				6 56								
			dep		10				6 56½								
20	30	Holsworthy	arr	78F	11				7 5½								
			dep		12				7 6								
25	27	Whitstone and	arr	82F	13				7 14								
		Bridgerule	dep		14				7 15								
30	73	BUDE	arr	73F	15				7 24								
17	44	Ashwater	arr	73F	16									7 14			
			dep		17									7 15			
21	13	Tower Hill	arr	73F	18									7 25			
			dep		19									7 26			
26	13	Launceston	arr	94R	20									7X36			
			dep		21									7 57			
30	36	Egloskerry	arr	80R	22									8 4			
			dep		23									8 5			
34	8	Tresmeer	arr	74R	24									8 12			
			dep		25									8 13			
38	78	Otterham	arr	73R	26									8 22			
			dep		27									8 23			
43	34	Camelford	arr	73F	28									8 30			
			dep		29									8 32			
45	63	Delabole	arr	74F	30									8 37			
			dep		31									8 38			
49	71	Port Isaac Road	arr	75F	32									8 45			
			dep		33									8 47			
52	42	St. Kew Highway	arr	73F	34									8 51			
			dep		35									8 52			
56	51	WADEBRIDGE	arr	75F	36	6 50							8X17	8X59		10 37	
			dep	132	37						7‖45	8† 0	8V20	9 5		10 39	
62	23	PADSTOW	arr	R & F	38						7‖54	8† 9	8V29	9 14		10 48	

ECS (3C62): To work 8.48 am to Exeter Central.
7.50 am Bodmin Road (2C62): V—Terminates at Wadebridge on Saturdays.

WEEKDAYS UP

Mileage M	C	UP		Ruling Gradient 1 in		ECS		To Bodmin Road	Freight to Bodmin North	Empty D M U to Bodmin North					To Bodmin Road	8.56 am Torrington	
						3C77		2C56	9B06	3Z01	2C77		2C61		2C56	2C68	2C69
						am		▽ am	am	▽ MX am	am		am		SX am	▽ am	▽ SX am
0	0	PADSTOW	dep	132	1										8 10		8 35
5	52	WADEBRIDGE	arr	R & F	2										8X19		8 44
			dep		3			6 50	7 10	7†25					8 30		
9	61	St. Kew Highway	arr	75R	4												
			dep		5												
12	32	Port Isaac Road	arr	73R	6												
			dep		7												
16	40	Delabole	arr	73R	8												
			dep		9												
18	69	Camelford	arr	74R	10												
			dep		11												
23	25	Otterham	arr	73F	12												
			dep		13												
28	15	Tresmeer	arr	73F	14												
			dep		15												
31	67	Egloskerry	arr	74F	16												
			dep		17												
36	10	Launceston	arr	80F	18												
			dep		19								7 52				
41	10	Tower Hill	arr	94F	20								7 59				
			dep		21								8 1				
44	59	Ashwater	arr	73R	22								8 7				
			dep		23								8 9				
0	0	BUDE	dep		24	6† 5					7 35						
5	46	Whitstone and	arr	73R	25						7 46						
		Bridgerule	dep		26	6 15					7 46½						
10	43	Holsworthy	arr	82R	27						7 55½						
			dep		28	6 23					7 56						
15	8	Dunsland Cross	arr	78R	29						8 5½						
			dep		30	6 30					8 6						
18	37	HALWILL	arr	88R	31	6†37					8 12		8 18			10 18	
			dep		32								8 19				
53	52	Ashbury	arr	78R	33								8 26½				
			dep		34								8 27				
57	33	Maddaford Moor Halt		78F	35								8a35				
59	51	Meldon Jn.		78R	36								8 40				
62	23	OKEHAMPTON	arr	—	37								8V46				
			dep		38												

2C61: V—Stops at Quarry Halt on Saturdays and arrives Okehampton 8.57 am (not advertised).

OKEHAMPTON, HALWILL, BUDE AND PADSTOW WEEKDAYS P67

		Freight	10.20 am Bodmin Road Freight			To Barns Junction			12.5 pm Bodmin Road		1‖11 pm Boscarne Jn. L E				2.22 pm Bodmin North Freight		1.19 pm Exeter Central		
	2C77	9C38	9C38		2C69	2C94		2C77	2C62		0C38		2C77		9C38		2C69	2C77	
	am	SX Q am	am		am	▽ am		am	▽ PM		PM		PM		SX PM		PM	PM	
1																	2 1		
2					10 0								12 10				2 4		
3					10 8								12 18				2 11		
4					10 13								12 23				2a15		
5					10 20								12 30				2 21		
6					10 21								12 31				2 22		
7					10X27								12 37				2 28		
8	8 53				10 35	10 35		10 40					12 50				2 32	2 42	
9	8 59							10 46					12 56					2 48	
10	8 59½							10 48					12 58					2 50	
11	9 6½							10 56					1 6					2X58	
12	9 7½							10 57					1 7					3 3	
13	9 15½							11 5					1 15					3 11	
14	9 16							11 6					1 16					3 12	
15	9 25							11 15					1 25					3 21	
16					10 42												2 39		
17					10 42½												2 40		
18					10 48½												2 46		
19					10 50												2 47		
20					10 57												2 54		
21					11 3												2 56		
22					11 10												3 3		
23					11 11												3 4		
24					11 18												3 12		
25					11 19												3 12½		
26					11 28												3 21½		
27					11 29												3 22		
28					11 36												3 29		
29					11 38												3 30		
30					11X43												3 35		
31		10 30			11 46												3 36		
32					11 53												3 43		
33					11 54												3 44		
34					11 58												3 48		
35					11 59												3 49		
36		11 0	11 25		12 6				12 32		1‖22				3 15		3X56		
37					12 8				12 33								4 0		
38					12 17				12 42								4 9		

2C77 (10 40 am): Portion off 10.0 am Okehampton.

		To Exeter Central	To Bodmin Road			Freight			To Bodmin Road	Freight to Bodmin Road		L E to Boscarne Jn.	To Bodmin Road					
	2C77	2C79	2C56		2C77	9C10		2C61	2C56	9B05		0B08	2C56			2C61		
	am	am	▽ am		noon	SX Q am		am	am	am		PM	▽ PM			PM		
1		8 48						11 5	11 20				12 45					
2		8X57						11 14	11 29				12 54					
3		9 0	9 15			9 30		11 20	11 30	11 45		12‖40	12 55					
4		9 8						11 28										
5		9 9						11 29										
6		9 15						11 35										
7		9 16						11 36										
8		9 25						11X44										
9		9 26				10 0		11 45										
10		9 32						11 51										
11		9 34						11 52										
12		9 41						11 59										
13		9 42						12 0										
14		9 49						12 7										
15		9 50						12 8										
16		9 56						12 14										
17		9 57						12 15										
18		10 4						12 22										
19		10 8						12 24										
20		10 15						12 31										
21		10 16						12 32										
22		10 22						12 38										
23		10 23						12 39										
24	9 40				12 0											2 40		
25	9 51				12 11											2 51		
26	9 52				12 12											2 52		
27	10 1				12 21											3X1		
28	10 3				12 22											3 2		
29	10 12				12 31											3 11		
30	10 13				12 32											3 12		
31	10 20	10X32			12 39			12 48								3 19		
32		10 38						12 50								3 22		
33		10 47						12 59								3 31		
34		10 48						1 0								3 32		
35		10 57						1 8								3 40		
36		11 2						1 14								3 46		
37		11 8						1 20								3 53		
38		11 10																

P68 WEEKDAYS OKEHAMPTON, HALWILL, BUDE AND PADSTOW

DOWN			2.45 pm Wenford Freight	3.55 pm Bodmin Road	4.30 pm Bodmin Road	4.40 pm Bodmin North Freight			5.50 pm Bodmin North
			9C38	2C62§	2C62	9C38	2C62	2C77	2Z01
			SX Q PM	PM	▽ PM	SX Q PM	PM	PM	▽ SX PM
OKEHAMPTON	arr	1							
	dep	2						4 30	
Meldon Jn.		3						4 37	
Maddaford Moor Halt		4						4 42	
Ashbury	arr	5						4 48	
	dep	6						4 49	
HALWILL	arr	7						4 55	
	dep	8						4 59	
Dunsland Cross	arr	9						5X5	
	dep	10						5 8	
Holsworthy	arr	11						5 16	
	dep	12						5 17	
Whitstone and	arr	13						5 25	
Bridgerule	dep	14						5 26	
BUDE	arr	15						5 35	
Ashwater	arr	16							
	dep	17							
Tower Hill	arr	18							
	dep	19							
Launceston	arr	20							
	dep	21							
Egloskerry	arr	22							
	dep	23							
Tresmeer	arr	24							
	dep	25							
Otterham	arr	26							
	dep	27							
Camelford	arr	28							
	dep	29							
Delabole	arr	30							
	dep	31							
Port Isaac Road	arr	32							
	dep	33							
St. Kew Highway	arr	34							
	dep	35							
WADEBRIDGE	arr	36	4 10	4 27	4 57	5 20			6 10
	dep	37		4 28	5 1		5 40		
PADSTOW	arr	38		4 37	5 10		5 49		

§ On Saturdays worked by Rail Bus—2Z01

WEEKDAYS UP				3.55 pm Torrington		Empty Rail Bus to Boscarne Jn.	E C S	To Bodmin Road	L E to Okehampton SX, Exmouth Jn. SO	Freight to Bodmin Road		To Bodmin Road
			2C77	2C68	2C61	3Z01	3C69	2C56	0C24§	9B05	2C77	2Z01
			PM	▽ PM	PM	▽ SO PM	PM	▽ PM	PM	SX PM	PM	▽ SO PM
PADSTOW	dep	1			3 45	4†40	4†50	5 15				
WADEBRIDGE	arr	2			3X54	4†49	4†59	5 24				
	dep	3			3 57	5† 0		5 25		5 40		6 15
St. Kew Highway	arr	4			4 5							
	dep	5			4 5½							
Port Isaac Road	arr	6			4 11½							
	dep	7			4 12							
Delabole	arr	8			4 20							
	dep	9			4 20½							
Camelford	arr	10			4 26½							
	dep	11			4 27							
Otterham	arr	12			4 34							
	dep	13			4 35							
Tresmeer	arr	14			4 42							
	dep	15			4 43							
Egloskerry	arr	16			4 49							
	dep	17			4 50							
Launceston	arr	18			4 57							
	dep	19			5 0							
Tower Hill	arr	20			5 7							
	dep	21			5 8							
Ashwater	arr	22			5 14							
	dep	23			5 15							
BUDE	dep	24	4 35						5‖45		6 53	
Whitstone and	arr	25	4 46								7 2	
Bridgerule	dep	26	4 47						5 57		7 2½	
Holsworthy	arr	27	4 56								7 11½	
	dep	28	4 57						6 7		7 12	
Dunsland Cross	arr	29	5X6						6XC17		7 21	
	dep	30	5 7						6C21		7 22	
HALWILL	arr	31	5 14	5 18	5 24						7 29	
	dep	32			5 27				6 30			
Ashbury	arr	33			5 36							
	dep	34			5 37				6 40			
Maddaford Moor Halt		35			5 45							
Meldon Jn.		36			5 51				6 55			
OKEHAMPTON	arr	37			5 58				7‖1			
	dep	38							7‖10			

To work 5.40 pm to Padstow (3C69)

§ 0C14 on Saturdays (0C24)

OKEHAMPTON, HALWILL, BUDE AND PADSTOW WEEKDAYS P69

		6.25 pm Bodmin Road		To Barns Junction	8.0 pm Bodmin Road			9†25 pm Bodmin Road Empty D M U
	2C69	2C62	2C77	2C94	2C62	2C69	2C77	3C62
	PM	▽ PM	PM	▽ PM	▽ PM	PM	PM	▽ PM
1								
2			5 45			6 55		
3			5 52			7 2		
4			5 57			7 7		
5			6 4			7 14		
6			6 5			7 15		
7			6 11			7 21		
8	6 18		6 13	6 20		7 31	7 40	
9			6X19				7 46	
10			6C20				7 47	
11			6 28				7 55	
12			6 29				7 56	
13			6 37				8 4	
14			6 38				8 5	
15			6 46				8 14	
16	6 25					7 38		
17	6 26					7 39		
18	6 32					7X45		
19	6 33					7 51		
20	6 40					7 58		
21						8 0		
22						8 7		
23						8 8		
24						8 16		
25						8 17		
26						8 26		
27						8 27		
28						8 34		
29						8 35		
30						8 40		
31						8 40½		
32						8 47½		
33						8 48		
34						8 52		
35						8 53		
36		6 52			8 27	9 0		9†55
37		6 53						
38		7 2						

		To Bodmin Road	To Bodmin Road
	2C61	2C56	2C56
	PM	▽ PM	▽ PM
1	6 20	7 5	
2	6 29	7 14	
3	6 33	7 15	8 50
4	6 41		
5	6 42		
6	6 48		
7	6 49		
8	6 58		
9	6 59		
10	7 5		
11	7 6		
12	7 13		
13	7 14		
14	7 21		
15	7 22		
16	7 28		
17	7 29		
18	7 36		
19	7 41		
20	7X48		
21	7 50		
22	7 56		
23	7 57		
24			
25			
26			
27			
28			
29			
30			
31	8 6		
32	8 10		
33	8 19		
34	8 21		
35	8 30		
36	8 36		
37	8 42		
38			

Appendix 4
Padstow Carriage Working Notice Summer Saturdays 13th June to 11th September 1960
By Glen Woods

What better place is there to start to explain the carriage workings on the North Cornwall line than a summer Saturday at Padstow? The accompanying table sets out the Saturday workings from 13th June to 11th September 1960. The workings are laid out in departure time order (the column headed 'Train') with the stock that berthed at Padstow following.

PADSTOW (SO)

Train	Destination	Formation	Previous Service		
			Time	From	Due
a.m. 8 10 …	Bodmin Road W.R.	2-set (P.)… … … …	7 30 a.m. …	Bodmin General WR. … …	8 3
8 30 **R** … …	Waterloo …	(	--	Berth (until 16/7) …	--
		1. S.K … … … (	12. 25 a.m. …	Waterloo (23/7 to 6/8)	7 26
		(	--	Berth (com. 13/8)	--
		2-set (R)… …) 1. S.K (com 2/7))	--	Berth	--
	Wadebridge	2-set (P.)… … …)			
9 8 … … …	Bodmin Road W.R. … …	2 W.R. set	7. 50 a.m. … …	Bodmin Road W.R.	8 50
11 0 **R** (until 11/7)	Waterloo	5-set ... … … …) 1. C.K. … … …) 1 R.C.O. … …) 1. R.K.B. (3)…)	--	Berth	--
		3-set (L.) (com 16/7) (	12 15/12 25 a.m.	Waterloo (until 3/9)	7 26
		(	--	Berth (10/9 only)	--
11 35	Bodmin Road W.R.	2 W.R. set	10. 10 a.m.	Bodmin Road W.R.	11 24
p.m. 12 10	Bodmin North	2-set (P) … … …	11 20 a.m. …	Bodmin North	11 55
1 0 **R**	Waterloo … Okehampton	3-set (L.) 2-set (P.)… … …	1. 25 a.m. 10. 12 a.m.	Waterloo Okehampton R.P.	9 27 12 30
2 52	Bodmin North	2-set (P) … … …	2 0 p.m. …	Bodmin North	2 34
3 13	Waterloo Okehampton	1 News Van B. 2-set (P.)… … …	1. 25 a.m. 1. 15 p.m.	Waterloo Wadebridge	9 27 1 29
4 40	Bodmin North	2-set (P.)… … …	4. 5 p.m.	Bodmin North	4 35
6 0	Okehampton Exeter Central	2-set (P.)… … … 1 B.Y.	10. 15 a.m. 10. 12 a.m.	Wadebridge Okehampton F.P.	10 24 12 30
8 4	Bodmin Road W.R.	2 W.R. set	6. 17 p.m.	Bodmin Road W.R.	7 9
8 30	Wadebridge	2-set (P.)… … …	5. 51 p.m.	Okehampton	7 58
10 5	Wadebridge	2-set (P.)… … …	9. 8 p.m.	Bodmin Road W.R.	9 52
(2/7 to 20/8	Berth	1 S.K. (com. 16/7)) 1 S.K.) 2-set (P.)… … …)	7. 30 a.m.	Waterloo	2 14
--	Berth	1 S.K.) 1 C.K.) 5-set)	10. 35 a.m.	Waterloo	5 0
--	Berth	2-set (R) 1 B.C.K. 2-set (P.)… … …	11. 15 a.m.	Waterloo	6 22

Notes

R	Seat Reservable Train
com.	Commencing
F.P.	Front Portion
R.P.	Rear Portion

Coach Sets

2-set (P)	BCK + BSK (Maunsell)
2-set (R)	BCK + BSK (Bulleid)
3-set (L)	BSK + CK + BSK
5-set	BSK + SK + CK + SK + BSK
	2 W.R. SetW.R. 'B' set

Coaching Stock

B.C.K.	Corridor Brake Composite
B.S.K	Corridor Brake Second
B.Y.	4-Wheeled Passenger Brake Van
C.K.	Corridor Composite
R.C.O.	Restaurant Composite Open
R.K.B	Restaurant Kitchen Buffet
S.K.	Corridor Second

The first entry is the 8 10 a.m. to Bodmin Road, on the Western Region, and was formed of a 2-set (P) which had worked into Padstow on the 7 22 a.m. from Bodmin North arriving at 7 55 a.m. The next departure was the first of the Waterloo bound trains formed of one S.K. and a 3-set (L) plus a 2-set (P) for Wadebridge. The previous service for the S.K. changed over the summer period, working down from Waterloo on the 12 25 a.m. during the peak; at other times the vehicles berthed overnight on the preceding Friday. The 9 8 a.m. to Bodmin Road was a W.R. 'B' set; most Southern Region Carriage Working Notices did not give much detail on the stock provided by other regions. The 11 0 a.m. 'ACE' to Waterloo consisted of a Bulleid 5-set, a loose C.K., a Bulleid Tavern set (R.C.O + R.K.B.) plus an additional 3-set (L) from 16th July 1960. **Note:** The number in brackets after the R.K.B. was the Restaurant Car working diagram number. The Tavern set worked down to Padstow (unstaffed from Exeter Central) on the 11 0 a.m. from Waterloo on Fridays only. The Bulleid 5-set (one of sets 823 to 849) were regulars on the Saturday only workings in the summer period. The set arrived on the 10 35 a.m. from Waterloo and, surprisingly, was booked to berth at Padstow until the next Saturday when it returned on the 11 0 a.m. The 3 13 p.m. departure included the returning News Van B. These were roof-boarded at this point in time "NEWSPAPER TRAFFIC" on one board and either "WATERLOO-WEST OF ENGLAND" or "WATERLOO-PADSTOW" on the other. Two vans from the "pool" S265S to S280S were used on diagrams 69 and 70. In previous years S266S and S279S had been allocated to the Padstow workings. The 6 0 p.m. to Okehampton included a B.Y. for Exeter Central which had worked down on the 10 12 a.m. from Okehampton. This also applied on weekdays when the incoming service was the 9 56 a.m. from Okehampton with the destination of the B.Y. being Nine Elms. The 2-set (P) shown as berthing after having worked on the 7 30 a.m. from Waterloo did work all the way from Waterloo but on the 11 15 a.m., due at 6 22 p.m., only the 2-set (R) and the B.C.K. originated at Waterloo, the 2-set (P) being an attachment at Launceston.

North Cornwall Carriage Workings commencing 2nd July 1939
2-COACH LAVATORY SET WORKINGS
(SETS NOS. 7 to 21, 42 to 46, 51 to 54 and 56.)

Working No. / Station	Depart	Notes
(167) WEEKDAYS.	a.m.	
Okehampton	10 0	
Padstow	--	
S.X.	p.m.	
Padstow	12 40	
Okehampton	3 30	
Bude	5 30	
Halwill	--	
S.O.		
Padstow	12 30	**23/9 only**
	2 20	**not 23/9**
Okehampton	7 47	
Delabole	9†35	
Launceston	--	
Sundays		
Launceston	--	

Working No. / Station	Depart	Notes
(168) M.O.	a.m.	
Bude	7 22	
Halwill	--	
DAILY	a.m.	
Halwill	8 15	
Bude	--	
S.X.	a.m.	
Bude	9 40	
	p.m.	
Halwill	12 20	
Bude	1 35	
Okehampton	3 30	
Padstow	6 35	
Wadebridge	7 0	
Padstow	8 50	
Wadebridge	--	
S.O.	a.m.	
Bude	9 40	
Halwill	10 39	**F.P.**
Bude	1 30	
	p.m.	
Okehampton	3 30	
Padstow	6 35	
Wadebridge	7 0	
Padstow	8 50	
Wadebridge	--	
SUNDAYS		
Wadebridge	--	

Working No. / Station	Depart	Notes
(169) WEEKDAYS	p.m.	
Wadebridge	1 45	
Padstow	2 20	
Okehampton	--	
S.X.		
Okehampton	5 50	
Padstow	--	
S.O.		
Okehampton	6 28	
Bude	9 10	
Holsworthy	9 37	
Bude	--	
SUNDAYS		
2/7 to 10/9	a.m.	
Bude	10 10	
Okehampton	11 45	
	p.m.	
Bude	2 5	
Okehampton	3 35	
Bude	7 30	
Okehampton	9 15	
Bude	--	

Working No. / Station	Depart	Notes
(170) WEEKDAYS	a.m.	
Bude	7 22	**F.P.**
Okehampton	10 0	
Bude	--	
S.X.	p.m.	
Bude	12 35	
Halwill	1 38	**R.P.**
Bude	3 4	
Okehampton	5 50	
Bude	--	
Th.O.		
Bude	9 10	
Holsworthy	9 37	
Bude	--	
S.O.		
Bude	3 4	
Okehampton	5 30	
Padstow	--	
SUNDAYS		
2/7, 13/8, 10/9	a.m.	
Padstow	9 45	
	p.m.	
Exeter Central	7 47	
Padstow	--	

North Cornwall Carriage Workings commencing 2nd July 1939 (continued)
2-COACH LAVATORY SET WORKINGS
(SETS NOS. 7 to 21, 42 to 46, 51 to 54 and 56.)

Working No. / Station	Depart	Notes
(171) WEEKDAYS	a.m.	
Padstow	8 40	
Okehampton	--	
S.X.	a.m.	
Okehampton	11 28	
	p.m.	
Exeter Central	12 35	
Broad Clyst	1 9	
Exeter Central	3 48	
Plymouth	--	
S.O.	a.m.	
Okehampton	11 8	
	p.m.	
Exeter Central	1 40	
Honiton	3 36	
Exeter Central	5 26	
Plymouth	9 15	
Okehampton	--	
SUNDAYS	p.m.	
Okehampton	9 6	
Plymouth	--	

Working No. / Station	Depart	Notes
(173) WEEKDAYS	a.m.	
Exeter Central	8 0	
Sidmouth	--	
S.X.	a.m.	
Sidmouth	12 20	
Exeter Central	--	
S.O.	a.m.	
Sidmouth	9 45	
Exeter Central	--	
DAILY	a.m.	
Exeter Central	11 37	
	p.m.	
Okehampton	1 0	
Padstow	6 0	
Okehampton	--	
SUNDAYS	a.m.	
Okehampton	8 30	
	p.m.	
Plymouth	9 15	
Okehampton	--	

Working No. / Station	Depart	Notes
(174) M.O.	a.m.	
Halwill	5 21	F.
Launceston	--	
M.S.X.	a.m.	
Okehampton	4 0	F.
Launceston	--	
S.X.	a.m.	
Launceston	7 44	
Padstow	9 14	
Wadebridge	9 47	
	p.m.	
Padstow	2 55	
Wadebridge	3 20	
Exeter Central	--	
S.O.	p.m.	
Okehampton	3 30	
Bude	7 7	
Exeter Central	--	
SUNDAYS	p.m.	
Exeter Central	1 0	
Honiton	1 50	
Exeter Central	--	

Working No. / Station	Depart	Notes
(175) WEEKDAYS	a.m.	
Launceston	7 42	
	p.m.	
Okehampton	1 0	
Bude	--	
S.X.	p.m.	
Bude	7 2	
Okehampton	--	
S.O.	p.m.	
Bude	5 0	
Halwill	--	
SUNDAYS		
Halwill	--	

Working No. / Station	Depart	Notes
(177) S.X.	p.m.	Part of
Exeter Central	6 0	Diagram
Okehampton	7 39	Only
Launceston	--	

Appendix 5

Carriage Working Notice

Supplied by Glen Woods

B.R. 31105/2

BRITISH RAILWAYS

SOUTHERN REGION

CARRIAGE WORKING NOTICE STEAM TRAINS

15th June to 13th September, 1959 inclusive

WESTERN DISTRICT

EXPLANATION OF REFERENCES

SUN.	Sundays.	C.A.	Adaptor Fitted.
M.O.	Mondays.	C.P.	Pullman Gangway and Automatic Couplings.
M.X.	Mondays Excepted.	F.	Freight Train.
M.F.O.	Mondays and Fridays.	F.P.	Front Portion.
T.W.T.	Tuesdays, Wednesdays and Thursdays.	L.M.	London Midland Region.
W.O.	Wednesdays.	M.P.	Middle Portion.
W.X.	Wednesdays Excepted.	Q.	Conditional Train.
W.F.O.	Wednesdays and Fridays.	R.	Reservable.
Th.O.	Thursdays.	R.P.	Rear Portion.
F.O.	Fridays.	S.R.E.	Shunt to release engine.
F.X.	Fridays Excepted.	V.	Van Train.
S.O.	Saturdays.	W.R.	Western Region.
S.X.	Saturdays Excepted.	†	Empty Train.
Cor. P.M.V.	Gangwayed bogie luggage van, 10 tons carrying capacity.	B.Y.	Guard's van, 4 wheels, 23 ft. 0 in. wheel base, 10 tons carrying capacity.
Van B.	Guard's van, 8 wheels, 10 tons carrying capacity.	P.M.V. (4)	Luggage van, 4 wheels, 21 ft. 0 in. or 22 ft. 0 in. wheel base, 10 tons carrying capacity.

It is important that all services are formed with correct types of stock as shown herein, and all concerned must give special attention to the matter.

All Passenger Stock is Corridor Type except where otherwise shown.

Alterations to the booked working must be advised to the Passenger Rolling Stock Dept., Exeter Central.

For details and type of Sets as indicated by suffix letter and Loose Vehicles, Seating and Restrictions, see Appendix to Steam Train Carriage Working Notice.

The Working Numbers of Restaurant Cars, Buffet Cars and Dining Sets (as shown in the Appendix to Steam Train Carriage Working Notice) are shown in brackets against each car, etc.

BARNSTAPLE JN. (SX)—*continued*

—	Berth	I B.C.K. ... ... I S.K. **FO**	8.24 p.m. ...	Torrington	8 56
—	Berth	I S.K. **MFO** ... ... I S.K. ... ... I B.C.K.	8.30 p.m. ...	Ilfracombe...	9 9

BERE ALSTON (SX)

a.m. 6 15 ...	Plymouth Nth. Rd.	3-set (L.)... ... ... I S.K. ... ... P. & P. set (373) ...	6. 0 a.m. ... 5.30 a.m. ...	Tavistock North ... Callington...	6 11 6 10
7 35 ...	Plymouth Nth. Rd.	2-set (100/110) 2-set (100/110)	7.20 a.m. ... 7. 8 a.m. ...	Tavistock North ... Gunnislake	7 31 7 29
8 24 ...	Callington	2-set (100/110)	7.16 a.m. ...	Callington	7 59
10 40 ...	Callington	2-set (100/110)	9.43 a.m. ...	Callington	10 26
p.m. 12 50 ...	Plymouth Nth. Rd.	P. & P. set (373)	8.46 a.m. ...	Tavistock North ...	8 57
1 58 **WTh**	Gunnislake	2-set (100/110)	1. 0 p.m. ...	Callington	1 46
3 15 ...	Callington	*I B.C.K.	1. 0 p.m. ... 2.26 p.m. ...	Callington **MTF** ... Gunnislake **WTh** ...	1 46 2 47
5 23 ...	Callington	*I S. ... ... P. & P. set (373)	1. 0 p.m. ... 4.14 p.m. ...	Callington... ... ... Plymouth N. Rd. R.P.	1 46 4 52
6 1 ...	Gunnislake	2-set (100/110)	5. 9 p.m. ...	Plymouth Nth. Rd. ...	5 43
7 10 ...	Callington	P. & P. set (373)	6.20 p.m. ...	Callington...	7 1
8 0 ...	Callington	*I B.C.K. ... ... (*of 2-set (100/110)) ...	4.23 p.m. ...	Callington...	5 6

BODMIN GENERAL (W.R.) (SX). (Trains to and from S.R. only)

a.m. 9 0 ...	Wadebridge ...	2-set (P.)... ... ... I S.K.	8.12 a.m. ...	Padstow	8 55
p.m. 4 8 ...	Wadebridge	2 W.R. set	—	ex W.R.	—
6 1 ...	Bodmin Road ...	2 W.R. set	4†43 p.m. ...	Wadebridge	5† 8
10 20 ...	Bodmin Road ...	2 W.R. set	7. 5 p.m. ...	Wadebridge	7 25

BODMIN NORTH (SX)

a.m. 7 22 ...	Padstow...	2-set (P.)... ... ... I S.K.	6.52 a.m. ...	Wadebridge	7 12

BODMIN NORTH SX)—*continued*

a.m. 8 43	Wadebridge	2-set (P.)	8. 1 a.m.	Wadebridge	8 21
11 20	Padstow	2-set (P.) 1 S.K.	9.48 a.m.	Wadebridge	10 8
p.m. 2 0	Padstow	2-set (P.) 1 S.K.	11.55 a.m.	Padstow	12 45
4 23	Wadebridge	2-set (P.)	2.52 p.m.	Padstow	3 29
5 48	Wadebridge	2-set (P.)	5.11 p.m.	Wadebridge	5 31
6 45	Padstow	2-set (P.)	6.18 p.m.	Wadebridge	6 38

BODMIN ROAD (W.R.) (SX). (Trains to and from S.R. only)

a.m. 7 50	Padstow	2 W.R. set	7.30 a.m.	Bodmin General	7 37
10 10	Wadebridge	2 W.R. set	9. 3 a.m.	Padstow	9 54
p.m. 12 20	Wadebridge	2 W.R. set	11. 7 a.m.	Wadebridge	11 41
2 30	Wadebridge	2 W.R. set	1.23 p.m.	Wadebridge	1 57
4 25	Wadebridge	2 W.R. set	3.24 p.m.	Wadebridge	4 1
6 17	Wadebridge	2 W.R. set	5.34 p.m.	Wadebridge	6 8
7 26	Wadebridge	2 W.R. set	—	ex W.R.	—
9 5	Padstow	2-set (P.)	8. 4 p.m.	Padstow	8 51
9 42	Bodmin General	2 W.R. set	8.42 p.m.	Wadebridge	9 32

BRENTOR (SX)

p.m. 5 31	Plymouth Nth. Rd.	3-set (L.) **FX** 2-set (P.) **FO** 1 S.K. **FO**	4.14 p.m.	Plymouth Nth. Rd.	5 22

BROAD CLYST (SX)

p.m. 1 43	Exeter Central	1 B.C.K.	12.35 p.m.	Exeter Central	12 45

BUDE (SX)

a.m. 6†20	Halwill	2-set (P.)	—	Berth	—
7 58	Okehampton	2-set (P.)	—	Berth	—

BUDE (SX)—*continued*

a.m. 9 30	Exeter Central	1 S.K. **MO** (22/6 to 13/7)	—	Berth	—
		2-set (P.)	7.15 a.m.	Halwill	7 49
10 20 **R**	Waterloo	*1 S.K. (20/7 to 4/9) 1 B.C.K.	—	Berth (*also **MFO** 7/9 & 11/9)	—
	Halwill	2-set (P.)	8.53 a.m.	Halwill	9 25
p.m. 1 55	Okehampton	2-set (P.)	9.56 a.m.	Okehampton R.P.	11 20
3 15	Waterloo Okehampton	1 News van B. 2-set (P.)	1.18 p.m.	Okehampton	2 18
		1 S.K. **TO** (until 14/7)	—	Berth	—
5 32	Halwill	2-set (P.)	11. 0 a.m. or 11.5 a.m.	Waterloo F.P.	4 18
7 5	Halwill	1 S.K.	— 9.56 a.m.	Berth Okehampton F.P.	—**MO** 11 20**MX**
		2-set (P.)	4.24 p.m.	Okehampton	5 30
	Nine Elms	1 van fit	—	Berth	—
	Exeter Central	1 B.Y.	2**F** 6 a.m.	Exeter Central	6**F**14
—	Berth	‡1 S.K. **MFO** 1 B.C.K.	11. 0 a.m. or 11.5 a.m.	Waterloo R.P. (‡also **TWT** 21/7 to 3/9)	4 18
—	Berth	2-set (P.) 2-set (P.) **TO** (25/8 & 8/9) 1 S.K. **FO** (14/8 to 28/8)	5.51 p.m.	Okehampton	7 0
—	Berth	2-set (P.) **FX** 2-set (R.) **FO**	7.45 p.m.	Okehampton	9 0

BUDLEIGH SALTERTON (SX)

a.m. 6 55	Exmouth	2-set (100/110)	6†38 a.m.	Exmouth	6†49
10 55	Exmouth	2-set (100/110)	10.30 a.m.	Exmouth	10 41
p.m. 3 20	Exmouth	2-set (100/110)	2.50 p.m.	Exmouth	3 1
6 38	Exmouth	2-set (100/110)	6.16 p.m.	Exmouth	6 29

CALLINGTON (SX)

a.m. 5 30	Plymouth Nth. Rd.	P. & P. set (373)	—	Berth	—
7 16	Bere Alston	2-set (100/110)	—	Berth	—

8

CALLINGTON(SX)—*continued*

a.m. 9 43	Bere Alston	2-set (100/110)	8.24 a.m.	Bere Alston	9 9
p.m. 1 0	Bere Alston	2-set (100/110)	10.40 a.m.	Bere Alston	11 24
4 23	Bere Alston	*1 B.C.K.	3.15 p.m.	Bere Alston	3 57
6 20	Bere Alston	P. & P. set (373)	5.23 p.m.	Bere Alston R.P.	6 5
—	Berth	*1 S.	5.23 p.m.	Bere Alston F.P.	6 5
—	Berth	P. & P. set (373)	7.10 p.m.	Bere Alston	7 53
—	Berth	*1 B.C.K. (*of 2-set (100/110))	8. 0 p.m.	Bere Alston	8 42

CHARD JN. (SX)

p.m. 7 35	Axminster Exeter Central	3-set (L.) **FX** 3-set (L.) **FO** 2-set (R.) **FX**	6.15 p.m.	Exeter Central	7 18

CREDITON (SX)

p.m. 5 1	Waterloo	1 News van B. 1 B.C.K. **MX** 2-set (R.)	3. 0 p.m.	Ilfracombe	4 58
5V35	Exeter Central	Milk vans 1 van B.	— 3. 0 p.m.	Berth Ilfracombe	— 4 58

EXETER CENTRAL (SX)

Formation of Exeter—Exmouth 5 sets (E)

1 S*
1 BS
1 C (Seats 32/480)
1 BS
1 S*
(*not stencilled with set numbers)

a.m. 2F 6	Exeter St. Davids Torrington Ilfracombe Torrington Tavistock North Bude	1 B.Y. **MX** 1 van B. 1 van B. 1 van B. 1 B.Y. (stove) (400/401) 1 van B.	—	Berth	—
3V50 MO	Exmouth Jn. (thence Axminster)	1 B.Y. (stove) (400/1)	3V20 a.m. (News)	Yeoford	3V47
3†53 MO	Exeter St. Davids	1 B.C.K.	3.20 a.m. (News)	Yeoford R.P.	3 47

9

EXETER CENTRAL (SX)—*continued*

a.m. 5 6	Ilfracombe Bideford (thence Torrington)	1 S.K. **MO** 1 S.K. **MO** 2-set (R.) **MO** 1 B.C.K. **MX** 1 P.M.V. (4) 1 News van B.	— 1.15 a.m.	Berth Waterloo M.P.	— 5 0
5 12	Plymouth Nth. Rd. Padstow	1 S.K. 1 B.C.K. **MX** 2-set (R.) **MO** 1 B.C.K. **MX** 1 B.C.K. 1 News van B.	— 1.15 a.m.	Berth Waterloo M.P.	— 5 0
5 21	Ilfracombe Torrington	1 B.C.K. 1 News van B. 1 News van B.	4.25 a.m. — 1.15 a.m.	Exeter St. Davids Berth Waterloo R.P.	4 28**MO** —**MX** 5 0
6 0	Sidmouth	*1 S.K. **MFO** 2-set (100/110)	—	Berth (*To be attached brake end of set)	—
6 30 **R**	Waterloo	2-set (R.) 3-set (L.) 1 R.B. (18) 1 S.O. 1 B.C.K.	—	Berth	—
6 37	Waterloo	1 cor. P.M.V. 3-set (L.)	—	Berth	—
6 45	Exmouth	2 S.K. **MO** (7/9) 5-set (E.)	—	Berth	—
6 50	Axminster	1 S.K. 3-set (L.) 2 S.K.	—	Berth	—
7 16	Exmouth	5-set (E.)	6.40 a.m.	Exmouth	7 8
7 30 **R**	Waterloo	4-set (400) 1 S.O. 1 R.F. (30) 2 S.K. 1 B.C.K.	—	Berth	—
7 34	Sidmouth Tipton St. Johns	1 P.M.V. (4) 2-set (P.) **MO** 2-set (100/110) **MX** 3-set (L.) **FO**	—	Berth	—
7 35	Plymouth Nth. Rd. Padstow Okehampton	2-set (R.) **MO** 3-set (L.) 1 cor. P.M.V. **MX** 1 B.Y. **MX** 1 P.M.V. (4) **MX**	— 5V26 a.m. 1.15 a.m.	Berth Exmouth Jn. Waterloo F.P.	— 5V29 5 0

10

EXETER CENTRAL (SX)—*continued*

a.m.					
8 0 ...	Honiton...	2-set (P.)...	—	Berth	—
8 17 ...	Exmouth	5-set (E.)...	7.16 a.m. ...	Exmouth	7 43
8 30 ...	Ilfracombe	1 S.K. ... ... 3-set (L.)... ... ... 1 P.M.V. (4)	6.25 a.m. ...	Yeovil Town F.P. ...	8 10
8 42 ...	Plymouth Nth. Rd.	1 S.K. **TThO**... ... 3-set (L.)...	8.10 a.m. ...	Exmouth R.P.	8 35
		1 P.M.V. (4)	6.25 a.m. ... —	Yeovil Town R.P. ... Berth	8 10**MX** —**MO**
8 50 ...	Exmouth	5-set (E.)...	7.47 a.m. ...	Exmouth	8 14
8 53 ...	Waterloo ... ... Salisbury	1 P.M.V. (4) ... ... 3-set (L.)...	6.15 a.m. ...	Plymouth Nth. Rd. ...	8 39
9 24 ...	Exmouth	5-set (E.)...	8.50 a.m. ...	Exmouth	9 15
9 35 ...	Templecombe ...	1 S.K.	7. 5 a.m. ... 8. 0 a.m. ...	Torrington ... ... Axminster R.P.... ...	8 58**MO** 8 49**MX**
		3-set (L.)...	7. 5 a.m. ...	Torrington	8 58
9 40 ...	Ilfracombe	3-set (L.)... ... ... 3-set (L.) **ThO** (com. 20/8)	7.50 a.m. ...	Yeovil Town	9 29
		3-set (L.) **FO** (28/8) ...	—	Berth	—
	Torrington	3-set (L.) **FO** (11/9) ...	7.50 a.m. ...	Yeovil Town	9 29
9 55 ...	Exmouth	5-set (E.)...	9.22 a.m. ...	Exmouth	9 49
10 17 **MO**	Waterloo	2 B.C.K. (22/6 only) 1 B.C.K. (29/6) ... 1 B.C.K.	—	Berth	—
			— —	Berth ... ... Berth	— —
		1 R.C.O.... ... ... 1 R.K.B. (4/26) ... 1 F.K. ... ... 3-set (L.)... ... ... 2-set (R.)...	8.10 a.m. ...	Ilfracombe...	10 11
10 17 **FO**	Waterloo	1 B.C.K. ... ... 1 R.C.O....	—	Berth	—
		1 R.K.B. (4/10) ... 5-set ... ... 2-set (R.)...	8.10 a.m. ...	Ilfracombe...	10 11
10 30 **MO**	Waterloo	2 B.C.K. (22/6 only)	—	Berth	—
		1 R.C.O.... ... ... 1 R.K.B. (5) ... ... 1 S.K. ... ... 3-set (L.)...	8.25 a.m. ...	Plymouth Nth. Rd. ...	10 23

11

EXETER CENTRAL (SX)—*continued*

a.m.					
10 30 **TWT**	Waterloo	3-set (L.)... ... ... 2-set (R.)...	8.10 a.m. ... 8.10 a.m. ...	Ilfracombe... ... ... Torrington	10 11 10 11
		1 R.C.O.... ... ... 1 R.K.B. (5)	—	Berth	—
		3-set (L.)...	8.25 a.m. ...	Plymouth Nth. Rd. ...	10 23
10 30 **FO**	Waterloo	1 R.C.O.... ... ... 1 R.K.B. (5)	—	Berth	—
		1 S.K. (until 7/8) ... 3-set (L.)...	8.25 a.m. ...	Plymouth Nth. Rd. ...	10 23
10 45 ...	Exmouth	5-set (E.)...	9.54 a.m. ...	Exmouth	10 21
11 12 ...	Salisbury	3-set (L.)...	8.55 a.m. ...	Ilfracombe F.P.... ...	11 7
11 15 ...	Exmouth	5-set (E.)...	10.44 a.m. ...	Exmouth	11 10
11 27 ...	Ilfracombe ... ... Torrington	2 S.K. ... ... 3-set (L.)... ... ... 1 P.M.V. (4)	8.10 a.m. ...	Salisbury F.P.	11 19
11 45 **MX**	Exmouth	1 News van B. ... ... 5-set (E.)...	8.55 a.m. ... 8.21 a.m. ...	Ilfracombe R.P.... ... Exmouth	11 7 8 42
11 45 **MO**	Exmouth	1 News van B. ... ... 5-set (E.) (15/6 & com. 29/6)	8.55 a.m. ... 8.21 a.m. ...	Ilfracombe... ... ... Exmouth	11 7 8 42
		5-set (22/6) ... ... 2-set (P.) (22/6)	— 10.20 a.m. ...	Berth ... ... Sidmouth	— 11 14
11 47 **MO**	Plymouth Nth. Rd. Bude	4-set ... ... 2-set (P.)...	—	Berth	—
		1 News van B.	8.55 a.m. ...	Ilfracombe M.P. ...	11 7
11 47 **MX**	Plymouth Nth. Rd.	1 S.K.	8.10 a.m. ...	Ilfracombe F.P.... ...	10 11
		1 S.K. **TThO**... ... 3-set (L.)...	—	Berth	—
	Bude	2-set (P.)...	—	Berth	—
		1 News van B.	8.55 a.m. ...	Ilfracombe M.P. ...	11 7
p.m. 12 15 ...	Exmouth	5-set (E.)...	11.15 a.m. ...	Exmouth	11 41
12 18 ... (20/7 to 4/9, also **MFO** 7/9 & 11/9)	Waterloo	1 B.C.K. ... ... 1 R.C.O.... ... ... 1 R.K.B. (4)	—	Berth	—
		2 B.C.K. ... ... 1 S.K.	9.35 a.m. ...	Padstow	12 12
		1 S.K. ... ... 1 B.C.K.	10.20 a.m. ...	Bude	12 12
		2-set (R.)...	10. 2 a.m. ...	Plymouth Nth. Rd. ...	12 12

12

EXETER CENTRAL (SX)—*continued*

p.m.					
12 30 (20/7 to 4/9, also **MFO** 7/9 & 11/9)	Waterloo	1 B.C.K.	—	Berth	—
		1 R.C.O.			
		1 R.K.B. (7)			
		1 S.K.	10.30 a.m.	Ilfracombe	12 24
		2-set (R.)			
		1 S.K. **MFO**	10.30 a.m.	Torrington	12 24
		1 S.K.			
		1 B.C.K.			
12 30 (until 17/7 & **TWT** com. 8/9)	Waterloo	2 B.C.K.	9.35 a.m.	Padstow	12 12
		1 B.C.K.	10.20 a.m.	Bude	12 12
		2-set (R.)	10. 2 a.m.	Plymouth Nth. Rd.	12 12
		1 R.C.O.	—	Berth	—
		1 R.K.B. (7)			
		2-set (R.)	10.30 a.m.	Ilfracombe	12 24
		1 S.K.	10.30 a.m.	Torrington	12 24
		1 B.C.K.			
12 35	Broad Clyst	1 B.C.K.	9.35 a.m.	Padstow R.P.	12 12
12 45	Exmouth	5-set (E.)	11.45 a.m.	Exmouth	12 12
1 0	Brighton	6 buffet set (19/20)	11.10 a.m.	Plymouth Nth. Rd.	12 52
	Portsmouth & S.	4-set			
1 10	Waterloo	1 P.M.V. (4)	8.10 a.m.	Salisbury	11 19
	Salisbury	3-set (L.)	—	Berth	—
	Seaton Jn.	1 S.K. **WO** (17/6 and 26/8)			
		2 S.K. **ThO** (until 6/8)			
		2 S.K. **FO** (com. 4/9)			
1 16	Exmouth	5-set (E.)	12.45 p.m.	Exmouth (not 22/6)	1 11
			8.21 a.m.	Exmouth (22/6)	8 42
1 16	Plymouth Nth. Rd.	4-set	9. 0 a.m.	Waterloo F.P.	1 8
1 25	Topsham	2-set (P.) **MO**	12.45 p.m.	Exmouth (22/6)	1 11
			10.20 a.m.	Sidmouth (15/6 and com. 29/6)	11 14
		2-set (100/110) **MX**	10.20 a.m.	Sidmouth	11 14
1 28	Ilfracombe	1 R.F. (26) **FO**	—	Berth	—
		1 S.O. **FO**			
		3-set (L.)	9. 0 a.m.	Waterloo M.P.	1 8
	Torrington	1 B.C.K.			
		1 B.C.K. (6669) **WO**	7. 5 a.m.	Torrington	8 58
	Lapford	1 van B. **FO**	—	Berth	—
1 45	Exmouth	5-set (E.)	12.15 p.m.	Exmouth	12 41
2 11 **MO** (also **TWT** 21/7 to 3/9)	Ilfracombe	1 S.K.*	8.25 a.m.	Plymouth Nth. Rd.	10 23
		1 S.K.	11. 0 a.m.	Waterloo F.P.	2 5
		2-set (R.)			
	Torrington	1 S.K.			
		1 B.C.K.			

13

EXETER CENTRAL (SX)—*continued*

p.m.					
2 11 (**TWT** until 16/7 & com. 8/9)	Ilfracombe	1 S.K.	8.25 a.m.	Plymouth Nth. Rd.	10 23
	Torrington	2-set (R.)	11. 0 a.m.	Waterloo M.P.	2 5
		1 B.C.K.			
2 11 **FO**	Ilfracombe	1 B.C.K.	1.43 p.m.	Broad Clyst	1 54
		2 S.K.	11. 5 a.m.	Waterloo	2 15
		1 R.K.B. (3)			
		1 R.C.O.			
		2-set (R.)			
	Torrington	1 S.K.			
		1 B.C.K.			
2 15	Exmouth	5-set (E.)	1.15 p.m.	Exmouth	1 46
2 21 **MFO**	Padstow	1 P.M.V. (4)	—	Berth	—
		1 S.K.	11. 5 a.m.	Waterloo F.P.	2 16
		2 B.C.K.			
	Bude	1 S.K.			
		1 B.C.K.			
	Plymouth Nth. Rd.	2 S.K.			
		2-set (R.)			
2 21 **TWT** (until 16/7 & com. 8/9)	Padstow	1 P.M.V. (4)	—	Berth	—
		2 B.C.K.	11. 0 a.m.	Waterloo R.P.	2 5
	Bude	1 B.C.K.			
	Plymouth Nth. Rd.	2-set (R.)			
2 21 **TWT** (21/7 to 3/9)	Padstow	1 P.M.V. (4)	—	Berth	—
		1 S.K.	11. 5 a.m.	Waterloo F.P.	2 16
		2 B.C.K.			
	Bude	1 S.K.			
		1 B.C.K.			
	Plymouth Nth. Rd.	1 S.K.			
		2-set (R.)			
2 30 **R**	Waterloo	1 S.K. **FO** (until 7/8)	11.46 a.m.	Plymouth Nth. Rd.	2 11
		4-set			
		1 B.C.K.	9. 0 a.m.	Waterloo R.P.	1 8
		1 S.O.			
		1 R.B. (15)			
		3-set (L.)	1 .20 p.m.	Ilfracombe	2 23
		1 S.K.	12.18 p.m.	Torrington	2 23
		1 B.C.K.			
2 51	Exmouth	5-set (E.)	2.15 p.m.	Exmouth	2 40
3 10 **MWO**	Exmouth	3-set (L.)	8. 0 a.m.	Axminster M.P.	8 49
		1 S.K.	8. 0 a.m.	Axminster	8 49**MO**
			—	Berth	—**WO**
		2 S.	8.10 a.m.	Exmouth	8 35
3 10 **TO**	Exmouth	5-set	—	Berth	—
		3 S.	(1) —	Berth	—
			(2)8.10 a.m.	Exmouth F.P.	8 35

14

EXETER CENTRAL (SX)—*continued*

p.m. 3 10 **ThO**	Exmouth	3-set (L.) 3 S.	8. 0 a.m. (1) — (2)8.10 a.m.	Axminster M.P. Berth Exmouth F.P.	8 49 — 8 35
3 10 **FO**	Exmouth	3-set (L.) 2 S. (com. 4/9)	8. 0 a.m. 8.10 a.m.	Axminster M.P. Exmouth F.P.	8 49 8 35
3 20	Yeovil Jn. Templecombe	1 B.C.K. 3-set (L.)	1.43 p.m. 11. 5 a.m. 11.18 a.m.	Broad Clyst Waterloo Templecombe	1 54 **FX** 2 16 **FO** 1 42
3 48 **MO**	Okehampton	2-set (P.) 2-set (P.)	8.30 a.m.	Padstow	11 58
3 48 **TWT**	Okehampton	2 S.K. **ThO** (27/8) 1 S.K. **ThO** (3/9) 3-set (L.) **WO** (9/9) 2-set (P.) 2-set (P.) 2-set (P.) **TO** (25/8 & 8/9)	— 8.30 a.m. 7.50 a.m.	Berth Padstow Yeovil Town R.P.	— 11 58 9 29
3 48 **FO**	Okehampton	*1 R.F. (24) 1 S.O. (until 10/7 & com. 28/8) 2-set (P.) 2-set (P.)	— 8.30 a.m.	Berth (*Not staffed) Padstow	— 11 58
4 0	Exmouth	5-set (E.)	2.49 p.m.	Exmouth	3 15
4 12	Plymouth Nth. Rd.	6 buffet set (19/20) 4-set	11.30 a.m.	Brighton	4 7
4 21	Torrington Barnstaple Jn.	3-set (L.) 1 S.K. 3-set (L.) **FO** (com. 28/8) 1 B.C.K. **MO**	12.46 p.m. 12.20 p.m. — 12.46 p.m.	Salisbury F.P. Ilfracombe Berth Salisbury R.P.	3 33 2 23 — 3 33
4 30 **MO**	Waterloo	2-set (R.) 1 S.K. 1 B.C.K. 1 R.C.O. 1 R.K.B. (1) 1 S.K. 2 B.C.K. 2-set (R.)	2.25 p.m. 11. 0 a.m. or 11. 5 a.m. 2.20 p.m. 2.15 p.m.	Plymouth N. Rd. F.P. Waterloo Ilfracombe Torrington	4 11 2 5/2 16 4 24 4 24
4 30 **MX**	Waterloo	2-set (R.) 1 R.C.O. 1 R.K.B. (1) 2-set (R.) 1 S.K. 1 S.K. **FO** (until 3/7) 1 B.C.K. 1 S.K. 2 B.C.K. 1 B.C.K.	7.26 a.m. 11.0 a.m. or 11.5 a.m. 2.25 p.m. 2.20 p.m. 2.15 p.m.	Plymouth Nth. Rd. Waterloo Plymouth N Rd. R.P. Ilfracombe Torrington	9 53 2 5/2 16 4 11 4 24 4 24

15

EXETER CENTRAL (SX)—*continued*

p.m. 4 35 **MO**	Portsmouth & S. Salisbury Templecombe	1 P.M.V. (4) 3-set (L.) 1 S.K. 1 S.K.	— 8. 0 a.m.	Berth Axminster F.P.	— 8 49
4 35 **MX**	Portsmouth & S. Salisbury Templecombe	1 P.M.V. (4) 3-set (L.) 1 S.K. 1 S.K. **FO** 1 S.K. **FX**	5V26 a.m. 8. 0 a.m. 1.55 p.m. 8. 0 a.m.	Exmouth J.N. Sdgs. Axminster M.P. Axminster M.P. Axminster F.P.	5V29 8 49**TO** 2 56**TX** 8 49
4 45	Exmouth	5-set (E.)	3.36 p.m.	Exmouth	4 2
4 48	Plymouth Nth. Rd.	1 S.K. 4-set	10.30 a.m. 1. 0 p.m.	Ilfracombe Waterloo F.P.	12 24 4 41
5 5	Ilfracombe Torrington	1 S.K. **MFO** (com. 17/8) 1 S.K. 2-set (R.) 1 B.C.K.	— 8.25 a.m. 10.30 a.m. 1. 0 p.m.	Berth Plymouth Nth. Rd. Ilfracombe Waterloo R.P.	—**MO** 10 23 **FO** 12 24 4 41
5 18	Exmouth	5-set (E.) 2-set (100/110)	4.40 p.m.	Exmouth	5 8
5 35	Honiton	1 S.K. **ThO** (until 3/7) 3-set (L.)	2.35 p.m.	Plymouth Nth. Rd.	5 5
5 45	Exmouth	5-set (E.)	1.45 p.m.	Exmouth	2 12
5 52	Okehampton	2-set (P.) 1 S.K. **FX** 2-set (R.) **FO**	1.46 p.m. — 7.26 a.m. 3.34 p.m.	Topsham Berth Plymouth N. Rd. F.P. Templecombe R.P.	1 58**MO** — 9 53 5 33
5 54	Waterloo	1 News van B. 2-set (R.) 1 B.C.K. **MX** (until 16/7) 1 S.K. **FO** 1 R.C.O. 1 R.K.B. (2) 4-set 1 News van B.	3. 0 p.m. 12.46 p.m. 2.25 p.m. 1. 0 p.m. 4. 2 p.m.	Ilfracombe Salisbury Plymouth N. Rd. F.P. Waterloo M.P. Plymouth Nth. Rd.	5 24 3 33 4 11 4 41 5 48
6 15	Chard Jn.	2-set (R.) **FX** 3-set (L.)	3.34 p.m.	Templecombe	5 33
6 18	Exmouth	5-set (E.)	5.15 p.m.	Exmouth	5 41
6 37	Plymouth Nth. Rd.	3-set (L.)	3. 0 p.m.	Waterloo F.P.	6 31
6 45	Exmouth	5-set (E.)	5.45 p.m.	Exmouth	6 13
6V48	Clapham Jn.	Milk tanks 1 van B. 1 News van B.	5V35 p.m. 3.13 p.m.	Crediton Padstow R.P.	6V 3 6 38

16

EXETER CENTRAL (SX)—*continued*

p.m. 6 52 ...	Ilfracombe ... ... Torrington	1 S.K. **FO** (4/9) ... ... 3-set (L.)... ... ... 2-set (R.)... ... ... 3-set (L.) **FO** (11/9) ...	7.26 a.m. ... 3. 0 p.m. ... —	Plymouth N. Rd. F.P. Waterloo R.P. ... ... Berth	9 53 6 31 —
7 20 ...	Exmouth	5-set (E.)...	6.20 p.m. ...	Exmouth	6 47
7 45 ...	Exmouth	5-set (E.)...	6.47 p.m. ...	Exmouth	7 18
7 50 ...	Waterloo ... ... Eastleigh ... ... Portsmouth & S. ...	1 P.M.V. (4) ... ... 1 P.M.V. (4) ... ... 3-set (L.)... ... ... 1 S.K. ... ... 1 cor. P.M.V.	4.48 p.m. ... 4.52 p.m. ...	Ilfracombe F.P.... ... Plymouth N. Rd. R.P.	7 3 7 23
8 7 ...	Plymouth Nth. Rd. Yeoford	1 S.K. ... ... 2-set (R.)... ... ... 1 B.C.K. **FO** ... ... 3-set (L.) **FO**... ... ... 1 S.K. **FO**	5.34 p.m. ... 6.38 p.m. ... 4.52 p.m. ...	Templecombe ... ... Honiton ... ... Plymouth N. Rd. F.P.	7 34 7 12 7 23
8 15 ...	Exmouth	5-set (E.)...	7.17 p.m. ...	Exmouth	7 45
8 45 ...	Exmouth	5-set (E.)...	7.45 p.m. ...	Exmouth	8 12
9 15 ...	Exmouth	5-set (E.)...	8.15 p.m. ...	Exmouth	8 44
9 50 ...	Exmouth	5-set (E.)...	9.15 p.m. ...	Exmouth	9 41
10 18 **FX**	Honiton...	1 S.K. ... ... 2-set (P.)...	7.21 p.m. ...	Plymouth N. Rd. F.P.	9 48
10 18 **FO**	Honiton...	2-set (R.)... ... ... 2 S.K.	7.21 p.m. ...	Plymouth Nth. Rd. ...	9 48
10 24 ...	Plymouth Nth. Rd.	1 P.M.V. (4) ... ... 1 B.C.K. **FO** ... ... 2-set (R.)... ... ... 1 S.K.	7. 0 p.m. ...	Waterloo F.P.	10 18
10 25 ...	Exmouth	5-set (E.)...	8.45 p.m. ...	Exmouth	9 12
10F30 ...	Exmouth Jn.... ...	1 B.Y. ... ... 1 van fit ... ... 1 van B.	7.21 p.m. ... 7.42 p.m. ...	Plymouth N. Rd. R.P. Ilfracombe R.P.... ...	9 48 10 7
10†35 **MO** (22/7 to 24/8)	Exmouth	9 L.M. corrs.	9†25 p.m. ...	Exeter St. Davids ...	9†28
11 10 ...	Exmouth	5-set (E.)...	9.45 p.m. ...	Exmouth	10 12
MX ...	Berth	1 B.Y. (stove) (400/1) ...	3V20 a.m.... (News)	Yeoford	3V47
—	Berth	1 van B.	6.25 a.m. ...	Yeovil Town	8 10

17

EXETER CENTRAL (SX)—*continued*

—	Berth	1 S. **MWF** ... ... 2 S. **FO** (until 28/8)	8.10 a.m. ...	Exmouth	8 35
—	Berth	1 B.C.K. **MO** (22/6 to 6/7) ... ... 1 S.K. **MO** (22/6 & 29/6) ... ... 1 S.K. **TO** (until 1/9) 1 S.K. **WThO** (22/7 to 3/9)... ... ... 3-set (L.) **FO** (24/7 to 14/8)	7. 5 a.m. ...	Torrington	8 58
—	Berth	3-set (L.) **WO** (com. 26/8) ... ... 1 R.B. (17) **TO** } com. 1 S.O. **TO** } 23/6	7.50 a.m. ...	Yeovil Town	9 29
—	Berth	5-set **MO** ... ... 1 S.K. **FO** (11/9) ...	7.26 a.m. ...	Plymouth Nth. Rd. ...	9 53
FO ... (14/8)	Berth	1 S.K.	8.25 a.m. ...	Plymouth Nth. Rd. ...	10 23
MO ...	Berth	2 S.K. (22/6) ... ... 1 S.K. (29/6 to 13/7)	8.55 a.m. ...	Ilfracombe...	11 7
—	Berth	3-set (L.) **MO** (6/7) 1 S.K. **TO** (until 4/8) 1 S.K. **TO** (30/6 to 14/7) ... ... 1 S.K. **MO** (22/6 to 13/7)	8.30 a.m. ...	Padstow	11 58
—	Berth	1 S.K. **TWT** (21/7 to 3/9) ... ... 1 B.C.K. **MX**... ...	9.35 a.m. ...	Padstow	12 12
—	Berth	3-set (L.) **ThO** (27/8 & 10/9) ... ... 3-set (L.) **FO** (17/7, 21/8 & 28/8) ...	11.18 a.m. ...	Templecombe	1 42
MX ...	Berth	2-set (100/110)	1.46 p.m. ...	Topsham	1 58
—	Berth	*1 R.K.B. (3) **MO** ... *1 R.C.O. **MO** ... ‡1 B.C.K. **ThO** ...	11. 0 a.m. ...	Waterloo ... ... (*also **TWT** 21/7 to 3/9) (‡23/7 to 3/9)	2 5
MO ... (also **TWT** 21/7 to 3/9)	Berth	1 B.C.K.	11. 5 a.m. ...	Waterloo	2 16

18

EXETER CENTRAL (SX)—*continued*

—	Berth	2-set (100/110) **MO** 1 S. **MO** 1 B.Y. (stove) (400/1) **MO** 3-set (L.) **TO**	1.55 p.m.	Axminster	2 56
—	Berth	1 cor. P.M.V. 1 B.C.K. **MX** (com. 17/7)	12.46 p.m.	Salisbury R.P.	3 33
TO	Berth	3-set (L.) (until 30/6)	2.20 p.m.	Ilfracombe	4 24
—	Berth	2-set (P.)	4. 0 p.m.	Honiton	4 32
—	Berth	3-set (L.) *1 R.K.B. (10) } **TO** 1 R.C.O. } com. 21/7 *1 R.F. (24) } **TO** 1 S.O. } com. 25/8 *1 R.F. (26) } **WO** 1 S.O. } com. 22/7 *1 R.F. (28) } **WO** 1 S.O. } com. 26/8 *1 R.F. (32) } **ThO** 1 S.O. } 9/7 to 3/9 *1 R.F. (23) } **ThO** 1 S.O. } com. 13/8	3. 5 p.m.	Salisbury (*unstaffed)	6 5
—	Berth	1 B.C.K. **FX** 1 S.O. 1 R.B. (18)	3. 0 p.m.	Waterloo M.P.	6 31
—	Berth	1 S.K. **TWT** 2-set (P.)	3.13 p.m.	Padstow	6 38
—	Berth	1 S.K. **MO** (29/6) 3-set (L.) 1 P.M.V. (4)	4.48 p.m.	Ilfracombe R.P.	7 3
—	Berth	3-set (L.) **FX** 1 S.K. **ThO** (until 3/9)	6.38 p.m.	Honiton	7 12
FX	Berth	1 S.K.	4.52 p.m.	Plymouth Nth. Rd.	7 23
—	Berth	2-set (R.) **FX** 3-set (L.) **FO** 1 B.C.K. **FO** (19/6 and 11/9)	7.35 p.m.	Chard Jn.	8 55
—	Berth	1 B.Y.	7.21 p.m.	Plymouth Nth. Rd.	9 48
—	Berth	2 S.K. 4-set (400) 1 R.K.B. (5) 1 R.C.O. 1 B.C.K. 1 S.K. **FO** (com. 14/8)	6. 0 p.m.	Waterloo	9 59

19

EXETER CENTRAL (SX)—*continued*

—	Berth	3-set (L.) 1 van B.	7.42 p.m.	Ilfracombe	10 7
—	Berth	1 R.K.B. (7) 1 R.C.O. 1 B.C.K.	7. 0 p.m.	Waterloo R.P.	10 18
—	Berth	3-set (L.) **FX** 5-set **FO** 1 R.F. (30) 1 S.O.	5. 0 p.m.	Waterloo	10 40
—	Berth	2-set (100/110) 5-set (E.)**FO**	10.17 p.m.	Exmouth	10 43
—	Berth	3-set (L.) Milk tanks 1 van B.	3V54 p.m.	Clapham Jn.	11V20
—	Berth	5-set (E.)	11. 5 p.m.	Exmouth	11 35
FX	Berth	2-set (P.) 1 S.K.	11.10 p.m.	Honiton	11 40
FO	Berth	2 S.K. 2-set (R.)	11.10 p.m.	Honiton	11 40

EXETER ST. DAVIDS (SX)

a.m. 4 25 **MO**	Exeter Central	1 B.C.K.	3†53 a.m.	Exeter Central	3†56
5V 0 **MX**	Exeter Central	Vans 1 B.Y.	— 2F 6 a.m.	ex W.R. Exeter Central	— 2F10
8 38	Ilfracombe	1 S.K. 3-set (L.)	8.30 a.m.	Exeter Central	8 33
	Torrington	1 P.M.V. (4) 1 W.R. van **MX**	—	ex W.R.	—
p.m. 9†25 **MO** (22/6 to 24/8)	Exmouth	9 L.M. cors.	—	ex W.R.	—

EXMOUTH (SX)

Formation of Exmouth—Exeter 5 sets (E.):—

1 S.*
1 B.S.
1 C.
1 B.S.
1 S.*

(*not stencilled with set numbers)
(Seats 32/480)

a.m. 6†38	Budleigh Salterton	2-set (100/110)	—	Berth	—
6 40	Exeter Central	5-set (E.)	—	Berth	—

22

EXMOUTH (SX)—*continued*

—	Berth	3-set (L.) **TX** 5-set **TO** 1 S.K. **MWO** 2 S. **FX** (also **FO** com. 4/9) 1 S. **TThO**	3.10 p.m.	Exeter Central	3 35
—	Berth	2-set (100/110)	5.56 p.m.	Tipton St. Johns	6 27
—	Berth	1 S.K.	8.30 p.m.	Sidmouth R.P.	9 12
FX	Berth	5-set (E.)	9.15 p.m.	Exeter Central	9 41
—	Berth	5-set (E.)	9.50 p.m.	Exeter Central	10 15
—	Berth	2-set (100/110)	10. 7 p.m.	Tipton St. Johns	10 35
MO (22/6 to 24/8)	Berth	9 L.M. cors.	9†25 p.m.	Exeter St. Davids	10†57
—	Berth	5-set (E.)	11.10 p.m.	Exeter Central	11 39

GUNNISLAKE (SX)

a.m. 7 8	Plymouth Nth. Rd.	2-set (100/110)	—	Berth	—
p.m. 2 26 **WThO**	Bere Alston	2-set (100/110)	1.58 p.m.	Bere Alston	2 18
—	Berth	2-set (100/110)	5. 9 p.m.	Plymouth Nth. Rd.	6 21

HALWILL (SX)

a.m. 5F17	Bude	1 van B.	2F6 a.m.	Exeter Central	5F14
7 15	Bude	2-set (P.)	6†20 a.m.	Bude	6†52
7 16	Padstow	2-set (P.) 1 B.C.K. 1 News van B.	— 1.15 a.m.	Berth Waterloo	— 6 58
8 49	Okehampton	2-set (P.) 2-set (P.)	8.20 a.m. 7.58 a.m.	Launceston Bude	8 44 8 36
8 53	Bude	2-set (P.)	—	Berth	—
10 28	Exeter Central	3-set (L.) **MO** (6/7 only) 1 S.K. **TuO** (until 4/8) 1 S.K. **TuO** (30/6 to 14/7) 2-set (P.)	8.30 a.m.	Padstow	10 22
		1 S.K. **MO** (22/6 to 13/7) 2-set (P.)	9.30 a.m.	Bude	10 10

23

HALWILL (SX)—*continued*

10 32	Padstow	*1 S.K. **TWT** 2-set (P.) 1 B.Y. **MX**	9.56 a.m.	Okehampton F.P. (*Also **Fridays** com. 10/7)	10 23
10 38	Torrington	1 B.C.K.	8.52 a.m.	Torrington	10 18
10 39	Bude	1 S.K. **MX** 2-set (P.)	— 9.56 a.m.	Berth Okehampton R.P.	— 10 23
11 9	Waterloo	2 B.C.K. *1 S.K.	9.35 a.m.	Padstow (*20/7 to 4/9, also **MFO** 7/9 & 11/9)	11 5
		*1 S.K. 1 B.C.K.	10.20 a.m.	Bude	10 55
p.m. 2 45	Waterloo	1 S.K. **FO** (until 3/7) 1 B.C.K.	12.58 p.m.	Padstow	2 41
	Okehampton	2-set (P.) 2-set (P.)	1.55 p.m.	Bude	2 35
3 39	Padstow	1 P.M.V. (4) *1 S.K. **MFO** 2 B.C.K.	11. 0 a.m.	Waterloo F.P. (*Also **TWT** 21/7 to 3/9)	3 36
3 43	Bude	2-set (P.) *1 S.K. **MFO** 1 B.C.K.	10.20 a.m. 11. 0 a.m.	Bude R.P. Waterloo R.P. (*Also **TWT** 21/7 to 3/9)	10 55 3 36
4 56	Bude	2-set (P.)	4.24 p.m.	Okehampton F.P.	4 53
5 1	Wadebridge	2-set (P.)	4.24 p.m.	Okehampton R.P.	4 53
6 24	Padstow	3-set (L.) **WO** (9/9 only) *1 R.F. (24) **FO** (until 10/7 & com. 28/8) *1 S.O. **FO** (until 10/7 & com. 28/8) 2 S.K. **ThO** (27/8) 1 S.K. **ThO** (3/9) 2-set (P.)	5.51 p.m.	Okehampton F.P. (*Not staffed)	6 21
6 27	Bude	2-set (P.) *1 S.K. **FO** 2-set (P.) **TO** (25/8 & 8/9)	5.51 p.m.	Okehampton R.P. (*14/8 to 28/8)	6 21
6 30	Torrington	1 B.C.K.	4. 0 p.m.	Torrington	5 23
8 0	Okehampton Exeter Central Nine Elms	2-set (P.) 1 P.M.V. (4) 1 B.Y.	6. 0 p.m.	Padstow	7 56
	Exeter Central	1 van fit 1 B.Y.	7. 5 p.m.	Bude R.P.	7 45
8 20	Launceston	2-set (P.)	7.45 p.m.	Okehampton F.P.	8 17

24

HALWILL (SX)—*continued*

p.m. 8 25	Bude	2-set (P.) **FX** 2-set (R.) **FO**	7.45 p.m.	Okehampton R.P.	8 17
—	Berth	2-set (P.)	5.32 p.m.	Bude	6 11
—	Berth	1 S.K. 2-set (P.)	7. 5 p.m.	Bude F.P.	7 45

HONITON (SX)

p.m. 4 0	Exeter Central	2-set (P.)	8. 0 a.m.	Exeter Central	8 35
4†35 **FX**	Sidmouth Jn.	1 S. 2-set (100/110)	4.20 p.m.	Sidmouth Jn.	4 28
6 38	Exeter Central	3-set (L.) 1 S.K. **ThO** (until 3/9)	5.35 p.m.	Exeter Central	6 8
11 10	Exeter Central	2 S.K. **FO** 2-set (R.) **FO** 2-set (P.) **FX** 1 S.K. **FX**	10.18 p.m.	Exeter Central	10 53
FO	Berth	2-set (100/110) 1 S.	4.20 p.m.	Sidmouth Jn.	4 28

ILFRACOMBE (SX)

a.m. 6 50	King's Nympton	2-set (R.)	—	Berth	—
8 10 **R MO**	Waterloo	1 F.K. 3-set (L.)	—	Berth	—
8 10 **R TWT**	Exeter Central Waterloo	1 S.K. 3-set (L.)	—	Berth	—
8 10 **R FO**	Exeter Central Waterloo	1 S.K. 5-set	—	Berth	—
8 55	Salisbury	3-set (L.)	—	Berth	—
10 30 **R**	Exeter Central	2 S.K.	1.15 a.m. —	Waterloo Berth	6 50**MO** —**MX**
	Waterloo	*1 S.K. 2-set (R.)	— 1.15 a.m. 8. 0 a.m.	Berth Waterloo Barnstaple Jn. R.P. (*20/7 to 4/9, also **MFO** com. 7/9)	— 6 50**MO** 8 45**MX**
p.m. 12 20 **R**	Exeter Central Waterloo	1 S.K. 3-set (L.)	— 6.25 a.m.	Berth Yeovil Town F.P.	— 10 52
1 30	Barnstaple Jn.	5-set **MO** 3-set (L.) **MX**	— 7.50 a.m.	Berth Yeovil Town	— 12 0

26

ILFRACOMBE (SX)—*continued*

—	Berth	1 S.K. **FO** (4/9) 3-set (L.)	3. 0 p.m.	Waterloo	9 6

KING'S NYMPTON (SX)

a.m. 8 30	Barnstaple Jn.	2-set (R.)	6.50 a.m.	Ilfracombe	7 52

LAPFORD (SX)

FO	Berth	1 van B.	9. 0 a.m.	Waterloo R.P.	2 13

LAUNCESTON (SX)

a.m. 7 5	Plymouth Nth. Rd.	2 W.R. set	—	Berth	—
8 20	Okehampton	2-set (P.)	—	Berth	—
10 15	Plymouth Nth. Rd.	2 W.R. set	7.10 a.m.	Plymouth Nth. Rd.	8 43
p.m. 5 40	Plymouth Nth. Rd.	2 W.R. set	3. 5 p.m.	Plymouth Nth. Rd.	4 39
—	Berth	2 W.R. set	6.20 p.m.	Plymouth Nth. Rd.	7 50
—	Berth	2-set (P.)	7.45 p.m.	Okehampton	8 42

LYME REGIS (SX)

a.m. 8 11	Axminster	2-set (100/110)	—	Berth	—
10 0	Axminster	2-set (100/110)	8.43 a.m.	Axminster	9 4
11 37 **R**	Axminster Waterloo	2-set (100/110) 1 B.C.K.	10.37 a.m. —	Axminster Berth	10 58 —
p.m. 1 10	Axminster	2-set (100/110)	12.33 p.m.	Axminster	12 54
2 16	Axminster	2-set (100/110)	1.48 p.m.	Axminster	2 9
3 53	Axminster	2-set (100/110)	2.48 p.m.	Axminster	3 9
5 10	Axminster	2-set (100/110) 1 B.C.K. **FO** (11/9)	4.43 p.m.	Axminster R.P.	5 4
6 7	Axminster	2-set (100/110)	5.40 p.m.	Axminster	6 1
8 22	Axminster	2-set (100/110)	6.45 p.m.	Axminster	7 6
FX (also **FO** until 4/9)	Berth	1 B.C.K.	4.43 p.m.	Axminster F.P.	5 4
—	Berth	2-set (100/110)	8.55 p.m.	Axminster	9 16

27

OKEHAMPTON (SX)

a.m. 4F25	Tavistock North	1 B.Y. (stove) (400/401)	1F38 a.m.	Exmouth Jn.	4F16
4F37	Bude	1 van B.	1F38 a.m.	Exmouth Jn.	4F16
6 6	Plymouth Nth. Rd.	1 S.K. 2-set (R.) **MO** 2 B.C.K. **MX**	1.15 a.m.	Waterloo R.P.	5 57
6 30	Padstow	1 B.C.K. 1 News van B.	1.15 a.m.	Waterloo F.P.	5 57
7 0	Plymouth Nth. Rd.	2-set (P.) 3-set (L.) **MO** 1 B.C.K. **MO**	—	Berth	—
8 54 **FX**	Exeter Central	1 S.K. 5-set **MO** 2-set (R.) **MX**	7.26 a.m.	Plymouth Nth. Rd.	8 51
8 54 **FO**	Exeter Central	1 S.K. (com. 4/9) 2-set (R.)	7.26 a.m.	Plymouth N. Rd. F.P.	8 51
9 56	Padstow	1 B.Y. **MX** 1 S.K. **TWT** 1 S.K. **FO** (com. 10/7)	7.35 a.m. —	Exeter Central R.P. Berth	8 40 —
	Bude	2-set (P.) 2-set (P.)	8.20 a.m.	Launceston	9 17
11 34	Waterloo	2 B.C.K. *2 S.K. 1 B.C.K.	9.35 a.m.	Padstow (*20/7 to 4/9, also **MFO** 7/9 & 11/9)	11 30
	Exeter Central	2-set (R.) ‡1 S.K. 1 B.C.K. **MO** 2 B.C.K. **MX**	10. 2 a.m.	Plymouth Nth. Rd. (‡**TWT** 21/7 to 3/9)	11 16
p.m. 12 59	Plymouth Nth. Rd.	4-set **MO** 1 S.K. **MX** 1 S.K. **TThO** 3-set (L.) **MX**	11.47 a.m.	Exeter Central F.P.	12 53
1 18	Bude	2-set (P.) 1 News van B.	11.47 a.m.	Exeter Central R.P.	12 53
3 14	Padstow	1 P.M.V. (4) *1 S.K. **MFO** 2 B.C.K.	11. 0 a.m.	Waterloo F.P.	2 59
	Bude	*1 S.K. **MFO** 1 B.C.K.		(*Also **TWT** 21/7 to 3/9)	
3 22	Plymouth Nth. Rd.	2 S.K. **MFO** *1 S.K. 2-set (R.)	11. 0 a.m.	Waterloo R.P. (***TWT** 21/7 to 3/9)	2 59

28

OKEHAMPTON (SX)—*continued*

p.m. 3 33	Exeter Central Waterloo	1 S.K. **FO** 2-set (R.) 1 S.K.	2.25 p.m.	Plymouth Nth. Rd.	3 29
		1 S.K. **FO** (until 3/7) 1 B.C.K.	12.58 p.m.	Padstow F.P.	3 13
4† 7 (stone empties)	Meldon Quarry	1 B.S.L.	—	Berth	—
4 24	Bude Wadebridge	2-set (P.) 2-set (P.)	12.58 p.m.	Padstow R.P.	3 13
5 6	Waterloo	4-set 1 News van B.	4. 2 p.m. 3.15 p.m.	Plymouth Nth. Rd. Bude	5 2 4 34
5 51 **MO**	Padstow Bude	2-set (P.) 2-set (P.)	3.48 p.m.	Exeter Central	4 46
5 51 **TWT**	Padstow	2 S.K. **ThO** (27/8) 1 S.K. **ThO** (3/9) 3-set (L.) **WO** (9/9) 2-set (P.)	3.48 p.m.	Exeter Central	4 46
	Bude	2-set (P.) 2-set (P.) **TuO** (25/8 & 8/9)			
5 51 **FO**	Padstow	*1 R.F. (24) *1 S.O. 2-set (P.)	3.48 p.m.	Exeter Central (*Until 10/7 & com. 28/8 (not staffed))	4 46
	Bude	2-set (P.) 1 S.K. (14/8 to 28/8)	7.26 a.m.	Plymouth N. Rd. F.P.	8 51
7 45	Launceston Bude	2-set (P.) 2-set (P.) **FX** 2-set (R.) **FO**	3.15 p.m. 5.52 p.m.	Bude M.P. Exeter Central R.P.	4 34 6 56
8 52	Exeter Central	1 S.K. **FX** 2-set (P.) **FX** 2-set (R.) **FO**	7.21 p.m.	Plymouth Nth. Rd.	8 46
	Nine Elms Exeter Central	2 S.K. **FO** 1 P.M.V. (4) 1 B.Y. 1 van fit 1 B.Y.	6. 0 p.m.	Padstow	8 29**MX** 8 32**MO**
9 15	Plymouth Nth. Rd.	1 S.K. 2-set (R.)	8. 7 p.m.	Exeter Central	9 10
		*1 S.K. **TuO**	3.15 p.m.	Bude (*Until 14/7)	4 34
—	Berth	2-set (P.) **FO**	3.15 p.m.	Bude	4 34
—	Berth	1 B.S.L.	5F10 p.m.	Meldon Quarry	5F18
FX	Berth	1 S.K.	5.52 p.m.	Exeter Central	6 56

29

OKEHAMPTON (SX)—*continued*

—	Berth	2-set (P.)	6. 0 p.m.	Padstow	8 29**MX** 8 32**MO**
FO	Berth	4-set	10†20 p.m.	Tavistock North	10†50

PADSTOW (SX)

a.m. 8 12	Bodmin General	I S.K. 2-set (P.)	7.22 a.m.	Bodmin North	7 55
8 30	Exeter Central	3-set (L.) **MO** (6/7 only) ‡I S.K. **TuO** §I S.K. **TuO** 2-set (P.)	—	Berth (‡Until 4/8) (§30/6 to 14/7)	—
9 3	Bodmin Rd. W.R.	2 W.R. set	7.50 a.m.	Bodmin Rd. W.R.	8 50
9 35 **R**	Waterloo	2 B.C.K. *I S.K.	—	Berth (*20/7 to 4/9, also **MFO** 7/9 & 11/9)	—
10 55	Wadebridge	2-set (P.)	10.30 a.m.	Wadebridge	10 39
11 55	Bodmin North	I S.K. 2-set (P.)	11.20 a.m.	Bodmin North	11 50
p.m. 12 58 **R**	Waterloo Okehampton	I S.K. **FO** (until 3/7) I B.C.K. 2-set (P.)	— 1.15 a.m.	Berth Waterloo	— 9 22
2 52	Wadebridge	I S.K. 2-set (P.)	2. 0 p.m.	Bodmin North	2 34
	Bodmin North	2-set (P.)	1.15 p.m.	Wadebridge	1 29
3 13	Exeter Central	I S.K. **TWT** 2-set (P.)	9.56 a.m.	Okehampton F.P.	12 14
	Waterloo	I News van B.	1.15 a.m.	Waterloo	9 22
5 15	Wadebridge	*I S.K. **FX** 2-set (P.)	4.30 p.m.	Wadebridge (*Also **FO** 10/7 to 28/8)	4 39
5†35	Wadebridge	2 B.C.K.	11. 0 a.m.	Waterloo R.P.	5 7
6 0	Okehampton Exeter Central Nine Elms	2-set (P.) I P.M.V. (4) I B.Y.	5.33 p.m. 11. 0 a.m. — 9.56 a.m.	Wadebridge Waterloo F.P. Berth Okehampton	5 42 5 7 —**MO** 12 14**MX**
6†35 **FO** (10/7 to 28/8)	Wadebridge	2 B.C.K.	6.13 p.m.	Wadebridge	6 22
8 4	Bodmin Rd. W.R.	2-set (P.)	6.45 p.m.	Bodmin North F.P.	7 19
8 30	Wadebridge	*I S.K. **FO** 2-set (P.)	9.56 a.m. 5.51 p.m.	Okehampton Okehampton R.P. (*10/7 to 28/8)	12 14 7 58

30

PADSTOW (SX)—*continued*

p.m. 10 5 **FO** (com. 4/9)	Wadebridge Berth	2-set (P.) I S.K.	9. 5 p.m. 9.56 a.m.	Bodmin Rd. W.R. Okehampton F.P.	9 51 12 14
FO (until 3/7 & com. 4/9)	Berth	I S.K.	4.30 p.m.	Wadebridge	4 39
MFO (also **TWT** 21/7 to 3/9)	Berth	I S.K.	11. 0 a.m.	Waterloo	5 0
FX (also **FO** until 3/7 & com. 4/9)	Berth	2 B.C.K.	6.13 p.m.	Wadebridge	6 22
—	Berth	2-set (P.)	6.45 p.m.	Bodmin North R.P.	7 19
—	Berth	3-set (L.) **WO** (9/9 only) 2 S.K. **ThO** (27/8) I S.K. **ThO** (3/9) *I R.F. (24) **FO** (until 10/7 & com. 28/8) I S.O. **FO**	5.51 p.m.	Okehampton (*Not staffed)	7 58

PETROCKSTOW (SX)

a.m. 7 55	Torrington	I B.C.K.	6.25 a.m.	Torrington F.P.	7† 4
p.m. 1F55	Torrington	I B.C.K.	1F0 p.m.	Torrington	1F45
4 35	Halwill	I B.C.K.	4. 0 p.m.	Torrington R.P.	4 34
4 37	Torrington	I B.C.K.	6.25 a.m. 4. 0 p.m.	Torrington R.P. Torrington F.P.	7† 4**WX** 4 34**WO**

PLYMOUTH FRIARY SIDINGS (SX)

Empties to and from Plymouth (North Road) unless otherwise shown.

a.m. 12F55	Exmouth Jn. **MO** Exeter Ctl. **MX**	I B.Y. (stove) (400/1)	—	Berth	—
6† 2 for 6 15	Waterloo Salisbury	I P.M.V. (4) 3-set (L.)	—	Berth	—
7†10 **FX** for 7 26 **FX**	Exeter Central	I S.K. 5-set **MO** 2-set (R.) **MX**	—	Berth	—

44

TORRINGTON (SX)—*continued*

p.m. 2 15 **R**	Waterloo	2-set (R.) **MO** 1 B.C.K. **MX**	11.23 a.m.	Barnstaple Jn.	11 58
	Barnstaple Jn.	1 S.K.	— 11.23 a.m.	Berth Barnstaple Jn.	—**MO** 11 58**MX**
2 47	Crediton Barnstaple Jn.	1 van B. 4 W.R. set **MO** 3 W.R. set **MX**	2F6 a.m. 1.10 p.m.	Exeter Central Barnstaple Jn. F.P.	6F 8 1 46
4 0	Petrockstow Halwill	1 B.C.K. (6669) **WO** 1 B.C.K.	9. 0 a.m. 1F55 p.m.	Waterloo R.P. Petrockstow	3 39 2F59
4 38	Exeter Central Barnstaple Jn.	1 P.M.V. (4) 1 B.C.K. 1 S.K.	1.10 p.m. 9. 0 a.m.	Barnstaple Jn. R.P. Waterloo	1 46 3 39
5 46	Paddington Barnstaple Jn.	1 P.M.V. (4) 1 B.C.K. 1 S.K. **FO**	10.18 a.m. 11. 0 a.m.	Barnstaple Jn. R.P. Waterloo	10 51 3 54
7 38	Barnstaple Jn. Exeter Central Paddington	3-set (L.) 1 van B. 1 W.R. van	4.28 p.m. 2F6 a.m. 10.18 a.m. —	Barnstaple Jn. Exeter Central Barnstaple Jn. R.P. Berth	4 58 6F 8 10 51**MX** —**MO**
8 24	Barnstaple Jn.	1 B.C.K. 1 S.K. **FO**	6.30 p.m. 1. 0 p.m.	Halwill Waterloo	7 56 7 9
MO	Berth	*1 S.K.	11. 0 a.m.	Waterloo (*also **TWT** 21/7 to 3/9)	3 54
FO (11/9)	Berth	3-set (L.)	4.28 p.m.	Barnstaple Jn. R.P.	4 58
—	Berth	1 B.C.K.	4.37 p.m.	Petrockstow	5 14
—	Berth	1 S.K. 3-set (L.) 3-set (L.) **FO** (com. 28/8)	4.21 p.m.	Exeter Central	6 24
—	Berth	2 B.C.K.	1. 0 p.m.	Waterloo	7 9
—	Berth	3-set (L.) **FO** (until 4/9) 2-set (R.) 3-set (L.) **FO** (11/9)	3. 0 p.m.	Waterloo	8 58

WADEBRIDGE (SX)

a.m. 6 52	Bodmin North	1 S.K. 2-set (P.)	—	Berth	—
8 1	Bodmin North	2-set (P.)	—	Berth	—

45

WADEBRIDGE (SX)—*continued*

a.m. 8 32	Bodmin General	1 S.K. 2-set (P.)	8.10 a.m.	Padstow	8 19
9 48	Bodmin North	1 S.K. 2-set (P.)	9. 2 a.m.	Bodmin General	9 21
10 30	Padstow	2-set (P.)	8.43 a.m.	Bodmin North	9 2
11 7	Bodmin Rd. W.R.	2 W.R. set	10.10 a.m.	Bodmin Road W.R.	10 55
p.m. 12 25	Bodmin North	2-set (P.)	11.55 a.m.	Padstow	12 4
1 15	Padstow	2-set (P.)	10.55 a.m.	Padstow	11 4
1 23	Bodmin Rd. W.R.	2 W.R. set	12.20 p.m.	Bodmin Road W.R.	12 57
3 9	Bodmin North	2-set (P.)	2.52 p.m.	Padstow R.P.	3 1
3 24	Bodmin Road W.R.	2 W.R. set	2.30 p.m.	Bodmin Road W.R.	3 6
4 30	Padstow	2-set (P.) 1 S.K. **FX**	2.52 p.m.	Padstow F.P.	3 1
4†43	Bodmin General	2 W.R. set	4. 8 p.m.	Bodmin General	4 28
5 11	Bodmin North	2-set (P.)	4.23 p.m.	Bodmin North	4 42
5 30	Bodmin Road W.R.	2 W.R. set	4.25 p.m.	Bodmin Road W.R.	5 9
5 33	Padstow	2-set (P.)	5.15 p.m.	Padstow	5 24
6 13	Padstow	2 B.C.K.	5†35 p.m.	Padstow	5†44
6 18	Bodmin North	2-set (P.)	5.48 p.m.	Bodmin North	6 7
7 5	Bodmin General	2 W.R. set	6.17 p.m.	Bodmin Road W.R.	6 49
7 10	Padstow	2-set (P.) 2-set (P.)	6.45 p.m. 4.24 p.m.	Bodmin North Okehampton	7 4 6 24
8 42	Bodmin Road W.R.	2 W.R. set	7.26 p.m.	Bodmin Road W.R.	8 2
FX	Berth	1 S.K.	5.15 p.m.	Padstow F.P.	5 24
FO (10/7 to 28/8)	Berth	1 S.K. 2 B.C.K.	6†35 p.m.	Padstow	6†44
—	Berth	*1 S.K. **FO** 2-set (P.)	8.30 p.m.	Padstow (*10/7 to 28/8)	8 39
—	Berth	2-set (P.)	10. 5 p.m.	Padstow	10 14

BARNSTAPLE JN. (SO)—*continued*

—	Berth	3-set (L.)	8.24 p.m.	Torrington	8 56
—	Berth	2 S.K. 4 W.R. set	8.30 p.m.	Ilfracombe	9 9

BERE ALSTON (SO)

a.m. 6 15	Plymouth Nth. Rd.	3-set (L.) 2-set (100/110)	6. 0 a.m. 5.30 a.m.	Tavistock North Callington	6 11 6 10
7 35	Plymouth Nth. Rd.	2-set (100/110) 2-set (100/110)	7.20 a.m. 7. 8 a.m.	Tavistock North Gunnislake	7 31 7 29
8 24	Callington	P. & P. set (373)	7.16 a.m.	Callington	7 59
10 40	Callington	P. & P. set (373)	9.43 a.m.	Callington	10 26
p.m. 12 50	Plymouth Nth. Rd.	2-set (100/110)	8.46 a.m.	Tavistock North	8 57
12 57	Tavistock North	3-set (L.) 2-set (P.)	12.18 p.m.	Plymouth N. Rd. R.P.	12 51
1 2	Callington	2-set (100/110)	12.18 p.m.	Plymouth N. Rd. F.P.	12 51
1 58	Gunnislake	P. & P. set (373)	1. 0 p.m.	Callington	1 46
3 22	Callington	P. & P. set (373)	2.26 p.m.	Gunnislake	2 47
5 23	Callington	P. & P. set (373) 2-set (100/110)	4.23 p.m. 4.14 p.m.	Callington Plymouth Nth. Rd.	5 6 4 52
7 10	Callington	2-set (100/110)	6.20 p.m.	Callington	7 1
10 5	Callington	2-set (100/110)	9.10 p.m.	Callington	9 53

BODMIN GENERAL (W.R.) (SO) (Trains to and from S.R. only)

p.m. 7 38	Bodmin Road	2 W.R. set	7. 5 p.m.	Wadebridge	7 25

BODMIN NORTH (SO)

a.m. 7 22	Padstow	2-set (P.)	6.52 a.m.	Wadebridge	7 12
8 43	Wadebridge	2-set (P.)	8. 1 a.m.	Wadebridge	8 21
11 20	Padstow	2-set (P.)	9.48 a.m.	Wadebridge	10 8
p.m. 2 0	Padstow	2-set (P.)	12.10 p.m.	Padstow	12 48
4 5	Padstow	2-set (P.)	2.52 p.m.	Padstow	3 29
5 36	Wadebridge	2-set (P.)	4.40 p.m.	Padstow	5 31
6 45	Padstow	2-set (P.)	6.18 p.m.	Wadebridge	6 38

BODMIN ROAD (W.R.) (SO) (Trains to and from S.R. only)

a.m. 7 50	Padstow	2 W.R. set	7.30 a.m.	Bodmin General	7 37
10 10	Wadebridge	2 W.R. set 2-set (P.)	9. 8 a.m. 8.10 a.m.	Padstow Padstow	9 54 9 5
p.m. 12 38	Wadebridge	2 W.R. set	11.35 a.m.	Padstow	12 30
2 30	Wadebridge	2 W.R. set	1.23 p.m.	Wadebridge	1 57
4 55	Wadebridge	2 W.R. set	3.24 p.m.	Wadebridge	4 1
6 17	Wadebridge	2 W.R. set	—	ex W.R.	—
7 26	Wadebridge	2 W.R. set	5.56 p.m.	Wadebridge	6 50
9 5	Padstow	2-set (P.)	8. 4 p.m.	Padstow	8 51
9 42	Bodmin General	2 W.R. set	8.42 p.m.	Wadebridge	9 32

BRENTOR (SO)

p.m. 5 32	Plymouth Nth. Rd.	2-set (P.) 1 S.K.	4. 14 p.m.	Plymouth Nth. Rd.	5 22

BUDE (SO)

a.m. 7 58	Okehampton	2-set (P.)	—	Berth	—
9 0 R (11/7 to 29/8)	Waterloo	2-set (P.) 1 S.K.	12.15 a.m. 12.25 a.m. — 12.25 a.m.	Waterloo (11/7 & 15/8 to 29/8) Waterloo (18/7 to 8/8) Berth (11/7 & com. 15/8) Waterloo (18/7 to 8/8)	6 34 6 34 — 6 34
9 30 R	Waterloo	1 S.K. 1 S.K. 2-set (R.)	7.15 a.m. —	Halwill Berth	7 49 —
11 45 R (until 11/7)	Waterloo	1 B.C.K. 2-set (P.)	— 7.15 a.m.	Berth Halwill	— 7 49
11 45 R (com. 18/7)	Waterloo	1 S.K. 2-set (P.) 2-set (P.) 2 B.C.K.	— 7.15 a.m. 8.53 a.m. —	Berth Halwill Halwill Berth	— 7 49 9 25 —
p.m. 2 1	Okehampton	2-set (P.)	10.12 a.m.	Okehampton F.P.	11 33
3 13	Waterloo Okehampton	1 P.M.V. (4) 1 B.S.L. 2-set (P.)	— 1.20 p.m.	Berth Okehampton	— 2 23

58

BUDE (SO)—*continued*

p.m. 5 32	Halwill	2-set (P.)	8.53 a.m. 7.33 a.m. — 12.15 a.m.	Halwill (until 11/7) Waterloo (18/7 to 22/8) Berth (29/8 & 12/9) Waterloo (5/9)	9 25 1 23 — 6 34
		1 B.C.K. (until 4/7) 1 S.K. (until 27/6)	10.35 a.m.	Waterloo R.P.	3 54
7 5	Exeter Central Okehampton Halwill	1 van B. 1 B.C.K. 2-set (P.)	2F6 a.m. 10.35 a.m. — 7.33 a.m. —	Exeter Central Waterloo R.P. Berth (20/6) Waterloo (27/6 to 22/8) Berth (com. 29/8)	6F14 3 54 — 1 23 —
—	Berth	1 S.K. (com. 4/7) 1 B.C.K. 1 B.C.K. (com. 11/7)	10.35 a.m.	Waterloo	3 54
—	Berth	1 S.K. 2-set (R.)	11.15 a.m.	Waterloo	5 9
—	Berth	2-set (P.)	5.51 p.m.	Okehampton	7 0
—	Berth	2-set (P.)	7.45 p.m.	Okehampton	9 0

BUDLEIGH SALTERTON (SO)

a.m. 6 55	Exmouth	2-set (100/110)	6†38 a.m.	Exmouth	6†49
p.m. 6 38	Exmouth	3-set (L.)	6.17 p.m.	Exmouth	6 29

CALLINGTON (SO)

a.m. 5 30	Plymouth Nth. Rd.	2-set (100/110)	—	Berth	—
7 16	Bere Alston	P. & P. set (373)	—	Berth	—
9 43	Bere Alston	P. & P. set (373)	8.24 a.m.	Bere Alston	9 9
p.m. 1 0	Bere Alston	P. & P. set (373)	10.40 a.m.	Bere Alston	11 24
4 23	Bere Alston Gunnislake	P. & P. set (373) 2-set (100/110)	3.22 p.m. 1. 2 p.m.	Bere Alston Bere Alston	4 4 1 46
6 20	Bere Alston	2-set (100/110)	5.23 p.m.	Bere Alston R.P.	6 5
9 10	Bere Alston	2-set (100/110)	7.10 p.m.	Bere Alston	7 53
—	Berth	P. & P. set (373)	5.23 p.m.	Bere Alston F.P.	6 5
—	Berth	2-set (100/110)	10. 5 p.m.	Bere Alston	10 49

59

CHARD JN. (SO)

p.m. 7 35	Exeter Central	3-set (L.) (20/6 & 12/9) 4-set (400) (27/6 to 5/9)	6.15 p.m.	Exeter Central	7 18

CREDITON (SO)

p.m. 5 3	Waterloo	2 News vans B. 1 News van B. 3-set (L.)	2.55 p.m.	Ilfracombe F.P.	5 0
5V35	Exeter Central	Milk vans 1 van B. 1 van B.	— 4V0 p.m. 2.55 p.m.	Berth Lapford Ilfracombe R.P.	— 4V27 5 0

EXETER CENTRAL (SO)

a.m. 2F 6	Exeter St. Davids Torrington Ilfracombe Torrington Tavistock North Bude	1 B.Y. 1 van B. 1 van B. 1 van B. 1 B.Y. (stove) (400/1) 1 van B.	—	Berth	—
4 20 (11/7 & 15/8 to 5/9)	Ilfracombe Torrington	2 S.K. (15/8) 1 S.K. (22/8 & 29/8) 3-set (L.) 3-set (L.)	12.15 a.m.	Waterloo	4 0
4.20 (18/7 to 8/8)	Ilfracombe Torrington	2 S.K. 3-set (L.) 3-set (L.)	12.15 a.m.	Waterloo	4 0
4 30 (18/7 to 8/8)	Padstow Bude	3-set (L.) 1 S.K. 1 S.K. 2-set (P.)	12.25 a.m.	Waterloo F.P.	4 23
4 30 (11/7 & 15/8 to 5/9)	Padstow Bude	3-set (L.) 2-set (P.)	12.15 a.m.	Waterloo	4 0
5 6 (until 22/8)	Ilfracombe Bideford (thence Torrington)	5-set 1 S.K. 1 van B. 3-set (L.) 1 News van B.	1.15 a.m.	Waterloo R.P.	5 0
5 6 (com. 29/8)	Ilfracombe Bideford (thence Torrington)	1 B.C.K. 1 B.C.K. 1 News van B.	1.15 a.m.	Waterloo M.P.	5 0

60

EXETER CENTRAL (SO)—*continued*

a.m.					
5 17 (until 22/8)	Plymouth Nth. Rd. Padstow	3-set (L.) 1 B.C.K. 1 S.K. 1 News van B.	1.25 a.m.	Waterloo F.P.	5 9
5 17 (com. 29/8)	Plymouth Nth. Rd. Padstow	3-set (L.) 1 B.C.K. 1 News van B.	1.15 a.m.	Waterloo M.P.	5 0
5 26	Ilfracombe Torrington Exeter St. Davids	3-set (L.) 1 News van B. 1 News van B. 2 W.R. set (18/7 to 8/8)	— 1.15/1.25 a.m. 5. 0 a.m.	Berth Waterloo R.P. Exeter St. Davids	— 5 0/5 9 5 3
5 30	Exmouth	2 S. 2-set (100/110)	—	Berth	—
6 0	Sidmouth	*1 S. 2-set (P.)	—	Berth	—
6 30 **R**	Waterloo	5-set 1 R.B. (18) 1 S.O.	—	Berth	—
6 37	Waterloo	1 cor. P.M.V. 3-set (L.)	5. 0 a.m. —	Exeter St. Davids Berth	5 3 —
6 45	Exmouth	1 van B. 3-set (L.) 1 S. } (com. 2-set (P.) } 5/9)	—	Berth	—
6 50	Axminster	5-set (E.)	—	Berth	—
7 16	Exmouth	2 S. 2-set (100/110)	6.40 a.m.	Exmouth	7 8
7 30 **R**	Waterloo	1 B.C.K. 3-set (L.) 1 S.O. 1 R.F. (30) 2 S.K. 1 B.C.K.	—	Berth	—
7 34	Sidmouth	2 P.M.V. (4) 2-set (100/110)	5. 0 a.m. —	Exeter St. Davids Berth	5 3 —
7 35	Plymouth Nth. Rd. Padstow	3-set (L.) 1 cor. P.M.V. 1 B.Y.	— 5V26 a.m.	Berth Exmouth Jn.	— 5V29
8 0	Honiton	3-set (L.) 2-set (R.)	—	Berth	—
8 17	Exmouth	5-set (E.)	7.16 a.m.	Exmouth	7 43

61

EXETER CENTRAL (SO)—*continued*

a.m.					
8 30	Ilfracombe	3-set (L.) 3-set (L.)	6.25 a.m.	Yeovil Town F.P.	8 10
8 30 **R** (27/6 to 5/9)	Waterloo	4-set (400)	—	Berth	—
8 41	Plymouth Nth. Rd.	2-set (100/110) 2 S. 1 P.M.V. (4)	8.10* a.m. 6.25 a.m.	Exmouth Yeovil Town R.P.	8 35 8 10
8 47	Templecombe	3-set (L.)	6.15 a.m.	Plymouth N. Rd. R.P.	8 39
8 50	Exmouth	5-set (E.)	—	Berth	—
9 24	Exmouth	5-set (E.)	8.50 a.m.	Exmouth	9 15
9 35	Ilfracombe	1 S.K. 3-set (L.)	7.45 a.m.	Yeovil Town F.P.	9 29
9 52 (until 29/8)	Manchester	5 L.M. cors. 4 L.M. cors.	9.18 a.m. 8.21 a.m.	Exmouth Exmouth R.P.	9 46 8 42
9 57	Exmouth	5-set (E.)	8. 0 a.m.	Axminster	8 49
10 18 **R**	Waterloo	1 B.C.K. 1 R.C.O. 1 R.K.B. (7) 1 B.C.K. 1 S.K. 3-set (L.) 2-set (R.) 1 S.K. 1 B.C.K.	7.45 a.m. — 8.10 a.m.	Yeovil Town R.P. Berth Ilfracombe	9 29 — 10 11
10 32 **R**	Waterloo	1 S.K. 1 B.C.K. 1 R.C.O. 1 R.K.B. (5) 2-set (R.) 1 B.C.K. 4-set	— 8.25 a.m.	Berth Plymouth Nth. Rd.	— 10 25
10 37	Salisbury	3-set (L.) 2-set (100/110)	6.15 a.m. 8.21 a.m. 9.18 a.m.	Plymouth N. Rd. F.P. Exmouth (until 29/8) Exmouth (5/9 & 12/9)	8 39 8 42 9 46
10 45	Exmouth	1 S. 5-set (E.)	9.18 a.m. — 7 47 a.m.	Exmouth (com. 5/9) F.P. Berth (until 29/8) Exmouth	9 46 — 8 14
11 0	Waterloo	3-set (L.) 3-set (L.) 5-set	8.50 a.m. 9.10 a.m.	Ilfracombe Torrington	10 50 10 50
11 15	Exmouth	5-set (E.)	9.54 a.m.	Exmouth	10 21

EXETER CENTRAL (SO)—*continued*

a.m. 11 16 (27/6, 4/7 & 11/7)	Padstow Bude	1 S.K. 3-set (L.) 2-set (P.)	7.33 a.m.	Waterloo F.P.	11 10
11 16 (18/7 to 22/8)	Padstow Bude Okehampton	2 S.K. 3-set (L.) 2-set (P.) 2-set (P.) 1 R.F. (24) 1 S.O. 1 B.C.K.	7.33 a.m.	Waterloo	11 10
11 18 (11/7 to 29/8)	Waterloo	2 S.K. 2 B.C.K. 2-set (P.) 1 S.K.	8.10 a.m. 9. 0 a.m.	Wadebridge Bude	11 12 11 12
11 26 (27/6, 4/7 & 11/7)	Ilfracombe Torrington	1 S.K. 3-set (L.) 1 B.C.K.	7.33 a.m.	Waterloo M.P.	11 10
11 26 (18/7 to 8/8)	Ilfracombe Torrington	2 S.K. 3-set (L.) 3-set (L.)	7.38 a.m.	Waterloo F.P.	11 20
11 39	Ilfracombe	2-set (100/110) 3-set (L.) 1 P.M.V. (4)	7.45 a.m.	Salisbury F.P.	10 57
11 40 (11/7 to 5/9)	Waterloo	1 S.K. 1 S.O. 1 R.F. (32) 3-set (L.) 2 S.K. 3-set (L.)	7.45 a.m. — 9.40 a.m.	Salisbury M.P. Berth Ilfracombe	10 57 — 11 33
11 45	Exmouth	5-set (E.)	10.46 a.m.	Exmouth	11 13
11 56	Waterloo	3-set (L.) 1 S.O. 1 R.F. (31) 1 S.K. 3-set (L.) 2 S.K. 2-set (R.)	10.14 a.m. — 8.30 a.m. 9.30 a.m.	Sidmouth Jn. Berth Padstow Bude	10 39 — 11 50 11 50
p.m. 12 10 (27/6 to 22/8)	Ilfracombe	1 S.K. 5-set	8.22 a.m.	Waterloo F.P.	12 4
12 12	Portsmouth & S.	2 S.K. 6-set (270/1)	10. 2 a.m.	Plymouth Nth. Rd.	12 6
12 16	Exmouth	1 S. 5-set (E.)	11.45 a.m.	Exmouth	12 11

EXETER CENTRAL (SO)—*continued*

p.m. 12 26 (until 5/9)	Ilfracombe Torrington	1 S.K. 5-set 1 S.K. 2-set (R.)	8.35 a.m.	Waterloo F.P.	12 20
12 30	Waterloo	2-set (R.) 2-set (R.) 1 F.K. 1 R.C.O. 1 R.K.B. (3) 1 S.K. 5-set	7.26 a.m. 10.30 a.m.	Plymouth N. Rd. F.P. Ilfracombe	9 55 12 21
12 45 **R** (until 4/7)	Waterloo	3-set (L.) 1 S.O. 1 R.F. (23) 1 B.C.K. 3 S.K. 3-set (L.)	— 7.33 a.m. — 10.48 a.m.	Berth Waterloo (27/6 & 4/7) Berth (20/6) Torrington	— 11 10 — 12 39
12 45 **R** (com. 11/7)	Waterloo	1 B.C.K. 1 S.O. 1 R.F. (23) 1 B.C.K. 2 S.K. 3-set (L.) 1 S.K. 3-set (L.)	7.38 a.m. — 7.33 a.m. 7.38 a.m. — 10.48 a.m.	Waterloo (18/7 to 8/8) Berth (11/7 & com. 15/8) Waterloo (11/7) Waterloo (18/7 to 8/8) Berth (com. 15/8) Torrington	11 20 — 11 10 11 20 — 12 39
12 48	Exmouth	1 S. 5-set (E.)	9.18 a.m. — 11.17 a.m.	Exmouth F.P. (com. 5/9) Berth (until 29/8) Exmouth	9 46 — 11 47
12 56	Plymouth Nth. Rd.	2 S.K. 6-set (270/1)	9. 3 a.m.	Portsmouth & S.	12 48
1 0 **R**	Brighton	4-set 6 buffet set (19/20) 2 S.K.	7.26 a.m. 11.10 a.m.	Plymouth N. Rd. R.P. Plymouth Nth Rd.	9 55 12 52
1 8	Yeovil Town	3-set (L.)	7. 5 a.m.	Torrington F.P.	8 56
1 12	Ilfracombe	2 S.K. 3-set (L.)	*8.57 a.m.	Waterloo F.P. (*8.54 a.m. 12/9)	1 5
1 15	Exmouth	1 S. 5-set (E.)	— 8.21 a.m. 12.15 p.m.	Berth Exmouth Exmouth	— (until 29/8) 8 42 (com. 5/9) 12 41
1 26	Plymouth Nth. Rd.	4-set 1 S.K.	*8.57 a.m.	Waterloo R.P. (*8.54 a.m. 12/9)	1 5

EXETER CENTRAL (SO)—*continued*

p.m. 4 0	Exmouth	1 S. 5-set (E.)	2.49 p.m.	Exmouth	3 15
4 5 **R** (27/6 to 5/9)	Waterloo	1 B.C.K. 1 R.C.O. 1 R.K.B. (9)	10.15 a.m.	Waterloo R.P.	1 40
		3-set (L.)	1.45 p.m.	Ilfracombe	3 58
		3-set (L.) 1 S.K. 1 B.C.K.	1.38 p.m.	Torrington	3 58
4 12	Plymouth Nth. Rd.	4-set 6 buffet set (19/20)	11.30 a.m.	Brighton R.P.	4 7
4 30	Waterloo	3-set (L.)	2.10 p.m.	Ilfracombe	4 11
		1 S.K. 1 B.C.K.	2. 7 p.m.	Torrington	4 11
		1 R.C.O. 1 R.K.B. (1)	11.15 a.m.	Waterloo M.P.	2 39
		3-set (L.)	2.33 p.m.	Plymouth N. Rd. R.P.	4 24
		2 B.C.K. (until 4/7) 2 S.K. (com. 11/7) 1 B.C.K.	1. 0 p.m.	Padstow	4 24
4 35	Portsmouth & S.	1 P.M.V. (4)	1.15 a.m.	Waterloo	5 0
	Salisbury	3-set (L.) 1 S.K.	2. 8 p.m.	Axminster	3 6
	Templecombe	1 S.K.			
4 45	Exmouth	1 S. 5-set (E.)	3.36 p.m.	Exmouth	4 2
4 48	Plymouth Nth. Rd.	4-set	1. 0 p.m.	Waterloo F.P.	4 41
5 5	Ilfracombe Torrington	3-set (L.) 2-set (R.)	1. 0 p.m.	Waterloo R.P.	4 41
5 18	Exmouth	2 S. 2-set (100/110)	2.45 p.m.	Plymouth N. Rd. F.P.	5 8
5 35	Honiton	3-set (L.)	12.56 p.m.	Salisbury F.P.	4 27
5 45	Exmouth	1 S. 5-set (E.)	4.45 p.m.	Exmouth	5 13
5 52	Okehampton	2-set (P.)	2.45 p.m.	Plymouth N. Rd. R.P.	5 8
5 54	Waterloo	1 News van B. (until 22/8)	2.55 p.m.	Ilfracombe	5 26
		1 News van B. 3-set (L.) 1 S.K. 1 R.C.O. 1 R.K.B. (2)	1. 0 p.m.	Waterloo M.P.	4 41
		3-set (L.) 1 P.M.V. (4)	4. 2 p.m.	Plymouth Nth. Rd.	5 48

EXETER CENTRAL (SO)—*continued*

p.m. 6 15	Chard Jn.	4-set (400) (27/6 to 5/9) 3-set (L.) (20/6 & 12/9)	3. 5 p.m.	Salisbury R.P.	6 5
6 18	Exmouth	1 S. 5-set (E.)	5.15 p.m.	Exmouth	5 41
6 37	Plymouth Nth. Rd.	1 B.C.K. 1 S.K. 2-set (R.)	3. 0 p.m.	Waterloo F.P.	6 31
6 45	Exmouth	1 S. 5-set (E.)	5.45 p.m.	Exmouth	6 13
6V48 (milk)	Clapham Jn.	Milk tanks 1 van B.	5V35 p.m.	Crediton	6V3
	Yeovil Jn.	3-set (L.)	1. 5 p.m.	Waterloo	5 37
6 52	Ilfracombe Torrington	3-set (L.) 1 S.K. 1 B.C.K.	3. 0 p.m.	Waterloo M.P.	6 31
7 20	Exmouth	1 S. 5-set (E.)	6.20 p.m.	Exmouth	6 47
7 45	Exmouth	2 S.K. 2 S. 2-set (100/110)	6.47 p.m.	Exmouth	7 18
7 50	Waterloo	1 P.M.V. (4)	4.48 p.m.	Ilfracombe	7 3
		1 P.M.V. (4)	4.52 p.m.	Plymouth Nth. Rd.	7 23
	Eastleigh	1 S.K. 3-set (L.)			
	Portsmouth & S.	1 cor. P.M.V.			
8 7	Plymouth Nth. Rd.	2 S.K. (not 12/9) 5-set	3. 5 p.m.	Waterloo	7 36
	Exeter St. Davids	1 P.M.V. (4)	6.38 p.m.	Honiton R.P.	7 12
8 15	Exmouth	1 S. 5-set (E.)	7.17 p.m.	Exmouth	7 45
8 45	Exmouth	5-set (E.)	7.45 p.m.	Exmouth F.P.	8 12
9 15	Exmouth	1 S. 5-set (E.)	8.15 p.m.	Exmouth	8 42
9 50	Exmouth	1 S. 2-set (100/110)	8.45 p.m.	Exmouth F.P.	9 12
10 18	Honiton	1 S.K. 2-set (P.)	7.21 p.m.	Plymouth N. Rd. F.P.	9 48
10 24	Plymouth Nth. Rd.	3-set (L.)	7. 0 p.m.	Waterloo F.P.	10 18
10 25	Exmouth	5-set (E.)	9.45 p.m.	Exmouth	10 12
10F30	Exmouth Jn.	1 B.Y. 1 van B.	7.21 p.m.	Plymouth N. Rd. R.P.	9 48

EXETER CENTRAL (SO)—*continued*

p.m.					
11 5 ...	Honiton...	1 S.K. 2-set (100/110)	2.33 p.m. ... 2.55 p.m. ...	Plymouth N. Rd. F.P. Sidmouth R.P.	4 24 4 23
11 10 ...	Exmouth	5-set (E.)...	9.15 p.m. ...	Exmouth F.P.	9 41
—	Berth	1 B.Y. (400/1)...	3V20 a.m....	Yeoford	3V47
(until 22/8)	Berth	1 P.M.V. (4)	1.25 a.m. ...	Waterloo R.P.	5 9
—	Berth	2 P.M.V. (4)	6.25 a.m. ...	Yeovil Town	8 10
Com. 5/9 ...	Berth	2-set (P.)...	8.21 a.m. ...	Exmouth	8 42
(until 4/7 & 12/9)	Berth	1 S.K.	7.45 a.m. ...	Salisbury M.P.	10 57
(until 11/7)	Berth	1 R.F. (25) ... ... 1 S.O. ... ... 1 B.C.K.	8.35 a.m. ...	Waterloo	12 20
(20/6) ...	Berth	1 R.K.B. (9) ... ... 1 R.C.O.... ... ... 1 B.C.K.	10.15 a.m. ...	Waterloo R.P.	1 40
—	Berth	1 B.C.K.	10.35 a.m. ...	Waterloo R.P.	1 55
—	Berth	2-set (R.)...	11.15 a.m. ...	Waterloo R.P.	2 39
—	Berth	2 S.K.	11.30 a.m. ...	Brighton F.P.	4 7
—	Berth	2-set (P.)...	2.55 p.m. ...	Sidmouth R.P.	4 23
—	Berth	2 S.K.	12.56 p.m. ...	Salisbury	4 27
—	Berth	1 B.C.K.	1. 0 p.m. ...	Waterloo R.P.	4 41
(27/6 to 5/9)	Berth	1 B.C.K. ... ... 1 S.K. ... ... 1 B.C.K.	1. 5 p.m. ...	Waterloo	5 37
—	Berth	1 cor. P.M.V....	3. 5 p.m. ...	Salisbury	6 5
—	Berth	1 R.K.B. (7) ... ... 1 R.C.O.... ... ... 1 B.C.K.	3. 0 p.m. ...	Waterloo M.P.... ...	6 31
—	Berth	1 S.K. (27/6) ... ... 3-set (L.)... ... ... 1 P.M.V. (4)	4.48 p.m. ...	Ilfracombe...	7 3
—	Berth	3-set (L.)...	6.38 p.m. ...	Honiton F.P.	7 12

EXETER CENTRAL (SO)—*continued*

p.m.					
(until 29/8)	Berth	1 B.C.K.	6.47 p.m. ...	Exmouth	7 18
—	Berth	1 S.	7.45 p.m. ...	Exmouth M.P.	8 12
—	Berth	3-set (L.) (20/6 & 12/9) 4-set (400/) (27/6 to 5/9)	7.35 p.m. ...	Chard Jn.	8 55
—	Berth	1 S. ... ... 2 S.K.	8.45 p.m. ...	Exmouth R.P.	9 12
—	Berth	1 S.	9.15 p.m. ...	Exmouth R.P.	9 41
—	Berth	4-set ... ... 1 B.C.K. ... ... 2-set (R.)... ... ... 1 R.K.B. (5) ... ... 1 R.C.O.... ... ... 1 B.C.K. ... ... 1 S.K. ... ... 2 B.C.K. (com. 18/7)	6. 0 p.m. ...	Waterloo	9 59
—	Berth	4-set ... ... 1 R.C.O.... ... ... 1 R.K.B. (10) ... ... 1 van B. ... ... 2 News van B. ... 1 van B.	7.42 p.m. ...	Ilfracombe...	10 7
—	Berth	1 S.K. ... ... 1 R.F. (31) ... ... 1 S.O.	7. 0 p.m. ...	Waterloo R.P.	10 18
—	Berth	3-set (L.)... ... ... 1 R.B. (21) ... ... 1 S.O.	5. 0 p.m. ...	Waterloo	10 40
—	Berth	5-set (E.)... ... ... 1 S. ... ... 1 R.F. (30) ... ... 1 S.O.	10.15 p.m. ...	Exmouth	10 43
—	Berth	1 S.K. ... ... Milk tanks ... ... 1 van B.	4V4 p.m. ...	Clapham Jn.	11V20
—	Berth	5-set (E.)... ... ... 1 S. ... ... 2-set (100/110) ...	11. 5 p.m. ...	Exmouth	11 35
—	Berth	2-set (P.)... ... ... 1 S.K.	11.10 p.m. ...	Honiton	11 40
—	Berth	5-set (E.)...	11.50 p.m. ...	Exmouth	12 19

73

GUNNISLAKE (SO)

a.m. 7 8 ...	Plymouth Nth. Rd.	2-set (100/110)	—	Berth	—
p.m. 2 26 ...	Bere Alston	P. & P. set (373)	1.58 p.m. ...	Bere Alston	2 18
4 43 ...	Bere Alston	2-set (100/110)	4.23 p.m. ...	Callington F.P.	4 42
—	Berth	2-set (100/110)	4.23 p.m. ...	Callington R.P.	4 42

HALWILL (SO)

a.m. 5F17 ...	Bude	1 B.Y.	2F6 a.m. ...	Exeter Central	5F14
5 41 ... (11/7 to 5/9)	Padstow...	1 S.K. (18/7 to 8/8) 3-set (L.)...	12.15 a.m. ...	Waterloo F.P.	5 36
5 48 ... (11/7 to 5/9)	Bude	1 S.K. (18/7 to 8/8) 2-set (P.)...	2.15 a.m. ...	Waterloo R.P.	5 36
7 15 ...	Bude	2-set (P.)... ... ... 1 S.K.	—	Berth	—
8 49 ...	Okehampton... ...	2-set (P.)... ... ... 2-set (P.)...	8.20 a.m. ... 7.58 a.m. ...	Launceston ... ... Bude	8 44 8 36
8 53 ...	Bude	2-set (P.)...	—	Berth	—
9 54 ... (11/7 to 29/8)	Waterloo	2 S.K. ... ... 2 B.C.K. ... ... 2-set (P.)... ... ... 1 S.K.	8.10 a.m. ... 9. 0 a.m. ...	Wadebridge ... ... Bude	9 49 9 42
10 27 ...	Waterloo	1 S.K. ... ... 3-set (L.)... ... ... 2 S.K. ... ... 2-set (R.)...	8.30 a.m. ... 9.30 a.m. ...	Padstow ... ... Bude	10 22 10 10
10 47 ...	Padstow...	1 B.Y. ... ... 2-set (P.)...	10.12 a.m. ...	Okehampton F.P. ...	10 44
10 52 ...	Torrington	1 B.C.K.	8.52 a.m. ...	Torrington	10 18
10 55 ...	Bude	2-set (P.)...	10.12 a.m. ...	Okehampton R.P. ...	10 44
p.m. 1 46 ...	Bude	2-set (P.)... ... ... 1 B.S.L.	1.20 p.m. ...	Okehampton F.P. ...	1 45
1 53 ...	Launceston	2-set (P.)...	1.20 p.m. ...	Okehampton R.P. ...	1 45
2 51 ...	Waterloo ... ... Okehampton... ...	2 B.C.K. (until 4/7) 2 S.K. (com. 11/7)... 1 B.C.K. ... ... 2-set (P.)... ... ... 2-set (P.)...	1. 0 p.m. ... 2. 1 p.m. ...	Padstow ... ... Bude	2 47 2 41

74

HALWILL (SO)—*continued*

p.m. 3 11 ...	Padstow...	1 C.K. 5-set	10.35 a.m. ...	Waterloo F.P.	3 7
3 16 ...	Bude	1 S.K. ... ... 2 B.C.K.	10.35 a.m. ...	Waterloo R.P.	3 7
4 29 ...	Padstow...	1 B.C.K. ... ... 1 S.K. ... ... 1 B.C.K.	11.15 a.m. ...	Waterloo F.P.	4 26
4 35 ...	Bude	1 S.K. ... ... 2-set (R.)...	11.15 a.m. ...	Waterloo R.P.	4 26
6 24 ...	Padstow...	2-set (P.)...	5.51 p.m. ...	Okehampton F.P. ...	6 21
6 27 ...	Bude	2-set (P.)...	5.51 p.m. ...	Okehampton R.P. ...	6 21
6 30 ...	Torrington	1 B.C.K. ... ... 1 S.K. (until 27/6) 1 B.C.K. (until 4/7)	4.40 p.m. ... 5.32 p.m. ...	Torrington ... ... Bude	6 6 6 11
8 0 ...	Okehampton ... Exeter Central ...	2-set (P.)... ... ... 1 B.Y. ... ... 1 van B.	6. 0 p.m. ... 7. 5 p.m. ...	Padstow ... ... Bude F.P.	7 56 7 45
8 20 ...	Launceston	2-set (P.)...	7.45 p.m. ...	Okehampton F.P. ...	8 17
8 25 ...	Bude	2-set (P.)...	7.45 p.m. ...	Okehampton R.P. ...	8 17
—	Berth	2-set (P.)...	5.32 p.m. ...	Bude (F.P. until 4/7)	6 11
—	Berth	2-set (P.)...	7. 5 p.m. ...	Bude R.P.	7 45

HONITON (SO)

a.m. 9† 3 ...	Sidmouth Jn.... ...	2-set (R.)... ... ... 3-set (L.)...	8. 0 a.m. ...	Exeter Central	8 35
p.m. 1 45 ...	Exeter Central ...	2-set (100/110) ... 1 S.	—	Berth	—
6 38 ...	Exeter Central ...	3-set (L.)...	5.35 p.m. ...	Exeter Central	6 8
11 10 ...	Exeter Central ...	2-set (P.)... ... ... 1 S.K.	10.18 p.m. ...	Exeter Central	10 53
11†47 ...	Sidmouth Jn. ...	2-set (100/110) ... 1 S.K.	11. 5 p.m. ...	Exeter Central	11 34

ILFRACOMBE (SO)

a.m. 6 50 ...	King's Nympton ...	1 S.K. ... ... 1 B.C.K.	—	Berth	—

ILFRACOMBE (SO)—*continued*

(12/9) ...	Berth	2-set (100/110)	11.39 a.m. ...	Exeter Central	2 5
27/6 to 22/8)	Berth	1 S.K. 5-set	8.22 a.m. ...	Waterloo	2 21
—	Berth	1 S.K. (20/6 & 4/7 to 5/9) ... ... 5-set (until 5/9) ...	8.35 a.m. ...	Waterloo	2 41
(until 5/9)	Berth	1 S.K. ... ... 1 F.K. 5-set	10.15 a.m. ...	Waterloo	3 40
—	Berth	2 S.K. ... ... 1 F.K. 5-set	11. 0 a.m. ...	Waterloo	4 38
—	Berth	5-set ... ... 1 R.S.O. ... ... 1 R.K. (37) ... ... 1 R.F.O. ... ... 1 B.C.K.	12. 5 p.m. ...	Waterloo	5 33
(12/9) ...	Berth	3-set (L.)...	5.50 p.m. ...	Barnstaple Jn.	6 35
—	Berth	3-set (L.)...	1. 0 p.m. ...	Waterloo	7 17
—	Berth	3-set (L.)...	3. 0 p.m. ...	Waterloo	9 6

KING'S NYMPTON (SO)

a.m. 8 30 ...	Barnstaple Jn. ...	1 B.C.K. ... ... 1 S.K.	6.50 a.m. ...	Ilfracombe...	7 52

LAPFORD (SO)

p.m. 4V0 ...	Crediton	Milk tanks ... ... 1 van B.	—	Berth	—

LAUNCESTON (SO)

a.m. 7 5 ...	Plymouth Nth. Rd.	2 W.R. set	—	Berth	—
8 20 ...	Okehampton... ...	2-set (P.)...	—	Berth	—
10 15 ...	Redruth W.R. ...	2 W.R. set	7.10 a.m. ...	Plymouth Nth. Rd. ...	8 43
p.m. 12 50 ...	Plymouth Nth. Rd.	2 W.R. set	10. 3 a.m. ...	Saltash	12 15
2 5 ...	Plymouth Nth. Rd.	2 W.R. set	12.12 p.m. ...	Plymouth Nth. Rd. ...	1 57

LAUNCESTON (SO)—*continued*

p.m. 4 56 ...	Padstow...	1 B.C.K. ... ... 1 S.K. ... ... 1 B.C.K. ... ... 2-set (P.)...	11.15 a.m. ... 1.20 p.m. ...	Waterloo ... ... Okehampton	4 51 2 15
5 40 ...	Plymouth Nth. Rd.	2 W.R. set	3. 5 p.m. ...	Plymouth Nth. Rd. ...	4 39
8 35 ...	Plymouth Nth. Rd.	2 W.R. set	6.23 p.m. ...	Plymouth Nth. Rd. ...	7 55
—	Berth	2-set (P.)...	7.45 p.m. ...	Okehampton	8 42
—	Berth	2 W.R. set	8.40 p.m. ...	Plymouth Nth. Rd. ...	10 10

LITTLEHAM (SO)

a.m. 9 38 **R** ...	Waterloo	3-set (L.)... ... ... 1 S.K. ... ... 1 B.C.K.	9†31 a.m. ...	Exmouth	9†36

LYME REGIS (SO)

a.m. 7 35 ...	Axminster	2-set (100/110)	—	Berth	—
9 0 **R** ...	Axminster ... ... Waterloo	2-set (100/110) ... *1 B.C.K. ... ... *3-set (L.)...	8.32 a.m. ... —	Axminster... ... ... Berth ... ... (*27/6 to 5/9)	8 53 —
10 5 ...	Axminster	2-set (100/110)	9.35 a.m. ...	Axminster...	9 56
11 5 ...	Axminster	2-set (100/110)	10.35 a.m. ...	Axminster...	10 56
p.m. 12 10 ...	Axminster	2-set (100/110)	11.35 a.m. ...	Axminster F.P.	11 56
1 12 ...	Axminster	2-set (100/110)	12.43 p.m. ...	Axminster...	1 4
3 5 **R** ...	Waterloo	5-set	10.45 a.m. ...	Waterloo	2 11
4 10 ...	Axminster	2-set (100/110)	3.40 p.m. ...	Axminster...	4 1
5 10 ...	Axminster ... ... Waterloo	2-set (100/110) ... ... 1 P.M.V. (4)	4.42 p.m. ... —	Axminster... ... ... Berth	5 3 —
6 7 ...	Axminster	2-set (100/110)	5.40 p.m. ...	Axminster...	6 1
8 22 ...	Axminster	2-set (100/110)	6.50 p.m. ...	Axminster...	7 11
(until 29/8)	Berth	3-set (L.)...	11.35 a.m. ...	Axminster R.P.... ... (8.5 a.m. Waterloo)	11 56
—	Berth	2-set (100/110)	8.55 p.m. ...	Axminster...	9 16

79

OKEHAMPTON (SO)

a.m. 4F37	Bude	1 van B.	1F38 a.m.	Exmouth Jn. R.P.	4F16
6 11	Plymouth Nth. Rd.	3-set (L.)	1.15 or 1.25 a.m.	Waterloo	6 2
6 30	Padstow	1 B.C.K. 1 S.K. (until 22/8) 1 News van B.	1.15 or 1.25 a.m.	Waterloo	6 2
7 0	Plymouth Nth. Rd.	4-set	—	Berth	—
8 45	Plymouth Nth. Rd.	3-set (L.) 1 cor. P.M.V.	7.35 a.m.	Exeter Central F.P.	8 40
10 12	Padstow Bude	1 B.Y. 2-set (P.) 2-set (P.)	7.35 a.m. 8.20 a.m.	Exeter Central R.P. Launceston	8 40 9 20
p.m. 12 6 (27/6 to 22/8)	Padstow	1 S.K. (com. 18/7) 1 S.K. 3-set (L.)	7.33 a.m.	Waterloo	12 2
12 18 (27/6 to 22/8)	Bude	2-set (P.) (com. 18/7) 2-set (P.)	7.33 a.m.	Waterloo	12 2
1 11 (until 11/7)	Waterloo	5-set 1 S.O. 1 R.F. (24) 1 C.K. 1 B.C.K. 2-set (P.)	11. 0 a.m. 11.45 a.m.	Padstow Bude	1 7 12 53
1 11 (18/7 to 22/8)	Waterloo	5-set 1 C.K. 3-set (L.) 1 S.O. 1 R.F. (24) 1 B.C.K.	11. 0 a.m. 7.33 a.m.	Padstow Waterloo R.P.	1 7 12 2
1 20	Bude Launceston	2-set (P.) 1 B.S.L. 2-set (P.)	—	Berth	—
3 39	Plymouth Nth. Rd.	3-set (L.)	11.15 a.m.	Waterloo F.P.	3 33
3 41	Exeter Central Waterloo	1 S.K. 3-set (L.) 2 B.C.K. (until 4/7) 2 S.K. (com. 11/7) 1 B.C.K.	2.33 p.m. 1. 0 p.m.	Plymouth Nth. Rd. Padstow F.P.	3 37 3 20
3 55	Padstow Bude	1 B.C.K. 1 S.K. 1 B.C.K. 1 S.K. 2-set (R.)	11.15 a.m.	Waterloo R.P.	3 33

80

OKEHAMPTON (SO)—*continued*

p.m. 4 14	Exeter Central	2 S. 2-set (100/110) 2-set (P.)	2.45 p.m. 1. 0 p.m.	Plymouth Nth. Rd. Padstow	4 9 3 20
5 6	Waterloo	3-set (L.) 1 P.M.V. (4)	4. 2 p.m. 3.13 p.m.	Plymouth Nth. Rd. Bude	5 2 4 37
5 51	Padstow Bude	2-set (P.) 2-set (P.)	1. 0 p.m. 3.13 p.m.	Padstow R.P. Bude R.P.	3 20 4 37
6 19	Waterloo Eastleigh Portsmouth & S. Waterloo	1 P.M.V. (4) 1 S.K. 3-set (L.) 1 cor. P.M.V. 1 News van B.	4.52 p.m. 3.13 p.m.	Plymouth Nth. Rd. Padstow R.P.	6 16 5 47
7 45	Launceston Bude	2-set (P.) 2-set (P.)	5.52 p.m. 3.13 p.m.	Exeter Central Padstow F.P.	6 56 5 47
8 52	Exeter Central	1 S.K. 2-set (P.) 1 B.Y. 1 van B.	7.21 p.m. 6. 0 p.m.	Plymouth Nth. Rd. Padstow R.P.	8 46 8 29
—	Berth	1 B.S.L.	3.13 p.m.	Bude M.P.	4 37
—	Berth	2-set	6. 0 p.m.	Padstow F.P.	8 29
—	Berth	3-set (L.)	9.26 p.m.	Plymouth Nth. Rd.	10 55

PADSTOW (SO)

a.m. 8 10	Bodmin Rd. W.R.	2-set (P.)	7.22 a.m.	Bodmin North	7 55
8 30	Waterloo Wadebridge	1 S.K. 3-set (L.) 2-set (P.)	— 12.25 a.m. — — 12.15/25 a.m. — —	Berth (until 11/7) Waterloo (18/7 to 8/8) Berth (com. 15/8) Berth (until 4/7) Waterloo (11/7 to 5/9) Berth (12/9) Berth	— 7 26 — — 7 26 — —
9 8	Bodmin Rd. W.R.	2 W.R. set	7.50 a.m.	Bodmin Rd. W.R.	8 50
11 0R (until 11/7)	Waterloo	5-set 1 S.O. 1 R.F. (24) 1 C.K.	—	Berth	—
11 0R (18/7 to 22/8)	Waterloo	5-set 1 C.K. 3-set (L.)	—	Berth	—

81

PADSTOW (SO)—*continued*

a.m. 11 0 **R** ... (com. 29/8)	Waterloo	5-set ... ... 1 S.O. ... ... 1 R.F. (24) ... ... 1 C.K. ... ... 3-set (L.) (29/8 only) 2 B.C.K. (com. 5/9)	—	Berth	—
11 35 ...	Bodmin Rd. W.R....	2 W.R. set	10.10 a.m. ...	Bodmin Rd. W.R. ...	11 24
p.m. 12 10 ...	Bodmin North ...	2-set (P.)...	11.20 a.m. ...	Bodmin North	11 55
1 0 **R** ... (until 4/7)	Waterloo	3 B.C.K.	(1) 1.25 a.m. (2) —	Waterloo ... ... Berth	9 27 —
	Okehampton... ...	2-set (P.)...	10.12 a.m. ...	Okehampton R.P. ...	12 30
1 0 **R** ... (com. 11/7)	Waterloo	2 S.K.	(1) — (1) 1.25 a.m. —	Berth ... ... Waterloo M.P. (until 22/8) Berth (com. 29/8) ...	— 9 27 —
		1 B.C.K.	1.25 a.m. ...	Waterloo F.P.	9 27
	Okehampton... ...	2-set (P.)...	10.12 a.m. ...	Okehampton R.P. ...	12 30
2 52 ...	Bodmin North ...	2-set (P.)...	2. 0 p.m. ...	Bodmin North	2 34
3 13 ...	Waterloo ... ... Okehampton... ...	1 News van B. ... ... 2-set (P.)...	1.25 a.m. ... 1.15 p.m. ...	Waterloo ... ... Wadebridge F.P. ...	9 27 1 29
4 40 ...	Bodmin North ...	2-set (P.)...	4. 5 p.m. ...	Bodmin North	4 35
6 0 ...	Okehampton... ... Exeter Central	2-set (P.)... ... ... 1 B.Y.	10.15 a.m. ... 10.12 a.m. ...	Wadebridge ... ... Okehampton F.P. ...	10 24 12 30
8 4 ...	Bodmin Rd. W.R....	2-set (P.)...	6.45 p.m. ...	Bodmin North	7 19
8 30 ...	Wadebridge	1 S.K. ... ... 2-set (P.)...	11.15 a.m. ... 5.51 p.m. ...	Waterloo ... ... Okehampton R.P. ...	6 22 7 58
10 5 ...	Wadebridge	2-set (P.)...	9. 5 p.m. ...	Bodmin Rd. W.R. ...	9 51
(until 4/7)	Berth	1 S.K.	1.25 a.m. ...	Waterloo M.P.	9 27
(27/6 to 22/8)	Berth	1 S.K. (com. 18/7)... 1 S.K. ... ... 3-set (L.)...	7.33 a.m. ...	Waterloo	2 14
—	Berth	1 C.K. 5-set	10.35 a.m. ...	Waterloo	5 0
—	Berth	2 B.C.K. ... ... 2-set (P.)...	11.15 a.m. ...	Waterloo	6 22

PETROCKSTOW (SO)

a.m. 7 55 ...	Torrington	1 B.C.K.	6.25 a.m. ...	Torrington F.P.... ...	7† 4
11 42 ...	Torrington	1 B.C.K. ... ... 1 B.C.K.	10.52 a.m. ... 6.25 a.m. ...	Halwill ... ... Torrington R.P. ...	11 41 7† 4

F

93

TORRINGTON (SO)—*continued*

p.m. 4 38 ...	Exeter Central ... Barnstaple Jn. ...	1 P.M.V. (4) ... ... 3-set (L.)...	**2F** 6 a.m. ... 10.15 a.m. ... 2.43 p.m. ...	Exeter Central ... ... Waterloo (until 5/9) R.P. Barnstaple Jn. (12/9)	**6F** 8 3 41 3 12
4 40 ...	Halwill	1 B.C.K.	10.15 a.m. 10.52 a.m.	Waterloo F.P. (until 5/9) Halwill R.P. (12/9) ...	3 41 12 18
5 48 ...	Paddington ... ... Bristol ... ... Barnstaple Jn. ...	1 P.M.V. (4) ... ... 1 P.M.V. (4) ... ... 2-set (R.)... ... ... 1 S.K.	— 10.12 a.m. ... 11. 0 a.m. ...	Berth ... ... Barnstaple Jn. ... ... Waterloo	— 10 45 4 30
7 38 ...	Barnstaple Jn. ... Exeter Central ... Paddington	2-set (R.)... ... ... 1 News van B. ... ... 1 News van B. ... ... 1 van B. ... ... 1 W.R. van	12. 5 p.m. ... 7.17 a.m. ... 7. 6 a.m. ... **2F** 6 a.m. ... 10.12 a.m. ...	Waterloo ... ... Bideford ... ... Barnstaple Jn. R.P. ... Exeter Central ... ... Barnstaple Jn.	5 29 7 26 7 48 **6F** 8 10 45
8 24 ...	Barnstaple Jn. ...	3-set (L.)...	5.40 p.m. ...	Barnstaple Jn.	6 10
(com. 29/8)	Berth	1 B.C.K.	7.17 a.m. ...	Bideford	7 26
(20/6 & 12/9)	Berth	1 S.K.	8.13 a.m. ...	Barnstaple Jn.	8 45
(20/6 & 12/9)	Berth	1 B.C.K.	10.52 a.m. ...	Halwill F.P.	12 18
(27/6 to 11/7)	Berth	1 B.C.K.	7.33 a.m. ...	Waterloo	1 27
(18/7 to 8/8)	Berth	3-set (L.)...	7.38 a.m. ...	Waterloo	1 27
(until 5/9)	Berth	1 S.K. ... ... 2-set (R.)...	8.35 a.m. ...	Waterloo	2 31
—	Berth	1 S.K. ... ... 2-set (R.)... ... ... 2-set (R.)...	1. 0 p.m. ...	Waterloo	7 9
—	Berth	1 B.C.K. ... ... 1 B.C.K. (until 4/7) 1 S.K. (until 27/6)	6.30 p.m. ...	Halwill	7 56
—	Berth	3 S.K. ... ... 1 B.C.K.	3. 0 p.m. ...	Waterloo	8 58

WADEBRIDGE (SO)

a.m. 6 52 ...	Bodmin North ...	2-set (P.)...	—	Berth	—
8 1 ...	Bodmin North ...	2-set (P.)...	—	Berth	—
8 10 **R** ... (11/7 to 29/8)	Waterloo	2 S.K. ... ... 2 B.C.K.	—	Berth	—

94

WADEBRIDGE (SO)—*continued*

Arr.	From	Formation	Dep.	To	Next
a.m. 8 32	Bodmin Rd. W.R.	2-set (P.)	8.10 a.m.	Padstow	8 19
8 45	Waterloo	1 S.K. 3-set (L.)	8.30 a.m.	Padstow F.P.	8 39
9 48	Bodmin North	2-set (P.)	8.43 a.m.	Bodmin Road	9 2
10 15	Padstow	2-set (P.)	8.30 a.m.	Padstow R.P.	8 39
11 15	Padstow	2 W.R. set	10.10 a.m.	Bodmin Rd. W.R. F.P.	10 55
11 55	Bodmin Rd. W.R.	2 W.R. set	11.35 a.m.	Padstow	11 44
p.m. 12 28	Bodmin North	2-set (P.)	12.10 p.m.	Padstow	12 19
1 15	Padstow	2-set (P.)	10.10 a.m.	Bodmin Rd. W.R. R.P.	10 55
1 23	Bodmin Rd. W.R.	2 W.R. set	12.38 p.m.	Bodmin Rd. W.R.	1 10
3 9	Bodmin North	2-set (P.)	2.52 p.m.	Padstow	3 1
3 24	Bodmin Rd. W.R.	2 W.R. set	2.30 p.m.	Bodmin Rd. W.R.	3 6
5 11	Bodmin North	2-set (P.)	4.40 p.m.	Padstow	4 49
5 56	Bodmin Rd. W.R.	2 W.R. set	4.55 p.m.	Bodmin Rd. W.R.	5 39
6 18	Bodmin North	2-set (P.)	5.36 p.m.	Bodmin North	5 53
7 5	Bodmin General	2 W.R. set	6.17 p.m.	Bodmin Rd. W.R.	6 49
8 42	Bodmin Rd. W.R.	2 W.R. set	7.26 p.m.	Bodmin Rd. W.R.	8 2
—	Berth	1 S.K. 2-set (P.)	8.30 p.m.	Padstow	8 39
—	Berth	2-set (P.)	10. 5 p.m.	Padstow	10 14

YEOFORD (SO)

Arr.	From	Formation	Dep.	To	Next
a.m. 3 20 (news)	Exeter Central	1 B.Y. (stove) (400/1)	12F55 a.m.	Plymouth Friary Sdgs.	3F16
p.m. 12 23	Plymouth Nth. Rd.	3-set (L.) 1 S.K.	—	Berth	—
—	Berth	1 B.C.K.	10.37 a.m.	Barnstaple Jn.	11 46

YEOVIL JN. (SO)

Arr.	From	Formation	Dep.	To	Next
a.m. 3V57	Yeovil Town	1 News B.Y.	1.15 a.m.	Waterloo R.P.	3 49
4 24	Exeter Central Yeovil Town	1 P.M.V. (4) 3-set (L.) 1 S.K.	1.50 a.m.	Eastleigh	4 17

100

BARNSTAPLE JN. (SUN.)—*continued*

Arr.	From	Formation	Dep.	To	Next
p.m. 9 49	Ilfracombe	2-set (R.) 3-set (L.)	4. 0 p.m.	Waterloo F.P.	9 44
9 54	Torrington	2-set (R.)	4. 0 p.m.	Waterloo R.P.	9 44
—	Berth	1 B.C.K. (19/7 to 23/8) 1 B.C.K.	5.15 p.m.	Exeter Central	6 38
—	Berth	3-set (L.)	7.50 p.m.	Torrington	8 18
—	Berth	1 B.C.K. 1 S.K. 1 B.C.K. (until 12/7 & com. 30/8)	9. 5 p.m.	Torrington	9 35
—	Berth	1 S.K. 3-set (L.)	9.10 p.m.	Ilfracombe	9 48

BERE ALSTON (SUN.)

Arr.	From	Formation	Dep.	To	Next
a.m. 9 18	Callington	2-set (100/110)	8.15 a.m.	Callington	8 57
p.m. 12 22	Callington	2-set (100/110)	11.12 a.m.	Callington	11 58
7 24	Callington	2-set (100/110)	6.32 p.m.	Callington	7 12
10 2	Callington	2-set (100/110)	9.10 p.m.	Callington	9 51

BUDE (SUN.)

Arr.	From	Formation	Dep.	To	Next
a.m. 9 45 **R**	Waterloo Okehampton	2-set (R.) 1 B.C.K. 1 S.K.	—	Berth	—
11 18	Halwill	2-set (P.)	10.29 a.m.	Halwill	11 2
p.m. 2 28	Okehampton	2-set (P.) 2-set (P.) (until 16/8)	11.40 a.m. —	Okehampton R.P. Berth	12 48 —
6 45	Okehampton	1 S.K. 2-set (P.)	11.40 a.m. 11. 0 a.m.	Okehampton F.P. Waterloo F.P.	12 48 5 23
—	Berth	1 S.K. 1 B.C.K.	11. 0 a.m.	Waterloo R.P.	5 23
—	Berth	2-set (P.) 1 S.K.	9.20 p.m.	Okehampton	10 26

CALLINGTON (SUN.)

Arr.	From	Formation	Dep.	To	Next
a.m. 8 15	Bere Alston	2-set (100/110)	—	Berth	—

101

CALLINGTON (SUN.)—*continued*

a.m. 11 12	Bere Alston	2-set (100/110)	9.18 a.m.	Bere Alston	10 0
p.m. 6 32	Bere Alston	2-set (100/110)	12.22 p.m.	Bere Alston	1 4
9 10	Bere Alston	2-set (100/110)	7.24 p.m.	Bere Alston	8 5
—	Berth	2-set (100/110)	10. 2 p.m.	Bere Alston	10 43

EXETER CENTRAL (SUN.)

Formation of Exeter—Exmouth 5 sets (E.):—

*1 S.
1 B.S.
1 C.
1 B.S.
*1 S.
(*not stencilled with set numbers)

a.m. 8V25	Exeter St. Davids	2 P.M.V. (4) 1 van B.	—	Berth	—
8 35	Honiton	3-set (L.) (com. 28/6) 2-set (R.)	—	Berth	—
9 55	Sidmouth	2-set (P.)	—	Berth	—
10 0	Exmouth	5-set (E.)	9.15 a.m.	Exmouth	9 47
10 0	Ilfracombe	1 S.K. 4-set	—	Berth	—
	Torrington	1 P.M.V. (4)	8V50 a.m.	Exeter St. Davids	8V53
10 15	Plymouth Nth. Rd. Okehampton	1 S.K. 3-set (L.) 1 S.K. 2-set (P.) (com. 23/8)	—	Berth	—
10 30	Exmouth	1 S. 5-set (E.)	—	Berth	—
11 0	Waterloo	1 News van B. 1 S.K. (not 13/9) 3-set (L.) 1 R.C.O. 1 R.K.B. (5) 2-set (R.)	— 8.30 a.m. — 9.23 a.m.	Berth Plymouth Nth. Rd. Berth Honiton	— 10 47 — 9 54
11 20	Exmouth	1 S. 5-set (E.)	—	Berth	—
11 57 (Excns. 5/7, 19/7, 16/8)	Paignton W.R.	5-set 1 S.K.	9.20 a.m.	Salisbury	11 45

102

EXETER CENTRAL (SUN.)—*continued*

p.m. 12 2 **R**	Waterloo	1 B.C.K. 1 S.K. 1 R.C.O. 1 R.K.B. (10) 5-set 1 S.K. 2-set (R.)	— 10.10 a.m.	Berth Plymouth Nth. Rd.	— 11 56
12 7	Exmouth	1 S. 5-set (E.)	— 11. 0 a.m.	Berth Exmouth	— 11 32
12 13	Honiton	1 S.K. 3-set (L.)	Pt.9.30 a.m.	Yeovil Town	11 26
12 30 **R**	Waterloo	1 B.C.K. 5-set 1 R.F.O. 1 R.K. (37) 1 R.S.O. 2-set (R.) 2-set (R.) (until 6/9) 2 B.C.K. (13/9 only)	— 10.30 a.m.	Berth Ilfracombe	— 12 24
12V45	Exeter St. Davids	1 van B.	8V50 a.m.	Exeter St. Davids	8V53
12 55	Exmouth	1 S. 5-set (E.)	12. 0 noon	Exmouth	12 26
12 56	Plymouth Nth. Rd.	3-set (L.)	9. 0 a.m.	Waterloo F.P.	12 50
1 0	Brighton Portsmouth & S.	6 buffet set (19/20) 4-set	11.10 a.m.	Plymouth Nth. Rd.	12 52
1 5	Ilfracombe Torrington	3-set (L.) 1 B.C.K.	9. 0 a.m.	Waterloo M.P.	12 50
1 16 Excn. (19/7 & 30/8)	Plymouth	9 S.R./W.R. cors. (incl. 1 C.A.F.)	9.13 a.m.	Portsmouth Hbr.	1 7
1 22 (28/6, 12/7, 2/8, 16/8, 23/8 & 6/9)	Exmouth	5-set	9.23 a.m.	Waterloo R.P.	1 17
1 57	Exmouth	1 S. 5-set (E.)	12.45 p.m.	Exmouth	1 12
2 2	Ilfracombe Torrington	5-set 2-set (R.) 1 S.K.	10.45 a.m.	Waterloo F.P.	1 56
2 15	Exmouth	1 S. 5-set (E.)	—	Berth	—
2 55	Exmouth	1 S. 5-set (E.)	1.45 p.m	Exmouth	2 15

103

EXETER CENTRAL (SUN.)—*continued*

p.m.					
2 55	Plymouth Nth. Rd. Bude	2 S.K. 3-set (L.) 1 B.C.K. 1 S.K.	11. 0 a.m.	Waterloo F.P.	2 43
3 7	Exmouth	2-set (100/110) 2-set (100/110) 2-set (P.)	9. 5 a.m. — — Pt. 9.30 a.m.	Ilfracombe R.P. Berth Berth (until 16/8) Yeovil Town (com. 23/8)	11 12 — — 11 26
3 12	Ilfracombe Torrington	1 P.M.V. (4) 3-set (L.) 3-set (L.)	1V15 p.m. 11.15 a.m.	Exeter St. Davids Waterloo F.P.	1V18 3 0
3 20	Salisbury	1 S.K. 3-set (L.)	1.17 p.m.	Honiton	1 47
3 45	Exmouth	1 S. 5-set (E.)	2.55 p.m.	Exmouth	3 25
4 12 **R**	Waterloo	1 B.C.K. (until 12/7)	—	Berth	—
		1 B.C.K. 1 S.O. 1 R.B. (15)	9. 0 a.m.	Waterloo R.P.	12 50
		1 S.K. 4-set	2. 0 p.m.	Ilfracombe	4 6
		1 B.C.K. 3-set (L.)	1.55 p.m.	Torrington	4 6
4 18	Plymouth Nth. Rd.	6 buffet set (19/20) 4-set	11.30 a.m.	Brighton	4 12
4 25	Exmouth	1 S. 5-set (E.)	3.40 p.m.	Exmouth	4 8
4 44 **R**	Waterloo	2-set (R.) 1 R.C.O. 1 R.K.B. (3)	10.45 a.m.	Waterloo R.P.	1 56
		2-set (R.) 1 S.K. 5-set	2.45 p.m.	Ilfracombe	4 38
4 56 **R**	Waterloo	3-set (L.) 1 R.C.O. 1 R.K.B. (1)	11. 0 a.m.	Waterloo R.P.	2 43
		1 S.K. (21/6 only)	—	Berth	—
		2-set (R.) 1 B.C.K. 1 S.K. 3-set (L.)	3. 1 p.m.	Plymouth Nth. Rd.	4 49
5 10	Exmouth	1 S. 5-set (E.)	4.20 p.m.	Exmouth	4 50
5 15	Ilfracombe Barnstaple Jn.	3-set (L.) 1 B.C.K. 1 B.C.K. (19/7 to 23/8)	11.48 a.m. —	Plymouth N. Rd. R.P. Berth	2 10 —

104

EXETER CENTRAL (SUN.)—*continued*

p.m.					
5 20 (milk & parcels)	Waterloo	Milk tanks Vans 1 News van B.	—	Berth	—
	Templecombe	1 S.K. 1 B.C.K.	11.15 a.m. —	Waterloo (21/6) R.P. Berth (com. 28/6)	3 0 —
	Lyme Regis Seaton	1 B.C.K. (com. 28/6) 1 B.C.K. (6/9)	—	Berth	—
5 25	Plymouth Nth. Rd.	3-set (L.)	1.33 p.m.	Salisbury M.P.	4 42
		1 S.K.	11.48 a.m. —	Plymouth N. Rd. F.P. (until 6/9) Berth (13/9)	2 10 —
		1 S.K.	11.15 a.m. — 9. 0 a.m.	Waterloo (21/6) Berth (28/6) Waterloo M.P.	3 0 — 12 50 (com. 5/7)
6 12	Exmouth	4-set (400) 3 S.K.	—	Berth	—
6 30 **R** (21/6)	Waterloo	3-set (L.)	9. 5 a.m.	Ilfracombe	11 12
		3-set (L.)	—	Berth	—
		1 R.C.O. 1 R.K.B. (2)	11.15 a.m.	Waterloo	3 0
		4-set	—	Berth	—
6 30 **R** (com. 28/6)	Waterloo	1 S.K.	— 7. 0 a.m.	Berth Waterloo M.P.	— (28/6 only) 12 50 (com. 5/7)
		1 S.K.	—	Berth	—
		2-set (R.) 1 S.K. 1 R.C.O. 1 R.K.B. (2)	11.15 a.m.	Waterloo	3 0
		4-set	—	Berth	—
6 52 (excn. 28/6, 12/7, 2/8, 16/8, 23/8, 6/9)	Waterloo	5-set	2†5 p.m.	Exmouth	2†28
		1 R.C.O. 1 R.K.B. (9) 3-set (L.) 1 S.K.	9.23 a.m.	Waterloo F.P.	1 17
7 10	Salisbury Yeovil Town	3-set (L.)	9. 5 a.m.	Ilfracombe F.P.	11 12
		3-set (L.) 1 S.K. (until 28/6)	—	Berth	—
7 15	Exmouth	1 S. 5-set (E.)	6.10 p.m.	Exmouth	6 40
8 9	Plymouth Nth. Rd.	5-set	4. 0 p.m.	Waterloo F.P.	8 1
8 20	Ilfracombe	2-set (R.)	—	Berth	—
	Torrington	3-set (L.) 2-set (R.)	4. 0 p.m.	Waterloo R.P.	8 1
8 25	Exmouth	1 S. 5-set (E.)	6.50 p.m.	Exmouth	7 23

105

EXETER CENTRAL (SUN.)—*continued*

p.m. 9 15 ...	Exmouth	1 S. ... ... 5-set (E.)...	8.15 p.m. ...	Exmouth	8 47
9 20 excn. (19/7 & 30/8)	Portsmouth Hbr....	9 S.R./W.R. cors. (incl. C.A.F.)	7.35 p.m. ...	Plymouth Nth. Rd. ...	9 14
9 32 ...	Salisbury	1 S.K. 5-set	9.20 a.m. ... 7.55 p.m. ...	Salisbury ... ... (not 5/7, 19/7 & 16/8) Paignton W.R.... ... (5/7, 19/7 & 16/8)	11 45 9 25
10 16 ...	Exmouth	2-set (100/110) ... ... 1 S. ... ... 5-set (E.)...	8.53 p.m. ... 7.50 p.m. ...	Exmouth R.P. ... ... Exmouth	9 17 8 17
11 0 ...	Exmouth	1 S. ... ... 5-set (E.)...	9. 0 p.m. ...	Exmouth	9 30
—	Berth	1 S.K. (28/6 & 5/7) 3 S.K. (12/7)	9. 5 a.m. ...	Ilfracombe F.P.... ...	11 12
—	Berth	2 P.M.V. (4) ... ... 1 B.C.K. (com. 16/8) 1 S.K. (5/7 to 19/7 & 16/8)	9.30 a.m. ...	Yeovil Town R.P. ...	11 26
—	Berth	1 van B.	1V15 p.m....	Exeter St. Davids ...	1V18
—	Berth	1 R.F. (26) ... ... 1 S.O. ... ... 3 S.K. (30/8 & 6/9)	1.33 p.m. ...	Salisbury F.P.	4 42
—	Berth	5-set (E.)... ... ... 1 S.	5.45 p.m. ...	Exmouth	6 17
—	Berth	3 S.K. 4-set (400)	7.10 p.m. ...	Exmouth	7 43
—	Berth	1 R.K.B. (4) ... ... 1 R.C.O.... ... ... 1 B.C.K.	4. 0 p.m. ...	Waterloo M.P.... ...	8 1
—	Berth	1 S.K. ... ... 1 S.K. (until 23/8)... 3-set (L.)... ... ... 1 S.K. ... ... 2-set (R.)...	6.15 p.m. ...	Ilfracombe...	8 22
—	Berth	3-set (L.)...	7. 0 p.m. ...	Yeovil Town	8 50
—	Berth	4-set	6.45 p.m. ...	Plymouth Nth. Rd. ...	9 1
—	Berth	2-set (P.)...	8.53 p.m. ...	Exmouth F.P.	9 17

106

EXETER CENTRAL (SUN.)—*continued*

p.m. —	Berth	3-set (L.)... ... ... 2-set (R.)... ... ... 1 R.K.B. (5) ... ... 1 R.C.O.... ... ... 3-set (L.)... ... ... 2 S.K. ... ... 1 B.C.K. (com. 19/7)	6. 0 p.m. ...	Waterloo	10 2
—	Berth	3-set (L.)... ... ... 3-set (L.) (until 28/6)	7.50 p.m. ...	Ilfracombe...	10 3
—	Berth	5-set (21/6) ... ... 3-set (L.) (com. 28/6)	10.15 p.m. ...	Exmouth	10 45
—	Berth	1 S.K. ... ... 1 B.C.K. ... ... Milk tanks ... ... 1 van B.	3V50 p.m....	Clapham Jn.	10V57
—	Berth	2-set (100/110)	10.30 p.m. ...	Sidmouth	11 11
—	Berth	2-set (P.)...	10.55 p.m. ...	Exmouth	11 25

EXETER ST. DAVIDS (SUN.)

a.m. 8V50 ...	Exeter Central ...	Vans... ... ... 1 van B. (stove)	— 8V25 a.m....	Ex. W.R. ... ... Exeter Central... ...	— 8V28
p.m. 1V15 ...	Exeter Central Ilfracombe ... Torrington ... Plymouth N. Rd. Exeter Central ...	Vans... ... ... 1 van B.	 12V45 p.m....	Ex. W.R. ... ... Exeter Central... ...	 12V48

EXMOUTH (SUN.)

Formation of Exmouth—Exeter 5-sets (E.):—

*1 S.
1 B.S.
1 C.
1 B.S.
*1 S.

(*not stencilled with set number)

a.m. 9 15 ...	Exeter Central ...	5-set (E.)...	—	Berth	—
10 35 ...	Tipton St. Johns ...	2-set (100/110)	—	Berth	—
11 0 ...	Exeter Central ...	5-set (E.)...	10. 0 a.m. ...	Exeter Central... ...	10 29
noon 12 0 ...	Exeter Central ...	5-set (E.)... ... ... 1 S.	11.20 a.m. ...	Exeter Central... ...	11 51

108

EXMOUTH (SUN.)—*continued*

p.m. —	Berth	2-set (100/110)	3. 7 p.m.	Exeter Central	3 39
—	Berth	1 S. 5-set (E.)	9.15 p.m.	Exeter Central	9 44
—	Berth	2-set (100/110) 1 S. 5-set (E.)	10.16 p.m.	Exeter Central	10 47
—	Berth	1 S. 5-set (E.)	11. 0 p.m.	Exeter Central	11 29

HALWILL (SUN.)

a.m. 10 29	Bude	2-set (P.)	9.50 a.m.	Launceston	10 14
p.m. 12 18	Launceston	2-set (P.)	11.18 a.m.	Bude	11 56
4 55	Launceston	2-set (P.)	2.35 p.m.	Launceston	2 58
7 30	Launceston	2-set (P.)	6.50 p.m.	Launceston	7 13

HONITON (SUN.)

a.m. 9 23	Exeter Central	2-set (R.)	8.35 a.m.	Exeter Central R.P.	9 6
p.m. 1 17	Exeter Central	3-set (L.) 1 S.K.	12.13 p.m.	Exeter Central	1 44
1 42 (com. 28/6)	Exmouth	3-set (L.)	8.35 a.m.	Exeter Central F.P.	9 6

ILFRACOMBE (SUN.)

a.m. 9 5	Exeter Central	1 S.K. (28/6 & 5/7) 3 S.K. (12/7) 3-set (L.) (21/6) 3-set (L.) 2-set (100/110) (13/9)	—	Berth	—
10 30 **R**	Waterloo	5-set 1 R.F.O. 1 R.K. (37) 1 R.S.O.	—	Berth	—
p.m. 2 0 **R**	Waterloo	1 S.K. 4-set 1 B.C.K.	10. 0 a.m. —	Exeter Central Berth	12 21 —

109

ILFRACOMBE (SUN.)—*continued*

p.m. 2 45 **R**	Waterloo	2-set (R.) 1 S.K. 5-set	10.45 a.m. —	Barnstaple Jn. Berth	11 26 —
6 15	Exeter Central	1 S.K. 1 S.K. (until 23/8) 3-set (L.)	— 9. 0 a.m.	Berth Waterloo	— 3 9
7 50	Exeter Central	3-set (L.) (until 28/6) 3-set (L.)	— 11.15 a.m.	Berth Waterloo R.P.	— 5 22
9 10	Barnstaple Jn.	1 S.K. 3-set (L.)	— 5.15 p.m.	Berth Exeter Central	— 7 25
—	Berth	5-set	10.45 a.m.	Waterloo	3 56
—	Berth	1 P.M.V. (4)	11.15 a.m.	Waterloo F.P.	5 22
—	Berth	2-set (R.) 3-set (L.)	4. 0 p.m.	Waterloo	10 30

LAUNCESTON (SUN.)

a.m. 9 50	Halwill	2-set (P.)	—	Berth	—
p.m. 2 35	Halwill	2-set (P.)	12.18 p.m.	Halwill	12 40
6 50	Halwill	2-set (P.)	4.55 p.m.	Halwill	5 17
—	Berth	2-set (P.)	7.30 p.m.	Halwill	7 52

LYME REGIS (SUN.)

a.m. 10 30	Axminster	2-set (100/110)	—	Berth	—
11 34	Axminster	2-set (100/110)	11. 7 a.m.	Axminster	11 28
p.m. 12 37	Axminster	2-set (100/110)	12.10 p.m.	Axminster	12 31
1 50	Axminster	2-set (100/110)	1. 6 p.m.	Axminster	1 27
2 55	Axminster	2-set (100/110)	2.22 p.m.	Axminster	2 43
3 57	Axminster	2-set (100/110)	3.31 p.m.	Axminster	3 52
4 56	Axminster	2-set (100/110)	4.27 p.m.	Axminster	4 48
6 45	Axminster	2-set (100/110)	5.42 p.m.	Axminster	6 3
7 44	Axminster	2-set (100/110)	7.16 p.m.	Axminster	7 37

LYME REGIS (SUN.)—*continued*

p.m. 8 50	Axminster	2-set (100/110)	8.16 p.m.	Axminster R.P.	8 37
9 57 (5/7, 19/7 & 16/8)	Axminster	2-set (100/110)	9.22 p.m.	Axminster	9 43
(com. 28/6)	Berth	1 B.C.K.	7.16 p.m.	Axminster F.P.	7 37
Except 5/7, 19/7 & 16/8	Berth	2-set (100/110)	9.22 p.m.	Axminster	9 43
(5/7, 19/7 & 16/8)	Berth	2-set (100/110)	10.27 p.m.	Axminster	10 48

OKEHAMPTON (SUN.)

a.m. 8 30	Plymouth Nth. Rd.	3-set (L.)	—	Berth	—
11 17	Waterloo	5-set 1 S.K. }	10.10 a.m.	Plymouth Nth. Rd.	11 12
		2-set (R.)	9.45 a.m.	Bude F.P.	10 57
11 19	Plymouth Nth. Rd.	1 S.K. 3-set (L.) 1 S.K. }	10.15 a.m.	Exeter Central F.P.	11 15
11 40	Bude	1 S.K.	9.45 a.m.	Bude R.P.	10 57
		2-set (P.)	—	Berth	—
		1 P.M.V. (4)	10.15 a.m.	Exeter Central R.P.	11 15
p.m. 3 49	Plymouth Nth. Rd.	2 S.K. 3-set (L.) }	11. 0 a.m.	Waterloo F.P.	3 43
4 15	Bude	2-set (P.)	2.28 p.m.	Bude F.P.	3 44
		1 B.C.K. 1 S.K. }	11. 0 a.m.	Waterloo R.P.	3 43
9 20	Bude	2-set (P.) 1 S.K. }	6.45 p.m.	Bude R.P.	7 56
—	Berth	1 B.C.K.	9.45 a.m.	Bude M.P.	10 57
(com. 23/8)	Berth	2-set (P.)	10.15 a.m.	Exeter Central M.P.	11 15
(until 16/8)	Berth	2-set (P.)	2.28 p.m.	Bude R.P.	3 44
—	Berth	3-set (L.)	9.25 p.m.	Plymouth Nth. Rd.	10 51

PLYMOUTH FRIARY SDGS. (SUN.)

Empties to and from Plymouth (North Road) unless otherwise shown

a.m. 8†17 for 8 30	Waterloo	1 S.K. (not 13/9) 3-set (L.) }	—	Berth	—

Appendix 6

Locomotive Diagrams

Supplied by Roger Merry Price

1951

BRITISH RAILWAYS
SOUTHERN OPERATING AREA

ENGINE WORKINGS
FOR
PASSENGER AND FREIGHT TRAINS
WESTERN DISTRICT

WEEKDAYS

12th February, 1951, and until further notice.

EXPLANATORY NOTES

A	... Engine prepared.	F	... Freight.	Q	... Conditional.
AR	... Assisting required.	M	... Milk Train.	SRE	... Shunt release engine.
ANR	... Assisting not required.	O/R	... On rear.	V	... Vans.
C	... Coaching.	P	... Passenger Train.	‖	... Light engine.
E	... Empty.	P/O	... Pull out.	**	... Time uncertain.

SUMMARY OF DEPOTS AND ENGINE DUTIES (COMMENCING NUMBERS)

Salisbury	430	Torrington	584
Yeovil	480	Ilfracombe	589
Templecombe	490	Okehampton	593
Lyme Regis	492	Launceston	598
Seaton	493	Bude	600
Exmouth Junction	494	Wadebridge	602
Exmouth	568	Callington	610
Barnstaple	572	Friary	614

Office of Supt. of Operation,
Waterloo.

Western Region Engines working over Southern Region—WEEKDAYS. 1

W.R. ENGINE.

—	Pen Mill ...	... 11.57 a.m.	F
12. 2 p.m.	Yeovil Town	... 1. 8 p.m.	F
1.13 p.m.	Pen Mill ...	... 8.45 p.m.	F
8.50 p.m.	Yeovil Town	... 9. 0 p.m.	F
9. 5 p.m.	Yeovil Jct. ...	... 9.32 p.m.	F
9.37 p.m.	Yeovil Town	... 9.47 p.m.	F
9.52 p.m.	Pen Mill ...	... —	

W.R. Men.

W.R. ENGINE.

—	Exeter (St. David's)	10.48 a.m.	‖
10.51 a.m.	Exeter Ctl. ...	... 11.46 a.m.	P
2.32 p.m.	Friary ...	... 2.38 p.m.	‖
2.45 p.m.	Loco. Yard ...	... 4.25 p.m.	‖
4.33 p.m.	Friary ...	... 4.40 p.m.	P
7.24 p.m.	Exeter Ctl. ...	... 7.45 p.m.	‖
7.48 p.m.	Exeter (St. David's)	—	

W.R. Men.

W.R. ENGINE.

—	Laira Loco. ...	... 1.55 p.m.	‖
2. 5 p.m.	Friary ...	... 2.35 p.m.	P
5. 8 p.m.	Exeter Ctl. ...	... 5.12 p.m.	‖
5.16 p.m.	Exmouth Jc....	... 6.20 p.m.	‖
6.24 p.m.	Exeter Ctl. ... (3.0 p.m. ex Waterloo.)	... 6.47 p.m.	P
8.51 p.m.	Friary ...	... 9.20 p.m.	‖
9.30 p.m.	Laira Loco. ...	... —	

W.R. Men.

W.R. ENGINE.
LAIRA DUTY No. 610.
(45 X.X. Class.)

As diagrammed then work.

	Liara Loco. ...	... 2.20 p.m.	‖
2.26 p.m.	Friary ...	... 2.48 p.m.	F
2.54 p.m.	Laira	... 3.15 p.m.	F
3.21 p.m.	Friary ...	... —	
	C. shunting 4.0 p.m. to 5.45 p.m.		
	Friary ...	... 6.16 p.m.	P
7.17 p.m.	Tavistock ...	... 8.25 p.m.	P
9.17 p.m.	Friary ...	... 9.30 p.m.	‖
9.36 p.m.	Laira Loco. ...	... —	

W.R. Laira Men.
Work first part.

Plymouth Friary Men.
1st Set. On duty 1.20 p.m., walk to Laira Loco. work 2.20 p.m.‖ etc., and relief at 9.17 p.m.
2nd Set. On duty 8.47 p.m., relieve 9.17 p.m., work engine to Laira Loco., then pass to Friary Loco., perform requirements on No. 616 duty, then dispose No. 617 duty **(S.X.)**.

W.R. ENGINE.

—	Bodmin (W.R.)	... 8.13 a.m.	P
8.50 a.m.	Padstow ...	... 9. 8 a.m.	P
9.40 a.m.	Bodmin (W.R.)	... 10.38 a.m. **(Mixed)**	
11.10 a.m.	Padstow ...	... 11.48 a.m.	P
12.20 p.m.	Bodmin (W.R.)	... 12.55 p.m.	P
1.12 p.m.	Wadebridge...	... 1.25 p.m.	P
1.45 p.m.	Bodmin (W.R.)	... 2.53 p.m.	P
3.10 p.m.	Wadebridge...	... 3.28 p.m. **(Mixed)**	
3.51 p.m.	Bodmin (W.R.)	... 4.50 p.m.	P
5. 7 p.m.	Wadebridge...	... 5.56 p.m.	P
6.16 p.m.	Bodmin (W.R.)	... 6.30 p.m.	P
6.47 p.m.	Wadebridge...	... 7. 5 p.m.	P
7.25 p.m.	Bodmin (W.R.)	... 7.43 p.m.	P
8. 0 p.m.	Wadebridge...	... 8.42 p.m.	P
9. 2 p.m.	Bodmin (W.R.)	... —	

W.R. Men.

W.R. ENGINE.
SATURDAYS EXCEPTED.

—	Bodmin (W.R.)	... 4. 8 p.m.	P
4.27 p.m.	Wadebridge...	... 4.43 p.m.	E
5. 8 p.m.	Bodmin (W.R.)	... —	

W.R. Men.

SOMERSET AND DORSET SECTION ENGINES WORKING OVER WESTERN DISTRICT.

TEMPLECOMBE DUTY No. 21.
2 F.T. (G.6 Class).

MONDAYS ONLY.

—	Templecombe Lr. Loco. ...	... 1.55 a.m.	‖
2. 0 a.m.	Templecombe Upper	—	

Continuous **C.** and **F.** shunting engine until 6.0 a.m. following Sunday.
(Less $1\frac{1}{2}$ hours daily engine requirements, meals, etc.)

—	Templecombe **(M.X.)** ...	... 9.30 a.m.	F
9.40 a.m.	Milborne Port **(M.X.)** ...	... 10.13 a.m.	F
10.20 a.m.	Templecombe ...	—	

(M.O.—C. 2 hours. **F.** 17 hours.)
(M.X.—C. 2 hours. **F.** $17\frac{3}{4}$ hours.)
(Sun. —F. $5\frac{1}{2}$ hours. **E.R.** 30 mins.)

—	Templecombe Upper	6. 0 a.m. **(Sun.)**	‖
6. 5 a.m.	Templecombe Lr. Loco. ...	... —	

EXMOUTH JCT. DUTY No. 537.

6 M.T. (West Country Class).

Arr.	Station	Dep.	
—	Loco. Yard ...	... 1.25 a.m.	||
1.28 a.m.	Exmouth Jct.	... 1.38 a.m.	F
4.55 a.m.	Tavistock ...	... 6. 0 a.m.	P
6.53 a.m.	Friary ...	... 7.15 a.m.	||

(Via Mount Gould Jct. and Cattewater Jct. to Turn.)

Arr.	Station	Dep.	
7.30 a.m.	Friary	—	
	C. shunting 7.30 a.m. to 8.45 a.m.		
—	Friary ...	... 8.45 a.m.	||

SATURDAYS EXCEPTED.

Arr.	Station	Dep.	
8.52 a.m.	Loco. Yard ...	... 11.20 a.m.	||
11.27 a.m.	Friary ...	... 11.35 a.m.	ANR
12.21 p.m.	Bere Alston ...	... 1.15 p.m.	F
2.40 p.m.	Okehampton	... 2.42 p.m.	||
2.45 p.m.	Loco. Yard ...	... 3.15 p.m.	||
3.18 p.m.	Okehampton	... 3.55 p.m.	P
6.22 p.m.	Padstow ...	... 6.35 p.m.	||
6.46 p.m.	Wadebridge Loco. ...	—	

Stable for No. 603 duty.

Friary to ensure that the engine is well coaled.

SATURDAYS ONLY.

Arr.	Station	Dep.	
8.50 a.m.	Loco. Yard ...	... 1. 5 p.m.	||
1.10 p.m.	Friary ...	... 1.21 p.m.	F
5.37 p.m.	Okehampton	... 6.50 p.m.	F
8.33 p.m.	Exmouth Jct.	... 8.43 p.m.	||
8.46 p.m.	Exmouth Jct. Loco....	9.50 p.m.	||
9.54 p.m.	Exeter ...	... 10.12 p.m.	P
	(6.0 p.m. ex Waterloo.)		
12.12 a.m.	Friary ...	... 12.20 a.m.	||
12.25 a.m.	Loco. Yard ...	... —	

Stable for No. 615 duty **(Sunday).**

Exmouth Jct. Men.

1st Set. On duty 12.25 a.m., work to Okehampton, change to No. 597 duty at 4.20 a.m., shunt until 7.25 a.m., then relieve on No. 614 duty (5.56 a.m. ex Friary) at 7.35 a.m., and work to Exeter.

2nd Set (S.X.). On duty 2.29 p.m., passenger to Okehampton, work 3.55 p.m. to Wadebridge, then change to No. 602 duty, work 6.14 p.m. to Okehampton and home passenger.

Friary Men.

1st Set. Of No. 542 duty, change at Okehampton 4.20 a.m., work to Friary and relief at 9.20 a.m.

2nd Set. Men of No. 624 duty relieve at 9.20 a.m. and **(S.X.)** prepare for 11.20 a.m. **(S.O.)** dispose.

[*continued*

EXMOUTH JCT. DUTY No. 537—*continued*

3rd Set (S.X.). On duty 11.5 a.m., work to Okehampton, relief at 2.40 p.m., then relieve on No. 597 duty, shunt till 4.56 p.m., change with No. 614 duty (4.12 p.m. ex Exeter) and complete.

(S.O.). On duty 12.5 p.m., work to Okehampton, relief 5.37 p.m., then relieve on No. 535 duty (4.50 p.m. ex Exeter) at 5.40 p.m. and work to Friary.

4th Set (S.O.). Of No. 540 duty, relieve 11.1 p.m. and complete and dispose.

Okehampton Men.

1st Set (S.X.). Off No. 548 duty, relieve at Okehampton 2.40 p.m., perform engine requirements and train for 3.55 p.m

(S.O.). Of No. 597 duty, relieve at Okehampton 5.37 p.m. and relief at Okehampton 11.1 p.m.

Wadebridge Men (S.X.).

Off No. 602 duty, change over at Wadebridge and work to Padstow and back and dispose.

EXMOUTH JCT. DUTY No. 538.

6 M.T. (West Country Class).

Arr.	Station	Dep.	
—	Loco. Yard ...	... 5.15 a.m.	||
5.18 a.m.	Exmouth Jct.	... 5.35 a.m.	F
9.57 a.m.	Friary ...	... 10. 2 a.m.	||
10. 7 a.m.	Friary Loco.	... 1.40 p.m.	||
1.53 p.m.	Millbay ...	... 2. 4 p.m.	E
2. 8 p.m.	Plymouth North Rd.	2.15 p.m.	P
3.33 p.m.	Newton Abbot ...	4. 0 p.m.	P
4.50 p.m.	Exeter St. David's		
	W.R. Loco. Yard		
—	Exeter St. David's ...	5.30 p.m.	P
6. 7 p.m.	Newton Abbot ...	7.30 p.m.	P
8.43 p.m.	Plymouth North Rd.	8.46 p.m.	E
8.50 p.m.	Millbay ...	... 9.15 p.m.	||
9.30 p.m.	Friary Loco. ...	... —	

Stable for No. 615 duty.

Engine must take water at Newton Abbot in both directions.

Exmouth Jct. Men.

On duty 4.15 a.m., work and relieved at Okehampton at 7.40 a.m., then to Loco., prepare No. 593 **(S.X.)** duty, work and relieved at 8.58 a.m., passenger per 9.35 a.m. to Exeter, relieve No. 539 duty at 10.23 a.m., work and dispose.

Friary Men.

1st Set. Of No. 614 duty (5.58 a.m. ex Friary), relieve at Okehampton 7.40 a.m., work to Friary and prepare for 1.40 p.m.||

2nd Set. On duty 1.25 p.m., complete and relief in Loco.

No. 3 P. & D. men dispose engine.

EXMOUTH JCT. DUTY No. 545.

4 M.T. (N. Class).

Arr.	Station	Dep.	
—	Loco. Yard ...	... 7.15 a.m.	||
7.18 a.m.	Exmouth Jct.	... 7.32 a.m.	Q (Stone)
9.41 a.m.	Meldon Quarry ...	9.55 a.m.	||
10. 0 a.m.	Okehampton (Turn)	10.45 a.m.	||
10.52 a.m.	Meldon Quarry ...	11.28 a.m.	(Stone)
12.51 p.m.	Exeter ...	... 12.55 p.m.	||
12.58 p.m.	Exmouth Jct. Loco....	—	

SATURDAYS EXCEPTED.

Arr.	Station	Dep.	
—	Exmouth Jct. Loco....	7.45 p.m.	||
7.49 p.m.	Exeter ...	... 7.58 p.m.	ANR
9. 1 p.m.	Okehampton (Turn)	—	
—	Okehampton ...	11.55 p.m.	(Stone)
1.10 a.m.	Exeter ...	... 1.15 a.m.	||
1.18 a.m.	Exmouth Jct. Loco....	—	

SATURDAYS ONLY.

Arr.	Station	Dep.	
—	Exmouth Jct. Loco....	9. 5 p.m.	||
9. 9 p.m.	Exeter ...	... 9.20 p.m.	F
	(6.8 p.m. ex Templecombe.)		
12. 0 mdt.	Okehampton (Turn)	12.56 a.m.	||
2. 0 a.m.	Exmouth Jct. Loco....	—	

Exmouth Jct. Men.

1st Set. On duty 6.15 a.m., work and dispose.

2nd Set. On duty **(S.X.)** 6.45 p.m., **(S.O.)** 8.5 p.m., work and dispose.

EXMOUTH JCT. DUTY No. 546.

2 P.T. (M.7 Class).

Exmouth Jct. to arrange for Bude change-over engine to work:—

SATURDAYS ONLY.

Arr.	Station	Dep.	
—	Exmouth Jct.	... 11. 0 a.m.	||
12.20 p.m.	Okehampton	... 1.18 p.m.	ANR
1.44 p.m.	Halwill ...	... 1.53 p.m.	P
2.15 p.m.	Launceston ...	... 2.48 p.m.	||
3.12 p.m.	Halwill ...	... 3.25 p.m.	||
3.53 p.m.	Okehampton	... 4.14 p.m.	ANR
5. 8 p.m.	Exeter ...	... 5.10 p.m.	||
5.13 p.m.	Exmouth Jct.	... —	

Exmouth Jct. Men.

(S.O.). On duty 10.15 a.m., complete and dispose.

EXMOUTH JCT. DUTY No. 547.

2 P. (T.9 Class).

Arr.	Station	Dep.	
—	Exmouth Jct.	... 11.25 a.m.	||
11.29 a.m.	Exeter Ctl. ...	... 11.46 a.m.	P ANR
12.53 p.m.	Okehampton	... 1.18 p.m.	P
2.23 p.m.	Bude	... 2.30 p.m.	||
2.35 p.m.	Loco. Yard ...	... 2.55 p.m.	||
3. 0 p.m.	Bude	... 3.13 p.m.	P
4.37 p.m.	Okehampton	... 4.40 p.m.	||
4.43 p.m.	Loco. Yard ...	... 5.15 p.m.	||
5.18 p.m.	Okehampton	... 5.51 p.m.	P
7.56 p.m.	Padstow ...	... 8.40 p.m.	Mixed
8.54 p.m.	Wadebridge...	... 9. 5 p.m.	||
9.10 p.m.	Loco. Yard ...	... —	

Stable for No. 602 duty.

Exmouth Jct. Men.

No. 2 P. & D. men prepare for 11.25 a.m. **(S.X.)**||

1st Set. (S.O.) On duty 10.40 a.m., work and relieve at Okehampton at 4.37 p.m. and home passenger per 5.6 p.m.

(S.O.). On duty 11.10 a.m., work and relieved at Okehampton at 4.37 p.m., and home passenger.

2nd Set. Of No. 535 duty, work 5.51 p.m. to Launceston, change to No. 608 duty **(S.X.)**, 594 duty **(S.O.)** (4.30 p.m. **F.** ex Wadebridge) at 6.46 p.m., and work to Exmouth Jct.

Wadebridge Men.

Of No. 608 or 594 duty, change over at Launceston 6.46 p.m. and complete, then **(S.X.)** dispose No. 606 duty engine.

Launceston Men.

(S.O.). Off No. 549 duty, relieve at Okehampton 4.37 p.m. and work until 5.51 p.m.

EXMOUTH JCT. DUTY No. 548.

4 M.T. (N. Class).

**	Loco. Yard ...	... 12.28 a.m. (M.O.)	‖
12.31 a.m.	Exmouth Jct.	... 12.38 a.m. (M.O.)	F
—	Loco. Yard ...	... 11.41 p.m. (S.X.)	‖
11.43 p.m.	Exmouth Jct.	... 12. 1 a.m. (M.X.)	F
3.20 a.m. (M.O.)	Okehampton	... 4.37 a.m.	F
3.10 a.m. (M.X.)	Okehampton	... 4.37 a.m.	F
6.14 a.m.	Bude	... 6.40 a.m.	‖
6.45 a.m.	Loco. Yard ...	... 8. 0 a.m.	‖
8. 5 a.m.	Bude	... 8.15 a.m.	F

SATURDAYS EXCEPTED.

2.14 p.m.	Okehampton	... 3. 4 p.m.	F
	(1.5 p.m. ex Bere Alston.)		
6.30 p.m.	Exmouth Jct.	... 6.40 p.m.	‖
6.43 p.m.	Loco. Yard ...	... —	

SATURDAYS ONLY.

2.14 p.m.	Okehampton	... 2.30 p.m.	‖
2.33 p.m.	Loco. Yard ...	... —	

Stable for No. 543 duty **Monday.**

Exmouth Jct. Men.

(M.O.). Men off No. 505 duty prepare.
(M.X.). No. 6 P. & D. men prepare.
1st Set. On duty 12.13 a.m. **(M.O.)** 11.26 p.m. **(S.X.)**, relief at Okehampton 4.15 a.m., then relieve on No. 542 duty (2.0 a.m. **F.** ex Friary) 4.20 a.m. and work to Exmouth Jct.
2nd Set (S.X.). On duty 1.8 p.m., passenger to Okehampton, relieve at 2.25 p.m. complete and dispose.

Okehampton Men.

1st Set (M.O.). On duty 3.15 a.m., prepare No. 597 and then as shown for **M.X.**
(M.X.). On duty 4.0 a.m., relieve **4**.15 a.m., work 4.37 a.m. to Holsworthy, change to No. 600 duty at 9.51 a.m. and work to Halwill, relief 10.25 a.m. and home passenger.

2nd Set. Of No. 543/544 duty (3.30 a.m. ex Exmouth Jct.), change at Holsworthy at 10.55 a.m. and work to Okehampton, relief 2.35 p.m. **(S.X.)**, relieve No. 537 duty at 2.40 p.m. and perform requirements.
S.O.—Dispose engine.

Bude Men.

Of No. 600 duty, change over at Holsworthy at 9.51 a.m. and perform shunting until changing back to No. 600 duty at 10.55 a.m., relief 12.35 p.m.

EXMOUTH JCT. DUTY No. 549.

4 M.T. (N. Class).

—	Exmouth Jct.	... 4.42 a.m.	‖
4.46 a.m.	Exeter ...	... 5. 9 a.m.	ANR
5.55 a.m.	Okehampton	... 6.20 a.m.	P
7.46 a.m.	Launceston ...	... 8. 5 a.m.	P
9.38 a.m.	Padstow ...	... —	
	F. shunting 10.0 a.m. to 11.0 a.m.		
—	Padstow ...	... 11.30 a.m.	F
11.44 a.m.	Wadebridge	... 11.50 a.m.	‖
11.55 a.m.	Loco. Yard ...	... 1. 6 p.m.	‖
1.11 p.m.	Wadebridge...	... 1.16 p.m.	P
	(1.0 p.m. ex Padstow.)		
3.19 p.m.	Okehampton	... 3.25 p.m.	‖
3.23 p.m.	Loco. Yard ...	... 4. 2 p.m.	‖
4. 5 p.m.	Okehampton (S.X.)	4.38 p.m.	E
4.50 p.m.	Meldon Quarry (S.X.)	5.10 p.m. (Stone)	
5.20 p.m.	Okehampton	... 5.30 p.m.	‖
5.33 p.m.	Loco. Yard ...	... 6.15 p.m.	‖
6.18 p.m.	Okehampton	... —	
	Meldon Stone Trips as required.		
—	Okehampton	... 7.47 p.m.	P
8.42 p.m.	Launceston ...	... 9.10 p.m.	‖
9.25 p.m.	W.R. Loco. Yard	... —	

Stable for No. 598 duty.

Exmouth Jct. Men.

(M.O.). Off No. 505 duty prepare.
(M.X.). No. 10 P. & D. men prepare.
1st Set. On duty 4.27 a.m., work to Launceston, relief 7.55 a.m., relieve on No. 594 duty, perform shunting, change to No. 603 duty (8.30 a.m. ex Padstow) at 9.50 a.m. and work to Exeter.

Launceston Men.

1st Set. Off No. 598 duty, relieve at 7.55 a.m. and relief at 2.20 p.m.
2nd Set. On duty 2.5 p.m., complete and dispose. **(S.O.)** relieve on No. 547 duty at Okehampton from 4.37 until 5.51 p.m.

OKEHAMPTON DUTY No. 593.

6 M.T. (W.C. Class).

M.O.—With engine of No. 595 duty **Saturday.**
M.X.—With engine of No. 540 duty previous day.

SATURDAYS EXCEPTED.

—	Loco. Yard ...	... 8.30 a.m.	‖
8.33 a.m.	Okehampton	... 8.58 a.m.	F
1.12 p.m.	Friary ...	... 1.20 p.m.	‖
1.25 p.m.	Loco. Yard ...	... 9.45 p.m.	‖
9.50 p.m.	Friary ...	... 10. 0 p.m.	F
2.45 a.m.	Exmouth Jct.	... 2.55 a.m.	‖
2.58 a.m.	Loco. Yard ...	... —	

SATURDAYS ONLY.

—	Loco. Yard ...	... 3.15 p.m.	‖
3.18 p.m.	Okehampton	... 3.55 p.m.	P
6.22 p.m.	Padstow ...	... 6.35 p.m.	‖
6.49 p.m.	Wadebridge Loco. ...	—	

Stable for No. 603 duty **Monday.**

Exmouth Jct. Men (S.X.).

Of No. 538 duty, prepare and train engine for 8.58 a.m. **F.**, then passenger to Exeter Ctl., relieve on No. 539 duty at 10.23 a.m.

Friary Men (S.X.).

Of No. 617 duty (7.8 a.m. ex Friary), relieve and work 8.58 a.m. **F.** to Friary.
No. 2 P. & D. men relieve in Loco. and dispose.

Friary Men (S.X.).

On duty 8.45 p.m., work 10.0 p.m. **F.** to Okehampton, change to No. 536 duty (9.20 a.m. **F.** ex Exeter) at 12.25 a.m. and work to Friary.

Exmouth Jct. Men.

(S.X.). Of No. 536 duty, change at Okehampton 12.25 a.m. and work to Yeoford, change to No. 543 duty or 544 duty at 1.20 a.m., shunt until 3.10 a.m. and home passenger per 3.20 a.m.
Off No. 543 or 544 duty, change at Yeoford 1.20 a.m. and work to Exmouth Jct.
No. 539 duty men dispose.

Okehampton Men.

(S.O.). Of No. 605 duty, prepare and train for 3.55 p.m.

Exmouth Jct. Men.

(S.O.). On duty 2.29 p.m., passenger to Okehampton, work 3.55 p.m. to Wadebridge, then change to No. 602 duty and work 6.14 p.m. to Okehampton and home passenger.

Wadebridge Men.

(S.O.). Of No. 602 duty, change over at Wadebridge 6.10 p.m. and work to Padstow and back and dispose.

OKEHAMPTON DUTY No. 594.

4 M.T. (N. Class).

Stabled off No. 533 duty **previous day.**

MONDAYS ONLY.

—	Loco. Yard ...	... 2.30 a.m.	‖
2.33 a.m.	Okehampton	... —	

Shunting 2.30 a.m. until 4.0 a.m. and as shown for **Mondays Excepted.**

MONDAYS EXCEPTED.

—	Loco. Yard ...	... 3.40 a.m.	‖
3.43 a.m.	Okehampton	... 4. 0 a.m. (Mixed)	
	(12.1 a.m. ex Exmouth Jct.)		
6. 0 a.m.	Launceston ...	... —	
	C. & **F.** shunting 6.0 a.m. to 10.0 a.m.		
	(**C.** 1 hour. **F.** 2½ hours. E.R. 30 mins.)		
—	Launceston ...	... 10. 0 a.m.	F

SATURDAYS EXCEPTED.

12.35 p.m.	Wadebridge...	... 12.40 p.m.	‖
12.45 p.m.	Loco. Yard ...	... —	

Stable for No. 605 duty.

SATURDAYS ONLY.

1.39 p.m.	Wadebridge	... 1.44 p.m.	‖
1.49 p.m.	Loco. Yard ...	... 2.20 p.m.	‖
2.25 p.m.	Wadebridge...	... 2.28 p.m.	ANR
2.37 p.m.	Padstow ...	... 2.55 p.m.	P
3. 4 p.m.	Wadebridge...	... 3. 9 p.m.	‖
3.14 p.m.	Loco. Yard ...	... 4.20 p.m.	‖
4.25 p.m.	Wadebridge...	... 4.30 p.m.	F
12.35 a.m.	Exmouth Jct.	... 12.45 a.m.	‖
12.48 a.m.	Loco. Yard ...	... —	

Okehampton Men.

(M.O.). On duty 1.30 a.m., work 4.0 a.m. to Launceston, then change to No. 598 duty and work 8.20 a.m. to Okehampton, requirements and train for 10.8 a.m. **F.**
(M.X.). On duty 2.10 a.m., prepare No. 597 duty and own engine, work 4.0 a.m. to Launceston, relief 7.55 a.m., then relieve on No. 598 duty and work 8.20 a.m. to Okehampton and train for 10.8 a.m. **F.**

Exmouth Jct. Men.

Of No. 549 duty, relieve at 7.55 a.m. and change to No. 603 duty (8.30 a.m. ex Padstow) at 9.50 a.m. and work to Exmouth Jct.

Wadebridge Men.

Of No. 603 duty, change at Launceston 9.50 a.m. and work to Wadebridge. **(S.X.)** dispose engine. **(S.O.)** relief at 2.28 p.m.
(S.O.). On duty 2.13 p.m., relieve 2.28 p.m., work to Launceston, change to No. 547 duty (5.51 p.m. ex Okehampton), work to Wadebridge and dispose.

Exmouth Jct. Men.

(S.O.). Of No. 535/547 duty, change at Launceston 6.46 p.m. and work to Exmouth Jct.
No. 9 P. & D. men dispose.

OKEHAMPTON DUTY No. 595.

2 P. (T.9 Class).
Stabled off No. 602 duty.

MONDAYS & SATURDAYS EXCEPTED.

—	Loco. Yard ...	...	6.40 a.m.	‖
6.43 a.m.	Okehampton	...	6.58 a.m.	P
7. 4 a.m.	Quarry Halt...	...	7. 6 a.m.	E
7. 9 a.m.	Meldon Jct. ...	...	7.16 a.m.	E
7.21 a.m.	Okehampton	...	7.22 a.m.	‖
7.25 a.m.	Loco. Yard ...	...	—	

EVERY WEEKDAY.

—	Loco. Yard ...	...	9.45 a.m.	‖
9.48 a.m.	Okehampton	...	9.56 a.m.	P
11.56 a.m.	Wadebridge...	...	12. 1 p.m.	P
12.10 p.m.	Padstow ...	...	1. 0 p.m.	P

SATURDAYS EXCEPTED.

1. 9 p.m.	Wadebridge...	...	1.10 p.m.	‖
1.15 p.m.	Loco. Yard ...	...	2.20 p.m.	‖
2.25 p.m.	Wadebridge...	...	2.28 p.m.	P
2.37 p.m.	Padstow ...	...	2.55 p.m.	P
6.38 p.m.	Exeter ...	...	6.52 p.m.	‖
6.55 p.m.	Exmouth Jct.	...	—	

SATURDAYS ONLY.

1. 9 p.m.	Wadebridge...	...	1.10 p.m.	‖
1.15 p.m.	Loco. Yard ...	...	2.20 p.m.	‖
2.25 p.m.	Wadebridge...	...	2.28 p.m.	P
2.37 p.m.	Padstow ...	...	3.15 p.m.	P
5.47 p.m.	Okehampton	...	5.50 p.m.	‖
5.53 p.m.	Loco. Yard ...	...	—	

Stable for No. 593 duty **Monday.**

Okehampton Men.
1st Set (M.O.). Off No. 543 duty, prepare and work 9.45 a.m.‖, work and relieved at 9.56 a.m.

(M.X.). On duty 5.55 a.m., work and relieved at 9.56 a.m., then as ordered.

2nd Set (S.X.). On duty 9.41 a.m., work to Padstow and back, relief 5.54 p.m.

2nd Set (S.O.). On duty 9.41 a.m., work to Port Isaac Rd., change to No. 605 duty (10.50 a.m. ex Wadebridge) at 11.44 a.m., work to Halwill, relief and home passenger.

3rd Set (S.O.). Off No. 598 duty, change at Camelford and work to Okehampton and berth engine.

(S.O.). No. 605 duty men dispose engine.

OKEHAMPTON DUTY No. 595—*continued.*
Wadebridge Men.
1st Set (S.O.). Of No. 605 duty, change over at Port Isaac Rd., work to Wadebridge, relief 2.15 p.m.
2nd Set. On duty 2.0 p.m., work to Camelford, change to No. 598 duty (10.8 a.m. **F.** ex Okehampton) at 4.6 p.m., work to Wadebridge, complete disposal and as ordered.
Exmouth Jct. Men.
1st Set (S.X.). Off No. 547 duty, relieve at Okehampton 5.54 p.m. and complete relief in Loco.
(S.X.). No. 5 P. & D. men dispose.

No. 596 SPARE.

OKEHAMPTON DUTY No. 597.

1 M.T. (L.11 Class).

—	Loco. Yard ...	...	5. 0 a.m.	‖
5. 2 a.m.	Okehampton	...	—	

F. shunting—9 hours 40 mins.
C. shunting—3 hours.
Meals and engine requirements—
10.25 a.m. to 10.45 a.m.
12.45 p.m. to 1.50 p.m.

—	Okehampton	...	7. 0 p.m.	‖
7. 3 p.m.	Loco. Yard ...	...	—	

Engine prepared by men of No. 548 duty **(M.O.)**, No. 594 duty **(M.X.)**.
Exmouth Jct. Men.
Off No. 537 duty, work 5.0 a.m.‖, shunt to 7.25 a.m., then relieve on No. 614 duty at 7.35 a.m. and work to Exeter.
Okehampton Men.
On duty 7.0 a.m., relieve 7.25 a.m., and relief 2.45 p.m.
Friary Men.
(S.X.). Off No. 537 duty, relieve at 2.45 p.m., shunt till 4.56 p.m., then change with No. 614 duty (4.12 p.m. ex Exeter) and work to Friary.
Exmouth Jct. Men.
(S.X.). Off No. 614 duty (4.12 p.m. ex Exeter), change over at Okehampton at 4.56 p.m. and complete and dispose, then change to No. 605 duty and work 9.25 p.m. Stone **Q.**
Okehampton Men.
(S.O.). On duty 2.30 p.m., relieve 2.45 p.m., and relief 5.0 p.m., then relieve on No. 537 duty at 5.37 p.m. (1.21 p.m. ex Friary), work to Exeter and back, relief 11.1 p.m.
Exmouth Jct. Men.
(S.O.). On duty 3.52 p.m., passenger to Okehampton, relieve 5.0 p.m. and complete and dispose, then get No. 605 duty engine and work to Exmouth Jct.

LAUNCESTON DUTY No. 598.

4 M.T. (N. Class).
Stabled off No. 549 duty.

—	W.R. Loco. Yard	...	7.30 a.m.	‖
7.45 a.m.	Launceston ...	...	8.20 a.m.	P
9.17 a.m.	Okehampton	...	9.18 a.m.	‖
9.21 a.m.	Loco. Yard ...	...	10. 0 a.m.	‖
10. 3 a.m.	Okehampton	...	10. 8 a.m.	F
7.13 p.m.	Wadebridge...	...	7.15 p.m.	‖
7.20 p.m.	Loco. Yard ...	...	—	

S.X.—Stable for No. 608 duty.
S.O.—Stable for No. 605 duty **(M.O.)**.

Launceston Men.
On duty 6.30 a.m., prepare and train engine, then relieve No. 549 duty at 7.55 a.m. and work as shown, relief at 2.20 p.m.

Okehampton Men.
Of No. 594 duty, work 8.20 a.m. **P.** to Okehampton.

Okehampton Men.
(S.X.). On duty 9.55 a.m., work 10.8 a.m. **F** to Tresmeer, change to No. 605 duty (11.35 a.m. ex Wadebridge) at 2.39 p.m., work to Halwill and home passenger.

Wadebridge Men.
(S.X.). Of No. 605 duty, change over at Tresmeer 2.39 p.m. and work to Wadebridge, relief 7.13 p.m.

No. 604 duty Men.
(S.X.). Relieve 7.13 p.m. and complete.

Okehampton Men.
(S.O.). On duty 9.55 a.m., work 10.8 a.m. **F** to Camelford, change to No. 595 duty at 4.6 p.m. (3.15 p.m. ex Padstow) and work to Okehampton and berth engine.

Wadebridge Men.
(S.O.). Of No. 595 duty, change at Camelford and complete duty, then work as ordered.

No. 599 SPARE.

Western District—WEEKDAYS. 61

WADEBRIDGE DUTY No. 602.
2 P. (T.9 Class).
Stabled off No. 547 duty.

Arr.	Station	Dep.	
—	Loco. Yard ...	... 1.35 p.m.	‖
1.40 p.m.	Wadebridge...	... 1.45 p.m.	P
1.59 p.m.	Padstow ...	... —	
	F. shunting 2.30 p.m. to 3.30 p.m.		
—	Padstow ...	... 3.40 p.m.	FQ
3.54 p.m.	Wadebridge...	... 4.15 p.m.	FQ
4.29 p.m.	Padstow ...	... 6. 0 p.m.	P
8.29 p.m.	Okehampton	... 8.30 p.m.	‖
8.33 p.m.	Loco. Yard ...	... —	

Stable for No. 595 duty.

Wadebridge Men.
On duty 12.35 p.m., change to No. 537 **(S.X.)**, No. 593 **(S.O.)** duty (3.55 p.m. ex Okehampton) at 6.10 p.m. and complete.

Exmouth Jct. Men.
Off No. 537 **(S.X.)**, 593 **(S.O.)** duty, change at Wadebridge at 6.10 p.m., work to Okehampton and home passenger.

Okehampton Men.
Off No. 605 duty, dispose.

WADEBRIDGE DUTY No. 603.
6 M.T. (W.C. Class).
M.O.—Stable off No. 593 duty.
M.X.—Stabled off No. 537 duty.

Arr.	Station	Dep.	
—	Loco. Yard ...	... 7.15 a.m.	‖
7.19 a.m.	Wadebridge...	... 7.20 a.m.	F
7.34 a.m.	Padstow ...	... 8.30 a.m.	P
10.59 a.m.	Okehampton	... 11. 2 a.m.	P
11.58 a.m.	Exeter ...	... 12. 2 p.m.	‖
12. 5 p.m.	Exmouth Jct.	... 2.15 p.m.	‖
2.19 p.m.	Exeter ...	... 2.36 p.m.	P
	(11.0 a.m. ex Waterloo.)		
4.32 p.m.	Ilfracombe ...	... 5. 0 p.m.	‖
5. 5 p.m.	Loco. Yard ...	... 5.30 p.m.	‖
5.35 p.m.	Ilfracombe ...	... 5.45 p.m.	P
6.28 p.m.	Barnstaple Jct.	... 6.51 p.m.	F
	(4.52 p.m. ex Torrington.)		
9.30 p.m.	Exmouth Jct.	... 9.40 p.m.	‖
9.43 p.m.	Loco. Yard ...	... —	

Wadebridge Men.
On duty 6.15 a.m., work to Launceston, change to No. 594 duty at 9.50 a.m. and work 10.0 a.m. **F.** to Wadebridge.

Exmouth Jct. Men.
Of No. 549/594 duty, change at Launceston 9.50 a.m. and work to Exmouth Jct.
No. 2 P. & D. men relieve at 12.5 p.m. and relieved at 2.15 p.m.
On duty 2.0 p.m., relieve at 2.15 p.m., work and relieved in Loco.
No. 5 P. & D. men dispose.

WADEBRIDGE DUTY No. 604.
0 FT. (0298 Class).

Arr.	Station	Dep.	
—	Loco. Yard ...	... 6.30 a.m.	‖
6.35 a.m.	Wadebridge...	... —	

Station and Quay **F.** shunting 6.35 a.m. to 5.30 p.m.
(**C.** 1 hour. **F.** 9 hours 35 mins.)
(Engine requirements 12.40 p.m. to 1.0 p.m.)

Arr.	Station	Dep.	
—	Wadebridge...	... 5.30 p.m.	‖
5.35 p.m.	Loco. Yard ...	... —	

Wadebridge Men.
1st Set (S.X.). On duty 4.45 a.m., prepare No. 606 duty and then own duty and relief 12.15 p.m.
2nd Set (S.X.). Of No. 605 duty, relieve 12.15 p.m. till 2.15 p.m.
3rd Set (S.X.). On duty 2.0 p.m., relieve and complete, then relieve No. 598 duty at 7.13 p.m. and complete.
1st Set (S.O.). On duty 4.30 a.m., prepare No. 506 duty and relief at 12.15 p.m.
2nd Set (S.O.). On duty 12.0 noon, relieve 12.15 p.m. and complete.

602—604

Western District—WEEKDAYS. 62

WADEBRIDGE DUTY No. 605.
4 M.T. (N. Class).
M.O.—Stabled off No. 598 duty **Saturday.**
M.X.—Stabled off No. 594 duty **previous day.**

Arr.	Station	Dep.	
—	Loco. Yard ...	... 7.40 a.m.	‖
7.45 a.m.	Wadebridge...	... 8. 3 a.m.	P
8.26 a.m.	Bodmin S.R....	... 8.45 a.m.	P
9. 4 a.m.	Wadebridge...	... 9.24 a.m.	ANR
9.38 a.m.	Padstow ...	... 10.15 a.m.	F

SATURDAYS EXCEPTED.

Arr.	Station	Dep.	
10.29 a.m.	Wadebridge...	... 10.35 a.m.	‖
10.40 a.m.	Loco. Yard ...	... 11.25 a.m.	‖
11.30 a.m.	Wadebridge...	... 11.35 a.m.	F
4.55 p.m.	Halwill ...	... 6.50 p.m.	F
7.30 p.m.	Okehampton	... —	
	F. shunting 7.40 to 8.55 p.m.		
—	Okehampton	... 8.55 p.m.	‖
8.58 p.m.	Loco. Yard ...	... 9.10 p.m.	‖
9.15 p.m.	Okehampton	... 9.25 p.m. (Stone)	
10.43 p.m.	Exeter ...	... 10.46 p.m.	‖
10.50 p.m.	Exmouth Jct.	... —	

SATURDAYS ONLY.

Arr.	Station	Dep.	
10.29 a.m.	Wadebridge...	... 10.50 a.m.	F
4.55 p.m.	Halwill ...	... 7. 0 p.m.	F
7.40 p.m.	Okehampton	... —	
	F. shunting 7.40 to 8.55 p.m.		
—	Okehampton	... 9.10 p.m.	‖
9.35 p.m.	Yeoford ...	... 10.11 p.m.	F
11.41 p.m.	Exmouth Jct.	... **	‖
**	Loco. Yard ...	... —	

Wadebridge Men.
1st Set (S.X.). On duty 6.40 a.m., relief at 11.35 a.m., then relieve on No. 604 duty 12.15 p.m. till 2.0 p.m.
2nd Set (S.X.). On duty 11.20 a.m., work to Tresmeer, change to No. 598 duty (10.8 a.m. ex Okehampton) at 2.39 p.m., and work to Wadebridge, relief 7.13 p.m.

Okehampton Men.
(S.X.). Off No. 598 duty, change over at Tresmeer 2.39 p.m., work to Halwill and home passenger.

Wadebridge Men.
(S.O.). On duty 6.40 a.m., work to Port Isaac Rd., change to No. 595 duty (9.56 a.m. ex Okehampton) at 11.44 a.m., and work to Wadebridge, relief 2.15 p.m

[*continued*

WADEBRIDGE DUTY No. 605—*continued*

Okehampton Men.
(S.O.). Off No. 595 duty, change at Port Isaac Rd. 11.44 a.m., and work to Halwill, relief at 4.55 p.m. and home passenger per 5.27 p.m.

Okehampton Men.
On duty 3.40 p.m. **(S.X.)**, 2.15 p.m. **(S.O.)**, prepare and train No. 593 duty **(S.O.)**, then passenger to Halwill, relieve 4.55 p.m., work to Okehampton and dispose No. 602 duty engine. Also dispose No. 595 duty **(S.O.)**.

Exmouth Jct. Men.
(S X). Off No. 614/597 duty, relief at 9.10 p.m., work and dispose.
(S.O.). Off No. 597 duty, relieve at 9.10 p.m., work and relieved in Loco.
No. 10 P. & D. men dispose **(S.O.)**.

605

Western District—SUNDAYS. 13

OKEHAMPTON DUTY No. 593.
4 M.T. (N Class).

SUNDAYS.

—	Loco. Yard	... 8.15 a.m.	||
8.18 a.m.	Okehampton ...	... 8.30 a.m.	P
10. 1 a.m.	Friary	...10.45 a.m.	||
10.52 a.m.	Loco. Yard	...11.25 a.m.	||
11.32 a.m.	Friary	...11.40 a.m.	P
2.10 p.m.	Exeter...	... 2.21 p.m.	||
2.25 p.m.	Exmouth Jc. ...	... 3. 6 p.m.	||
3.40 p.m.	Exeter Ctl.... ...	... **	||
**	St. Davids	... 4.46 p.m. (Bank)	
4.49 p.m.	Exeter Ctl.... ...	... 5.25 p.m.	P
8. 0 p.m.	Friary	... 8. 5 p.m.	||
8.12 p.m.	Loco. Yard	... 9. 0 p.m.	||
9. 7 p.m.	Friary	... 9.15 p.m.	P
10.51 p.m.	Okehampton ...	...11. 0 p.m.	||
11. 3 p.m.	Loco. Yard	... —	

Okehampton Men.

1st set on duty 7.15 a.m. and relief at 1.1 p.m.

2nd set on duty 12.50 p.m. and relief at 6.29 p.m.

3rd set on duty 6.15 p.m., work and dispose.

Nos. 594 to 597—SPARE

LAUNCESTON DUTY No. 598.
4 M.T. (N Class).

SUNDAYS.

(W.R.)	Loco. Yard	... 2.20 p.m.	||
2.35 p.m.	Launceston... ...	... 2.40 p.m.	P
3. 4 p.m.	Halwill	... 4.52 p.m.	P
5.14 p.m.	Launceston... ...	... 5.20 p.m.	||
5.35 p.m.	Loco. Yard (W.R.) ...	—	

Launceston Men.

On duty 1.20 p.m., work and dispose.

No. 599—SPARE

BUDE DUTY No. 600.
2 P.T. (M.7 Class).

SUNDAYS.

—	Loco. Yard	... 2.15 p.m.	||
2.20 p.m.	Bude	... 2.35 p.m.	P
3.47 p.m.	Okehampton ...	... 4.12 p.m.	P
5.18 p.m.	Bude	... 5.45 p.m.	||
5.50 p.m.	Loco. Yard	... —	

Bude Men.

On duty 1.30 p.m., work and dispose.

Nos. 601 to 610—SPARE

CALLINGTON DUTY No. 611.
1 P.T. (O.S Class.)

SUNDAYS.

—	Loco. Yard	... 8.10 a.m.	||
8.13 a.m.	Callington	... 8.15 a.m.	P
8.57 a.m.	Bere Alston ...	... 9.26 a.m.	P
10. 8 a.m.	Callington	...11.30 a.m.	P
12.11 p.m.	Bere Alston ...	...12.24 p.m.	P
1. 6 p.m.	Callington	... 1.25 p.m.	||
1.28 p.m.	Loco. Yard	... 6.20 p.m.	||
6.23 p.m.	Callington	... 6.30 p.m.	P
7.10 p.m.	Bere Alston ...	... 7.21 p.m.	P
8. 2 p.m.	Callington	... 9.10 p.m.	P
9.51 p.m.	Bere Alston ...	...10.20 p.m.	P
11. 2 p.m.	Callington	...11.25 p.m.	||
11.28 p.m.	Loco. Yard	... —	

Callington Men.

1st set of men on duty 7.25 a.m. and complete first part.

2nd set of men on duty 5.35 p.m., work and dispose.

Nos. 612 to 613—SPARE

593—613

Western District—WEEKDAYS. 63

WADEBRIDGE DUTY No. 606.
1 P.T. (O.2 Class).

—	Loco. Yard ...	... 6.40 a.m.	||
6.45 a.m.	Wadebridge...	... 6.55 a.m.	P
7.15 a.m.	Bodmin S.R....	... 7.22 a.m.	P
7.41 a.m.	Wadebridge...	... 7.43 a.m.	P
7.55 a.m.	Padstow ...	... 8.10 a.m.	P
8.55 a.m.	Bodmin W.R.	... 9. 0 a.m.	P
9.18 a.m.	Wadebridge...	... 9.46 a.m.	P
10. 6 a.m.	Bodmin S.R....	... 11.28 a.m.	P
11.47 a.m.	Wadebridge...	... 11.50 a.m.	||
11.55 a.m.	Loco. Yard ...	... 12.28 p.m.	||
12.33 p.m.	Wadebridge...	... 12.38 p.m. (Mixed)	
1. 2 p.m.	Bodmin S.R....	... 2. 0 p.m.	P
2.23 p.m.	Wadebridge...	... 2.25 p.m.	||
2.30 p.m.	Loco. Yard ...	... 3. 3 p.m.	||
3. 8 p.m.	Wadebridge...	... 3.12 p.m.	P
3.35 p.m.	Bodmin S.R....	... 4.23 p.m.	P
4.53 p.m.	Padstow ...	... 4.58 p.m.	P
5. 7 p.m.	Wadebridge...	... 5.10 p.m.	P
5.30 p.m.	Bodmin S.R....	... 5.36 p.m.	P
5.55 p.m.	Wadebridge...	... 6.12 p.m.	P
6.32 p.m.	Bodmin S.R....	... 6.43 p.m.	P
7.17 p.m.	Padstow ...	... —	
	F. shunting 7.25 p.m. to 7.40 p.m.		
—	Padstow ...	... 8. 2 p.m.	P
8.11 p.m.	Wadebridge...	... 8.13 p.m.	P
8.50 p.m.	Bodmin Road W.R.	9. 5 p.m.	P
9.48 p.m.	Padstow ...	... 10. 5 p.m.	P
10.14 p.m.	Wadebridge...	... 10.25 p.m.	||
10.30 p.m.	Loco. Yard ...	... —	

Wadebridge Men.

Engine prepared by men of No. 604 duty.

1st Set. On duty 6.25 a.m.

2nd Set. On duty 2.15 p.m. **(S.X.)**, 2.50 p.m. **(S.O.)** and dispose.

Engine disposed **(S.X.)** of by men of No. 608 duty.

WADEBRIDGE DUTY No. 607.
O.P.T (0.298 Class).

WEDNESDAYS AND SATURDAYS EXCEPTED.

—	Loco. Yard ...	... 9.50 a.m.	||
9.55 a.m.	Wadebridge...	... 10. 0 a.m.	F
12.41 p.m.	Wenford ...	... 1.20 p.m.	F
3.58 p.m.	Wadebridge...	... 4. 3 p.m.	||
4. 8 p.m.	Loco. Yard ...	... —	

WEDNESDAYS ONLY.

—	Loco. Yard ...	... 9.50 a.m.	||
9.55 a.m.	Wadebridge...	... 10. 0 a.m.	F
10.15 a.m.	Boscarne Jct.	... 11. 0 a.m.	F
11.15 a.m.	Wadebridge...	... 11.20 a.m.	||
11.25 a.m.	Loco. Yard ...	... 1.35 p.m.	||
1.40 p.m.	Wadebridge...	... 1.45 p.m.	F
2. 0 p.m.	Boscarne Jct.	... 2.25 p.m.	F
2.40 p.m.	Wadebridge...	... 2.45 p.m.	||
2.50 p.m.	Loco. Yard ...	... —	

Wadebridge Men.

On duty 9.5 a.m. and complete.

WADEBRIDGE DUTY No. 608.
4 M.T. (N. Class).

Stabled off No. 598 duty.

SATURDAYS EXCEPTED.

—	Loco. Yard ...	... 10.40 a.m.	||
10.45 a.m.	Wadebridge...	... 10.50 a.m.	F
11.22 a.m.	Delabole ...	... —	
	F. shunting 11.35 a.m. to 12.50 p.m.		
—	Delabole ...	... 1. 5 p.m.	F
1.15 p.m.	Port Isaac Rd.	... 1.45 p.m.	F
1.49 p.m.	Toms Sidings	... 2. 6 p.m.	F
2.58 p.m.	Wadebridge...	... 3. 5 p.m.	||
3.10 p.m.	Loco. Yard ...	... 4.20 p.m.	||
4.25 p.m.	Wadebridge...	... 4.30 p.m.	F
12.35 a.m.	Exmouth Jct.	... 12.45 a.m.	||
12.48 a.m.	Loco. Yard ...	... —	

Wadebridge Men.

1st Set. On duty 9.40 a.m., work duty till 3.35 p.m.

2nd Set. On duty 3.20 p.m., work to Launceston, change to No. 547 duty (5.51 p.m. ex Okehampton) at 6.46 p.m. and work to Wadebridge and dispose.

Exmouth Jct. Men.

Of No. 535/547 duty, change over at Launceston 6.46 p.m. and work to Exmouth Jct.

No. 9 P. & D. men dispose.

No. 609—SPARE.

606—609

BRITISH RAILWAYS

SOUTHERN REGION

B.R. 31051

ENGINE WORKINGS

FOR

PASSENGER AND FREIGHT TRAINS

(WESTERN DISTRICT)

MONDAYS TO FRIDAYS

15th JUNE, 1959, and until further notice

EXPLANATORY NOTES

AR	Assisting required.	M ...	Milk Train.	SRE...	Shunt release engine.
ANR	Assisting not required.	O/R...	On rear.	V ...	Vans.
C ...	Coaching.	P ...	Passenger Train.	‖ ...	Light engine.
E ...	Empty Train.	P/O	Pull out.	** ...	Time uncertain.
F ...	Freight.	Q ...	Conditional		

FAST—LOCOMOTIVES Nos. 15211—36 and D. 3665 UPWARDS.

SUMMARY OF DEPOTS AND ENGINE DUTIES. (Commencing Numbers.)

Salisbury	491	Barnstaple	636
Yeovil	512	Torrington	641
Exmouth Junction	524	Wadebridge	645
Exmouth	626	Callington	650

Operating Officer's Office.
WATERLOO STATION.

1959

Western Region Engines Working over Western District—(MONDAYS TO FRIDAYS) 7

FRIARY DUTY No. 12.

O.P.T. (O.2 Class)

—	Friary Loco.	5.28 a.m. ‖
5.39 a.m.	Devonport	—

F—Shunting 6.15 a.m. to 9.0 a.m.

Engine requirements 9.0 a.m. to 9.30 a.m. and work Q trips to Stonehouse Pool.

—	Devonport	9.35 a.m. F
**	Keyham	** F
10.45 a.m.	St. Budeaux	11.15 a.m. F
11.22 a.m.	Devonport	—

F—Shunting 11.30 a.m. to 12.20 p.m.

Engine requirements 12.20 p.m. to 12.40 p.m.

F—Shunting 12.40 p.m. to 4.20 p.m.

Engine requirements 4.20 p.m. to 4.40 p.m.

F—Shunting 4.40 p.m. to 6.0 p.m.

—	Devonport	6.30 p.m. ‖
6.42 p.m.	Friary Loco.	—

Friary Men.

ST. BLAZEY DUTY No. 24.

4 M.T. (45 XX Class)

—	Bodmin Road	7.50 a.m. P
8.50 a.m.	Padstow	9. 3 a.m. P
9.54 a.m.	Bodmin Road	10.10 a.m. M.X.D.
10.55 a.m.	Wadebridge	11. 7 a.m. P
11.41 a.m.	Bodmin Road	12.20 p.m. P
12.57 p.m.	Wadebridge	1.23 p.m. P
1.45 p.m.	Bodmin General ...	—
—	Bodmin General ...	4. 8 p.m. P
4.27 p.m.	Wadebridge	4.43 p.m. E
5. 8 p.m.	Bodmin General ...	—
—	Bodmin Road	6.17 p.m. P
6.49 p.m.	Wadebridge	7. 5 p.m. P
7.35 p.m.	Bodmin General ...	—

W.R. Men.

BODMIN DUTY No. 1.

4 M.T. (45 XX Class)

—	Bodmin General ...	11.40 a.m. F
11.53 a.m.	Boscarne Jc.	12.15 p.m. F
12.29 p.m.	Bodmin General ...	12.45 p.m. P
12.52 p.m.	Bodmin Road	1. 5 p.m. P
1.13 p.m.	Bodmin General ... (1.23 p.m. Wadebridge)	1.50 p.m. P
1.57 p.m.	Bodmin Road	2.30 p.m. P
3. 6 p.m.	Wadebridge	3.24 p.m. M.X.D.
4. 1 p.m.	Bodmin Road	4.25 p.m. P
5. 9 p.m.	Wadebridge	5.34 p.m. P
6. 8 p.m.	Bodmin Road	7.26 p.m. P
8. 0 p.m.	Wadebridge	8.42 p.m. P
9.32 p.m.	Bodmin Road	—

W.R. Men.

EXMOUTH JC. DUTY No. 581

7 P/5 F. (W.C. Class)

—	Loco. Yard	2.55 a.m. ‖ (M.O.)
2.58 a.m.	Exmouth Jc.	3.15 a.m. F (M.O.)
—	Loco. Yard	3.10 a.m. ‖ (M.X)
3.14 a.m.	Exeter Ctl.	3.25 a.m. F. (M.X.)
	(10.15 p.m. ex Nine Elms)	
6.37 a.m.	Friary	6.50 a.m. ‖
	(Via Laira Jc. and Lipson Jc. to Turn)	
7.15 a.m.	Friary Loco.	7.40 a.m. ‖
8. 7 a.m.	Friary	8.12 a.m. E
8.20 a.m.	Plymouth	8.25 a.m. P
10.23 a.m.	Exeter Ctl....	10.35 a.m. ‖
10.38 a.m.	Exmouth Jc.	1.46 p.m. ‖
1.50 p.m.	Exeter	2.21 p.m. P
5. 7 p.m.	Padstow	5.36 p.m. ‖
5.45 p.m.	Wadebridge	6.13 p.m. P
6.22 p.m.	Padstow ... ...(B)	6.35 p.m. ‖
6.44 p.m.	Wadebridge Loco. ...	—

Stable for No. 582.

B—6.35 p.m. **E (F.O.)**.

Exmouth Jc. Men.

(1) **Sun.**—No. 7 P. and D. men, prepare(**M.O.**).

(2) **M.X.**—Off No. 563, prepare.

[*continued.*

EXMOUTH JC. DUTY No. 581—*continued.*

Exmouth Jc. Men.

(3) 1st set on duty 2.40 a.m. (**M.O.**) 2.55 a.m. (**M.X.**), relief 10.23 a.m.

(4) Off No. 620, relieve at Exeter 10.23 a.m., work and relieved in depot.

(5) No. 3 P. and D. men, perform requirements for 1.46 p.m.‖.

(6) 2nd set on duty 1.31 p.m., work to Launceston, change to No. 591 at 3.57 p.m., work to Halwill, change to No. 589 at 5.0 p.m. and work and relieved in depot.

Wadebridge Men.

(7) Off No. 591, change at Launceston 3.57 p.m., work and relieved in depot.

(8) Off No. 645, part dispose.

(9) Off No. 587, complete disposal.

EXMOUTH JC. DUTY No. 582

M.O.—22/6 and from 31/8.

4 P/5 F. (N. Class)

Off No. 590, **Friday.**

M.O.—29/6 to 24/8 (7 P/5 F W.C. Class).
Off No. 581 **Sat.**

M.X.—7 P/5 F (W.C. Class).
Off No. 581 **(S.X.).**

—	Wadebridge Loco. ...	7.10 a.m. ‖
7.14 a.m.	Wadebridge	7.20 a.m. F
7.34 a.m.	Padstow	—
	F—Shunting 7.35 a.m. to 7.50 a.m.	
—	Padstow	8.30 a.m. P
11.58 a.m.	Exeter...	12. 0 noon ‖
12. 4 p.m.	Exmouth Jc.	1.46 p.m. ‖
1.50 p.m.	Exeter...	2.11 p.m. P
	(11.0 a.m. Waterloo)	
4.11 p.m.	Ilfracombe	4.40 p.m. ‖
4.45 p.m.	Ilfracombe Loco. ...	5.30 p.m. ‖
5.35 p.m.	Ilfracombe	5.50 p.m. P
6.28 p.m.	Barnstaple Jc.	6.41 p.m. F
	(5.25 p.m. Torrington)	
9.33 p.m.	Exmouth Jc.	9.40 p.m. ‖
9.43 p.m.	Loco. Yard...	—

Wadebridge Men.

(1) 1st set on duty 6.10 a.m., work to Halwill, change to No. 599 at 10.24 a.m., work and change to No. 590 at 11.44 a.m. at Port Isaac Rd., work and dispose.

Exmouth Jc. Men.

(2) Off No. 599, change at Halwill 10.24 a.m. and work and relieved 1.46 p.m., dispose No. 9.

(3) 1st set on duty 1.31 p.m., work and relieved in depot.

(4) No. 6 P. and D. men, dispose.

EXMOUTH JC. DUTY No. 583

7 P/5 F. (W.C. Class)

—	Exmouth Jc.	1.46 p.m. ‖
1.50 p.m.	Exeter	2.21 p.m. P A.N.R.
3. 8 p.m.	Okehampton	3.50 p.m. ‖
4.23 p.m.	Halwill	5. 1 p.m. P
6.31 p.m.	Wadebridge	**‖
**	Wadebridge Loco. ...	—

Stable No. 584.

Exmouth Jc. Men.

(1) Prepare for 1.46 p.m.‖.

(2) 1st set on duty 1.31 p.m., work to St. Kew Highway, change to No. 598 at 6.23 p.m., work and relieved Okehampton 8.30 p.m., relieve No. 567 at 8.50 p.m. and work and relieved Exeter 9.48 p.m.

Wadebridge Men.

(3) Off No. 598, change at St. Kew Highway 6.23 p.m. and work and dispose.

Engine Workings—Western District—(MONDAYS TO FRIDAYS) 60

EXMOUTH JC. DUTY No. 590

4 P/5 F. (N. Class)

M.X.—Off No. 589.

Arr.	Station	Dep.	
**	Loco. Yard...	...12.10 a.m. (M.O.)	‖
12.14 a.m.	Exmouth Jc.	...12.20 a.m. (M.O.)	F
—	Loco. Yard...	...11.41 p.m. (F.X.)	‖
11.43 p.m.	Exmouth Jc.	...12. 1 a.m. (M.X.)	F
6.56 a.m.	Launceston...	—	

C. & F.—Shunting 7.0 a.m. to 8.15 a.m.
C—Shunting ½ hr., **F**—Shunting ¾ hour.

Arr.	Station	Dep.	
—	Launceston	... 8.15 a.m.	F
12.23 p.m.	Wadebridge	...12.34 p.m.	‖
12.40 p.m.	Wadebridge Loco.	—	

F.X.—Stable No. 591.

F.O.—19/6 and from 28/8 stable No. 582

Monday.
F.O.—26/6 to 21/8 stable No. 591 **Saturday.**

Exmouth Jc. Men.

(1) **M.O.**—Sunday No. 7 P. and D. men, prepare and work and relieved Exeter 12.25 a.m.

(2) 1st set **(M.O.)** on duty 12.10 a.m., work and relieved Okehampton 5.35 a.m., prepare No. 599 and home pass. per 7.39 a.m.

(3) **F.X.**—Off No. 594, prepare for 11.41 p.m. ‖.

(4) 1st set **(F.X.)** on duty 11.26 p.m., work to Yeoford, change to No. 577 at 1.30 a.m., work to Okehampton, change to No. 574 at 4.20 a.m., and work and relieved in depot.

[*continued.*

EXMOUTH JC. DUTY No. 590. *continued.*

Okehampton Men.

(5) **M.X.**—Off No. 577, change at Yeoford 1.30 a.m. and work and **(M.S.X.)** relieved Okehampton 5.40 a.m., train No. 593, prepare No. 599, **(S.O.)** relieved Okehampton 5.35 a.m. and prepare No. 571.

(6) 1st set on duty; 5.25 a.m. **(M.O.)**; 4.35 a.m. **(M.X.)** prepare No. 593, work to Camelford, change to No. 584 at 10.11 a.m., work and relieved Okehampton 11.30 a.m., relieve No. 596 in Loco. and work and relieved 1.0 p.m.

Wadebridge Men.

(7) Off No. 584, change at Camelford 10.11 a.m., work and change to No. 599 at Port Isaac 11.44 a.m.

(8) Off No. 599, change at Port Isaac 11.44 a.m. and work and dispose.

590

Engine Workings—Western District—(MONDAYS TO FRIDAYS) 61

EXMOUTH JC. DUTY No. 591.

4 P/5 F. (N. Class)

Off No. 590.

Arr.	Station	Dep.	
—	Wadebridge Loco.	... 7.40 a.m.	‖
7.45 a.m.	Wadebridge	... 8. 1 a.m.	P
8.26 a.m.	Bodmin S.R.	... 8.43 a.m.	P
9. 2 a.m.	Wadebridge	... 9.10 a.m.	‖
9.15 a.m.	Loco. Yard...	...10.15 a.m.	‖
**	Wadebridge	...10.30 a.m.	P
10.39 a.m.	Padstow	...10.55 a.m.	P
11. 4 a.m.	Wadebridge	...11.35 a.m.	F
7.42 p.m.	Okehampton	—	

C—Shunting 8.30 p.m. to 8.55 p.m.

Arr.	Station	Dep.	
—	Okehampton	... 9.25 p.m. Stone	
10.43 p.m.	Exeter...	...10.46 p.m.	‖
10.49 p.m.	Exmouth Jc.	—	

Wadebridge Men.

(1) 1st set on duty 6.40 a.m., work and relieved 11.5 a.m., prepare No. 598, prepare No. 588 and as ordered.

(2) 2nd set on duty 10.50 a.m., relieve 11.5 a.m., work to Launceston, change to No. 581 at 3.57 p.m., work and relieved in depot.

Exmouth Jc. Men.

(3) Off No. 581, change at Launceston 3.57 p.m., work to Halwill, change to No. 589 at 5.30 p.m. and work and relieved in depot.

Okehampton Men.

(4) Off No. 589, change at 5.30 p.m. and work and relieved Okehampton 9.0 p.m., dispose Nos. 593 and 598 and **(F.O.)** finish disposal No. 549.

Exmouth Jc. Men.

(5) Off No. 592, relieve 9.20 a.m., work and relieved in depot.

(6) No. 12 P. and D. men, dispose.

[*continued.*

EXMOUTH JC. DUTY No. 592

4 P/5 F. (N. Class)

Arr.	Station	Dep.	
—	Loco. Yard...	... 7.15 a.m.	‖
7.18 a.m.	Exmouth Jc.	... 7.32 a.m. (Stone)	Q
9.41 a.m.	Meldon Quarry	... 9.55 a.m.	‖
10. 0 a.m.	Okehampton (Turn)	10.20 a.m.	‖
**	Okehampton	...10.40 a.m. (Stone)	
10.47 a.m.	Meldon Quarry	...11.35 a.m. (Stone)	Q
1.24 p.m.	Exmouth Jc.	... 1.35 p.m.	‖
1.38 p.m.	Exmouth Jc. Loco.	... 3.25 p.m.	‖
3.28 p.m.	Exeter	... 3.48 p.m.	P
4.46 p.m.	Okehampton	—	

F—Shunting 4.50 p.m. to 7.0 p.m.

Arr.	Station	Dep.	
—	Okehampton	... 7. 0 p.m.	‖
**	Okehampton Loco. ...	—	

Stable for No. 593.

Exmouth Jc. Men.

(1) **M.O.**—Off No. 545, prepare.

(2) **M.X.**—No. 11 P. and D. men, prepare.

(3) 1st set on duty 7.0 a.m., relieved 2.45 p.m.

(4) 2nd set on duty 2.30 p.m., work and dispose, then relieve No. 598 at 8.30 p.m., work to Loco., relieve No. 391 at Okehampton 9.0 p.m., work and relieved in depot.

591—592

EXMOUTH JC. DUTY No. 593.

4 P/5 F. (N. Class)

M.O.—Stabled off No. 587 **Saturday.**

M.X.—Stabled off No. 592.

Arr.	Station	Dep.	
—	Okehampton Loco. ...	6. 0 a.m.	‖
6. 5 a.m.	Okehampton ...	6.30 a.m.	
9.22 a.m.	Padstow	—	
	C—Shunting 9.30 a.m. to 9.45 a.m.		
	F—Shunting 9.45 a.m. to 10.5 a.m.		
—	Padstow	10.10 a.m.	F
10.32 a.m.	Wadebridge	—	
	F—Shunting Q 10.55 a.m. to 11.30 a.m.		
—	Wadebridge ...	11.30 a.m.	‖
11.35 a.m.	Loco. Yard... ...	12.49 p.m.	‖
12.54 p.m.	Wadebridge ... (12.58 p.m. ex Padstow).	1.14 p.m.	P
3.13 p.m.	Okehampton ...	3.15 p.m.	‖
3.18 p.m.	Okehampton Loco. ...	4. 0 p.m.	‖
4. 5 p.m.	Okehampton ...	4.24 p.m.	P
5.30 p.m.	Bude	5.40 p.m.	‖
5.45 p.m.	Bude	6. 0 p.m.	‖
6. 5 p.m.	Loco. Yard... ...	6.50 p.m.	‖
6.55 p.m.	Bude	7. 5 p.m.	P
7.45 p.m.	Halwill	8.30 p.m.	F
		A.N.R.	
9. 0 p.m.	Okehampton ...	9. 3 p.m.	‖
9. 6 p.m.	Okehampton Loco. ...	—	

Stable No. 594.

[continued.

EXMOUTH JC. DUTY No. 593—*continued*

Okehampton Men.

(1) 1st set (**M.O.**) on duty 5.0 a.m., work to Launceston, relieved 7.55 a.m., work No. 587 and relieved Okehampton Loco. 11.0 a.m. and as ordered.

(2) **M.X.**—Off No. 590, prepare for 6.0 a.m.‖.

(3) **M.X.**—Off No. 590, train engine for 6.25 a.m.

Exmouth Jc. Men.

(4) 1st set (**M.X.**) on duty 4.57 a.m., pass. per 5.12 a.m. to Okehampton, relieve 6.5 a.m., work and relieved Launceston 7.55 a.m., work No. 587 to Okehampton, relieved 11.0 a.m. and home pass per 11.15 a.m.

Launceston Men (W.R.).

(5) Off No. 587, relieve 7.55 a.m., work and relieved Launceston 2.15 p.m.

(6) 1st set on duty 2.0 p.m., relieve 2.15 p.m., change at Halwill with No. 586 at 8.17 p.m., work and dispose.

Okehampton Men.

(7) Off No. 586, change at Halwill 8.17 p.m. and work and relieved in depot.

(8) Off No. 591, dispose.

EXMOUTH JC. DUTY No. 598.

3 P.T. (T.9 Class)

Off No. 597.

Arr.	Station	Dep.	
**	Wadebridge Loco. ...	1. 0 p.m.	‖
**	Wadebridge	1.15 p.m.	P
1.29 p.m.	Padstow	—	
	C—Shunting 2.0 p.m. to 2.15 p.m.		
	F—Shunting 2.15 p.m. to 2.50 p.m.		
—	Padstow	2.52 p.m.	P
3. 1 p.m.	Wadebridge	4.30 p.m.	P
4.39 p.m.	Padstow	5.15 p.m.	P
5.24 p.m.	Wadebridge	5.33 p.m.	P
5.42 p.m.	Padstow	—	
	C—Shunting 5.45 p.m. to 6.0 p.m.		
—	Padstow	6. 0 p.m.	P
8.29 p.m.	Okehampton	8.32 p.m.	‖
8.35 p.m.	Okehampton Loco. ...	—	

Stable No. 599.

Wadebridge Men.

(1) Off No. 591, prepare.

(2) 1st set on duty 12.45 p.m., work and change to No. 583 at St. Kew 6.23 p.m., work and dispose.

Exmouth Jc. Men.

(3) Off No. 583, change at St. Kew 6.23 p.m., work and relieved Okehampton 8.30 p.m., relieve No. 567 at 8.50 p.m.

(4) Off No. 592, relieve 8.30 p.m. and work to Loco., relieve No. 591 at 9.0 p.m.

Okehampton Men.

(5) Off No. 591, dispose.

EXMOUTH JC. DUTY No. 599

3 P (T.9 Class)

Off No. 598.

Arr.	Station	Dep.	
—	Okehampton Loco. ...	7.50 a.m.	‖
7.55 a.m.	Okehampton	—	
	F—Shunting 7.55 a.m. to 8.40 a.m.		
	C—Shunting 8.55 a.m. to 9.45 a.m.		
—	Okehampton	9.56 a.m.	P
12.14 p.m.	Padstow	12.58 p.m.	P
1. 7 p.m.	Wadebridge	1.15 p.m.	‖
1.20 p.m.	Loco. Yard... ...	2.20 p.m.	‖
2.25 p.m.	Wadebridge	2.28 p.m.	P
2.37 p.m.	Padstow	3.13 p.m.	P
6.38 p.m.	Exeter...	6.52 p.m.	‖
6.55 p.m.	Exmouth Jc.	—	

[continued.

EXMOUTH JC. DUTY No. 599—*continued.*

Exmouth Jc. Men.

(1) **M.O.**—Off No. 590, prepare for 7.50 a.m.‖.

Okehampton Men.

(2) **M.X.**—Off No. 590, prepare.

Exmouth Jc. Men.

(3) Off No. 572, work and relieved 9.56 a.m., prepare and work No. 597.

(4) 1st set on duty 8.26 a.m., pass. to Okehampton, relieve 9.56 a.m., work to Halwill, change to No. 582 at 10.24 a.m., work and relieved 1.46 p.m. and dispose No. 9.

Wadebridge Men.

(5) Off No. 582, change at Halwill 10.24 a.m., work to Port Isaac Rd., change to No. 590 at 11.44 a.m., and work and dispose.

(6) Off No. 590, change at Port Isaac Rd. 11.44 a.m., work and relieved Wadebridge 3.22 p.m.

(7) 1st set on duty 3.7 p.m., relieve 3.22 p.m., work to Otterham, change to No. 587 at 4.16 p.m., work and dispose, complete disposal No. 581 and dispose No. 597 and 646.

Okehampton Men.

(8) Off No. 587, change over at Otterham 4.16 p.m., work and relieved at Okehampton 5.54 p.m.

Exmouth Jc. Men.

(9) Off No. 569, relieve at Okehampton 5.54 p.m., and work and dispose, then to Exeter and relieve No. 567 at 9.48 p.m.

No. 600 NOT USED

WADEBRIDGE DUTY No. 645.

0 P.T. (0298 Class)

—	Loco. Yard...	6.30 a.m.	‖
6.35 a.m.	Wadebridge	—	

Station and Quay **F** Shunting
6.35 a.m. to 8.0 a.m.
8.20 a.m. to 11.40 a.m.
12.10 p.m. to 5.30 p.m.
(Less 1 hr. **C** Shunting)

—	Wadebridge	5.30 p.m.	‖
5.35 p.m.	Loco. Yard...	—	

Wadebridge Men.
(1) 1st set on duty 4.30 a.m., prepare No. 646 duty and then own duty and relief 12.15 p.m.

(2) 2nd set on duty 12.0 noon work and dispose and part dispose No. 520.

WADEBRIDGE DUTY No. 646.

O. P.T. (O. 2 Class)

—	Loco. Yard...	6.40 a.m.	‖
6.45 a.m.	Wadebridge	6.52 a.m.	P
7.12 a.m.	Bodmin North	7.22 a.m.	P
7.55 a.m.	Padstow	8.12 a.m.	P
8.55 a.m.	Bodmin Gen.	9. 0 a.m.	P
9.18 a.m.	Wadebridge	9.48 a.m.	P
10. 8 a.m.	Bodmin North	11.20 a.m.	P
11.50 a.m.	Padstow	11.55 a.m.	P
12. 4 p.m.	Wadebridge	12. 5 p.m.	‖
12. 8 p.m.	Loco. Yard...	12.20 p.m.	‖
12.23 p.m.	Wadebridge (11.55 a.m. Padstow)	12.25 p.m.	P
12.49 p.m.	Bodmin North	2. 0 p.m.	P
2.23 p.m.	Wadebridge	2.25 p.m.	‖
2.30 p.m.	Loco. Yard...	3. 0 p.m.	‖
3. 3 p.m.	Wadebridge (2.52 p.m. Padstow).	3. 9 p.m.	P

[continued.

WADEBRIDGE DUTY No. 646—*continued.*

3.29 p.m.	Bodmin North	4.23 p.m.	P
4.42 p.m.	Wadebridge	5.11 p.m.	P
5.31 p.m.	Bodmin North	5.48 p.m.	P
6. 7 p.m.	Wadebridge	6.18 p.m.	P
6.38 p.m.	Bodmin North	6.45 p.m.	P
7.19 p.m.	Padstow	8. 4 p.m.	P
8.50 p.m.	Bodmin Road W.R.	9. 5 p.m.	P
9.51 p.m.	Padstow	10. 5 p.m.	P
10.14 p.m.	Wadebridge	10.25 p.m.	‖
10.30 p.m.	Loco. Yard...	—	

Wadebridge Men.
(1) Off No. 645, prepare.

(2) 1st set on duty 6.25 a.m. and perform requirements for 3.0 p.m. ‖.

(3) 2nd set on duty 2.15 p.m., work and relieved in depot.

(4) Off No. 587, dispose.

WADEBRIDGE DUTY No. 647.

O P.T. (O. 298 Class)

—	Loco. Yard...	9.50 a.m.	‖
9.55 a.m.	Wadebridge	10. 3 a.m.	F
12.41 p.m.	Wenford	—	

F—Shunting 12.45 p.m. to 1.20 p.m.

—	Wenford	1.20 p.m.	F
3.58 p.m.	Wadebridge	4. 3 p.m.	‖
4. 8 p.m.	Loco. Yard	—	

Wadebridge Men.
( ) 1st set on duty 9.5 a.m., work and dispose.

Nos. 648 & 649 NOT USED

EXMOUTH JC. DUTY No. 578.

2 P.T. (L.M.R. Class)

—	Callington Loco.	8.10 a.m.	‖
8.13 a.m.	Callington	8.15 a.m.	P
8.57 a.m.	Bere Alston	9.18 a.m.	P
10. 0 a.m.	Callington (B)	11.12 a.m.	P
11.58 a.m.	Bere Alston (C)	12.22 p.m.	P
1. 4 p.m.	Callington	1.25 p.m.	‖
1.28 p.m.	Loco. Yard...	6.20 p.m.	‖
6.23 p.m.	Callington	6.32 p.m.	P
7.12 p.m.	Bere Alston	7.24 p.m.	P
8. 5 p.m.	Callington	9.10 p.m.	P
9.51 p.m.	Bere Alston	10. 2 p.m.	P
10.43 p.m.	Callington	10.50 p.m.	‖
10.53 p.m.	Callington Loco.	—	

B—1/11/59 to 24/4/60 start 11.30 a.m. and arr. 12.16 p.m.

C—1/11/59 to 24/4/60 start 12.45 p.m. and arr. 1.22 p.m.

Callington Men.
(1) 1st set of men on duty 7.25 a.m. and work and dispose.

(3) 2nd set of men on duty 5.35 p.m., work and dispose.

Nos. 579 to 586 NOT USED.

EXMOUTH JC. DUTY No. 587.

4 P./5 F. (N. Class)

Off No. 592 **Sat.**

—	Launceston Loco.	2. 5 p.m.	‖
—	Launceston	2.32 p.m.	P
2.55 p.m.	Halwill (Turn)	4.55 p.m.	P
5.17 p.m.	Launceston...	—	‖
—	Launceston Loco.	—	

Stable No. 587 **Monday.**

Launceston Men.
(1) 1st set on duty 1.5 p.m., work and dispose.

Nos. 588 to 593 NOT USED

EXMOUTH JC. DUTY No. 594.

4 P. (N. Class)

Stabled off No. 592 **Saturday.**

—	Okehampton Loco.	8.15 a.m.	‖
8.18 a.m.	Okehampton	8.30 a.m.	P
9.46 a.m.	Plymouth	9.49 a.m.	E
10. 1 a.m.	Friary	10.45 a.m.	‖
10.52 a.m.	Loco. Yard...	11.20 a.m.	‖
11.27 a.m.	Friary	11.31 a.m.	E
11.33 a.m.	Plymouth (B)	11.48 a.m.	P
2.10 p.m.	Exeter...	2.21 p.m.	‖
2.25 p.m.	Exmouth Jc.	3.33 p.m.	‖
**	St. Davids	4. 3 p.m. (Bank)	P
4. 6 p.m.	Exeter Ctl.	**	‖
**	St. Davids	4.46 p.m. (Bank)	P
4.49 p.m.	Exeter Ctl.	5.25 p.m.	P
7.47 p.m.	Plymouth	7.51 p.m.	E
8.30 p.m.	Friary	8. 5 p.m.	‖
8.12 p.m.	Loco. Yard...	9. 0 p.m.	‖
8. 7 p.m.	Friary	9.11 p.m.	E
9.23 p.m.	Plymouth	9.25 p.m.	P
10.51 p.m.	Okehampton	11. 0 p.m.	‖
11. 3 p.m.	Okehampton Loco.	—	

Stable for No. 594 **Mondays.**

B—Arr. 2.22 p.m. **up to 24/4/60.**

Okehampton Men.
(1) 1st set on duty 7.15 a.m., and relief at 1.10 p.m.

(2) 2nd set on duty 12.55 p.m., relieve 1.10 p.m. and relief at 6.29 p.m.

(3) 3rd set on duty 6.14 p.m., work and dispose.

Nos. 595 to 599 NOT USED

Above. Halwill, the final hurrah! *Below*. Not dead but sleeping... Malcolm Briggs